A Complete History of Dripping Springs and the P. A. Smith Survey

(As Best I Can Tell)

A Complete History of Dripping Springs and the P. A. Smith Survey

(As Best I Can Tell)

CARL WAITS

Fort Worth, Texas

Dedication

To my wife, Susie,
for her patience during the many hours
consumed by research and computer time.

And to
Our son, Tim, his wife, Cristina,
and daughters, Emily and Allison,
because they make us proud.

And to
the community of Dripping Springs.

Book design and typography by Pat Molenaar

FIRST EDITION
Copyright © 2003
By Carl Waits
Manufactured in the U.S.A.
By Nortex Press
A Division of Wild Horse Media Group
Fort Worth, Texas
www.WildHorseMedia.com
ALL RIGHTS RESERVED.
ISBN 978-1-940130-35-4

Contents

Preface v

PART ONE
The Beginnings 1
Genealogy 11
The History of the Town of Dripping Springs 27
Governing Entities 41
Public Services 47
History of Business Buildings 72
History of Businesses 99
History of Houses 110
Gone But Not Forgotten 127
Transportation 147
Places to Go and Things to Do 154
Forms of Entertainment 161
Things Heard or Read 165

PART TWO
History of Land Ownership 187
Property Maps
   Dripping Springs, x; Northwest Quarter, 191; Original Plat, 192; Road Changes, 195; First Addition, 205; Fourth Addition, 215; Fifth Addition, 216; Academy Block, 218; R. E. Spaw Addition, 220; P. L. Turner Addition, 223; Smith-Ragland Addition, 227; Smith-Crow Subdivision, 230; J. W. Wilson, Jr., Subdivision, 234; Northeast Quarter, 243; Stephenson 100 Acres, 245, Southeast Quarter, 250; J. D. Robert Addition, 255, Southwest Quarter, 258; Phillips Cemetery, 259

PART THREE
Good People 265
Good Churches 277
Good Schools 291
    School Programs, 309, The Basics, 314, School Spirit, 323, Athletic Programs, 325, Things Read or Heard, 333, School Faculties, 340, Teaching Careers, 356, School Trustees, 366, Student Honors, 369

Sources of Information. 381
About the Author 385

Preface

The path leading to the completion of this literary document was almost as adventurous as the trip the leading characters must have taken to begin their lives in Dripping Springs, Texas. I first came to Dripping Springs in the spring of 1965 to meet with the Dripping Springs ISD school board to interview for a teaching/coaching position. That trip almost made me change my mind about staying but it was my fault. I foolishly did not take a map with me because I thought I knew where I was going. All I knew about Dripping Springs was it was near Lake Travis, so when I got to the "Y" in Oak Hill I followed the road that pointed to Lake Travis. After a few miles I decided I was probably lost and at the time there were few houses along Highway 71 to stop and ask. Finally I pulled in at Johnson's Trading Post and asked directions to Dripping Springs. They explained how to get there from the Hamilton Pool road. This brought me to Dripping Springs through the narrow and winding road that was to be RR 12 and Old Fitzhugh Road. At that point I was saying to myself "if this is the only way to get to Dripping Springs, then I don't know if I really want this job." It was then I discovered that if I had simply stayed on 290, the probable route taken by the original founders, I would have had plenty of time to stop and eat before going to the school board meeting. It was nice to know there was a better way to get to Dripping Springs.

Being a coach was not the area of work that usually allows one to stay in any one place very long. I was lucky. Certainly it was not because my skills were good enough as a coach to stay around but that things worked out to where I was able to complete a 30-year teaching career at Dripping Springs before retiring. History has always been one of my favorite subjects. One of my early reasons was because I thought it never changed. Once you learned something, then you did not have to worry about it moving around on you. Well, what a false assumption. We all know how modern technology and new discoveries have changed things that we always thought were rock solid. The same can be said about the history of Dripping Springs and the Phillip A. Smith survey.

Like so many others, I have driven by most of the buildings in and around Dripping Springs hundreds of times without really noticing them or having more than a mild curiosity about their history. As a history teacher, there would be times I would

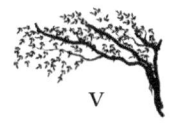

read or hear stories about them and get the urge to delve deeper into the subject but it always seemed that other interests would consume the time needed to pursue the curiosity. Finally in the fall of 1990, the urge became very strong and I set out vigorously to do a video history of the buildings. My idea was to give a history of Dripping Springs through a brief synopsis of each of the buildings, especially the businesses. I thought this would not only be interesting but easy and not take too long to complete. Boy, was I wrong on the last two. I set about the task expecting to finish the video by Christmas. As usual with my projects, as I interviewed people to get information to go with the pictures, it became obvious there was more to this community than met the eye. I was hooked. Their stories opened all types of new ideas and suddenly the scope of my project broadened to a point where I knew it was going to take much more time to do it proper justice than first I thought. My sense of urgency waned and I did not spend as much time on the project as I should have. Hence, the months have evolved into years. Part of my problem is my perfection complex. I just wanted to make sure that I got everything as close to correct and complete as possible. I just did not want to miss a fact, if at all possible. Every time I thought I was sure of something, sure enough, more information would come to me and off I would have to go in search of that clue. It never seemed to end.

One of my early premises was "if these old walls could talk, what tales they could tell." Well, that is probably true but in talking with many of the long-time natives of the area, it became obvious they, too, had some very interesting tales to be told. It also became obvious that all the information I was obtaining could not be included in the limited space of a video. I decided a supplement to the video would be needed and that is how this book became a reality. Researching for a book is definitely an eye-opening experience. I now know why you read about professional authors going away into seclusion for many months to write their book. The time and solitude needed to research and put your thoughts in order is tremendous. Without that luxury, it does evolve into years. Spending a day a week and an hour or two here and there does not make for fast progress. You get on the trail of something and time runs out on the day and you have to wait a week to get back at it. This was frustrating and meant a lot of time-consuming backtracking to get to go forward, making a wasteful situation. I thought originally it would be easy. Just compile the stories I had read and the ones being told to me and I would have the history of Dripping Springs. That's what I started out to do and I'm glad I did not complete that task because I would have only continued the inaccuracies that were rampant in previous writings.

After the research began, one of the truths learned early on was "you cannot believe everything you read or hear." Recollections are mostly good for substance but not always for accuracy. Even the short span of time I have lived here, there are things that I cannot recall accurately about bygone days. Neither is it a good idea to assume facts without proper research, because you might be like me and find yourself way off base. A major problem I have encountered is the contradictions and inaccuracies that frequently occur in the information, especially in the area of dates. The mathematics of times and dates and other details would not always add up. It is my belief the misinformation occurred through typographical errors, forgetfulness, embellishment, carelessness, and assumptions without research. It is a shame because when people read or hear the information, quite naturally they assume it is valid and repeat the misinformation as truth, perpetuating the problem. Hopefully, my research will not contribute to that tradition.

I would like to stand here and tell you that everything you read in this book is 100 percent correct, and it might be, but I can-

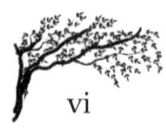

not, with certainty, verify all the information given here. I do believe it to be close. This brings us back to my warning about not believing everything you read or hear. This book includes material that I am passing on at the face value of someone else. Also my interpretations of what I have read may not be correct. So again, do not take everything that I report as gospel unless you so desire. Feel free to research and correct anything that I may have gotten wrong. Certainly that is what I am doing with someone else's history.

My data has come through many, many questions to a lot of patient people around Dripping Springs, reading many books and articles, plus spending many hours in the Hays County Courthouse Annex, going through deeds, commissioner court minutes, tax records, census forms, election results, and school minutes. At the San Marcos Library, there were many more hours going through microfilm of all the newspapers of Hays County. I just did not want to miss a chance to get the facts as close as possible. I do regret that I did not get the urge in the '80s because in that time span I lost many of the people who could have given me some firsthand knowledge of Dripping Springs around the turn of the century.

This whole thing has been like putting a large jigsaw puzzle together without having a definite, clear picture to go by. Slowly but surely the pieces began falling into place and the picture became much clearer. History has always been a fascinating subject to me and I really did enjoy working on this. I was like the child just starting to school. It was so exciting to learn new pieces to the puzzle, even though I might later find out that someone already knew what was a new discovery for me. It continually amazed me to find out how little I did know about this area even though I had lived here since 1965. So I hope the natives, as well as relative newcomers get as much enjoyment out of finding out about the history of Dripping Springs and the P. A. Smith survey (as best I can tell) as I did in gathering it.

Part One

—Photo by Mark Myers

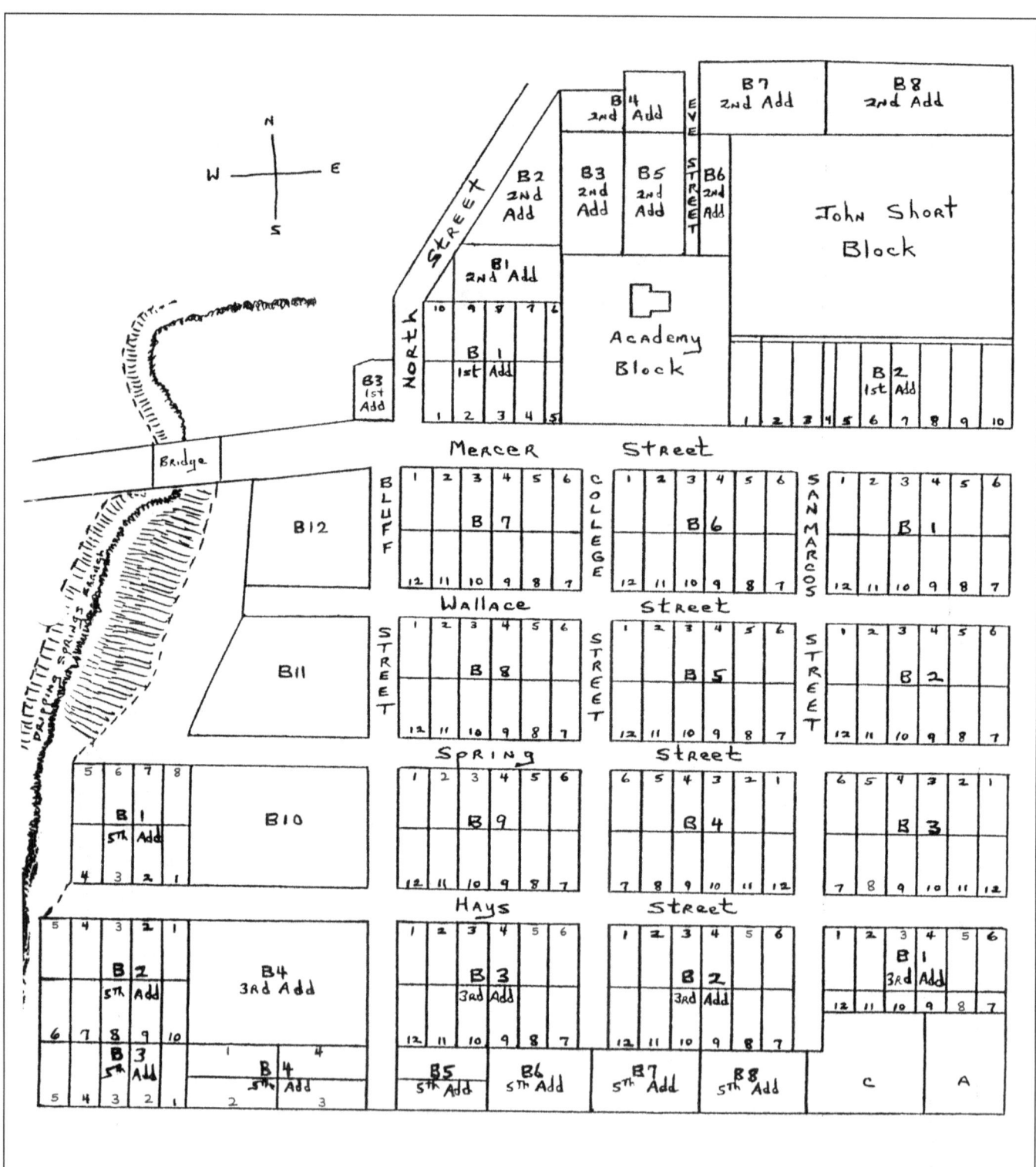

The Beginnings

Stephen F. Austin, known as the "Father of Texas," got the ball rolling with three hundred, while Dripping Springs would make do with three. In 1821 Austin received a charter from the Mexican government that allowed him to bring in 300 families to begin the white settlement of Texas. They became known as the "Old Three Hundred." Thirty-two years later and eight years after Texas became the 28th state of the United States, Dripping Springs would have a more modest beginning with its "Old Three." In late 1853 and early 1854, three families bound by kinship and friendship would make their way to this area from Mississippi to put down their roots. Even though it was located less than thirty miles west of the state capital of Austin, it was still a bold move because the area was still considered a part of the Texas frontier. A line of forts had been established in the late '40s and early '50s that included sites at Fredericksburg and Burnet. Still, Indians roamed the area to provide a menace and danger, plus the difficulty of travel left most families isolated.

The Dripping Springs area was included in an eleven-league land grant in 1826 to empresario Benjamin R. Milam. This contract, like all other empresario contracts, was terminated by the April 6, 1830, law. Texas gained its independence from Mexico in 1836 and became a republic until gaining statehood on December 29, 1845. Dripping Springs was a part of Travis County until Hays County was formed from part of Travis County on March 1, 1848.

Following their independence, Texas rewarded its citizens with grants of land. Those heads of families, known as headrights, who were in Texas prior to Texas gaining its independence received a league of land. Phillip A. Smith received a league of land by virtue of Certificate No. 56 issued by the Board of Land Commissioners of Jasper County on March 3, 1838. Evidently Mr. Smith did not or could not collect on his grant. According to records at the Texas Archives Genealogy division, there was a Phillip Smith from Sabine on the census of 1832 but no Phillip Smith showed up on the 1840 census. On April 27, 1850, the Phillip A. Smith league of land (4,428 acres), which encompasses Dripping Springs, was surveyed and assigned to George W. Glasscock by Governor P. H. Bell and attested by the Commissioner of the General Land Office, George W. Smith. Mr. Glasscock got involved with a lot of land around the Central Texas area. In fact, Georgetown, Texas, was named after him. Anyway, Fielding S. Roy bought

the league of land from Glasscock on September 19, 1853. It did not take Mr. Roy long to start selling off his league. Dr. W. H. Howard bought the southern half of the league on October 3, 1853. Willis Fawcett would buy the northeast quarter of the league on November 13, 1853.

Records appear to indicate that Mr. Fawcett was one of the earliest settlers of the general area, living somewhere along or near Barton Creek but not in the P. A. Smith survey. Research done by several members of the 1999 DSHS freshman class revealed that Mr. Fawcett would later move to Blanco County and marry into the Johnson family that later had Lyndon B. Johnson in it. He bought the quarter league on the same day the Pounds were married in Mississippi and some months later would sell it to the Pounds and Wallaces. For the P. A. Smith league and Dripping Springs, the families of Dr. Joseph McKegg Pound, John Lee Wallace, and John Lauter Moss would be the ones to give it prominence. The bulk of the history centers around the Pound family due to their many years of leadership in the community, the survival of a part of the original home and the large number of direct descendants in the area who had the foresight to preserve the historical value of the Pound artifacts. However, after this research began, it was discovered there was much more about the Wallace family than had earlier been thought as relatives outside the general area had been involved in doing research that helped enlighten the history of the Wallaces as well. The Mosses were a moving family and did not stay in the area very long.

As you might expect, there are many conflicting reports concerning the beginnings of these three families, even as to their correct names. One of the first is that they all came together. We do know that Carrie Wallace was born December 29, 1853. I assumed this meant she was born on the way to Texas, but a great-granddaughter, Mrs. Patricia Lawshe Barton, said that every census she had seen listed Carrie's birthplace as Kentucky and my research also proved the same thing. This meant that either Mr. Wallace came alone with the other two to find land or stayed with his wife and they came later when she was able to travel. After all, they had lost four children prior to Carrie's birth.

The general story is that the families came in the late fall of 1853. It is known the Pounds were married in Hinds County, Mississippi, on November 13, 1853. Another document on the same page with the marriage license was a contract with the governor's office that was dated November 26, 1853. The distance from Hinds County, which is the site of the state capital, Jackson, to Dripping Springs, following the Old San Antonio Road, is approximately 610 miles. Averaging fifteen miles a day by wagon would mean a good forty days to get here, maybe more. Of course taking the water route, which was much more expensive, could have cut some days off that. John Moss bought the northwest quarter of the P. A. Smith survey from Mr. Roy on January 23, 1854. Dr. Pound bought his first property near Henly, the Jesse Massey survey, one day later on January 24, 1854. In all probability, John Wallace bought his acreage in June of 1854. When Dr. Pound finally bought his 700 acres from Mr. Fawcett on December 21, 1854, it stated in the deed of trust that the property to the south was already sold to Mr. Wallace.

It has been generally circulated that the Pound house was built in 1853. Given the fact that the property it was erected on was not even purchased until late December of 1854, this is unlikely. They would have to hustle to build it in the last ten days of 1854. Of course, it could have already been there. An archeologist told me that usually one cures the logs used in the buildings for one year. The exact date confusion of coming here and the house certainly does not change the history of Dripping Springs. When you are talking nearly one hundred and fifty years, a few months difference does not seem that significant to me.

John Lee Wallace
—Courtesy Patricia Barton

Malvina Wallace
—Courtesy Patricia Barton

Mr. Wallace, a nephew of the Confederate general, Robert E. Lee, is referred to in some of the writings as Robert Lee Wallace. His real name is John Lee Wallace. He is indeed kin to Lee and the Lee signifies the family link to the Lee family of Virginia. It is probable that someone thinking of the connection to Robert E. Lee was not careful and inadvertantly transposed the name Robert for John, and others not knowing just followed suit without researching to make sure. Likewise, Mr. Moss has been referred to as Joe in several articles I have read. Joe was the name of his son.

Joseph McKegg Pound was born on October 26, 1826, in Jefferson County, Kentucky. He was one of eleven children in the family of Jonathan and Mary Risley Pound. At the age of nineteen, he enlisted in the army to fight in the U.S.–Mexico War. He served under General Zachary Taylor and had his first physical contact with Texas in 1846 when he marched from Corpus Christi and fought in the Battle of Palo Alto near Brownsville and later Buena Vista.

After the war, he returned to Kentucky where he enrolled in the school of medicine at the University of Louisville. It was one of the more progressive medical schools of its time. After receiving his medical education, he ended up in Mississippi where he met and married Sarah Dunbiben Ward on November 13, 1853. It was thought by colleagues that Dr. Pound was suffering from tuberculosis. The usual recommendation for this was to move to a drier climate. During 1851-52, according to his great-grandson, Charles Hammack, he went on a journey to the western states. He followed the Oregon Trail until he reached Utah and then veered into Wyoming where he met the famous frontiersman, Jim Bridger. Mr. Hammack did not believe this trip cured his tuberculosis and he had to consider drier climates. Whether for this reason or just a pioneering spirit, the newlyweds joined the families of

Sarah Pound
—Courtesy Marjorie Owens

Dr. Joseph M. Pound
—Courtesy Marjorie Owens

John Lee Wallace and John L. Moss on an excursion that ended up in Texas and the rest, as we say, is history.

No one really knows for sure what brought this group of families to this part of Texas. The reasons are always as varied as the people who made the decision. Perhaps there was kin in the area. Or maybe they had read advertisements about the area. In talking to another great-granddaughter, Mrs. Mary Louise Patton Labenski, she recalled asking her mother, when she was young, why the Wallaces came to Texas. Her mother replied "that Mr. Wallace liked the horses too much." This could have indicated that he may have run up a debt from betting and needed to get away or it was a great opportunity to raise and trade or sell horses, which was a thriving business in the area. Another possibility was the fact they had lost four of their children in Kentucky and wanted a change of scenery. It is always only speculation why anyone would leave what would look like a comfortable situation to try the unknown.

It is quite easy, if you have taken the time to drive through the area that has not been changed by urbanization, to realize why they would want to settle in this area. You can start with the beauty of the streams and the countryside. What the pioneers wanted along with that were the necessities of life. They needed water, building materials, and a source of food. All of those were available. Even though the land was not the best for making a living from it, the early days were of a subsistent nature and there was enough arable land to generate this without much problem. Also the wild game of the area provided another good food source.

Most certainly, the climate and the Hill Country must have agreed with the Pounds. Their marriage lasted 61 years and produced nine children. From these offspring there are still many descendants living in and around

the area. Dr. Pound died in 1914 and his wife, Sarah, in 1915. They, along with most of their children, are buried in the Wallace Mountain Cemetery.

John Lee Wallace, a nephew of the Confederate general, Robert E. Lee, and his wife, Malvina Louise, came from Kentucky, where they were good friends with the Pounds and Mosses. John was born on March 23, 1821, and Malvina Louise Gillespie on December 14, 1823. They were married June 28, 1842, by the Reverend Nathan L. Rice. John was the second of nine children born to Samuel McDowell Wallace and Matilda A. Lee Wallace. Matilda, his third wife (the other two had died), descended from the famous Lee family of Virginia. In particular, Henry "Light Horse" Harry Lee, the father of Robert E. Lee. John's grandfather was Judge Caleb Wallace of Woodford County, Kentucky. He was married to Rosanna Christian. He was a prominent Appeals Court judge, as well as a Presbyterian minister. He helped found Hampden-Sidney College, Transylvania University and Washington College, now Washington and Lee University, prior to his death in 1814. Malvina's parents were G. E. and Louise F. Gillespie of Kentucky.

According to Mrs. Barton, there was a general migration of Wallace kin to Texas and more specifically to the Central Texas area. John's niece, Mary Frances Wallace, a daughter of a half-brother, married the Reverend J. H. Zivley who helped to reorganize the Presbyterian church in San Marcos in 1854, according to Dobie's history of Hays County. John's sister, Cornelia, married Samuel Redd and lived near Austin. A nephew, Charles Harvey Wallace married Sally Schaefer of Texas and lived around the Cypress Mills area. Another brother, Thomas Henry Wallace, married a Miss Redd of Woodford County, Kentucky, and moved to Texas, too.

In all probability, the Wallaces came to the Hill Country a few months after their friends. Courthouse records indicate the deed to the Wallace's 377½ acres purchased from Willis Fawcett for $255 was recorded on June 28, 1855. A deed of trust recorded December 21, 1854, for Dr. Pound's purchase of 700 acres indicates that this was the final portion of Fawcett's quarter league with Wallace owning the land to his south. The recorded deed for Dr. Pound was done in December of 1855. What this tells me is that the distance to the County seat, San Marcos, delayed taking deeds to be recorded and they probably did not bother to record the deeds until they were actually paid for. My guess is it took the Wallaces about a year to pay for the land, thus they probably bought it around June 1854. So far I have not turned up a deed of trust for the Wallace land, only the recorded deed date.

It has been reported that during his stay in Texas as commander of a U.S. cavalry regiment between the years of 1855-61, Robert E. Lee visited relatives in the area, including the Wallaces. There is known to be one family with the surname of Lee who lived in the Cherry Springs area just southwest of Dripping Springs and there were probably more.

It must have been something in the water because the Wallaces enjoyed marital bliss for more than a half century too. The Wallaces had eleven children. As reported before, four died before they made the trip to Texas. Carrie was born in Kentucky and the other six were born in Texas. One son died in infancy. Mr. Wallace died February 27, 1893, and his wife on January 19, 1912.

At one time the Wallaces ran a stagecoach stop at their place. A reconstructed rock corral is a reminder of those days. Until I started this work, the story was that Mr. Wallace was a Dripping Springs postmaster before the Civil War and because he fought in the war, could not continue the job after the war. An official list of Dripping Springs U.S. postmasters does not include Mr. Wallace. According to this list, when Texas became a member of the Confederacy, Mr. Wallace was appointed as the Dripping Springs postmaster on July 12, 1861, and served in that capacity during the war. He was the postmaster for the Confederate States of America, not the United States. When the CSA was no more, neither was his job as postmaster. His affiliation with CSA negated any chance that he could be appointed a U.S. postmaster. That cleared up another mystery for his great-granddaughter, Patricia Barton. She had wondered why Mrs. Wallace had been turned down for a Confederate veteran's pension when she applied.

Another mystery that was cleared up for me by Katherine Cannon concerned the Wallace family cemetery plot. It is located a hundred yards south of their home midway up Wallace mountain on the south side of Highway 290. Today the fenced family plot contains the graves of Mr. Wallace, his infant son John, and daughter Mattie. My question was, "Why not the wife and mother, Malvina?" Mrs. Cannon gave me information that showed Mrs. Wallace was buried in the San Marcos Cemetery along with her oldest daughter, Carrie, and her husband and two of their children. Mrs. Wallace lived in the old homestead for six years after her husband's death before selling it in 1899. At that point, she lived with her children, moving from time to time. She evidently lived with the Voights in her final days. The Voights had moved to San Marcos in 1893 and Mr. Voight died in 1902. It would be my guess, that in those days of transportation, it was much easier to have Mrs. Wallace buried in the Voight family plot than transport her back to Dripping Springs for burial.

Another thing is Wallace Mountain, one of the highest points around Dripping Springs. I just assumed it was a part of the Wallace 377 acres until studying the deeds. The summit where the Wallace Mountain Cemetery is located was not a part of his property. Certainly he owned enough of it for the name to be appropo.

The site of the Wallace home is located on the north side of Highway 290 about a third of the way down the mountain. The house was destroyed by fire on August 7, 1953. All that remains is the rock rubble of the home and several buildings plus the restored rock corral where stagecoach horses were once penned. Dennis and Katherine Cannon now own this land.

Although one of the original three, the John Moss family would not stay around long but would leave a permanent mark on the area. Mr. Moss was the first of the three to purchase land in the P. A. Smith survey. He bought the northwest quarter (1,107 acres) from Fielding S. Roy on January 23, 1854, for $1,350 that included land on both sides of the Dripping Springs branch. No one I have talked to were quite sure as to the location of their home but some believe it to be northwest of the present Intermediate school campus. By 1860, the Moss family had left Dripping Springs. He was still on the 1860 Hays County tax roll with 1,107 acres but not on the poll tax list. Mr. Moss had become a nonresident owner and had already moved to the Round Mountain area in Blanco County. They would sell their Dripping Springs property to Phillip H. Raiford on May 1, 1860, for $3,000, which should indicate improvements having been made.

Army records indicate that at the age of 44, John Moss enlisted in the Confederate army on May 1, 1863, and joined Captain Lewis Maverick's Company of Texas, this being in Blanco County. Later it was reported they moved to Arizona and even later, according to the great-granddaughter of Dr. Pound, Mrs. Marjorie Owens, they moved to Alpine, Texas, where both are buried. Mrs. Owens said the two families kept in touch throughout the years and she believes the Mosses only had one son, Joseph, who never married. He was 17 when he joined the Confederate army in 1863.

The Moss history, like the Wallace history, is why I am glad that I did not hurriedly finish my book. If so, the history would once again be distorted. Thanks to Rebeccah Haralson, a freshman in the class of 2000, and her grandmother, Ethel Spillar, the Moss history was brought up to date and changed what we had believed to be true. She took on the Moss history as a project in her English class and her research was thorough and invaluable for correcting past assumptions. It allowed me to correspond with a grandson, Mr. Gloyd Moss, who lives in Alpine. He, in turn, gave me the address of a great-grandson, Dr. Robert Kokernot, of San Antonio. He was able to really fill in some major voids of what had happened to the Moss family after they left Dripping Springs.

Indeed, Mrs. Moss and son, Joseph, ended up in Alpine, where they are both buried. Instead of Arizona, the Moss family ended up in Ozona, Texas. Information given by Dr. Kokernot, shows that the Mosses had a penchant for moving. We know that they left Dripping Springs and moved into Blanco County in 1860. Dr. Kokernot said the 1870 census has John, Indiana, and Joseph (24) living in Bosque County, in and around Meridian, Texas, near where John's brother lived. From there they moved to Crockett County with Ozona as the county seat, but actually lived in that part of the county that would become Schleicher County with El Dorado as the county seat. A book on the history of Schleicher County published in 1930 related a story of Mr. Moss drilling a water well during the winter of 1882-83. Dr. Kokernot has sworn statements signed by Mrs. M. L. Wallace and Sarah D. Pound on November 21, 1911, attesting that Mr. Moss died in 1883 in what was Crockett County at the time. No doubt, he is probably buried in Schleicher County.

Another thing we can be grateful for from Dr. Kokernot is what the initial L. stood for in John Moss's name. At no time could I find any material that gave me the middle name. It always read John L. Moss. Dr. Kokernot is one of those individuals researchers are always looking for. He had the presence of mind to take notes when he was interviewing an aunt before she died. In looking back through his collected material on the family to help me, he discovered the initial stood for Lauter. Not being a common name, one would believe it was a family name.

Joseph Moss married at the age of 46 and raised a large family, so there are living descendants of all three original families of the P. A. Smith survey. Mrs. Owens had a letter written from Joseph to Dr. Pound shortly after Mrs. Moss's death in 1911, to verify that he was the only heir to the Moss estate. This seemed to indicate that Joseph was not married—in reality it only meant that he was the only child of the marriage and he wanted to have his claim to his mother's property upheld. He was 65 at the time and had a family. He died in 1920.

It was John's wife, Indiana (Nannie), who would leave the lasting imprint of the Moss family on Dripping Springs. Nannie was Sarah Pound's sister and this might have been how the Pounds ended up here. Nevertheless, it was Nannie Moss who is given credit for selecting the name Dripping Springs. A name became a necessity when a

A young Joseph Moss
—Courtesy Robert Kokernot

Joseph Moss
—Courtesy Robert Kokernot

Indiana "Nannie" Moss
—Courtesy Robert Kokernot

post office was set up and John was named the first postmaster of Dripping Springs on June 5, 1857.

There are those who claim the site had already been designated as Dripping Springs on early maps and she may have already known this. This would not be unusual for mapmakers to identify certain natural features for better accuracy of their maps. Others claim the many springs in the area and especially the slowly dripping ones off the limestone ledges at the head of what would become the Dripping Springs branch made her choice a natural. Certainly, it was more poetic and distinctive than say Mossville, Pound City, or Wallaceburg.

Studying the tax rolls brings up some interesting facts about the three families which puts all three in the slave-owning category. The first tax roll that has the three on it is the 1855 one. Usually these tax rolls were completed around May to September, so I'm not sure how this affected the three who had bought land in 1854, or what constituted the 1855 tax year. Willis Fawcett was the only one listed in the 1854 tax roll.

John Moss definitely had the higher tax value with a total of $11,165. He would have the 1,107 acres valued at $3,330, eleven Negroes valued at $8,000, five horses at $100, two wagons, etc., at $450, but oddly enough, no cattle. By the time they left Dripping Springs in 1860 the acreage value had dropped to $1,500 and their eleven Negroes had dropped in value to $7,700. They had three horses at $325, 75 head of cattle at $450, plus hogs, corn, and buggy valued at $600, for a total of $10,475. They would sell their land to the Raifords for $3,000. The Raiford's 1861 tax roll included four Negroes, six horses, 50 head of cattle, and 451 head of sheep. It's possible they may have obtained some of this from the Moss's.

Joseph Pound's first rendering for 1855 included his 700 acres $900, one Negro,

$500, one horse, $50, 16 cattle, $80, a wagon, $100, for a total of $1630. By 1862 the Pound's had acquired three Negroes, had 24 horses, 25 cattle. He had sold off 300 acres.

John Wallace's 377 acres were valued at $750. He had two Negroes, $1000, three horses, $140, and a wagon and team, $210, for a total of $2100. By 1866 the land value had dropped to $565 but he had added 40 horses, $800, 50 cattle, $200, 30 sheep, $22 and miscellaneous, $100, for a total of $1,657.

There is one other family that might need to be considered. We know that Dr. William H. Howard purchased the southern half of the P. A. Smith survey in October 1853. I have no proof that he moved onto this property at this time. The only proof that he lived here was in a recollection by one of the Marshall boys who recalled the families of Dr. Pound, John Wallace, and Dr. Howard lived within two miles of his family's house when they moved to Dripping Springs in 1870. Dr. Howard would sell, what I believe to be their homestead, in 1874. Deeds gave his name as the seller until 1878 as he sold off more of his acreage, but by 1881 the remainder of his land was being sold by his heirs. Someone else may have the complete story on the Howard family. There were other Howards in the history of Dripping Springs but I'm not sure if any were kin down the line.

McCuistion Drugstore. L-R: Anna Crenshaw (married Frank Sansom), Dora P. Crenshaw (married Bruce B. Mading), William Hill Crenshaw (owner of drugstore), Dr. Berkley, Dave Wesley Crenshaw, Webb Hudson, Caudential Waite Crenshaw. On the left in the background is the blacksmith shop.

—Courtesy George Bruce Mading

Genealogy

When I first arrived in Dripping Springs in the fall of 1965, one of the first pieces of advice I received, in what I thought was a joking manner, was "Don't talk about anyone here to someone else because they are probably kin to each other." Well, I came from a small town and that seemed to be a standard joke there too, so I really did not think about that advice all that much. After starting this project, I realized the advice was truly a fact. Until the 1970s when the influx of immigrants really began to take over, it is amazing how many families were actually kin somewhere down the line. The major reason lies with the need for large families to carry on the business of farming and other businesses before the advent of machinery. You couple this with the small community and intermarriage of families was a natural. Some of the families that have been around for a century or more include the surname of Pound, Wallace, Crow, Glosson, Garnett, Shelton, Spaw, Roberts, Davis, Robbins, Norwood, Sorrell, Stephenson, Harmon, and many others we will try to explore in the following pages. This in no way will be a complete list. I did not go to any extremes trying to trace down the family trees, only repeating what my research gave me but it should be enough for you to get the idea of how the intermixing took place. Also it will help to familiarize you with names that you will see mentioned in various ways throughout this book. Many of the names were obtained from deeds, obituaries, and newspapers that I researched, therefore the spelling might not be correct and I will not have all the dates of birth and death. Again, it will give a starting place for researching a family tree.

First of all, I thought a study of the Hays County census taken for the years from 1860 through 1920 might be interesting. The 1890 census records were destroyed by a fire. The names on the census were just those that were a part of the P. A. Smith survey at one time or another. These census lists are no doubt incomplete and the spelling might be incorrect because reading the writing on the sheets was not a walk in the park in many instances.

1860 Census (Taken in June)

Moss, John L., 40 (farmer), Georgia; Indiana, 30, Mississippi; Joseph, 14, Mississippi.

Pound, Joseph M., 34 (farmer), Kentucky; Sarah, 27, Mississippi; Indiana, 5, Texas; Mary, 4, Texas; Olive, 2, Texas.

Wallace, John L., 38 (farmer), Kentucky; Malvina, 34, Kentucky; Carrie, 6, Kentucky; William, 3, Texas; Edwin, 1, Texas.

1870 Census (Taken in August)

Collins, Stacy 46; Allia, 44 (keeping house); Eli Harvey, 21; Herman F., 19 (farm laborer); Warren J., 17 (farm laborer); Richard M., 15.

Davis, Francis N., 30 (farmer), New Jersey; Artellia, 28, New Jersey; Charles, 7, New Jersey; Isaac, 1.

Davis, Kate, 15 (student).

Gibson, Bleu M., 32 (farmer); Martha, 27 (keeping house; James, 7; Daniel M., 5; Calvin, 3; Mark, 1.

Lienneweber, Pedernales, 14.

Marshall, Burrell J., 44 (farmer), Alabama; Martha, 35; George W., 12; Jefferson D., 10; Jasper N., 7; Robert L., 5; Francis, 1.

McKellar, Hector, 55 (merchant), North Carolina.

McKellar, Sock, 50 (farmer), North Carolina; Anna M., 40 (keeping house); Walter, 12 (at home); Henrietta, 10 (at home); Anna, 8 (at home); Mary, 4 (at home).

McLendon, B. H., 38 (farm laborer), Louisiana; Mahala, 32 (keeping house); Martha J., 10 (at home); Elizabeth, 9 (at home); Thomas H., 8 (at home); S.W., 6 (at home); William S., 5 (at home).

McLendon, Jesse, 67 (farmer), North Carolina; Jane, 40, London, England; Charles Seal, 7.

Moore, Lorenzo, 49 (farmer), Illinois; Mary, 48, New Jersey; Eli F., 14 (stockhand); Sarah A., 12, Mary M., 10; George B., 8; Polly, 83.

Pound, Joseph M., 44 (physician); Sarah, 38 (keeping house); Mary B., 14 (attending school); Mittie V., 10 (at home); Louisianna, 7 (at home); Charles, 3 (at home); Georgia, 1 (at home).

Pounds, Adelia, 15 (student).

Riley, E. J. 35; Martha J., 33; Otmanda, 12 (attending school); Willis P., 9 (at home); William E., 5 (at home); Celita, 3, John F., 1.

Riley, Nancy, 61 (keeping house).

Roy, Fielding S., 50 (stonemason); Jane, 40; John, 21 (stock dealer); William, 18 (stock dealer); Albert, 17 (stonemason); Charles, 15 (farm laborer); Henry, 12 (farm laborer); Mary, 11 (attending school); Josephine, 9 (attending school); Francis, 8 (attending school); Martha, 5; Rufus, 3.

Voight, Thomas, 25 (carpenter), Mississippi.

Wallace, John L., 49 (farmer); Malvina L., 45 (keeping house); Carrie, 16 (teaching school); William, 14 (at home); Edward, 11 (at home); Andrew, 9 (at home); Mattie, 7 (at home); Charles, 4 (at home).

1880 Census

Chapman, W. T., 45 (farmer and grocery sales); Martha, 45; Willie, 6; Mercer, 1; Jeff Marshall, 19, stepson (farmer); Ben Marshall, 18, stepson; Levi Marshall, 16, stepson; Fanny Marshall, 10, stepdaughter; Dooley Chapman, 17, half-brother (farmer); Bettie Chapman, 14, half-sister; Henry Pearcy, 57 (clerk in the store).

Collins, Newton, 50; Elizabeth, 38; Martha, 14; Sarah, 10; Mary, 8; Lydia, 4; Virginia, 2.

Collins, Theron, 28; Martha, 26; Lora, 3; Greg, 2; Stacy Collins, 55, father.

Collins, Warren, 26; Jane M. (Riley), 40 (wife); Celita Riley, 13; Nellie Riley, 8; Nora Riley, 5; Willis P. Riley, 15; John Daniel, 22, brother-in-law (school teacher); Minerva Daniel, 65, mother-in-law; William Daniel, 19, brother-in-law (cowboy).

Cook, Wesley C., 43 (farmer); Tulia, 35; James, 17.

Daniels, Aaron K., 29; Missouri R., 27; Alva P., 1; John Riley, 10, nephew.

Davis, Albert Lawson, 55; Nancy Jane, 37; Jeff, 21 (cowboy); A. L. Jr., 18; Addison, 12.

Dye, Albin, 50; Priscilla (wife); Logan, 17; James, 10; Mary E., 1.

Fairchild, Jackson, 31; Mary, 28; Sarah, 13; Nancy, 11; Samuel, 8; William, 6; Katie, 2; Nancy Riley, 72, grandmother.

Gibson, Bleu, 42; Martha, 38; James, 18; Daniel, 15; Calvin, 13; Mark, 11; Effie, 6; Andrew, 4; Blue, 2; Isabella, 1.

Gibson, Richard, 48; Lucy, 46; Sarah, 13; Mitchell, 10; Sanford, 8; John, 7.

Lienneweber, Pedernales, 24 (blacksmith).

McLendon, Isaac, C.P., 42; Sallie, 36; Bessie, 10; Birdie, 8; William S., 3.

McLendon, Jesse, 77; Jane, 45; Charles Seal, 17.

Needham, James, 35; Carsolona, 27; James M., 14; Nancy A., 12; Rebecca E., 5; Francis, 8; William, 6; Millie S., 2.

Norwood, William, 33; Ellen, 23; Emma, 6; Kate, 4; Rosa, 1.

Phillips, John W., 50; Nancy, 42; John W., 17; Sarah, 16; Lucy, 14; Hattie, 11; Soloman, 7; Thomas, 5; Minnie, 2.

Pound, Joseph M., 53; Sarah, 45; Mary, 22; Minnie, 18; Louisianna, 15; Charles, 13; Georgia, 9; Lavonia, 7.

Riley, William, 16, boarder with Dooley Chapman and Jeff Marshall.

Roberts, Jacob, 45; Brazoria, 42; Frank, 18; Ida, 13; Maud, 10; Stella, 8; Katie, 1.

Rowe, James C., 38, blacksmith; Mary, 36; James E., 16; Alice, 9; Mathilda, 6; Alzada 3.

Rowland, James, 32; Mattie, 20; William, 3; Leila, 1.

Sampson, Edwin, 34; Roksie, 27; Lura, 10; Emmitt, 6; Simpson, 4; Ina, 2.

Sorrell, Fountain, 27 (farmer); Sallie S., 23; Flora F., 5; Gillis, 3; John, 1.

Sorrell, A. Melvina, 50; Lee, 16 (going to school); Oliver, 12; Mattie, 7; Laura Bailey, 16, niece.

Sorrell, Nancy Rebeccah, 33; Eddie, 10; William, 8; James, 6; George, 4; Lizzie, 1.

Spaw, Beverly L., 43; Sisrelda, 41; William, 14; John, 12; Robert, 9; Lula, 4; Louissa, 1; William Hobdy, 77, boarder.

Stephenson, Ben, 28; Nanny, 24; Frank, 6; Carrie, 4; Joseph, 3, Nettie, 1.

Voight, Thomas, 32; Carrie, 26; Wallace, 6; Louis, 4.

Wallace, John L., 59; Malvina, 55; William, 23; Andrew, 18; Mattie, 17; Charles, 14.

Womack, Ed, 62; Virginia, 43; Ella, 20; Thomas, 18; Louissa, 15; Daniel, 13; Achilles, 10.

Womack, George, 22; Susie L., 21; Robert, 1.

1900 Census

Adams, Sam W., 43 (farmer); Mary, 59 (wife); Tandy, 20; Wm. C. Stewart, 37 (boarder/dentist).

Banks, William H., 50 (farmer); Nancy R. (Sorrell), 62 (wife); John T., 18; Dilla M., 14; Miles H., 14; Fred A., 12; James Sorrell, 26 (stepson).

Cavett, Moses C., 67 (farmer); Annie L., 27; Richard M., 25 (teacher); Moses S., 22; Dove J., 19 (teacher); Maye E., 15; Oma A., 10.

Cavett, Thomas, 29; Flora, 25 (wife); Dewitt, 3.

Chapman, W. T., 65 (merchant); Martha, 65; R. L. Marshall, 34; Fannie M. Burkett, 30 (widow); Willie P. Chapman, 26; Mercer Chapman, 21 (general store salesman); Mabel W. Burkett, 7 (granddaughter)

Collenbach, C. M., 34 (rock mason); Alma, 32 (wife); Lizzie R., 11; Francis P., 8; Ottie May, 1.

Crow, MacCreary, 27; Stella, 26 (wife); Paul M., 6; Louella, 4; Bessie, 3.

Daniel, Aaron K., 49; Missouri, 47 (wife); Iva J., 20 (teacher); Elva D., 18 (music teacher); Willie L., 13; Ira E., 12; Frank, 10.

Darroh, David, 54 (farmer); Mattie E., 50 (wife); Nannie B., 23 (teacher); Maggie E., 21; Ella L., 18; Lula M., 14; Lorie R., 17; Ethel, 15; Fannie, 12; George R., 8.

Davis, A. L., 38 (merchant); Willie H., 34 (wife); Ethel M., 13; Hallie E., 8; Howard H., 5; William Sherman, 2.

Davis, I.V., 32 (cattle raiser); Katie May, 29; Lanier K., 7; Howard T,. 4; Walton J., 3; I.V., 1.

DeLaune, R. J., 28 (son/farmer); Linda

DeLaune, 50 (mother); Annie R., 18 (sister); Myrtle L., 13 (sister).

Dye, Alton, 71; Priscilla, 46 (wife); Mary, 20; Cordella, 12; Lucy, 10.

Dye, William L., 36 (rock mason); Rushie R., 26 (wife); James E., 8; Lester, 4; Hobson, 2; Armour, 9 mos.

Evert, Ann, 62.

Gibson, John, 26 (son/farmer); Lucy, 66 (mother).

Glosson, James, 62 (farmer); Susan, 59 (wife); Thomas J., 28; Agatha, 22; Solon B., 19.

Graham, Hiram, 32 (minister); Weltha, 32 (wife); Walter J., 7; John M., 5; Ethel, 3.

Hudson, W. P., 48; Melvina R., 45 (wife); Asbury, 21; Wm. M., 18; Mary B., 11; Webster R., 7.

Hughes, David, 45 (merchant grocer); Margaret, 38 (wife/sales lady); Sadie Mary, 19; Jessie B., 17; Annie, 15; Lora E., 11; James T., 8; Emma, 5; Nellie D., 2.

Jones, Dave G., 38 (grocer); Maud, 29 (wife); Wharton R., 3; Joe S., 2; Frand, 5 mos.

Kirk, Frank M., 41 (farmer); Mary E., 42 (wife); Annie B., 15; Buford H., 12; Albert F., 8.

Lienneweber, Pedernales, 43 (blacksmith); George, 20; Thomas D., 17; Basheba, 16; Elizabeth, 14; Lydia M., 9; Ethel M., 1.

Martin, William, 55; Mary Robbins Martin, 47 (wife); Thomas Robbins, 18; Webster Robbins, 17; Jennie Robbins, 15; Louisa Robbins, 14; Daisy Robbins, 13; Minerva Robbins, 11; Pearl Robbins, 10; Wallace W. Robbins, 7.

Mayne, William R., 48 (farmer); Sallie S., 39 (wife); Delta, 19; Lou E., 18; Thurman, 16; Grover C., 14; Willie E., 11; Clyde R., 9; George T. Roberts, 21 (boarder).

McCuistion, George, 41 (druggist); Joe E., 32 (wife); Emma R., 14.

McKellar, Walter P., 41 (ginner); Florence, 36 (wife); Edward J., 16; Annie Lois, 15; Hallie B., 12; Walter M., 10; James Howard, 7.

McLendon, I.C.P., 63 (farmer); Jacob L. Riley, 50 (boarder).

McLendon, Sallie, 56 (mother/music teacher); William S., 23 (son).

Moore, Hiram, 35 (farmer); Maggie, 29 (wife).

Norwood, William, 52 (farmer); Ellen, 43 (wife); Kate B., 26; Samuel J., 18; Minnie E., 15; Malvina, 13; William D., 6.

Phillips, John W., 70 (farmer); Nancy, 62 (wife); Soloman A., 27; Etta Lyle, 18; Van W. Clark, 26 (son-in-law); Minnie L., 21; Beatrice, 1 (granddaughter).

Pound, Joseph M., 73 (physician); Sarah D., 60 (wife); Mary E. Pound Walters; 40 (widow), Charles W., 30; Lovonia, 24; Georgia Cavett, 27; Marguerite Cavett, 5 (granddaughter); Mittie L. Walters, 12 (granddaughter).

Puckett, Joseph, 56 (farmer); Mary L., 46 (wife); Edward E., 20; Joseph A., 14.

Raines, R. H., 59 (blacksmith); Elizabeth, 54 (wife); Russell R., 26; Robert E., 15; Roy F., 13; Renard T., 10; Milton Lloyd, 17 (nephew); Ollie M. Lloyd, 15 (niece); Ann Galloway, 60 (boarder).

Roberts, Jacob, 64; Brazoria, 61 (wife); Katie K., 20; Berta B., 16.

Roberts, Wm. P., 42; Alice, 40 (wife); Emery, 19; Hester, 14; Iva, 8; Wm. T., 4; Nellie May, 3; Unnamed daughter, 5 mos.

Rowland, James O., 52 (farmer); Mattie E., 40 (wife); Leila D., 21; Jesse W., 18; Annie F., 16; Charles J., 14; Ella B., 12; Marena A., 8; Albert D., 5; Willie May, 2.

Sansom, Thomas, 56 (farmer); Parlee M., 52 (wife); Robert R., 21; Frank L., 15.

Seal, Charles, 38 (farmer); Dilla M., 30 (wife); Pauline, 18; Oscar, 6; Edith W., 4; Jane, 69 (mother).

Shelton, E. P., 33 (physician); Lula, 24 (wife); John E., 6; Neva, 5; Robert H., 4; Ora May, 2; Maud, 2 mos.

Sorrell, Manor, 2.

Sorrell, Amanda, 71 (head); Jacob P., 41; Willie D., 16 (granddaughter); Madie M., 15 (granddaughter); Stella, 10 (granddaughter); Ruth, 5 (granddaughter).

Sorrell, Ollie, 33 (farmer); Sallie L., 30

(wife); Leslie B., 12; Clyde L., 6; Novella 1.

Spaw, Beverly L., 62 (farmer); Louisa, 55 (wife).

Spaw, John T., 32; Ella M., 28 (wife); Willie E., 11; George B., 10; Robert T., 7; John E., 5.

Spaw, Robert E., 29 (farmer); Ida M., 24 (wife); Eura May, 1; Davis S., 5 mos.

Stephenson, Ben, 50 (farmer); Nannie E., 45 (wife); Antoinette, 22; Keaugh, 19; Allen P., 12; Leta E., 10; Sidney P., 8.

Stephenson, Frank, 26 (farmer); Maggie, 26 (wife); Clayton R., 4.

Stephenson, James M., 23 (farmer); Sallie R., 23 (wife); Curtis B., 2.

Turner, Peter L., 24 (farmer); Annie, 22 (wife); Wade C., 4 mos.

Walker, Daniel, 39; Annie L., 41 (wife); Fred, 14; Thomas P., 13; Carr, 7; Otis, 6; Mach, 1; Tennie Roy, 19 (stepdaughter).

Walker, F. M., 61 (farmer); Martha, 59 (wife); Elon, 26; Mary A., 23; Ruth, 21; Gertie, 18; Nora M., 15.

Wilhite, B. R., 58 (farmer); Mary L., 55 (wife); Sam S., 21; William S., 25; Mary E., 16; Mabel G., 12; B. K., 19.

Wilhite, Thomas, 29 (farmer); Mollie L., 27 (wife); Claude, 2.

1910 Census

Applewhite, Alex, 49 (general store merchant); Lizzie, 37 (wife); Alex, 17; Lillian, 13; Clyde, 11; Mary, 9; Ruby Lee, 5.

Baird, William R., 43.

Breed, Carter, 28; Emma, 21 (wife); Cecil, 2; D. B., 11/12.

Chapman, Mercer, 31 (general store merchant); Berta, 26 (wife); ?? son, 7.

Chapman, W. T., 75; Martha, 75 (wife).

Cockrill, Will, 43; Della, 37 (wife).

Crenshaw, William H., 54 (druggist); Cecilia, 53 (wife); Waite, 19; David, 16.

Crow, McCreary, 37; Stella, 35 (wife); Paul, 16; Louise, 14; Bessie, 12; Allie, 9; William, 7; Maurine, 6.

Davis, I.V., 42 (rancher); Katie, 39 (wife); Lanier, 16 (teacher); Howard T., 15; J. Walton, 13; IV Jr., 11; Mae, 9; Lucille, 8; Bessie, 4; Elbert H., 3; Bradley 3/12.

Davis, Mrs. N. J., 87.

Fairly, Hugh J., 35; Lula, 25 (wife); Dan, 8; Wilson, 2.

Ferrell, Will, 35; Florence, 34 (wife); Lizzie, 15; James, 1.

Garnett, W. S., 39 (blacksmith); Emma, 36 (wife); Paul, 9; William, 7; Mary Lou, 5.

Gibson, John M., 32; Annie, 26 (wife); Richard, 4; Lonnie, 4; Wallace, $1^{10}/_{12}$.

Glosson, James W., 41; Mary, 40 (wife); Olivas, 17; S. B., 16; Paula?, 13; Solon, 11; Johnnie, 9; George, 2.

Glosson, Solon, 29; Lou, 25 (wife); Jimmy, 6; John, 3; Thelma, 1.

Glosson, Mrs. Susan, 69; Agatha, 33 (daughter).

Haydon, Charles, 21; Beulah, 18 (wife).

Horner, James A., 39; Minnie, 29 (wife); Wallace, 10; William E., $^7/_{12}$.

Hudson, Am??, 80; Lizzie, 27 (wife); Arlin, 10.

Hudson, William P., 57; Melvina (wife), 56; Webster 16.

Lawrence, Young L., 38; Kittie, 32 (wife); Melvina, $1^5/_{12}$.

Lyle, William R., 47; Sarah, 38 (wife); Robert, 16; Inthaberry, 14; Johnny, 12; Willie, 10; Roseia?, 8.

Malott, John W., 33; Ellie?, 35 (wife); Bessie?, 12; Wesley, 10; L.O., 5; Holly, 8; Millie & Mattie, 2.

McClendon, William S., 25 (telephone operator); Effie, 19 (wife); Erlene, 2; Mittie, 20 (telephone operator)

McMackin, William, 55; Leah, 50 (wife).

Norwood, William J., 61; Maria E., 53 (wife); Melvina, 21 (teacher); William, 14; Malvina Sorrell, 80 (mother-in-law)

Peal, Henry T., 50 (clergy); Amanda, 48 (wife); ??daughter, 18 (school teacher); ??daughter, 13; Hillie, 9.

Pound, Joseph, 83; Sarah, 75 (wife); Georgia Cavett, 45 (teacher); Marguerite Cavett, 16.

Puckett, Edward A., 29; Katie, 28 (wife); Albert, 5; M.T., 3; Mattie, 2.

Puckett, Joe A., 24; Mattie, 25 (wife)

15

Puckett, J. L., 66; Mary, 56 (wife).
Randerson, Fletcher, 63; Hattie, 38 (wife) (music teacher); Lucille, 17; Luther, 16; Robert, 12; William, 9; Catherine, 8; Hattie Irene, 3.
Robbins, Thomas, 28; Priscilla, 21 (wife).
Roberts, J. K., 75; Beatrice, 71 (wife).
Rowland, Charles, 24; Beulah, 20 (wife).
Rowland, James, 62; Mattie E., 50 (wife); Alice, 18; Albert, 15; Millie May, 12.
Sansom, Frank, 25; Anna, 26 (wife).
Sansom, Thomas, 66; Pauline, 62 (wife).
Seal, Charles, 48 (meat market butcher); Dilly M., 40 (wife); Garland, 16; Edith, 14; Charlie Mae, 8; Jane, 78 (mother).
Spaw, Beverly K., 72; Louisie, 64 (wife); Minnie, 54 (sister-in-law).
Spaw, Robert E., 39; Ida, 34 (wife); Cora M., 11; Beverly H., 7; Millburn C., 6; Robert L., 2.
Stephenson, Frank, 36; Maggie, 36 (wife); Robbin, 13; Ida, 8.
Stephenson, Mrs. Nannie, 55; Allen, 22; Leta, 20.
Stubbs, William A., 47; Annie, 35 (wife; music teacher); Virgil, 17; Wade H., 14.
Thurman, Henry G., 87; Edward Milam, 36 (son-in-law; mill griller); Ella, 38 (wife); Arnella, 9; Amanda, 8; Floyd, 7; Daniel?, 5; Ollie, 2; Amzie?, 1.
Turner, Peter L., 34; Annie, 33 (wife); Worth, 11; Wallace, 8; Mabel, 5.

Family Trees

JOSEPH MCKEGG POUND

Dr. and Mrs. Sarah Dunbiben Ward Pound had nine children after coming to Texas. It is through the offspring of these children that many of the Pound descendants still live in and around the Dripping Springs area.

(1) Indiana Adelia (b. 1-18-1855, d. 8-11-39) married Benjamin F. Stephenson (b. 2-17-1850, d. 3-10-1902) on 10-8-1872. They had ten children.
- Frank M. Stephenson (1-19-1874) married Maggie M. Robbins (1-4-1875) on 7-3-1895. They had a son and a daughter.
  - ❶ Clarence Robbins (Robin) (b. 9-12-1896) married Cordia Hancock and they had a son before she died in January 1933. He then married his wife's sister, Louise. They had two sons and a daughter.
  - ❷ Their daughter, Ida Adelia (b. 12-16-1900), married William Glosson.
- Carrie Mae Stephenson (b. 4-25-1875) married Daniel Watson (b. 11-16-1864) on 9-28-1893. Their first daughter, Mary Porter (b. 7-10-1894), lived only two days. A son, Robert Daniel Watson, was born 6-14-1896. The other three children were Indiana, Lleta Ruth, and Reaugh Landis.
- Joseph Moss Stephenson (b. 2-4-1877), married Sallie Robbins (b. 1-16-1877) on 12-9-1896. They had two children, son, Curtis Burton (b. 11-1-1897) and daughter, Verna May (b. 1-1-1900).
- Antoinette (Lanette) Stephenson (b. 12-4-1879) married Lon Perry (b. 5-16-1879) on 11-29-1900 and moved to Oklahoma.
- Reaugh Stephenson (b. 11-13-1881).
- Clarence Stephenson (b. 1-10-1883, d. 2-24-1890).
- Temple Taylor Stephenson (b. 12-28-1884, d. 12-8-1886) lived only two years.
- P. Allen Stephenson (b. 11-18-1887) married Hazel Bohl and they had two children. Allen Dixon was born in 1923 and died in 1938, the result of gangrene setting in from a broken leg received in a baseball game. The new high school built in 1939 was dedicated to his memory. The daughter was Dorothy Louise.
- Lleta Stephenson (b. 4-10-1890) married a Mr. Lewis.
- The Stephenson's final child, Sidney Pound (b. 3-15-1892) married Lillian (b. 11-3-1896).

(2) The Pound's second child was Mary Elizabeth (b. 3-20-1856), who married Samuel T. Walters on 12-17-1885. They had one daughter before the death of Mr. Walters on 1-6-1890. She took George Arthur Hunt as her second husband on 9-1-1901. Mary died on 10-1-1933 from cirrhosis of the liver. The Walters' daughter, Mittie Lou (b. 9-20-1886) married a fellow named Brackenridge and died in January 1915 from tuberculosis while staying in Silver City, New Mexico.

(3) Olive Allen Pound (b. 2-7-1858, d. 1861).

(4) Mittie Violet Pound (b. 12-12-1861, d. 1-1-1954) married Jake Sorrell and they moved

to Oklahoma. When Jake died from injuries when a tree fell on him, Mittie moved back to Dripping Springs. Her brother-in-law, Ollie Sorrell, lost his wife, and he and Mittie married and moved back to Oklahoma.

(5) Louisianna Pound (b. 12-4-1863, d. 3-25-1885) never married.

(6) Charles Ward (Bud) Pound (b. 9-4-1866, d. 5-3-1911) also never married.

(7) Georgia Virginia Pound (b. 10-15-1868, d. 2-3-1968) lived nearly one century. It was through this lineage that most of the Pound artifacts have been saved and handed down through the generations. She married Mose Columbus Cavett on 10-10-1890. Their only child, before divorcing, was daughter, Marguerite Ruperta (b. 1-21-1895, d. 8-26-1983). She married Charles Ross Hammack and they had three children: Marguerite, Charles, and Mittie.

- Marguerite (Marjorie) Virginia (b. 8-11-1921) married Clifton Cameron Owens. They had three children.
  ❶ Wanda June married Richard Mauldin and they have one son, ☆Charles Ross Thomas.
  ❷ Clifton Ross is unmarried.
  ❸ Wilma Ruth married Christopher Long. They have three children: ☆Zebulon Stephen, ☆Caleb Jonathan, and ☆Josiah Thaddaeus.
- Charles Joseph married Gladys Lorene Mann. They had three children.
  ❶ Charles Randall married Lenore Lawlor and they have one child, ☆Charles Matthew.
  ❷ Cynthia Lorain married Rodney William Tierman. They had no children. She then married Dr. Bernd L. Steinbach and this marriage produced three children: ☆Eric Charles, ☆Jan Joseph, and ☆Christina Lorain.
  ❸ Kelly Joseph married Linda Gay Bailey. They had four children: ☆Kelly Joseph II married Kelly Marie Ransom and they had one child, Carrie Nichole; ☆Daniel Zacharias; ☆Angela Marie, and ☆Aaron Kirk.
- Mittie Ruth married William Edward Simpson and they had four children.
  ❶ David William,
  ❷ Edward Charles married Bernice Amelia Martin and had two children: ☆Natasha Lana and ☆Israel. Edward then married Susan Trilo and had five children: ☆Dessie Renee, ☆Dannon Marguerite, ☆Joshua Charles, ☆Selah Marie, and ☆a little girl who lived only a few days.
  ❸ James Michael married Leslie Black.
  ❹ Franklin Matthew married Debbie Kae Parker.

(8) Lovonia Pound (b. 8-6-1870, d. 7-19-1944) married Ove Oldham, and they had one daughter, Sarah Edith, who never married.

(9) The Pound's last child, Jonathan Kester, was born in August of 1872, but only lived two months.

JOHN LEE WALLACE

The bulk of this genealogy was provided by research done by a great-granddaughter, Mrs. Patricia Barton of Salado, Texas. The Wallace's, John and Malvina, had four sons and two daughters survive infancy out of eleven births. The sons were mostly interested in the cattle industry and moved to the Blanco and Llano counties to follow that trade. A diary kept by Mrs. Wallace from 1889-92 revealed that much time was spent with members of the family coming and going and using the old homestead as a stopover on these trips.

Prior to coming to Texas, the Wallaces had four children who did not survive to make the trip to Texas. They were

(1) Lewis Lee (1843-1852)
(2) Emma Louise (1845-1848)
(3) Crittenden D. (1847-1848)
(4) Frank (1850-1851)
(5) Caroline Watkins (Carrie) Wallace (12-29-1853) was born in Kentucky. The rest were born in Texas. Carrie married Thomas Fielding Voight, who gave his occupation as carpenter in the 1870 census. He ran two separate gins during his stay in Dripping Springs. The couple had three children: Wallace, Louis, and Mattie.

They moved to San Marcos in 1893. Thomas, Carrie, her mother, Wallace, and Mattie are buried in the family plot in the San Marcos Cemetery. A marker on his grave indicates that Thomas served in the Civil War for the Confederacy from 1861-1865. Mattie Voight Winston died within a month of her mother at the age of 27 in 1913. Wallace was 57 when he died in 1931.

(6) A son William Crittenden (Will) Wallace (1856-1923) married Ida Roberts on 9-2-1878. They had eight children.
- Kitty (1879-1945) married Vollie Richardson and they had no children.
- Mallie (1880-1895).
- William Hayes (1882) married Elizabeth Mayes and they had two children.
  ❶ William M. married Pat and they had no children.
  ❷ Joe Thomas Wallace married Mary Faye Richardson and had three children. ☆Joe Thomas Jr. married Rebecca Wehmeyer and they had three children: Thomas Cullen, Bryson Cade Wallace, and stepson Dustin Cade Kramer. ☆William Marshall married Mary Kathryn Gesell, and they had two children: Kathryn Elizabeth and Amelia Noble. ☆Charles Warren married Bernice Ann Castilla.
- Claude Roberts (1885) married Ruth Hamilton and they had five children.
  ❶ Loretta May married Joe Warren and they had two girls, ☆May and ☆Gertrude. Gertrude had four children.
  ❷ Virginia married Walker Jordan, and they had four children, ☆Jennie Ben, ☆Ruth Elizabeth, ☆Walker, and ☆Jill.
  ❸ Dorothy married Wilburn Lemburg and they had three children. ☆Amy Lou married Bob Capps, ☆Bill never married, and ☆Kathy married Bill Groce.
  ❹ Claude Hamilton married Mildred, and they had two children. ☆Claude Hamilton Jr. married Dona and had three children: Zachary, Ryan and Danvielle. Danvielle married Andrew Cantrells. ☆Anita married Darryl Stegenmoeller.
  ❺ Bobby Ruth married Humphrey Price, and they had two children. ☆Humphrey Wallace married Sandy Kel and had two children, Mason and Emma. ☆Jessamine Wallace married Martin Weilbacher and had two children, Clayton and Katherine.
- Howard Gillespie (1892-1978) married Mary Miller and they had no children.
- Charles Lee (1895) married Elizabeth and they had no children.
- Ida Maude (1897-1990) married Sam Harold Nivens, and they two children.
  ❶ Billie Marie married Harry Nichols and had three children. ☆Penny Kay married Lloyd Cupp and they had two children, Lloyd G. Cupp III and Amy Kathleen who married Paul Avery Hundredmark and had one son, Brett. ☆Charles Harold married Susa Jordan and they had two children, Heather Elaine and Hunt Edward. ☆Pamela Ann married Richard Leiter.
  ❷ Hal Wallace married Betty Jo Steinmeyer and had four children. ☆Hal Michael married Beatrice Simmons and they had two children, Diana and Meredith. ☆Stepdaughter Angela Espinosa married Danny Shouse and they had two children, Isaac and Gallin. ☆Robin Nivens married Michael Norley and they had four children, Michael, Sarah, Laura, and David. ☆Tammy Nivens married Don Downey and they had two children, Aubrey and Autumn. ☆Reneé Nivens married Jim Allred and they had two children, Madison and Carson.
- J. Frank was the eighth child of Will and Ida Wallace.

(7) Edwin Henley Wallace (1859-1928) married Ada B. Crow in 1886. They had seven children—six sons and one daughter.
- John Lee (1887-1965) married Anne Morgan and had two children.
  ❶ Addeleen (1909-1998), Anne's daughter by a previous marriage, married Dr. Roy Bowen. They had one child, ☆Eleanor Anne Bowen. Eleanor married a Mr. Paulle and they had one son, Bowen Paulle. His marriage produced a grandchild in 2002.
  ❷ John Lee Jr. (1915-?) married Anne Windham and had three children. ☆Roger was a son by Anne's first marriage. ☆Selden Anne (1952) married Mr. Morales and they had no children. ☆John Lee III (1954) married Debra Warner and they had no children.
- Charles Crow (1888-1949) married Gladys and had one child, Charlene Jeanette (1928), who married a Mr. Miles and had one son.
- Edwin Henley Jr. (1890-1923) married Christi Stevenson and had two children.
  ❶ Edwin III (1915-1979) married Edith and had two children, ☆Edwin H. IV (1938) and ☆John Lee (1944), who married Karen and they had one daughter,

Dana. Dana married Jason Brocks and they have one daughter, Holly (2002).

❷ Jackson Stevenson (1918-?) married Lillian Strand (–1971) and had three children. ☆Christie Lee (1943) married John Castanon and had two children, Sonia (1970) and Emiliano (1977). Sonia married Shane Michael Olton and they had two children, Christina Marie (1997) and Victoria (2001). ☆Terrell J. married Georgia and they had no children. ☆Cynthia married Bruce Jansen and had two children, Brian Robert Lee (1987) and Steven Wallace (1985).

After Lillian's death, Jackson married Susan Navis and they had one son, ☆Andrew J. Wallace (1980).

- Gillis Gillespie "G.G." (1892-1964) never married.
- Bess Louise (1894-1952) married Frank Louis Lawshe and had one child,
  ❶ Patricia Anne (1933) who married John Allen Barton, Jr. They had three children. ☆Karen Ann (1956) married Thomas Lon Curtis and they had no children. ☆Beth Lynne (1962) married Thomas A. J. Schweiger and they had one daughter, Margaret Eleanor (1993). ☆Nancy Claire (1966) married Jeffrey James Tuck and they had three children, Jeffrey Jonathan (1993), Emry Anne Elisabeth (1996), and William Kellen (1998).
- Andrew Jackson "Jack" (1896-?) married Mozelle and had one child, Bobby Joe Wallace (1923). He had no children.
- Joseph Sayers (1899-?) married Marie, and then Maude Ledbetter and had no children.

(8) Mattie Louise Wallace (1863-1885) married Charles Seal in 1881 and had a daughter.

- Pauline (1882-1979). Pauline Seal married Arthur Patton, who would run the Dripping Springs Telephone company from 1918-1921, before they moved to Buda in January 1922. They would have one daughter, Mattie Louise Patton.
  ❶ Mattie Louise, a long time beautician in Buda, married C. T. Labenski, but had no children.

(9) Charles Moorhead Wallace (1866-1940) married Dellua (Lula) Dudley. They had three children.

- Louis Lee (1907-1976).
- Mallie (1901-?) married R. O. Moss.
- Dudley married Arlene and they had two sons.

(10) Andrew Zivley Wallace (1861-1942) never married.

(11) John Lee Wallace II lived less than a year after being born in 1868.

JOHN LAUTER MOSS

Thanks to Rebeccah Haralson and her research during her 2000 freshman English class, we now have a much better and accurate history of the Moss family. John Moss's father was a captain of a British naval ship and he first saw the United States when he sailed to Florida. The United States must have impressed him because he moved his family to New Orleans from England. Like many others of the time, staying in one spot did not happen. According to the 1860 census, John Moss was born in Georgia. His date of birth is not known at this time and the year is uncertain. He would have been born in 1820, if you believe the June 1860 census, but his age of enrollment into the Confederate Army in June 1863 was given as 44, which would have meant the year of birth was 1819. Sometime a little later, the Mosses would find Vicksburg, Mississippi, to their liking and it became their permanent home. The children included John, his brother Robert, and his sister Ethel.

Indiana Jane Ward, who would later became the wife of John Moss, was born in Mississippi. Again the date of birth is not known, and the year is uncertain as well. The 1860 census indicates 1830, but her death age in October 1911 was 80, indicating an 1831 year. Her parents were W. F. and Mississippi Terrell Ward. She had at least two siblings—brother Charles G. Ward, and sister Sarah Dunbiben Ward Pound. They grew up in Vicksburg, Mississippi, and met their spouses there.

John and Indiana would only have one son, Joseph, which seemed to be rare in those days. He was seven years of age when they arrived in Texas. At first it was believed that Joseph never married, but Miss Haralson's research proved that he waited until he was 46 before he tied the knot with

20-year-old Gertrude Kimball in 1892. Before his death in October 1920, Joseph and Gertrude would have 11 children, seven of whom would survive to adulthood. The children were Ethel, Ivan, Nell, Lucy, John, Joe, Mary, Clifton, and Gloyd. Gertrude died in 1957.

(1) Ethel (1893-1986) married Jim Nail and together they had two children, Jim and June.
(2) Ivan (1895) did not marry before his death in April 1920.
(3) Nell was born in 1898 and died in 1911.
(4) Lucy (1900-1993) married Robert L. Kokernot (1898-1930). They had one son.
   * Robert H. Kokernot, born in 1921, who married Edith Babcock and had four children—Jan, Peggy, Walter H., and Diana. He is presently married to Marlene Pierce Kokernot.
(5) John Moss was born in 1902 and died in 1911.
(6) Joe Moss (1904-1998) married Edna Mae Wheat and had two children, Joe Wesley and Nellie Mae.
(7) Mary married Frank Adams and had two daughters (names unavailable).
(8) Clifton Moss (1911-1965) married Annie Burger and had two boys, Clifton Jr. and David.
(9) Gloyd (1913-) married Ann Lange and they had two daughters, Sylvia and Patsy Lee.
(10)(11) Two other Joseph Moss children died in infancy.

Dr. William H. Howard

He first bought property in 1853, but I'm not sure when he actually moved on it. I did not find his wife's name, but his four children were Frank, Kate, Ellen "Nellie" Howard Gillian, and Susan "Sue" Howard Davidson.

Beverly L. Spaw

It is uncertain when B. L. Spaw and his wife, Sisrelda Emmerine Dye, moved their family to the Dripping Springs area. He served in the Union army, first settled in Goliad, Texas, and then came to Dripping Springs in the 1870s. They had five children:

(1) William was born in 1866.
(2) John T. (1868) married Ellie Blue and produced eight offspring.
   * Will E. married Rosa Lyle and had three children, Billie, John Reagan, and Landon.
   * George Beverly married Willie Mae Peal and had two children, Chester and Elliott.
   * Robert T. married Bessie and had four children, Thomas, Virginia, and twins Nellie and Rachel.
   * John E. married Mary Applewhite and they had two daughters.
      ❶ Marie married Jones Eckols and they had two children, ☆Merrie Jean and ☆Elizabeth Jo.
      ❷ Clydene
   * Nellie married Ben Pearson and had one son, Bennie.
   * Mozelle married Otis Walker and had three children, Beverly, Joe Sid, and Sears. Later, she married John McGee.
   * Leah married Lewis Brooks.
   * Serelda married Van Spinks and they had one child, Vaniece.
(3) Robert E. "Bob" (1871) married Ida Robbins and they had four children, Eura May, Beverly H., Milburn C., and Robert L.
(4) Lula (1876) married E. P. Shelton and had thirteen children (named later).
(5) Callie (1879) married Dave Brack and they had six children.
   * Dove married Robert Bigelow
   * Lila
   * Howard
   * David
   * Genevieve married Bill Byers
   * Bernice.

Edgar Poe Shelton

Dr. Shelton married Lula Spaw and they had thirteen children.

(1) John Elbert married Lillian Applewhite. They had one son.
   * Robert Francis married Ima Lois Breed. They had five children.
      ❶ Robert Francis Jr. married Beverly Green of Buda. They had four children: ☆Robert Francis III, ☆Ryan, ☆Clay, and ☆Megan.
      ❷ Becky married Bobby Burke, both DS grads, and they had three children, ☆Robin, ☆Robert, and ☆Carter.
      ❸ James "Jimmy" Shelton had two children, ☆Tammy and ☆Toby.
      ❹ Poe Shelton married Tami Gillis, both DS

grads, and they had three daughters: ☆Heather, ☆Haylie, and ☆Holli.
- ❺ Lisa Shelton married Mike Robertson and they had one daughter, ☆Lindsey.

(2) Neva married John A. Garner. Their children were John Elbert, Alma Lanier, Robert Borden, and Ovela Fay.

(3) Robert Horace married Mabel Morris. Their children were Hazel and Dorothy.

(4) Ora Shelton married James Powell. Their children were Lula Blanch and James Jr.

(5) Maude married Granvel Huey. They had five children before her death in 1928.
- Dorothy Nell married O. L. Fisher.
- Lois Erlene married Travis Garnett.
- Marvin Elbert Huey.
- Jack married Ruthie Mae Crumley.
- Joyce married James R. Pridemore.

(6) Beverly Ellison married Ellen Brotmarkel. Their children were James and Beverly.

(7) Fay married Alex Cox. Their children were:
- Alex Jr.,
- Patricia
- Bobby
- Mildred Lois

(8) Ralph, twin to Roy. Ralph married Wilma Gray, and they had Ralph Gordon and Barbara Ann.

(9) Roy, twin to Ralph. Roy married Norma Woods. Their children were Dorothy, Audrey, Seth Edgar, and Douglas.

(10) Lois Shelton married Latham Boone. They raised Dollene, Mary Lois, Latham III, Shelton, and Laura Jean.

(11) Willie Edna married Oscar Banta and after he died she married Erby Wolfe. With Oscar she had Joe and Jaxena, and with Erby were Seba, Fay, Erby, Hugh, and Jimmie.

(12) Clarence T. married Merle Thomas Glosson. Their children are Eddie, Donnie, and Karen.

(13) The last was Edgar Vaughan, who remained a bachelor all his life.

JAMES W. GLOSSON

James W. married Susan and they had seven children.

(1) Pulaski A. Glosson married Sarah Jane Sinclair on 9-24-1885. They later divorced in February 1902. This marriage produced six children.
- Andrew Walter who married Dora.
- Bertha Agatha married Mercer Chapman
- William married Ida Adelia Stephenson
- Lelia married a Mr. Freeman
- Zula married Mr. Henslee
- Mary married Jim Waley.

P. A. then married Anne Bell on 12-16-1908. This marriage produced two children.
- Susan married John Foster Harmon and they had three children.
  - ❶ O. C. married Joy Jernigan and this union produced two childen, Todd and Stacy.
  - ❷ Ann Ella.
  - ❸ John.
- Vaughn married Wilena.

(2) James Walter married Laura and they had five children: Olivia who married Mr. Peal, Solon B. Glosson, I.V. Glosson, John W. Glosson, and Eula Glosson who married Mr. McGaughy. By his second wife, Mary, were reared two more children, George W. Glosson who married Lois E., and Marvin Glosson.

(3) Thomas Jefferson.

(4) Izzy married Mr. Roland.

(5) L.O. Glosson.

(6) Agatha Glosson.

(7) Solon Bell married Lou Robbins and they had eight children.
- E. B. "Pete" Glosson married Naoma Black and had three children.
  - ❶ Minnie Lou Glosson married Enoch "Buzzy" Needham and they had three children, Sherry, Aaron, and Enoch.
  - ❷ Merlene Glosson married Marvin Myers and they have two sons, Michael and Mark.
  - ❸ Patricia Glosson has one daughter, Patty.
- James "Jimmy" Glosson married Tula Quick and they had six children.
  - ❶ Carroll Glosson married Mae Frances Sansom and they had three children: Guy, Greg, and Sherry.
  - ❷ Jerry "Woody" Glosson married Judy Hoard and they had two daughters, Karen and Patty Loyce.
  - ❸ James S. "Shot" Glosson married Nancy Spillar and they had two children, Kathy and Larry.
  - ❹ Dean Glosson married Jay Spillar and they had three children, Connie, Sid, and Debra.
  - ❺ Lucy Glosson married Bill Moore.
  - ❻ Bonnie Glosson married Jim Pearson and they had two children, Tommy and Terry.

- Johnny Franklin Glosson married Hazel Puryear and they had three children.
  ❶ J. F. Jr. married Cleo Lowden and they had two children, ☆Monte and ☆Mitzi. Monte married Bridgette Billings and they have two sons, Chris and Monte, Jr. Mitzi married Gary Wiedeker and they have two children, Justin and Courtney.
  ❷ Martha Jane.
  ❸ Jo Ann.
- Merle Thomas Glosson married Clarence Shelton.
- Jerry Lee Glosson married Louise Johnson.
- Solon D. "Curly" Glosson married Jessie Lee Arnold.
- Thelmata Glosson married Doyle Moore.
- Wilma Gayle married Temple Collins.

WILLIAM HUDSON ROBBINS

W. H. Robbins married Mary Jane Cockrell. He died in the 1890s and left her with fifteen children. She then married William Martin. The fifteen children were: J. R. who married Bashie; Thomas; Wallace Walker; J. S. who married Jennie; Daisy who married W. I. King; Minerva Robbins; Pearl who married A. B. "Bud" Watson and their daughter Della Mae married Raymond Jenkins; Sallie who married Joseph Moss Stephenson; Ida who married Robert E. Spaw; Maggie who married Frank M. Stephenson; Webbie Robbins; Della who married J. W. Cockrill; Jennie who married Jessie Rowland; Louisa who married Solon Bell Glosson; and Mamie who married Charles Frierson.

GEORGE WASHINGTON CHAMPION

George married Ella McKelvey and they had seven children. Ernest Champion died single in 1900, J. S. "Sam" Champion married Anna Mae, J. W. "Worth" Champion married Sadie J. Spillar, Annie May Champion married Mr. Wagner, Myrtle Champion married Garland English, and Mabel Champion married Ade Justice.

WILLIAM J. ROBERTS

W. J. Roberts married Alice M. Haydon and they had five children. They were Ivy who married Ila Roena, Nellie "Nell" M. married Ross Earl Shahan, Zula Ruth married A. W. Powell, W. T. who married Jennie May, and Hester.

JACOB F. ROBERTS

J. F. Roberts married Brazoria Beatrice Lincoln. They had six children. Stella married McCreary Crow, Ida married William C. Wallace, Frank Worth, Maud, Katie, and Ava who married Sidney Smith.

IKE D. ROBERTS

Ike married Ella Darroh. They had six children.
(1) Dayton married a Perry and they had a son, Perry, who married Martha Jo Maul and had two sons, Tommy and Marty.
(2) Elsie married a Johnson.
(3) Blanche married Hunter Smith.
(4) Leroy married Katherine King. They had a son, Bobby, who was killed in Vietnam, and a daughter, Kay who married Marvin Hohmann. They in turn had two daughters, Kim and Bobbie.
(5) Another son, Oliver, was married to Lily.
(6) Katie Marie married Robert Shrader.

JOHN W. PHILLIPS

He married Nancy E. Parks. They had eight children: Thomas B., Soloman Alpha, Minnie L. married V. W. Clark, Etta Lyell married George Temple Roberts, Lizzie E. married W. P. Riley, John W. Jr., Hattie O. married George H. Cooke, and Lucy Emma married J. W. Graham.

ALBERT LAWSON DAVIS, SR.

He married Nancy Jane. They had three children.
(1) A. L. Jr. married Willie Herndon. They had five children. Hallie married C. H. Bass, Howard Herndon, Ethel May, Carol who married Harold G. Smith, and William Sherman.
(2) Addison married Fannie Dickey.
(3) Jeff.

I.V. DAVIS, JR.

I.V. married Katie Howard and from this

marriage produced ten children. The first was daughter Lanier who married John Dement. Then came three sons, Howard, James Walton, and I.V. III, then three daughters, Mae who married Elgin Arnold, Lucille who married Lucas Harvey, and Bess. Finally three more sons, Elbert Hudson, Bradley, and Charles.

A. H. Sorrell

He married Amanda Melvina. They had seven children.

(1) Bascom G. married Nancy Rebeccah, and they had five children before his death in 1880. The five Sorrell children were Ed F. who married Maggie, Lizzie who married John Dickey, James "Jim," George, and William. Nancy Rebeccah then married W. H. Banks and they had four children who survived birth. They were John T., twins Dilla M. and Miles H., and Fred A.
(2) Flora married Thomas Cavett.
(3) Jake married Mittie Pound.
(4) Oliver "Ollie" took Mittie Pound as his second wife.
(5) Lee.
(6) Mariah E. married W. J. Norwood.
(7) Mattie married Tom Willhite.

William Robert Lyle

He married S. E. Robbins and they had six children.

(1) Robert T.,
(2) John R.,
(3) Rosa married Will E. Spaw,
(4) William A. married Lura Branum. They had two children. Jack Lyle married Mary Sue Young and they had three children, LouAnn, Lura, and Trenton. Dean Lyle married Robert Kumlacky.
(5) Inthaberry married I. C. Ferrell.
(6) Sarah May Lyle.

Mose Columbus Cavett

The seventh child of Richard Savannah and Virginia Martin Cavett first married Georgia Virginia Pound on 11-10-1890. They had one child, Marguerite Ruperta. This marriage dissolved and he married Pearl Cannon on 6-22-1898. They had two children.

(1) Guy Oran married Gladys Fruend and they had three children, Mary Louise, Peggy, and Robert Milton.
(2) Kathryn married John Elbert Shelton and they had three children.
- Dan Robert married Joy Miller and they had two children, Kay Nell and Reynolds Miller.
  - ❶ Kay Nell married Howard Hallum and had two children, John Howard and James.
  - ❷ Reynolds married Jaqueline Ann Zidd and they had one child, Susan.
- Jack Cavett married Virginia Campbell and had one child, Jack C. Jr.
- Gayle Adele married Kleber C. Miller.

Thomas Samuel Cavett

He was the ninth and youngest child of Richard Savannah and Virginia Cavett. He married Flora Field Sorrell, and they had six children.

(1) Dewitt married Etta Mae Dulaney.
(2) Burkett lived less than a month.
(3) Dennis lived a year.
(4) Aletha married Olga H. Cobb. They had two children.
- Joe Harold married Yvonne Bell Evans and they had two children, Shannon Lea and Kimberly Sue.
- Clarence Collins married Betty Dean Burrier and they had one child, Codie Collins.
(5) Newt was born in 1914 and died in 1930.
(6) Rex Wilkes married Hazel Evans and they had one child, Karen Aletha.

William J. Norwood

He married Mariah Ellen Sorrell. They had six children.

(1) Vina Ann
(2) Rosay L.
(3) Kate married Y. L. Lawrence. They had two children before she died.
- Melvina
- Beulah Marie who married Enoch Needham. They had nine children: Bobby, Norwood Enoch "Buzzy," Shirley, Peggy, Eddie, Joey, Minnie, Cherry, and Donna.
(4) S. J.
(5) Mary Ethel married a Gibson
(6) Marjorie.

GALEN CROW

He married Cordelia Price and they had a son, McCreary Crow. He married Stella Roberts and they had six children.

(1) Paul married Vennie
(2) Will P. married Faye Conn and they had a son, William McCreary. He married Agnes Martin and he would die before his son, William McCreary Crow was born. William "Mac" Crow married Elizabeth "Betty" Ashley and they had two sons, Travis and Morgan.
(3) Allie B."Pete"
(4) Maurine married a Biles
(5) Bess married Tom Chapman
(6) Louise married a Searight.

JAMES L. PATTERSON

J. L. Patterson married Ellie Hill. They had four children.
(1) Joel M.
(2) Mattie married Edwin McKellar.
(3) Edith L. married Willie Sam Butler, and had three children.
  - James P.
  - Eloise .
  - Billie Barbara married Nathan Hall and they had three children, James "Sandy," Kay, and Barbara.
(4) Barbara L. married Earl Wood, then Ben Everett.

THOMAS W. RAGLAND

Thanks to the work of Frances Ragland Rhodes, it became obvious how intertwined the Ragland clan was to the history of Dripping Springs. Thomas Walter Ragland and his wife, Paulina Fidelia Davidson, the daughter of Nalium Davidson and Ottawa Hoy, produced eleven offspring, ten of which survived to adulthood.

(1) Willie Bell (1896) married Harvey Henderson King. They had one daughter, Hazel Bell. She married E. E. Myers and they had one daughter, Virginia Ann. She married Ernest Tipton and they had two children.
(2) Jesse Edward (1898) married Thelma Conn. They had three children, Denton, Gerald and Merle.
(3) Verda Edith (1900) married Albert Borders. They had one son, A. J.
(4) Bessie Beatrice (1901) married Ray Blackwell Wilson. They had two children, Ray Blackwell and Marjorie Rae. Ray Blackwell "R.B." married Thelma Doris Carson and they had three children, Janie, Connie and Judy. Marjorie married Clifton Laverne Odell and they had three children, Juanita Marie, Eddie Ray and Roy Gene.
(5) Ottie Anna (1903) married Jessie Monroe Langston. They had two children, Samuel Monroe and Jessie Milton. Samuel married Dosia Mae Rippy and they had two daughters, Frances Cherrie and Janet Vida. Jessie married Dale Lynn Holtzclaw and they had two children, Karen Sue and Kenneth Wayne.
(6) Marguerite Deeldra (1906) married John Bushnell. They had one child, Viola. Viola married Wilford Pannell and they had two daughters, Rita and Diane.
(7) Baby Boy (1909).
(8) Mable Loleet (1910) married Harvey Kullenberg. They had three children, H. S., Edith and Walter.
(9) Thomas Walter, Jr. (1912) married Bessie Louise Walker. They had nine children.
  - Thomas Fred married Linda Elliot and they had two children.
    ❶ Elizabeth Lynn married Tonie Matthews, then Michael Odis Drake and they had one son, ☆Cody Michael. After Michael's death, she married Mike Pinner.
    ❷ Jeanna Evon married John Hurnsburger and they had one son, ☆Timothy Jacob. She then married Dean Thompson and they had one son, ☆Christopher Lane. She recently married Perry Don Henson. Thomas Fred then married Bobbie Wright and they had two children, Wayne and Missy.
  - S. A. married Janet May Monzingo and they had two children.
    ❶ Mary Denice married Larry Havenridge and they had three children, ☆Kara Blake, ☆Erick James and ☆Shana Elizabeth. She recently married William Gulzow.
    ❷ Scott Anthony.
  - Texanna
  - Louisanna
  - Tonie Lee
  - Diana Sue
  - Deanna Ruth
  - Carl Allen
  - Kenneth Allen.
(10) John Deliva (1914) married Willie Edna

Puryear and they had one child, Betty Jean. She was killed in an auto accident during the summer prior to her senior year at Dripping Springs.

(11) Roy James "Skeet" (1917) married Eva Louise Bradshaw and they had three children.
- Roy James, Jr., married Connie Diane Goodman and they had two children, James David and Summer Dawn.
- Frances Louise married Terry Joe Balch. They had two sons, Jason Duane and James Robert. Frances would then marry Walter Russell Rhodes and they had one daughter, Stacy Renee.
- Roger was killed in an automobile accident just a couple of years after his graduation.

MEXICAN POPULATION.

A *San Marcos Record* report written in the September 1, 1939, edition concerning the history of Dripping Springs at that time closed with this notation. "Dripping Springs is strictly a white settlement. No Negroes or Mexicans." This would change dramatically in the next half decade when Sesario and Concepcion Falcon Garza would bring their extensive family to Dripping Springs to buy property and make their homes. Their background work was that of migrant workers who would start in South Texas harvesting crops, moving on through Dripping Springs to shear sheep and goats and possibly end up in faraway places like Michigan, picking the crops up there before returning and starting the cycle all over again. The Garza clan put a stop to their nomadic ways and found a home where they could be productive members without moving all the time. It has been Dripping Springs' gain that they made their decisions. Until Geronimo Garza worked up the Garza genealogy for me, did I ever realize the Garza thread ran through the Nevarez, Ramirez, Castor, and Beltran families. I had always looked upon them as separate families. At the same time, the Felix Cruz family would also settle in Dripping Springs.

SESARIO M. GARZA

Mr. Garza and two of his sons bought two acre lots from P. L. Turner on the north side of Dripping Springs in 1944 and built houses. Grandson Geronimo said he was told that early on several families lived in Mr. Garza's house. Each assigned a room until the families got too large to stay. Mr. Garza's wife's maiden name was Falcon and to honor this, each of his son's middle name is Falcon. They had four sons and five daughters.

(1) Remedios married Genoveva and they had six children.
- Raymond married Janie and they had three children: Patrick, Amanda, and Tommy.
- Adolpho married Julia and they had two children: Diane and Adolpho Jr.
- Alfredo married Margie and they had three children: Linda, Rene, and Alfredo Jr.
- Cristella married Lupe Alvarado and they had a daughter, Maria.
- Angie married Ernesto Cordova and they had two children: Ernesto Jr. and Christopher. She also married Joe Sell and they had one child, Stephanie.
- Amy married Daniel Cisneros and they have no children.

(2) Felipe and his first wife had a son, Richard, who married Rosa and had two children, Ricky and Joanna.

After his wife's death, he married Mercedes and they had four sons and two daughters.
- Juan (Johnny) married Deanna and they have three children, Johnny Jr., Dillon, and Katie.
- Eduardo (Eddie) married Rebecca Rendon and they had three children, Marcus, Vincent, and Marissa.
- Felipe married Stella and they have a daughter, Abigail.
- Sesario married Cindy and they have a daughter, Marina.
- Modesta married Kevin Alcorn and they have three children Michael, Jessica and Kevin.
- Victoria married Chris Sanders and from this marriage came three girls, Christina, Lisa, and Teri.

(3) Epifanio married Francis Riza Garza and they had nine children.
- Lucia married Leon Hernandez and they had three children, Jose, Lori Ann, Jennifer.
- Andrea has not married to date.

- Teresa married Jose Salazar and they had three children, Justin, Steven, and Sierra Jo.
- Sylvia married Kevin Skrupa.
- Rogerellio has not married to date.
- Roberto married Patricia Balderas and they had two children Rebecca and Jordan Robert.
- Geronimo married Josie and they had three children Christin, Geronimo E., Samantha.
- Oscar married Deana Salazar and he has three stepchildren, Stephanie, Kristie, and Paul.
- Alehandro (Alex) has not married to date.

(4) Benito married Florencia and they had one son, Ramiro (Ramsey), who married Sandra Blaney.

(5) Gregoria married Cleofas Ramirez and they had seven children.

(6) Casimira married Gilberto Nevarez and they had nine children.

(7) Juanita married Bartolo Navarro and they had two sons, Juan and Nasario.

(8) Beta married Antanacio Boconegra and they had five children.

(9) Tanes married Jose Gutierrez and they had thirteen children.

Cleofas Ramirez

Cleofas married Gregoria Garza and they had two sons and five daughters.

(1) Israel married Rosa Rios and they had one child, Lorie.

(2) Jose Ysmael (Joe) married Sally and they had two children, Veronica and Roland.

(3) Cruz married Ramon Beltran and they had four children, Nora, Rosemary, Raymond, and David.

(4) Eva married Ramon Torres and they had two children, Joe and Sonia.

(5) Hortencia married Armando Prouty. They had four children, Armando, Mark, Orlando, and Adrian.

(6) Mary Delia married Paul Ozuna. They had three children.

(7) Carmen had two children, Fatima and Gabriel.

Gilberto Nevarez

Gilberto married Casimira Garza. They had five sons and four daughters. When Casimira died in March 2001, at the age of 89, she left behind 33 grandchildren, 57 great-grandchildren and 12 great-great grandchildren.

(1) Daniel married Olivia Chapa and they had three children.

(2) Gilberto Jr. married Odelia Castro and they had three children, Angela, Liza, and Felicia

(3) Ernesto married Elidia and they had five children, Gilbert, Yolanda, Erma, Bertha, and Lorrie.

(4) Rudolpho (Rudy) had four children.

(5) Antonio married Eva and they had seven children, Rudolpho (Rudy), Olivia, Rosendo, Relles (Ray), Antonio (Tony), Otilia, and Romaldo.

(6) Dora married Augustine Castor and they had two children, Bonnie and Belinda.

(7) Aurora married Mike Scarbroughs and they had two children.

(8) Guadalupe (Lupe) married Jimmy Moreno and they had two children.

(9) Beatrice. married Guadalupe Alvarado and they had one child, Maria.

Felix Cruz

The Cruz family had four sons. They were Edward, Juan, Concepcion, and Antonio.

Barney Castor

Barney and his wife, Santos, had three children. They are Augustin, Guadalupe, and Helen.

The History of the Town of Dripping Springs

The community of Dripping Springs had its small beginnings in 1854, as we have noted before. It would get its official name in 1857. However, it would be 27 years before it would get its definition. This would be left up to one W. T. Chapman, who would seem to have been in the right place at the right time. The town of Dripping Springs would be carved out of the original John L. Moss quarter league of land in the Phillip A. Smith league. The property would change hands a couple of times before Burrell J. Marshall purchased the property in 1870.

In February of 1872, Mr. Marshall became ill and died. He left behind a wife, Martha Ann Box Marshall, and five children. They were George Washington, Jefferson Davis, Jasper Newton, Robert Lee, and Frances Mary. He had already sold 386 acres of the 1,107 acres he had bought. Since all of the children were minors, the mother had to file for the estate of B. J. Marshall on behalf of her children. This she did on October 19, 1872. By this time she was already married to W. T. Chapman. On November 22, 1872, Martha A. Marshall, as guardian of Estate, had to post a $7,000 bond and B. M. Gibson, M. McKellar and Jacob Roberts were appointed appraisers.

Each year after that she had to file a report and get it approved by the court. Finally in 1880, George W. Marshall came of age and wanted his share of the inheritance. On May 17, 1880, the guardian's final account as to George W. Marshall was examined, approved, and ordered of record. The application for partition was approved. John L. Wallace, Jake Roberts and J.W. Phillips were appointed as commissioners to partition same and report at next term of court. On September 23, 1880, the report of the commissioners appointed to partition land between the heirs was approved and ordered of record. George received 81 acres, Jeff 85, Jasper 73, Robert 98, and Frances 150. This left Martha Ann 234 acres, including the house.

As her husband, Mr. Chapman shared in the use of the land. He was a businessman and a land speculator. At the time of the partition, he was running a general merchandise store on the property. Previous to this, it has been reported that Charles Poteet and Alex Young operated stores, presumably on the Wallace land. Ben Manor was reported to have run a small mill in the late '60s, most likely the one described near Walnut Springs when the DS–San Marcos road was being built. L. McKellar's store was mentioned as being west of Dripping Springs in one of the Austin–Fredericksburg road improvement decisions.

With the partition done, definite plans could be made with the land, and Chapman saw his chance and took advantage of it. The first opportunity came when W. M. Jordan talked about building the Dripping Springs Academy. The Chapmans donated a block of land for the building of this church/school. The cornerstone to the Academy was set August 6, 1881. Chapman filed his original plat of twelve blocks for the town of Dripping Springs on September 24, 1881, which bordered south of the Academy. He would quickly add three more additions and later a fourth.

The September 7, 1878, edition of the San Marcos *Free Press* (SMFP) gave a history of Hays County. A synopsis of Dripping Springs was given as "A settlement through which runs the Austin–Fredericksburg road; is an attractive region with good land, fine range, wild game and easy living."

The early growth of the town is chronicled by newspaper articles and I will give them in the order in which they were written. It is not easy to determine exactly where some of these buildings were, but at least we know they were built.

January 26, 1882 (SMFP): The writer signed his article with the name Solon. He extolled the village of Dripping Springs. Said he could call it that because it has been laid off for a town. Says since the first of October, five new buildings have been erected, one of them a boarding house kept by Mrs. Caperton who offers to take boarders at a reduced rate. Families moving into Dripping Springs included Dr. Myers of Bastrop and Rev. Mr. Wallace from Blanco who bought land a few hundred yards of the school building.

May 25, 1882 (SMFP): Farmers happy after good rains. Business reported lively. Mr. Chapman, an accommodating merchant greatly increased his stock of goods and gave his customers good bargains. Mr. Fairchild put up a store. His house was near completion. Mr. H. C. Pearcy, former partner of Chapman & Pearcy, was visiting old home in Missouri. The high school classes were being held in Jordan's house.

June 7, 1883 (SMFP): The *Free Press* editor, I. H. Julian, visited Dripping Springs on the previous Friday and Saturday to check out the growth of Dripping Springs, along with the commencement exercises. On the way over he noticed the absence of prickly pears and mesquite. He spoke of merchants Chapman and Davis, staying overnight with Davis. Businesses: Chapman & Davis, general merchandise (post office in their store with A. L. Davis, Jr., in charge); Crow & Estille, general merchandise; Major Wortham, general merchandise; A. D. Gilpin, druggist; G. W. Womack, saddles and harnesses; Carpenter & Lincoln, blacksmiths and woodworkers; J. C. Rowe, blacksmith and woodshop. The town had daily stage line and tri-weekly mails. A gin was about to be established. Baptists dominate. Rev. Mr. Martin of Kyle was the pastor and Jordan was the superintendent of Sunday School.

September 27, 1883 (SMFP): Mr. Durar reported that a large hotel was being built. Mr. Wortham was building a handsome new store. Four private residences were going up. Dr. Harrison was about to begin building his house in town. Dr. Pound had gone with a car load of horses to Kentucky.

October 4, 1883 (SMFP): Hotel was nearing completion, one new store was completed, lumber was on the way for another. Lumber for a Masonic Lodge had been purchased. Carl Pearcy began the erection of a large and commodious building for the purpose of an agricultural implement depot, which was much needed. New gin was doing a big business.

November 8, 1883 (SMFP): Alex Smith was reported moving to his ranch in Dripping Springs. Sold his property in San Marcos.

November 15, 1883 (SMFP): Among the businesses listed, W. C. Roy had the livery stable. Mentioned the hotel. Masonic Lodge going up.

February 14, 1884 (SMFP): Mr. Granger bought property at or near Dripping Springs and was to move there.

April 24, 1884 (SMFP): *Blanco Star* reports that the W. H. Greer family had moved to Dripping Springs and will be a valuable acquisition for the town. William Pursley wrote that Dripping Springs was alive. Three new buildings well nigh completed the past three weeks.

May 8, 1884 (SMFP): Creeks had been this high only once in 30 years. Grass fine, stock doing well, corn and grain look well. Cotton predicted to be a failure. Too much cold and wet.

July 3, 1884 (SMFP): A reporter wrote about making his first trip to Dripping Springs. He was amazed at Walnut Springs. Between there and Dripping Springs, he saw the finest field of cotton this year. He ate breakfast at the hotel. He bragged on the beauty of Onion Creek and Walnut Springs.

August 14, 1884 (SMFP): Alex Smith and W. T. Walters down from Dripping Springs. Also met Thomas W. Hofheinz of the vicinity of Dripping Springs where he sold improved farms.

October 9, 1884 (SMFP): Main churches were Baptist, Methodist, and Christian, plus many members of others. Said only two years earlier, the place was only a country store.

January 22, 1885 (SMFP): W. R. McMillan went to Dripping Springs to engage in the saddle business.

October 29, 1885 (SMFP): H. H. Marshall now was running a boot and shoe shop. Some of the lumber for the new school wing was on the ground. Workmen would commence the erection of the new room soon. Farmers were busy picking cotton.

December 17, 1885 (SMFP): Reverend Hollis lately completed a commodius two-story residence. Addition to Academy nearing completion. Chapman & Davis had a 7½ foot stuffed rattlesnake in the store that was killed west of town. S. D. Gilpin, the druggist, was burned out about a year ago, but his new building was a grand improvement over the old. C. S. Graham was running the steam gin here. Charley Herndon was the acting postmaster. Businesses listed: General merchandise: Crow & Short; Chapman & Davis; J. T. Wortham; Dickey & Herndon; Drugs: S. D. Gilpin; Blacksmiths: W. A. Hogan; J. C. Rowe; Shoemaker: H. H. Marshall; Feed stable: W. Herndon. Town estimated to do about $100,000 worth of business a year. Population estimated at 300.

In the *Hays County Times & Farmers Journal* (HCTFJ) published by David McNaughton, the following advertisements were in the July 3, 1886 edition. (1) Dripping Springs Hotel, Home Comforts, Good Meals, Good Beds, and Ample accommodations, healthy locality, fine schools. Charges very reasonable. Good stabling, shooting and fishing. Favorite for invalids. C. S. Graham, proprietor. (2) Dr. Harrison, Physician and Surgeon, Dripping Springs. (3) S. D. Gilpin, Druggist and Apothecary, Dripping Springs, Texas. Dealer in Drugs, medicines, paints, oils, fancy articles, lotions, perfumery, sponges, fine soaps, tobacco & cigars, garden seeds, diamond dyes and dye stuffs, jewelry, a fine assortment of spectacles and eyeglasses of every description, pure wines and liquors for medical use. Physician prescription carefully compounded day and night.

September 18, 1886 (HCTFJ): Ginners are Graham and McMillan. Mr. McMillan moved to town where he could be near his business and the school.

December 2, 1886 (SMFP): Dickey & Carey have just received a fine lot of Christmas goods (vases, toilet sets, cups, saucers, etc.)

January 8, 1887 (HCTFJ): Advertisement: Z. I. Williams, Dripping Springs, Texas, general dealer in groceries and other merchandise. Fine lot of saddles and harnesses and saddletry hardware on hand. Boot and shoemaking and repairing a specialty. "Give me a call and examine my goods."

January 20, 1887 (SMFP): Dickey & Carey selling goods at less than cost.

March 5, 1887 (HCTFJ): Corn was being shipped from Kyle to Dripping Springs. Chapman and Davis still in the lead as mountain merchants. Eggs selling for 20-25 cents a dozen.

April 16, 1887 (HCTFJ): C. S. Graham sold his livery stable to John Hamilton, the mail contractor.

June 4, 1887 (HCTFJ): "If readers want a pleasant time, then put up in our hotel where Mrs. Hamilton has everything in apple-pie order."

July 16, 1887 (HCTFJ): Mr. Cook of Austin purchased the storehouse of S. D. Gilpin, formerly occupied by Williams and Gilpin as a saddleshop. Also, the blacksmith shop of Mr. Hogan. Mr. Cook was to put the houses together and open a general merchandise business at his place.

July 23, 1887 (HCTFJ): Someone set fire to Mr. J. C. Rowe's plank building house across the street from the hotel and next to the Masonic Lodge/A. L. Davis building. They were able to save the other buildings by gaining rapid access to Mason's room and pouring water out the windows that were already broken from the heat. The pine rosin was already beginning to melt and bubble from the heat. In all probability, the sparks would have destroyed the hotel and drugstore. The slight dew and light rain during the previous afternoon helped prevent the shingles of the hotel from catching on fire as the sparks landed on them. Mr. Rowe was the Justice of the Peace and he also used the building as his wood workshop. Everything was a total loss to him. Mrs. Hamilton was awakened by the glare and crackling of the flames through her window. She woke her husband and a patron to send the alarm. Mr. Cook's store was about ready for the stock of goods to come.

September 17, 1887 (HCTFJ): Last Sunday night, Crow and Short store burned to the ground. Mr. Graham's gin kept busy.

October 22, 1887 (HCTFJ): H. W. Cook began at once to rebuild a fine erection as a store in place of that lately destroyed by fire. J. C. Rowe again commenced to work and erected a handsome workshop, office, etc. Short and Crow also will rebuild at an early date. Twelve wells have been dug around Dripping Springs. H. C. Durar's was the latest. S. D. Gilpin was still the leading druggist. His success was due to his willingness to advertise (especially in their paper).

October 29, 1887 (HCTFJ): Mr. Cook had the lumber on the ground to rebuild his store.

November 19, 1887 (HCTFJ): Charlie Wallace was hauling the lumber for his new home.

December 9, 1887 (HCTFJ): Major Cook bought the store house of the Grange. John Short will open a store about six miles from this place on Barton Creek. John Hamilton bought the residence of J.R.B. Fairchild. John Hamilton was always on the trade and never let a good deal pass. J. M. Livingston drilled a well for W. A. McMillan and hit plenty of water at 62 feet. Now was drilling a well in rear of Major Cook's storehouse.

December 16, 1887 (HCTFJ): The Grange rented Mr. Dickey's store house and moved their goods in. Joe Williams to open a saddle shop in 7-10 days.

February 2, 1888 (SMFP): George Marshall, the postmaster at Dripping Springs, established himself and the letter boxes in new quarters. Dripping Springs now blessed with daily mail.

February 9, 1888 (SMFP): Changes in the business world of Dripping Springs in the past year. Five houses were doing business. They were Chapman & Davis; Crow & Short; S. D. Gilpin, Mr. Dickey and Major Wortham. First Major Wortham retired and the Grange took his place. Next Major Cook opened up a good stock of merchandise in Gilpin's old place. Then Crow & Short's store destroyed by fire. Shortly afterwards, so was Major Cook's. Major Cook moved into the Grange store and the Grange moved into Mr. Dickey's, who was retiring from the mercantile business. Now the Grange shut down their shop. Mr. Short moved down on the Barton. Major Cook's business will pass to other hands. Only A. L. Davis, Jr., and S. D. Gilpin remained. Mr. Joe Williams settled down to take care of our soles (shoes that is).

April 12, 1888 (SMFP): Mr. John Hamilton leased his stage route between Dripping Springs and Blanco.

May 10, 1888 (SMFP): Town crowded. A. L. Davis and Mr. Gilpin had their hands full at their stores. Mr. Hamilton moved to Austin and gave his stable and place into Mr. Davis's charge during his absence.

October 11, 1888 (SMFP): Joe Williams moved to Blanco and when asked why? replied, "There's nothing like leather." A. L. Davis put in best stock of goods and the smiling postmaster's stock of sweets was largely augmented.

October 17, 1889 (SMFP): Mr. Rowe retired from the blacksmith business and sold his business to Stapleton and Loman, who were now running the shop. Stapleton also bought lots opposite the shop.

February 6, 1890 (SMFP): Mr. Ed Wallace sold his business to Dave Jones and Dr. Gilpin. The latter moved his drugstore up to the dry goods store. Mr. Durar bought out Mr. Marshall's stock and was established in the building next to the A. L. Davis store. It was rumored that a furniture warehouse would be established in the old hotel building.

May 2, 1890 (HCTFJ): For sale: A good dwelling house and six lots, beautifully situated in village of Dripping Springs and occupied by Mr. Stapleton, blacksmith. Property in good order and located close to church and schools. Price only $350. (This is Block 7, 2nd addition.)

May 29, 1890 (SMFP): Squire Rowe getting his shop in order to work.

October 9, 1891 (HCTFJ): Mr. A. L. Davis expected to have his new store house in shape to move into in a couple of weeks. (This is the building on Lot 6 of Block 7.)

September 28, 1894 (HCTFJ): Mr. McKellar's gin in full force. There was an ice cream supper at the hotel (Mr. Mading's) last Saturday night. Proceeds went to fixing up the school. It was in bad need of repairs. Dripping Springs well supplied with doctors—Pound, Steel, Russell, and Shelton. Also a dentist, Stewart. School opens first of October. Families are moving into town.

August 19, 1904 (HCTFJ): Advertisement: Vines and shrubbery from the Sylvan Nursery, Dripping Springs. Agents wanted. D. Garner, proprietor, Dripping Springs, Texas.

May 11, 1905 (DS *Pointer*): An editorial by editor, W. E. James, continued the pursuit of getting help to do the needed work on the school, which he described as being in poor condition. The improvements needed should be done now and not wait until next fall when school is to begin. He believed there was at least 50 to 60 patrons of the community who could donate at least one dollar each and many others, being the young men of the community, who would eagerly do the work. The windows needed screening to protect the glass and there was enough wire on hand to finish the screening. Year before last, $4.50 was expended for glass alone. This year, $16 for glass and window frames. There are a few panes to be put in this year. A new floor was the most needed improvement of all. Good flooring cost about $22 per M feet. The approximate cost on one room would be about $16. New blackboards are greatly needed. If he were a teacher and asked to use the smeared side of the wall for blackboard purposes, he would get highly insulted. There is no reason these things should exist. The children were entitled to the best in public school life and we should see that they got it.

May 25, 1905 (DSP): The Dramatic Club held a meeting in Dripping Springs to elect M. E. Chapman as vice-president of the club to finish out the unexpired term of the resigning vice-president. During the meeting, they also addressed the problem of school repair improvements. They voted to donate $40 to the repair fund with the stipulation the money would be handed over to the Trustees when the community had raised $80 for the said fund.

November 17, 1905 (*Kyle News*), T. F. Harwell, editor and publisher: Mr. D. G. Jones already displaying Christmas goods. W. A. Stone sold his ranch property. Mr. Lyle bought the Howard farm. Mr. Garnett was putting a new fence around his premises. R. M. McCall left with two loads of fruit trees from Garner nurseries.

June 22, 1906 (KN): The hotel was to be painted soon. The telephone company was now constructing a line to San Marcos via Wimberley. R. E. Spaw intended putting in a switchboard at Driftwood in the near future.

March 24, 1922 (*San Marcos Record*): Last Sunday, the home of J. F. Roberts, 87, burned to the ground and all its contents. He did not have insurance at the time and the property was valued at $3,000.

April 6, 1923 (SMR): Quite a few changes taking place in Dripping Springs. Mrs. Mayne Roberts sold her home to Waite Crenshaw and moved to Austin. Madames Glosson and Breed bought the Perry place and opened a hotel, where the travelling public can find first class accommodations. Mr. Gilbert Searight bought Lou Breed's house and on Wednesday would marry Miss Erma Elsner. Mr. Searight was a popular young merchant.

June 11, 1926 (SMR): The Fredericksburg–Austin highway near Dripping Springs was being straightened. There were some dangerous curves.

September 23, 1927: W. C. Crenshaw installed a Delco light plant in his garage and residence.

March 30, 1928 (SMR): W. R. Baird lost his barn and contents to fire the previous Sunday night.

November 9, 1928 (SMR): Mr. Earl Wood was retiring from the mercantile business in Dripping Springs and was having a new residence erected on his ranch near Dripping Springs.

April 4, 1930 (SMR): Dave Crenshaw purchased the grocery store from W. H. Kitchens at Dripping Springs the previous week.

November 14, 1930 (SMR): Dr. Baskett moved his drug and optical business into the building known as the Meat Market, which had been vacant for several months. Mr. Dave Crenshaw opened up a new drugstore in the building formerly occupied by Dr. Baskett.

November 21, 1930 (SMR): Dr. Baskett moved into one of the apartments with Will Crow. Mr. and Mrs. O. S. Brumley went to Dallas to purchase their holiday goods.

January 30, 1931 (SMR): There was a new doctor in town—Doc Wilkerson.

February 6, 1931 (SMR): Dripping Springs formed a Chamber of Commerce last month and had 65 members which included businessmen and ranchers from the surrounding area.

February 20, 1931 (SMR): The rock tank and windmill on the school grounds would soon be removed. Billie Garnett was doing some improving on his garage—building a large shed at the rear that would house several cars. It would be constructed mostly out of iron welded together and would have a gravel floor.

February 27, 1931 (SMR): Dave Crenshaw moved his stock of groceries to the drug store where he would be in charge of both. The grocery store had been managed for the last year by Will Crow.

March 6, 1931 (SMR): Will Crow, who had formerly managed the grocery business for D. W. Crenshaw the past year, opened a grocery store in the building formerly occupied by Crenshaw. The building had been overhauled, newly painted, and had a neat appearance. Opening day was Wednesday. Mr. Charles Haydon installed a lighting system from his gin and lighted the school house. Mr. Grady Walker brought his movie picture machine to Dripping Springs and put on a show.

June 19, 1931 (SMR): Dr. E. P. Shelton had just given his house a new top of sheet iron. Dr. C. L. Baskett was having a new front added to his drugstore, having a new plate glass front and finishing off with rock work. Charles Haydon was building a new shed to his gin building for corn crushing. Mr. D.C. Jones had his new store front trimmed up with a new coat of paint.

July 17, 1931 (SMR): Billie Garnett had a new front built to his garage. He tore away a few feet and replaced it with rock. It had a drink stand when finished. Dr. Baskett had a new pen made for his wild fowl zoo.

June 3, 1932 (SMR): Two Dripping Springs stores were robbed. The mercantile store of O. S. Brumley and the drugstore of D. W. Crenshaw were entered on Monday night (5-30-32). At Brumley's they did not get into the safe, took a few dollars, and a side of bacon. At Crenshaw's they got three dollars from the safe and took a sack of sugar, sack of beans, and a side of bacon.

May 8, 1936 (SMR): L. P. Scheh completed his new building in Dripping Springs. Last Thursday, while John Spaw was out for supper, his oil stove overheated and caused quite a little blaze in the barber shop. Luckily the bucket brigade of the fire department came from all over and put it out with only minor damage incurred. Saturday, the new barber shop of Mance Cockrell also caught fire when his stove overheated. Again the fire department came to the rescue.

March 26, 1937 (SMR): James Ferrell and C. W. Crenshaw were building an up-to-date theater located on the ball ground. Hoped to have it completed in the near future. Charles Haydon was building a new service station and garage north of the gin.

June 25, 1937 (SMR): Work on Highway 20 was completed. Road from Austin to Fredericksburg was in fine shape. New theater was near completion.

July 30, 1937 (SMR): Harvey King and Hazel Bell King were in charge of the Roberts Cafe while the Leroy Roberts family was attending the Driftwood Reunion.

August 6, 1937 (SMR): A new barber shop was being erected by Johnny Spaw. The new garage and filling station that was to be opened to the public this week was being built by Charles Haydon and son Bill.

October 1, 1937 (SMR): Mrs. Scheh opened the West End Cafe.

November 11, 1937 (SMR): O. J. Bean bought the D. W. Crenshaw place in town. Sam Byars and wife moved to their place in town last week.

December 10, 1937 (SMR): Virgil Conn leased the Haydon service station.

July 29, 1938 (SMR): The O. S. Brumley general store and the post office in the same building was consumed by fire around 3:00 A.M. last Thursday (7-21). The two-story rock building was one of the oldest in Dripping Springs. Only the walls remained.

October 28, 1938 (SMR): The new residence of Mr. and Mrs. W. P. Crow was near completion.

November 4, 1938 (SMR): Work on the new high school building was started the previous Friday.

December 9, 1938 (SMR): A large crowd gathered in town Saturday afternoon for the grand opening of O. S. Brumley's new store.

February 24, 1939 (SMR): The King Cafe caught on fire last Friday night (2-17) but was extinguished before it received too much damage.

April 21, 1939 (SMR): W. P. Crow's warehouse was completely destroyed by fire on Wednesday night (4-12).

May 5, 1939 (SMR): Mrs. Fannie Coopwood moved back to her home in Dripping Springs.

September 1, 1939 (SMR): An article about the history of Dripping Springs said it had two stores, three garages, a beauty shop, a barber shop, theater, two cafes, post office, drugstore, blacksmith shop, wool and mohair warehouse. Will Crow is the owner of the largest store and warehouse. Samp McLendon is the postmaster. It is strictly a white settlement. No Negroes or Mexicans.

November 10, 1939 (SMR): W. P. Crow handled 125,000 lbs. of 12-month wool, 50,000 lbs. of short wool, and 125,000 lbs. of mohair.

November 17, 1939 (SMR): Mr. and Mrs. Tom Ragland moved into their new home. Alva Haydon finished drilling a well at his service station. C. W. Crenshaw had his station well dug deeper, too.

January 1, 1940 (SMR): C. W. Crenshaw changed his station from Texaco to Sinclair.

January 26, 1940 (SMR): Mr. and Mrs. Ben Everett purchased the I. D. Hedge ranch last week.

June 28, 1940 (SMR): Harvey King accepted employment in Austin and gave up King's Cafe.

July 12, 1940 (SMR): Postmaster W. S. McLendon was building a new home. Mr. and Mrs. John Killen would occupy the old one that they bought.

September 20, 1940 (SMR): Quite an excitement was caused early Friday morning (9-13) when the Dripping Springs gin and mill burned.

November 8, 1940 (SMR): Dripping Springs lost its one source of amusement when James Ferrell moved his moving picture equipment to Moulton. Mrs. Mary Spaw became acting postmaster at Dripping Springs, taking the late W. S. McLendon's place.

January 17, 1941 (SMR): Sam Byars was building a new rent house and I. D. Roberts just finished building one.

March 7, 1941 (SMR): Citizens of Dripping Springs contributed funds to build a seven-foot ornamental fence between campus and main highway to be completed in a short while. Added much to the appearance of the school ground.

April 4, 1941 (SMR): The State Highway Department donated enough wire to enclose the entire school grounds.

April 11, 1941 (SMR): Mrs. Della Cockrell sold her ranch in Mt. Gainer and was building a house on a lot purchased from P. L. Turner.

July 18, 1941 (SMR): J. E. Spaw bought the W. C. Crenshaw house and moved in last week.

July 25, 1941 (SMR): The new home of K. C. Whisenant was nearing completion. It was purchased under the FST plan.

August 1, 1941 (SMR): Mrs. I. V. Davis was having a house built next door to Mr. Tilley. Work was beginning on a new Church of Christ.

August 8, 1941 (SMR): The W. A. Lyle home has been purchased by a Mr. Graves of Austin. P. A. Glosson was having a rent house built on his property. Mrs. Arthur Keesee was purchasing the boarding house owned by Lou Breed of Austin.

August 15, 1941 (SMR): The school must have a new pump for the well and plans were being made to raise the necessary funds.

August 22, 1941 (SMR): Taking advantage of the prices, Mr. and Mrs. Ray Volmering sold their goats and sheep and were building a home. Mrs. Vanda Volmering was having a home built on a P. L. Turner lot.

September 12, 1941 (SMR): W. C. Goslin was remodeling and enlarging his drugstore. Ed Howard of Kyle moved the old store 22 feet and did the job so smoothly that Mr. Goslin carried on his business while the moving was done.

October 10, 1941 (SMR): J.W. Wilson took over the Texaco station formerly run by Tommie Turner.

October 17, 1941 (SMR): Mary Spaw received definite appointment as postmaster.

November 14, 1941 (SMR): Seven huge trucks of wool left the warehouse of W. P. Crow.

November 21, 1941 (SMR): Mr. and Mrs. J. W. Butler moved into Mrs. I. V. Davis's new house. Would celebrate their 50th anniversary next week. Mr. and Mrs. Jesse Ragland were building a new rock veneer home in the P. L. Turner addition. The W. C. Goslin store was practically complete with an attractive light-colored rock. The school received a new flag from the Austin American Legion Post.

December 5, 1941 (SMR): W. C. Goslin moved into the new store. Baptist Church being re-shingled. Dripping Springs post office being moved into the J. E. Spaw barbershop.

January 2, 1942 (SMR): Mr. and Mrs. J. E. Ragland moved into their new home. Mr. and Mrs. W. A. Lyle moved into the Ragland house which Mrs. S. E. Lyle purchased. Church of Christ building rapidly nearing completion.

February 20, 1942 (SMR): Mr. and Mrs. Andrew Herwig moved here and opened a store in the Brumley building.

March 13, 1942 (SMR): Miss Mayne Kroll purchased the cafe formerly owned by Leroy Roberts.

June 12, 1942 (SMR): Lee Smith purchased part of the Chapman estate and would build a house and other improvements.

August 7, 1942 (SMR): Mr. Bowling and Mr. Mills rented the vacant cafe building and would be buying tomatoes, potatoes, and onions.

September 18, 1942 (SMR): Mr. and Mrs. Lee Smith moved into their new home.

June 25, 1943 (SMR): The Bill Garnetts were completing the rock house they started several years before. It was built of unusual rocks, with curios and other old timey things decorating it. The house was interesting as well as attractive.

September 3, 1943 (SMR): Mr. and Mrs. Alva Haydon were having their home rebuilt. It would be an attractive rock house when completed.

October 8, 1943 (SMR): Alva Haydon closed his garage here which leaves Dripping Springs "garageless."

June 2, 1944 (SMR): Mr. and Mrs. John Ferrell moved to Dripping Springs and were living in the Methodist parsonage. Members of the Baptist church purchased lots near the church and would build a parsonage on them at an early date.

September 15, 1944 (SMR): The new Baptist parsonage was soon to be completed and ready for the pastor to move in.

July 19, 1946 (SMR): School bond election passed 137-24 and was used to build a new school and buy two new buses. Arrangements were made for remodeling a building for school lunch service to make more room for classes.

Mercer Street, 1956

January 10, 1947 (SMR): Dripping Springs started the new year with several new buildings being erected. Billie Garnett was constructing a new tile building to be used as an electric appliance and repair shop. Mrs. Robert Shelton opened a dress shop and variety store and the Watson brothers, recently discharged from the army, were in the garage and filling station business. Ten new homes were built in the last few months and the school's plan was on display with the school to be completed the same year.

August 8, 1947 (SMR): Mrs. Ola Butler moved to town and was taking care of the phone office.

January 23, 1948 (SMR): Baptist church is to be remodeled and enlarged in the near future. The Methodist parsonage has been sold and a new one on the highway is planned.

April 23, 1948 (SMR): The Methodist parsonage is almost finished and expecting a resident pastor by June.

May 21, 1948 (SMR): The formal opening of the new auditorium at the First Baptist church was on Sunday.

October 22, 1948 (SMR): The cornerstone to the new school will be laid with appropriate ceremony on November 1 and is expected to be finished in late January.

November 26, 1948 (SMR): Dripping Springs is selling bonds for the lighted football field. The PTA gave $100 toward the lighting of the field.

May 13, 1949 (SMR): Mr. and Mrs. Jimmy Glosson bought a house and plan to move it to a lot west of Dripping Springs and move in as soon as it can be remodeled.

March 24, 1950 (SMR): The Methodist church has improved their building with a new foundation and other repairs. Among other things, the church is being turned around to face the Wimberley highway. A new rock barbeque pit has been added.

September 22, 1950 (SMR): The Methodist church looks very nice after being repainted. The inside has been cleaned and the grounds are being worked on.

November 8, 1950 (SMR): Mrs. Minnie Horner moved into her lovely new home.

March 2, 1951 (SMR): Mr. and Mrs. James Ragland leased the old Puckett place and expect to move in shortly.

March 23, 1951 (SMR): We have a new beauty shop operator at Willie Mae's Beauty Shop. Mrs. Vaughan Glosson has the task of making the ladies of Dripping Springs beautiful. Mrs. Haydon is still the owner but is at home resting.

April 6, 1951 (SMR): Mrs. Dosia Hohman is having a home built in Dripping Springs.

June 29, 1951 (SMR): Mrs. John Ferrell has moved to her new home. The Murphy family of San Antonio gave the Methodist church a beautiful old piano. The other has gone in the Sunday School rooms.

July 13, 1951 (SMR): Dosia Hohman is being honored with a housewarming party. She recently moved into her new home.

August 17, 1951 (SMR): The Central Service Station was robbed on the 12th, a Sunday night.

October 5, 1951 (SMR): Construction work at the Methodist parsonage is progressing nicely. The foundation for the garage and storage space has been poured and the men are ready to begin the walls.

October 19, 1951 (SMR): Construction work on the Methodist parsonage is progressing rapidly. John Baird is doing the work with the help of volunteers.

November 23, 1951 (SMR): Fire totally destroyed the two-story Masonic Lodge/grocery store early Monday morning (11-19).

February 1, 1952 (SMR): Mr. and Mrs. Andrew Herwig sold their interest in the Herwig and Jennings Lumber-Feed store to Lewis Jennings and moved to a turkey ranch near Johnson City.

February 22, 1952 (SMR): The Dripping Springs Community Council met on Thursday (2-14) to discuss a bond election to build a gym.

March 21, 1952 (SMR): Mr. and Mrs. Alfard Hohman were honored with a housewarming on March 14.

May 16, 1952 (SMR): The Community Council is trying to interest a doctor in establishing an office in Dripping Springs.

June 6, 1952 (SMR): Mr. and Mrs. Dayton Roberts are building an addition to their home.

September 5, 1952 (SMR): P. A. Glosson and W. F. Rippy purchased the old Scheh cafe building and are now in the feed business.

October 17, 1952 (SMR): The Baptist church is buying new pews and making other repairs.

January 2, 1953 (SMR): Construction on the educational building for the Methodist church has been started. Alfard Hohman is in charge of the work.

March 6, 1953 (SMR): Dripping Springs is without a dress shop and variety store since Mrs. Robert F. Shelton moved hers to Austin.

March 20, 1953 (SMR): It is announced the 12th of May is the date for the opening and dedication of the recently constructed educational building at the Methodist church.

April 17, 1953 (SMR): Dripping Springs adds a new business with the opening of a BBQ stand by Garland Seal.

May 15, 1953 (SMR): Dripping Springs boasts of another grocery store in the Billie Garnett building. Billie and Alma Garnett are to run it and there will be an open house June 6.

January 22, 1954 (SMR): Alfard Hohman purchased the drugstore owned by Dayton Roberts. He is remodeling it and hopes to be in this week.

July 9, 1954 (SMR): Dripping Springs has a new cafe, serving barbeque lunches. Mr. Garland Seal opened his cafe for business on Saturday, June 26. He barbeques the meat he serves.

September 10, 1954 (SMR); Mr. and Mrs. Travis Garnett held open house on Saturday, September 4, when opening their new Humble service station.

September 24, 1954 (SMR): Will Crow bought the Garland Seal cafe. It closed for repairs and reopened with Katherine Roberts running it.

January 7, 1955 (SMR): Mr. and Mrs. Virgil Conn purchased the contents of the Drug & Grocery store from Alfard Hohman and are in business there.

January 14, 1955 (SMR): Mr. George Wiest purchased the cafe formerly operated by Katherine Roberts and owned by Will Crow. It is now run by George and Lorene Wiest.

Wiest Cafe
—Courtesy James Felps

January 21, 1955 (SMR): Mrs. Allie Mae McClaferty was having her service station remodeled. It was to be operated by Ira Ruston.

February 10, 1956 (SMR): Pete Glosson took over the feed store from Lewis Jennings. George Wiest was having a new addition added to his cafe.

May 16, 1956 (*Hays County Citizen*): Mr. and Mrs. George Wiest added an all-night service station to their business and as of the previous Friday began keeping their cafe open all night.

September 7, 1956 (HCC): Mr. and Mrs. Thoma Crow moved into their new home in Dripping Springs.

September 28, 1956 (HCC): Mr. and Mrs. E. E. Myers are building a house on land recently purchased from S. J. Moore. Billy Ray Rippy just moved into the house vacated by Billie Garnett. Mr. and Mrs. Jim Fulton and Mr. Willie Tschoeppe have moved to the house they just purchased from Mrs. Allie Mae McClaferty.

October 3, 1956 (SMR): Marvin Odell

purchased the Wilson Fairly place and is to move there. The Fairlys are moving to Abilene.

November 9, 1956 (HCC): Mr. Hitchcock and Mr. Roberts of San Marcos are to open up a cedar post yard.

November 16, 1956 (HCC): The E. E. Myers house is almost complete and they are to build a new home on the lot where their present home is located for Mr. and Mrs. Harvey King.

December 14, 1956 (HCC): Mr. and Mrs. Wooten moved into their new home on the Fredericksburg highway.

January 18, 1957 (HCC): Mr. and Mrs. Harvey King's home has all but been torn down and the new one is ready to begin.

January 25, 1957 (HCC): Mrs. Lewis Jennings opened up the Rock Cafe. It has been closed for a while. Katherine Roberts is helping in the cafe.

March 8, 1957 (SMR): A housewarming has been held for Mr. and Mrs. J. C. Harmon, who recently completed their new home.

June 23, 1957 (HCC): Johnny Ireland bought the O. J. Bean place and moved in.

August 1, 1957 (HCC): The Church of Christ moved from where it was built to give right of way for the Super Highway.

August 8, 1957 (HCC): Mr. and Mrs. Elmo Hall bought the Schlortt home.

September 12, 1957 (HCC): Mrs. Mattie Volmering opened up the cafe on the highway owned by W. P. Crow. It has been closed for a while. Last run by the Wiests. Mr. and Mrs. Sorrell opened their cafe near the school.

October 17, 1957 (HCC): Mrs. Carrie Jo Latson bought the East End Cafe. She took over the cafe the previous Monday. Mr. Wiest had run the cafe until recently.

November 14, 1957 (HCC): Lou Glosson bought the Mt. Gainer Baptist Church, moved it to a lot in Dripping Springs, and remodeled it for a residence.

January 16, 1958 (HCC): The Wallace Horners have been living in the Brenizer place until it sold. They are moving back to their home in Dripping Springs.

February 27, 1958 (HCC): Mrs. Lou Glosson moved into her new home in Dripping Springs. Mrs. Carrie Jo Latson sold the East End Cafe to Mr. and Mrs. Stephenson of Austin. They took over the previous week.

March 6, 1958 (HCC): The E. L. Russells moved to their new home across from the Brenizer place.

August 14, 1958 (HCC): Mrs. Mattie Volmering sold the cafe she has been operating for some time to Mrs. Chester Davis. The new highway is almost complete.

September 18, 1958 (HCC): Mr. and Mrs. Stephenson of Houston, who owned and operated the East End Cafe, sold it but bought it back and are to open it up again Tuesday. It has been closed for the past two weeks since Mrs. Chester Davis closed it.

October 16, 1958 (HCC): The new highway is nearly finished. The ditches are being cleaned out.

November 6, 1958 (HCC): Alva Haydon is building a new filling station on the new highway.

February 5, 1959 (HCC): Mr. and Mrs. Billy Rippy moved into their new home. So did Mr. and Mrs. William Glosson. Raymond Whisenant has his new home ready for Coach Daugherty to move into.

February 26, 1959 (HCC): Noah Edwards bought the P.L. Turner home.

April 9, 1959 (HCC): E. E. Myers opened up the new Magnolia station owned by the Haydons. Garland Seal is almost ready to move into his new home.

May 28, 1959 (HCC): Marvin Hill is moving from the Dayton Roberts house to the one they recently bought from John Spaw.

June 11, 1959 (HCC): Fred Garnett and family moved into the Dayton Roberts house. E. E. Myers had a grand opening at the Magnolia station.

June 18, 1959 (HCC): Polly Goslin sold her old plank store building behind her rock store to Lewis Jennings who is using it for his lumber business. Mrs. Goslin expanded her rock store.

July 30, 1959 (HCC): The Charlie Neal Haydons are moving to their new home, which was the old Bill McNair place. The Ray Kelleys are to move to their old house where the Haydons had lived for four years.

November 5, 1959 (HCC): The new Sinclair station is completed and now in operation. It is owned by Ed Felps and run by L. B. Wooten.

December 5, 1959 (HCC): Skeet Ragland is building a new home near theirs but on the new highway. Travis Garnett is building a new station on the new highway.

January 14, 1960 (HCC): Dial telephones have been installed. Mr. and Mrs. Bill McNair moved into their new home. W. P. Crow moved back into his home that the McNairs had been living in.

January 28, 1960 (HCC): Mr. and Mrs. Gourley moved from Katherine Roberts' house and Mrs. Massey moved in.

February 25, 1960 (HCC): The James "Skeet" Raglands moved into their new home.

March 17, 1960 (HCC): The Conns sold their drug and grocery business to the Wiests.

October 27, 1960 (SMR): The D. R. Mulhollens recently moved into their new home on Fitzhugh Road. They had been living in the old John Gibson place.

January 3, 1961 (SMR): Bids are being let for the new U.S. Post Office.

March 23, 1961 (SMR): The contract for the new post office went to J. W. Glosson. The post office formula is to have private ownership of the land so it would stay on the tax rolls. The building is to be leased by the Post Office for five years with one five-year option renewal. The building is to have 800 square feet and all new equipment.

May 11, 1961 (SMR): The Civic Club is assisting in building the rodeo pen on the school ground. Hopes to have it completed in the near future.

July 13, 1961 (SMR): The Jimmy Hoards were honored with a housewarming for their new home.

August 17, 1961 (SMR): Nut's Hobby Shop formally opened on Saturday the 19th. Mr. and Mrs. Virgil Conn are the owners.

August 24, 1961 (SMR): Mr. and Mrs. Ira Ruston and family moved to the Oran Rippy house recently occupied by Minnie Matthews. He is to be employed as a barber.

November 30, 1961 (SMR): The Dripping Springs Lumber Company, owned by O. B. McKown, is to have its grand opening on December 2. A turkey is to be given away. The Post Office opens for business for the first time on Thanksgiving morning.

December 28, 1961 (SMR): Mr. Felix Rippy purchased the Billy Ray Rippy house and moved in.

April 5, 1962 (SMR): Skeet Ragland recently completed his Conoco service station at the Village Center. Melvin McNair is to be the proprietor.

April 19, 1962 (SMR): Mr. M. Z. Piland is soon to have his office open at the former Texaco station. He is in the real estate business.

May 17, 1962 (SMR): The John A. McNairs were honored with a housewarming party at their new home.

June 14, 1962 (SMR): The U.S. Civil Service Commission is taking applications for the Dripping Springs postmaster. Pay is $4,975. July 3rd is the cutoff date.

September 13, 1962 (SMR): Work is beginning on a new Methodist Church. Charlie Oldham is the contractor.

January 24, 1963 (SMR): The formal opening of the Methodist church is to be February 10.

February 21, 1963 (SMR): The cornerstone has been laid for the new Methodist church. Charlie Oldham and Willie Lyle, who assisted with the rockwork, laid the stone.

February 22, 1963 (HCC): The Dripping Springs Methodists held opening services in their new church. The Baptists did not hold services so all could come to the opening.

March 23, 1963 (HCC): The Grady Moores moved to Dripping Springs on the Alfard Hohman place near the school. The Hohmans are building a new home.

April 4, 1963 (SMR): Mr. and Mrs. John Clower and two daughters, Deanne and Judy, moved into their new home on Fitzhugh Road.

May 24, 1963 (HCC): Mr. and Mrs. Elbert Shelton bought the old Dave Jones house from the Gibson children.

June 27, 1963 (SMR): J. W. Wilson opened a new TV shop. The old one was destroyed by fire several weeks previously.

July 11, 1963 (SMR): Mr. and Mrs. Alfard Hohman moved into their new home. They were living on the Will Crow ranch.

July 25, 1963 (SMR): Calvin Knauth is named Dripping Springs ISD superintendent. Mr Robert Shelton took a job in Roma, Texas.

October 17, 1963 (SMR): The Pound house received its Historical Medallion in ceremonies held at the house on October 12. Mr. and Mrs. Clarence Cobb are now living in Dripping Springs. They purchased the home previously owned by Mrs. Wiedebusch.

November 28, 1963 (SMR): Mr. and Mrs. Woody Glosson were honored with a housewarming for their new house. Also, Mr. and Mrs. Bradshaw completed their new home in the same subdivision.

December 5, 1963 (SMR): Bradley Davis and his sister, Mrs. Lanier Dement, moved into the home owned by Dayton Roberts.

April 2, 1964 (SMR): The Dripping Springs Civic Club sponsored a fish fry at the school. It was attended by 400 people. The occasion was the opening of the new wing to the school. The high school band entertained.

May 21, 1964 (SMR): Mrs. Lura Womack and son, Bobby, took over the cafe at the Village Center.

July 17, 1964 (HCC): W. P. Crow, president of the Dripping Springs Water Supply Corporation, announced that construction is underway.

July 23, 1964 (SMR): O. B. McKown purchased the home owned by the Lou Glosson heirs.

August 27, 1964 (SMR): Mr. and Mrs. George Wiest are now at their new location next door to the Sinclair station. A new electric scoreboard is installed at the football field. The Community Recreation Club held its first meeting of the year. They elected officers and planned the first party to be held on Saturday, September 12.

September 17, 1964 (SMR): Mrs. Daisy King and Mrs. Katherine Roberts are moving to Mrs. Roberts' house on Fitzhugh Road, across from the Masonic Lodge.

October 15, 1964 (SMR): The new fence and gates are installed at the Phillips cemetery.

October 22, 1964 (SMR): Bersha McIntyre and Joy Whisenant are in business together at Bersha's Beauty Shop. They renamed it B&J's Beauty Shop.

April 8, 1965 (SMR): Mr. and Mrs. J. E. Murrah purchased a lot from Alva Haydon's block and started building a house. Mrs. Mae Watson bought a lot from Virgil Conn and intends to begin building soon.

April 29, 1965 (SMR): Burglars broke into Glosson's Grocery, Gay Harris Feed, McNair's Hardware, and Rippy Wool and Mohair. Cash was taken at Glosson's and McNair's, but nothing at the other two.

July 15, 1965 (SMR): Mrs. Mae Watson is expected to move into her new home the next week.

August 5, 1965 (SMR): Mr. and Mrs. Ernest Williamson recently completed their new home and moved in.

It was at this point that I moved to Dripping Springs and so I did not feel much like continuing the process of reading all the newspapers of the area. The history of Dripping Springs in the last 35 years can be pieced together by reading other chapters in this book. I'll leave that up to you.

Governing Entities

As all other citizens of the State of Texas, the residents of Dripping Springs and Phillip A. Smith league are governed by several governmental bodies. The people of Texas are also unique in the type of governments that have had control over them in their history. They had to follow the laws of Spain and then Mexico before gaining their independence and becoming the Republic of Texas. After a decade of independence, Texas became one of the states of the United States of America. Fifteen years later, they would cast their lot with the Confederate States of America before returning to the fold. Each of these steps along the way would put the citizens under a higher set of laws, as well as their local ones.

Commissioner's Court

Beginning with the Texas Constitution of 1845, a framework of government for the counties was put in effect. The business of the county was to be taken care of by a county judge and four commissioners. It was known as the Commissioner's Court. They would be assisted by other officials of the county. These would be the Sheriff, Tax-Assessor-Collector, County Clerk, District Clerk, and County Treasurer. Until 1848, the people of what is now Hays County, were a part of Travis County. All of that changed when the county of Hays was carved out of Travis County. Even then, the P. A. Smith league did not exist. This would not occur until April 27, 1850. We will only concern ourselves with the commissioner who served the P. A. Smith survey.

According to an article written and published in the *Times of Hays County*, a special edition newspaper depicting the history of Hays County until 1880, the four commissioners were not elected by geographical precincts for the first six years. That is understandable when one understands the sparsity of population, especially in the northern half of the county during that span. With that in mind, the commissioner chosen was the one closest to the Dripping Springs area. The first election was held on March 8, 1848, with only fifty people voting in the election. **Shepard Colbath** was one of those elected. He was listed in an 1856 school census from the school precinct that included Dripping Springs. Therefore, it is my opinion he was the first commissioner for our area. The best I can tell, the nearest person elected from 1850-1854 was **Ulysses A. Young** of Wimberley. From the beginning, the commissioners met quarterly, with a few special meetings thrown in, and were paid three dollars a day for their services. The county judge was called the Chief Justice.

At this point, the county was divided into four precincts. As the population of Hays County grew, the precincts had to be adjusted to make the voting populace more representative. Dripping Springs was in Precinct 3. **L. M. Gatlin**, of the Gatlin Community, represented the precinct from 1854-1858. **T. P. Roundtree** held the office from 1858-1860. The best I can tell, **U. A. Young** became the commissioner for Dripping Springs for the term of 1860-1862. This time span included the joining of the Confederacy by Texas. Although the state was a part of the Confederacy, few things changed for the local governments. It was business as usual—the usual business of trying to support the war effort.

Ranson G. Blanton, who had earlier served as the Dripping Springs postmaster, was elected a commissioner in 1862 and served in that post until his resignation in January 1867. Texas messed up by not ratifying the Amendments to the U.S. Constitution and the second Reconstruction Era began under military control. This also changed the name of the court. It was now called the Police Court and its members were Police Commissioners. Commissioners were paid four dollars a day. **William Adams** of Fitzhugh served as commissioner from 1867-1870.

During this span of time, the Constitution of 1869 was ratified. As a part of the Texas Constitution that was convened under the Construction laws of Congress passed March 3, 1867, and as directed by General Order No. 27 from Headquarters 5th Military District dated March 7, 1869, it is ordered and decreed that the territory of Hays County be divided into five justice precincts, each having specific boundaries. Dripping Springs fell within Precinct 4. Precinct 1, which was San Marcos, elected the Presiding Justice. The other four were now called Justices of the Peace, instead of commissioners. It was still known as the Police Court.

Lorenzo Daw Moore, who lived northwest of Dripping Springs on present-day CR 187, was elected in 1870. His term of office would end in tragedy. As he went out to look for some of his horses on May 19, 1872, he was attacked by a band of Indians. After giving a good account of himself, he was slain by them. At their July 29, 1872, court meeting, a resolution was written into the minutes, which read, "Whereas it has been made known to us that our esteemed brother, Lorenzo Moore, was brutally murdered near his house in the county on the 19th day of May, 1872, by a band of savages. Be it resolved that by his sudden death it forcibly reminds us of the uncertainty of life and that we, too, will soon be called away and that his loss calls forth our warmest sympathies for this family, in their deep distress. And while we regret this loss of his reason and sound judgment on the administration of the duties of the court, yet we humbly bow to Him who rules over the destinies of us all. Resolved that by the death of our brother, the county has lost an efficient officer and honest and upright citizen."

B. F. Cady, of Bear Creek, took Moore's place on September 30, 1872, and served one term. **J.R. Brown** was elected in 1874 and served to 1876. During this term the JPs were called associate justices. The laws under the Constitution of 1876 were now in effect and under this constitution, each county would have a commissioner's court, one from each of four precincts and presided over by a county judge. The precinct that would include the Dripping Springs area would remain Precinct 4. Each commissioner's pay reverted back to three dollars a day and would stay that way until around 1918.

J. L. Blazemore of the Cedar Valley area was the first to serve under the new constitution. He would serve two years and **Peter Schmidt** of the Salem area came on to serve from 1878-1882. **W. R. Wood** was elected two terms, serving from 1883-1886. **Peter**

Schmidt would return to the office for 1887-1888. **B. R. Wilhite** of Dripping Springs held the office from 1889-1894. **J. R. Wuthrich** was elected for the 1895-1896 term. **J. M. Morris** was elected for the 1897-1898 term but resigned his post November 12, 1897. **M. L. Reed** of Henly served out his term. **Ben F. Stephenson** of Dripping Springs was elected for the turn of the century term, 1899-1900.

D. P. Fairley was elected in the November 1900 election but by February 1901 had died. **Ben F. Stephenson** was appointed to take his place and evidently stayed in office until an election was held later in the year. **W. C. Day** served from 1902 until 1904. **J. W. Glosson** of Dripping Springs held the office for two terms, 1905-1908. **J. R. Wilhelm** of Driftwood was elected and served 1909-1912. **P. L. Turner** served from 1913-1916; **John T. Spaw** from 1917-1920, and **J. W. Champion** from 1921-1924. They were all from Dripping Springs. **E. H. Martin** stepped in to serve 1925-1928. After that, **J. D. Rust** of Henly held the position until 1934. **Charles Haydon** served from 1935 until his death in May of 1938 and his wife, **Beulah**, was appointed to serve out his term. **Reid Hollingsworth** of Henly took up the banner and served from 1939 to 1941. He was seriously injured in an automobile accident and circumstances surrounding the accident caused a group to file charges of incompetency against him. He resigned effective February 1, 1942. **A. A. Elsner** of Dripping Springs was appointed to serve during 1942.

Lewis B. Jennings of Dripping Springs took over for the years 1943-1946. He handed the reins over to **Virgil Conn**, also of Dripping Springs, who held the office for the next fifteen years. This was the second longest tenure of anyone. The longest belongs to his successor, **Lynn C. McCarty** of Henly, who took over in January of 1963 and served until 1984. His last term held a few out of the ordinary events. Around the election in November of 1982, he was accused of taking county gas for personal use. After winning the election, he decided to resign his position. **Oran Hill Rippy** of Dripping Springs resigned his teaching position at Dripping Springs ISD to take the appointment. In the meantime, McCarty's lawyer convinced him to come back and serve the term he was elected to because the lawyer felt the act of resigning would put the aura of guilt on him in the upcoming trial. So he took the oath of office on January 1, 1983, and began to serve his new term of office. This left Rippy a very short-term commissioner. At least for the time being.

The trial exonerated McCarty of guilt. However, in the summer of 1984, Lynn decided to retire. Oran Rippy was again appointed to finish the term. The reason for early retirement was to give Rippy a leg up in the coming election, since he would be running as an incumbent. Rippy won the election and two more, the last two for four-year terms. In November of 1994, **Russell Molenaar**, of Paul's Valley, surprised Rippy and ousted him from the court. Molenaar won reelection in the 1998 and 2002 elections.

Commissioners traditionally have been thought of as having mostly road duties. In the early days, they appointed people to view and locate roads, oversaw the actual building of the roads, and then later reviewed them for possible improvement. Each precinct had its own barn to store road equipment. Each year commissioners were required to give a report on the conditions of the roads in their precincts. In those days, the commissioners took a lot of flack over roads in their precincts. It seems that more road improvement took place around election time than any other.

Some of the funds they had to administer in the old days that seem unusual to us today were the Lunatic and Pauper Fund and the Estray Fund. The Estray Fund were the proceeds received from the sale of stray animals. Of course, they needed the Road and Bridge Repair fund. They would also determine the amount of money to be given to

Precinct 4 County Commissioner's Office/Road Department, 1930s

each school district from the county coffers. Anything that had to do with the county had to be approved by the commissioner's court and still does. They would appoint the people in charge of elections, name the individuals to serve on the petit and grand jurys, etc. They had to oversee the building of four courthouses and the renovation of the last one. Today they take care of one of the fastest growing counties in Texas. No more quarterly meetings. It is now a salaried occupation that takes a commissioner's full-time attention.

There were some interesting things that showed up in the minutes of their meetings. At least they struck me as interesting.

In the November 1865 meeting they commissioned the Assessor-Collector to collect a poll tax for each male of the age of 21 in Hays County. Freedmen, idiots, and persons non compos mentis excepted.

In the September 29, 1873, meeting, Thomas G. Voight presented an account for $10 for one coffin for William Allen, a pauper.

In April 1882, Dr. Joseph Pound was paid five dollars from the Lunatic and Pauper fund for medical treatment of Mrs. McLendon, a lunatic.

In September 1882, W. P. Riley and N. Harris were paid $10 to transport Bob Thompson, a lunatic, from Dripping Springs to San Marcos.

At the August 1890 meeting, an election was ordered to be held in Dripping Springs on September 27, 1890, to determine if the people wanted hogs, sheep, and goats to run wild.

November 1899: Commissioner B. F. Stephenson made the motion and it passed that dancing in the Courthouse would be positively prohibited.

February 1901: Commissioner Stephenson made the point that dancing in the Courthouse has injurious effect on the building. Violators to be fined $25.

November 1906: It was ordered that there be erected a justice courtroom in Dripping Springs for the use of the Justice of the Peace, provided a suitable lot be donated upon which to build it.

January 8, 1908: Commissioner's Court met in Dripping Springs. Leslie Sorrell was found to have a case of smallpox and was living with B. L. Spaw. The Spaws and Charles Livingston family were quarantined and citizens of Dripping Springs warned to watch themselves for symptoms.

City Government

For almost a century after W. T. Chapman laid out the plan for Dripping Springs and filed it on September 24, 1881, the little town of Dripping Springs remained a sleepy farm and ranch community. Suddenly, all of this came to an end. The town's big neighbor to the east, Austin, was responsible for waking the people and prodding them into action. Austin was planning for future growth by expanding its ETJ (Extra-Territorial Jurisdiction). Eventually Austin expected its jurisdiction to reach Highway 281 in Blanco County. When the people of Dripping Springs got wind of Austin's expansion plans to the west, the alarm went off. What this meant to unincorporated areas like Dripping Springs was captivity. Any future plans or decisions would have to comply with the rules set by the Austin government. The citizens of the area organized to do battle.

Much like the United States in a couple of its wars with England, Dripping Springs got lucky. It was a time when Austin was being dogged on several fronts because they had overextended themselves. They could little afford more bad publicity nor had the time to really exert their power in the matter. In the meantime, Dripping Springs came to the realization that one of their chances for success was to incorporate the town. An election was called and the deed was done on April 4, 1981. Much of the surrounding area had owners who petitioned to be a part of the ETJ of Dripping Springs, plus others who wanted to be within the city limits. The result was boundaries of varying shape.

After numerous meetings with officials of Austin, an agreement was reached. One of the main meetings included one in which Gonzalo Barrientos, the Austin mayor, and other dignitaries met with Dripping Springs residents on a rainy day where umbrellas were needed. One of Austin's reasons for extension was to control the growth of the area by administering Austin's more strict regulations to it. They agreed to back away from Dripping Springs and its ETJ, as long as Dripping Springs would pass and enforce some strict subdivision laws of their own. This delayed Austin's expansion to the west for the time being.

The historical first election took place on August 8, 1981. Becoming the first official mayor of Dripping Springs was retired businessman, James W. "Jimmy" Glosson. He was the winner over Bradley Davis and Alva Haydon. Joining the mayor in forming the first City Council were Alva Haydon, E. L. Russell, Oran Hill Rippy, and Joy Whisenant.

Like other small towns that get into the business of governing themselves and experiencing growth, turnover in the council became common. The 1990s proved to be more stable in that area. The second mayoral election took place April 3, 1982, and Mr. Glosson was re-elected. Seven days later the community mourned his death.

Alva Haydon was appointed mayor and served the two-year term plus an additional two-year term of his own. Bob Burke was elected mayor in the April 5, 1986, election and was re-elected in May of 1988, but he would resign in October of 1989. Galen Dodson was appointed to finish out Burke's term, then he ran for and was elected to the position in May of 1990. He turned in his resignation in September of 1991. David Houston was elected mayor on May 2, 1992, but had to resign in December when he moved outside the city limits. Carroll Montague took over the top spot until May 1, 1993, when Terry Garnett was elected to finish out the term. He was re-elected in 1994 and 1996 but was defeated by Wayne Smith in the 1998 elections. Smith was re-elected in 2000 without opposition. In May of 2001, Mr. Smith suffered a serious heart attack with subsequent operations necessary. Because of these health problems, he resigned his position as of July 1, 2001. Todd Purcell, a council member, was appointed by the City Council to fill out Mr. Smith's term. Purcell received no opposition for his bid as mayor in the 2002 election.

Dripping Springs has experienced a tremendous growth since early in the 1990s. The Council has the responsibility of governing all of this growth and the problems growth brings. Just about all of the P. A. Smith survey has fallen to the subdivision/commercial interests. The same can be said for all of the land in the ETJ of Dripping Springs as well. No doubt, tremendous change will take place in the local government in the next decade, as the sleepy little town is transformed into a large urban area that will match that of communities west of IH 35, from Round Rock to San Marcos. More change will take place in the next ten years for the Dripping Springs community and P. A. Smith survey than it did in all of the previous 149.

Dripping Springs Post Office, 1961

Public Services

Many people take for granted the many public services that take place within a community that makes living here much easier and better. In the following pages we are going to try and give you a little enlightenment about these services.

United States Post Office

In frontier times, when an area had enough individuals to warrant it, the United States Postal Service would appoint a postmaster and establish a post office. Dripping Springs was certainly no different from others. However, it probably did not hurt that Dripping Springs was on the established Austin-Fredericksburg road. The three families who settled in the immediate area came in 1854. They had to wait for three years before they could receive mail from their own post office. This would come on June 5, 1857, when John Moss (one of those three) was appointed as the first postmaster of Dripping Springs.

Prior to this act, an area had to have an address, that is, a name. John's wife, Indiana "Nannie," the sister of Dr. Pound's wife, Sarah, is credited with officially giving Dripping Springs its name. It seems to be a natural with all the many springs that were and are in the area. There are those that contend there were earlier maps that already had the name Dripping Springs on them for this area and she did not need to be given credit. The term on those maps could have been used as a description rather than as a designation. Whatever, someone had to fill out the application for a post office and the name on the application becomes the official name of the town. Dripping Springs it was, and Dripping Springs it remains.

In the early days, the house of the designated postmaster would usually serve as the post office. Later on when the town began to develop, business locations served the purpose. Mail would not be delivered daily, more like a couple of times a week. Either the patrons would come in and check or possibly if the postmaster could catch someone headed that way, get them to deliver it to the people it was destined for. The *San Marcos Free Press* listed the individuals who had mail and had not picked it up. It is known that post office sites included the Marshall-Chapman house, the Chapman-Masonic Lodge building (on site of Rippy Ranch Supply), the A. L. Davis building, the Dripping Springs hotel, the J. L. Patterson building and the John Spaw barbershop.

It would not be until 1961 that Dripping

Springs would have a post office built especially for that purpose. The town was beginning to grow and postal business became more difficult to conduct from business locations. The location chosen was the southeast corner of the Academy Block, which is bordered by Old Fitzhugh Road and Mercer Street. A small, red-brick structure of 800 square feet, with a flat roof was built. It would open for business for the first time on Thanksgiving morning in 1961. This would serve the people of Dripping Springs for two decades before the continued growth of the area forced the Postal Service to think about larger quarters.

The site chosen was just across the parking lot. It was the old Glosson grocery store. The building had been vacant for a couple of years. The building was renovated, remodeled, and turned into the newest post office facility for Dripping Springs. The exterior was rocked with limestone blocks to match the older buildings around it. The moving date was February 14, 1984. The little red brick building became only a memory as it was razed to provide more parking space for the new post office.

Since its inception, the Dripping Springs post office has had twenty U.S. postmasters and one Confederate postmaster. Any time the subject of John Wallace comes up, it is usually mentioned that he once served as the Dripping Springs U.S. postmaster but was not allowed to keep his job after the Civil War. Actually, he never served as a U.S Postmaster. Instead, he was appointed as postmaster by the Confederate States of America government while Texas was a member of the Confederacy. The CSA government was carried on much like that of the USA. He served in that capacity from July 12, 1861, until the war's end in May of 1865. Because of his affiliation with the Confederacy, he was ineligible to continue or hold the post under the rules of Reconstruction set out by the United States government. For a couple of years after the war, the United States tried to allow the Southern states to carry on their business as before. When the Southern states began to fall back into their pre-war ways, a new set of Reconstruction rules were administered and the military took over the governmental duties. As part of this, the postal service to Dripping Springs was discontinued from June 26, 1868, to July 10, 1871. The route took a detour through Mt. Gainer to Blanco and the mail was either picked up there or brought in by the military.

In 1976, the United States celebrated its bicentennial. As a part of that, the United States Post Office sent each postmaster an official list of the people assigned as postmaster to that post office. Mr. Oliver Ponder

U.S. Post Office, 1987 Previously Glosson Grocery, 1952

was the postmaster at the time and later shared the list with me. Early on, postmaster assignments did not appear to last long. It could have been because of death, moving, or any number of reasons. At best, they were serving as a convenient dropping off spot for letters and other mail. Articles in the 1880's newpapers mentioned names as postmasters that did not coincide with this official list, which means the appointed postmaster did not always serve in that capacity himself but had someone else do it for him. Certainly, the handing out of a few letters could be handled by most anyone. The date following the postmasters' names is the date of their appointment. Sometimes there is a time span between the time one leaves and the next one is officially appointed.

John Moss (6-5-1857)
Thomas S. Caperton (9-12-1857)
Ranson G. Blanton (10-4-1858)
William Pursley (2-4-1867)
Burrel J. Marshall (7-10-1871)
Jacob F. Roberts (4-1-1872)
William T. Chapman (10-29-1872)
Harold Durar (11-1-1889)
David G. Jones (11-4-1893)
Morgan H. Howard (10-18-1897)
Mercer E. Chapman (2-27-1906)
Charles Seal (3-20-1919)
William S. McLendon (1-1-1938)
Mary L. Spaw (11-1-1940)
Doris B. Davidson (7-6-1962)
Marion E. Summers (9-30-1963)
Oliver L. Ponder (1-8-1972)
Ray Dalhbeck (9-1-1980)
Rene Hollers (6-9-1984)
Carole Futch (11-20-1998).

Tale of Two Cemeteries

As most rural areas with pioneer backgrounds, Dripping Springs has many little family plots that dot the area. In the early days, families had to bury their own and this was usually done on the property near the homesteads. If possible, gravestones would mark the spots but it was not out of the ordinary for graves to be unmarked or, at the least, unidentified. Three burial sites known to me that fall within the P. A. Smith survey are John Wallace, Marshall-Chapman, and the unknown graves under the trees on the DS triangle. Dripping Springs has two major cemeteries that serve the community and are open to families of Dripping Springs and they both have a long history. They are the Wallace Mountain Cemetery and the Phillips Cemetery.

The Wallace Mountain Cemetery is considered the oldest by some, but that may not be true. According to lore, it was started quite by accident in the 1860s. The story given by Mr. Bradley Davis and others was this. A family was traveling through Dripping Springs when their eight-year old daughter died. The distraught parents had no idea where to bury their child when John Wallace came to the rescue. He suggested the top of his mountain as an ideal location because it wasn't good for anything else anyway. This is supposed to be the first burial but it is unknown where the unmarked grave is located. Later Mr. Wallace donated one-quarter acre of land on top of the mountain for a cemetery.

Although the story of the little girl's death and the subsequent burial might be true, the rest of it has some holes in it. First of all, Mr. Wallace never owned the land on top of Wallace Mountain and could not donate the acreage. At that time, Dr. William H. Howard owned the land. On October 13, 1881, A.L. Davis, Sr., and W. T. Chapman, doing business as partners, purchased the property from the Howard heirs. A couple of years later, they sold the land with the stipulation that one acre on top of Wallace Mountain be reserved for a community cemetery. So it is my guess it was actually Davis/Chapman that established the cemetery. That does not mean that graves were not already there. Most likely there were, or why would they decide to designate it, except for the exquisite beauty of the spot overlooking Dripping Springs? However, the oldest marked grave is that of William

Hobdy in 1881 which would coincide with the purchase. To mark the cemetery, the people fenced it in by nailing boards and wire to existing trees. By 1938, the old fence was deemed useless for keeping out the livestock. The present rock post fence was built inside the old one. A survey in the 1960s revealed the present site to be two acres instead of one. This meant the original fenced area was even that much larger than the original donation.

John L. Wallace Family Gravesite

Many prominent members of the community have been laid to rest overlooking the town of Dripping Springs, including the Pounds. It is definitely one of the more scenic views around. In the 1930s, Alva Haydon and Haskell McNair, only teenagers, were given the task of moving to the mountain the graves of the Marshall-Chapman families, which were located in the grove of trees within the old lumber yard on Block 6. The four people buried in this plot were B. J. Marshall (b. 9-9-1828, d. 2-28-1872), D. W. Burkett, Marshall's son-in-law (b. 2-29-1868, d. 4-17-1900), Infant Egerton, Chapman's grandchild (1901), and T. H. Egerton, Jr., Chapman's grandson (b. 5-31-1905, d. 6-2-1907). Mack Crow and his DSHS History Club did likewise to graves located near the grove of trees on the county triangle in the early 1970s.

The Wallace family plot is located south of Highway 290, about halfway between their home site and the Wallace Mountain Cemetery. It contains John Wallace (1821-1893), daughter Mattie (1863-1885), and infant son John Lee (1868-1869), who lived less than a year. On June 8, 2002, the Wallace descendants had a ceremony at the gravesite to place a historical marker on the cemetery. The three-person plot is fenced in and now is a part of the Robert Shelton property.

Dr. J. M. Pound Family Gravesite
Wallace Mt. Cemetery

The Phillips Cemetery, located about two miles south of Highway 290 on Ranch Road 12, was formerly known as the Methodist Cemetery and can definitely pinpoint its beginnings in 1880. The cemetery lies in the southeast corner of the southwest quarter of the P. A. Smith survey and spills

First graves at Phillips Cemetery were Sorrell (on left) and Norwood (on right) in 1880.

over a little into the southeast quarter. On January 10, 1880, the trustees of the Methodist church purchased one and one-third acres of land from John W. Phillips for five dollars. The property line was given as beginning some 600 feet north of the south quarter line. The congregation completed the small Walnut Springs Methodist Church by March of that year.

The Reverend O. A. Fisher recorded the first burial in the diary he kept. He notes on March 12 that he is going to the church near Dripping Springs to hold the Second Quarterly Conference. A cool norther was increasing as the day advanced. March 13—"No service on account of the cold and mist. Quarterly Conference at brother Phillips' residence. A brother Sorrell died and was buried near the new church." The next day the storm intensified to sleeting and freezing. The grave is still there with a low rock wall surrounding it and a marker inscribed "B. C. Sorrell, Born August 29, 1848, Died March 13, 1880." Many of the early graves had fences or rock walls around them. It was more for protection of the body than for ornament. The lack of equipment to dig deep enough into this rocky soil meant shallow graves. Members of the loved one's families would often construct these barriers to protect the bodies from being dug up by wild animals. Although, no doubt, the Sorrell family must have gotten permission, as the land he was buried on was not theirs. A couple of other graves joined him in a short while.

On March 3, 1882, Hays County paid John W. Phillips and Ed Womack two dollars for land to establish a public burying ground. It would contain 4,200 square varas (.73 acres) of land adjacent to the Methodist Church property and would encompass the several graves already there, including Sorrell's. Because it was next to the church, it came to be known as the Methodist Cemetery. It was expanded by an acre in 1922 when Mrs. A. D. Heierman and Mr. A. A. Elsner each gave a half-acre to the cemetery. In August of 1942, Cecil Breed, R. T. Hadley and W. P. Crow were named as a committee to raise funds for more land. All the lots had been used. The result was a donation of 2.3 acres from Felix Lindsey later that month. Other additions included .53 acres in 1975 by Mrs. Alice Elsner, and 1.16 acres in 1981 from the Burl E. Eastup estate. The site grew to 7.72 acres when a 2-acre addition mistake was allowed by M. K. Hage in the early 1990s.

Although the Methodist church would relocate to Dripping Springs in 1901, the cemetery continued to be called the Methodist Cemetery. In 1940, the Methodists decided to turn the cemetery over to the community. Finally, a Cemetery Association was formed in 1962, with Virgil Conn as the first president. At that first meeting, it was officially named Phillips in honor of the original owners of the land. Although many believe that the originally purchased land to build the church on is now a part of the cemetery ground, my research does not bear this out. According to deed records, the cemetery land always has been separate and apart from the church property. The land described as the church property (as best that I can tell) is now a part of the original Phillips property, just north of the cemetery where the grove of liveoaks survive. I believe my research was borne out in Miss Ennis Follis's, *History of Phillips Cemetery*, published in 1993. She had always assumed the church property was a part of the cemetery and had this contention when a Leroy Bush survey in 1965 showed there to be 3.88 acres in the cemetery. She contended that it should have been 4.63. She got this number by adding up the 1.3 acres of the church, 2.3 of Lindsey, and .50 acres each of Elsner and Heierman. It is correct when you take away the church property and add in the Hays County purchase of Phillips and Womack. Anytime you see a deed, you have to remember the final phrase of more or less. Even the 210x426 donation of Lindsey does not come out as 2.3 acres but less.

In the early days of burial, several men of the community would dig the grave, go home to get dressed for the funeral, then after the burial, take turns putting the dirt back on the grave, while the mourners watched. Much of the area, as we know, has a deep shelf of rock, making it hard to dig through. There came a time when dynamite had to be used to blast out the holes. Later, the County would lend their jackhammers to the funeral homes to dig the graves. Later, the funeral homes would buy their own jackhammers. Today, there is machinery that can do the job cleanly and quickly.

There have been some milestones along the way for the Phillips Cemetery. In October 1964, the Austin Fence Company set the posts and built the fence and gate along RR 12. In 1973, John A. and Jay Spillar completed and erected a metal sign at the entrance. On 9-10-1987, there was a ceremony whereby the Methodist church turned over deeds to the Cemetery Association, that included a deed for the 1.3 acres of the original Methodist Church. The flagpole was erected in 1989. Finally, on 5-30-1991, Memorial Day, Phillips Cemetery received its Historical Marker.

Telephone System

Although the people of Dripping Springs had been clamoring for a telephone line since the mid-1880s, the first line I can find being established was in 1895. The people in the newspapers were pushing for a telephone line to run from Kyle through Driftwood, then to Dripping Springs and on to Blanco. Upon putting the question to a banker who might be involved in financing such a venture, they did not find the answer they were looking for. His reply was that there simply were not enough people along the proposed route to make the investment worthwhile.

The first lines around anywhere tended to be by individuals. In the Hays County Commissioners Court minutes of May 13, 1895, A. L. Davis, Jr., was granted permission to run a telephone line along the Austin-Fredericksburg road from Dripping Springs to the east Hays County line as long as it did not impede travel. It did not specify whether the line went to his house on block 10 or to his store on block 7. Most likely the store. Mrs. Georgia Pound Cavett substantiated this when in her recollections in the May 14, 1954, edition of the *San Marcos Record* she said one telephone was finally installed at the A. L. Davis store. Around 1902-1903, J. R. Wilhelm put in a telephone line from Driftwood to Dripping Springs according to the book on the history of Driftwood.

Sometime after 1900 (because the census listed him as a farmer) and most likely after 1903, Robert E. "Bob" Spaw established the Dripping Springs Telephone Company. He had a telephone exchange at Dripping Springs, plus lines to Austin, Driftwood, and Henly. According to the deed date, he sold his entire business to Inter-Urban Telephone Company on June 13, 1905. This new setup would make Spaw the President/Treasurer with 98 shares of stock in the company. A. L. Davis, Jr., was the vice-president and George H. McCuistion the secretary and the manager of the company. McCuistion was the local druggist and the switchboard was housed in his drugstore on Mercer Street. It was obvious the sell had taken place a little earlier because in the May 11, 1905, issue of the *Dripping Springs Pointer*, the company was already being advertised as having connections of 100 miles without extra charge. It also had a connection with the Martin System at Dripping Springs and Liberty Hill.

In December 1905, McCuistion sold his drugstore to the Crenshaws. Evidently the switchboard stayed there and it is believed that Dora Crenshaw Mading became the switchboard operator. It is not known who was the first operator, but Thelma Houchin and Mattie Campbell were early switchboard operators as well. There could have been several firsts depending on which we are talking about. After all, someone had to operate the switchboard when R. E. Spaw first started the company.

With the added revenue, the company began to expand. His first expansion was to Blanco. The *Blanco News* was full of this expansion. As early as the February 22, 1906, edition, the paper reported Mr. Spaw was in town putting up telephone posts and arranging for putting in an exchange. It was reported he already had 24 people signed up and many others wanting them. He closed the gap between his Henly line and Blanco by the end of April. The people of Blanco could then call to Austin. The switchboard was located in the Blanco bank building. At the same time, Dave Martin, who was the owner of the Martin Telephone System, was putting in lines for his company. Mr. Spaw even moved his family to Blanco to run the company from there. Residential phones cost $12 a year and commercial phones $18. In the June 22, 1906, issue of the *Kyle News* it was reported that the telephone company was constructing a line to San Marcos via Wimberley. "R. E. Spaw intends putting in a switchboard at Driftwood in the near future." In the July 26, 1906, edition of the *Blanco News*, it said Mr. Spaw was in town visiting his family. "He is at work on his telephone line from Dripping Springs to Wimberley at which place he will connect with the Wimberley, Purgatory, and San Marcos line." He purchased that line and as soon as he made the connection, the people on the Dripping Springs telephone system were able to call San Marcos.

At some point in the next four years, William Sampson "Samp" McLendon took charge of the company. Probably around 1908 because Mr. Spaw had moved to Arizona by then. In the 1910 census, McLendon listed his occupation as telephone operator. It is said that for a while he had the switchboard in his parents' house, located on the north half of block 6, second addition. This was around 1910. He bought property a little farther north on Fitzhugh Road and built his house in 1912. It was designed with the telephone company in mind. The rounded style front room was designed to serve as the switchboard room. In the 1912 tax records, the Dripping Springs Telephone Company was listed with a value of $1,500.

A telephone company is quite restrictive on your time. In 1918, McLendon sold his house and the business to Arthur Patton. According to the 1913 poll tax rolls, Patton was listed as the telephone manager. Patton was married to Pauline Seal, the granddaughter of John Lee Wallace. McLendon moved to Brownsville where he worked as a customs agent. A year later he resigned from the job because the climate did not agree with his wife, and moved back to the area. In late 1921, McLendon reacquired the property from Patton, who moved to Buda and bought the Buda Telephone Company.

At some point in the early 1920s, a small

house was built just north of the McLendon's house. This allowed the switchboard to be located there and the operator could live there as well. In 1923 the beginning of a new era emerged. This was the year that Wallace and Ila Mae Horner moved into the little house and Ila Mae took over as operator. She relinquished that position for only one week in the next 37 years. By this time Mid-Continental Telephone Company was in charge of the Dripping Springs service. In 1928 McLendon sold an acre of land to Mid-Continental that included the small house.

A short time later Mid-Continental was taken in by a larger umbrella company known as Mid-West States Utilities Company. However, these were the times of the Depression and that meant times were hard. Mid-West filed for bankruptcy on June 22, 1934. After being in receivership for two years, the Mid-West States Telephone Company emerged the owner on September, 29, 1836. On August 28, 1940, the United Telephone Company became the owners. In the 1950s the Southwestern States Telephone Company became the boss, and in 1968 Southwestern States merged with General Telephone and has been under their wing until Verizon bought out GTE in 2000.

There are always eras in anything that lasts. Some good and some bad. One remembered, with not much fondness, was what happened when the dial system came to Dripping Springs in 1959. Prior to that, telephones were big wooden boxes that mostly hung on the walls. Each customer's telephone number had to do with long and short rings. These were administered by turning a handle. Several rounds for a long and maybe one turn for the short. Most everyone were on party lines. You had to go through the operator to make calls outside your party line. All of these boxes were taken up and replaced by dial phones. The telephones were owned by the company. All of the boxes were stored at the phone office. Fearing that someone might use these old phones to set up a rival company, a decision was made to set the pile of telephones on fire. A Mr. Lacy was sent down from Brownwood and he struck the match that destroyed all the old telephones. Can you imagine what those antiques would be worth in today's market? Betty Butler Haydon, who had worked as an operator at one time, was able to salvage one for herself.

There might be some argument as to who was the first operator but there has never been an argument as to who held the post the longest. Ila Mae Horner holds that distinction hands down. She and her husband moved into the house in 1923 and made it their home for more than a quarter of a century. This meant much of the time they had to live with that switchboard day and night. Finally it got to the point where she received the help she needed. For $90 a month she worked eight hours a day, mailed the toll tickets each day, collected the bills, robbed the pay stations, and mailed the collections report once a month. In 1949 she decided she wanted to try the city life of Austin and took a job there as a PBX operator at the Stephen F. Austin Hotel. It only took a week for her to come back to her senses and resume her rightful place in Dripping Springs telephone history. She continued serving Dripping Springs until the summer of 1960 when she took her last call and pulled the plug on a long and rewarding career in telephone service.

At one time or another, quite a few people got to experience the art of switchboarding. The list looks like a who's who of Dripping Springs. Early on Willie Mae Ragland was the day operator while the McLendons took care of the night. It was kept in the family too, as Odie McLendon, Dilly McLendon Seal, and Erlene McLendon took their turns. Others on the list over the years were Doris Nell Arnold, Inella Breed, Ola Butler, Gertrude Clayton, Delores Conn, Doris Davidson, Rena Tetley, Francis Glass, Polly Goslin, Betty Butler Haydon, Dosia Hohman, Merle Ragland Hohman, Erma

Horner, Willie King, Ottie Langston, Minnie Ferrell Mathews, Lillie Susan Miles, Hazel Bell King Myers, and Thelma Ragland. No doubt there were more we have missed.

With today's modern methods of telephone communications, it is hard to imagine the problems people encountered before the 1960s. Phones were hard to come by in the more remote areas. Lines did not always go from pole to pole but from tree limb to tree limb. The operators often laughingly called it the 4-H system: Hoop and Holler and Hope they could Hear you. The operators were the recipients of much knowledge because all the calls had to come through them. They might have information that no one else had. Sometimes when a person wanted to make a call to someone, the operator would let them know where they could find this particular person. They were the first ones to meet newcomers. If they had the time they could listen in on calls being made from different phones around the community, sometimes being called from there because they did not want others to know what they were doing. Those who had no phones would sometimes come to the phone office to make the call and then have to wait around most of the day waiting for the return call, meanwhile visiting with the operator. Sometimes the operator would receive an emergency message for someone who did not have a phone and they would have to find someone to take the message to them. For many years this service fell on Wallace Horner. He seemed to be the most available for Ila Mae to summon.

People always seemed to share their good times and bad times with the operators. They were the sounding board for many. Mrs. Horner recalled that one man would always call in and bawl her out every time that his horse threw him. Operators were always afraid they were going to be subpoenaed at various trials. Can you just imagine in this day of "tell-all" books just how many millions an operator could make by detailing the interesting tidbits they had gleaned from their job?

Volunteer Fire Department

Until 1958 Dripping Springs had no formal fire department. They had "bucket brigades" that would do their best to get to the fire and use every means at their disposal to put the fire out with a minimum of loss. Seldom were they very successful. Over the years, fires destroyed many buildings in the community. Thanks to the Grange's donation of $200, the community was able to purchase a fire truck from the Buda Fire Department. It was truck #12, a 1921 Seagraves, that Buda had bought from the city of Austin. This was the start. There was no firehouse and in the early days, the fire truck was housed in Short Mama's garage. Finally in the early 1960s, E. G. Kingsbery came to the rescue. He was a big landowner west of town and owned the Feather Lite Cinder Block Company. He donated the cinder blocks to build the fire station. It was built on the north corner of the Hays County Triangle, next to the County Barn. Excited by the thought of having a fire station of their own, the community wanted to honor Mr. Kingsbery by naming the building after him. He quickly let them know that if this was their intention, then he would rescind the offer. Suffice it to say, an unnamed building was erected.

Alva Haydon served as the fire chief for the first 17 years. He also ran Central Garage at the same time. Part of the job description for working with him was you had to be a member of the Volunteer Fire Department. This assured him of having some help in case of fires. He could always depend on Dripping Springs native, Travis Garnett. Travis was a steady member and recalled that many times he would be the only one available at fires. Finally, when Travis retired after more than 40 years of dedicated service, the station received a name. In honor of his longtime service, the station was named the Travis Garnett Station.

The growth of the area dictated that the fire department needed to expand as well.

Volunteer Fire Department House, 1960

An addition was erected on the east side of the present building. Growth continued and the space was not sufficient to take care of the services needed. Plans were made to relocate. Land was donated along Sportsplex Road and funds were solicited to finance a new building. The goal was met and materials were acquired to put up the building. Since much of the work was done by volunteers, it was slow to be finished. As 2000 neared an end, the fire department had not yet moved into their new quarters, but the time was near.

A volunteer fire department takes a lot of dedication from its members. Dripping Springs has been very fortunate in this area. Dedication means when the fire alarm goes off, you drop what you are doing and go fight the fire. There have been years when high school students have been members and got to leave school when called upon to do so. The community cannot begin to appreciate the time and effort these volunteers put forth to help protect those in need of a helping hand, even those thoughtless souls who set burn piles afire and then drove off and left the resultant grass fire to volunteers to bring under control. From the beginning, volunteers have battled the scarcity of money, equipment, and sometimes help, to get a credible job done. Heading up this group were the individuals who were elected to serve as fire chiefs. Serving as fire chiefs for the department since Haydon gave up the post were George Turner, Grady Southwell, Billy Brooks, Joe McCarthy, Rod Holloway, Leroy Boessling, and Joe Felkel. Because of the many hours of dedicated work as fire chief and construction, the members voted to name the new facility Holloway Central after Rod Holloway. The dedication ceremonies were held on January 20, 2001.

The growth of the area has put a tremendous strain on the department, with two or three calls a day, mostly for car accidents. To help out, the department now has a couple of people who are paid to stay at the station and take care of some of the more mundane calls that do not require the attendance of a lot of volunteers.

Dripping Springs Water Corporation

The idea for a water system for Dripping Springs was born in 1963. W. P. Crow was the first president of the water corporation. The other members of that original board were Alva Haydon, E. E. Myers, Bill McNair, and Jimmy Glosson. By July 1964, a grant was obtained and work began. Wells were drilled and pipe lines laid. Water began running through those pipes on April 1, 1965. Since then the Dripping Springs Water Supply Corporation has expanded its services to the citizens in and around Dripping Springs. The Water Supply made plans to install a sewer system for much of the original area of the town of Dripping Springs. This project met opposition due to the nature of the plant and its location. An earlier attempt in the late 1980s to put in a sewer system was met with defeat at the polls. Also, in 1999, there began a tug of war between the water corporation and the city for control of the water system. Finally, late in the year, a vote of the members of the corporation was obtained. Overwhelmingly, the members voted to retain the corporation as it was and not turn it over to the city. Part of the struggle has been because the water system is needed for the sewer system. In 2001, the water corporation contracted with the Lower Colorado River Authority (LCRA) to put in a water line from Lake Travis to supplement the area with much-needed extra water. As 2001 came to an end, the city and water corporation reached an agreement with Erik Howard, who owned the land between RR 150 and North Onion Creek, bordering RR 12, for acreage to locate a waste disposal site for Dripping Springs. The agreement between the city and the water corporation was signed in June 2002. It remains to be seen as to when the sewer system will become a reality.

Emergency Medical Service

It is hard to imagine a time when Dripping Springs did not have the services of an EMS unit. Despite the long history of doctors in Dripping Springs, there came a time when there was a scarcity of such. After Dr. A.E.O. Pope retired in the 1950s, Dripping Springs did not have a permanent in-residence doctor until the late 1980s when Dr. L. M. Cartall set up a practice here. Shortly after I arrived in 1965, so did Margaret Williamson and she was our EMS for many years. Without a doctor in town it was a scary thing to be the football coach and have to think about administering to injuries. We did not have athletic trainers either. I was lucky. Margaret and Ernest Williamson had three boys and they all played sports and that guaranteed the parents would be at the games. Margaret was a professional nurse and her expertise was sorely needed. She came through too many times to count. Fortunately for me, Dr. D. B. Houle and Dr. Don Connell volunteered their time to be on the sidelines as well. We also were able to partake of the UT trainer program where they would assign one of their student trainers to schools around the area to get hands-on experience. We had the good fortune to have the services of Bruce Dumler for several years.

Even with these capable people during the years prior to the establishment of the EMS, professional transportion to hospitals for the serious injuries was non-existent. Someone with a station wagon was usually called upon to transport a player if the injury called for the student to be prone during the trip. Other times the injured player was piled into a car and carted there. It was much the same with the members of the community when they became ill or injured. Then EMS came to the rescue.

The North Hays County Emergency Medical Service actually got its jumpstart in 1974 when Chuck Morrison, the son of

EMS building, 1998

Charles and Janet Morrison, of Wimberley, was involved in a motorcycle/automobile accident. When it took medical services almost an hour to be available in the life threatening injuries, it started Morrison on a crusade. He recognized the need for an EMS organization and started doing something about establishing one for the northern part of Hays County that included Wimberley and Dripping Springs. He headed up a committee that would make their report to the County Commissioners Court in May 1976. The court approved $30,000 to purchase an ambulance and they had to raise another $15,000 to outfit it. Next came the training. That first class included Bob Burke, Homer Cearley, O. C. Harmon, Harrell Robinson, and Ed Thomassen from Dripping Springs. Each year the participation from Dripping Springs continued to grow. That second class included Patti Haffelder, Dave Fields, and Hazel and Bill Bassett. The intensity of the work burned workers out in a few years and new ones took their places, but Patti Haffelder has stayed with the program throughout. She even survived her first experience with not being able to save the patient. It was a true test because she was told that the devastation and reality of not being able to save every life causes many to lose heart.

In the beginning, the EMS headquarters were in Wimberley and had only one ambulance. Response time to Dripping Springs was not as fast as having an ambulance in Dripping Springs. The Dripping Springs group began to solicit pledges for a substation at Dripping Springs. Patti recalls her first loss was Mr. Kuykendall who had already pledged. After his death, his widow doubled that pledge and it was enough to get them over the mark to purchase an ambulance early in 1981. They shared the volunteer fire department building. Volunteers immediately began to add extra bays to accommodate all the vehicles. Even with expansion, the town's growth made this facility too small for one group, much less two. First, they were given land next to the fire department along Sportsplex Road. Next was their quest to raise the necessary funds to erect a building. They met their goal and erected a building on their land. It was completed in 1998 and they moved in and have been operating out of it since.

The EMS, like the VFD, is a volunteer organization. The members have to go through extensive training courses and can advance in degrees in their training. When the alarm is given, the response by the volunteers is tremendous and many lives over those years have been saved by their expertise. Because of the need for someone to stay at the facility most of the time, in the recent past, a paid employee has been used.

Community Library

Dripping Springs has long had an interest in library opportunities for the community. Back in the 1960s and 1970s different stores in the community acted as branch libraries for the San Marcos Library. They transported books from San Marcos, making several trips a month to renew the supply. Lester Brenizer, a prominent man of arts, donated many books to the school library in the early 1950s. Volunteers of the community were determined to make programs available to those not in school and used the school library for their programs.

When the new high school was moved into in 1985, it had a fairly large library at the time. With a grant from the city, the community formed the Dripping Springs Community Library Association and became partners with the high school and staffed a community program. Charlotte Rhodes, Mike Davidson, Lynette Ritter, and Dr. Paula Renfro served on the first Board of Directors. This worked okay until the growth at Dripping Springs continued to soar and the library became inadequate for the high school, much less the community. A new high school library was planned and built but it just was not feasible to continue the shared arrangement.

Dripping Springs Library, 1998

At this point the community got busy and began looking for land on which to build a community library. This was secured when John Baird donated a portion of his land. Now funds had to be raised for a building. Thanks to a very active and creative library board, giant fundraisers were held and well received. So much so, that ground was broken and the dedication of the new facility was held on June 25, 1998. The library continues to be funded by a huge fundraiser each year. The library board was also successful in getting a portion of the city's sales tax dedicated to the library, which gives them some stable funding. The person who has spent the most time as the librarian has been Nora Wouters. She has been very instrumental in giving the library a stable influence during her years of service.

Physicians

A major plus from the very beginning has been Dripping Springs' access to a doctor. Not all areas can make that claim. In some of the early surveys of Hays County, only a couple of doctors were listed. Although there were others, Dripping Springs had the services of two prominent men. Dr. Joseph M. Pound was one of the original three families. He attended one of the most modern medical schools of its time in Kentucky. He would live in the Dripping Springs community until his death in 1914. Several doctors came to Dripping Springs to work around Dr. Pound. One of those was Dr. Edgar Poe (E. P) Shelton. It is said he came to spend a few years to gain experience and move on. Instead, Dr. Shelton followed in Dr. Pound's footsteps. He married a local girl and remained until his death.

Prior to Dr. Shelton, Dripping Springs had another prominent doctor. He was J. W. Harrison. In newspaper articles, he was plying his trade in the area in the early 1880s and possibly earlier. In 1883, he bought block four of the third addition from W. T. Chapman and built one of the more elegant houses which is now owned by Joan Crosswell. He stayed in Dripping Springs until 1891. His wife was not in good health and suffered from rheumatism. I believe they moved to Kerrville. He sold his house to Dr. S. G. Shaw in January 1891, and then in October of that year Dr. Shelton purchased the house. In an 1894 article, it listed a Dr. Steel and a Dr. Russell, along with Shelton and Pound, as doctors in Dripping Springs.

In the early 1900s Dr. Pound and Dr. Shelton were joined by Dr. C. H. Berkley and Dr. A. V. Duncan. Dr. Berkley came to Dripping Springs in 1909 and ended his career here around 1934, when a broken hip curtailed his active life. Dr. A.E.C. Pope moved to the Dripping Springs area in 1947 and began practice here. By September 1948, he had his office in the W. W. "Buddy" Williamson house (now Alfard Hohman's rent house). He also had offices in the Garnett house next to the DS Butane building and the Goslin rock rent house, next to the Veranda. His health caused early retirement before his death in 1960. After this, Dripping Springs suffered a drought of doctors. A few doctors made short stops in Dripping Springs in the early 1980s but did not make it a permanent home. This changed when Dr. L. M. Cartall, who came to Dripping Springs to retire, found the town without a doctor and decided to open an office in the Veranda in 1987. He turned

Dr. J. W. Harrison House, 1883

his practice over to Dr. Todd Buchanan in the mid-1990s. Dr. Mike Sharman joined Dr. Buchanan in 2001 and then took over several of the vacated rooms in the Veranda to set up a clinic of his own.

Newspapers

Newspapers are the heart and soul of a community's history. Unfortunately for Dripping Springs there was little heart and soul from a local standpoint. Even though the community was good enough to support several doctors at a time, it evidently was not good enough to support newspapers. Prior to 1982 Dripping Springs had only three short-time papers published.

The first paper was called the *Pedernales Baptist* and was begun in the Spring of 1905. The editor was A. L. James, the Baptist minister. He turned the paper over to W. Erick James, possibly his son. W. E. James renamed the paper, *The Pointer*. It would only last until October 1905 when James sold his subscriptions to the *Kyle News* and moved to Hondo, Texas. It is a shame that the paper didn't last longer and the copies of the ones published did not survive. The two copies I have are chock full of the things that would have made my research much easier.

It would not be until 1972 that another attempt would be made. Jeanine Lewis, the owner of the old Glosson Grocery, started up a little mimeographed newspaper called *The Roadrunner*. It would blossom into a full-fledged production a little later on. Hughleen Preslar was her editor. Mrs. Preslar said that Mrs. Lewis was not as interested in printing the news of the community as she was trying to get dirt on people. One of her reasons for the paper was to try and get a wet vote for Dripping Springs so they could sell alcoholic beverages at the store. This paper too was short-lived. She sold her subscription list to the Blanco newspaper. The only real long lasting paper was the school's *Tiger Cry* that began publishing twice a month in October 1941. The students would be responsible for the school news and the paper was continued into the 1960s, maybe 1970s. From time to time since, the school paper has been started up and presently one has been published for a number of years as a part of a local newspaper. The *Tiger Cry* kept a pretty good history of the goings on of the school but not so much the community, except through the business advertisements. Just like all the other papers, few copies have been saved for posterity.

Bryan Jones decided to try his luck in the

newspaper business and started up the *Dripping Springs Dispatch* in 1983. He and his wife, Deborah Fey, were owners of the paper and a graphic arts business. They divorced and Jones kept the paper and Fey the graphics art business. Mack Crow, who owned the Crow Hardware store, began going with Jones' ex-wife. As a matter of vendetta, Mr. Crow decided to start up a newspaper in direct competition with the *Dispatch* and tried to run them out of business. He called his paper *The Springer* and it began publishing in 1985. For most of five years they carried on a vicious battle. They alternated between giving the papers away and subscriptions as a way of getting the upper hand. So much so, their story was the subject of an article in *The Texas Monthly*. Finally, Mack had to blink. He moved to New Mexico and the final copy rolled off the press on July 11, 1990. Jones would limp along until 1992 when he sold the paper to Dale Roberson. Roberson would keep the paper in Dripping Springs for several years and finally decided to make the paper a regional edition instead of mainly a local paper. He moved it to the middle of the county and changed the name to *News Dispatch*.

In the meantime, Jack Mynier of Wimberley decided to expand his newspaper holdings. In 1990 he had newspapers covering Wimberley and Kyle and thought it was the right time to move into Dripping Springs. The *Springer* had demised and the *Dispatch* was hurting. Mynier named his paper *The Century-News*. It started out being a weekly for 51 weeks of each year with the copies being mailed free to the people living on a Dripping Springs rural route and subscriptions by others each Wednesday. In 1999 it began to be published twice weekly with the Saturday edition going subscription only. Starting in November 1999 all editions were subscription only. In January 2002, it was decided to make the Wednesday edition free again.

So to fill in the many gaps, the people of Dripping Springs had to go to other sources to find out about the news of their fair community. The *Austin American* began being published in 1874 and has been a choice since then. San Marcos has also provided Dripping Springs with coverage. The first major one was the *San Marcos Free Press* billed as the "Official Paper of Hays and Blanco Counties" by the editor, I. H. Julian. He came to San Marcos in 1873 and shortly thereafter purchased the *San Marcos Times* from F. J. Manlove. At first he named it the *Free Press*. This was November 22, 1873. In December he decided to rename it the *West Texas Free Press* before settling on the *San Marcos Free Press* in November of 1877. He tried to sell it one time but ended up publishing it until his retirement in 1890. Dripping Springs was pretty well covered in this paper and we are fortunate that most of the copies were preserved for our view and study.

David McNaughton founded the *Hays County Times & Farmers Journal* and it, too, covered Dripping Springs from 1886 to 1904, although the copies from 1894 to 1904 were scarce. The *Kyle News* was started April 13, 1903, by Maurice Bell. In November 1905, T. F. Harwell was the editor. About the only time it mentioned Dripping Springs was when it had something to do with Kyle sports. In 1955, the *Kyle News* was renamed the *Hays County Citizen*. *The San Marcos Record* also began in that time-span. Unfortunately, few editions from 1900-1920 were preserved. The *Record* covered Dripping Springs the best. The big problem was getting someone from Dripping Springs to send in weekly reports as to what was going on in the community. Sometimes it would be months, if not a year, before someone would do it for a while. The news from Dripping Springs columns would deal primarily with people. If you wanted to know about each of the church's goings on, who was giving showers, who attended, who was going where to visit, and other organization meetings information, then you were covered. These items were completely covered and for sure were of interest to the readers of the day. I was surprised to find that school activities and sports events, unlike today, were almost nonexistent in the reporting. When they did have a sports section, it covered only the San Marcos schools and only at district or county meets did Dripping Springs receive mention. One of the most frustrating things that frequently happened was that the paper would have a big leadup story about a coming event that would have something to do with Dripping Springs, mostly in the school or sports arena, and then in the next issue would not even mention the event. The *Onion Creek Free Press* came into being in the 1980s and covered Dripping Springs until the mid-1980s when a lack of advertising support and the two Dripping Springs papers forced them to drop that area of coverage and concentrate elsewhere.

Community Service Organizations

Throughout the history of Dripping Springs, there have always been groups of people working toward the betterment of the community. Probably the first to come along would be the group of people who came together to get the Dripping Springs Academy built. It was not a formally organized activity but it met the early criteria for a community service group. The first organization that really had a following in Dripping Springs had to be the Farmers Alliance, a group of people who were formed to do battle with the evils of the railroads. Dripping Springs did not have a railroad to worry about but the charges did affect them. Another subject of debate during those years was Prohibition. The Dripping Springs chapter was called the Wallace Farmers Alliance. It was only mentioned like this a few times so I'm not sure if it was named after the John Wallace family or not, but it would make sense for it to be. It was an active chapter for a couple of decades.

The next organization mentioned in the paper was the Chamber of Commerce, which formed in January 1931. It had 65 members, which included businessmen and ranchers from the surrounding area. Dr. Clell Basket, doctor and druggist of Dripping Springs, was the first president. Leonard Twidwell was elected secretary, J. D. Rust was vice-president, and C. O. McCarty was treasurer. One of their main projects in the early days was to see that dams were put across Onion Creek to prevent flooding. The Chamber must have faded into the woodwork, or least it was not mentioned in later years.

Next came civic clubs with the same basic idea—to work for improvements in the community. The Dripping Springs Community Council was formed in late 1951 by Robert Shelton, the superintendent of schools. He used it as a forum to get support for passing a bond issue to add the gym and cafeteria to the high school campus. With that accomplished, the Council became intent on getting a doctor to come to Dripping Springs and become a permanent resident. Quite possibly, the volunteer fire department and water corporation were outgrowths of civic club concerns. A Recreational Council was formed in February 1958 designed to provide well-chaperoned and wholesome recreation for youth. They entered into an agreement to use the old high school building and gave a BBQ to raise funds to repair the building. The first year officers were B. E. Daugherty, president; C. V. Phillips, vice president; and Mrs. Rufus Johnson, secretary. This organization was still meeting and electing officers in 1964, although I don't recall it when I came here in the fall of 1965. On July 12, 1960, a group of men met to form the Dripping Springs Civic Club. The first officers elected were: O. B. McCown, president; Alva Haydon, 1st vice president; E. E. Myers, 2nd vice president; Jimmy Hoard, 3rd vice president; James Glosson, treasurer; and E. E. Kingsbery, secretary. Meetings were held the third Monday of each month at 8:00 P.M. at Hoard's Cafe, the Western Kitchen. The Civic Club was still an organization when I arrived in 1965 and was active for a few more years. The problems with many of these type organizations is they will go strong as long as they have an active leadership. Eventually, a few have to carry the major load and they tire out and so does the organization.

School booster clubs have been around for some time. The first were the QB Clubs which would meet once a week to watch the football films and discuss ways to raise funds to aid the expenses of the athletic program, volunteer for many of the side duties necessary to carry on a game, and take care of the concession stand. In my early years it meant a big BBQ served on the day of the homecoming game. Eventually they became Athletic Booster Clubs to cover the entire sports scene. Almost every active organization in our schools has a booster club with a major goal of raising funds to help offset expenses.

The incorporation of Dripping Springs gave the people a group to take their concerns to, but as the area began to grow and more businesses were moved in, a new Chamber of Commerce was formed in 1984 and have worked for the betterment of the community. Their mission statement is "To further the commercial and civic welfare of the greater Dripping Springs area by fostering economic growth through the support of existing businesses and attraction of new business consistent with the community." Other groups that fit this description include the Founders Day committee and the Greater Dripping Springs Community Foundation founded in 1999.

Druggists

As soon as Dripping Springs was formed, it had a certified druggist. He was Samuel D. Gilpin, who had a small drugstore built on Block 12, which is across from DS Butane. His first building burned to the ground, and he not only rebuilt with a rock building, but later had another building next to where the Patterson Store now stands. He went into partnership with David G. Jones and moved to the Wortham Business House in 1890, only to see the business fail two years later. I'm not sure if he tried to get into business again or not.

The next druggist was George McCuistion. He bought Lot 5 of block six and built a drugstore on it in 1901. He sold it in 1905, but the new owners were not druggists and could not do prescriptions.

The next certified druggist was probably Clell Basket in 1929. He bought the business and then had to let it go back, although he moved next door into the Breed Market building for several years.

Then like doctors, Dripping Springs would be shy of druggists for decades to come. One of the reasons was probably the improvement in transportation and the nearness of Austin. Finally, with the growth of Dripping Springs and the additions of business centers, there became a need for a pharmacy again. The Senior Citizen complexes were going strong and Wayne Holloway opened up the U-Save Drug Mart in the Redwood Center in August 1984. Although he was a pharmacist, he left most of the work to Nancy Snowden. He moved his business to the Commons in 1986 and renamed it the Dripping Springs Pharmacy. It was a good move because the Redwood Center was consumed by fire a little later. He sold his business to Snowden in 1992, and she has been a mainstay since.

Dentists

Dentists were not as plentiful in Dripping Springs as doctors, probably because, just like today, people put off going to a dentist or use home remedies. One of the first dentists mentioned in newspaper articles was in May 1886 and concerned a traveling dentist. His name was Beckton and he caused quite a stir around Dripping Springs. It seems that he was staying at the local hotel, where one of the teachers at the Academy, 22-year-old Miss Branch, was also staying. By the end of the month they decided to get married. This they did at the

Hofheinz Hotel in San Marcos and then left on a railroad car. He left his dental chair and some articles with Mr. Patterson in San Marcos to send to him when they found a place. In the meantime, word came to Dripping Springs that he was already married and had a wife and two children living in Brownwood. The sheriff was called on to look into the incident. The newspaper made the comment that Miss Branch stood high where she lived but has proven herself wanting in sound judgment. Months later Beckton was caught and charged with bigamy. He received a light sentence.

The first local dentist mentioned was in 1894. He was Dr. Stewart. Not sure how long he stayed but he was still listed in the 1900 census. In the 1910-1911 school catalogue, L. Stipp was advertised as a dental surgeon. Dripping Springs, like most small communities, was just not large enough to support fulltime dentists. Instead, dentists moved from town to town, possibly on a circuit. They advertised in the local paper the length of time they would be in a town, usually a couple of weeks, and if you needed a dentist that would be the time to get it done. Then it would be on to another town. The growth of Dripping Springs in the 1970s and 1980s gave us the necessary population to support a local dentist. Dr. Joe Miller was the first to make the move when he purchased the W. P. Crow house on Creek Road in 1983 and converted the garage into his office. In early 2002, he moved into new quarters on Hwy. 290 and named it the Lone Star Dental Center. The Promenade Center was completed in the mid-1980s, and Dr. Clay Lasiter moved an office into the building in July 1987. He incurred a hand injury on May 10, 1995, that ended his career as a dentist. His business was bought out by the husband and wife team of Allen and Laura Adair. By January 1, 2000, they moved into new quarters a few miles east of Dripping Springs on Hwy. 290. Rob Smith set up his practice in another section of the Promenade Center in the fall of 2000.

Senior Citizen Complex

Following World War II, many changes took place in American society. There was a migration from rural to urban living. Improvements in farming equipment made it unnecessary for so many to be involved in that industry. With the increased mobility and job opportunities, families became more scattered. It became common for both parents to go into the work force. Another outcrop of all the research and discovery of medicines was the extended life expectancy into the 70s. This meant an increasing population of elderly. As this group increased in number, there became a need for activities and care. More and more, family members were incapable of doing as much for their parents and grandparents as in the past. To add to that, senior citizens craved independence.

Hill Country Senior Citizen Activity Center. When it becomes apparent there is a need, you can bet there will be someone capable of stepping in and providing the leadership for that service. For Dripping Springs, that person was Rose Duvall. Rose was the wife of the Dripping Springs First Baptist Church pastor, Don Duvall. Brother Duvall became concerned about the needs of the elderly of the community after reading an article in the *Baptist Standard* about an elderly lady who died three days prior to being found. He appointed his wife to head up a committee to make a study. She saw that the elderly did not have a place to meet or carry on activities of interest to them. Also the elderly did not always get to eat as regularly or as properly as they needed. Mrs. Duvall would lead the remedy for this.

On November 3, 1976, she formed the Hill Country Senior Citizens organization and they began meeting in the Annex of the Baptist Church. They met once a week for activities and a meal. By the first anniversary in 1977, there were a hundred active members, 60 years and older. It was obvious their surroundings were becoming too small for them and it was time to look for prop-

Hill Country Senior Citizens' Center, 1980

erty. The land was the easy part. Frances and Foster Harmon owned land in the strip between the old 290 highway and the new 290, known as the Ragland subdivision. They sold the senior citizens an acre of this land for a reduced price. Now it was time to get busy and raise the money to erect a building. Through money gained from loans, grants, donations, and fundraisers, the dream became a reality. On March 29, 1980, the new Hill Country Senior Citizens Activity Center was dedicated. Mr. R. K. Howell was the contractor in charge of building the facility. The Board of Directors for the facility were Donna Thomassen, chairperson; Lynn McCarty, vice-chairman; Frances Harmon, Gladys Shults, Don Duvall, Cleve Phillips, and Grady Roe.

Mrs. Duvall was well known for her work with the aging. In November 1880, the center hosted the Texas Farmer's Union's State Forum on Aging. As a result, in 1981 she was invited to Washington D.C. to participate in a conference on the problems of the aging. She was able to hobnob with all the big-wigs, including Speaker of the House Tip O'Neill. Being the wife of a pastor leaves one with a tenuous position. Finally in 1987, her husband decided to make a career change and in so doing, would leave Dripping Springs. This would leave the Activity Center without its director. Soon Ruth Bennett was chosen to continue and improve on the growing facility. The mantel was passed to Ruth on July 1, 1987, and she held the position until April 1,1998, when she retired and the reins were turned over to Dixie Wells. The Pavillion was completed shortly after Ruth Bennett took over, and another addition has been added to the Activity Center. One of the many activities that members are active at is quilting. This takes additional space to do it right. A room dedicated to this purpose was erected on the southwest corner of the building. It was completed before the end of 2000.

Hill Country Cottages Inc. The industrious senior citizens and their leaders were not ready to stop with a center. They knew there were other areas of need and they had a plan to see that those were met. The next facility they would complete would be the Hill Country Cottages. This would allow some of the elderly to live closer to the services of the center and still be independent. They would buy three acres of land adjacent to the center from O. C. and Joy Harmon. Money was raised by charging a $5 membership fee and obtaining a fifty-year loan in the amount of $333,000 from the Farmers Home Administration. The finished product would include twelve single apartments, two double apartments and one handicapped unit. These facilities opened in December 1981. Board members that first year were Rose Duvall, John P. Burke, Jr., Ruth Bennett, John Henry Cauthen, Clarence Cobb, Don Duvall, J. F. Harmon,

W. E. McNair, J. D. Spillar, and Ray Whisenant, Jr.

Hill Country Care Inc. With the first two projects complete, it was time to look toward the final step in taking care of the elderly, a nursing home. When Rose Duvall completed her study in 1976, the need most mentioned by the interviewed elderly was a nursing home. Her vision was to reach this goal in the third step instead. They found some available property just west of their other two facilities. The problem was to get the money in time to purchase the property before it could be sold to someone else. Eugene and Jean Reimers came to the rescue. They would purchase the five acres from Sam C. Roberto on April 6, 1982, for $10,000 and then hold it until the senior citizens could raise the necessary funding. This funding would come in the form of $100 membership fees, a grant from the Lola Wright Foundation for $25,000, a grant from the Houston Foundation, donations of money or room furnishings from individuals in honor or memory of a loved one, plus a thirty-year Community Facility Loan from the Farmer's Home Administration for $1.5 million.

On June 27, 1983, they were able to purchase the land from the Reimers for $30,000. This was made possible by the Lola Wright grant, Houston grant, and individual donations. The facility was completed on March 15, 1986, and the dedication ceremony occurred March 29, 1986. It includes sixty beds and three apartments for the frail elderly. Sharon French became the first director of the facility. The first Board of Directors were Horace Eckols, chairman; Oran H. Rippy, vice-president; Rose Duvall, Mattie Bryant, John P. Burke, Jr., Betty Dunn, Celest Dye, and Delores Conn.

It was not known until after her death in April of 2001, but the nursing home housed a person whose history goes back to the beginnings of Dripping Springs history. Annie Irene Burger Moss spent the last six months of her life in Dripping Springs. She was born in Manchaca, Texas, and married Clifton Moss, Sr., who was the son of Joseph Moss, and the grandson of John L. Moss, one of the original three families.

In all three senior citizen facilities, the group would get much needed support from County Commissioner Lynn McCarty, Congressman J. J. "Jake" Pickle, and County Judge Walter "Bud" Burnett. It still would not have been possible without the tremendous support of the senior citizens themselves.

Fundraiser Organizations. Since the senior citizens organization is nonprofit, much of their operating funds come from their fundraisers. Early on, the Methodist Church ran a Thrift Shop from a building in downtown Dripping Springs. When the senior citizens group organized, the Methodist women offered the Thrift Shop to them. They accepted and have run the store since 1978. In the late 1990s they bought the lot and razed the old wooden building that had just about become unusable. They then built a nice white stone building to continue selling their goods. The store is run by volunteers. They also hold an arts and craft sale each May and raffles are favorites as well.

From the beginning of the completion of the nursing home facility, a fundraising organization was formed to support the nursing home for the future. Rose Duvall enlisted the assistance of an intern from the University of Texas School of Social Work to organize. It was named the Bluebonnet Auxiliary. Since then they have conducted fundraising activities throughout the year. These include bake sales, a Pampered Chef event, and their best known event, the big eat-out hosted by the Salt Lick. Under the guidance of the current president, Betty Cobb, the organization was able to get a small building on the property of Security State Bank and Trust donated and moved across the road to the nursing home acreage. It became a gift shop and the proceeds go toward the nursing home as well. In early 2000, the nursing home began searching for funds for a serious problem. The roof on the facility began to need extensive repair and so the senior citizens, in no time, raised the necessary funds to put on a new roof and complete other needed repairs.

Rambo Masonic Lodge #426

Freemasonry is the largest and oldest fraternity in the world with its roots in England, coming to America with the colonists. Freemasonry is a charitable fraternity whose members focus on the importance of improving themselves and the world around them, mainly through education. They support continuing education and intellectual growth for its members and believe that public education in the community is equally important. They raise money and award scholarships to deserving seniors each year. One of those projects for the past several years has been headed up by John Hudson and friends. Over the holidays of Memorial Day, July 4th, and Labor Day, they set up a barbeque station on the corner of 290 and RR 12 and serve barbeque and other fixings to anyone who would like to drop by and chow down. A donation jar is there to put in whatever you want to give. One of my most cherished awards was the Mirabeau B. Lamar Award of Excellence medallion presented to me on July 3, 1993, by the Rambo Masonic Lodge recognizing my 28 years in the teaching profession at the time. Lamar is known as the Father of Public Education in Texas.

The Rambo Masonic Lodge #426 was chartered on June 5, 1875. Lodges are usually named after someone prominent in the area or in the chartering. It was named after the R. J. Rambo family. They owned land in the area and quite possibly were responsible for organizing the original Friendship Baptist Church or even the Lodge. Onion Creek had a thriving Lodge and several members of that Lodge petitioned to establish the Lodge at Cedar Valley, possibly because it was closer to their homes. Joe D. Sayers, who would later become a governor of Texas, W. L. Young, W. M. Wilford, and J. W. Anderson were the organizers. Cedar Valley was in Travis County and the charter was filed in that county. They began meeting in the second story of the Friendship Baptist Church. Another member was W. T. Chapman, who later founded the town of Dripping Springs in 1881.

Possibly for the same reasons that Rambo Lodge was formed out of the Onion Creek Lodge, W. T. Chapman was able to convince Rambo Lodge to move into quarters that he built in the town of Dripping Springs for that purpose. It was the second story of his mercantile store built on Lot 3 of Block 7. The Rippy Ranch Supply business now rests on that site. They signed the deed to the second story on January 1, 1884. Outside stairs led to the meeting room. The deed stipulation was that no business could be carried on downstairs that would interfere with Masons meeting. The move was not as uneventful as it may seem. Since it was chartered in Travis County and they wanted to move to Hays County to meet, they had to get permission to do this. They could only do this by getting special permission to meet in the other county by the Grand Lodge of Texas. Permission granted. Move made.

The Lodge continued to grow and the ceremony to install members called for big celebrations in the town. In November 1907, J. W. Glosson, who owned the store now, added a 20x26 foot addition to the upstairs. Finally, in June 1920, they purchased four lots in block 7 that included the Davis store. It was a two-story edifice and they used the upstairs room as their meeting place. Again stairs on the east side of the building led up to their meeting room. They sold the property but retained the ownership of the second story. In November 1951, the building burned to the ground, destroying all their records and the original charter. When the owner, W. P. Crow, decided to not rebuild the second story, the Masons were without a permanent meeting place. They did not have to look far to find another ideal building and location. It was just across the street on the Academy block—the old Academy building itself. In 1949, the public school vacated the building to move to their new site. The Masons were able to negotiate the sale of the town's most historic building. Its two-story structure was just right for the history of the Masons as well. They had always met in a second story and this had been a house of education for all of its life. This was July 1952, and they have occupied this building ever since.

Rambo Lodge has always been steeped in history and it continues to follow part of its past. In the days prior to electric lights, the Masons all around came up with a unique practice to provide light for their comings and goings to the meetings. They used the lights provided by nature. That is, moonlight. They had their meetings when there was a full moon. That way they could make their way home following the meetings with ample light to see where they were going. When electricity took hold, most masonic lodges dropped this practice and began meeting on a specified time and day. The Rambo Lodge chose not to follow. Even today, the full moon determines their meeting day—the first Saturday of, or following, the full moon. Dripping Springs is one of just a few lodges that abide by this meeting time. That is why it is known as a Moon Lodge and that is declared on their sign post. Driftwood formed Masonic Lodge #1221. When it began to struggle during the war years, it merged with Rambo Lodge on September 14, 1943.

Throughout its 125-year history, Rambo Lodge #426 has had many Masters. To become a member of the Rambo Lodge a person has to pass three steps of tests. After that there are fourteen phases that a person can go through to reach the stage that would allow them to serve as a Master. According to John Hudson, there are seven stations up for election each year. While there are offices that do not change much over the years, there are three, including the Master, that usually rotates among the members qualified. By the rules of the Masonic Lodge, the elections must take place before June 21 of each year. The installation of these officers must take place between June 22 and September 1. In the old newspapers of the 1880s, the installation of these officers called for big celebrations in Dripping Springs. After the installation ceremonies at the lodge, the officers and other members would march to a big field in town and there would be a community picnic, ballgame, and a concert. There was a small charge for the concert that went to the Lodge, otherwise the proceedings were free of charge. Since the elections fell in the middle of the year, a master's term would cover two years, much like a school term, and it will be given as that in the list below of those who have served the Rambo Lodge as master. As you might expect, there are some repeaters. Below is the list of those who served. My thanks go out to John Hudson who researched and gave me the list. It is always interesting to me to study the leaders of the different organizations because you will see these same names in other areas of the history as well.

W. L. Young (1875-77)
Jonathan Wilford (1877-78)
W. L. Young (1878-79)
A. C. Hardin (1879-80)
J. D. Cady (1880-82)
J. Wilford (1882-83)
S. L. Walters (1883-84)
J. Wilford (1884-85)
Rolland Christal (1885-86)
B. F. Stephenson (1886-88)
J. Wilford (1888-89)
J. W. Crow (1889-91)
B. F. Stephenson (1891-93)
J. A. Garrison (1893-94)
B. F. Stephenson (1894-96)
W. G. McKellar (1896-97)
B. F. Stephenson (1897-99)
Not Available (1899-1904)
E. P. Shelton (1904-06)
H. R. Harmon (1906-11)
E. P. Shelton (1911-12)
C. M. Gilmore (1912-13)
H. R. Harmon (1913-21)

H. G. Schubert (1921-22)
H. R. Harmon (1922-23)
Charles Howard (1923-24)
W. S. McClendon (1924-25)
E. C. Glimp (1925-26)
C. M. Gilmore (1926-27)
H. R. Harmon (1927-29)
W. C. Goslin (1929-31)
E. C. Glimp (1931-33)
J. W. Champion (1933-34)
D. W. Crenshaw (1934-35)
C. C. Haydon (1935-36)
H. R. Harmon (1936-37)
E. P. Shelton (1937-38)
P. L. Turner (1938-39)
J. Y. Holt (1939-45)
C. F. Southwell (1945-46)
T. S. Presley (1946-47)
G. C. Herring (1947-48)
L. T. Roberts (1948-49)
D. L. Holliday (1949-50)
E. E. Robinson (1950-51)
L. B. Jennings (1951-52)
A. B. Cocke (1952-53)
Alva Haydon (1953-54)
E. E. Myers (1954-55)
Virgil B. Conn (1955-56)
Dayton Roberts (1956-57)
John W. Glass (1957-58)
Marvin H. Odell (1958-59)
E. E. Myers (1959-60)
Glenn G. Maddox (1960-61)
Wm. H. Goslin (1961-62)
Wm. R. Smith (1962-63)
Joe W. Strickland (1963-64)
Clarence Cobb (1964-66)
Charlie Neal Haydon (1966-67)
Leonard McCarty (1967-68)
Clarence A. Campbell (1968-69)
James Cristal (1969-70)
J. S. Breed (1970-71)
I. A. Applewhite (1971-72)
D. W. Cauthen (1972-73)
Dayton Roberts (1973-74)
J. A. Hudson (1974-75)
Boone Kemp (1975-76)
J. C. Spears (1976-77)
Daniel Galloway (1977-78)
C. E. Bankston (1978-79)

W. R. Leonard, Jr. (1979-80)
Glenn Steed (1980-81)
J. P. Steele (1981-82)
Kirmon C. Smith (1982-83)
Ellis Linsey (1983-84)
W. A. "Cotton" Hudson (1984-85)
Harry D. Hainline (1985-86)
Lowell H. Hudson (1986-87)
Bennie L. Hudson (1987-88)
David W. Houston (1988-89)
S. Mac Belk (1989-90)
Earl Hays (1990-91)
Walter Hudson (1991-92)
John M. Hudson (1992-93)
Joe A. New (1993-94)
William T. Reeves (1994-95)
Timothy Ford (1995-96)
John Henry Cauthen (1996-97)
Charlie Melear (1997-98)
Ernest Levingston (1998-99)
Howard Bryan, Sr. (1999-00)
Roy Schuster (2000-01)
Porter Laird III (2001-02)
Frank Wawak (2002-03)

Order of the Eastern Star

The Order of the Eastern Star is the sister organization to the Masonic Fraternity and is dedicated to kindness, truth, and charity. It was conceived, written and taught by a Master Mason to provide a place where both men and women could work and serve side by side. Originally, all daughters, widows, wives, sisters, and mothers of Master Masons, along with Master Masons themselves, could become members. Dripping Springs had to be jump-started twice before it finally took hold on the third try. The first chapter was formed shortly after the movement began. They received their charter on October 10, 1895. It was called Chapter #68 and it is thought that Dr. Pound, a charter member, and his daughters were a driving force in its establishment. Just having that group would have made it have good membership alone. For whatever reason, this chapter demised in 1898.

They would try again in 1919. This

charter was issued on October 15, 1919. This chapter was named the B. F. Stephenson Chapter #365. Ben Stephenson was the son-in-law of Dr. Pound and a charter member of the first chapter. Due to the times that left most of the members without enough money to support the organization, this chapter demised in 1926. Undaunted, they would try again. This time it was chartered on October 31, 1940. The Pound influence was still there as his daughter, Georgia Pound Cavett, and P. L. "Pete" Turner were responsible for much of the organization of this chapter. Several periods of low membership brought a fear that this chapter would be forced to demise as well. A small spurt in membership in each case saved the day for the chapter. Recently, eligibility has been expanded and the local chapter has experienced tremendous growth. A few years back, 28 members were initiated in one year. The Dripping Springs chapter meets in the Masonic Lodge building.

Lions Club

The Dripping Springs Lions Club was established February 9, 1978. They were sponsored by the Lions Club of Wimberley. There were 45 charter members, some of which are still active in the club in the year 2002. In 1987, the Dripping Springs Breakfast Lions Club sponsored another Dripping Springs club known as the Noon Lions.

Like all Lions Clubs, they contribute to many international services such as Lions Eye Bank, Leader Dogs for the Blind, international aid funds and, in Texas, to the Texas Lions Camp. They collect used eyeglasses, which are recycled and provided to those who cannot afford them. Both organizations have also been very active in assisting the community throughout the years, donating funds to Hill Country Care, Hill Country Senior Citizens Activity Center, the youth sports association, 4-H, and FFA projects, scholarships, and many other worthwhile causes. To raise the funds for their charitable contributions, the clubs have held barbecues, sponsored carnivals, worked in the concession stands at UT football games, manned booths at Founders Day, sponsored the cook-off contestants' booths and many other activities. A "Star Party" held in conjunction with the Austin Astronomical Society, brought telescopes to Dripping Springs for children and their families to view constellations and individual planets up close and personal. The Lions secured the location and provided concessions and the organizations divided the admission fees. In the past few years, the Breakfast Club has sponsored a highly successful golf tournament.

The year 2001 was also a milestone year. It was at this time that the two Lions Clubs decided they could be of greater service if they were unified once again. The merger was completed at mid-year and the Lions Club of Dripping Springs now has approximately 60 members on its rolls. It presently meets at the Methodist Church, serving breakfast at 6:00 A.M. and beginning its meetings at 6:30 A.M. During 2001 the club underwrote construction to double the size of the local Helping Hands Food Pantry, provided two scholarships to deserving high school graduates, and contributed funds to 12 other organizations in the Dripping Springs area to help with their ongoing financial needs. They have entered into an agreement with the Dripping Springs Chamber of Commerce, providing the land known as Lions Field to build a permanent Visitors and Community Center at the corner of RR 12 and Mercer Street.

Today the Dripping Springs Lions Club is positioned to make even greater contributions of time and funds, both to the Lions International charities and to local groups. Its members are representative of the citizens of this area who regularly demonstrate their big hearts and their strong sense of community.

Helping Hands

In 1986 another need was taken care of by local citizens. This was to make sure that the people of the Dripping Springs area would not be going hungry. Led by Patty Hastings and others, space was found around the community to house food supplies to be distributed to those in the community that were in need. The people called their organization The Helping Hands. They now have a permanent location on the Senior Citizens Activity Center property, where volunteers distribute food a couple of times a week.

Rotary Club

On May 13, 2002, the Dripping Springs Rotary Club received its charter from Rotary International at a banquet held at the Stone Mountain Events Center. District Governor Dick Baggett presented the charter. This charter was pushed through by Bonnie Rose and others, with the Wimberley Rotary Club acting as the sponsor. There were 25 charter members. The Rotary Club is made up of professional and business leaders of the community who volunteer to improve the quality of life in their home communities and in the world community. These volunteers build goodwill and peace, provide humanitarian service and encourage high ethical standards in all vocations. The Rotary motto is "Service Above Self." Rotary clubs are autonomous and determine service projects based on local needs. However, they are encouraged to base their projects on the following: children at risk, disabled persons, health care, international understanding and goodwill, literacy and numeracy, population issues, poverty and hunger, the environment, and urban concerns.

Dripping Springs Volunteer Fire Department, 2000.

History of Business Buildings

Businesses are the glue that holds communities together. Those enterprising people who attempt to make their living serving a need of others are to be commended. For many, the road is very rocky and wrought with financial peril. Dripping Springs has had its fair share of all this. Many hung on through the slow growth years as Dripping Springs remained a small rural community until the growth spurt took place and others could help out. Most businesses are located where they can attract the most customers with a minimum amount of effort, usually along main roads.

Before the town was laid out in 1881, any businesses in the area had to be leased out by the land owners because no deeds could be found showing change of ownership. When the early settlers arrived in 1854, they probably used the road winding from Austin to Fort Scott in Fredericksburg, known as the Austin-Fredericksburg Road. In the late '60s, another road was developed that connected Dripping Springs to the county seat in San Marcos, roughly RR 150 today. It is known that John Lee Wallace ran a stagecoach stop at his house. It has been noted in some accounts that I have read that the first store was operated by Charles Poteet and Alex Young and later by Hector McKellar. The site was given as the open area just east of RR 12, south of Hays Street. McKellar's store was probably down the Creek Road aways instead of in the P. A. Smith survey. Ben Manor was said to have a small mill in the late sixties that was located on Howard property near north Onion Creek and the site is now a part of the Enoch Needham property. We do know that Thomas F. Voight, a son-in-law to Wallace, had a gin in the late '70s located on his property just north of the Dairy Queen.

One thing we should remember was that in the early days, the people lived by subsistence farming. This means they made, grew, hunted, and fished for most of the essentials of life. Money was scarce and even if things might be available to them, they might not be able to afford them. Other essentials could be obtained by occasional trips to Austin or San Marcos, by stage or traveling salespeople who had the products with them. Mills would probably be the most useful in turning out shingles and lumber or grinding grains into flour or meal. Water power in the area made these feasible.

William Thomas Chapman seized the moment in 1881. He had already been running a general merchandise store for several years. My best guess is the store was located on the property across from his house, now owned by the Church of Christ or possibly across from the DS Butane property on Block 12. Either would have put it on the Austin–Fredericksburg Road. He donated the land for the Dripping Springs Academy that opened its doors in January 1882. Being the land speculator and shrewd businessman that he was, he immediately began to draw up a plat for Dripping Springs and had it surveyed so that he could take advantage of the growth that the Academy would bring. He soon added four more additions and began selling the lots that would form the present town of Dripping Springs.

Dripping Springs Academy

The Dripping Springs Academy was the brainchild of one William M. Jordan. He was visiting one of his kinfolk in Dripping Springs, Jesse McLendon, and became convinced that Dripping Springs would be an ideal location for a boarding school. His enthusiasm carried over to others and before you knew it, several of the leaders of the community, W. T. Chapman, A. L. Davis and Dr. Pound, got behind the project and made it a reality. Mr. Chapman donated the land, not an altogether altruistic deed when you know of his plans to develop the land around it. Dr. Pound allowed his patients to pay off their debts to him by working on the building. Limestone from a nearby quarry provided material to erect the original two-room, one-story edifice. The cornerstone was laid with much fanfare on August 6, 1881, and it was expected to be ready to open its doors by October 1, 1881. Instead, it was the middle of January 1882.

Originally the plan was to build a rock structure with a main room 30x50 with 30x30 wings on the east and west sides. The main room was to double as the First Baptist Church and the two wings would give it the appearance of a cross. Whether that was intended or not, I do not know. It was estimated the project would cost $4,000, plus the volunteer workers. Times were hard and the donations and volunteers were not as plentiful as was hoped for. It was decided to only complete the main room and east wing and hopefully add the other later. The school enjoyed the success that it was believed would be as it enrolled 150-200 students at its height. There became a need for the other room and a wooden one-room wing was added to the west side in December 1885. In a newspaper article in the 1947 *San Marcos Record*, Robert Lee Marshall recalled the building of the Academy. He said that W. T. Chapman, Jasper Newton and Robert Levi Marshall, Ed Womack and sons Tom, Dan and Will, A. L. Davis, Sr., and sons A. L., Jr., and Addison, Samuel Gilpin, H. C. Pearcy, J. M. Pound and W. M. Jordan were responsible for the bulk of the labor. A nice touch to the building was the flat limestone slate used to engrave

Dripping Springs Academy. Bottom was built in 1882, top in 1922.

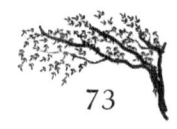

Right: Dripping Springs Academy after 1886
—Courtesy Hazel Bell Myers

Below: Dripping Springs Academy, 1905-15. Georgia Cavett stands second from left.
—Courtesy Travis Garnett

the important details of the Academy. Carved into this stone was the words Dripping Springs curved on top, 1881 in the middle and Academy on the bottom. In the upper left corner is a star and in the upper right is an open book.

Dr. Jordan would stay for two years before moving over to Kyle and establishing another school. One of the reasons for the move may have been the loss of his son. The Academy was originally set up with a military curriculum. His son was practicing some of the manuevers when he was accidentally killed. The military curriculum was dropped and Dr. Jordan turned the administration of the school over to the newly formed Pedernales Baptist Association. The Dripping Springs Baptist Church assumed control in 1889, as per agreement, when the school had to drop their religion curriculum to get state funds. In 1921, the site was deeded over to the public school system. Improvements needed to be made and a bond issue was finally passed after two failures. The money went to tearing down the wooden wing and building a second story above the original limestone building. The stairs were added to the outside as well. The building continued to serve as an educational facility until 1949. In 1952, the Masonic Lodge, who had recently lost their lodge due to fire, purchased the building from Dripping Springs ISD. They have continued to make improvements and keep the building in good shape. The upstairs is their meeting room and the east room on the first floor is their eating and social meeting place. The west side rooms have been let out to various businesses over the

Dripping Springs Academy, now the Visitors' Center, in 2002.

years, including a Montessouri school, the *Dispatch* newspaper, various dance groups, and even a church. In early 2001 the Chamber of Commerce moved their Visitors Center to this location.

A. L. Davis, Jr., Store

Although not the first business to be built along Mercer Street, the Davis general merchandise building was the first built to last. A. L. Davis purchased lots 5, 6, 7, and 8 of block seven in 1891 and built the two-story rock structure on lot six. The bottom floor was used as the store and the upper story was used as a meeting room by different groups. There were stairs leading up to the second story located on the east wall. On the west side was a large cistern to catch rainwater. Mr. Davis used this water supply for his home. He ran a water line over to his house located on block ten (site of Alva Haydon's house). Later, when he sold his home, the water rights stayed as part of the deed. In subsequent sales, that stipulation remained.

The W. T. Chapman Firm, composed of Chapman, his son Mercer, and son-in-law Thomas Egerton bought the business in 1901 and ran the general merchandise store until 1920. The Masonic Lodge took over ownership of the property in 1920 and made their meeting place the second story room. In 1922, David G. Jones, who had run several other businesses in town before, bought the first floor to continue to run the merchandise store. Reports are that he had stuff stacked to the ceiling everywhere, and it was hard to get around in there. Pete Glosson said that Jones ran one of the first help-yourself establishments. He would get drunk and people would come and get what they wanted, hopefully pay, and leave.

Will Crow bought the business in 1934. He got into several enterprises in the next few years, including the wool and mohair business. Also, the coming of electricity in the late '30s–early '40s opened up other possibilities for items that needed to be refrigerated. Until that time stores could not

A. L. Davis Mercantile Store, 1891.
In the background on the left is the Haydon Gin, Huey House, and the Baptist Church steeple. On the right is Short Mama's house.
—Courtesy of Travis Garnett

A. L. Davis Mercantile Store, 1950s. Notice Minnie Horner's icehouse on the far right, and the cistern standing next to the mercantile.

A. L. Davis Mercantile Store, 2002

carry products that were highly perishable unless they could be sold quickly. Solon Glosson leased the building from Crow and ran the Red & White Grocery there until the building burned to the ground early Monday morning on November 19, 1951. Only the rock walls remained. Mr. Crow decided to rebuild only the first floor and moved his hardward business into the building. This left Glosson and the Masonic Lodge looking for new sites.

In 1962, longtime employee, W. E. "Bill" McNair purchased the business from Mr. Crow. He, in turn, sold the business to O. C. Harmon in 1976, who added the rock addition to the west side of the building. W. M. "Mac" Crow continued the hardware business when he bought it in 1982. Hard times in the '80s caused financial problems for Crow and in 1990, Pedernales Electric Coop bought the property. Presumably, PEC had plans to restore the building to its original two-story days. This did not happen. For a while it appeared a winery would buy the building but this did not materialize when an election to make Dripping Springs wet did not pass. Finally, Bob Purcell and family purchased the property in 1994 and set up their electrical business in the rock addition. The main floor was leased out to an auction company for a short while and then the Dripping Springs Community Fellowship Church began using it for their meeting place. It became too small for them and they moved out in 2000. Other businesses, including an antique store and a pattern shop have occupied the building.

George McCuistion Drugstore

In December of 1900, George McCuistion bought Lot 5 of block six. McQuistion was a druggist and built a drugstore on the site. He kept the business for five years before selling it to W. H. Crenshaw. Crenshaw was not a druggist and when doctors prescribed medicine, they would have to go down to the drugstore and fill the prescription themselves. The building went through several owners but remained a drugstore. Mr. W. C. Goslin decided to replace the building with a larger rock structure in 1941 and this started an odyssey of nomadic life for three decades. It was first moved to the side by Ed Howard of Kyle and continued to serve as a working store while the new building was being erected. After that, it was moved to the back of the new building. Lewis Jennings bought it in November of 1958 from Mrs. Goslin and used it as a storehouse for his lumber company. Its last move was in 1972. Hilton Lewis, the new owner of Glosson's Grocery, bought the building and moved it to its final resting place between the J. L. Patterson building and the Allen Stephenson

high school building. The Lewises plastered the exterior of the old wooden structure and used it for a production room where they produced a newspaper called the *Roadrunner* for several years. This old vine-covered structure with the rusting tin roof continues to be a well kept secret and gives no outward hint of its importance in the history of Dripping Springs.

J. L. Patterson Building

In 1903, J. L. Patterson moved to Dripping Springs from Rice's Crossing, near Hutto, Texas. He was a man of means and with a propensity to invest it. In 1906, he bought the 50x100 foot lot located on the north side of Mercer Street, directly across from the Davis store, and built the story-and-half limestone rock building. It too was built to be a general merchandise store. Stairs led up to the loft area that allowed one to walk around and was used mostly for storage. General merchandise stores carried a little of everything and were the early version of the one-stop shopping centers that are prevalent in today's world.

Mr. and Mrs. Patterson ran the store but they needed some help. Their son, Joel, and his family were still living in Rice's Crossing. They talked them into moving to Dripping Springs and running the store for them. The deal was, if they did not like it, they were free to return to Rice's Crossing. They gave it a try but the wife in particular was not enthralled with life in Dripping Springs and after six years returned to their old homestead. The aging Pattersons did not wish to continue the responsibility of this store and sold it to P. A. Glosson in 1914. Mr. Glosson and his wife, Annie, ran the store for seven years. At some point, it is said that Earl Woods, a son-in-law of the Pattersons helped run the store in the '20s.

The Searights, Gibb and Irma, bought the building in 1921 and in 1925 sold it to Will Ella Searight. Apparently they had other people run the store for them, at least part of the time. It is known the Corrie Smith family was in charge in the late '20s. One source said they used the loft area for their living quarters. A 1928 advertisement in the *Kyle News* had this to say: "On the Lone Star Highway" "New Orleans to San Francisco Route" "Tourists invited to Stop With Us" "Groceries, Candies, Fruits, Drinks" "Cash Paid for Chickens and Eggs" "Corrie Smith" "Dripping Springs."

O. S. Brumley, Sr., ran the Brumley Cash Grocery throughout the '30s until his death in 1940. On Thursday, July 21, 1938, around 3:00 A.M., fire completely consumed the building. It burned out two businesses because the store also doubled as the post office. The two-story building was rebuilt as a one-story only. The grand opening occurred on December 2, 1938, a Saturday. A large crowd attended. Ellis McCullough, with Admiration Coffee Company, served hot coffee. Cakes were donated by Brown Cracker Company. Butter Krust gave out samples of

James L. Patterson Mercantile Store, 1906
—Courtesy Travis Garnett

James L. Patterson Mercantile Store, 2002

bread. Pioneer Flour Mills of San Antonio furnished delicious cakes, served by their hostess, Mrs. Ethel Deen of Austin. Mrs. Brumley would buy the building after his death and try to run the store for a while before finally selling it to Will Crow in 1942. This would be the end of this building's use as a food supply for humans.

Not so for animals. Andrew Herwig and Louis B. Jennings opened a feed store and lumber yard in 1942. Mr. Jennings went it alone beginning in January of 1952 when the Herwigs decided to move to a turkey ranch near Johnson City. Jennings finally sold his feed business to Pete Glosson in 1956 and moved his lumber business across the street. Ed Fine took over from Pete in 1961 and then sold it to Gay Harris in 1962. He would stay in business until 1966. Then the building went silent. Enter Joan Crosswell, Susan McFarland, and Carla Allen in 1977. They ran an antique furniture store called Country Homes International and kept it open until 1981, when they leased the building to Rex Miller for his real estate office. After his departure, in 1984-85, a local thespian group called The 290 Playhouse was allowed to use the premises for their productions. The Benji Larance architectural firm opened an office there in 1986. The pitter patter of little feet began to make their presence known in 1989. Cheryl de los Santos was looking for a place to start a dance studio and saw the possibilities afforded by this place. She parlayed her talents and those of her students into a successful business known quite appropriately as Cheryl's Dance Studio. In 1997, Anton Allen decided to move his real estate business back to this site. In its early days there was a covered partition that extended over the two doors and entranceway for protection from the elements. It was missing for many years but Mr. Allen replaced it. The wooden addition at the back was said to be used at one time to test the butter fat of milk that had been bought before it was sent on.

C. Waite Crenshaw Garage

Located on the corner of Mercer and San Marcos, the wooden and tin garage was built by C. W. Crenshaw some time after buying the lot in November of 1924. At this time, the main road from Austin to Fredericksburg (Texas Highway 20) came down Wallace Mountain and took a right on San Marcos at Spring and then left onto Mercer. Because of this, the driveway was angled so that cars could easily enter and exit from either street. An April 1928 advertisement in the *Kyle News* for the C. W. Crenshaw Garage touted "Texaco Products," "Mobil Oil," and a "Complete repair department." There was also a request for the "Tourists on the Austin-Fredericksburg Highway," to "Give us your trade."

By 1938, the through-route had once again changed along with its name. This time the roadway (now Highway 290) was diverted as it came down Wallace Mountain and took the path that is basically Loop 64 today. If the road could change, so could the Crenshaw Garage, now owned by D. W. Crenshaw. The front was given a facelift. It was given a rock exterior and the driveway was rearranged to become parallel to Mercer Street, as it is today.

C. W. Crenshaw Garage was built in 1926, rocked in 1937. It became the Travis Garnett Humble station in the 1950s. Pictured above are Bobby Needham and Gary Garnett.
—Courtesy Travis Garnett

Crenshaw Garage operated as a Ritter Station in 1955.
—Courtesy James Felps

Crenshaw Garage in 2002

In 1937, Crenshaw put into motion the plans to build a movie theater across the street and took out a loan using the garage as collateral. John McClaferty held the deed of trust and by the end of 1940, it became his property when Crenshaw had to default on his debt. Crenshaw decided to change his station from Texaco to Sinclair in January of 1940. Later in that year H. F. Severn signed a lease through 1943. McClaferty would honor Severn's lease. McClaferty died suddenly in 1942. Felix Rippy ran the Humble station in 1945-46 and also sold feed there. It became Robinson Brothers Garage in 1946. Ed McIntyre ran the station from 1950-52. Travis Garnett wanted to have the Humble franchise at his place but had to run this one from 1952-54 to get the move done. Pearl and Ira Ruston ran the Ritter's station for about eight months in 1955. Walter Price continued the building's career as a gas station when he ran the Ritter's Service Station from 1956-60. At that point Highway 290 had already been re-routed to its present location and all the service stations that were located along Mercer Street had soon closed their doors and made the move over to where the traffic was.

For most of the next quarter century, the building was not used commercially. It has remained the property of the McClaferty heirs. At one point, a Mr. Abel used the building for his living quarters. In 1980, Todd Cearley opened Todd's Cycle Center for a while. Finally, in the mid '80s, it was remodeled and turned into a barbershop. Alex Applewhite opened and ran it until 1992 when Charles Edwards took over.

William S. "Bill" Garnett Garage

The Garnett Garage was an example of how the winds of change are met by people. Beginning in 1884, this site, located on the north side of Mercer Street and near the west end, was used as a livery stable. After W. S. Garnett, Sr., bought land, including this one in 1904, it continued to be used as such with Will Garnett running the business. It was the days of the horse and buggy and you could rent them for a date or any other purpose or leave your animal there to be tended to. With the coming of cars, this type of business became obsolete. So the next step was to get in line with the next mode of transportation.

Garnett, Sr., ran the blacksmith shop next door and it was right to expand. In 1925 a Gulf station and garage was built. It was operated by Bill Garnett, Jr. He bought it in 1934. As most buildings with any age to them, this one has undergone a few changes since its creation. Originally it had a tin portion for the garage and two driveways for attending cars. The tin portion was expanded to the north. On the south end, changes also took place. The arrival of Highway 20 in the late '30s and the widening of Mercer Street caused the outside driveway to be eliminated. In the mid '60s, when it was no longer a service station, the lone driveway was rocked in to make a foyer and display area. A little later, a rock office addition to the west was added.

Bill Garnett was a master mechanic and continued to run his business until his untimely death in 1948. At that point John D. Herwig, his son-in-law, took over the business and ran it throughout 1949. Next Jay Spillar and his brothers ran it for another year. The building remained vacant for most of the next four years, except for a spell when the telephone company leased it. Bill's son, Travis, returned it to a garage and service station in 1954. Travis and Lois held their open house on September 6 to commemorate the occasion. Travis wanted to have a Humble station there but the rules forbid him from going straight to that as long as Gulf still had the lease. Instead he had to run one at another location until the lease expired. It was a Humble station until 1960 when he, like all the others, moved to a new 290 location.

Again the building would lie dormant for five years when Fred Garnett, another son, moved his DS Butane business to the premises. Over the years the business was expanded to include DS Electric and Mechanical and DS Hardware. In 1983 those two businesses moved over to a site on RR12 N. Ever since, DS Butane has maintained its headquarters in the building.

Charles Haydon Central Garage

Charlie C. Haydon bought the lot on the corner of Mercer and College in 1925. A wooden building, probably built from the remains of the old Applewhite store, was on the property and served as a barbershop for Johnny Spaw. It also had a lean-to added to it that would serve as a hamburger and pancake place run by Piggy Roberts. This arrangement would stay in place until 1935, when it was decided to build the rock building that now stands there. Traffic was building and Highway 20 was getting ready to make its debut to bring even more. It took a couple of years to complete. The rockwork was done by masons Wimberley and Hughes. Mr. Haydon's son, Alva, and his good friend, Haskell McNair, poured the concrete for the floor and walls. The rocks for the walls were gleaned from around the Central Texas area. The petrified wood came from

Travis Garnett and a battery salesman stand before Travis Garnett's Gulf Station/Garage. —Courtesy Travis Garnett

McDade, Texas. Alva said the farmer who owned the land said he would be glad to let them have all the rocks they could carry off, since the rocks were a nuisance to him. Granite and other rocks came from the Llano and Marble Falls area. The shinier types came from the rockmason's place near Flite Acres in Wimberley. There is a big rock in front. It was dug up by Alva while he was plowing land on the Lyle place they were leasing. He asked his dad if they could put it in the rockwork and his dad told the masons to put it in the front.

Another story was in the roof. At that time, there was a tomato shed located next to the Creek Road that had once been run by a Cooperative. It was just south of where the Church of Christ now stands and in the middle of present 290. The decision was made to use the shed's roof for their new building. That decision was not as easy as it may seem. Getting it from point A to point B was not easy. It was on the opposite side of the big ravine, that is Dripping Springs Branch, with only a narrow bridge with bannister railings to get across. The roof was secured with cables and a winch truck held it in place while the four support poles were taken away. The front of the roof was then lowered down onto a couple of vehicles and the back was secured to a couple of barrells. Being careful, the adventurous journey was completed in about two weeks. That roof served its purpose until the mid '80s when it was replaced.

This building with unusual rockwork opened for business the second week of August 1937. It served as a garage and Mobil gas station. James Ferrell ran the garage until December 1939 when Alva Haydon took over. The service station was leased to Virgil Conn in December 1937. Virgil Conn ran the service station for about a year and it was taken over by Leroy T. Roberts and his wife, Katherine. They had previously run the Roberts Cafe next door in

Central Garage/Mobil station opened for business in 1937. On the right is the A. L. Davis store, 1891. —Courtesy Travis Garnett

Central Garage, 1964

Mobil Station/ Central Garage, 1937 L-R: unknown, Leroy Roberts, Mr. King, Ollie Sorrell
—Courtesy Katherine Roberts

the old Breed Market Place. Mrs. Roberts put in a cafe in the east end of the station. They catered to a very good truck trade that made its way through Dripping Springs at this time. For a while the business stayed open 24 hours a day.

Mr. Roberts' health began to fail and he was forced to give up the business. He asked E. E "Nookie" Myers if he wanted to take over and in September of 1951, he accepted the offer. The cinder block portion of the building was completed in 1954-55. It was needed to protect the workers from the elements as they serviced the cars. Until then, the racks that held the cars being worked on, were on the outside of the building. Alva Haydon got an early jump on the move to the new 290 location and built a new station in 1959, and Mr. Myers made the move and left the front of the building vacant.

After taking over the garage in 1939, Alva Haydon ran this business until 1964 when he, too, would move to another location along 290. The old building would not stay in mothballs very long. In 1967, Jake Spears leased the garage for his repair shop and remained in the business until his retirement in 1991. The more prominent business to occupy the front of the building was a glassworks business owned by Drew Patterson in the late '80s. In the spring of 1993, Buddy Lewis leased the building and the lot behind it to open up his rental enterprise and small engine repair. A woodworking business now occupies the cinderblock portion of the building.

Crenshaw/Ferrell Movie Theater

It was probably a good idea, but the timing proved to be all wrong. D. Waite Crenshaw owned the garage across the street and James Ferrell worked as a mechanic for him. Dripping Springs was growing and the new highway was to come in front of it, instead of beside it. Austin was still a good trip in for any type entertainment. They recognized what they thought would be a good business opportunity—to build a movie theater. They bought Lot 12 of block one and built a rock structure in 1937 that would hold up to 300 patrons at a time. Years ago this site housed a blacksmith shop.

Wade Turner and Leland Lyle lent their skills in putting up the rock on the stylish building. Unfortunately for the owners, despite the accommodations, it was not a money-making proposition. The country was just coming out of the Depression and this may have had something to do with it. Within a couple of years the business went bankrupt. James moved his moving picture equipment in November of 1940 to Moulton for a couple of years and Waite moved permanently to Austin. In 1941 creditors bought the building in a sheriff's sale. It changed hands again but it was not used as a theater. Finally in 1945, the building was

Crenshaw/Ferrell Movie Theater, now a Wells Fargo bank

purchased by Joe K. O'Bryant of Austin. He already owned two theaters in Austin, one being the Ritz, and was looking to expand. He named the theater DisTex. Some remember it as Dixie. Movies were shown only on the weekends. During his senior year in high school, Raymond Whisenant managed the theater for its final hoorah. He recalls showing movies on Friday and Saturday nights. He would then pack up the receipts and films and ship them by bus to Austin on Sunday. That was the last time the building was used for the purpose it was built.

In 1948 James Lumpkin came to town to set up a business named the Texas Insulation and Manufacturing Company where Central Garage now resides. In doing so, he purchased the old theater building to be used, among other things, as a warehouse. He removed all the seats and converted the building into a feed store and warehouse for his insulation supplies. One of the problems they encountered was the sloping floor that was necessary for all to see the movie from the seats. When it rained, water would stand at the bottom of the slant and workers would have to wade through water. Luckily they could use the stage to store the feed on and it would not get wet. Others remember getting to use this big floor for roller skating. This should have offered some exciting challenges for them.

Lumpkin coaxed Felix Rippy to run the feed store for him and he did so until around 1950. At that time Leland Lyle tried his hand at it. M. Z. Piland, who was a partner with Lumpkin, was a part of the business with Lumpkin. Lumpkin ran the feed store for a while himself, when the insulation business began to falter. The building fell vacant again. O. B. McKown bought the building in 1962 to be used as a warehouse for his lumber business across the street. In 1969, it would see life as a business again. A company called Porta Craft made portable buildings there for a while. It went back to being a warehouse when the King Feed Company took over the old lumber yard. James Hurlbut rescued the storied building in 1977 and sent it into an even more exciting future. He remodeled the building into an office complex and leased it out to several entrepreneurs. Another golden opportunity for service was afforded the old building in 1981. Dripping Springs was in line to get its first bank ever. So James went about this new remodeling job. In September of 1981, it officially became the property of the Dripping Springs National Bank. The only major change to the exterior of the building was the annex built on the east side to house the vault. Unfortunately the bank was caught up in the great land bust of the mid-80s and finally failed in 1991. The Texas Bank took over the operation on July 12, 1991. On April 18, 1997, Norwest bought out the interest of Texas Bank and took charge. Wells Fargo bought out the Norwest banks in 1998 and the bank took that name officially in 2000.

J. E. Spaw Barber Shop

When the Haydons decided to move the

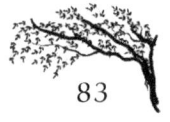

Johnny E. Spaw Barber Shop was built in 1937

building off the lot and replace it with the Central Garage, Johnny Spaw lost his barber shop. He immediately began to look for a suitable place to build a new barber shop. He bought a 12½x100 foot strip that was available from the east side of Lot 4 in block seven. This was not enough to build on but it was a start. He worked a deal with Will Crow to exchange land owned so that he would have the front portion of that lot measuring 25x50 feet and Mr. Crow would then have the back 25x50. Now he had room to build the little rock barbershop. This was in September 1937. He was free to ply his trade until his retirement December 31, 1963. This small building served a dual purpose during this era. Johnny's wife, Mary, was the postmistress for 21 years, officially beginning November 1, 1942. Within the month she moved from across the street and the building served as the post office too. Naoma Glosson said Mary had a little trapdoor in the floor where she kept money and valuables in a safe. Mrs. Glosson ended up with the little metal window that served as the post office window to make it look official.

Ira Ruston bought the shop and moved his business there as of January 1, 1964, and continued its career as a barbershop. Ira decided to cut back and sold his business to John Bender in 1978 but continued to help out several days a week. A bad back forced Mr. Bender from the business in less than a year. In 1981 the little rock building changed its clientele although hair was still the business. At this time Nita Jernigan leased the building and opened Nita's Clip and Curl. She turned the business over to Mary Garnett in 1984 and the name changed to Artistic Cuts. Mary gave up the business in 1993 and the building stayed vacant for a little while. In May 1994, Joy Purcell bought the property. In November of 1995, Wild Bill & Company relocated his hair business there and remained there until the spring of 2001. A little remodeling and the Royal Treatment moved in. They moved out by October 2002 and it once again became vacant.

Will Crow Wool and Mohair

Will Crow built a wooden building on

Will P. Crow Wool & Mohair Store opened in 1937

Rippy Wool & Mohair, 1939

the back portion of Lots 3 and 4 of block seven and started up his wool and mohair business in 1937. It burned down while full of wool on April 12, 1939. He quickly rebuilt in practically the same place. Later another wooden addition was added that faced Mercer Street. He opened up the town's first hardware store in this new addition in 1946. It continued to serve as a wool and mohair center even after Crow moved his hardware store over to the A. L. Davis building next door. He eventually sold the business to the Rippys and these two buildings have survived over the years. They now house a feed business with wool and mohair occupying the building next door.

Allen Stephenson High School

The advent of school growth, due to the beginnings of consolidations with Dripping Springs, left the Dripping Springs Academy building woefully lacking in space. It was decided to purchase land. Although 35 acres were purchased that would have put the campus elsewhere, it was decided to build adjacent to the west side of the existing school and build a new high school addition. Under the auspices of the Works Progress Administration (WPA) and using local laborers, the rock structure was completed prior to the September 1939 school term. It was also decided to dedicate this building to the memory of a popular student, Allen J. Stephenson. Allen was a 15-year-old student who had broken his leg in a baseball game in late April 1938. Complications arose because the cast was too tight and gangrene was the result. He died on May 2, 1938.

An interesting addition to the rock work can be found near the top of the south wall. A star is embedded in the wall just below a limestone block looked to be intended for word inscription, although none was ever added. Two plaques are attached to the front entrance wall—one concerning particulars about Allen Stephenson and the other recognizing the contributions of the WPA. This building ceased to be a haven for education in 1949 when the new school was completed. Since the new school did not include a gymnasium or auditorium, the auditorium in this building continued to serve as a host for graduations and other meetings until the gym was completed in 1953. For the next 20 years, it would be used mostly for community activities, including Grange meetings, elections, church services, and get togethers.

In 1972, Cynthia Snider began using the building for her school program and then in 1976, it came alive as a school once more. DSISD was growing so rapidly, the space was needed for the kindergarten classes. It was remodeled to fit the occasion. It was school as usual until 1985. The new high school along 290 west was completed and this afforded room at the old high school site. This did not mean the sturdy building would be relegated to mothballs again. It was remodeled again, this time to accommodate the DSISD administration offices, tax office, and board room. The stage area on the north end became the superintendent's office. In 1990, the board room was eliminated to make more room for needed office space, including the superintendent's office in the southwest corner. A window was added to the windowless northside wall and an entrance door to the superintendent's office on the south wall.

Allen Stephenson High School, 1939

Allen Stephenson High School building in 2002, currently serving as county offices.

Changes continue to be made. As the original high school became vacant due to a new intermediate school being built on the north end of the campus, the original building was converted into an administration complex for the growing district. They made this move in the summer of 2000. The Stephenson building was leased to Hays County for their offices. This transition also took place in the summer of 2000.

Rinky Dink Domino Hall

Presently nestled among the trees and buildings and practically hidden from all view is the fabled Rinky Dink Domino Hall. It is located down the alley between the Post Office and Patterson building. You have to know where to look to actually find it. On the south side is the Patterson building and Rock Cafe. Almost in front of it on the east side is the old vine-covered McCuistion drugstore. On the north side is a warehouse and the DSISD administration building. The name is probably derived by the smallish nature of the building. The name stuck and someone obliged with a sign over the door so declaring. J. N. Rippy gave credit to Ollie Sorrell for making the sign.

Dominoes has always been a popular game to play and probably everyone who has ever lived in a small community can remember where the domino hall was located—where one could always find a game going on at almost any time of day or night. For Dripping Springs, the year was 1939. The men of the community wanted a place to play their beloved game of dominoes. Until then, they had set up their games under the oak tree by the A. L. Davis building. John Butler purchased the supplies necessary to erect this small building for about fifty dollars. R. B. Wilson said the lumber came from the old hotel located nearby. Ed Felps and A. B. Cauthen are credited as the carpenters who built the building for the players. It is said patrons of the games would pay 25 cents to play until the cost of the materials had been repaid. According to J. N. Rippy's

Rinky Dink Domino Hall was established in 1939.

recollections, a domino club was formed and the players paid one dollar a month to play until the debt was repaid. Mr. Butler received his investment back.

The small building has not always resided at its present site. Originally it was located on Mercer Street between where the old Texaco Station and Rock Cafe now reside. It was moved to its present site in the mid 1960s. It seems Mrs. Zadie Lumpkin, who had converted the little Rock Cafe into a home and business, protested that playing moon constituted an act of gambling. Of course, it was remembered that Mrs. Lumpkin was not the only one occasionally unhappy with the playing. Some wives have been known to get a little anxious about the prolonged absences of their menfolk to this game.

The building was moved as a compromise but Mrs. Lumpkin was not a total grinch to the players. She allowed an extension cord to be run from her house to the building so the players could have a lightbulb shining overhead. Today that electricity comes from Anton Allen's building. A wood stove affords the only warmth in the winter. The new location has not proved a detriment to its patrons either. Almost any day of the year, you could find a hotly contested game of dominoes being played inside. Only in recent years have the number of games diminished, partly because many of the regulars have died and replacements have started playing their games elsewhere, most notably the Senior Citizens building.

The little building has always been a squatter. It has never been on land it could call its own. At the present the site is probably sitting on three separate properties. Its site is so inconspicuous that it seems unlikely anyone in the near future will force its removal. Even then it seems only right that it would be moved to some place of prominence, quite possibly Founders Park, so that future generations could still get a glimpse of an important part of Dripping Springs history.

F. W. Miller Texaco Station

Located on the north side of Mercer Street across from the Spaw barbershop, the Texaco station was built by F. W. Miller in 1940. Fritz Miller lived in Kyle and was the Texaco dealer in this area. Up until January 1940, the Crenshaw Garage sold Texaco gas and products. In that month C. W. Crenshaw decided to change his station from Texaco to Sinclair. This left Mr. Miller without a market outlet in Dripping Springs. The new Highway 20 had just been completed a few years before and he wanted to continue a Texaco market in Dripping Springs to compete with the other major oil companies. To do this, he built the station and leased it out to various takers. This site on Lot 3 of block one of the first addition was made available when the old hotel was razed in the late 1930s.

F. W. Miller Texaco Station, 1941
—Courtesy Travis Garnett

F. W. Miller Texaco Station today

E. B. "Pete" Glosson had the honor of opening the Texaco station and running it until 1941. In October of 1941, J. W. Wilson, Sr., took over the reins from Tommie Turner until his retirement in early 1950. Bill Watson was in charge until Marvin Burrier took over in November of that year. He would operate the business until 1960, when that location would meet the same fate as all the other stations along the old 290 route. This new 290 would leave all the stations high and dry when it came to major traffic and they all had to meet a different calling to keep their history alive.

However, there was life after death for the ex-station, just like all the others. In May of 1962, M. Z. Piland moved in to set up his real estate office there. From 1967-70, it became the DS Quick Car Wash owned by Jack Lyle and Homer Cearley. In the early '70s Clem Best, Tommy Gray, and Bill Leonard had insurance offices there, plus it served as a community library, too. In the '80s Sonny Rippy ('83-'84) had his DS Cable TV office there, 1986-88 Staudt Surveying, and DS Recycling began their community service at the site in 1988-89. It was rented as the Republican headquarters for the 1990 campaign. The year 1991-92 found G Darling owned by Gail Frederick thriving. Short stays by Wardlow Stained Glass and a Whole Foods store have been the only occupants since 1992 until the Staudts returned to Dripping Springs and in May of 1998 returned to the building to headquarter their surveying business. They moved to larger quarters in 2000 and it was vacant only a short time before being occupied by other businesses. Presently, it is occupied by Calvin Myers' Grapevine signs and designs.

Like the others, the Miller Texaco station has retained its physical qualities throughout the years and allows one a look into the past when the town was smaller and the pace a little slower.

F. W. Miller Rock Cafe

A few months later, Fritz Miller bought Lot 5 of the first addition, only yards away from his Texaco station, and proceeded to build a small rock cafe in 1940. No doubt he believed this would be a good investment, too. While husband Pete was taking care of the Texaco station, his wife, Naoma, ran the Rock Cafe. When Pete stopped working at his job in 1941, so did Naoma. This launched James W. "Jimmy" Glosson and his wife, Tula, into a fourteen-year excursion into the cafe business. They would name it Bonnie's Cafe in honor of their daughter. After his father's death in 1956, the Glossons closed their doors and moved two buildings east and took over the family grocery business. After a few months of vacancy, Mrs. Lewis Jennings opened up the Rock Cafe with

Inside F. W. Miller Rock Cafe. with Tula Glosson and Edna Monroe.

Hattie and Lois Garnett stand in front of Bonnie's Cafe

The Rock Cafe, 2002

Katherine Roberts assisting her and ran it for a while before its final meal was served to the public.

Mrs. Zadie Lumpkin purchased the property in 1965. She converted the little cafe into an office for her insurance business and later converted it into living quarters. She lived in the building until her death in 1992. Since then several businesses have located there for a spell including the Blackjack Gallery. It has even played a part in a movie. Now Joy Purcell has her offices in the building. It never ceases to amaze present day people when they look at this building and find out that it once served as a cafe. You think of how big the restaurants are around town today and you cannot envision that the Rock Cafe was big enough to do the job in its time.

W. C. Goslin Drugstore

The Goslins owned the property on Lot 5 of block six since 1934 and ran the drugstore that had previously been run by McCuistion and Crenshaws. Finally in 1941 the Goslins decided they needed to expand. To do this they decided to build a new building. He got Ed Howard of Kyle to move the old building over 22 feet to the west. He did the job so smoothly that Mr. Goslin carried on his business while the moving was being done and proceeded to build a new stone building. The project was begun in September of that year and by December they had moved in. Mr. Goslin died in 1944 and the Goslin family continued to run the store for another year. At that time George Prather and Pinkerton took over.

Dayton Roberts leased the store in 1946 and ran the grocery and drugstore through 1953. In January 1954, Alfard Hohman tried his hand at the business. This brief adventure lasted until January 1955 when Virgil Conn bought out the future Hays County sheriff and stayed until 1960. In late 1959, the cinder block expansion on the

W. C. Goslin Drugstore was built in 1941.

south end was completed and used as a meat market space. They even held a grand opening and gave away twelve baskets of groceries. George Wiest moved in for a short stay in May 1960. As soon as the building was completed on Highway 290, the Wiests moved their drug and grocery enterprise there. The longtime drugstore ended up another victim of the new 290. The site also served as a bus stop for many years.

The Goslins returned to the building after a 15-year hiatus. Mrs. Polly Goslin opened up a specialty shop and her son, Harvey, had his insurance office there. A daughter, Edith Cauthen also helped run the store. Polly died in 1973 and Harvey in 1976. Finally, the Goslin heirs leased the building to Bill Bassett in 1981. He converted it into a machine shop named the Brass Works and has occupied the building ever since, although it has not been an active business for some years. One of the products turned out by Bill were bullets to be used in movies. Joy Purcell bought the property from the Goslin heirs in March 1997.

Billie Garnett Complex

Located on Lots 1 and 12 of block seven, this complex of three sections faces Mercer Street on the north and stretches along Bluff Street to the south. Billie Garnett built this cinderblock structure in 1946. Basically, the commercial addition faces Mercer. The middle section is a garage area used by Mr. Garnett to service and repair the machinery that he worked with for many years. The southernmost part is used as their home. The first business to occupy the building was Ima Lois Shelton's Ready-To-Wear shop in 1947. By 1951 she had relocated to another site. After the A. L. Davis building caught fire and burned to the ground in November of 1951, Solon Glosson, whose grocery occupied the first floor, moved his grocery to Garnett's while he was building on another site. After the Glossons moved out in late 1952, it gave Billie and Alma Garnett the urge to continue using the space for a grocery. They opened in May of 1953 and had their grand opening on June 6. They stayed in business until June of 1956. They also served as a sub-station for Tucker's Cleaners. This ended the building's career as a grocery store.

In the late '50s, Rippy's Feed used the space for offices and storing feed. In the late '60s, Garnett Electric made it a storage area for their parts. It stayed mostly vacant after that until the '80s when Grace Broussard had a combination flower shop and dance studio there. Slim Hendricks moved his Slim's Upholstery shop in the building in 1989. Except for a small break in 1994, Slim has held fast to the spot. His wife opened a collector's shop in part of the room.

Billie Garnett recalls that sometime between 1949-52, the middle section was used for a GI Vocational training school. Otherwise, as mentioned, the area has been used mostly for personal use.

James Lumpkin Insulation Company

James Lumpkin moved to Dripping Springs and, with M. Z. Piland as a partner, purchased the west half of block two in 1948. He saw the need for insulation in buildings and opened the Texas Insulation Company on these lots. The insulation process included using newspapers as part of the material. The insulation business never really caught on and in the '50s it ceased to operate. In 1959, Alva Haydon bought the property from the owners. It was not until January of 1965 that Alva Haydon converted the property into his new location for Central Garage. The area where they kept their parts was a section of the insulation company. The rest he built on to provide for his business. In November of 1976, Ben Metcalf bought the business and property from Alva, kept the name, and has operated it since.

Solon Glosson Grocery

Solon Glosson operated the Red & White

Glosson Grocery, 1952

Grocery since 1942. It was located on the bottom floor of the A. L. Davis building, then owned by W. P. Crow. In November of 1951, the two-story edifice burned to the ground. All that could burn that is. Mr. Crow decided to rebuild only the first floor and move his hardware store into it. This left Mr. Glosson looking for a new site. He moved temporarily into the Billie Garnett building down the street. Meanwhile, DSISD had already moved to their new site west of town. This left some of their Academy property available. He was able to obtain a lot that fronted Mercer Street, next to the Patterson Store and was a part of the old school playground. Mr. Glosson erected a cinder block building. The new store was officially dedicated November 1, 1952.

When Mr. Glosson died in 1956, his son, Jimmy, took over management of the store. The heir apparent to the store was Jimmy's son, Woody. When Woody's lifespan was halted by cancer in 1970, Jimmy decided to retire. He sold the business to Hilton and Jeanine Lewis. It is not always easy to come into a small town and fit in neatly. The Hill Country Superette started to decline. A major cause in the Lewis's loss of popularity was their support of a wet election for Dripping Springs. They sold the store a couple of times but it kept coming back to them when the buyers could not pay for it. At various times it was named Val-U-Mart, Rose Imports, and finally Poor Boys Superette in 1979. When these businesses failed, the building went vacant and its life as a grocery store was no more.

The 1980's growth spurt finally worked in the Lewis's favor. The population explosion was fast making the little red brick post office located in the southeast corner of the Academy block way too small and a new location became necessary. A deal was struck whereby Roger Hanks bought the property from the Lewises and remodeled it into the newest Dripping Springs Post Office. The outside exterior included limestone blocks much like many of the surrounding buildings, plus a metal roof. Otherwise, the outside kept its basic integrity. The attractive building became occupied with its new tenant on February 14, 1987.

J. W. Wilson TV & Appliance

After four years of running their television business, mostly from their own home, J. W. and his wife, Lurline, decided to build a building to house their business in the southwest corner of their home lot. It was located on Highway 20, just west of town. This was 1953. At the time, the roadbed of Highway 20 was below the structure but five years later, when Highway 290 was completed, the roadbed was above it and this caused some drainage problems for the Wilsons. In the early part of 1963, lightning struck the store and it burned to the ground. By June of that year the present building was completed. When the old wooden Methodist Church was replaced with the rock one at the corner of 290 and RR12 in 1963, the wooden structure was moved behind the store and used for additional storage. The old church caught on fire and burned in the '80s but luckily the original building was spared. Also in 1964, a laundromat was added to the east side of the building. It survived for many years. After

Wilson TV & Appliance

more than thirty years, the building became woefully small for the expanding business and in 1987, a new and larger building was built on the southeast corner of the same property. The old building has remained a useful member of the family as a storage facility, although many inquiries about leasing it have been proffered.

Haydon Mobil Station

The rerouting of Highway 290 to go straight through on Spring Street caused a stampede of new businesses that depended on traffic for their livelihood and previously had been on Mercer Street. Alva and Charlie N. Haydon already owned the land in block five that bordered 290. This allowed them to get the jump on others. The first thing they did was to build a new Mobil station on the corner of San Marcos and 290, where the old gin stood a couple of decades before. E. E. "Nookie" Myers, who had run the Mobil station on Mercer, moved over to the new facility in June 1959. They had a grand opening complete with music, coffee, and cake. Myers ran the Mobil station until his retirement in December of 1972.

Clyde Gillis took over the station and ran it until 1976. At that point Dan Triesch of Blanco took over management of the station. In 1982, Dan converted it to a Texaco Station. In 1985 Ray and Gibb Duvall bought out Triesch and then turned over the business to Thomas Brownson in 1987. One year later, Glenn Louvier took over and ran the business until late 1995 when he closed the doors. After being vacant for a while, Jones Eckols leased the premises for the purpose of selling used cars. That business lasted until Jim Powers bought the property from the Haydons in 1997. He immediately remodeled the facility into a combination Texaco Station and Popeyes Fried Chicken. It opened February 25, 1998.

Felps Sinclair Station

It was definitely an advantage to already

Mobil Station, 1959

own the land alongside the new 290 route, if you wanted to get a head start on building. Mr. and Mrs. Ed Felps owned the southeast corner lots in block two. They built a Sinclair station on the old route and proceeded to build the new station at the corner of 290 and now RR12 north, finishing their building just a few months ahead of the Garnett-Glosson Humble Station across the way. It opened in November of 1959. L. B. Wooten moved over from the other Sinclair station to be the first operator.

Unlike the other two service stations, the Sinclair station had a string of operators during its career. In 1961 it became Fulton's. From there it was Jennings (1962), Bowmans (1963-64), Wiests (1965-66), John Glass (1967), Rhodes (1968). Faye Dee James ran the station when it was a Fina in 1973-74. J. F. Glosson recalls that the last person to run the station was a Mrs. Sinclair who drowned while driving back to her home in Johnson City. In 1976, James McCrocklin put an end to its original use, when he purchased the property and converted the building into his headquarters for the Dripping Springs part of his real estate business. It remains in that capacity today.

Garnett/Glosson Humble Station

Travis Garnett, who had been running the Humble station on Mercer Street, was next to make the move. He asked J. F. Glosson, Jr., to be his partner and they bought the land on the corner of San Marcos and 290 from the Charles Seal family in late 1959. It was located diagonally from the Mobil station. By July 1960, the place was ready for business.

Part of the interesting history was in the holes for the gasoline storage tanks. As most around here knows, there is a lot of solid rock. It is not easy to get holes put into the ground. In this case, it was necessary to blast out the holes with dynamite. Travis set 52 sticks of dynamite, expecting them to be set off in intervals. Instead, when Louis Gourley came in to set them off, he decided to set them all off at once. He was afraid he would not be able to find the other wires after the first blast. The battery he was going to use to detonate the charge was not strong enough to do the job. They had to run an extension cord over from the Mobil station across the street and this worked.

At the same time, the Sinclair station was being built across the street, now McCrocklin's. Travis went over there to warn the worker on the roof that a blast was eminent. He was unconcerned, thinking he was far enough away to not be in any serious danger. When Travis mentioned the 52 sticks, the worker could not get down fast enough. The blast blew chunks of rocks through the roof of the Methodist parsonage next door. That was the only damage attributed to the blast.

In 1973, Travis offered his share of the business to J. F. At that point, J. F. and his wife, Cleo, became the sole owners. They purchased the six lots of that block and expanded the building to meet the growing population, selling gas plus car repair. Over the years, the name of the product changed but not the first name on the sign. The gas company went from Humble to Enco to Exxon. On June 1, 1999, when Cleo and J. F. decided to close the doors for the last time and enjoy retirement, there still was not a name change. Son, Monte, who worked alongside his dad for most of his adult life, carried on the Glosson tradition. He and his wife Bridgette now own the business. J.F. is

Garnett-Glosson Humble Station, 1960

still seen around with his wrecker helping out cars in trouble.

Haydon Complex

Alva and Charlie Neal Haydon owned all of block five or what was left of it after 290 went through. They had already built the Mobil station and in 1960 they built the first of three sections to it. The first building, located on the west end of the block, was a restaurant. It was named the Western Kitchen. It was opened in 1960 by Jimmy and Martine Hoard. They operated this very popular eating place until their retirement in 1975. It would not open again until 1976 when Bonnie Pearson reopened it as Tiger Den. Bonnie's parents were Jimmy and Tula Glosson, who had named the little rock cafe on Mercer Street, that they had operated in the '40s and '50s, after her. Blackie and Jeanne Cutrer retained the name when they took over in 1979. Bert Reid changed it to Bert's Restaurant for his 1981-83 stay. In 1983, high school student Louie Alvarez managed the eating place for one year and brought back the name Tiger Den.

Name changes continued with Oak Shadows Restaurant (1984), Texas Traditions (1986) and finally Green Mesquite (1988) managed by Dart and Gail Hyde. In 1989, the restaurant string came to an end. Sherry Burke leased the building and converted it into a flower shop she named Flowers To Go. In 1992, Flowers To Go was purchased by Sylvia McCaslin. She ran the business until late 1999 when she sold it to Dawn Fultz Kidd. Brenda Smith would purchase the business from her in February 2002.

In 1962 a second building was erected to the east of the Western Kitchen. Its first tenant was Virgil Conn. He had a small business down the street in the old insulation building now owned by Haydon. He kept pushing the Haydons to put in a building for his business and Alva obliged. Virgil's nickname was Nut so he called it Nut's Hobby Shop. He was just ahead of his time as he had all types of objects to satisfy the curious. Unfortunately this type of business had not hit its stride in small towns and he struggled with it for eight years before having to give up his love. Nell Graham opened an antique store called The Gallery in 1971. In the late '70s it had a short life as an amusement center. By 1987, Ben Woodland was managing Aunt Nell's Attic. In 1989, antiques gave way to coffins when Harrell's Funeral Home took over the area. They stayed until 1993. For a short time a children's store called the Little Rascals was in there. In 1995, Nancy Haffelder moved her store over from the Veranda and named it the Gateway Emporium, having a variety of gift ideas, much like its predecessor so many years before. A runaway trailer, loaded with a band's musical instruments, crashed into the building in June 1999 and destroyed much of the building and its contents. The building was repaired by late July but the owners of Gateway Emporium decided not to continue. Other businesses have since moved in.

1984 saw the gap between the two buildings closed in to make another business room. In its career each of the two other buildings have used it to enlarge theirs. At first it was used as one of the dining rooms for the restaurant. When they ceased to be, it turned to other uses in combinations. When Harrell's Funeral Home took up residence, this area became the visiting room. It has spent time as an antique store as well and the headquarters for an insurance agent.

Ragland's Village Center

Alva Haydon was not the only one who took advantage of the new Hwy. 290 to start a thriving complex. Louise and Skeet Ragland chose an excellent spot on the south side of 290 just west of the Creek Road. They purchased the small strip of land that included a four-room house and put together

Village Center, 1961

the forerunner of the one-stop shopping center for Dripping Springs. The center included a cafe, grocery, beauty and barber shop. The house became the west end of the main building. The front two rooms became the barber and beauty shops and the back two rooms were used as living areas or storage. When the grocery was expanded to include the rooms previously being the barber and beauty shops, the portion that was the house could be noted by the slanted floor leading to those rooms. The grocery and cafe was run by the Raglands. Bersha McIntyre had the beauty shop and Ira Ruston the barber shop. It opened in August 1961. A Conoco station was separate from the rest of the center and located on the east side of the property. The station was completed by April 1962, and Melvin McNair was the first to run it. Later Fisher would take over. The cafe occupied the east end of the main building with the grocery in the middle and the barber/beauty shops on the west end.

The Conoco station was managed in its early years by the Raglands (1963-64), Corky Pendleton (1965) and John Glass (1966). The cafe was handled by Womack in 1964 and J. W. Hunnicutt in 1965. Oscar Vineyard took over in 1966 and ran it until the McCartys took over in 1970. The station and cafe were phased out and the space used for other things. Today, the entire complex is one building dedicated to the grocery and market business. The station portion housed feed for animals. There are Shamrock self-serve gas pumps out front.

The Dietchers took over the Village Center in 1967. The next year Bill Tracy purchased the establishment and ran it until 1982. His health was failing him and Mack Crow took it off his hands. Billy Peters bought the store from Mack in 1987 and renamed it Dripping Springs Grocery & Market. In January 1992, the title went to Jim Powers. He sold it to Jeff Harris and Keith Askey and they sold it to an Arab group headed by a man named Amir in 1994. On 9-15-2001, they sold the business to El San, Inc.

Felps Drug & Grocery

Mr. and Mrs. Ed Felps were still in the building mood after completing the Sinclair station. Next door they built a cinder block building that stretched almost the entire length of the lot. This was still 1961 and this building was one of the last to be built during this year of growth for Dripping Springs businesses. George Wiest, who had run the cafe and Sinclair station for the Felps in the '50s, was biding his time with a grocery business on Mercer Street and quickly moved into the building and ran his drug and grocery business from there. This association lasted until 1966 when the business closed. For several years in the late '60s and early '70s, Marion Jackson used the facility for his antique auctions until it simply grew too small for his large crowds. In 1975, it became the home of Dripping Springs Auto Parts with Walter Tharp being one of the partners. DS Auto Parts closed its doors in 1991. It did not have another permanent occupant until Elvie Richardson and his partner, Tom Buttrum, moved their Showstopper Video Rental business there in April 1993. Since then they have also added an amusement room for video games.

Dripping Springs Lumber Company

O. B. McKown decided to purchase lots 7 and 8 in block six from L. B. Jennings in August 1961. Mr. Jennings had been in the lumber business in several locations for many years. The last was out of a small building on this property. Mr. McKown visualized a much larger version for this community. He also bought Lot 9 to give him plenty of room, and founded the Dripping Springs Lumber Company. The main building faced San Marcos Street and took up the northern portion of Lot 7. The sheds for storing the lumber were facing south and built along the northern side of the lots and connected to the main building. This allowed plenty of parking and moving around space on the south side. He would have his grand opening on December 2, 1961. A turkey would be given away. King Feed and Lumber occupied the premises beginning in late 1973. King ceased to run the business from this location a few years later. In March of 1978, the property was leased to General Telephone. GTE had offices and supplies stored there. Reorganization plans caused GTE to vacate in 1988. The vacancy sign did not stay out very long. C.K. Automotive Supply opened their doors to the public in 1989 and stayed there until they moved to another location in 1992. Since then it has been mostly vacant. A family lived there for a very short while. In January 1996, the Dripping Springs Community Fellowship Church was formed and chose this as their home. In 1998, they chose to move out and it began a life of vacancy again until an environmental business began occupying it in 2001.

Spurgeon Breed Milling & Feed

J. N. and Oran Rippy purchased Lots 1, 2, 6, 7, 8, 9, and 10 of block one in the first addition. This was property formerly owned by Will Garnett. He had his blacksmith business located here. The Rippys tore down all the buildings and moved their feed grinder there as part of the process of moving part of their feed business there. In midstream they decided to get out of the feed business and concentrate on wool and mohair. Spurgeon Breed liked the idea of a feed store and bought the property in 1963 and built the portion located on lot 1. He had scales and the works. He ran a thriving business until 1973 when he sold it to Sims Feed and Milling. They ran into problems and sold the property to Raymond Whisenant and Wayne Mathewson in 1974. They shared the space for their respective businesses. Whisenant ran a well drilling enterprise called ROWSCO and Mathewson had a cabinet company. The tin building was later expanded north to almost double its capacity. In 1983, Whisenant decided to move his company out west on 290 and Mathewson bought him out. The Mathewsons added a large warehouse running east and west on their lots in 1988. They ran into the same financial problems that others were having about the same time. Millwood took up residence there in 1989 and lasted a few years. Kevin Bogan purchased the property and relocated his C.K. Automotive Supply to this site in 1992. They leased it out to A-Line Auto Parts in 1996. A-Line moved to a location on 290 in June 2002. At the present this building is vacant.

The 1980s and 1990s

It was the best of times and the worst of times for Dripping Springs businesses in the '80s. Times were good and money was being thrown around like there would be no to-

morrow. Land prices just soared giving some settlers the opportunity to take the money for their land and run. Many others were left holding a mighty big bag when the law of gravity sent everything spiraling down to earth from whence it came. Dripping Springs had gotten the first bank in 1981 and they, as well as many other loaning businesses, were willing to dole out big loans using the high price of land as collateral. When those values came tumbling down in the mid-'80s, the loans could not be repaid and this caused a mighty crash heard round the country as businesses hit bankruptcy in droves. Very few in Dripping Springs were left unaffected and it took well into the '90s for many to get things settled down so they could start all over again.

Business centers sprang up all over the area. The Loop 64 Joint Venture group headed up by Knox Williams, Mark McManus, John P. Burke, and Robert Peerman built the Drippin' Office Center on Loop 64. Dan McMahon built The Commons just east of Drippin' Office Center. J. P. Tate built an office complex and rental buildings on Ranch Road 12 south called Oakwood Plaza, plus the Promenade on Ranch Road 12 south near 290, and a smaller office building and rental building on 290 West called Oakwood Plaza Too. James Hurlbut built Pioneer Plaza facing Hays Street. Dayton Roberts used his property on Loop 64 to build the Veranda. Randy Garnett raised a four-office complex called Bluff Center on 290. Walter Tharp opened up Redwood Center, also on 290 West. Dairy Queen was the first fast food establishment along 290 and this occurred in the 1980s. Many owners were forced to give up their enterprises as they went through bankruptcy proceedings.

The boom reinvented itself in the mid-'90s for Dripping Springs. Property along 290 began being turned into commercial enterprises once again and the many subdivisions of the area were being maxed out. Sonic Drive-In, Cattleman's Bank, Jack Brown Cleaners, Popeye's Fried Chicken, Taco Bell, Diamond Shamrock, Ace Hardware, Central Texas Drilling, Hamburger Hill, Bolton Works Nursery & Country Landscape, and Dripping Springs Car Wash are just a few new businesses.

In the first couple years of the 21st century other businesses continue to make their presence known. Along 290 the following have made their appearance: PEC (Pedernales Electric Co-operative), Sophie's Garden, Lone Star Dentistry, Country Living Furnishings, Aromatheraphy Skin Care, The Arbor Center, Westview Building, Eye Care Associates, and Security State Bank & Trust. Brown-Karhan built a new campus just off old Highway 290. On Ranch Road 12 north, The Ole Hen House eatery, Gateway Landscaping Materials, and Another Roadside Attraction opened for business. Ole Hen House did not last very long. Traveling RR 12 south, you will find The Springs Fitness Family & Fun Center and the Outpost Motel, Dripping Springs' first such lodging establishment since the '20s. More is planned on this road. If the Caliterra development follows through with its plans for the 600-acre location on the west side of RR12, then they will have a golf course, a convention center, and a major subdivision.

Clockwise, from top left: Harvey Goslin and Pete Glosson at Glosson's Grocery, 1968; Bill Garnett Garage/Gulf Station, 1925; Outpost Motel, RR12 S; McNair's Hardware. Pictured are Bobby Roberts, Ina Mae "Skeet" Gilmore, Melvin and Bill McNair, 1964; PEC building, 2000.

History of Businesses

Wilson TV & Appliances

Despite what many of our citizens under forty may believe, television has not always been around. Dripping Springs had one person who had the foresight to see it coming and was prepared when it did. J. W. Wilson, Jr., went to TV repair school so that he would be ready to get into the business when the first TV station in the area, Channel 4 in San Antonio, came on the air. This was in 1949.

J. W. and his wife, Lurline, leased the old Breed Meat Market building located on Mercer street next to the Mobil Station to open up their radio and TV store. It had recently closed as a cafe. However, having to endure one winter in the airish building was all he wanted. He said the air conditioning worked too well during the winter months. They made the decision to move the business to their house on Hwy 290 W. They had built it in 1948. The move was made in 1950.

J. W. was the only qualified repairman in the area and soon locked up all the surrounding area towns to do TV repair. This was their main revenue while TV sales were limited. In the beginning, they only sold Admiral TVs. When the quality of this brand started declining, J. W. was quick to go to a different brand that he could depend on. This legacy of honesty and dependability was his trademark. The quality of the product and work provided a reputation that has brought customers from near and far to do business.

Finally in 1953, a building was built in the front yard to house the growing business. J. W. said when they first built, the 290 roadbed was below the structure, but when the expanded 290 was built in the late '50s, the roadbed was raised and it caused him drainage problems. Lightning caused a problem as well. In the Spring of 1963, lightning struck the building on a Sunday afternoon and the building burned to the ground, leaving nothing but the foundation. The present building was completed by June of 1963. A laundromat was added to the east side in 1964. For over two decades, the small building served the purpose but as the business grew, space became a problem. They bought the old Methodist church for more storage space in 1963. The old church would later burn down in the '80s.

In 1987 it was decided to build a much larger structure just east of the Wilson home. It would have the space to display, repair, and store. The business not only included appliances and televisions but air-conditioning installation as well. In 1993, J. W. lost his battle with heart disease and passed away. His son, J. W. III (Trey), who had handled the service department since 1982, and his wife Gay Lynn, took over the entire business and continued the tradition. However, part of the tradition that was the anchor and original reason for being, the television business, has not survived. J. W. was the kingpin in television repair and upon his death, no one was capable of continuing that phase of the business with the same quality and tenacity. That and the fact that the television business had become a competitive and consuming thing. Trey decided to get out of that phase of the business in 1995 and concentrate on the air conditioning and appliance part of it. They made the decision to point this out by renaming the business Wilson AC and Appliance. The habit is hard to break. Even today, customers come in and expect to see televisions and want theirs repaired.

Rippy Ranch Supply

This third generation family business dates back to 1952. Located on Mercer Street, it started out in humble surroundings and has expanded into several buildings. Much of the appeal is derived from an appearance that dates back to another time and generation. Instead of a modern building, customers and visitors are treated to surroundings that have changed little over the decades of use. There are probably some original cobwebs still lurking in the corners of the old building. Since the area around Dripping Springs made the change from farming to ranching in the '30s, feed stores have been plentiful and constant in the community. The Rippy name has been the most prominent through most of those years and has withstood the competition in good stead.

The Rippy name first got into the feed business in 1945. At this time W. F. "Felix" Rippy was operating the Humble station located on the corner of Mercer and San Marcos. Being an old rancher, he decided to begin selling feed out of the garage area of the station. He continued this arrangement until 1947. After the movie theater closed that year, Mr. Rippy moved his feed business across the street into that building. His son, J. N. Rippy, recalls a problem with the new site. Being a theater, the floor was slanted to below ground level and when it rained, water accumulated. The feed was stacked on the stage and the workers had to slosh through the water to fill the orders. In 1948, Jim Lumpkin bought the theater building and the present Central Garage site. He put in an insulation business and continued the feed business with Mr. Rippy managing it for him until early 1950.

Mr. Rippy's retirement lasted until 1952. He and P. A. Glosson were sitting around one day and the price of feed became the topic of conversation. They became incensed that the feed stores were making a profit of fifty cents per one hundred pounds of feed. They decided they could do something about the situation. With Mr. Rippy's feed business experience and Mr. Glosson's capital, a partnership was formed. They found a site they liked. It was an old cafe that Mr. L. P. Scheh had moved from Buda in the '30s, located between the Billie Garnett store and the Will Crow Wool and Mohair building. It was a small wooden building and they got Pete Glosson to lay cinder block walls to expand it to about a 30x50 foot area. They were now ready to open the Rippy and Glosson Feed Store.

Their strategy was to make a twenty-five cent profit on one hundred pounds and let the volume make the money. It proved to be a sound policy. They had taken on turkey feed accounts, as well, and had feed sacks stacked to the ceiling. Business was booming as sacks of feed were moved in and out of the store. The problem proved to be age. The age of the owners, that is. Mr. Rippy was 65 and Mr. Glosson was 87 and the physical exertion needed to carry on the business was difficult to maintain. Son J. N. Rippy remembers coming in during that first year and helping out in his spare time.

After a year, Mr. Glosson was ready to get out of the business and sold his share to Oran Rippy, another son. Within a year, J. N. Rippy bought into the business too. During this time, wool and mohair was added to the business. At first, Mr. Howard Ragsdale of Johnson City, a wool and mohair warehouse dealer, approached them about setting up a wool and mohair warehouse at their place. Their building was just too small to accommodate this offer but they did agree to buy it in Dripping Springs and truck it to Johnson City. To their amazement, they bought over 30,000 pounds that first year. At this point, Will Crow wanted the Rippys to buy out his wool and mohair business. They did not have the capital, so had to decline. They did agree to lease the business and have Hollis Blackwell of Goldthwaite supervise it for three years. Oran Rippy managed the business until 1963. According to J. N. Rippy, Oran's main interest did not lie in the running of the business. He loved to trade animals and of this, J. N. interjected "Oran held a doctor's degree in livestock trading."

In the meantime, both businesses continued to prosper. J. N. had to lease the Garnett building next door for office space. Tiring of the walk back and forth to the other two buildings, J. N. decided to approach Will Crow about building office space in his building for them. Mr. Crow declined but said he would sell the building to the Rippys. J. N. replied, as before, that he did not have enough money to buy the place. To this, Mr. Crow countered "If you can pay the rent, you can buy the building." So that is how the Rippys acquired the Crow building. The first thing they did was to build the needed office space and apply plywood to the west wall. In the years to follow, the feed store and Crow building were made one by enclosing the alley between the two. The floor covered a well located in the alley. Another wooden addition was added behind the old feed store and in the '80s, a second story storage area was added over the original feed store.

More changes came in the early '60s. A decision to expand further was on the drawing board. The land across the street where the old Garnett blacksmith building stood was purchased and the feed grinder moved over there. The idea was to build a building and move the feed store business there. Upon further review, J. N. decided against the venture. He had grown tired of the slow-pay habits of some of his biggest customers and grown fond of his wool and mohair business. So, instead, Spurgeon Breed built and opened the feed store and the Rippys specialized in wool and mohair. J. N. bought out Oran's share of the business in 1963 and when their father died later that year, he became the sole owner. The Rippys re-entered the feed supply business in 1974. It became a third generation business in 1984, when Oran Hill Rippy bought the business from his uncle. J. N. still handles the wool and mohair portion. Along with the usual feed and ranch supplies, the new owners diversified with a western apparel section for a few years.

Some of the feed stores over the years have been Herwig & Jennings, Pete Glosson, Ed Fine, Gay Harris, Spurgeon Breed, Sims Feed, and King Feed. Also, various types of stores have carried feed as a part of their merchandise.

S. P. Breed Feed Store, 1963

Wool and Mohair Industry

The early settlers of Dripping Springs selected the area because of the plentiful supply of water, materials for building, and soil sufficient to make a subsistence farming existence. By the 1920s, the people had begun to realize the poor quality of the land was not suitable for making a living by farming crops. Cattle ranching provided an answer but even this was not ideal. It just took too much land to support cattle. It became obvious to some that sheep and goats could provide the answer. Early pioneers in this style of ranching, according to J. N. Rippy, included J. L. Patterson, B. F. Quick, W. F. Rippy, Glenn Key, Wolf Cobb, Roger Parker, and Tom Joy. Even earlier than this group was P. H. Raiford, who bought the John Moss place in 1860. In the 1861 tax rolls, the Raifords counted among their possessions, 451 head of sheep valued at $1,358.

Over the '20s and '30s, the sheep and goat industry became prominent in Dripping Springs. A report in the *San Marcos Record* said that between the years of 1925 to 1927, Angora goats had increased from 2,150 to 25,690 in Hays County. Thousands of miles of goat fences had been built by the late '30s. With the increased interest, a market opened up for the fleece of the sheep (wool) and the hair of the goat (mohair).

The earliest wool and mohair magnate of Dripping Springs was Will Crow. Around 1937 he built a wooden warehouse approximately 30x50. It was located where the east wing of the Rippy building is today. He had torn down the old Masonic Lodge/merchandise building on Lot 3 of block seven and erected the warehouse on the back of the property. On April 12, 1939, it burned to the ground while it was full of wool and mohair. He rebuilt it on the same spot. By November of that year he reported that he had handled 125,000 pounds of 12-month wool, 50,000 pounds of short wool and 125,000 pounds of mohair. By 1946, he built a similarly sized building running north and south, facing Mercer Street. This gave the complex an L-shape. In 1946, he used the front portion, facing Mercer, to open the first hardware store. He was unchallenged in the wool and mohair business in Dripping Springs until the Rippys got involved in 1952.

At this time, the Rippy and Glosson Feed Store was getting underway next door. Howard Ragsdale, a wool and mohair dealer from Johnson City, tried to get the Rippy-Glosson business to go in competition with Crow. With no room in their building and no money to expand it, they had to graciously decline the offer. Not one to give up easily, Mr. Ragsdale proposed they collect the product at Dripping Springs and truck it to Johnson City. He would pay them a set price per pound to do this. They accepted. To their amazement, they trucked 30,000 pounds to Johnson City. This was the beginning of the Rippy's involvement in this end of the wool and mohair business.

At this point, Will Crow was not much interested in getting into a competitive situation. Instead he offered to sell his business to the Rippys. They were still not in a position financially to accept the offer. So Mr. Crow said he knew someone who was interested in opening a subsidiary in Dripping Springs. It was Hollis Blackwell of Goldthwaite. At this time, there were three major dealers in the huge Central Texas area. Along with Blackwell, there was Weldon Cloud of Lampasas and Mickey Stephens of Lometa. According to J. N. Rippy, this area was known as the "Land of the Forty Thieves." Cloud already had a business located in Johnson City and Blackwell did not want to get in direct competition. He proposed that Cloud supervise the Dripping Springs location and they split the profits. Cloud agreed to a three-year deal. The financial backing came from Leon Stone of the Austin National Bank. Most of their dealings went through his secretary, Allene Breed, a native of Dripping Springs. J. N. Rippy said another prominent lady in the wool and mohair business was Skeet Gillmore. Miss Gillmore handled all of Will

Crow's financial payments in his business for years.

After the three years were up, J. N. Rippy was in a position to take over the business and leased the building from Will Crow. The business continued to flourish. So much so, office space had to be rented in the Billie Garnett building next door. Tiring of the constant trips between the warehouse and office to conduct business, J. N. approached Mr. Crow about making some improvements in his building, including office space. Mr. Crow balked at the suggestion but instead offered to sell the building to him. Mr. Crow contended that if he could afford to pay rent, he could afford payments and allowed J. N. to make his rental payments until the building was paid for.

Improvements and changes to the Rippy enterprise have taken place over the years, beginning with the office space and plywood walls on the west side of the Crow building. The feed store and Crow building were made one by enclosing the alley between. The alley floor was built over a well. Another warehouse was built behind the feed store. The last change was made in the '80s when a metal second floor building was erected over the old feed store portion where now the grading and separating of wool and mohair takes place.

From 1962 to 1974, the Rippys were out of the feed business. They concentrated entirely on the wool and mohair business. Like most businesses, there are highs and lows. A proud moment came in 1964. That year Texas marketed thirty million pounds of wool and mohair. Of that total, 1.1 million pounds passed through the Rippy establishment. That peak was followed by a five-year slide before another upswing took place. It is always a gamble in the buying and selling game. J. N. recalls there were times when he has bought at a low price, held the hair in storage a year or two before doubling or tripling his profit. On the otherhand, he can remember times when he lost that gamble too.

Times began to change in the '70s. The trend away from ranching had started. Difficulty in making a living from the land, rising property taxes, and few wanting to follow in the footsteps were factors. Increases in the population opened up the need for land to expand the cities through the suburb system, and subdivisions out in the countryside became popular. The sale of land to speculators and parcels to people wanting to enjoy country living became more profitable than what they were doing and many ranchers began to sell off some or all of their acreage. J. N. delights in recalling that at one time he bought thousands of pounds from the Davenport Ranch, which is now the Austin Country Club, as well as from acreage now inside Loop 360 in Austin.

J. N. sold the entire business to his nephew, Oran Hill Rippy, in 1984. Even after the sale, he continues to be involved in the wool and mohair phase of the business. His pride in what he has accomplished over the years and the knowledge that his is a dying breed keeps him involved to make sure a part of Texas history continues. Of all the many like businesses that thrived throughout the area in years past, only Rippy's still buys and sells wool and mohair.

DS Butane

In 1962, Fred Garnett, his wife Betty, and their children Terry and Theresa, were living in Dayton Roberts' house on Mercer Street (now behind the Veranda). It was here the Garnett family started up the DS Butane business. Across the street was the old Sinclair station that had relocated in 1960 and O. B. McKown, Sr., had upgraded the building to a residence by remodeling and expanding the size of the building. So in 1963, the family and business moved across the street. This looked like a very convenient arrangement with the office up front where the station was. Fred said he found out that looks could be deceiving. What frequently happened was customers would just walk back into the living quarters without thinking about it being someone's home. This lack of privacy was a concern to the family.

Come 1965, the family moved back into Dayton Roberts' house and the business down to the other end of Mercer. It would find a permanent home in his dad's old Gulf station and more recently, brother Travis's Humble station. The station and garage had been vacant since 1960. Part of the remodeling process was to rock the old driveway and make it a foyer and display area of the business. Later office space was added to the west side. The back area held the parts and supplies.

The family continued to expand beyond butane. Electrical, air conditioning, plumbing, and finally hardware all headquartered from this building. It was DS Butane, DS Plumbing and Mechanical, and DS Hardware all under one roof. They rented out Billie Garnett's store across the street to house some of their supplies. Finally, in 1983, a large metal building was built on RR12 N to house DS Hardware and DS Plumbing and Mechanical. At the present, Fred runs the DS Hardware store while son, Terry, is in charge of the DS Butane business.

Raymond Oran Whisenant & Son Company (R.O.W.S.C.O.)

Raymond Whisenant, a 1947 Dripping Springs graduate, had tired of the various jobs he had held since graduating and wanted to settle down to something permanent. He had worked for a well drilling company and decided he would like to give it a try. This was in 1963. At the time, he owned and lived on property on RR12 S, just beyond the town plat. He first ran his business from a building on the property. As the business began to prosper, more space was needed. He purchased land and erected a shop on the hill just beyond the Springlake subdivision entrance on RR12 N in 1970.

The shop area stayed on the hill but the business office was moved to the old Breed feed store on Mercer Street. The building was shared with the Mathewson cabinet warehouse. This arrangement was kept until 1983, when the growth of both businesses necessitated a change. ROWSCO expanded its business into paving and other road work, as well as well drilling. They relocated to property along Hwy 290 W, next to the Dripping Springs Heights subdivision. The building and the space were ample for all their needs.

A couple of years after his graduation in 1969, Raymond Oran Whisenant, Jr., joined his father in the business. In 1994, Raymond Whisenant, Sr., retired and left his son in charge of the business. The company decided to divest itself of the paving and road work sections of its business by selling them to others and went back to their roots, well drilling. Like many businesses that need to expand and do not have the ready capital to do so, ROWSCO looked for ways to remedy the situation. In 1998, ROWSCO came under the umbrella of Aqua Source, with the running of the business remaining under the auspices of the Whisenant leadership. It has since been renamed Aqua Utility. Recently, Ray and Pat Lyle bought the business back.

Mike's BBQ

The story of Mike's BBQ reminds you of the saying "From small acorns large oaks grow." It certainly had its small beginnings. Actually, in the beginning, Mike Poston was not even involved in the site where the business would make its mark. Oscar Vinyard still had some cooking fever left in him after giving up his reins at the Village Center Cafe in 1970. In 1972, he moved a little portable building to the northeast corner of 290 and College Street and began selling hamburgers. John Harmon bought the place in 1974. He poured a cement slab and attached a couple of screened in lean-to rooms with picnic tables for the customers. John stayed with the business until the summer of 1975. The building remained vacant until June 1976 when Alfred Garza re-opened the enterprise and named it Taco Hut. In the meantime, July 4, 1978, was the date Mike Poston made his move into the world of DS BBQ. He moved a little portable building under the tree on the east side of the, then, Mobil station and served BBQ and hamburgers out of it.

This went on for a couple of months. The owner of the Tiger Den, a restaurant on the same block, began to complain about this competitive situation to the property owner, who owned both properties. Rather than cause a hassle, Mike began to look for another spot to continue his business. By 1978, Garza tired of his business and Mike bought him out. Mike dragged his portable over and put it next to the other buildings and set up shop. He expanded by adding rooms to the existing structures. Finally, he decided against the hodgepodge look and built the present building in 1983. He did it by building over the original structure and at the last minute pulled the portable buildings out from under the new facility—all of this without ever having to close down or miss a single day of business.

He tired of the long hours and sold the business to Jack Davis and associates in 1984. They renamed it J.R.'s Steaks. They stayed in business for three years before returning it to Mike. Remodeling took place and Mike's BBQ was up to speed again. He tried to turn the business over to Jack and Mary Brown in 1987 but that lasted less than a year. No one had the magic touch of a Poston. They thought the third time might be the charm in turning the business over to James Bartels in 1990. It wasn't, and this time the Postons vowed to keep the business in the family. It cost too much to renovate and start over each time. This time, son Ottis and his wife Bambi were in charge.

Just when things were going great again, another disaster struck. On November 15, 1994, a fire destroyed the serving and front dining area of the building. Undaunted, Ottis and Bambi decided to continue in the business. They came back to their roots by building a small building east of the main building and began serving meals again. In the meantime, a decision was made to remodel the three dining areas not directly affected by the fire. A metal roof was installed to protect the area around the kitchen to the main building. Now a person could enjoy the food in at least three ways. They could use the drive-through window, walk up and order, or go into the dining area to order and be served. After the fire, Ottis and Bambi became sole owners of the business and renamed it Mini Mike's.

A split in the marriage of Ottis and Bambi in 1996 closed the business again. Glenna McIntyre moved her Mexican Louie's Restaurant over to the site. She, in turn, sold her business in the summer of 1997. Finally in the summer of 1998, Mexican Louie's bit the dust. Mike Poston re-modeled again, to ready the site for another tenant, and in November of 1998, Don Diego's opened its doors to continue the eating site started so many years ago. In the spring of 2002, it became Primo's.

Hamburger Hill Plus Restaurant

When the Redwood Center was erected on Highway 290 in 1984-85, it included a building apart from the rest of stores meant to be an eating place. The first tenant would be Hamburger Hill. There was already one in Oak Hill. The owners, Richard and Evelyn Silwedel, expanded by opening one in Dripping Springs. John and Martha Wright became the managers. Their marriage did not survive and John ran the business for a while longer. The Silwedels sold the Dripping Springs business to Bill and Judy Schlueter in 1988. They added the Plus to the name, so that others knew this was their business. They ran a thriving business. Bill was a lawman and one of his hobbies was collecting the patches of law agencies around the country. He had hundreds of them that decorated the walls of the dining room. The Redwood Center was in the process of a change of ownership and a name change to Trail Head.

Hamburger Hill survived a fire that burned most of Redwood Center on December 5, 1987. In 1994 a new owner was going to raise the terms of the lease for the Schlueters. They began to look around and found the location they wanted on the corner of Highway 290 and the DSYSA road, and bought it. By December of that year, they were open for business in an attractive white stone building. A favorite of the patrons was the Friday night "all you can eat" catfish dinners. Restaurant hours are tough on the people running them and by 2001, the Schlueters were tiring of the hours and needed a rest. They sold the property to Steve Axelrod and Melanie Stanford in April, who remodeled and opened the Que Pasta. This did not go over and by March 2002, the owners had leased it out to another hopeful. After remodeling, it opened under the name of Great Dane. It met the same fate, only quicker. The Schlueters bought the property back in June 2002, remodeled, and reopened the Hamburger Hill Plus on July 9.

John Glass Drilling

This business had its beginnings in Bee Caves where its founder John W. Glass lived at the time. This was during the war years of 1943-44. The next year he teamed up with James B. Tucker and it became known as Tucker and Glass Drilling. In 1948, John Glass made a career decision. He felt that in a few years the Bee Caves area would become a part of the Dripping Springs school system. With this in mind he decided to move to Dripping Springs where his kids would be nearer the school they would be going to. Sure enough he was right. He bought acreage from Sam Strong on 290 and just across the street from Wilson AC & Appliance. He built his house there and had his business in the back yard of his house.

By 1955, Mr. Tucker had decided to go into other areas of work, most notably Brown and Root. John then teamed up with his son under the name of J. W. Glass & Son. This association would end around 1962 when he mangled his hand in a cable rig accident. Being unable to do the drilling work, he sold his business to Duck Glass. Duck would hook up with Raymond Whisenant in 1963.

Tucker & Glass Drilling

James B. "Jimmy" Tucker, Jr., went to work in Austin for the *Austin American* newspaper. He worked there nights and worked days helping the Whisenants do drilling. After a few years of this, he decided to start up a drilling business in Dripping Springs. He asked his uncle, John Glass, if he wanted to work for him or become his partner in this new enterprise. John, since his retirement, had worked at the State Hospital in Austin and then, with his son, first ran the Conoco station at the Village Center and later moved up the street to run the Sinclair station. His reply was that if he was going to work with James, it was going to be as a partner. So, in October of 1968 they bought a cable tool rig and got back into the well drilling business.

At first the company was housed at Jimmy Tucker's place on Mt. Gainer Road southwest of Dripping Springs. John Glass bought a lot just east of his property in 1951. In 1970 the partnership built a building on the site. They bought their first air rig in the same year. On February 24, 1972, the partnership was incorporated and

Glass-Tucker Well Drilling, 1970

bought the lot. Their business grew and in 1978 they added a second air rig. By 1984 John Glass was ready to retire for good. On June 1, 1984, James and his wife, Ora Mae "Scooter," bought out their longtime partner and the business became officially known as James Tucker Drilling, Inc., after the incorporation papers were signed on November 13, 1985. Tucker's death in late 2002 leaves its future unknown.

Well Drilling

Even though Dripping Springs was known for its springs and surface water supply, there would come a time when wells were also a necessity. The first chronicle of people digging wells for others that I found was written in the *Hays County Times & Farm Journal*. In the June 18, 1887, issue, it noted that artesian wells were being dug. The modern equipment of today was not available in those days. It said that W. W. Caldwell dug one for Sallie McLendon and drilled another for Captain McLendon. Matt Livingston dug one at Mrs. J. M McLendon's at 154 feet and one at C. S. Graham's residence. In the July 9, 1887, edition, the comment was that the operators found water at 85 feet at the Graham's. Later in the July 30, 1887, issue it was noted the local citizens were trying to raise money so they could form a company to buy machines to dig artesian wells with the comment that the area needs the water. In the next issue they were cheerleading for the well company with the comment to "Whoop up the artesian well scheme." By October 22, 1887, twelve wells had been dug around Dripping Springs. The December 9, 1887, issue said J. M. Livingston drilled a well for W. A. McMillan and hit plenty of water at 62 feet. He also drilled a well in the rear of Major Cook's storehouse. Well drilling was not mentioned after that and it is not known whether the company was ever formed or not.

Well drilling was surely a necessary profession throughout the history of Dripping Springs. Charles C. Haydon, in addition to his other occupations, also dug wells for a living. As noted elsewhere John W. Glass started his well drilling business in 1943 and Raymond Whisenant and Duck Glass began their business in 1963. The Glass name has been synonymous with well drilling in the Hill Country for many decades. B&B Drilling has been around since 1965 but moved to Dripping Springs only a couple of years ago. With the continued growth of the area and the scarcity of good water available, there is no doubt that all the well drillers of the area will have more than enough to keep them busy for years to come, whether it is in the form of new wells or deepening existing ones.

Eating Places

Due to the problem of storing food supplies and the like, not many eating places could be found in and around Dripping Springs. If you believe the movies, most of the early stagecoach stops provided a meal when the stage made its regular stop. If so, the first such eating place might have been at the Wallace house where they had a stagecoach stop, where they kept horses, etc., associated with the stage line. Otherwise the first mentioned place was the Dripping Springs hotel. In several articles, the writer mentioned the good meals that could be had there.

The next mentioned was the Breed Meat Market. Mr. Breed bought the lot in 1914 and it is believed he opened the building soon thereafter. Although, it was primarily for the sale of fresh butchered meat, it is said he would also serve chili there too. The building was used as a cafe until 1949. Ivy "Piggy" Roberts sold hamburgers out of a portion of the building, prior to 1935, that the Haydons owned in block six. L. P. Scheh moved a building over to Lot 2, block seven and opened the West End Cafe in 1936. The business did not last but a couple of years. Next to enter the competition would be the Rock Cafe beside the Patterson building on Mercer Street in 1940. It served food until

1957. Meanwhile, Katherine Roberts opened a cafe in a portion of the Central Garage in the early '40s. The Sorrells built a cafe on a lot in front of the new high school in 1948 and Mrs. Volmering ran it as the West End Cafe for a while and then the Sorrells ran it until the early '60s. Garland Seal opened a barbeque business in 1954 on block one. He built a cafe on Lot 1 and sold it to W. P. Crow, who had several people try to run this eating establishment. It survived into the early '60s. The building that survived the longest as an eating place was built by the Haydons on block five. It was called Western Kitchen for the 14 years the Hoards ran the place. It ceased being one of the better places to eat in the late '80s. R. J. "Skeet" Ragland opened the Village Center in 1961 and it included a cafe that would last into the early '70s. The forerunner to Mr. Mike's location was a small building and lean-tos that served meals. The building craze of the mid-'80s opened up other opportunities to have eating places. Hamburger Hill opened at the Redwood Center and stayed there until moving to another location in 1994. Its place was taken by the Sidesaddle Bakehouse. The Commons had room for a restaurant and Mexican Louie's opened. Several owners tried to keep the restaurant open but finally in the late '90s, the last moved out and it was taken over by Your Growing Child daycare center. Across the street, a pizza place opened up and is still going strong. Knox Williams' real estate office was turned into an eating place and several tried to stay in business there. Just above DS Hardware on RR12 N, a building was built for the purpose of housing One-Eyed Jack's Pizza. It did not last, but Perry and JoAnn Alba opened the Mi Tierra restaurant there for several years. As traffic increased through Dripping Springs, so did businesses catering to your eating habits. Coming down Wallace Mountain on Highway 290 from Austin, people have the choice of stopping at Dairy Queen, Sonic, Taco Bell, Popeye's Chicken, Primos, Taco Hut, Hamburger Hill, Jerez' Place, Sidesaddle Bakehouse, and Subway. Expect more in the future.

Gas Stations

With the onset of the automobile age in the early '20s, there would be a need to sell gasoline for those mechanical horses. Many of you have probably seen the early gas pumps. The first gas stations were not like the ones we experience today. The old pumps, with glass tanks so you could see the gas, were pumped by hand and set outside the place of business. The earliest places were the Crenshaw Garage on block six and Garnett Garage on the other end of Mercer street. Crenshaw sold Texaco and Garnett sold Gulf. Crenshaw and W. P. Crow sold gas

Sinclair Station, 1958
—Courtesy James Felps

at their location on block seven. I have seen the gas pumps in pictures of the Patterson store and the A. L. Davis, Jr. hardware building. There were probably others along Mercer street. In 1937, the Haydons opened the Mobil station on the corner of block six and F. W. Miller opened a Texaco station in 1940, on the north side of Mercer, when the Crenshaw garage began selling Humble gas. A Sinclair station opened in the '50s in block one where the drive-in bank location is now. When the new 290 came through in 1958, the gas stations quickly moved to new locations. Mobil, Humble, and Sinclair moved and the others closed down. The Village Center offered Conoco. Today, coming down Wallace Mountain, one has the choice of Mobil, Exxon, Shell, Shamrock, Chevron, and Shamrock.

Garages

The coming of automobiles spelled the demise for the blacksmith industry but opened up another in the form of garages, with mechanics, to work on the cars. Repair garages did not necessarily have to be located where there was a lot of traffic, but early ones combined with the gas stations. The first two were located on Mercer and were the Crenshaw and Garnett garages. In 1937 Haydon's Central Garage joined the group. When Garnett and Glosson opened their Exxon station in 1960, so did the Garnett garage. Finally in 1964, Central Garage moved over to 290 and has been there since. In 1973 Glosson bought out Garnett and continues to have a garage business there. Garnett opened his 5G Garage at his home site just off Mercer street. Straley's Garage on Creek Road has been in business since the early '80s. The new kid on the block is Touchstone Automotive. They are located next to DS Butane on Mercer and have been in business for a couple of years now.

Dripping Springs Triangle, 2003

History of Houses

People who moved to an area wanted to have three things available to them. Materials to build their houses from, a water supply, and a source of food. The Dripping Springs area qualified in those areas. In most cases, the people who came to the area were not necessarily skilled in building elaborate homes. Early homes were mostly to protect the family from the elements, as well as from other dangers. Therefore, many were quite crude by our standards. Many were log cabin pens. As lumber mills came into being, houses were also made of boards, and cypress shingles were in demand and available in the area. Limestone was later quarried to make even more substantial living quarters.

The design of the log cabin was usually simple. Cut the logs, let them cure and then erect them in a stacked manner with doors hewn out and most likely a fireplace. The spaces between the logs were filled with objects, usually rocks, and then plastered to cover up any cracks that would let the weather come in. Then the roof would be put on. It was all pretty simple but still difficult to do without help. In those days it was not unusual for the neighbors to get together and help raise the house. If the family was small, then probably only one log pen was built. Others would be added as needed. The thick logs provided a measure of insulation for the building.

Later, when lumber became available, another simple construction was popular. A pier and beam would be used for supporting the floor. Then a framework of maybe two by fours were nailed to the floor. The walls were one by sixes or possibly one by twelves nailed vertical to the framework. The gaps where the boards met were closed by nailing slats over them. That was all that kept one from being outside. Newspaper, magazines, cardboard, and later wallpaper were used to try and insulate the inside from the outside elements. Later, outside walls would have overlapping boards and an inside wall. Still no insulation between the walls. Wallpaper and papers were still the best substitutes for insulation. In my early years, my family lived in just such a house. I never realized until sometime later why the rooms were so cold and more blankets were needed or why the walls appeared to be breathing as the wallpaper moved when the wind blew. That's just the way it was for most and you adapted to survive the winter.

Besides wooden structures, abundant rock and limestone were also used to construct buildings in later years when rock-

masons were more prevalent in the area. In doing research on the age of buildings, it appears that when you see a building constructed of old limestone blocks, it was most likely built around the turn of the 20th century. Dripping Springs had a run of good rockmasons in the '30s and '40s and for this reason most of the rock buildings were built between 1935-45.

One must understand that many of the early houses that still survive, in all likelihood, do not survive in their original form. As changes take place in the family and times, the residences are adapted to those needs; so additions are common.

Pound House

The log pen portion of Dr. Joseph M. Pound's house is the oldest surviving building in the P. A. Smith league. There is some confusion as to when it was built. Some accounts say it was in the fall of 1853. If so, it was built before Dr. Pound actually bought the land. A deed of trust gives the purchase of the property as December 21, 1854. If Dr. Pound actually erected the log cabin pen, it is more reasonable that it was probably completed in early 1855. Maybe some of our modern inventions will be able to pinpoint a reliable time. Nevertheless, a few months or even a year will not alter the storied history of this residence that was occupied by members of the Pound family until 1983.

Being a slave-owning family, it has always been assumed that slaves helped construct Dr. Pound's log cabin. The two that Dr. Pound owned were not even teenagers at the time the house was first being built. However, his brother-in-law, John Moss, owned eleven and next door neighbor, John Wallace, one. With the common practice of neighbors helping to "raise" each others houses to hasten an otherwise laborious task, it would be expected that everyone pitched in, with the slaves possibly doing much of the hard labor involved. There is no concrete evidence, either way, of the makeup of the construction crew.

John Moss and John Wallace bought their land months before the Pounds and their homes would have been built before the Pound House. The Mosses left Dripping Springs by 1860 and it is not known what happened to their house, unless it was the one that was later moved by Burrell J. Marshall to its site overlooking the Dripping Springs. Again, the house of choice appeared to be log cabins and not made of lumber. The Wallace home survived until the 1950s when the home was destroyed by fire.

The history of the Pound house was similar to most others, in that, as the occasion called for, it was changed to meet the situation. As time permitted and families grew, so did the additions to the house. The Pound house began as one log pen, the west one. It had the usual fireplace, this one on the west side. Three doors were placed on the north, east, and west sides and a window on the south side. The height of doors rarely reached higher than six

J. M. Pound House, 1855

feet and one has to be careful entering these. A closer look at this log pen reveals how really crude the construction was. It did not take a master carpenter to build. It looks much like structures I used to build as a kid with cedar posts. The logs were all shapes and sizes instead of being perfectly straight. The gaps between the logs might be as much as a foot or more. These gaps were chinked with many rocks and then plastered to fill in the gaps. One usually thinks of logs being notched so there is very little space between logs but that is not the case here. There was need for long, straight logs that spanned the entire length of the 16x16 room on the north, east, and south sides above the doors and window plus on the bottom of those three sides. Otherwise, the section of log was less than half that length for the rest of the walls. Rocks were used to keep the logs spaced so that the window and door frames could be nailed to the sawed logs. Saws and axes were used to trim two sides of the logs that would form the inside and outside surface of the walls. The bark was left on much of the rest of the log. You can see the axe marks on the logs where the blade caught wood instead of shaving the wood smooth as intended. Cedar posts were angled north and south to a point with other cedar posts fashioned as support posts on the east and west sides. A post stretched the length of the crest and other posts tied in with this center beam. Then cypress shingles were used for the roof and to fill in the east and west ends of the log pen. It is quite possible the first floor was simply dirt with the wood being added later.

In January of 1855, their family had expanded by one with the birth of Indiana. Within the year, a second log pen to the east was probably added with a dogtrot in between. At some point, a round rock cistern about ten feet deep and maybe eight feet wide at the base was built about fifteen feet west of the cabin to hold rainwater. Either then or later, a charcoal filter system to help purify the rainwater was built. On the northside of the west pen room, a rock walled cellar was built for storage, as well as a safe haven during storms or possible attacks.

As the family and Dr. Pound's practice grew, some major expansion renovations were made. Unfortunately, it included the dismantling of the east log room. It would have been nice if he had decided to just add on to the east log room rather than replace it. In its place, two larger wooden rooms were built that narrowed the dogtrot somewhat. Each had a fireplace. The northeast room was used for his office and the other doubled as a hospital room for sick patients. It was constructed of boards on the outside and board walls on the inside, but no insulation. When these two rooms were dismantled in the restoration project, the person in charge, George Gendron, remarked that part of the original log pen was used to construct the new rooms. The floor log beams were used to support the floor on part of the north room and other logs were used as the perimeter of the entire two rooms.

A kitchen was built to the east side of the remaining log room. It was designed in such a way as to incorporate the cistern into the west wall. The people inside could simply go to the window and draw their water from the cistern without having to go outside. The fireplace to the log room was rebuilt, so that each room would have access to it. A ledge near the top of the fireplace was designed to hold up and support ceiling beams. The kitchen was of simple construction. The floor was on wooden beams that rested on rock piers. It was made of grooved one by fours and pretty well airtight. Not so for the walls. It was typical one board wall. The main boards were 1x12s nailed to the framework. One by fours were nailed over the cracks between the main boards. That was all that kept one from living outside.

Insulation was whatever one could find, mostly paper products. Newspapers, magazines, rags, and cardboard were the common materials found in this room. When the kitchen was torn down on February 26, 1994, to prepare for reconstruction, the ceiling was found to be layers of cardboard cartons mixed with pages of magazines. This was sealed off with wallpaper. Layer upon layer of wallpaper was applied to the walls. The floor had three layers of linoleum on it and the papers and magazines spread out between the layers to prevent sticking, dated their installation. The first was applied to the wooden floor in 1942, while the second was put down in 1949, and the third in late 1952.

Later additions to the building included a small washroom just off the north side of the kitchen. In the 1950s, the stone cellar was deemed unsafe and was filled in and a room built over it. The southside porch was enclosed too. Other interesting things about the house include a rock storehouse just north of the building. On the southeast side of the house is an earthen plant cellar. Also, in the front yard is a rosebush that was supposed to have been brought from Mississippi with them and has survived all these years.

A project to return the house to its appearance at Dr. Pound's death in 1914 has been underway since 1988 when the family donated the home and three acres to the city for the purpose of turning it into a museum. The task for actually getting the job done was turned over to a group known as The Friends of the Pound House, headed up by Dr. Dennis and Katherine Cannon. The restoration was completed by the Fall of 2002. The grand opening was held in early 2003. The Pound House Museum is located near the northeast corner of Founders Park. The entrance to the park is on Ranch Road 12 north.

Marshall-Chapman

This house, located just above the limestone ledges that helped Dripping Springs get its name and near the west end of Loop 64, is the second oldest surviving building. It is possible the wooden portion of this building was built by John L. Moss, and if so, then it would be older than the Pound

Marshall/Chapman House, pre-1870

House. My guess, since the other two pioneers built log cabins, is that the Mosses probably did too. I'm not sure how easily lumber was obtained in this area in the early 1850s. We do know that Mr. Moss had much more worth than his two neighbors, including eleven slaves. This might have meant he could afford a little more. They were ranchers and did not stay long, but they had to live in some type of structure and one has to believe their house could have survived as long as the others.

John Moss sold his property to Phillip Raiford in May of 1860. Possibly because of the onset of the Civil War, the Raifords did not stay long and sold the property to Joseph Steiner in November of 1861 for $1,500 more than they paid for it. This usually means some type of improvement took place.

We do know that Burrell Jackson Marshall and his wife, Martha Ann, and their five children bought the land in January of 1870. They moved the wooden structure to its present site and added the rock rooms to it in 1871. Mr. Marshall was appointed postmaster and the house was used as the post office. Unfortunately, Mr. Marshall became ill and died on February 28, 1872, at the age of 49, leaving a widow and five children.

Enter William Thomas Chapman, 37. He was a land speculator who had come to Dripping Springs around 1872. He wooed the recently widowed Marshall, and in less than a year they were married. They resided in the Marshall home and had two children of their own, Mercer Ernest and Willie Pearl.

The Marshall heirs divided what was left of their one-quarter league in 1880. Chapman and his wife kept the house property and the land that would later become the town of Dripping Springs.

Mr. Chapman died in 1917 and his wife, Martha Ann, in 1924. Family members continued to live at the residence until it was sold in 1942 to John and Clara Wilson. They purchased the 76-acre parcel and sold most of it early on. Mrs. Wilson lived in the house until 1983. It was accorded a historical marker and remained vacant until 1996 when Alva Haydon, a son-in-law of the Wilson's, and his son, Charlie, renovated the building to usable condition. Charlie's daughter, Laura, and husband, John Russell, resided there until late 2000. Charlie's youngest daughter, Lea Anne, and husband, Brad Schroeder moved in during the summer of 2001.

Dr. J. W. Harrison

Dr. Pound was a well-known doctor and many people in the medical profession wanted to get their early training under him. Dr. J. W. Harrison may have been one of them. He had been engaged in the profession for quite some time in the area before he decided to buy land and build a home in the recently formed town of Dripping Springs. He bought a portion of block four in the third addition in 1883 and built a two-story home on it. In 1891 he retired, moved to Kerrville and sold it to another doctor, S. G. Shaw. Twenty months later the property was sold to a third doctor. This doctor only stayed in this house a few years, but he lived in Dripping Springs for the rest of his life. He was Dr. E. P. Shelton. D. G. Jones purchased the house in 1895, and in 1905 added a porch with columns. After numerous owners throughout the following years, John Elbert Shelton purchased the property in 1963. He was the eldest son of Dr. Shelton and was born in that house. The house is now owned by Mrs. Joan J. Crosswell, who bought it in 1977. The landscape of this property shows that this has always been an elegant showplace. The house is located on the corner of Hays and Bluff streets.

Chapman Boarding House

The opening of the Dripping Springs Academy in 1882 also opened up the need for places to stay for the students who were enrolled at the school. W. T. Chapman was an opportunistic businessman and shortly after donating the land for the Academy, went about drawing up the plat for the town of Dripping Springs and selling lots. This two-story house is located on the northeast corner of the Academy block, scarcely 10-20 feet from the property line. It was specifically built as a boarding house. The upstairs had a couple of rooms and a porch that students could rent out. This building was built in 1881, making it the third oldest building in Dripping Springs.

W. T. Chapman Boarding House, 1881
102 Old Fitzhugh Road

Mrs. Caperton ran the house the first year and Mrs. W. M. Jordan, wife of the school principal, the second year. Eventually, this building became a residence when its use as a boarding house waned. It basically kept its original look until Paul Allen, the high school principal, purchased the property in 1969. He liked to fix up old houses and he went to work on this one. On the outside he rocked up the walls. On the inside, he ripped out the stairs that led to the upstairs rooms, and to gain space, inserted a spiral staircase. He also added a shower upstairs. Galen Dodson, also a teacher and later a principal, purchased the property in 1973 and resides there now with his wife, Jerry Lou.

I.C.P. McLendon

I.C.P. McLendon purchased the northern half of the sixth block in the second addition in 1884. It is presumed the house was probably built about then as well. It is said that the house was used to house the telephone exchange for a while. It continues to be a residence.

I.C.P. McLendon House, 1884

C. S. Graham

This house was first built in 1884 when C. S. Graham bought the first two lots in block two of the first addition. Originally it

C. S. Graham House, 1884

faced the Academy block. Two versions popped up about its history in the mid-'20s. One version says it burned down, the other that it was simply remodeled. Whichever is true, the building was rebuilt using the same fireplace, and this time with the front door facing Mercer Street. The Crenshaws lived in it at the time and it has changed little since then. Johnny Chase has owned the property since 1976.

George Dickey

This two-story rock structure located on the sharp curve about eight-tenths of a mile from Highway 290 on RR12 south was built by George Dickey. He was a rock mason and carpenter with good skills. He bought the property in 1884, began the rock work in December 1885, and completed the project in June 1887. He was a businessman as well and doing the work in his spare time was probably what took him so long to get it completed. The site is a very beautiful location with Walnut Springs flowing just south of the building. He built the dam so that he could raise fish. There is known to have been a mill in the 1870s where Walnut Springs and Onion Creek intersect. Its remains and the site is now located on the Needham

Mr. and Mrs. J. L. Patterson and family, 1905, stand before the George Dickey House built in 1886-87. —Courtesy Carla Allen

property and never was a part of the Dickey property. There must have been several houses in and around the Walnut Springs area because several newspaper articles divulged that a couple of families were moving to the Walnut Springs property before the Dickey house had even been completed. It is also possible that the wooden building said to have been on the southwest corner of this house may well have been where the Dickeys lived until its completion.

As was common for the times, the front had a gabled porch over the second story outside door. The gate entrance with his name and the date was flanked with a wooden picket fence on a low rock base. A wooden room was added on the southwest corner of the house, probably for a kitchen area or perhaps servant's quarters.

J. L. Patterson bought the property in 1903 because he thought the house should be able to withstand a strong windstorm. He replaced the picket fence with a stacked rock fence. He also decorated the front yard with flowering plants. Even though the rock structure might have been able to withstand a storm, the wooden portion was unable to withstand a fire. The house burned in 1917 or 1918. They rebuilt before he and his wife died in 1921.

It was Lester Brenizer who made the site a real showplace. He was an accomplished singer who liked arts and antiques. He transformed the property into the form that you mostly see today. He remodeled the house to add a large screened-in porch on each floor and carved stone panels on each side of the front. He had the stone fence around the place built. He added a large pigeon house (that was torn down in the mid-'90s because of its hazardous condition), and many statues, including the pony express rider that was broken into many pieces by an out-of-control car in 1990. It has since been restored. He ran an antique business called Pony Express Antiques. In March of 1943, the caretaker's headquarters burned to the ground and almost took the life of the caretaker when he tried to rescue a dog inside. Mr. Brenizer died in an automble accident in 1954.

O. B. McKown came into the property in the '50s and he enlarged the house by building a large stone section perpendicular to the west wall. When Anton and Carla Allen, the

George Dickey House, 2002

present owners, purchased the property in 1975, they decided to remodel the McKown addition by tying it to the original wall a little better. Instead, part of the new walls collapsed and it was decided it was more prudent to raze the addition than to repair it. So the building was returned to its original stone structure of 1887.

For years the Allens worked toward getting the building recognized as an historical building. They were unable to meet the criteria and finally decided to make a change. In late 1995, they began to add a section to the west wall that would triple the size of the house with two identical sections. These two sections were built in the same form as the original and did not compromise the orginal at all. In fact, it is believable that they could have all been built at the same time.

This house, like most others, is known to people by who lived in it when they were growing up. With that in mind, you might hear it referred to as any one of the above names and they will be talking about the same house. It is definitely one of the most visible showplaces historically, as well as for its elegance in the Dripping Springs area.

J. B Smith

W. A. Lyle and daughter-in-law Mary Sue Lyle stand before the J. B. Smith House, also known as the Mercer Chapman House, 1883.   —Courtesy Jack Lyle

The best guess when this house was built on Lots 1 and 2 of block nine is 1883-84. The 1884 Hays County tax roll had J. B. Smith paying taxes on lots 1, 2, 11, and 12 with a tax value of $300. This value usually indicates a house. In 1885 the property was sold for taxes to W. T. Chapman and A. L. Davis, Sr. They sold the property to Indiana Weber in 1886 for $290. Probably there were additions over the years. The house has been in the Lyle family since 1941. After being used as a residence for all these years, it was leased in 1997 to Ron Bolton, who converted the premises into headquarters for his nursery, called the Bolton Works. Mr. Bolton sold his business to Sunshine Garden Nurseries in the summer of 2002.

W. G. McKellar

This home, better known as "Short Mama's," located on lots 4, 5, and 6 of block 8 was probably built by W. G. McKellar shortly after he purchased the property in 1899. It is a two-story wooden frame house that originally had a gabled upstairs porch. Lou Breed bought the house in 1923 and turned it into a boarding house. In 1929, she had her brother-in-law, Worth Champion, build the porches that stretch all the way across the front of the house. The house stayed in the Haydon family from 1934 until 1995 when they sold it to Wanda Graham. The deteriorating structure was smartly remodeled in basically the same style and turned into a bed and breakfast place appropriately named "Short Mama's House." It has since been turned into an office building. "Short Mama" was Beulah Crumley Haydon. She lived in that house until her death in 1989 at the age of 97. The little house out back proved to be one of the first public washaterias in Dripping Springs. It seems Short Mama got the first washing machine around, a two-cycle Maytag. After she got through washing her clothes, she would allow others to come by and use it. A. K. Daniel bought the entire block in 1881 and by 1883 the block was appraised at

W. G. McKellar Home, better known as Short Mama's.
—Courtesy Charlie Haydon

$300 on the tax rolls. Most likely he had a house on the property, but possibly not the one standing today. He sold the block to McKellar in 1899 for only $100.

W. M. Collenback

In all probability this house, hidden by dense growth in the lot behind the Pioneer Plaza on RR12 south, was built by W. M Collenback in late 1901 or early 1902. The Peal family lived in it the longest. Collenback sold the property around it to the Baptist Church, and it may have been used as the Baptist parsonage in the early years.

I.C.P. McLendon

Like others around the area, I.C.P. McLendon bought property, built, and then sold. He bought the block of land in 1903 and built a small wooden structure. The house, located at the south end of San Marcos Street, and the land were then sold to Jane Nicholson. The house was rocked in the early '40s by Ray Kelley to give it the look that so many others built in that period of history. It was nicknamed the "newlywed house" because many newlyweds of the area made it their first residence.

W. S. McLendon

William Sampson McLendon was the owner of the Dripping Springs Telephone Company. The telephone exchange had been housed in several buildings. He purchased property just above town on Old Fitzhugh Road in 1911 and proceeded to build his home with the telephone company in mind. The front room, nearest the road, was designed to be the telephone office. It is a rounded room with many windows and still shows the marks on the outside

*I.C.P. McLendon House, 1903.
It was rocked in 1945 by Ray Kelley.*

*W. S. "Samp" McLendon House/Telephone Office, 1911
250 Old Fitzhugh Road*

of the room where telephone equipment was installed. It was used as the office until the '20s when another building was built for just that purpose. The house continued to be used as a residence and was allowed to run down with age and nonuse in later years. Charlie Haydon, who bought the property in 1995, took it on as a restoration project, returned it to an earlier stage of its life, and it is back to being used as a residence again.

John T. Spaw House, 1913

George W. Houchin House, 1913

G. W. Houchin

This was the first deed I came across in which the seller dictated what the buyer was to do with the purchase. George W. Houchin bought this ten-acre piece of property from A. L. Davis, Jr., in May 1913. The stipulation was that Houchin must drill a well and build a three-room house by January 1, or the property would go back to Davis. Evidently the deadline was met. This house can be reached by going to the south end of College Street and take the right-of-way road. Like so many other early houses, it has been updated and expanded to meet present-day situations.

J. T. Spaw

J. T. Spaw bought property from W. S. McLendon located just above his house. Today, the Spaw house is next to the GTE telephone building. Mr. Spaw purchased the land in December 1912 and finished the house in 1913. It was a wooden frame house in the beginning but Rosa Lyle Spaw said she remembered the rock exterior being added. It seems the rock enjoyed a second life. It was originally a part of the Middlebrook school/church. John Spaw walked down Creek Road and brought the rock back to put on the house.

Will P. Crow

Will Crow's house is the rock house surrounded by a rock fence on the left as you start down Creek Road (CR 190) from Hwy. 290. The property overlooks the Milkhouse Branch. The rock fence really served two purposes. W. A. Lyle was the rockmason for the house. Mr. Lyle's son, Jack, said that his dad was just getting started in the business and Mr. Crow wanted proof that he was good enough to build his house. To do this, he made him build the fence first and if it passed the test then he would have the job. It must have been good enough because Mr.

W. P. "Will" Crow House, 1938

Lyle did the rock work on the house. The second purpose of the fence was to divert the stream of water that made its way to the branch from flooding into his yard and house. The house was built in 1938.

Tom Ragland

Tearing down buildings and reusing the lumber to make other structures is a fairly common practice. It was decided to tear down the old Dripping Springs hotel, which was in a very dilapidated state. Tom Ragland contracted to do this for the lumber. With the lumber from the hotel, he built his residence at 501 Old Fitzhugh Road, just across from the old caliche pit and the Mac Belk house. It is built in the old style of having the outer wall constructed of one by twelves nailed to a framework and then one by fours nailed over the seams between the one by twelves. They moved into the house in November of 1939.

P. D. Lindsey

This is the first residence on the right as you exit Highway 290 onto Creek Road (CR 190). Roy Volmering purchased the property. In August 1941 he sold goats and sheep and used the money to build the house. Prior to the concrete dance floor being poured at Camp Ben McCullough, each year in preparation for the big reunion activities, a wooden floor was installed. After the close of the reunion, the floor was dismantled and the lumber sold. In 1941 Roy Volmering bought the lumber and used it to build the front couple of rooms. Emma Maude Lindsey said it took a little longer to complete than usual because the builder liked to imbibe spirits and therefore was not a regular worker. The Lindseys bought the house and property in 1954 and it has been in the Lindsey family since. The Lindseys added a room on the west side of the house with lumber they got from a barn on the Maude Traylor ranch west of town.

"Mama" Glosson

Located on the northwest corner of Hays and Bluff streets, the center of the house that faces Hays Street once served as the Mt. Gainer Baptist Church. It was moved to the site and rooms on the east and west sides added in 1957. The house was occupied by the widow of Solon B. Glosson until her death in 1964.

Jonathan Clower

This house now serves as the Fun

*T. W. Ragland House, 1939.
501 Old Fitzhugh Road*

Factory today. Jonathan worked for James Hall, who owned the land. He bought the land from Mr. Hall and built the house, completing it and moving in by April 1963. Before he got to enjoy it too much, he took a job in New Braunfels and let it go back to Mr. Hall and his two partners, Colonel Jack Payne and Mr. Ja Warman of Wimberley. One day John Greiner came by and looked at the house and inquired of Mr. Hall if it was for sale. Mr. Hall assured him that it was but he would have to check with his partners. One came over immediately and after the deal was made, Mr. Greiner inquired as to whether Dripping Springs had a bank. When the answer was no, he said "I will just pay cash then" and he immediately shelled out the money right on the spot. He also informed the pair that his furniture was on a truck downtown and he was ready to move in. They pitched in and helped him move in. Calvin Knauth, long time DSISD superintendent, bought the property in 1966 and added a room before he left in 1979. Aileen Gillis then bought the property and Jodie Gillis Hudson opened up the Fun Factory Day Care Center. A few years later, Jodie turned the business over to Betty Whitaker.

James Hall's Mother

For some time, James C. Hall had been on the lookout for a house for his mother. Around 1959-60, he found the ideal building in Austin. It was to be moved to make room for a street. Mr. Hall bought the house, had the foundation poured, then moved the house to Dripping Springs and placed on the foundation. He added a carport. This house is located on the lot just north of the Fun Factory house. After Mrs. Hall's death, the house was sold to the owners of the Fun Factory.

A. A. Elsner Rent House

This little house, a quarter of mile north of the Phillips Cemetery on RR 12, was built in 1921 for George and Vonny Elsner

A. A. Elsner Rent House, 1921

Moffett by Mr. Elsner. Vonny was a cousin. It changed hands several times over the years before coming vacant. The Allen-Crosswell-McFarland group purchased the strip of land that included the house in 1978. Mrs. McFarland chose to make it her home until late in 2000 when the property was swapped for other land to make room for a large subdivision in the area. After 80 years, this house was moved to another location on RR 165 in Blanco County in the spring of 2002.

Allen-Crosswell-McFarland Loghouse

This group purchased this eleven-acre strip of land just above the Phillips Cemetery in 1978. They had recently moved from Houston and had been involved in Transcendalism meditation. It was their intention to build this loghouse and have their guru move to Dripping Springs. The deal fell through after the house was completed. Since then it has been used as a rent house. In 2000, the house was part of a land swap with a 600-acre subdivision by the ACM group. Its future is not known at this time.

Lomis Slaughter

Built by the Slaughters in 1947, this

house is located on the north fork of Onion Creek just before the creek road takes the sharp turn along Onion Creek. It is a nice looking building in the style of houses built at that time.

D.W. Crenshaw

This house is located on the John Short block off Old Fitzhugh Road. The Crenshaws bought the property from W. L. Dye in 1925. The house on the property was the old Jordan two-story house. The Crenshaws tore that house down and built this one in 1925. The Spaws bought it in 1941. It is still being used as a residence by a member of the Spaw family.

D. W. Crenshaw/ Johnny E. Spaw House, 1925

Thomas F. Voight #1

When Carrie Wallace married Thomas Voight, they bought 124 acres from her father, John Wallace, in 1874. Mr. Voight was a carpenter by trade and probably built the house at that time. They lived there until 1883 when they sold the property and moved to Blanco. Many people owned the property until Dr. C. H. Berkley bought the property in 1909 and lived in the house until his death. The property is now owned by his granddaughter, Katherine Berkley Cannon, and her daughter Susan and husband, have made it their home. Just across the way is a typical tenant's house. It is not known when this might have been built. The house is northeast of the Wallace homesite.

N. J. Jones

I'd have to guess at the date of construction for this house by looking at the price paid for the property. It is located in the easternmost 200 acres of the Pound property. Mrs. Jones paid Dr. Pound $800 for the property in January 1884, which could indicate a building on the land but she turned around and sold the property to R. S. Cavett in September of that year for $1,500. My guess she built a house on it before selling. Mr. Cavett lived there for 20 years before selling to Fletcher Randerson, who lived there 38 years. W. R. and Bessie Ireland Scott have owned and lived in this house since 1957.

Thomas F. Voight #2

After their stay in Blanco, the Thomas Voight family moved back to Dripping Springs and ended up buying another 67-acre tract of the Wallace property. I suspect he built this house around 1890. In Mrs. John Wallace's diary, she talked about

Thomas Voight House, 1890

Carrie walking over to her house. There are other members of the Wallace family who could have built this residence prior to the Voights' moving back. But there is no proof either way. The Voights moved again, this time to San Marcos, and the property was sold. In 1912, it was bought by T. L. Sansom and stayed in the Sansom family until the Robert F. Shelton family bought it in 1949. The Sheltons have owned the property since. The house is located across 290 from the Wallace homesite.

I. D. Roberts

After living in the M.C. Cavett house since 1916, the Roberts family decided to build a new rock home on the site in 1939. It would be their home until their deaths. The Cecil Jenkins family bought the house in 1971. It is located next to the Sonic on 290.

I. D. Roberts House, 1939

L. B. Milam

Mr. Milam bought 65 acres from W. T. Chapman in 1884 and built his house on part of that property. W. R. Baird bought 32½ acres from him in 1888 that included the house. The house has been in the Baird family since, with the exception of a couple of years in the 1980s when it was sold to a family who had to let it go back when they decided to leave the community. The house,

L. B. Milam/W. R. Baird House, 1884

now in poor condition, is northeast of the DSYSA ballfield complex.

I. V. Davis Addition

The Davis family bought the house that was on block four, second addition, in 1902. In 1916, two of the older sons built a two-room addition on the east side of the house. Mr. Davis died in 1911. In 1941, Mrs. Davis decided to tear down the orginal house and use the materials to build another house on her property next door. The two-room addition was left behind and still stands today. For many years, Bradley Davis used this building to store many of his science projects and other varmints he used in his exhibitions at camps, etc.

I. V. Davis, Jr., House Addition, 1915

Katie Davis

Katie Davis House

I. V. Davis bought four acres next to his home in block four, second addition. After his death, the family continued to live in the house. When Bradley Davis went to Austin in 1935 to embark on his teaching career, his mother went with him. In 1941, she decided to build a house on the four acres. She tore down the old homestead, except for the two front rooms, and constructed a new house. She never lived in the house but rented it out for a few years before selling it. An addition to the north, done in the 1980s, greatly expanded the size of the residence. The house is located at 215 Old Fitzhugh Road.

P. L. "Pete" Turner

Mr. Turner purchased 171 acres from J. L. Patterson in March 1920, and not long after that, he built a house on part of that property and lived there until his death in 1956. The house is located on Old Fitzhugh Road.

J. L. "Lee" Smith

Mr. Smith bought 140 acres along the Creek Road in 1942 and shortly thereafter built his house on the property where the Oran Rippy house now stands. In 1960 this house was moved to another section of the Rippy property on the Creek Road and continued as a residence for renters.

Willie Sam Butler

Mr. Butler married the daughter of J. L. Patterson and she inherited 391 acres that fronted RR12 S in 1925. They built a house on the property and lived there for the rest of their lives. The house stood where Oakwood Plaza now stands. The property was sold in the early '80s, and Dave Edwards had the house moved to 500 Springlake Drive in 1985, where it is still housing families.

Sam Strong

Mr. Strong bought three acres from J. L. Smith in late 1947. He was a contractor and built the house in 1948. He sold the land to John Glass in 1950 and they lived there for three decades. The house is located across the street from the Wilson AC & Appliance store on Hwy. 290.

P. L. Turner House, 1921
Old Fitzhugh Road

Sam Strong House, 1948

Clockwise, from top left: Lou "Mama" Glosson House, 1956, 315 Hays Street, formerly Mt. Gainer Church; L. J. Sorrell House (moved there), 1943; Jesse E. Ragland House, 1942; Alva Haydon House, 1943; W. A. Roberts House, 1945, Old Fitzhugh Road; Minnie Horner House, 1950.

Clockwise, from top left: Della Cockrell House, 1941. 731 Old Fitzhugh; W. W. Williamson House, 1945; John Killen House, 1943; Mercer Street, 2003 (Courtesy Mark Myers); *Sophie's Garden, 1999; W. C. Goslin Rent House, 1940.*

Gone But Not Forgotten

As the years go by, various buildings and businesses of the community do not survive. This may be due to disaster, old age, or in the name of progress. Nevertheless, these buildings have been an instrumental part of the community's history and need to be remembered. The way the community looks today is certainly not the way it has always looked, and with all the growth taking place, its future look will not be recognized by those of today.

Although the town of Dripping Springs was laid out in the fall of 1881, the buildings of today are young, comparatively speaking. This is because, while other towns had more durable rock or brick buildings, most of the early buildings in Dripping Springs were constructed of wood. Most of the surviving buildings were built in the late '30s and early '40s.

Dripping Springs Hotel

One of the first questions you will get from natives when inquiring about the history of Dripping Springs is "Did you know we had a hotel here at one time?" And it was true that Dripping Springs had a hotel almost from the beginning. It was another one of those W. T. Chapman enterprises.

The Dripping Springs Academy that opened in January 1882, proved to be a successful venture. Students enrolled from near and far. This meant the students and sometimes their parents needed a place to stay for the school term. Chapman had already built a boarding house near the campus, and he proceeded to build a hotel on Mercer Street. It was located on the same property where the little Texaco station now stands.

The building was two-story, 36 feet square, with eight rooms. Outside stairs led to the upper-floor hallway that divided the rooms. It was completed in October 1883. It prospered for the rest of the 1880s but as changes took place in the boarding school and fewer students needed boarding, the rooms began to be used for other purposes. Some rooms were transposed into office space. Possibly the *Dripping Springs Pointer* newspaper had its office there in 1905. In 1910, Dr. A. V. Duncan, who came to Dripping Springs from Blanco, advertised that his office was in the Burleson Hotel. That was the only time I could find that it was given a name. It was also used as a post office by Charles Seal, possibly for his entire 18 years that spanned 1919-38.

In one newspaper article I read, it said the hotel was being readied for painting.

Whether at this time or later, some described its walls as being painted a mustard yellow. By 1938 the building was in a pretty run-down state. Tom Ragland tore the building down and used the materials from it to build his house on the Old Fitzhugh Road location. The house, located just across the road from the Mac Belk residence, is still standing today. R. B. Wilson said the Rinky Dink Domino Hall was also built from the remains of the hotel. This means the old Dripping Springs hotel lives on.

Garnett Blacksmith Shop

As it evolved, the Will S. "Grampy" Garnett blacksmith business was a complex of buildings. He bought the property in the first addition of Dripping Springs in 1904. The main shop was located on Lot 1 of block one on Mercer Street, where the old Breed Feed Store now stands. In the early days, another blacksmith shop was located just west of this one. Just to the east of the main building was the workshop building where the forge was located. He also entered into the funeral business and he built a small building behind the main building to be used as an embalming room. Another building behind the present-day DS Butane was used to store the caskets. A 1925 Dodge hearse was kept in the back of the main blacksmith shop.

Mr. Garnett continued to run his business until about a year before his death in 1950.

After his death, the buildings stayed mostly vacant. During the 1950s, Bob Fulton, a keymaker, rented the embalming building for a residence until his death. In 1961, J. N. Rippy purchased the property from the Garnetts with the intent of moving the feed portion of his business across the street. He tore down the buildings in preparation for the move but ended up selling the property to Spurgeon Breed to build his feed store.

Cotton Gins

Like many rural areas around the state, cotton was the main cash crop for the people of Dripping Springs. The soil was not great for high yields per acre but everyone seemed to grow as much as they could. There appears to have been three gin locations in the history of Dripping Springs.

The first was built by Thomas F. Voight on land just north of the Dairy Queen. He married Carrie Wallace, the daughter of John Lee Wallace. Carrie was deeded 124 acres of the Wallace property and they built the gin on the most western three acres of this tract. He built a steam-powered gin about 1877, and ran the gin until selling it in September of 1882 to F. D. Henry. Henry paid $1,400 for three acres and all the gin and machinery consisting of the gin house, engine and fixtures, two gin stands and fix-

Will S. and Emma Garnett, 1948
—Courtesy Travis Garnett

tures, one press, one set of platform scales, and all other machinery and fixtures pertaining thereto. F. D. Henry probably ran the gin for the 1882 season only. When he sold the property in 1885, the price paid could not have included any improvements.

The second gin was built in the summer of 1883 by C. S. Graham. There is some question as to where it was actually located. Some believe that it was located on the Dripping Springs branch about where the John A. McNair house is located. Other reports had one located just east of RR12 South. It would make sense to me that a steam engine needing water would be located on the edge of the Dripping Springs branch. However, a better location would have been east of the branch in the area where Hwy. 290 crosses the ravine. That would give it a better location and better access, too. Charlie Haydon said he remembers a little dam-like structure on the branch that could have held the water needed to run the engine. I just did not find any proof as to where it was located. It is known, however, that a second one existed. It was described in an 1887 newspaper article as being one of the best gins and meal mills in the county. In 1885 Graham expected to gin about 230 bales. In the 1887 article, he had already ginned 100 bales by the middle of October. It was not unusual for the gin to run all night during the peak season.

A third gin is the one best remembered and stayed in place the longest. Tom Voight, who built the first one, also built this one. In between gins, he and his family moved to Blanco and ran a successful gin there. In a February 1888 issue, he said he was expecting to gin 1,000 bales during the coming season. Don't know the reason he left the area to come back, unless it was because Carrie's parents were getting up in years and they wanted to be near.

Voight bought Lots 6 and 7 in block five. Mrs. Wallace kept a diary about the goings-on in Dripping Springs. In it she made several entries concerning her son-in-law's gin. On June 11, 1891, she made the notation that "he had most of the woodwork done on his gin." Later on June 24, she noted that "Tom is putting up the chimney to his engine." By September 8, he had ginned 100 bales and by October 1, the total had eased up to 182. She wrote in the August 23, 1892, entry that Tom Voight had ginned his first bale at the Dripping Springs gin. He bought adjoining Lots 4, 5, 8, and 9 in March 1892, so that he could expand the business. However, the 1892 season would be his last—for any of a number of reasons. Mr. Wallace died that year, or maybe he tired of the strenuous work that ginning represented, or maybe for health problems. He died in 1902 at the relatively young age of 54. The Voight family sold the gin property to W. C. McKellar in July of 1893 and moved to San Marcos where both are interred in the San Marcos Cemetery.

When Voight sold to McKellar, the property included the gin and a grist mill. By the time McKellar sold to A. B. Egger in 1905, a saw mill had been added as well. The property changed hands several times in the next twenty years, most notably to J. L. Patterson and Peter A. Huey. In 1924 Huey sold it to its last owner, Charles Haydon, who had previously owned a gin in Driftwood before moving to Dripping Springs.

According to the son, Alva Haydon, the gin was steam powered. It had a big boiler, fired by wood. In 1925 the Haydons purchased a Tips, twin-cylinder engine. It was run by kerosene but it had to be started with gas first. Later in 1928, they upgraded their power plant with a Fairbanks-Marsh engine. Alva said it was a very good power plant.

Cotton crops in the area were on the downswing as ranching began to take over. Actually, in 1939 the Haydons did not even run the gin for the season. On September 13, 1940, as they were getting it ready to make another season, it caught on fire and burned to the ground. That ended the history of cotton gins for Dripping Springs. Only distant memories remain.

Horner Ice House

There were days of yore when the people did not have the luxury of electric refrigerators to protect their perishables. They had to find other methods. In the beginning, the cold springs in the area sufficed for some things such as milk. Later on, the most common cooling device was the use of iceboxes. They were well-insulated boxes with doors on them. One could put a block or two of ice in them and this would keep everything inside cool—for a short while. Blocks of ice usually came in 50 pound units or were cut up in quarters or halves. I can remember growing up in a rural area where the iceman delivered ice on a regular route two or three times each week. The ice stacked on the truck was covered with a heavy tarp to keep it from melting too fast. The ice company was located in town and more could be purchased there, if needed.

In Dripping Springs, the source of ice was Mrs. Minnie Horner's icehouse. She bought her ice supply from the Southland Ice Company in San Marcos. Mrs. Horner's icehouse was a small insulated wooden building, approximately 10x12 feet, located between an oak tree and the A. L. Davis building—just about where the corner of the new west rock addition is today. Mrs. Horner not only sold ice from her building but also milk, cream, and butter, as well. Charlie Haydon recalls that she let him and some of his friends run a little snow cone stand beside her. They did not have a grinder, so had to chip the ice with an ice pick, making a pretty chunky snow cone. He remembers that she drove a 1926 Model T coupe and transacted her business many times from the car. She stayed in business from the '40s to the early '50s.

Now you know when you hear someone refer to a refrigerator as an icebox, they are probably dating themselves.

Marshall-Chapman Cemetery

It was not unusual in the early days to have family burial plots somewhere on the homesite rather than in a community cemetery. Burrell J. Marshall purchased the original Moss property, which was an 1,100 acre northwest quarter of the Phillip A. Smith league survey, in 1870. He moved a wooden house to the plot of land just west of the ledge above the head of the Dripping Springs branch and added a couple of rock rooms. Unfortunately, Marshall became ill and died in February 1872, at the age of 49.

Whether true or not, there is a story about his selecting his gravesite. It is said as he lay in his bed dying, he looked southeast out of his window and pointed to a grove of live oak trees in the distance and said that was where he wanted to be buried. Those trees are located on Lots 7 and 8 in block six, where the old lumberyard is now located. You have to realize that in 1872 there were none of the big trees along the branch to block his view. Either that or he had already chosen the spot.

His grave was marked by a large gravestone. His son-in-law, D. W. Burkett, was buried in the plot in 1900. Two of W. T. and Martha Chapman's grandchildren were also buried there. The first was an Egerton infant, 1901. The other was T. H. Egerton, Jr., 1905-07. People coming to town on their horses or in wagons tied their horses to the tombstones so they could enjoy the shade while their masters shopped in town.

Charles Haydon purchased Lots 7, 8, and 9 from the Chapman heirs in 1936 with the graves intact. Part of the bargain was the Haydons would see to it that the graves were moved to the Wallace Mountain Cemetery. Shortly afterwards, teenagers Alva Haydon and his good friend, Haskell McNair, had the task of exhuming the graves and relocating them to the Wallace Mountain Cemetery. Alva Haydon recalls that Mr. Marshall's tombstone had been toppled over years before and broken into many pieces. Mr. Dye was able to cement the pieces back together when they moved to the mountain. They are now displayed in a prominent site on the southeast corner of the cemetery, along with the rest of the W. T. Chapman-Marshall graves.

Red Brick Post Office

For 104 years, Dripping Springs never had a post office that was built for that specific purpose. It was always located in the postmaster's house or a place of business. Finally in 1961, a growing community decided it was time to have a post office to call their own. Bids were let on January 1, 1961. The site chosen was a part of the old Academy Block owned by J. W. Glosson. During its school days the site was a part of the playground, including the outdoor basketball court. It later became a part of the parking lot for the Glosson Grocery. The building was located in the southeast corner of the Academy Block, bordered on the east by Old Fitzhugh Road and on the south by Mercer Street.

The building itself was an 800 square foot red brick structure with a flat roof. The Post Office leased the building for five years with a five-year option renewal. It opened for business for the first time on Thanksgiving morning. A glass door opened directly into the foyer, with Post Office boxes on the north wall and a table on the south wall. Another glass door was positioned between the foyer and the post office desk. There was a large plate glass window on the south wall of the desk area. Each area was woefully small but still sufficient for the population at the time.

The increasing number of people who began to move into the Dripping Springs area affected the post office as well. By the 1980s, the building just was not large enough to handle the volume. More space was needed and they had to look no farther than across the parking lot to the abandoned grocery store. That building was remodeled and the move to larger quarters took place on February 14, 1987. The little red brick building was razed and the space where it had served its purpose for a quarter of a century was relegated to parking lot duty once again.

Garland Seal Cafe

Garland Seal owned Lot 6 of block one and started out with a small barbeque stand on the property which he opened in April 1953. He then built a cafe on the lot and on Saturday, June 26, 1954, opened for business, serving barbeque lunches. He barbequed all the meat he served. Will Crow bought Lot 6 from Garland Seal on September 24, 1954.

Will Crow closed the business for repairs and then opened it with Katherine Roberts operating the cafe. He sold it to George and Lorene Wiest in January 1955. The building was located just off Highway 290 and the gravel road that would later become RR 12 north. The Wiest family operated the cafe called George and Lorene's Cafe, although most knew it simply as Wiest's Cafe. The Wiests added to the cafe in February 1956. For a while, the cafe and the Sinclair station next door were open 24 hours a day. In 1957 the Wiests tired of the arrangements and got out of the business.

In September 1957, Mrs. Mattie Volmering opened the cafe. That did not last long as Mrs. Carrie Jo Latson took over in October and it was called the East End Cafe. Latson sold the business to Mr. and Mrs. Stephenson in February 1958. Possibly the Stephensons sold the cafe to Mattie Volmering as the Dripping Springs column in the *Hays County Citizen* related that Mrs. Volmering sold the cafe to Mrs. Chester Davis in August 1958. Mrs. Davis ran the cafe about two weeks and then closed it down. The Stephensons bought it back and operated it for a while, the final time of operation as an eatery.

Pete Crow, the brother of owner W. P. Crow, worked out an agreement with his brother that allowed him to live in this building until his death. In 1984 the property was then sold to the Dripping Springs National Bank and it was razed to make room for a drive-through. The building was located where the most eastern drive-through lanes are now.

Wiest Sinclair Station

A small service station was built in 1956 by Mr. and Mrs. Ed Felps on Lots 4 and 5 of block one. It was located about where the parking lot for the drive-in bank building is today. The Wiests were already running the cafe next door and contracted to add this business to their responsibility. At that time Highway 290 still followed Loop 64.

The service station was a small cinder-block building. L. B. Wootton ran the station during its final year of service from 1959 until it closed in 1960. By 1962, it had been remodeled and expanded into a residence. The first residents were the Fred Garnett family. They were just beginning the DS Butane business, and used the front of the station as their business office and lived in the rest of it. It did not work out as a dual purpose facility for the Garnetts and by 1965, they moved out.

The next occupant was the Bertha Hill family. She had been hired as the home economics teacher at Dripping Springs High School, and she and her family moved in prior to the fall of 1965. She lived there for two years before finding other living quarters.

E. R. Jones bought the property in 1967 and moved his family into the house. Mr. Jones was the custodian for DSISD. The family lived there until 1979. At this time James Hurlbut was in the process of developing much of the block. He bought the old theater and converted it into a complex of business office spaces. He traded property with the Joneses. He owned a lot on Old Fitzhugh Road and swapped it for the block one property. He then remodeled the building into a duplex. Five years later Hurlbut sold the property to the Dripping Springs National Bank as they prepared to put in a drive-through bank facility.

Sorrell Cafe

Mr. and Mrs. L. J. Sorrell purchased an acre of land from the J. W. Wilson, Sr., family in 1942 and moved a house on the property. When the school purchased twenty acres beside and behind their property, the Sorrells decided they had a great location for a business. Not only did they have a ready source provided by the school population, but Highway 290 passed right in front. They built a small cafe on the southeast corner of their property, around 1948. The school opened in the fall of 1949.

The initial chief cook and bottlewasher was Inez Volmering. She ran Inez's Cafe until November 1950. A column in the *Hays County Citizen* said that the Sorrells opened up the cafe near the school in September 1957. Mrs. Sorrell took over the grill and renamed the establishment the West End Cafe. The cafe closed its doors in the early '60s. Charlie Haydon remembers that as soon as the bell rang for lunch each day, the students would break and run for the cafe so they could get their order in first.

Ira Ruston began the building's off and on career as a clip joint in 1962. He moved his barbering business across the street from the Village Center in 1962 and set up in the front portion of the building. Within the year, Bersha McIntyre moved her beauty shop over from the Village Center as well. She took up residence in the back portion of the building. When Ira moved down to Mercer Street in January 1964, Bersha moved to the front room. By the next year Bersha had a partner—Joy Whisenant. They called their partnership the B&J Beauty Shop. Bersha changed locations the next year and Joy went it alone until 1968 as Joy's Beauty Shop.

At that time, S. J. Moore bought the property and made it his residence. After his death, another Joy would come into the life of this building. It was Joy Harmon, and Harmon's Hair Fashions. Bersha returned. Peggy Kugle came on board in 1972, while Opal Glass took Bersha's place in 1973. Joy Whisenant re-entered in 1974. Mr. and Mrs. L. O. Jackson, Jr., acquired the property in 1975, and it became DS Hair Fashions. Bersha worked for them and Pamela Barger ran the shop for several years until the end of 1978.

Enter Lynette Ritter. The Ritters recently moved to Dripping Springs when she looked for a site to open her beauty shop. She purchased the property in May 1979 and opened Lynette's Stylin' Salon. She stayed in the building until December 1982 when she decided to build a larger building on the most northern portion of her property and moved into her new headquarters. The old building's hairrazing days were at an end and, as it turned out, its existence was getting there too.

Almost immediately, Faye Wallace opened up a knick-knack and flower shop called the Bluebonnet Florist. It flourished but she eventually moved to a larger facility in the newly constructed Redwood Center in 1985. Sulcer Construction used the building for their office until 1986 when their business failed. The septic system was a problem and the need for a better entrance to her thriving business allowed Lynette to make the easy decision to call for its demise. It was torn down in 1986.

Breed Meat Market

In 1914, Carter Breed bought Lot 4 of block six and built himself a building that would house his meat market. Mr. Breed was the father of Ima Lois Shelton and Doris Davidson. From early on the meat market was open on Saturdays only. He butchered the animals late Friday night and kept the meat in a screened-in section in the back. On Saturdays he met the demand of his customers ordering meat. At the same time he prepared chili to be sold. It is said he also sold some barbeque. Maybe it depended on the time of year.

For most of the next thirty years the meat market was a place where food was served. After Mr. Breed tired of the business in early 1930, Dr. Clell Basket, who could not meet payments on the building next door and had to let it go back, leased the meat market building, and moved his drugstore into it. In June 1931 he added a new front to the building, which included a plate glass front and was finished off with rock work.

Others leased the building to run cafes. In the mid-'30s L. T. Roberts opened Roberts' Cafe. Harvey King ran King's Cafe from 1938-40, then it was Cecil Breed (son) giving it a try from 1940-41. Miss Mayne Kroll purchased the cafe in March 1942. Inez Volmering took it for the next two years. Otto Schluetter, a veteran Austin cafe owner, remodeled the building and opened shop in 1946. Ollie Williamson took the reins over in 1947 and ran Tiny's Cafe until his death in October 1948. For a short while Mrs. Monroe carried on the business.

Mr. and Mrs. Ollie Williamson in Tiny's Cafe in 1948.
—Courtesy Ernest Williamson

J. W. Wilson was the first to change the life of the building. He opened up his Radio & TV business in the fall of 1949. He did not like how well the air conditioning system worked during the winter months and moved out in 1950. Next Ima Lois Shelton, who had been running a ready-to-wear store down the street, relocated to her father's building in 1950. She stayed there until February 1953 when she moved her business to Austin. It is said that Margaret and O. T. Hodges ran a cleaners in the back of the building, maybe in the early '50s.

L. B. Jennings moved his lumber company across the street in 1956, where he leased the meat market for office space. He ran his business from here for the next five years. After that, the building went vacant and stayed that way until the Methodist women began looking for a building to move their infant Thrift Shop into. They approached the owner of the run-down building and he allowed them to move in at no charge. The Methodist women worked the store for the next eight years until they offered the opportunity to the newly-formed Senior Citizen organization. The building continued to fall into disrepair despite the efforts of the Senior Citizens. When they outgrew the little building and felt they could not keep holding it together with repairs and with no other option, they bit the bullet and bought the lot from the owner. The little meat market was torn down in May 1996 to make room for the Senior Citizens' new and roomier rock edifice.

Senior Citizens Thrift Shop, 1996

Rock Tank and Windmill

In 1906 it was decided to raise funds to build a rock tank with a windmill for the purpose of a public watering place. These were erected on the southwest corner of the Academy Block where the post office is now located. They remained there until 1931. In February of that year, Mr. O. V. Stubbs, the school principal, purchased the two and moved the windmill to his place.

Chapman Store and Masonic Lodge

This two-story building was built on Lot 3 of block seven. The Rippy Ranch Supply entrance stands there today. W. T. Chapman built this building in late 1883. He had been running a store at an unknown location prior to his laying out the town of Dripping Springs in 1881. The reason for building this building was two-fold. The bottom floor was to be for mercantile purposes. Also he was a member of the Rambo Masonic Lodge that was holding its meetings in the Friendship Baptist Church building. He was able to convince them that if he built a place for them in Dripping Springs they would make the move there. On January 1, 1884, the Rambo Lodge bought the one-half interest to acquire the top floor. The stipulation in the deed for anyone buying the bottom floor was they could not have any type of business that would intefere with the Masons.

Chapman ran his mercantile store from this location. Later he turned the business over to A. L. Davis, Jr., who ran it until 1891 when he bought four lots on the east of block seven and built a two-story rock mercantile building on the corner.

I'm not sure who ran the Chapman store from that point, possibly Chapman himself. Chapman bought out Davis in 1901, so someone else had to run this store after that.

The Chapman store almost had a very short history. In July 1887, someone torched the building of J. C. Rowe next to the store. The firefighters were able to gain entrance to the Masonic Lodge and pour water on the other building and at the same time save the store.

In 1905 J. W. Glosson and W. G. McKellar bought the property from Chapman. They ran the store until McKellar's death in 1907. Glosson then bought out McKellar's share from his widow, Florence. In November 1907 Glosson added a 20x26 foot section to the rear of the building. Rambo Lodge paid $115 for an addition to their second floor. Glosson stayed in business until George Houchin bought him out in 1913. Houchin sold his half of the property to J. W. Carter in February 1915. In 1920, Carter sold his property to J. A. Patton. In September 1920, the Masonic Lodge sold their share of the property to Mt. Camp #243 of the Woodmen of the World.

I'm not sure who ran the store while Patton owned it in the 1920s. One man, however, was John Howard Kitchen. He may have run the store for most of the decade. A newspaper article in 1941 said he was visiting Dripping Springs after a thirteen year absence, which would have been 1928. D. W. Crenshaw leased the building and ran a grocery store for much of 1929-30. Magnolia signed a lease with him in June 1930 to sell gas. When Crenshaw was forced to take his old store back down the street, Will Crow, who had managed the store for Crenshaw the past year, took over the store and ran a grocery there, as well as signing a lease with Magnolia, too. He called it Crow Service Sta-tion. To get ready for his opening on March 4, 1931, Crow's building was overhauled and newly painted. Crow ran the business until December 1936 when he bought the property from Patton. At the same time, Crow bought out the half interest of the Woodmen of the World. Shortly thereafter, Crow tore down the old building and constructed another building on the back of the lot to house his wool and mohair business.

Wortham Business House

It was September 4, 1882, when J. T. Wortham purchased Lots 1, 2, 11, and 12 of block six. On Lots 1 and 2 he built a wooden two-story building that stretched across most of the front of those two lots. The building was located basically where the old Central Garage now stands (DS Rentals). Mr. Wortham ran the business until September 1886 when he sold out to C. B. Hollis, Ed Womack, and L. B. Milam, known as Hollis, Milam and Company. By December 1887 they sold the business to H. W. Cook. He died a short while later and Edwin H. Wallace bought the business from Mary Cook in

Wortham Business House —Courtesy Charlie Haydon

September 1888 and tried his hand at it. He did not make a career out of the business. He headed to Llano County and sold the business to S. D. Gilpin and D. G. Jones in February 1890.

Gilpin was a long-time druggist in Dripping Springs and moved his drugstore to the building while Jones ran the grocery part of the business. By January 1892, they found themselves deep in debt and had to file for bankruptcy. The Nelson Davis Co. bought the property on June 29, 1892, because they were owed the most money. They turned around and sold it to Nannie M. Jones three days later. I'm not sure who ran the business for the next four years, probably not Ms. Jones. She sold the property to H. W. and M. E. Griffin in October 1896. They sold the property to David and M. E. Hughes in January 1899. In November 1901, W. P. Hudson and W. H. Crenshaw bought the property from the Hugheses and ran the store for most of the next four years.

W. M. Hudson bought out Crenshaw's share of the business in February 1905, and the business became known as W. P. Hudson & Son. A year later I. T. Applewhite purchased the property. The Applewhites held down the fort for the next 16 or 17 years. I'm not sure when they finally closed down the business. During the 1921-22 school year, when the second story was being added, classes were held in this building. One paper report talks of having to pull counters and desks around in order to make a makeshift stage to practice their play. Bradley Davis, who attended classes in the building, recalls that it was no longer being used as a store at the time. By the time Charles Haydon purchased the property in January 1925, the old building had been torn down and a smaller one built in its place. Alva Haydon recalls finding many old square nails on the property.

Courthouse

In November 1906 the County Commissioners Court decided that a justice courtroom should be erected in Dripping Springs for the use of the Justice of the Peace, provided a suitable lot could be found and donated. That lot was provided by W. T. Chapman on Lot 2 of block one. I'm not sure how long this building survived. In their August 1909 meeting, Commissioner J. R. Wilhelm asked the Commissioners' Court for $27.50 to be paid out of the Repair Fund to help replace the Justice Court hall at Dripping Springs. Whether it was used to expand and repair or rebuild, I'm not sure, but replace to me means just that. There are those around town who remember it as a long building where they could go to roller skate when it was not in use. It, too, was used for classroom space during the 1921-22 school year. Virgil Conn bought the property in 1946, so the building had been torn down by then.

Barton Livery Stable

In the days prior to automobiles, instead of parking garages for cars, there were parking garages for horses called livery stables—places where you could store your animal and have it attended to or rent one for a trip. They also had buggies and wagons to rent, very similar in purpose to the rental businesses of today.

In November 1883, O. C. Barton bought block three of the first addition, which is where the DS Butane building rests today, and opened a livery stable for Dripping Springs. Mr. Barton did not stay in the business very long as he sold the property to Galen Crow in April 1884. William Herndon bought the business in January 1885 and expanded it by buying the adjoining property from W. T. Chapman. He then sold it to C. S. Graham in February 1886. A year later J. W. Hamilton bought the property. Not only did he run the livery stable but he also ran a mail route from Dripping Springs to Blanco. It is probable that this site was a stop for the stages that went through the town. Ten years later, Mr. Hamilton moved out of town and sold the property to

Pedernales Lienneweber. I don't know who ran the business for the next seven years until Lienneweber sold the property to W. S. Garnett, Sr., in May 1904. He ran the business until cars became the major mode of transportation in the early 1920s. Around 1925 he built the garage building that now houses DS Butane and the livery stable business faded into the sunset.

County Barn

In May 1926 the county bought what is known as the triangle from Mr. T. D. Walker. It is not known when the first county barn was constructed on the southwest corner of the property, although I have seen pictures in the early '40s with the small building in the background. At one point more sheds were constructed to house the equipment used by the County Commissioner of precinct four, as well as a small office. The volunteer fire department built a fire station on the northwest corner.

In the '90s, the County Commissioners authorized a unitized road system. They established a Road Department and made its manager responsible for the roads and equipment in all four precincts. This eliminated duplication of equipment and ensured that all roads in the county were built and repaired on an equal basis.

At some time in the early part of the new century, the operation will be moved to county property on RR 150, and the old precinct four barn will be torn down. There are several options being considered on what to do with the land. Beautification groups started landscaping the eastern half of the triangle. Presently, the city has an option to buy the triangle for a possible city hall site.

Haydon Building

Charles Haydon bought Lots 1, 2, 11, and 12 of block six from I. T. Applewhite in January 1925. The old Wortham Business House had been torn down by that time. The small wooden building on the corner of Mercer and College had already been built from store remains. The building came to house two businesses. Johnny Spaw opened a barbershop in a portion of the northwest corner, and Ivy "Piggy" Roberts built a small lean-to shed off the east side of the building and sold hamburgers there. Sometimes he even slept there as well. In 1935 Charles Haydon decided he wanted to build the present rock Central Garage on the site, so the old wooden building was moved to the southwest corner of Lot 12. It was used at times as a residence by Granny Herwig and the Ed Felps family. For a while Willie Mae, the wife of Alva Haydon, used the building for her beauty salon business. Finally, the old wooden building was torn down and that lot has been vacant since.

Blacksmith Shops

In the horse and buggy days prior to the advent of automobiles and the days of mass production, the forerunners to our present-day garage and mechanic were the blacksmith and his shop. It was small and crude compared to today's garages but it certainly served the purpose. Horses had to be shod and the shoes made, parts to buggies and wagons had to be shaped and made, as well as repairing farm machines. It was definitely hot and hard work. The blacksmith and his shop were an integral part of any society and they were the early inventors because, at times, their ingenuity was the only thing between something working and not.

Just like today's commonality of garages, in the olden days blacksmith shops were as frequent. The only blacksmith listed in the Dripping Springs area in the 1870 census was Pedernales Lienneweber's father, whose shop was probably not within the P. A. Smith survey.

In the 1880 census, Pedernales was listed as a blacksmith, as well as James C. Rowe. Both were instrumental in the history of Dripping Springs. Of course, others could have been blacksmiths in this census but they were not listed.

The earliest blacksmith shop mentioned in the deeds after W. T. Chapman laid out the town in 1881 was one operated by a man named M. G. Caperton. His shop was located on the east side of DS Butane, basically where the road runs between the DS Butane and the old Breed feedstore building.

George Womack was listed as a blacksmith and woodworker, who owned lots six and seven of block five (the old gin property).

W. A. Hogan had a shop on property where the big warehouse now stands to the west of Academy Block. It is not known when he bought the property from Chapman but he sold it back to Chapman in 1889. He had already sold his business to Major Cook in 1887.

To the best of my research, George Dickey bought Lots 1 and 12 of block seven in 1885 and built a shop on the property. He sold it to James C. Rowe who ran the blacksmith shop until he retired in 1889. A newspaper article stated that Stapleton and Loman would take over Rowe's business upon his retirement. What made location a little difficult to ascertain is an article that said Stapleton bought property across from his blacksmith shop, and in 1890 an advertisement for the sale of his property appeared to be block seven of the second addition. They did not stay in business much longer than a year.

I'm not sure where he was located but an 1883 article listed J. C. Rowe as a blacksmith and woodworker, as well as Carpenter and Lincoln being blacksmiths and woodworkers. In an article in the May 14, 1954, edition of the *San Marcos Record*, Mrs. Georgia Pound Cavett recalled that there was a blacksmith shop where the Alva Haydon house now stands. A. L. Davis, Sr., built his house on that block in 1882, so maybe before then. By October of 1884, the paper said Dripping Springs had two blacksmiths which were probably Rowe and Hogan who were listed in an 1885 article. According to deed records Rowe sold Lots 1 and 12 to Pedernales Lienneweber, who was a blacksmith by trade himself. He may have operated the shop until he sold most of his Dripping Springs holdings to W. S. Garnett, Sr., in 1904. Mrs. Cavett also recalled that Lienneweber had a grist mill near the Travis Garnett home, which is the house next to the DS Butane building.

Mr. Garnett had the more famous of the shops and also the longevity record, as he kept the shop, located on Lot 1 of block one, first addition, open until near his death in 1950. Another site with a fairly long history of having a blacksmith shop was Lot 12 of block one. Most likely, the first person to open a blacksmith shop there was R. H. Raines, Sr., early in 1901, and he sold the property to R. H. Raines, Jr., by December of that year.

H. B. Harmon bought the property in 1905 and sold it to McCreary Crow in 1907, who sold it to W. A. Chesher. In October of that year he took on Sam Byars as a partner, and they operated under the business name of Chesher and Byars. W. M. McElyea bought them out in September 1908, then sold the business to M. A. George within two weeks. One month later it was in the hands of L. T. Guttery. He held onto the property for four years before selling it to P. A. Glosson in 1912. Glosson sold it to J. W. Champion in 1913. Most likely, for most of these owners, it was an investment with someone else running the shop. A school publication in 1910 advertised W.H. Dement, as a blacksmith and woodworker, specializing in horseshoeing. Most likely he carried on the business until the shop was deserted and finally torn down around 1918.

With the popularity and affordability of automobiles, blacksmith shops began to fade from the scene. It was a slow fade in the rural areas, where people still had need of their talents. As I was growing up in the '40s and early '50s, I remember going with my dad to blacksmith shops to get some things repaired. My dad, like many farmers and ranchers, had a small blacksmith-type shop to do some of the blacksmith chores.

Even today, some are still carrying on the trade to keep the art of blacksmithing from going the way of the dinosaurs.

W. M. Jordan Home

When Dr. W. M Jordan came to Dripping Springs to visit relatives and stayed to establish the Dripping Springs Academy boarding school, he purchased two acres of land adjacent to Academy Block. The school began in August 1881 and was not completed until January 1882. Dr. Jordan bought his two acres in November 1881. He built a two-story house on the property. It is not known if he and his family first lived in the Chapman boarding house or not, but an early article said that the high school students of the Academy held their classes in Dr. Jordan's living room. This was further substantiated by an article written by an Academy student, Robert Lee Marshall, in 1947. If so, this house must have been built before January 1882.

When Dr. Jordan left Dripping Springs abruptly in August 1883, he sold the property. Known residents of the house were John Short, J. W. Hamilton, R. H. Raines, J. B. Middlebrook, Mary J. Cavendar, and W. L. Dye. Mr. Dye would own the house from 1916 to 1925 when it was sold to D. W. Crenshaw. The Crenshaws tore the house down and built the present one on the property, now owned by Mr. and Mrs. Jones Eckols.

W. P. Hamilton Store

W. P. Hamilton bought Lot 2 of block seven in October 1883 and built a store on it. In September 1884 George Dickey purchased the lot and building. He ran a mercantile business out of it for several years, for a while with a partner, Carey.

Dave Jones ran the store a number of years around the turn of the century as well. It is not known if the building was still there in 1919 when L. P. Scheh bought the lot.

L. P. Scheh Cafe

Louis Scheh bought Lot 2 of block seven in 1919. It is not known if the other building had survived until then. However in 1936, Scheh moved a building from Buda and converted it into a cafe by May of that year. By September 1937, Mrs. Scheh was running the West End Cafe. Nina Tschoepe, stepdaughter, said she tried to run the cafe for a while. Later, Bill Dewey gave it a try as well.

A couple of men, Bowling and Mills, rented the building to buy onions, tomatoes, and potatoes in August 1942. It is believed the O. T. Hodges family ran a cleaning business from the building, too. Finally, in 1952, P. A. Glosson bought the building and the lot to open a feed store. Pete Glosson laid cinder block walls to expand it, and they began business. Over the years it has been modified somewhat but remains part of the Rippy Ranch Supplies complex.

S. D. Gilpin Drugstore

Actually there were several drugstores. Shortly after the town was laid out in 1881, S. D. Gilpin built a wooden building on his property, which was block twelve. It later burned to the ground. He then built a stone building on the spot which was just across from DS Butane. He sold the store in 1887 and moved to a building that I believe was next to the hotel building, or possibly within the hotel. The rock building burned down in 1888. He moved to the Wortham Business House in 1890. The third site was probably torn down later.

John Lee Wallace House

John Wallace was one of the original three settlers to build in Dripping Springs. He bought property in June 1854 and built a log cabin just below the crest of what would become Wallace Mountain. It was on the north side of the Austin-Fredericksburg Road. It was probably the second house built

John Wallace House was built in 1854. These pictures were taken circa 1930. The right one was taken from the back of the house.
—Courtesy Patricia Barton

in the P. A. Smith survey behind the one the Mosses built. As the family grew, so did the size of the house. It probably fell along the same lines as did the Pound house. It may have started out as a two log-pen cabin with a dogtrot. The Wallaces already had a child when they arrived in Dripping Springs.

A picture taken in 1930 showed the cabin looking a lot like the Pound house with the siding and the end room. According to Cecil Griffin, whose mother lived in this house a long time, it had a log room, approximately 18x24, that came equipped with rifle port holes. To the west of this room was the dogtrot, which probably meant there was a log pen on the other side. The way Cecil remembers it, there was a bedroom the same size as the log room on the east side. The bedroom had a fireplace. A porch on the south side spanned the length of the two rooms and dogtrot. Eventually, the portion of porch that fronted the two rooms was enclosed and made into a kitchen.

On each side of this building were rooms that were as wide as the house. The one on the east was a bedroom with the fireplace being shared with the adjacent bedroom. The room on the west served as a bedroom and living room. The porch in front of the dogtrot needed a step up to the level of the dogtrot and the room on the west was a step down from the dogtrot. The bedroom/living room also had a fireplace.

This house burned to the ground on August 7, 1953, while the Huggins family was living in it. Today, some rock rubble and the restored rock corrall are the only signs of its existence.

C. B. Hollis Home

The Reverend C. B. Hollis had completed what was described as a commodious two-story residence by December 1885 on a site about a half mile south on RR 12, across from the 40-acre park entrance. He moved to Louisiana shortly afterwards and sold the house to J. H. Morrow. The property changed hands several times until 1902 when the W. J. Norwood family purchased the home and moved in.

It eventually became the residence of the Enoch Needham family. Mrs. Needham was a Norwood granddaughter. The Needhams made a decision in the mid-'70s to tear down the old house and build a brick home in its place. It had been home to the nine Needham children, but all had left home by this time.

J. A. Smith Home

J. A. Smith bought block seven of the second addition in November 1883 and quickly built a residence on the property. He sold the property in 1888 and moved to San Marcos. In 1898 Dr. E. P. Shelton purchased the property and made it his home for the rest of his life. He added a room on the west side facing Old Fitzhugh Road that became his office. The house never had the modern conveniences of running water and bathrooms during its use as a residence. One of the more unique things about the house was the porch that faced south. There were many Sheltons. Dr. Shelton had 13 children himself. This porch was chockfull of names, dates, and height marks of various people. His last surviving son, Clarence, moved back to Dripping Springs in the '70s and built a home on block eight of the second addition which connected with block seven. He had intentions of renovatiing the old house but probably the cost was prohibitive. As the years passed by, the old house became more and more in disrepair, the front room almost falling off. Finally in 1999, Dr. Shelton's grandson, Jack Huey and his wife, moved back to Dripping Springs, bought the property, and built a house on the lot that necessitated the razing of the old home.

F. D. Henry Home

This home was built on a four-acre tract where Creek Road makes its first right curve after leaving Hwy. 290. It changed hands many times over the years after F. D. Henry purchased the tract in 1884. The one living the longest in the house was Miss Agatha Glosson who lived in it until her death in 1939. It burned while the Domingo Alba family was living in it in the early '70s. Today, the chimney and other rubble are all that survive.

Ben Manor Mill

This mill was located near North Onion Creek. It was first mentioned in the Commissioners' Court minutes in 1869 when it decreed that a road from San Marcos to Dripping Springs would be built. The second half of the road was to run from the Rio Blanco to the steam mill near Dripping Springs. Later in 1872, when A. L. Davis, Sr., bought a 400-acre tract from M. H. Howard, two acres were held out because it included the steam mill. In 1874, Davis purchased these two acres. No document, other than recollections by people, proves that Ben Manor owned or ran this mill but at least we know there was a mill there. The site now is a part of the Enoch Needham property.

Ben F. Stephenson Home

In 1874, when Dr. Pound's oldest daughter married Ben Stephenson, he sold them 100 acres from his place. They built a house on it and raised ten children. The house, located just east of the Fun Factory, found itself in the path of the construction of RR 12 N and, in the late 1960s, was razed to make way for the road.

A. L. Davis Home

This elaborate house, located on block ten, was built around 1883 by one of the prominent men of early Dripping Springs, A. L. Davis, Sr. Alva Haydon, who now owns the property, says he can remember the house when he first moved to Dripping Springs. It had a huge wrap-around porch. One of the interesting facts about the house was that it had water piped to it. A. L. Davis, Jr., built a two-story hardware store on Mercer Street and it included a big cistern to catch the runoff water. From this cistern, a line was run the couple of blocks to the house. For several exchanges of this property it was written into the deed that the house would continue to receive its water from the cistern. In the early '30s fire wiped out this historic house and nearly took the one across the street with it. Alva remem-

bers firefighters working hard to keep the shingles on the house from catching on fire, and taking it down too.

Dr. William H. Howard Home

It is not known exactly who built this house located on the south side of the north fork of Onion Creek. Most likely it was Dr. William H. Howard, who bought the property in 1853. In an article written by Robert Lee Marshall, whose family moved to Dripping Springs in 1870, he recalled that Dr. Howard lived within two miles of their home. It was sold to T. M. Caldwell in 1873.

John W. Phillips Outhouse

John W. Phillips House was built in the 1860s.

For sure the one who lived in it the longest was J. W. Phillips. He bought the 600 acres from Caldwell in 1876. He lived there for 33 years and raised his family. The Felix Lindsey family lived in the house another 30 years between 1924-54. This house has been vacant for many years and will probably be lost when a 600-acre subdivision is developed in the early 2000s.

Moses Columbus Cavett Home

Moses Cavett bought this 19 acre tract from John Wallace in 1884 for $386. We have to assume, if a house was already on the property, it was located beside the present Sonic business. Mr. Cavett married Georgia Pound, the daughter of Dr. Pound. He lived in this house until shortly before his death when he sold it to J. H. Gary in 1907. Mr. Gary's widow sold the property to I. D. Roberts in 1916. The Roberts lived in this house until 1939 when they built the present rock house that the Cecil Jenkins family has lived in since 1971. The Cavett site was known for a pear tree, a hand dug well, and a rock building for the purpose of making cheese. In an article in the paper in 1958, the Roberts commented that the pear tree had bore fruit for the 45 years they had lived on the property. Talking to the present owner, Minnie Jenkins, she said the pear tree was still alive and bearing fruit. She said the well was still there and the rock building too, in another form.

H. C. Pearcy Home

This house, now in a pretty dilapidated condition, is located in block one of the second addition of Dripping Springs. H. C. Pearcy bought the property in late August 1883, and soon afterward built the house. Pedernales Leinneweber bought the

H. C. Pearcy/W. S. Garnett House, 1883
—Courtesy Travis Garnett

property in 1890. I'm not sure if he lived in the home. He sold the property to W. S. Garnett in 1904. The Garnetts lived in the house and raised their family there until their deaths in 1950. Mary Lou Haster inherited the property and lived there until her death. The old house is now in an unliveable condition.

W. H. Robbins House

Mr. Robbins bought block four of the second addition in July 1893 and built a five-room house at that site soon after. It was this house that I. V. Davis, Jr., bought from Robbins' widow in 1902 to move his family closer to the school in Dripping Springs. Mr. Davis died in 1911 and two of his sons added two more rooms on the east side of the house. Mrs. Davis moved to Austin in 1935 with her youngest son, Bradley, when he began his teaching career. She did not move back. In 1941, she had the original house dismantled to build another one just north of it on other land that she owned. She rented it out for several years before selling the property and the house on it.

One-Eyed Jack's Pizza

Although the building is still there, it is now being used as a residence. The building is located on the northwest corner of Summit and RR12 N in the North Forty subdivision. It was built by one of the Bielkes in the 1980s to house One-Eyed Jack's Pizza.

It was not a success and closed its doors. Perry and JoAnn Alba leased the building and opened a Mexican restaurant called Mi Tierra. It operated successfully for some years before they tired of the business. Other owners changed its name and operated an eatery there for a while before the owner decided to terminate the lease and remodel it into a residence in the late '90s.

James Glosson House

Glosson bought block three of the second addition in 1883. In 1884 he sold the same lot to J. A. Smith for $300, which probably means that Glosson built a house on it. The house was certainly ideal for being close to the Academy, but was probably torn down by the time the property was sold to the school in 1931.

McLendon Barn

Mrs. Sallie McClendon came into block five, second addition in 1893. This block lies beside the Old Fitzhugh Road and across the street from the McLendon home on block six. Bradley Davis said he can remember the family talking about the building of the barn. Their house was located on block four, with an unrestricted view toward downtown. The Davis family tried to get the McLendons to build the barn a little farther back on the block, but they insisted on building it close to the road so that Mrs. McLendon would not have to walk too far to tend to her animals. The barn was gone by the time the school bought the property in 1938.

Edward J. Riley House

This site is just conjecture on my part. Mr. Riley bought 193 acres from Burrell J. Marshall in 1871. This is the land that is

now Meadow Oaks and Hidden Springs Ranches subdivisions. When my wife and I were touring houses being built in Hidden Springs Ranches, I discovered a hand dug well covered with a huge stone with a hole in the middle of the top. I could not find anyone who knew anything about it. This area was property just north of the Puckett place, which is now owned by Jim Karhan. Later, when we were touring the house on the cul-de-sac next to the well lot, I noticed the rock formations around it. It was then that it struck me that this could be the site of the Riley's home. It was certainly an ideal location for a home. The H. L. Moores bought this property in 1901 and owned it until 1939. I'm not sure if they lived at this site or not. It just makes sense to me that this was the Riley home site.

Old well on Hidden Springs Ranch

A. K. Daniel House

This is another conjecture. A. K. Daniel purchased 193 acres from Marshall, adjacent to the Riley's. When talking to Mrs. Willie Baird Crow, she related that a Mr. Rowland, with a long white beard, lived just northwest of her dad's place. The Rowlands owned the property next to Mr. Baird and I was trying to figure out where they might have lived. In talking to Teddy Draper, who now owns that property, he said he had to clear away rocks and things as if a house might have been on his homesite. This got me to thinking and it is my opinion that this could very well have been the Daniel house site as well. Again it is a very good location to have a house on. I think the Rowlands probably lived in it as well. Again, just a guess.

First Methodist Church

The first official Methodist church was built on the 1.3 acre tract bought from J. W. Phillips in January 1880. The building was completed on 3-12-1880. It also doubled as the Walnut Springs Academy. It met the same fate that other churches and schools during that time span. Someone deliberately set fire to the building on 2-2-1881 and it burned to the ground. The site is adjacent to the northern border of the Phillips Cemetery.

Second Methodist Church

Dismayed but not discouraged, the Methodists raised the funds to build another church on the same site. This one survived and served the congregation until 1901, when a new church was built in Dripping Springs. The old church was resurrected as a residence. O. G. Shockley bought the building and moved it to block one of the third addition. Ironically, it was situated just across the street from the new Methodist church. It was used as a residence until 1984 when James Hurlbut bought the property to build Pioneer Plaza, a business complex. The old church met its match in the name of progress.

Third Methodist Church

The first church built on the site on block three served as a church until 1962, when its condition became unsafe. J. W. Wilson, Jr., bought the building and moved it to the back of his place of business to serve as a place for storage. It burned down in the 1980s.

S. J. Moore House

Mr. Moore bought property along RR12 S and built his house in 1947. He lived there until selling it to Robert Terry in 1966, who rocked the house and lived in it. Mike Rose bought the place and lived in the house until 2001 when a mold problem became evident, and the house ended up being completely torn down. The Roses built a real estate office on the same site. It was completed in June 2002.

Millseat School

After the Millseat school district voted to consolidate with Dripping Springs in 1943, the old school became expendible. J. W. Wood bought the building in April 1944 and moved it to the lots in the third addition that he had previously bought. He converted it into his home, but the house burned to the ground in 1956.

J. L. Puckett House

When Mr. Puckett bought 85 acres in 1883, he built his home on the property, in the vicinity of where the Shamrock/Sub complex is now located. I am not sure when the house was finally torn down, but I do know the R. J. Ragland family lived in it during the 1950s. It probably served the purpose for another couple of decades.

J. A. Puckett House

When J. L. Puckett divided the property between his two sons in 1924, Joseph built a little three-room house on the 36-acre plot he was given. It is probable that he and his wife, Mattie, built the house years before, because Bradley Davis recalls it being there around 1916. The house was still there in 1966 when C. B. Draper bought the property and lived in the house until he could build a new house a couple of years later. The Draper house was converted to business offices that housed the Karhan offices. There are still remnants of several old rock sheds along the fence line.

M. E. Peal House

In 1908 M. E. Peal bought this property, which was a 1.3 acre part of the R. E. Spaw subdivision, along Old Fitzhugh Road. This house was sold several times but Sam Byars owned the property the longest. Bill and Clarene McNair bought the property in 1985 and later tore down the deteriorating structure.

Sam Byars Rent House

In 1941 Sam Byars built a rent house on his 1.3 acre lot in the R. E. Spaw subdivision. It was in a rundown condition when Bill and Clarene McNair bought the property in 1985. They later cleared the lot by tearing down the buildings on it and moved in a doublewide home on the property before selling it.

Sam Byars House

M. M. Caperton House

Mr. Caperton bought all of block eleven in 1881 and no doubt built his house on the north one-half of the block. He eventually sold the home to J. F. Roberts in 1898, who lived in the house for the rest of its days. It completely burned in March 1922. One could still see some evidence of the fire, when I moved here in 1965.

Charles Seal Barn

This barn was located on the corner of Spring and San Marcos streets where the Glosson Exxon station now stands. It was on the major thoroughfare of traffic in Dripping Springs. Mr. Davis can remember it as being one of those structures the circus liked to use to advertise their coming attraction. It was torn down before the property was bought to build the Exxon.

Garland Seal House

Mr. Seal built the little four-room house on his lot on the corner of San Marcos and Hays streets. It was conveyed with the property when J. F. Glosson acquired the half block for his Exxon station. It was used as a residence and a place of business. Bersha McIntyre had a beauty salon in it for a time. Finally, as it stayed vacant and J. F. Glosson found out that he was being taxed for the house, even though it was no longer being used for anything, he decided it would save him money to tear it down and he did.

Mrs. Ella O'Pry House

Located on Lot 10 of block seven, it was built in 1884 and was described as a neat little home in one newspaper article. It is uncertain when it was torn down, but a big storage barn was built on the property in the early 1980s by Mack Crow.

Ivy "Piggy" Roberts House

This house was located on the west half of block eight, facing Wallace Street. I can remember Mr. Roberts sitting on his front porch after I came here in 1965. I'm not sure when it was built or when it was torn down.

W. J. Sheppard A-Frame House

Mr. Sheppard bought the two acres now housing Promenade Center in 1963. He built a fancy A-frame style house on it and lived in it for a while. He then rented it out. My wife and I actually looked at it as a possible residence when we came here in 1965. It was torn down in the '80s to make room for the Promenade.

W. J. Hall House

This house was built on the eastern half of block three, second addition, by Mr. Hall in late 1883 or early 1884. It changed hands several times before the Methodists bought the property in 1892 for the purpose of having their first parsonage. It housed preachers until 1911, when one wife died of tuberculosis. It was decided to tear the house down as a health precaution.

Second Methodist Parsonage

Immediately, the Methodists erected another parsonage on the land in block three in 1912. This house was the home of the Methodist pastors and their families until 1948, when the property was sold to J. N. Rippy. The house was torn down before Rippy sold the property to the First Baptist Church in the 1950s.

Third Methodist Parsonage

Prior to selling their second parsonage property to J. N. Rippy, in 1948 the Methodists decided to build their next parsonage on the site of their church on block three of the original plat. There came a time when it was not used as a residence for the pastors, but remained a viable building. Finally, in the mid-'80s, when the church property was sold, the parsonage was torn down to make more room for parking for the funeral home. The house was located on the north side of the property, facing Highway 290.

Transportation

Generally, most towns can trace their beginnings, growth, and changes around modes of transportation. For many of the early towns, this involved railroads. For a while there was speculation that a railroad would come to Dripping Springs and fuel the already growing community. While the capitol of Texas was being built in the mid-1880s, a railroad was built to Oatmanville to bring back quarried limestone. Oatmanville was present-day Oak Hill. Since it was only 10-12 miles away, people just expected that it would eventually be extended to Dripping Springs and those beliefs were expressed by some of the newspapers at the time. As you well know, this did not happen.

Dripping Springs was never blessed with travel by rail, air, or water, so a land route served the purpose. Prior to the founding three families making their homes in Dripping Springs, a road from Austin to Fredericksburg had already been established to carry supplies to Fort Scott, which was built around 1849 and was a part of a line of forts built on the edge of the frontier to protect settlers from Indians. More than likely, families used this road to get to Dripping Springs. Until near the end of the first quarter of the twentieth century, distance was covered mostly on foot, horseback, or horsedrawn vehicles. Roads were mere trails and usually followed the paths of least resistance to nature's barriers. Mud posed problems and many a road's pathway was changed due to mudholes and the need to get around them.

In the early days, roads were the responsibility of the local people to build and to upkeep. The Commissioners Court minutes are full of naming committees charged with laying out the roads, then naming overseers and particular people in the area to actually build the roads. These appointments were a serious matter. If an appointed person failed to carry out the duty, the court would then prosecute them. People were always appealing to the Court to build roads in their area or to change them for various reasons. There were actually three groups that were appointed to get a road established. First, people had to view and locate the road. It was their job to actually lay out a proposed route by marking it. Next would come the road builders—an overseer and his named crew and anyone else he would choose to help out. It certainly was not the type of road construction we think of today. It was simply a matter of clearing a path by removing rocks and trees that would obstruct a wagon. Nothing more. The roadbed was still native ground, which meant mud when it rained. Reviewers were appointed to go over the roads from time to time and possibly suggest improvements, change the route or whatever else they might see during their inspections. Local citizens continued to be responsible for the upkeep of the roads in their area.

Dripping Springs, over the years, has been the hub of roads coming in every direction. The earliest road was first commissioned at a February 1857 meeting. Dr. J. M. Pound was among five men appointed to review the road from Willow Springs to Cannonville, intersecting the Dripping Springs-Fredericksburg road. At the August meeting, the group that included Dr. Pound did not report on their review, giving the reason as several of the men having moved out of the county. A new group that included John L. Moss and John L. Wallace were appointed and required to report to the November term. In August 1858, Frederick Voight was appointed the overseer of the road from the county line at Long's old place, then by way of Capt's Mill to Cannonville and on to Dripping Springs. Moss and Wallace were among the workers. By November, Wallace was appointed to oversee the road. Moss was still on the work list. In August 1859, Wallace gave his report and it was approved. At the November 1859 meeting, Peter Wuthrich headed up the work force that included Wallace. Today, that road is basically FM 1826 and County Road 150.

At the April 26, 1869, meeting, it was determined that a road from San Marcos to Dripping Springs needed to be located. William Smith, Ezekial Nance, and Ed Burleson were appointed to locate the road from San Marcos to Ezekial Nance's residence on the Rio Blanco. From there, John Butler, John R. Brown, and John L. Wallace were to locate it to near Dripping Springs. On September 6, 1869, it was ordered by the Court that a road be opened from San Marcos to the steam mill near Dripping Springs. Nance and S. B. Bales appointed commissioners of road from San Marcos to the Rio Blanco and Butler, Brown, and Wallace to lay it from Rio Blanco to the steam mill.

At the May 29, 1871, meeting, it was ordered that F. S. Roy, George Bell, B. J. Marshall, W. H. Howard, and L. McKellar be appointed to view out and locate a road beginning at the Travis-Hays County line where the Austin-Fredericksburg road crosses the line, then by the Dripping Springs to McKellar's store, then to the Blanco-Hays County line near the Hendley ranch. This was a change of the then Austin-Fredericksburg road which was to be done away with.

It is my opinion that the present Creek Road that comes out near Henly was the original Austin-Fredericksburg route. On January 26, 1874, J. B. Middlebrook and others were allowed to change the Fredericksburg road as per their petition. At the August 14, 1876, meeting, Thomas Voight was put in charge of the road from Travis County line by way of G. W. Click's to Dripping Springs. E. J. Riley would take it from Dripping Springs to the Blanco County line. B. F. Stephenson was appointed to oversee a portion of the Austin-Fredericksburg road leading from Dripping Springs to 22-mile post by the February 1879 court. His helpers included Thomas Voight, Mr. Spaw, George Spaw, Bas Sorrell, Jake Sorrell, Mr. Norwood, W. T. Chapman, G. W. Marshall, Pomp Sorrell, I.C.P. McLendon, Ed Wallace, and William Wallace. In February 1880, J. O. Rowland was made the overseer of the road from 22-mile post. His helpers stayed about the same, but also included A. J. Wallace, Jeff Marshall, and Jeff Davis. In February 1882, Rowland was still overseeing, and his help included A. K. Daniels, W. E. Daniels, W. P. Riley, Warren Collins, Matt Livingston, J. Young, B. F. Stephenson, Ed Wallace, Andrew Wallace, Henry Banks, J. M. Norwood, J. C. Rowe, B. L. Spaw, A. J. Meers, Elisha Sanders, M. Livingston, and H. C. Durar. He also had the authority to summon anyone else he needed.

Meanwhile, changes were taking place

on the San Marcos-Dripping Springs road. In November of 1879, B. M. Gibson, W. C. Collins, E. Nance, A. L. Davis, and J. F. Roberts were appointed reviewers for a road from San Marcos (1st class) to Nance's on the Rio Blanco, then from Nance's to Dripping Springs. The Court heard the report of J. M. Pound, Bleu M. Gibson, W. W. Caldwell, and others appointed to view and locate a change in the San Marcos to Dripping Springs road. In August 1882, it was agreed to change the route. They were to leave the present road at South Onion and then in a straight line to the Methodist Church, crossing North Onion about half a mile below the present crossing.

In May 1883, W. T. Chapman asked for changes in the DS-San Marcos road so that it turned 100 yards north of Walnut Springs to run northwest to the southwest corner of what is known as the Howard survey and then north on the west line of the survey to its northwest corner near Dripping Springs. Also, he asked that the settlement road from DS be changed at the south line of the Howard tract and run west on said line to connect with San Marcos-DS road at the west corner of Howard land. A committee composed of J. B. Wallace, Sam Gilpin, W. H. Banks, Dick Gibson, and W. T. Chapman were appointed to view out and locate changes and report back the second Monday of August 1883. In February 1891, the route was changed to run by the graveyard, intersecting the present road at Dickey's line.

For the average citizen, the trip to Austin was usually a three-day excursion. The first day would get them to Oak Hill where they spent the night. The next day was spent traveling to Austin, taking care of business, and returning to Oak Hill. The third day found you back home.

Many early families would only plan a couple of trips to Austin a year and one of these would probably coincide with the circus coming to town. The circus people came through surrounding communities and trade tickets for the right to post advertisement on the sides of barns and other visible buildings. Bradley Davis recalls that his was a typical family and he looked forward with great excitement to getting to make the trip to Austin. One of his biggest disappointments occurred on one of these planned trips. After viewing the circus posters plastered on the walls around town, Mr. Davis could hardly wait to see the real thing. The family boarded the wagon and only reached halfway up Wallace Mountain before bogging down in mud. It was decided to cancel the trip and some mighty disappointed kids had to return home and miss the circus.

Not all trips to Austin would take three days. Some people, making a living from these trips, had a system to beat the three-day turn around. One such person was Alex McGowan, a black man who lived near the Hays-Travis County line around Cedar Valley. Until 1918, he brought the mail, supplies and sometimes passengers to Dripping Springs on a daily basis. He owned four very fine teams of horses that could travel at a high rate of speed for long distances. He would leave his home and race to Austin. There he would pick up the mail and supplies, change teams and race back to his house were he would once again change teams and finish the race to Dripping Springs. Once the mission was completed, he changed to a fourth team to make a leisurely trip back home where the rested fourth team could lead off the next day's relay trip. Mr. McGowan also bought rabbits from the youngsters for a nickel and took them to Austin for resell.

Automobiles were not prevalent in Dripping Springs for a while, probably due to a lack of suitable roadways as much as anything else. Bradley Davis recalls seeing the first automobile in Dripping Springs around 1915. It was a Stanley Steamer. His oldest brother borrowed it from a cousin and had driven it to Dripping Springs from Austin to show it off. Mr. Davis remembers the ride was very bumpy, which could be attributed to road conditions. It would still be a few years before Dripping Springs would see roads capable of encouraging automobile travel.

As the road from Austin wound its way toward Dripping Springs and on to Fredericksburg, its course took several variations over the years. Long before the town of Dripping Springs was laid out, the trail made its way down Wallace Mountain beside the Wallace residence. The stagecoach stop was there for years. The road came on down the mountain and to cross the Dripping Springs branch ravine, one had to go around its northern edge and then go on its way much like the Creek Road does today. The original plat set out by W. T. Chapman in 1881 had the town of Dripping Springs blocked on the western edge by the ravine. The twelve blocks were divided by six streets, three running east and west and three north and south. The northern-most street running east and west was named Mercer after Chapman's son and was meant to be the main street because it was 75 feet wide while the others were only 50 feet. The middle street was named Wallace, most assuredly after the Wallace family. The southern-most street was named Spring because it ran to the spring-fed Dripping Springs branch. The eastern-most street running north and south was San Marcos because that was the road that would take you to San Marcos. The middle street was College, so named because it intersected at the Academy Block and schools in those days were known as colleges even though they were not the higher learning that we think of today. The western-most street was called Bluff Street because it ran parallel to the bluffs of the Dripping Springs branch.

In the next couple of years Chapman added four more additions to his original plat. When he added the third addition on the south side of town, he had to add another street. This one ran east and west and was named Hays Street after the county and connected on the east end with the road to San Marcos. In platting the first and second additions, two streets were penciled in. One was called North Street. It was opposite Bluff Street and went between present-day DS Butane and the Old Breed Feed Store and angled northeast to the end of the addition which later became the property line of the I. V Davis property, then was probably meant to head east and connect up with Eve Street. Eve Street was named after the County surveyor, Prof. Joseph C. Eve, who surveyed the plat. It stretched from Academy Block's northern boundary to the north boundary of the second addition, a distance of around 300 feet. It was fifty foot wide and split blocks four and five on the west from six and seven on the east. It was a dead end road on both ends with the Academy to the south and private property to the north.

It just made sense to drive the short distance to Mercer street through the Academy property, especially as the road north extended toward the Fitzhugh community. Over time this is what happened, and the road cut off the northeast corner and went along the east boundary to make the road. Depending on your destination, the road has been called Shingle Hill Road, Fitzhugh Road, and now either Post Office Road or Old Fitzhugh Road. North Street never did catch on. Part of the problem I'm told was that the land was a little marshy during wet weather and not really good for consistent travel, plus it was just more convenient to take the Fitzhugh road. Surveys did not always mean much when convenience and tradition got in the way.

After the plat, the road to Dripping Springs from Austin connected on the east end with Spring Street. If you were going to San Marcos, you would take a left on San Marcos Street, another left on Hays and then a right on what is now Ranch Road 12. If you were headed to Fredericksburg or downtown Dripping Springs, you would take a right on San Marcos and then a left on Mercer. As mentioned before, in the early days one had to skirt the branch on the northern side and come back to take either the Creek Road or go on to Johnson City. In August 1884, W. T. Chapman and others petitioned the Hays County Commissioners to build a bridge across the branch at the end of Mercer. They agreed to appropriate $200 dollars to build an earthern bridge across it. It was built in 1885. They had a lot of problems with it washing out and later an old wooden bridge would be built that would suffice until Highway 290 was built in 1937.

Within three years after Dripping Springs was platted, businesses popped up along Mercer Street. There were at least three general merchandise stores, the same number of blacksmith shops, a livery stable, drugstore and hotel. Later shoe repairmen, saddlemakers, photographers, dentists, and doctors were available to the populace. A meat market was added in 1914. A change in the times occurred by the end of the first quarter of the twentieth century when automobiles started to make their presence known. Garages for repairs and stores began to sell gasoline as well.

Gravel was the best topping on the roads of Dripping Springs until about 1935. As automobiles became more popular, the roads had to be upgraded for the increased travel. The road from Austin was called Texas Highway 20, but when the road was paved, it became Highway 290 and it changed the look of the town. This time it veered off its old course near the bottom of Wallace Mountain, near where Loop 64 begins now and connected with Mercer Street to proceed through the downtown area, crossing Dripping Springs branch and heading to Johnson City. Immediately, businesses that catered to the increase of traffic began to spring up along Mercer. Most of the buildings, still remaining today, were built in the late 1930s for this purpose. The only buildings surviving the pre-'30s period are the A. L. Davis building, Patterson building, Garnett Garage, and Crenshaw Garage. There were four service stations, three garages, and several eating places along the two blocks of main street, plus the general merchandise stores.

The lack of modern roadbuilding equipment meant most roads simply followed the course of their predecessors. Highway 20 was no exception. It was a very crooked excursion for its travelers. Those with experience recall that there were places where it seemed that you were meeting yourself coming and going. When it was paved in 1937, it became Highway 290, but even though the roadway was improved, it remained its same old crooked self.

By the 1950s, the size and speed of automobiles demanded better and safer roadways. With improvement in roadbuilding equipment, natural barriers were no longer an impediment to progress and safety, and straight roads were much easier to achieve. How much so can be observed by noticing the old highway 290 roadbeds along the way, both used and unused, between Austin and Johnson City. Circle Drive was a part of old highway 290, as well as Tiger Lane in front of the high school. You can still see old bridges and other remnants of the old road. It is hard to imagine that these were once the best roads around, but then the cars did not go the speed they are capable of doing today.

The present Highway 290 was completed through Dripping Springs by 1958. It not only changed the look of the town but surrounding fields as well. Clearing the rocky land around Dripping Springs meant something had to be done with the rocks. Mostly they were used to make rock fences. In building 290, a good roadbase was needed. The highway department bought up many of the old rock fences to be turned into roadbase. The road also took a different path through the town. It came straight down Wallace Mountain, once again connecting with Spring Street and going straight on through. All streets except Mercer were only fifty feet wide. The road would take at least one hundred feet. This meant property would have to be taken to accomplish the feat. In the very early days, roads remained a part of the person's property they went across. That changed as the state and counties bought property and it became theirs. Probably because there were fewer buildings to contend with, most of the land came from the blocks on the north side of Spring Street. It took almost half of blocks two, five, eight, and eleven. It also meant building a bridge across the Dripping Springs branch. Highway 290 severed the old Creek Road route that immediately cut left after crossing the Mercer Street bridge, leaving entrance to Creek Road from 290 only. The old 290 route through Mercer became known as Loop 64.

Immediately, the businesses depending on traffic made the move. By 1962, four service stations—Mobil, Sinclair, Humble, and Conoco—were open for business. Others were Wiest Grocery, Nut's Hobby Shop, Western Kitchen, and the Village Center.

Over the years, what is now Ranch Road 12 went through some changes. The original road coming from Wimberley turned at Hays Street to get to Dripping Springs. The Wimberley-Dripping Springs road was only gravel until 1945 when the state decided to pave it and make it a farm-to-market road. By August of that year all the right-of-way had been secured. By October 1947 the road had been completed. It now took a straight path in front of the Methodist church to connect with the road that would later become 290. Because of this change, the Methodist church moved their building to face the new RR12 road. A gravel road continued it to Highway 290 which is Loop 64 today. By 1970, right-of-way had been attained and a straight portion north was built to connect with Old Fitzhugh Road just above the Nelson Davidson homestead. Prior to this, all traffic coming from the north had to go down the narrow path known as Old Fitzhugh Road that connected at Mercer Street. The speed of the cars was a definite hazard to the residents living along this road. To show the signs of the times for this stretch of the road, the old Fitzhugh Road in the '30s and '40s was nicknamed Kid's Street, but in the '60s and '70s, it became known as Widow's Lane.

Transportation played a huge role in the next phase of growth for the community. In the late 60's and early 70's, farming and ranching were no longer profitable operations for most families around the area and taxes on the land began to put them between a rock and a hard spot. The solution to this problem was to begin selling off acreage. For some this became a very profitable solution. And being less than thirty miles from Austin and having a good highway to travel on, many locals began making their living in Austin while living the country life in Dripping Springs. This same lure appealed to those city folks who had a yearning to live in the country. As people began to move out to the countryside, realtors seized the opportunity, bought huge tracts of land, and converted them into subdivisions. Dripping Springs took on the look of a bedroom community. Only the lack of availability of good water in the area has kept the density of the houses down.

The gasoline crisis of the '70s put a small damper on the growth, making people worry about being able to get back and forth to work. In the early '80s, land prices began to soar and the building explosion again was on its way up. Speculators borrowed money and paid excessive prices for land as if the spiral would never end. New buildings for businesses went up left and right.

The mid-'80s witnessed a big crash in the fortunes of many. Bankruptcies were the rule rather than the exception. During this decade, Redwood Center (now Trail Head), The Commons, Promenade, Pioneer Plaza, Dripping Office Center, Bluff Center, and The Veranda became new kids on the block. Many went through bankruptcy proceedings in the early '90s, even the bank that loaned much of the money.

This proved to be just a temporary lull to the growth of Dripping Springs. Many of the businesses changed hands. Real estate ground to an almost standstill with many looking for other ways to make a living. After a couple of years going through financial problems, things began to pick up, with new money and people acting as if nothing had happened before. People who owned property along 290 were offered big bucks to turn loose of it and they did. Such businesses as Jack Brown Cleaners, Sonic Drive-In, Cattlemen's Bank, Taco Bell/Mobil have joined Dairy Queen to help greet people that come down 290 to enter the Gateway To The Hill Country, Dripping Springs. No doubt, transportation, and the improvement thereof, will continue to play a large part in the growth of Dripping Springs and the surrounding area far into the 21st century.

Subdivisions that cropped up in the P. A. Smith survey prior to the land busts of the late '80s included a part of Springlake, North Forty, Dripping Springs Heights, R. J. Ragland, Springwood, Blue Ridge, Grand Prairie, Cannon West Estates, Butler Ranch, and Meadow Oaks. In the '90s the trend continued with Hidden Springs Ranch, Hidden Springs Ranch II, Legacy Trails, and the new 600 acre development in the southwest quarter on RR12 S presently called Caliterra. Very little land remains in the survey that has not been designated for development.

As necessary as roads are to travel and community, nothing disfigures the uniqueness and originality of an area than an expanded road system. The growth of the Dripping Springs area and the expansion of the road system to accommodate is a testament to this fact. As this book goes to press, construction has already begun to put in a 290 turn lane from Wallace Mt. through most of the town. This is taking a little more of the right-of-way and putting residences closer to the roadway. Expanding from a two-land to a five-lane highway has put many buildings without any buffer zone at all. Businesses are left with little parking space. Probably within the next ten years, there will not be any residences along 290 or Ranch Road 12. The land is too valuable as commercial property. The face of Dripping Springs will be forever changed as the 1881 plat will become less and less recognizable. Without a good record of history for people to follow, how things were in the past will be lost for those who come later and have no knowledge of Dripping Springs history.

The Myers brothers
Herman, F. M. "Kite," Juel, J. W. "Buster," and E. E. "Nookie"

Places to Go and Things to Do

Like most frontier areas limited by methods of travel and hampered by the amount of available time free from the daily routine of coping with the perils of making a living and staying alive, the early settlers of Dripping Springs had to entertain themselves with surrounding events or places. Most certainly, the natural facilities of the area lent itself to hunting, fishing, swimming and picnics. You can believe plenty of this went on. Any chance for families to get together and visit was welcomed. Such events as the circuit preacher, revivals, school events, political picnics, elections, ceremonies, ballgames, harvests, quilting bees, hog-killing, and dances filled the bill. These events were not just limited to the 1800s. Very little changed for the rural areas of Texas until the late 1940s when electricity finally made its presence known and more convenience things were available to the people. Dripping Springs started getting electricity in the late '30s and early '40s.

I feel fortunate that I was born in the early '40s, because it allowed me to experience first-hand many of the types of events that the early settlers had to deal with. As a history teacher, I know how hard it is to get students to understand things that happened beyond their lifetimes. They think the whole world has always been the way it is in their day. I can remember not having electricity, enduring outdoor toilets, owning an icebox, and looking for the iceman to bring the blocks of ice to go in it. They had regular routes and ours came three days a week. I can remember my family's first indoor bathroom with a tub, looking forward to the cold winter days when it was hog-killing time, getting to eat cracklings, chopping cotton, picking cotton when you had to take the cotton out of the bolls, and picking cotton when you could grab bolls and all. I also remember gathering around a neighbor's living room each Saturday night to watch an eight-inch TV screen and marvelling at how big it was, getting our own first television set, going to ice cream and domino parties and playing with the other kids while the parents played and visited. A special treat was getting to go into town, even if I was wearing a shirt made out of feed sacks.

As I read old newspaper articles from the 1800s about the goings on of Dripping Springs, it pointed out how little had changed from that time until the time of my youth. It brought to mind the old saying, "The more things change, the more they remain the same." People were on the move all

the time. It was nothing for them to take off for places far and wide and all the time I wondered how could they do that without automobiles or airplanes. Except for the basic hardships put on them by the events of the times, they coped with everything much as we do today.

One of the largest gatherings of all times occurred with the ceremony of the Masons laying the cornerstone of the Dripping Springs Academy on August 9, 1881. The end of school terms each May brought many to town as do our graduations today. The Masons had their installation ceremonies in June, and this, plus political candidate speeches, made for big days.

Another event happened when the Dripping Springs Red Stocking baseball team played teams from around the area, including making a trip, by train, to San Antonio. There were many other events as well. Weddings were well attended and there never seemed to be a shortage of dances at people's houses. Fishing trips to Onion Creek and the Pedernales River were also favorites.

One opportunity for neighbors to work together was hog-killing time. Due to the fact there were few ways to preserve meat in the days of pre-electricity, it was a big occasion. On a cold winter day, neighbors gathered and got fires started, boiling big pots of water. As the water was being readied, someone killed the hogs to be butchered that day. The hogs were brought to a tree or some type of stand to be hung up and allowed to bleed out. The boiling water was poured in a big barrell, and the hog was lowered into boiling water. This was necessary to get the hide in the condition where the hair could be scraped off. When this process was completed, the butchering began. The fat was stripped off the hog, cut into small pieces and thrown into the big metal pots that had been used for boiling water. The fires were stoked and continued to blaze. This process was called rendering the lard. As the fat melted into a liquid, a cloth was put over lard cans that were as large as five gallons or more. The cloths were used as strainers. The melted fat was dipped out of the pots and poured over the cloth with the liquid going through and the rinds staying on top. This method continued until all the lard had been rendered. The big buckets of lard were stored and allowed to harden. This became the cook's supply of cooking oil for the year. The skin of the hogs back is what produced the rinds, also called cracklings. They really tasted good, especially when they were fresh. The rest of the meat was cut up into different sections, some made into sausage, others cured as hams and salted down to preserve as long as possible. Little remained of the hog, much like the buffalo to the Indian. There was always someone who wanted the hogshead to make tamales or something. Some people liked pickled pigs feet and the tongue. Even the intestines were used to stuff the sausage in. So you see, the hog was a major food source. During the time when I participated in the hog-killing process, we had locker plants to take the butchered products to and store in huge freezer rooms. I can remember how cold it was to walk in there with my parents to open our locker and get out the meat we wanted.

The neighbors who helped were often repaid at the next cold spell or even within a few days when everyone once again gathered to go through the same process. For kids, it was just a fun day and we did not look upon it as work or a necessity.

As the area grew in population, other forms of entertainment or pleasure were added to the mix. The longest running man-made event of the area is the Camp Ben McCulloch Reunion held each year in June. It was first organized in 1896 for the purpose of getting the Confederate soldiers of Hays County and their families together for a reunion. Among the organizers were W. T. Chapman and Dr. J. M Pound of Dripping Springs. The reunion was named for General Ben McCullouch, who had been a Texas hero at the Battle of San Jacinto, and a Texas Ranger who fought in the U.S.-Mexico War. On March 7, 1862, he lost his life while serving with the Confederate forces at the Battle of Pea Ridge, Arkansas.

The first meeting may not have numbered more than seventeen but it grew to the point where one year a record attendance of six thousand was reached. Today, I don't know if they have a way of counting how many come and go for the proceedings. The reunions are held on a forty-acre site on Onion Creek near Driftwood. It has been held every year since 1896, and the festivities today last eight days. In the early days people came in their wagons or on horseback and camped out. Today, the camping has more of a modern flavor as commercial campers provide the opportunity to "rough" it. Many long-time campers, such as Naoma Glosson and Mary Sue Lyle, eagerly set up their camps several days in advance and stay until it is over and maybe a little longer, if the visiting is good. Many have camped at the same spot for decades. They even post their names on trees or in other ways to let people know the spot is reserved. Even though Naoma and Mary Sue have made it an annual habit for more than fifty years, they do not hold a candle to Fannie Crumley McIntyre. Before her death in 1996 she had attended the first 100 reunions. Planned activities, besides visiting, include dances, group singing, fiddling contests, tennis tournaments, races, ball games, raffles, bingo, swimming in Onion Creek, a carnival, and many other types of activities, plus the business of the United Confederate Veterans organization.

Most of the things to do or places to go around Dripping Springs have to do with the beauty and natural phenomenon of the Hill Country. Just a drive around the countryside can be a very relaxing experience well worth the time involved. I love to drive down Creek Road (HC 190) and observe the beauty of the creeks and the peaceful water flowing over the numerous small dams. Most certainly, before the ease of transportation and other modern conveniences, the natural landmarks provided plenty of opportunities for things to do. Unfortunately, an influx of people and developing subdivisions is slowly robbing the area of its pristine beauty. It won't be many years before driving in the area will look like any other place that one can see driving from Austin—nothing but housetops and driveways so close together that nothing of nature's beauty can be seen.

Before electricity, one of the more popu-

Dripping Springs namesake

lar meeting places mixed business with pleasure. Prior to the days of refrigeration, people had to find a way to keep dairy products from quickly ruining. This meant keeping them cold or at least cool. Usually this meant a cold spring. Dripping Springs had many such springs but one seemed to fill the bill better than others. Located about a quarter of a mile from the town's namesake (Dripping Springs Branch) is a box canyon with rocky ledges that form a natural amphitheater at its head. At its base is a natural cave-like spot formed by a thick stone slab resting on two rock walls with a rock bottom. This natural room with cold spring water flowing through it was ideal for storing milk, hence the name Milkhouse Branch. This branch connects with the main

Dripping Springs Branch about two hundred yards from its head which is just behind the old Will Crow house on Creek Road.

The Milkhouse branch gave the people a chance to meet and it was an excellent place to hold picnics. There were other spring pools that have since filled in and calcified from dripping water, that also provided a place for a very cold dip or shower. Bradley Davis recalls that a pipe was placed so the spring water ran out over a ledge and provided a cold showering place. I have heard it was used for shock treatment as well.

There are several pictures I have seen showing whole groups posing in and around the amphitheater. If you have ever noticed the big rock ledges and rock walls along the ravines of the branches and can imagine what it looked like in a less vegetated state, then you can understand what a haven for play and exploration it must have been for the children of the community.

Another favorite spot for many was located maybe a quarter mile down Dripping Springs Branch from Milkhouse—a huge rock that became known as Initial Rock. Long before water towers were around to provide a place for people to paint their names and initials on, the people of Dripping Springs loved to leave their imprint in the form of initials as a monument to history. Time has weathered the surface to gray and it is difficult to decipher much of the carvings in its present condition. No doubt someone with the patience and correct tools could bring much of it back to life. The most visible initial reads J.E.G. 8-7-34. Today, the Dripping Springs, Milkhouse, and Initial Rock are located on private property and should not be observed without proper permission of the owners.

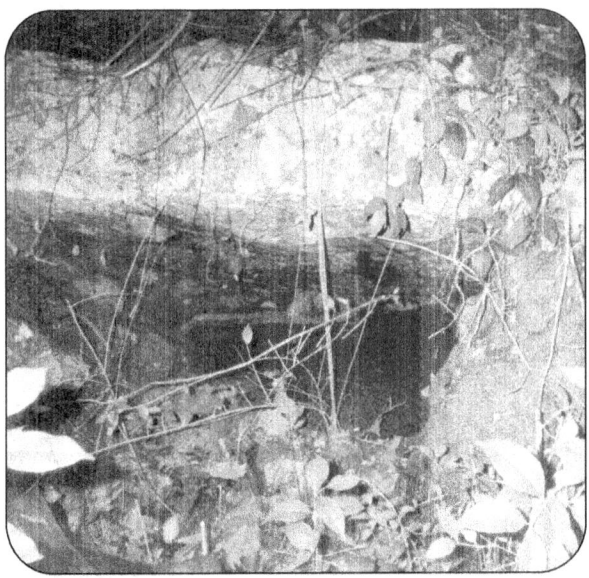

Milkhouse Springs Cave, where people kept dairy products cool.

Milkhouse Springs
—Courtesy Hazel Bell Myers

Initial Rock on Dripping Springs Branch

During the first half of the 1900s was a building known as the Courthouse. The County paid for it to be built, so the County and Dripping Springs had some place to conduct business when necessary. The first one was built in 1906. Evidently, it was either not well built or a larger one was needed. In 1909, the County Commissioners donated $27.50 to replace the old Courthouse. It was a large room used, among other things, as a classroom by the school. When not in official use, some remember using the big room for a skating rink. By 1937, the old Courthouse, which was located on Lot 1 of block one, and a blacksmith shop located on Lot 12 of the same block, had long been removed. The area became the site for the Dripping Springs Theater, and today as a bank. The theater turned out to not be a profitable adventure for what it was designed and in 1948 was gutted to become a warehouse and feedstore. Much like the skateboarders of today, there were no places that skaters couldn't use to have fun. Jack Lyle recalls skating in the old theater. It is imagined that the slanted floor used for good seating in the theater provided its share of challenges for those skaters.

Several grottos in the area present very scenic and enjoyable areas to picnic, swim, and relax. A grotto is a big hole in the ground where an underground cavern collapsed many thousands of years ago to form a small area of calm. One of these, located on private property and formerly a part of the huge Hurlbut Ranch, is known as Dead Man's Hole. Of course, the name is derived by an unsuspecting someone who fell over the edge and died from the fall. But legend provides us with several versions as to how the name was earned, and fact tells us there are those who dangerously jump off the edge and plunge to the water many feet below. Some have been seriously hurt and probably felt they were going to become a part of the name's legend. A waterfall cascading into a pool below, plus giant cypress trees provide the backdrop for the very serene surroundings. For my part, the best way to get there is to take the trail down the side of the ravine downstream and then walk alongside the stream until you get to this little bit of paradise.

The best known grotto in the area is Hamilton's Pool, located near the western tip of Travis County near the Pedernales River on Ranch Road 3288. This beautiful natural wonder was named after the tenth governor of Texas, Andrew J. Hamilton. The story goes that at one time he owned the property and spent some time there. For most of the 1900s it was owned by the Reimers family. They charged admission for its use and it became a favorite retreat for college and public school students alike. Although highly discouraged, there are known survivors of the 50-foot leap from its rim to the water below. At one time there was a lift erected from the top to the bottom. It could be used to lower supplies but it probably gained some use hauling battered divers up. Again, the safest way to enjoy the sights around the pool is to take the trail that led you there. In 1985, a bond issue was passed by the citizens of Travis County that allowed the County to purchase Hamilton Pool and 232 surrounding acres from owner Eugene Reimers. A good road has been built all the way from Highway 71 and today, the grotto is the focal point of the Hamilton Pool County Park. There are places to camp and park RV's, hike, or do other outdoor activities.

Just across the Pedernales River from Hamilton Pool is the Westcave Preserve. It is another grotto that has a wide variety of flora and fauna that is being protected for the enjoyment of visitors. Guided tours are the only way to view the exquisite beauty of the area.

Pedernales Falls State Park opened up in 1974, located, naturally, on the Pedernales River. The best way to get there is to take Ranch Road 3232, which is about two miles west of Henly on Highway 290. The park has a scenic stretch of the river, plus ideal places to camp, picnic, backpack, and ride horses. But the area can be as deadly as it is beautiful to the naive. High rising water and closed-to-the-public areas have caused more than a few deaths. Pedernales Falls' story is one of bureaucratic messups. It seemed the owner realized the beauty of the place she owned and wanted others to enjoy it as well. She offered to give it to the state for a park, but for some reason, she was turned down. Years later the bureaucrats turned around and bought the land to make this park.

There are several annual events that have cropped up in the last two decades that have a tendency to draw large crowds. The first of these is the Senior Citizens May Fair. Held each year as a fundraiser for the Senior Citizens Center, the members may be found in period dress giving demonstrations on making products long since a memory of the past. Various arts and crafts booths are available with items they have made. As usual, there is good food and drink to be consumed. The Senior Citizens had a large pavillon built beside the Center's parking lot for this purpose and have recently enclosed it.

In 1987, a group of citizens got together and brainstormed for something to put Dripping Springs on the map like those in other communities around the area. They came up with a three-day celebration that had arts and crafts, cookoffs, and entertainment. It is called Founders Day and is held the third weekend of April each year. It has grown into a huge event. As you might expect, the opening ceremonies on Friday include a parade complete with emergency vehicles, bands, horses, old and new cars, bicycles, go carts, kids, and floats. A few days earlier, the carnival pulls into town and gets into full swing, drawing the interest of many school kids. On Saturday and Sunday, Mercer Street is blocked off from traffic and the streets are lined with various types of booths, including arts and crafts, food, drinks, etc. A stage is erected and area bands and musicians entertain throughout the day and night. A street dance is held on Saturday night, usually with a name band playing. You can enter various tournaments including horseshoes and washers. The first major cookoff was chicken but the cook-offs have become so popular that all types are now part of the event. Saturday is the big day but Sunday afternoon is filled with entertainment and the booths are still there, not to mention the carnival.

In 1990 the city of Dripping Springs opened Founders Park using funds from a matching grant from the Texas Parks and Recreation Department. The entrance is located a little over a quarter of a mile from 290 on RR12 N. This thirty-acre park was bought and donated from lands formerly owned by two of the first founders of Dripping Springs, Dr. Pound and John Wallace. The name of the park was submitted by Lee Forister.

The focal point of the park is the swimming pool, adjacent pavillon, and a playscape. A larger playscape was added in 1999. Picnic tables and a walking trail are also close by. Just a few hundred yards from the entrance is a landscape donated by Gerald Brumley and his family.

Dripping Springs youth have used the park for a soccer league for several years.

Initial plans for the park included softball fields, a soccer field, and other types of recreational sports such as basketball and volleyball, and some wilderness study areas. Most of those plans have been shelved as youth football has taken the northern end and the rest contains soccer fields.

Bordering on the northeast corner of Founders Park is a three-acre site donated in 1988 by descendants of Dr. Joseph McKegg Pound to hold the future Pound House Museum. Funds and work to do the needed restoration of the place got off to a slow start but by the end of the '90s, a major surge took place. The Friends of the Pound House worked hard to raise the needed money. Each September they sponsored a fundraiser on the grounds. The work was completed and the museum opened in 2003. The house is restored to the way it was in 1914, the year Dr. Pound died. The original log pen is still a part of the house. Thanks to very thoughtful family members, much of Dr. Pound's belongings have been preserved for use in the museum. The restoration of the Pound homestead is a valuable and powerful reminder to the community of the heritage of our area.

Also in 1990 Damon McIntyre and other merchants in The Commons shopping center decided that the people of Dripping Springs needed something to entertain and keep them in Dripping Springs on the Fourth of July—a Fourth of July party. It included good food and drinks at low prices, a very informal parade, horseshoe and washer tournaments, closest to the pin contests, music and other forms of entertainment. There were Civil War demonstrations as well. As night fell on the community a fireworks display took place. This took place for just a few years before all the events fizzled except one. Huge crowds gathered in Founders Park with chairs, blankets, and refreshments for a picnic-like atmosphere around dusk. They were prepared for a big fireworks display that has seemed to get bigger and bigger each year. The event has gotten so large that in 2000 the event was moved to the 40-acre sports park on RR 12.

In 1998, Dripping Springs ISD, who owned 40 acres just off RR 12 South, entered into a plan with the City to convert this into a park. They applied for and qualified for a matching grant from Parks and Recreation to develop this acreage. It was named the Sports and Recreation Park, but many still refer it to the 40-acre park. The high school has their UIL baseball and softball fields there and dibs on more practice fields. The rest has been developed into soccer fields and a recreational area that includes a playscape, volleyball-basketball courts, horseshoe pits and a hiking trail around the entire park.

In 1999, there was another donation of land to the city to be developed into a park. Fourteen acres was donated by Jim Karhan and is appropriately named Karhan Park. It is being used primarily for adult activities. Much of the labor required to build facilities is being done by the Adult Softball Association. One softball field is completed, and another is nearing completion. Other plans will include either more fields or possibly a touch football field and soccer field.

Activities relating to the Dripping Springs school system have always provided the citizens plenty of opportunities to have a place to go and things to do. There is always a wide variety of chances ranging from UIL activities to other class projects of grades K-12. School activities alone provide places to go almost every day of the year. If that is not enough, then the Youth Association provides other opportunities for youngsters of all ages to participate in various sports activities throughout the year. The Scout and Church programs are also very strong in the area. Adults get the opportunity to participate in the men's and women's slowpitch leagues that have been in place since 1975.

Forms of Entertainment

As it has been noted in other places, the types of entertainment that prevailed in Dripping Springs over the years has not really changed very much. They may have changed their environment a little bit but it is interesting how the substance has never changed very much. Events that still bring people together include athletic events, dances, weddings, school functions, town celebrations, organizational ceremonies, picnics, movies, fishing, hunting, and such. Even though we like to think otherwise, there really isn't anything new. It seems everything has already been tried in some form or fashion. What never gets old is having fun and you can bet whatever the form or the fashion, the participants are having a good time.

Baseball

Such things as church revivals, house-raisings, dances, and other forms of gathering gave early pioneers an opportunity to visit. This helped break the monotony of the daily routine. For most rural communities, baseball was the central form of entertainment for 75-80 years. Baseball was first introduced in 1839 by Abner Doubleday and the Civil War helped to spread its popularity. The National League was formed in 1876. No doubt Dripping Springs had earlier teams but the first mention of a baseball game was in 1883 as part of the closing ceremonies of the school. Everytime any type function took place, a baseball game seemed to take center stage.

In the August 16, 1935, edition of the *San Marcos Record*, there was an interview with A. L. Davis, Jr., a graduate of the Dripping Springs Academy and a prominent merchant in Dripping Springs until 1902 when he moved to San Marcos. He was a pitcher for a baseball team that he also sponsored from 1884 to 1896. A part of the article included the 1896 team picture. The players in that photo were Rufus Smith, Ed Lindeman, Will Richie, Cal Brown, Jim Eckols, Albert Sprouse, A. L. Davis, Jim Richie, Sam Trautwein, Chester Harrison, and Arthur Bagley. He claimed they dominated the area for those twelve years. The main focus of this article was his recall of a June 13, 1884, game with Kyle. He said the real reason they were invited to play Kyle was to match him up with Jake Burkett in a footrace. Davis weighed 208 and Burkett 165. Davis did not feel he had a chance in a short dash but might if longer, so he agreed to a 100 yard dash. He spent time trying to get in shape and sure enough, was able to outlast Burkett in the longer race. Dripping Springs also won the game 8-4. (Articles written in the 1884 *San Marcos Free Press* gave the score as 11-9 and another 11-7.)

In July of that year, the Dripping Springs Redstocking baseball team caught a train at Kyle to go to San Antonio to play the Sunsets. After a day of being treated well, they were mistreated in the game by the Sunsets 22-0. Other scores given were Dripping Springs defeated by the Mountain Nine of Cedar Valley 20-17 (7-21-1887). In July 1889, they beat Round Mountain 52-1. In a September game of that year, DS defeated the Kyle Lone Stars 21-17. Kyle blamed the loss on the umpire but a DS supporter reminded them in a letter that they did not blame this same man in last year's win over Dripping Springs. Dripping Springs players on that team were Charlie Malott–1B, Cooke–SS, Davis–P, F. Graham–C, Garrett–CF, W. Graham–3B, Marshall–2B, Roberts–LF, Stone–RF. The Dripping Springs lineup in a 1926 game with San Marcos Bobcats and won by the Tigers 4-2 were J. Shelton–2B, Robert Shelton–1B, Shahan–3B, Ratliff–LF, E. Shelton–SS, Searight–C, Ralph Shelton–RF, Roy Shelton–RF, Crenshaw–CF, R. Smith–P. Sunday games continued to be popular in small communities until the late 1950s when adult baseball leagues tended to wane. In the mid-'50s Dripping Springs had a team that entered the CenTex Baseball League that included teams from Kyle, Wimberley, Dripping Springs, Austin, and Maxwell. They even won the league title in 1954.

Volleyball

Volleyball has long been a popular sport, not only at school, but among adults as well. In the early 1960s, Gerald Brumley, a 1950 DSHS graduate and avid volleyball fan, began to organize adult teams and holding tournaments. Volleyball night was a big event in Dripping Springs. My first experience was in the spring of 1966. As soon as the school basketball season was over, the volleyball season began. Every Monday night from 7:00 to 10:00 P.M. the gym was full of adults playing on the two courts provided. Everyone rotated so that all got to play. Tournaments were held all around the area, with the Methodist and Baptist teams acquitting themselves quite well. As Monday Night Football and other distractions took over, the event started to wane in the 1970s. However, there is a group of adults who still gather each Monday night at the primary school to spend a couple of hours playing the game.

Softball

In 1975, a new brand of ball was introduced to the adults of the community by Carl Waits. It was called slow-pitch softball. Rules were made so that the participants who played were somehow connected to the school district, whether living, working or paying taxes in the district. That has changed in recent years. The men's league was the first to be formed and eight teams signed up for that first spring league season. It has continued to flourish for over a quarter of a century and in 2002, twenty teams were entered in league play. The women let it be known they would not be left out of the fun and petitioned to have a league of their own. The women's league began in the spring of 1976.

In 1989, a men's summer league was formed to continue play for another season.

Youth Sports

Little League baseball was introduced in Dripping Springs in the '50s and continues to be a growing sport among the young people of the community. In the '80s as high school, college, and professional sports escalated, so did the offering of youth sports. Today youth has the option of playing football, basketball, soccer, swimming, and softball, to mention a few. Most are so well

organized that the winning teams can end up playing for a national championship, if they so desire and can raise the funds. The Dripping Springs Youth Sports Association was formed in the '80s to bring all the different youth activities under one umbrella. They acquired land and built baseball fields around 1987. Until that time they had built fields on available school grounds in the district and used the baseball field.

School Activities

From the early days of school history, it seems putting on plays and musical presentations was very popular, especially in the 1880s and '90s. Until the 1960s, junior and senior plays were put on as fundraisers—the juniors to pay for the junior-senior prom and the seniors to raise money for the senior trip. Other plays were put on by different groups to raise money for letter sweaters of the different sports. The UIL one-act play seemed to take the place of class plays. Of course, the growth of the schools made it more difficult to find the time to have class plays.

It did not mention sports in the old newspaper articles that I read, but it is probable they had at least a baseball team in the 1880s. For sure, Dripping Springs played baseball in the '20s. Until the 1930s the Dripping Springs school mostly had classes with less than ten pupils, so it was difficult to have many team sports. Basketball was one of the early sports. A team picture in the possession of the Pound family, gives the date for the girls team as 1911-12. One article I read had Dripping Springs playing Driftwood in 1921. The games had to be played outside because there were no gyms. Dripping Springs did not begin to play regularly in the county tournament held each year until the 1930s. Whether a formal sport or not, you know there were some type of races taking place, and certainly, tennis was an early sport.

Football got its start in 1938 when Dripping Springs joined the six-man ranks. Track has been around, too, and Dripping Springs competed in county meets in the '20s. Volleyball was a popular sport especially during the span when girls basketball was not sponsored by the UIL. Today all the sports, including soccer and powerlifting, are offered in the schools and each has its season.

The band program has been around since 1963 and the drill team has added another activity. Cheerleaders have been around since the 1940 football season and they were accompanied by pep squads.

Dominoes

For a long time dominoes have been one form of family entertainment. I can remember my parents going to a neighbor's house and playing dominoes for several hours while the kids played in another room. The favorites were the regular game of dominoes, 42, and moon. Every chance the men got they broke out a set of dominoes and began to play. Most small towns had small domino halls or tables in a business where a game of dominoes was going on almost any time of the day.

In Dripping Springs avid players finally pitched in enough money to build a little building dedicated solely to dominos. At first it was located on Mercer Street but later moved back near the old Academy building. It was an especially busy place at lunch time. Dominoes do not hold the prominence in today's generation as before but it is still a popular game of entertainment.

Halloween Night

Halloween was always a time for the kids to have their type of fun besides the trick or treat aspect of it. Prior to indoor restrooms, a big deal was made of either turning over the outhouses or moving them to another site. Other tricks, such as putting a cow in the upstairs room of the Academy school building or taking people to haunted (empty) houses, were ingenious and mostly nondangerous. Tootie Felps says in addition to some of the above, they used to stack old tires across Highway 290 between the school fence and Central Garage. Of course there was not as much traffic in the '40s as there is today. He can also remember stacking old tires in the stairwell of the old school building.

When we arrived here in the fall of 1965, that first October found us in the middle of a water balloon war. Not too many Halloweens later, the kids got a little bored with water balloons and decided to take it a step further, using eggs instead of water. Each year kids bought up all the eggs from the stores of the surrounding area plus those of the egg farm owned by the Hildreths. It evolved into a huge mess as they bombed cars and buildings. The streets and buildings looked like one big omelet. Eggs have to be removed fairly quick or they can do damage to whatever they are on, not to mention the smell. The last hurrah occurred when the parking lot of the Glosson Grocery (now the Post Office) took the hits of many dozens of eggs. Even deputy sheriff Alfard Hohman was the target of a couple while sitting in his car. Kids had to come down and clean up the mess and, fortunately, the practice of throwing eggs ceased after that.

Adult Organizations

In reading various newpaper articles, Dripping Springs residents organized activities that seemed to be well attended. In the 1920s and '30s, prior to athletics, a favorite activity seemed to be debates. They picked a subject, more times than not politics, and two or more people debated the issue or candidates. There have always been thespians among the populous. Plays were popular at every age and stage. In the 1980s there was a group who periodically put on plays under the name of 290 Playhouse. There was a Community Recreation Club in the '60s. A rodeo club was formed in the '40s and acreage bought by the members and held ropings each week. We cannot overlook the ice cream parties, Tupperware and Stanley parties, as well as canasta and other types of card and board games. Today Bunco parties are popular.

Anytime there was a mutual interest among a group of people then you could look for an organization being formed to meet those needs. These groups could be informal as well as formal in organization. Hunting and fishing groups are included and in the early days, the newspapers were full of dances taking place, mostly in someone's home.

Things Heard or Read

Part of what makes history so interesting are the tidbits of information that you glean along the way. Newspaper articles often tell the human side of events, and native Springers can tell some stories that are really amusing and show how little things change through the years. A few people cannot resist embellishing facts for entertainment. Facts or fiction? I leave that to your discernment in the following stories.

Grandchildren Charles Hammack and Marjorie Hammack Owens related some stories passed down to them about Dr. Pound.

• Just after completing his medical courses Dr. Pound was diagnosed with tuberculosis. It was believed the only cure was to go to a drier climate. So in 1851-52 he ventured west. He followed the Oregon Trail until he got to Utah and then headed toward Wyoming.

Snow was on the ground and it kept balling up on the horse's hooves, requiring Dr. Pound to stop and remove the snow. He happened to look back at one of these stops and saw a pack of wolves pursuing him with intentions of making meals of him and his horse. He adopted the strategy of shooting the lead wolf as the pack started closing in. The hungry wolves then devoured the fallen leader and after a time chose a new one to continue the pursuit. Dr. Pound had to carry out this strategy several times before he made it to Fort Bridger, the fur trading post that legendary scout Jim Bridger had established in southwestern Wyoming. Fort Bridger had a cluster of tents where Indians stayed. Bridger himself was married to an Indian woman.

When Dr. Pound arrived at the trading post, Bridger was not there. One of the Indians showed him to the Bridger teepee. Dr. Pound pulled back the flap to reveal an Indian lady who beckoned him to come sit by the fire which was a welcome sight after spending days in the cold. Within the hour Bridger arrived, and was very glad to see Dr. Pound. Whether it was because he knew Dr. Pound or was just glad to have someone to converse with in English is not known. Bridger had his wife prepare something for Dr. Pound to eat—a small cake and a glass of water. It hit the spot because he had not eaten that day, but then he felt really bad when he found out he had eaten half their rations with that meal. He made it safely back home later that year.

Being a doctor, the Indians looked upon Dr. Pound as one of the honored "Medicine Men" and seldom bothered him, but that did not keep him from being leery. On one trip he spotted a tree that was loaded down with mustang grapevines ready to be picked. He got down off his horse to see about picking a few as he returned home. Shortly after getting on the ground he spotted a very big moccasin track. Fearing the owner of the track may still be around and not know that he was a doctor, Dr. Pound quickly remounted and hurried home without any grapes.

Those who knew Dr. Pound said he always loved life and enjoyed a good joke. This humor showed through when he was taking a friend home to meet his parents prior to his marriage and trip to Texas. He convinced his friend to go along with his prank. Dr. Pound dressed up like a woman and borrowed a baby. They made it to the Pound house posing as a young couple. The Pounds took them in and offered them a meal, not recognizing Dr. Pound. He chose not to say anything during the meal in the fear it might give him away. After the meal, the neighbor who had loaned the baby came over and the Pounds began to introduce their guests. At this point the lady spilled the beans telling them it was their son Dr. Pound and not a woman. His dad chased Dr. Pound out of the house and into a muddy field outside but was unable to catch him. The mud probably ruined his boots.

• George E. Womack and Susan L. McCown marriage license was announced in the May 1878 issue of SMFP.

• John Lee Wallace and Ike McLendon were among 18 Democratic delegates appointed to attend the state convention from Hays County. In 1878, Hays had 1,568 white kids between 8-17 (200 were eight-year-olds. There were also 448 black kids. (SMFP, July 1878)

• In the September 7, 1878, edition of the *San Marcos Free Press*, was a history of Hays County. The description they gave of Dripping Springs stated that it was "a settlement through which runs the Austin-Fredericksburg road; is an attractive region with good land, fine range, wild game and easy living."

• W. C. Wallace and Ida Roberts marriage license was issued. W. T. Chapman, J. W. Phillips, W. J. Norwood, and B. L. Spaw were elected delegates from Pct. #4 to the Democractic District convention to be held in Luling on 9-24-78. (SMFP, September 1878)

• Marriage licenses were issued for A. K. Daniel and Missouri Runnels, and Wm. M. Crow and Laura A. Lyle. Peter Schmidt was elected commissioner of Pct. #4. Results: Schmidt 67, R. B. Fairchild 34, H. L. Brown 6. (SMFP, November 1878)

• John L. Wallace was chosen to serve on a petit jury in September 1879. (SMFP, August 1879)

• Elder McCarty married P. M. Massey and Miss M. J. Secrest on 9-17-79. (SMFP, September 1879)

• Thomas Voight was selected to serve on the March grand jury. W. T. Chapman served on a petit jury. (SMFP, March 1880)

• I.C.P. "Ike" McLendon wrote an article that said the Walnut Springs Academy (Methodist Church) was consumed by fire around 10:00 P.M. on February 2, 1881. It was deliberately set on fire. Two years earlier the Baptist Church was burned and later the little school house was set on fire but failed to burn. McLendon wanted the culprits found and punished. Also the marriage license of Jeff D. Marshall and Laura Bailey was issued. (SMFP, February 1881)

• Dr. Harrison and his wife visited San Marcos on the 28th. Thomas Voight and W. T. Chapman was selected for grand jury duty. (SMFP, March 1881)

• Rev. Mr. Jordan of Dripping Springs, principal, said the new school building will soon be ready for occupancy. Results of the election for the County seat site were announced. The choice was San Marcos or Hays City. San Marcos 816, Hays City 160, Center 59. Dripping Springs voted 88-0 for Hays City. (SMFP, January 1882)

• Ike McLendon was on a soap box in a report dated 1-18-82. He said a Robert Ross was found frozen to death under a bluff on the Rio Blanco. He claimed the man drank and not being sober was the reason. He blamed the government that would allow the sale of this poison. Three days later he adds that upon further investigation, Mr. Ross evidently was thrown from his mule and he walked off the bluff, breaking his back, ribs, and leg. (SMFP, January 1882)

• The editor of the *Free Press* noted in an 1882 edition that he had received some nice letters extolling the greatness of the new school but the *Free Press* would appreciate them going to work and getting a dozen or two subscribers. That would be the fair thing to do.

• About the middle of January, we moved into our new chapel. The high school department, up to that time, had occupied a room in Rev. Jordan's house, until Academy ready for use. Father Morrell was present when the new chapel was dedicated. He made the talk. (SMFP, May 1882)

• Dr. J. M. Pound, Thomas Voight, and John W. Crow were the delegates from Precinct #4 in the Democratic County convention. (SMFP, July 1882)

• A marriage license for J. P. Sorrell and Hattie McKellar was issued. (SMFP, December 1882)

• Henly was getting ready to build a new store house, gin, and school. (SMFP, April 1883)

• Dr. Harrison saved Mrs. Pursley after a rattlesnake bite. (SMFP, August 1883)

• Ada Ola, daughter of J. A. and R. A. Smith, died on 1-28-84. Mr. Granger bought property at or near Dripping Springs and will remove there. For the construction of the new capitol, a railroad has been built to the Oatmansville quarries, some ten miles from Dripping Springs. It carries passengers, etc. It is a great present convenience and will no doubt be extended to Dripping Springs and insures its future as a flourishing town. (SMFP, February 1884)

• In an 1884 edition of the SMFP, someone wrote an anonymous letter to gig one John Short. John was a local merchant and was by no means short at 6'4". "There was a ball about two miles from Dripping Springs on 2-27-1884. Mr. Short was the musician. During one of the breaks, he stepped out on the porch. He took an extra step and off the porch he went, probably expecting no more than a two-foot drop. But there was a cistern being dug that was another five or six feet deep. Luckily he was unhurt and went back in to play the rest of the night. The letterwriter said that John, a merchant, later sold his violin and concentrated on his mercantile business."

• Peter Schmidt, C. O. Barton, E. H. Wallace, B. F. Stephenson, T. B. Ford, and Dr. J. M. Pound represented Precinct #4 at the Hays County Democratic convention held 7-26-84. (SMFP, July 1884)

• In June of 1885, Eli Justice, a four-year old, was bitten by a rattlesnake on a Monday and died on Tuesday. (SMFP)

• A marriage license was issued for A. L. Davis, Jr., and Miss Willie Herndon. J. W. Crow opened a grocery store three miles from Henly. (SMFP, January 1886)

• Ed Wallace was married to Ada Crow last Wednesday at Mr. Crow's residence. (SMFP, February 1886)

• A marriage license was issued for F. W. Capt and Carrie Bell. (SMFP, September 2, 1886)

• A young man, Wilburn Woods, the stepson of Mr. Reasus, tried to ride a wild horse. It fell on him with the saddlehorn, crushing him so badly that he died. It happened on Saturday and he died on Tuesday. He was buried in the Wallace Mountain Cemetery. (SMFP, November 1886)

• The biggest excitement was Mrs. Fosselman coming to town last Monday and reporting her husband tried to whip her. He was arrested and had to pay a fine. Mr. A. L. Davis had a great party attended by many young people. Rev. Hollis conducted a meeting at the church. (HCTFJ, July 1886)

• Mr. O. Sorrell and Sallie Livingston were married at the bride's father's house a few days ago. (HCTFJ, Sept 1886)

• Thomas Wilhite, son of B. R. Wilhite, was jerked off a horse while roping a steer, and broke his leg below the knee. Some young men in the community have been breaking out window lights with slingshots. Mr. and Mrs. J. A. Smith, now of San Marcos, were visiting. (SMFP, December 1886)

• Some young men were working on the streets and sidewalks under the supervision of Dr. Pound and W. T. Chapman. Ed Wallace sold his ranch at Flat Creek and is moving to Dripping Springs. Ben F. Stephenson lost his youngest child last week to croup. Sam D. Gilpin has a nice stock of Christmas toys. Marriage licenses were issued to W. P. Riley and Lizzie Phillips, and G. W. McCuiston and Nora Simous. (SMFP, December 1886)

• Mr. Banks killed a hog that weighed 358 pounds. Hog law passed in the election. William Reeves died and was given a Masonic funeral at his home. Fireworks went off on Christmas Day, mostly by kids. Graham, Chapman, Davis, Pound, and others practiced shooting a target gun. Dr. Harrison fell off a scaffold while putting paper on the ceiling and broke his ankle. Sam Gilpin had a boy and said it would grow up to be governor of Texas. The A. L. Davises had a girl, the Seborn Stones, a boy, the John McCowans, a boy, the Brookshires, a boy. Mr. L. Jennings died at age of 76. (SMFP, January 1887)

• J. S. Killian, a San Marcos merchant, said he would pay fare to and from home for those who bought a minimum of $10 worth of goods. Mr. Dickey's house was almost complete at Walnut Springs. (HCTFJ, April 1887)

• A. L. Davis reports business was slightly improving. J. N. Marshall opened school on Monday. Professor Horsley returned from a trip to northern part of Texas and reported crops were doing well. Professor G. J. Buck of DuPre was in town with the object of opening an undenominational school at the request of a number of our people. W. A. Mayne left Thursday for Oregon with prospects of making a home there. Others, including W. T. Chapman, spoke of moving to fields anew. (HCTFJ, May 1887)

• Miss Mattie Redd, who had been visiting her uncle, J. L. Wallace, has returned to her home near Austin, leaving some of our boys in mourning. Mrs. Dellah Wallace and Mrs. O'Pry returned from Temple last week visiting friends. Three schools were in session. W. T. Chapman, G. W. Dickey and W. A. Mayne left for the land of milk and honey (California) last Tuesday. G. W. Dickey's new residence at Walnut Springs is all but finished. When occupied, it will be one of the most substantial and commodious in this section of the state. Janet, wife of Mitt Stone, after long suffering, died of consumption, leaving husband and three children to mourn. Artesian wells were being dug. W. W. Caldwell dug one for Sallie McLendon and was now drilling for Captain McLendon. Matt Livingston dug one at Mrs. J. McLendon's at 154 feet and was now drilling one at C. S. Graham's residence. Next Friday the Masons will have a big day. J. L. Wallace and lady have returned from Blanco city where they were visiting. Dick Cruze has moved to Williams ranch. W. T. Chapman wrote a letter about his railroad trip to San Diego, California, dated June 15, 1887. (HCTFJ, June 1887)

• W. T. Chapman wrote another letter, this time from Los Angeles, dated June 24, 1887. He was not too impressed with the area. When he asked one person what their best crop was, the reply was the "Yankee crop." A. Z. Wallace sends good news from California. Operators found water at 85 feet on the Graham's. Professor J. G. Buck returned to Dripping Springs and reopened school on Wednesday. Dripping Springs hosted the Alliance convention. They had a picnic, speeches on prohibition, lemonade in great demand. The hotel was doing a big business. The other stores were closed. A baseball game was played with Dripping Springs beating Cedar Valley 24-6. There will be another game on the 15th. After visiting California and other areas, Mayne, Dickey, and Chapman decided that Dripping Springs is a good place to stay after all. Deputy Sheriff Charley Seal arrested John

Riley on a charge of assault and battery. Mrs. Blyth died just a few days short of her 100th birthday. Mr. Addison R. Davis was in a shooting scrape last Saturday. No one was hurt but he was put under $1,000 bond. There was a baseball game at Cedar Valley on the 15th. Big barbeque. Then after dinner the game commenced. Old Mountain reliable nine outlasted Dripping Springs 20-17. A dance followed the game. Miss Eva Roberts was visiting her sister, Mrs. Ida Wallace, Llano County. Mrs. Voight and family, of Blanco, were visiting relatives. A bright social party was held at the residence of Charles Wallace. It was well attended by the beauty and musical talent of this city and Martindale. C. W. Pound and sister, Mattie, have returned from spending the summer in Green County. The local citizens are trying to raise money so they can form a company to buy machines to dig artesian wells. Area needs the water. (HCTFJ, July 1887)

• Business is looking up. What has become of the mail robber? Telephone communications with Kyle is wanted. Whoop up the artesian well scheme. Mr. Phillips is said to have gotten water by digging out the gravel in Onion Creek. Miss Maude Roberts gave a select musical entertainment last Saturday night. Young Mr. Cook is becoming popular even though he has not been here very long. Miss Emma Phillips is teaching the art of painting. Miss Etta Dibble is again smiling upon her host of friends here. (HCTFJ, August 1887)

• Charles Wallace was kicked by a horse last week. Not as serious as first thought. John Short, of Crow and Short, left for the north with a load of horses. Ed Wallace returned home from the north where he had been with a herd of horses. T. Gilpins had a boy. Professor Cook of Waco was here in interest of the school. It was thought Professor G. J. Buck had been secured for the school but he already had a contract with Science Hall. Miss Jessie McLendon gave a musical entertainment last Wednesday night. Dr. Pound gave a party. Mrs. White, Misses Calhoun and Hollingsworth of Austin visited Mrs. Ed Wallace. School will open soon with Professor Cook heading it up. (HCTFJ, September 1887)

• Sam Pursley and Mattie Wallace were married last Sunday in the home of the bride. Reverend McCarty officiated. J. T. Gilpin's child died and was buried in Wallace Mountain cemetery. Mrs. Wortham of Temple visited her daughter, Mrs. Charles Wallace. (HCTFJ, Oct. 1887)

• Mrs. E. H. Wallace returned from Austin where she was visiting friends. Milam and Mayne have returned from Louisiana where they went with horses. Milam was robbed of $86 by a pickpocket when he was changing cars. E. H. Wallace has returned from Jacksonville, Alabama where he went with horses. Masons had a big time last Saturday night. Successful dance was held at J. M. Livingston. H. C. Wallace was visiting from Llano. School has around 115 students. Masons had a big time last Saturday night. Mrs. Walters is visiting parents in Dripping Springs. (HCTFJ, Nov. 1887)

• Mr. and Mrs. J. L. Wallace went to Llano to visit W .C. Wallace. D. W. Phillips has returned from Indian Nation where he went with cattle. (HCTFJ, December 1887)

• Entertainment was provided at Walter McKellar's on Saturday night. A big supper on Friday was given by John Hamilton. William Martin held a dance. Lee Samuels and Miss Martin were married. Mr. Gilpin put a dynamite cartridge on top of his stove and it blew up taking the stove with it and damaging Frank Graham's ear. Mr. Hobdy died 12-31-87. A Mr. Shults, while looking at land in the area, killed himself with a shotgun. Mrs. Lee, a relative of W. T. Chapman, died. Had some extremely cold weather that froze chickens on the roost. Marriage licenses were issued for W. L. Sorrell and Lizzie Martin, and J.B. Stephenson and Ora Martin. Major Cook is quite ill. Mr. Frank Roberts is laid up with a sore throat. Bleu Gibson is dangerously ill. Major Cook's condition has improved. Mr.

Gibson died as well as a Mrs. Robinson. (SMFP, Jan. 1888)

• Last fall, A. K. Daniel and family, W. P. Collins and wife, W. P. Riley and wife, Nellie and Nora Riley, and several others took 200 head of cattle to New Mexico. It was reported they had lost all the cattle in a freeze. It turned out to not be true. Mr. Hartwig gave an enjoyable party on Friday night. Noticeable were Mrs. McKellar, Mrs. John Spaw, Misses Mittie and Georgia Pound, Misses McKellar, Howard, McLendon, Livingston, Riley, and young ladies of the house. Most of the boys from south Onion Creek to Flat Creek were in attendance. The best was the waltz by Mrs. Hartwig and Mrs. Evart. John Hamilton was the musician. Two young neighbors, Will Graham and Andrew Wallace, went to California some time earlier. Wallace has returned saying he was sick of it and with a bad case of typhoid fever. Says a person can live pleasantly there if they are worth five to ten million dollars. Says Los Angeles is swarming with beggars. Major Cook died. Mr. Crow gave a big party at Millseat. Tom Voight, who formerly ran a gin here, is doing the same in Blanco. Expects to do 1,000 bales this season. (SMFP, Feb. 1888)

• A Colonel Cunningham is pushing grain sorghum as the best coming crop in Texas. Mrs. M. H. Howard is touted for bringing the *Ladies Home Journal* to the area. Miss Willie Chapman is the most lively piano player of the Dripping Springs young ladies. With practice she could be a good musician. Dr. Pound and a Mr. Brooks got into a heated argument. Mr. Brooks could not understand English very well. Pound was talking about cities. Brooks fish. Each thinking they were talking about the same thing. Mrs. Gilpin had to come to the rescue. Miss McLendon and Walter Phillips got married. Will reside on the near side of Onion Creek. On Wednesday evening Mrs. Ed Wallace gave a party at which oysters were the *pièce de résistance*. William Daniels will go up the trail again this year but it is a good bet that Walter Phillips won't. Norther blew in on Saturday night and ice has formed on water. There is fear for the peaches. Mitchell Stone and the widow Sorrells joined their fortunes. Parson Garrison brought the license with him and performed the ceremony and then went 100 yards to Mr. Sieb's house and informed him. It was the first he knew of it. The young men's farmers conference met, as usual, at Dripping Springs. The subject was "How to get shed of crows." Two methods were discussed. (1) Attach horse hairs to grains of corn and strew them over the field. (2) Put tacks in the grain. The writer commented that he thought putting a tax on the crows would drive them out. (SMFP, March 1888)

• Mr. Torrey Gilpin has taken up his residence at Walnut Springs. Says if summer turns dry, he wants to be at a place where he can get a cool drink. Mr. Henry Hunter and Mr. McTice died. (SMFP, April 1888)

• Mrs. O'Pry was known for her sewing talent. The J. Rowland's had a baby girl last Saturday. The rush for Austin has begun. It is a week of drill and dedication of the new capitol. Hacks are filled with bright faces. Miss Sallie Nuckols, Miss Danny Crow, Misses Katie and Cinthy Crow went to Austin. Dr. Pound entertained at his hospitable mansion. Among the ladies were Misses Phillips, Roberts, Williams, Dilly Graham, and Fannie Marshall. Boys were L. Cavett, W. Graham, Tom Livingston, Will, John and Robert Spaw and J. Williams. (SMFP, May 1888)

• Mr. Dye lost a child last week. Mr. John Crow's child swallowed a bean and despite Dr. Harrison's efforts, died a week later in an Austin hospital. The bean had lodged in Allie Crow's windpipe. He was buried in Dripping Springs. (SMFP, June 1888)

• Brother Womack, Misses Pound, Mr. and Mrs. Ed Wallace were all disappointed when they went to New Hope church at Millseat expecting a camp meeting and the preacher did not show up. Jake Sorrell and mother from Red Rock are visiting Lee Sorrell and family. Miss Celita Riley married

John Smith at the home of H. C. Durar. Her mother is Mrs. Warren Collins and they had moved to New Mexico a while back. Miss Riley had been staying with the Durars. Will Spaw was the best man and Dilly Graham the bridesmaid. They were married by Rev. Bell. It was estimated 100 attended. Among those were Mrs. Chapman and her two daughters, the Pounds, Gilpins, Pucketts, Walter McKellars, Mrs. J. Sorrell, Mr./Mrs. Walter Phillips, Mr./Mrs. Spaw, Katie Howard, Jim Roe, I. V. Davis, Herbert Howard, and Jim Howard. After the wedding, dancers were invited to the Hartwig's. Short and Hamilton provided the music. W. T. Chapman presented himself to the Farmers Alliance as a candidate for the state legislature. Major Wallace and family returned home today. (SMFP, July 1888)

• W. T. Chapman is limping and smiling. He has been ailing for four months. There were two parties. A dance at the hotel and later at Major Wallace's. Seems there were more devotees to the ice cream than the floor. Mr. A. L. Davis, Sr., died. Malarial fever rampant. Speaks of a game between Dripping Springs and Cedar Valley. Seems Cedar Valley picked up four players from Austin, but Dripping Springs picked up three from Lockhart. A. L. Davis, Jr., was absent due to his father's death. Cedar Valley won the game played on the 9th. Dripping Springs complained of poor umpiring. (SMFP, August 1888)

• Torrey Gilpin died after a long illness. Younger adults lost a cherished schoolmate. Mrs. Addison Davis is improving after a sick spell. (SMFP, October 1888)

• H. C. Durar had his third son. M. H. Howard returned just before Thanksgiving after being gone for seven months. William Cavett, son of R. S. Cavett, died of typhoid fever. His grandmother died seven weeks prior. Mr. Baird bought the Milam place and moved there with his mother and sister. Mr/Mrs. John Smith moving to the Thurman house. Mr. Kirk and family will occupy the Lincoln place. Will Daniels expected to visit his niece, Mrs. Smith. Miss Etta Wallace is visiting Miss Estelle McKellar. (SMFP, Dec. 1888)

• Big entertainment party was held at Mrs. McLendon's last Wednesday. Misses McKellar, Etta Wallace, Garrett, Tina and Louise Hartwig, Kate Howard, Mattie Redd, Ava and Maud Roberts, Mollie Livingston, Cinthy Crow, Mrs. Walter Phillips, Ollie Sorrell, Walter McKellar, and gentlemen attended from near and far. Jennie Williams died from her illness. Dr. Pound was able to save her sister, Vishta. Miss Georgia Pound has returned. Ed Wallace said he would whip any man that said he was not the happiest man in the world. It's a boy. Florence, the sister of Jennie Williams, also died of typhoid fever. Alpha Caperton is sick with the fever. Mr./Mrs. Walter Phillips had a girl. S. D. Gilpin sick. John Garrett severely cut his foot with an axe. (SMFP, Jan. 1889)

• A Mr. William Adams on Barton Creek died at the age of 89. He was one of the first settlers in the area. Mrs. Sprousett, Cook, Hartwig, Stapleton, and George Moores all had babies. Alpha Caperton has a new piano. A musical and literary society had been formed but failed after a couple of weeks, possibly due to a ten cent initiation fee. Mr./Mrs. John Smith are heading to Wyoming Territory to make their new home. Gilpins are off to Missouri for a visit. (SMFP, Feb. 1889)

• Among the buggies noticed was Mrs. Wallace's neat turnout. She was accompanied by her daughter, Carrie Voight, who had just moved back from Blanco. (SMFP, March 1889)

• Jim Livingston and family are going to New Mexico. Mr. Powell and I.V. Davis are going too. Mr. Bunn Daniel has moved into the Hamilton house. His mother is quite ill. Mr. H. C. Durar shot his arm off a month ago while taking a shotgun out of the wagon. He is improving. A. L. Davis has a fine assortment of summer goods. Dr. Gilpin has returned. (SMFP, May 1889)

• Mrs. Garrett shut up her town house and moved back to the ranch, now that school is out. Shortly after arriving in Lusk,

Wyoming, John Smith died. His wife survived the disease and now has an infant son she named after his dad. Supposed to have a grand concert here next Friday. The concert was well received. Mrs. Plummer, Miss Jones, and Mrs. Estelle returned from their fishing trip on the Pedernales River, attended the concert and stayed with the John Wallaces. The teacher for the concert was Mrs. McLendon. Mr. Hamilton sang and played the guitar. After Mr. Williams and family left the hotel, it is closed up. They moved to Blanco. (SMFP, June 1889)

• Dripping Springs baseball team beat Round Mountain 52-1. Mrs. John Hamilton fell and broke her ankle. Rev. Jordan preached at the Academy. Mrs. Boardman has been staying with Mrs. Wallace. Had a circus in town that included prairie dogs, badgers, trained goats and tight rope dancer. Had a big band. Dr. Pound and family returned from a trip. (SMFP, July 1889)

• Dr. Gilpin and wife had a girl. One of Mrs. Gibson's sons was dragged to death by a horse. He got caught in the stake rope when the horse spooked. Matt Livingston did not like the West and returned. He is staying with his mother, Mrs. C. S. Graham, on Barton Creek. Mrs. John Smith has rejoined her mother, Mrs. Collins, in Washington Territory. Will O'Pry is successful in Asia of Polk County. His mother still resides in a pretty little house in Dripping Springs. Jake Sorrell is in town. Dripping Springs nine beat Cedar Valley-Driftwood 16-1. The Boiling Springs nine beat the Dripping Springs Kids 17-9. (SMFP, August 1889)

• Mr and Mrs Loman have moved back to town. Mrs. A. L. Davis is entertaining her sister, Miss Herndon, from Weimar. Mr. Mayne is making molasses at home. Robert Caldwell received a badly broken arm from the kick of a horse. Miss Georgia Pound is off to Fredericksburg for a visit. Miss Love Pound is going to Blanco to stay with her sister, Mrs. Walters, and go to school there. On Friday night the gin ran all night. Miss Byus married Mr. Patterson. A Mr. Sanders, a young man, died and was buried in Wallace Mountain Cemetery. Dripping Springs beat the Kyle Lone Stars 21-17 in a baseball game. A letter from a Dripping Springs ballplayer derides the Kyle team for blaming their loss to Dripping Springs on the umpire. Said they did not blame this umpire last year when Kyle won. George W. Dickey and I.C.P. McLendon were named to an executive committee to help raise funds for the Confederate Home of Texas. (SMFP, September 1889)

• Daily bell reminds us that school is in session. More than half the students who should be in school are missing due to picking cotton. They are earning money for needed articles. Gay music resounded last Friday as young people danced a blithe measure at Mr. Ed Wallace's pleasant home. Mrs. John Hamilton presented Mr. Hamilton with a son. Mrs. Rose from outside Dripping Springs added another little one to the family. Entertainment last Friday was given at Mrs. Howard's to celebrate the return of Mr. Jim Howard, who had been traveling in the north for the past several months. Mrs. Harrison has been ill. Miss Della Mayne has been quite ill and has been unable to attend school. Miss Herndon started on Sunday to return to Weimar. (SMFP, Oct. 1889)

• H. C. Durar was appointed postmaster. A double wedding took place for the daughters of J. W. Phillips. Emma became Mrs. Will Graham and Hattie, Mrs. George Cooke. Rev. J. A. Garrison performed the ceremonies. The C. S. Grahams gave a reception and dinner for the couples. Many locals attended the reception. Chapmans, Phillips, A. L. Davises, McMillans, H. Howards, Matt Livingston, Ollie Sorrell, H. C. Durar, Mr. Murphy, Jim Rowe, Charley Seal, Birdie McLendon, I.C.P. McLendon, Walter Phillips, Herbert, Jim and Katie Howard, Miss Roberts, Alice Rowe, Miss McMillan, Mrs. Scroggins, and Mrs. McLendon. Will Graham rented the Williams place and Cookes will spend the winter in Dripping Springs. Addison Davis married Fannie Dickey. (SMFP, Nov. 1889)

• Dripping Springs is well-filled. Schools are giving great satisfaction. Occasionally someone goes to Austin. Miss Etta Wallace visited for a brief while. Miss May Herndon was visiting her sister, Mrs. A. L. Davis. She was enjoying a drive in a new buggy behind two matched horses. Miss McMillan also has a new buggy. They are having a great time carting their friends around. Mr. Loman's mother, brother, and family have moved to Dripping Springs. Mr. Phillips and family moved into their Dripping Springs residence last week. Mrs. Sorrell has moved to town. Tom Cavett cut his foot with an axe. People getting ready for Christmas. Had concerts on Thursday and Friday to raise funds for school repair. Had a Christmas tree at the Academy on Christmas Eve. Fireworks everywhere were scaring the horses. One casualty was Mrs. Wallace's buggy when the horse bolted and broke it into pieces. Parties were numerous. Mr. Ed Wallace had one Christmas Eve. Others during the week were at the McLendon's, Crow's, John Wood's, Bill Martin's, and Dr. Harrison's. (SMFP, Dec. 1889)

• Dave Jones has returned and is about to settle permanently. I. V. Davis has also returned. Herbert Howard will be helping his dad ship horses north and west in the spring. Mr. Garrett moved his family back to the ranch for spring and summer. Baseball player Charlie Malott had a girl. Katie Howard is staying with Miss Caperton. Since the death of her husband, Mrs. Walters of Blanco has been staying with her father, Dr. Pound. Mr. and Mrs. Ed Wallace had a son. Mrs. Will Wallace and family are visiting Mrs. John Wallace. (SMFP, Jan. 1890)

• A cold snap took care of the gardens and fruit trees. Mrs. Caperton has been very sick. Mrs. Cooke is also ill. Mrs. B. Stephenson lost seven year old son, Clarence. Dr. Pound and Dr. Harrison have been ill. Kate Harrison has been visiting. Tom Loman is quite sick. Mrs. Sparr is improving after her sickness. (SMFP, March 1890)

• Big rain last night. Ed Wallace has decided to settle in Hye, Blanco County. Dr. Herndon preached at the Academy. Mr. Biggs has been preaching at the Methodist Church. (SMFP, April 1890)

• Reverend Jasper Newton Marshall is to be married to Miss Kemp of Johnson City. Mr. Lienneweber has moved into the house just vacated by Ed Wallace. Mr. Durar's bookkeeping class is progressing. Dr. Harrison and party caught 90 fish on Onion Creek. M. C. Cavett sent east for some Jersey Red pigs that grew much larger than others around. His neighbors had scoffed at his enterprise but he soon had made his expenses back when he sold their offspring. He also sent off for Longshanks and Plymouth Rocks which have produced larger and heavier eggs. McKellar and Sorrell own some fine stallions that make others look like ponies. Mrs. Harrison is suffering from rheumatism. Squire Rowe is getting his shop in order to work. Dripping Springs citizens were urging Blanco to push for a railroad from Austin to Blanco. Colonel Crow came through to go fishing on the Pedernales. He left his wife at the Wallace's and took Major Wallace, Andrew and Charley Wallace, and Mr. Roberts. Mr. Roberts took ill and Dr. Pound was summoned to the house of M. W. Howard. Mr. Herndon paid a short visit to daughter, Mrs. A. L. Davis, but did not take Effie Herndon with him. Writer advocated getting the money together to get railroad through Dripping Springs. (SMFP, May 1890)

• Mrs. William Livingston, not yet 21, died leaving two small children. She was the daughter of the late Mr. Walters of Blanco. Mr. Massey fell off the roof of his two-story house but luckily suffered only bruises. Mr. Bryant's one year old child was kicked in the head by a horse. Dr. Harrison is attending. Dr. Pound and his daughter, Mrs. Walters, took off for a month long trip out west. Several cattle drives have been made to Llano. A. L. Davis bought a lot of horses for shipment. Mr. and Mrs. Will Graham will be making their home in Buda. Started there June 23. (SMFP, June 1890)

• Miss Fannie Marshall will marry D. W. Burkett at the W. T. Chapman residence.

Jim Livingston died suddenly at his son, Matt's house. Marshall-Burkett wedding took place July 15. The writer said as he got ready to go, a gentle shower fell and there were claps of thunder. Most of the town was there. He named 43 people other than the wedding party and said there were others. Reverend Bell married the couple. Dr. Stewart and the bride's sister, Willie Chapman, assisted. The couple will be living near Fischer store. Dr. Pound and Mrs. Walters have returned. Miss Estelle McKellar expected home shortly. Traveling neighbors returning. Mrs. Caperton is back. Mr. Loman and Mr. and Mrs. Stapleton are enroute. Mr. and Mrs. Tom Loman have moved into the Garrett house. (SMFP, July 1890)

• School progessing under Professor A. L. Stubbs and R. L Marshall. The Walter Phillips family is heading for Mason County where they expect to make their home. W. P. Riley and J. W. Graham families started for Eddy, New Mexico, to make their home. (HCTFJ, October 1891)

• School opened September 7 and after a two-month successful private term, began November 2 with 90 students. During private term, all students received good grades in written and oral work in recitations and examinations. (HCTFJ, November 1891)

• State law stated after 9-1-1898, the textbooks will be introduced and used to the exclusion of all others. (*Blanco County News*, August 1898)

• Dr. A.V. Duncan, MD, advertised his office as being in the Blanco High School. (BCN, December 1898)

• Mr. Garrett of Dripping Springs bought the barber shop in Blanco from J. C. Neill. (BCN, September 1904)

• The party at Mr. and Mrs. Marvin Hudson's was quite an enjoyable occasion. The hypnotic power of Mr. Lamar, when applied to two of the young men, created much sport and amusement for those present. In all, everyone had a good time. Rev. Peal and family are now domiciled at the hotel. D. G. Jones' residence is nearing completion and when finished, will be the nicest building in town. He is having the gallery built in Colonial style, which adds much to the appearance all together. (DSP, 5-11-05)

• The entertainment given by Miss Emma McCuistion last Thursday night was greatly enjoyed by all the young people. Just arrived at D. G. Jones, a nice line of glassware, such as butter dishes, sugar bowls, molasses, pitchers, and other nice things. W. J. Norwood sold $2,000 worth of trees last week to Will Green of San Marcos. This was the largest order ever turned in to the Ramsey nursery at this time. Bob Spaw has discovered a worm that kills the boll weevil. Charley Smith and family are preparing to move to Dallas. Miss Babe Livingston has gone to Hill Country on a visit. B. L. Spaw and wife took her to Austin. The member of the library having volume 1 of the *Conquest of Mexico*, will, if through with it, please return it to the library and oblige a member. Mr. Jones' house is completed and is the finest house in town. It has modern conveniences in the way of water system and etc., the water being supplied from a large rock cistern. (DSP, 5-25-05)

• Dave Martin and W. T. Shugart were in town a short while looking to their telephone interests. R. E. Spaw, president of the Inter-Urban Telephone Company was here this week putting up telephone posts and arranging for putting in a telephone exchange. He already had 24 phones spoken for and others wanting them. He has gone to order the phones and start work on the gap in his line between Blanco and Henly. (BCN, February 1906)

• Mr. Spaw is preparing to put up his wires here in town and will soon have his exchange in. He will also have the gap between Blanco and Henly closed and the Blanco people can speak directly to Austin. For the present, Mr. Spaw will have his switchboard in the Blanco Bank building. (BCN, March 1906)

• The telephone men are pretty busy now. The Martin line is being wired and Mr. Spaw is stringing the lines for his company. Won't be long now. (BCN, April 1906)

• Talk is cheap if you have one of Spaw's lines. Residence phones are $12 a year, commercial $18. Marvin Hudson of Dripping Springs is visiting his old Blanco home this week and assisting in the telephone. The private neighborhood telephone line up the river is now running into town and connected with our exchange. R. E. Spaw is here this week with hands putting in phones and arranging the exchange. His switchboard is in the bank building. (BCN, April 1906)

• Telephone exchanges are both being put up and wires strung. Talk has already begun and no telling when it will end. (BCN, April 1906)

• Mr. Spaw informs us he expects the gap to be closed between Blanco and Henly by next week and we can talk directly to Austin. (BCN, April 1906)

• Advertisement: Sylvan Nursery of Dripping Springs—P. M. Ross, Blanco representative. Mr. Spaw, the telephone man, has moved his family to Blanco. (BCN, May 1906)

• R. E. Spaw was here on a visit to his family last Sunday. He is at work on his telephone line from Dripping Springs to Wimberley at which place he will connect with the Wimberley, Purgatory, and San Marcos line. He has purchased that line and as soon as he makes connection will be able to give telephone service direct to San Marcos. He thinks inside of a month the line will be in operation. (BCN, July 1906)

• Dr. Pound came by with Mr. and Mrs. Palmer on his return from the Confederates reunion at Mason. Next year it is to be held in Fredericksburg. (BCN, August 1906)

• Miss Mattie Voight left Thursday to visit Austin friends. (SMTJ, August 1906)

• Misses Herndon, Ethel Davis, Lucy Holmes, and Pallie McGehee returned from touring California and Colorado. Return delayed 14 hours because of a train wreck. (SMTJ, August 1906)

• Ed Day and Mrs. C. H. Berkley will teach in Wimberley school another year. (SMTJ, August 1906)

• A. B. Egger of Dripping Springs was in Wimberley on Monday for business. (SMTJ, August 1906)

• J. W. Phillips and wife of Dripping Springs returned home after a pleasant visit with Van Clark of San Marcos. (SMTJ, September 1906)

• W. J. Norwood of Dripping Springs was in San Marcos Tuesday with his daughter who is entering Normal for another term. Robert Spaw, the hustling telephone man of Blanco City has nearly completed his line from Dripping Springs to this place (Wimberley). He will extend it straight through to San Marcos. He is also talking of constructing a line from Fisher's Store to Wimberley. Mrs. O. V. Ward has returned home after lengthy stay in Wimberley. (SMTJ, September 1906)

• First automobile ever seen in Henly was here the last day of August. Misses Lois McKellar and Mamie Hudson returned to their home in Dripping Springs. (BCN, September 1906.

• W. J. Norwood, the fruit tree man, is here today taking orders for Ramsey's Nurseries of Austin. (SMTJ, October 1906)

• Mrs. Jane McLendon of Dripping Springs is visiting here in Mt. Sharp. (SMTJ, August 1907)

• People of Dripping Springs were getting excited about the prospects of hitting oil. One was being dug on W. J. Norwood's place and another to be dug on J. L. Patterson's. (SMR, April 1920)

• The Woodman of the World had a barbeque last Saturday. An estimated 2,000 attended. Candidates spoke and there was a baseball doubleheader between Dripping Springs-Blanco and Driftwood-Cedar Valley. There was also dancing and other amusements. Jake Riley, 60, died of acute indigestion. He was buried in the Methodist graveyard. About 50 children marched from the cemetery to the grave scattering flowers ahead of the funeral procession. Several carloads came from Austin. (SMR, July 1920)

• Edwin Waller, a Hays County politician, ran for many offices in his career, winning few, if any. He always had some comment as to why not. He accused his opponents of dirty politics. Community picnics were the avenue for most politicians' campaigning. At the Henly picnic Waller was the last of the candidates who spoke. It was agreed among them that at the Dripping Springs picnic, the order would be reversed. When his opponents found out there would be a baseball game at DS that would begin before all the speeches were made, they changed their minds and had Waller speak last again. This left him speaking to mostly empty seats. He accused the other candidates of going through the crowd making sure they knew the game was starting. (SMR, June 1922)

• George Conn, who accidentally shot himself during Christmas week, is improving fast. He was not expected to live at first but is now doing nicely. Mrs. R. L. Sansom died last Saturday. She was the daughter of A. C. Applewhite. She was survived by her husband, two-year old child, and an infant baby. Clyde Applewhite was her brother. (SMR, Jan. 1928)

• W. R. Baird lost his barn and contents to fire last Sunday night. Leon Moffatt broke a collarbone while playing baseball. Olga Cobb and Miss Aletha Cavett of Driftwood were married March 31 at four o'clock at the residence of Rev. and Mrs. A. D. Rogers, with Rev. Rogers, pastor of First Christian Church reading the ceremony. The witnesses were Hudson Dildy and Miss Leona Eckols, Horace Eckols, and Miss Nell Wallace, Frank Hall, and Miss Clara Williamson. (SMR, March 1928)

• Four members of the W. F. Rippy's family and two others fell victim to arsenic poisoning from a bucket of arsenic being thrown in their well. On July 18, Mrs. Rippy, her three children and two small children of Oris Anderson became violently ill after drinking water from the well. The bucket was discovered when the well was cleaned out. Rippy had been a witness in a goat theft case. This might have been the impetus. The Rippys moved to Mt. Sharp from Bandera two years earlier to engage in goat and sheep ranching. (SMR, July 1928)

• Mr. and Mrs. H. E. Pantermuehl purchased a new Chevrolet from Wade Crenshaw of Dripping Springs. Miss Vida Ada Quick visited Miss Myrtis Earp in Dripping Springs. Mr. Earl Wood is retiring from the mercantile business in Dripping Springs and is having a new residence erected on his ranch near Dripping Springs. Mr. and Mrs. Billie Garnett bought a new Dodge sedan Tuesday in Austin. (SMR, Nov. 1928)

• Mrs. Granvel Huey, the daughter of Dr. E. P. Shelton died last Monday. She is survived by her husband and five small children. (SMR, Jan. 1929)

• Oran Rippy was shaken but not seriously injured when the horse he was loping got his leg caught in the fender of a car they were meeting. Tore the fender right off the car. Mr. and Mrs. W. F. Rippy purchased a new Whippet car this week in San Marcos. (SMR, Feb. 1929)

• The Dripping Springs school gave a benefit play Saturday night and raised $64.50. (SMR, March 1929)

• The Elsner oil well #1 caved in last Friday night. They will continue drilling in a few days. (SMR, Sept. 1929). The Elsner well is now down to 1,075 with splendid indications of oil. (SMR, Dec. 1929). The Elsner well is down to 2,300. Prospects looking good. (SMR, Feb. 1930)

• W. H. Crenshaw, 75, died at his home in Dripping Springs after 1:00 P.M. Wednesday. He is survived by his wife and six children: sons: D. W. Crenshaw, C. W. Crenshaw. daughters: Mrs. Frank Sansom, Mrs. B. F. Mading, Mrs. A.V. Etheridge, Mrs. Mance Cockrill. (BCN, January 1931)

• The San Marcos PTA defeated the Dripping Springs PTA women 12-8. Playing for Dripping Springs were Brooks, A. Follis, Brumley, Lawrence, Kennedy, Spaw, Glimp, V. Follis, Stubbs and Baskett. (SMR, June 1931)

• Earl E. Woods was found dead in his bed last Tuesday by his wife, Barbara

Patterson Woods. He was 39 and lived one mile north of town. He had played in a baseball game on Saturday. He went fishing with relations and came home feeling a little bad. However, he went to bed feeling a little better. Doctor said he died from a stroke of appoplexy. He had been in the stock and mercantile business. A big picnic attended by 2,500-3,000 netted the school $93. The ballgame results were the school boys lost to Goforth, the Dripping Springs men beat Fitzhugh, and the Wimberley women beat Dripping Springs. The music was provided by Professor Peavy, the assistant principal. (SMR, July 1931)

• Commissioner J. D. Rust reports the bridge over Onion Creek on the Mr. Gainer road has been completed. It is 198 feet long with five openings. It was built mostly by community labor and cost the county about $500 for material. It is on the way from the main highway to the dam built last year. (SMR, March 1932)

• Mrs. Carter Breed died May 20. She is survived by her husband and five children: Cecil, D. B., Norman, Doris, and Ima Lois; parents, Mr. and Mrs. Jim Spillar; three brothers: Henry, Jim, Sam; four sisters: Mrs. Mary Eggers, Mrs. Lou Breed, Mrs. Sadie Champion, and Mrs. Liddie Thielepape. (SMR, May 1932)

• Dripping Springs announced a big free barbeque on June 23. There will be ball games, speaking, old fiddlers contest, etc., and a negro minstrel and other activities at the school that night. (SMR, June 1932)

• Mrs. Katie Davis received a broken collarbone and shoulder bone in a car wreck in Austin on November 17. Her daughter, Mrs. H. O. Lucas received a fractured skull and serious cuts and bruises about the head (she died of her injuries). Mrs. Lucas's son, Harvie, Jr., received minor cuts. A daughter, Margaret, and Bradley Davis escaped injury. (SMR, November 1932)

• A play was given at the school to raise funds for playground equipment. Despite the bad weather, it raised $13.50. There was a large crowd. Taking part were Annie Follis, Opal Brumley, Lillie Susan Miles, Merle Elsner, Vivian Thielepape, Mrs. Cecil Breed, Nellie Pierson, Nola St. Clair, and Elbert Davis, Ulmer Follis, Norman Breed, and Harvey King. Music was provided by P. L. Turner, Jarrell Galimore, and Harvey King. The play was prompted by Mrs. Peters. (SMR, December 1932)

• Mr. and Mrs. John Spaw had all their children at home for Christmas. Mr. and Mrs. Will Spaw and children of Floresville, Mr. and Mrs. Johnny Spaw and children, Mrs. Nellie Pierson and son Bennie, Mr. and Mrs. Lewis Brooks, Mr. and Mrs. Tom Spaw and children, Mr. and Mrs. John McGee, Mr. and Mrs. Van Spinks and Mr. Beverly Spaw of Austin. (SMR, December 1932)

• On Monday, January 9, Mrs. Robin Stephenson died. She was the primary teacher at the school. (SMR, January 1933)

• H. H. King and O. S. Brumley announced plans for the big barbeque picnic to be held June 14. Expected to be the biggest gathering in Hays County this year. Proceeds of the sale of refreshments will go to benefit the school. An estimated crowd of 2,000 attended the picnic. Dr. E. P. Shelton was the emcee and at least 25 candidates for public office spoke. (SMR, June 1934)

• The boys coach for Dripping Springs was Champion Callihan. He played football for San Marcos and Southwest Texas. He made the Ripleys "Believe It or Not" column for his 105 yard punt in a game. (SMR, September 1934)

• Clarence T. Shelton of Dripping Springs made the starting team at shortstop for the Baylor University freshman. Miss Margaret Stewart, a teacher of home economics and the sixth and seventh grades, resigned to take a county home demonstrator job for Clay County. Bradley Davis was hired to finish out the year. (SMR, March 1935)

• In an article about A. L. Davis, Jr., and the baseball teams he played on and sponsored at Dripping Springs, was a picture of the 1896 team. Members of that team were Davis, Rufus Smith, Ed Lindeman, Will Richie, Cal Brown, Jim Eckols, Albert

Sprouse, Jim Richie, Sam Trautwein, Chester Harrison, and Arthur Bagley. Davis was the pitcher. (SMR, August 1935)

• Charles C. Haydon was found dead in his automobile about four miles east of Dripping Springs. He died of a heart attack on May 2. He had made a trip to San Antonio with his daughter, Nina, to get tractor parts on Monday. He dropped her off in Austin after assuring her he felt well enough to drive home. Enoch Needham, WPA worker, found him slumped in the seat and his coat acting as a pillow on the back of the seat. Funeral services were held in Dripping Springs for Allen Stephenson, Jr., 15, who died Monday at 5:30 P.M. following complications of injuries received in a baseball game on April 26. He suffered fractures in both bones and it damaged blood vessels causing gangrene. (SMR, May 1938)

• The outside playground girls baseball team beat Buda Friday evening 10-5. Members of the team were Willie Mae Haydon, Delores Conn, Evelyn Brumley, Edith Goslin, LaRue Sansom, Juanita Schneider, Marie Spaw, Lillian Hollingsworth, and captain Opal Brumley. Evelyn Brumley broke a finger in the game. B. C. Mann of Thomas Drilling has moved his machinery to Frank Reeder's place. Will begin to drill for oil in a few days. The Night Owls girls club went to Corpus Christi. Those going were Marie Spaw, Laverne Crenshaw, Evelyn and Elois Brumley, Grace Conn, Bettie Mae Black, Freddy Ray Elsner, Opal Brumley, Mrs. W. P. Crow, Mrs. James Ferrell, Mrs. Virgil Conn, Mrs. Ralph Owens and Mrs. Alva Haydon. (SMR, June 1939)

• An article about the history of Dripping Springs said it had two stores, three garages, a beauty shop, a barber shop, theater, two cafes, a post office, drugstore, blacksmith shop, and wool and mohair warehouse. Will Crow is the owner of the largest store and warehouse. Samp McLendon is the postmaster. Eldridge "Pete" Glosson and Naoma Black were married last Saturday night. (SMR, September 1939)

• W. S. McLendon died suddenly on Monday night at the age of 63 from a stroke of apoplexy while driving back from a neighbors. He was the postmaster for two years. He is survived by his daughter, Mrs. E. H. Davis and one sister, Mrs. Frank Graham. W. S. Malott and Mrs. Beulah Haydon were married last Thursday in Austin. (SMR, October 1940)

• J.W.T. "Snooks" Goslin was killed in an accident while going to the Del Valle airport to work. The truck turned over and he was suffocated by the gas fumes. (SMR, August 1942)

• The year 1948 was not good for prominent men in Dripping Springs. Three died of gunshot wounds. Bill Garnett, 45, owner of the Gulf station and garage, was shot in the chest with a rifle in Austin on December 29 by Raymond S. Turner, 33, of Dripping Springs. Mr. Turner was charged with murder when Mr. Garnett died on January 3 but pleaded self-defense. Mr. Garnett had hid in the trunk of the car while his wife had driven to Austin. She stopped and he got out of the car when two guys were approaching the car to talk to Mrs. Garnett. Mrs. Garnett, who claimed she did not know her husband was in the car tried to drive off. In the meantime, Mr. Turner shot Mr. Garnett in the chest with a small rifle from about 30 yards. Mr. Garnett had a tire tool. Mr. Turner was found not guilty of murder. (SMR, January 1948)

The next to fall was McCreary "Buck" Crow, 21, the only son of W. P. Crow. He was killed on Sunday, July 18, at an address on old Fredericksburg road. Mr. Crow and his bride of eight months went out for the evening with Mr. and Mrs. C. H. Roper. After getting back, an argument ensued. The argument elevated to the point that Dr. Roper, a dentist, ended up shooting and killing Mr. Crow around 3:30 in the morning. Mrs. Crow was pregnant at the time and Mr. Crow never got to see his only son, William McCreary Crow. Dr. Roper was sentenced to five years. (SMR, July 1948)

On October 6, 1948, O. M. Williamson, 54, a cafe operator, was shot and killed by

Bill Kuykendall as he and friends were headlighting on Mr. Kuykendall's ranch. Mr. Kuykendall called a couple of people and when they arrived they found Mr. Williamson alive but unable to talk. He died a few minutes later. Mr. Kuykendall was charged but was no-billed by the grand jury. (SMR, October 1948)

• A blizzard is in its fifth day. School has been out for a week. The trees are weighed down to the ground. Buses can't make their runs. Only the mailman, Earl Pursley, is making it each day. (SMR, January 1948)

• J. W. Wilson tells this story about a traveling salesman who stopped at the cafe located in the old Breed Meat Market, known as Tiny's Cafe, and bought a cup of coffee. He complained about the cost of the coffee. At that time, Ernest Williamson, the son of the owner, Mr. O. M. Williamson, said that a cup of coffee was a nickel and if you wanted cream, seven cents. The owner explained that the coffee was free, the charge was for dirtying the cup. In that case, the salesman replied, I want the cup saved and that way the next time I come through, the coffee will be free. The cup was placed high upon a shelf. J. W. said the cup was still there in 1949 when he moved his radio and TV business into the building.

• Mrs. E. P. Shelton died of a stroke after having been ill for several years. Mr. Maxwell of the Church of Christ conducted the service. A. B. Tiner, one of the owners of what would become the Lomis Slaughter place, was killed on his ranch when the guard on his tractor power saw came loose and hit him in the head on January 11, 1951. (SMR, January 1951)

• The Central Service Station was robbed on August 12, a Sunday night. In an unrelated incident, Leroy Roberts, the owner of the Central Service Station, suffered a stroke last week. (SMR, August 1951)

• Mr. and Mrs. W. Tiner of San Antonio but owners of a ranch in Dripping Springs were killed in an automobile crash near Manor. He was the brother of A. B. Tiner, who had been killed in January. Four year old Mike Davidson was stricken with polio two weeks ago. He is in an iron lung but not critical. (SMR, October 1951)

• W. R. Baird, 91, died Friday, August 8. He was born in 1861 and came to Dripping Springs in 1884 and has lived here since. (SMR, August 1952)

• Lester Brenizer, the owner of the Dickey place on RR12 S, was killed in an automobile accident on March 30 while returning from Ft. Worth. (KN, April 1954)

• Mrs. Georgia Pound Cavett recollected about the early life of Dripping Springs. She said they got their logs from Jackson Branch located south of Dripping Springs to build their log cabins. At first the children were taught in private schools and then a one-teacher school was built. The roads were poor with the maintenance being done by the locals. The first telephone was installed in the A. L. Davis store. A blacksmith shop was located where the Alva Haydon house now stands. Pedernales Lienneweber had a grist mill near the Travis Garnett home. Tom Boyett (Voight) had a windmill to grind corn on the old Berkley place. (SMR, May 1954)

• Mr. and Mrs. W. F. Rippy escaped serious injury when their pickup, loaded with feed, hit a bridge and overturned near Bastrop. They received minor but painful injuries. (HCC, April 1956)

• Mrs. Georgia Cavett broke her hip several weeks ago. (SMR, September 1956)

• The people are busy setting back their fences in preparation for the Super Highway getting ready to be put through Dripping Springs soon. Ike Roberts is having another well drilled. The other one that furnished water for many the past 70 years went dry. Mrs. Gertrude Clayton was transferred to Hallettsville by the telephone company. Mr. and Mrs. Felix Lindsey celebrated their Golden anniversary. (HCC, April 1957)

• While oiling a truck on a rack in his service station on Monday, Charlie Neal Haydon was crushed against the wall when the truck slipped off the rack. His leg was broken between the knee and hip. He is doing nicely now though. George A. Wiest was involved in a wreck that killed his 13-year-old son, George R., and broke the leg of 11-year-old David. Construction work on the new highway is making progress. Plenty of noise and dust. Two cars were washed off the Onion Creek bridge while trying to cross. K. C. Whisenant and his son, Raymond, rescued the passengers. (HCC, June 1958)

• The old pear tree belonging to Ike Roberts has never failed to produce pears in the 45 years he has owned the place. Produced ten bushels so far this year. (HCC, September 1958)

• Harrell Robinson, a recent DSHS graduate, had a couple of fingers blown off when a dynamite cap exploded in his hand. A group of M. C. Cavett relatives came to visit the Ike Roberts' place. Cavett owned that place many years ago. They came to see the hand dug well and rock building where cheese was made. The Roberts had torn down the old Cavett home and built a rock one in its place. (HCC, June 1959)

• The Virgil Conn's car was stolen from their store. It was found in San Antonio. (HCC, September 1959)

• Dial telephones have been installed. (HCC, January 1960).

• Marvin Burrier was killed when a truck tire he was fixing a flat on at the Garnett-Glosson Humble station blew up and the rim hit him. (HCC, March 1963)

• Jimmy Shelton, a sophomore at Southwest Texas and son of Mr. and Mrs. Robert Shelton, had his design for all SWT academic publications chosen from among 25 designs submitted from the art students of Dr. Ted Franks, head of the Art Department. Shelton was also chosen to be the cartoonist for the campus newspaper, *The College Star*. (HCC, July 1963)

• Mrs. Lou Glosson died at the age of 78. She was survived by five sons, three daughters, and three sisters (SMR, January 1964)

• W. P. Crow, president of the Dripping Springs Water Supply Corporation, announced that construction was underway. It included a 600-foot well. (HCC, July 1964)

• No history of any town would be complete without a story of hidden treasure. Katherine Cannon tells the story of a hidden treasure on the John Lee Wallace place she now owns. It served as a stagecoach stop in the early days between Austin and Fredericksburg and places farther west. One man who carried large sums of gold or silver frequently traveled back and forth along the route. One time he became afraid he was going to be robbed, so he found a hollow in one of the oak trees and stashed the money there, to be picked up on his return through. He drove a nail in the tree to mark it. As fate would have it, the man was killed while away. Many have searched the area, including Mrs. Cannon, in the hopes of finding the infamous hollow with the treasure in it. If there ever was a treasure, more than likely it was found quite early and not reported. Nevertheless, there is always hope.

• Ed McKellar lived across the road and back up the hill from the J. L. Patterson place. They had a big pear orchard.

• Alva Haydon recalls a two-story house once existed on the block where he now lives. It had big curved porches upstairs and downstairs. It was the old A. L. Davis house. It burned in the early '30s nearly taking the house across the street with it. After the Charles Haydons purchased the Lou Breed house (now Short Mama's), they moved their other house (the old Huey house) to the site of the present Alva Haydon house. It was rented out to workers helping to pave Highway 290. Was pretty dilapidated by the early '40s.

• Once while taking communion at church where they used real wine, Logan Dye bypassed the little cup and drank out of the pitcher. His comment was "if this little cup can do me some good, then this pitcher should do me a whole lot of good."

• W. R. "Buddy" Baird used to brag that he held his wife, Edna, in his arms when she was a baby. This was probably true because he was 35 years old when she was born.

• W. R. "Buddy" Baird, who raised watermelons and drove a Model T Ford, was known as "One Shot Buddy" at the Garnett Gulf Station because he never bought more than one gallon of gas at a time. He would get out his measuring stick and put it in the gas tank located under the seat. He would not buy gas until it fell below a certain mark and then only one gallon.

• Dripping Springs got its first traffic light at the intersection of 290 and RR12 in December 1987. Until then, a blinking caution light sufficed.

• According to Bradley Davis, Earl Woods and Barbara Patterson, the daughter of J. L. Patterson wanted to get married but Mr. Patterson would not give his consent. They decided to elope. Barbara went into the house while Earl kept the buggy nearby. Barbara threw her clothes out the window of her room and off they went to get married.

• According to Doris Davidson, the big tree near the road at her house on Old Fitzhugh Road was called the Hanging Tree. Purportedly it got its name, not from the hanging of people, but because it was used to hang animals that were being butchered. Also rumored was that a band of Indians left a man scalped under the tree.

• Doris Davidson, the daughter of Carter Breed who owned the Meat Market, said her job as a child was to stay at home and answer the telephone. Invariably, P. H. Bell, the Mt. Gainer postmaster, would call each Saturday morning. As Doris would answer the phone Mr. Bell would say "Tell Mr. Carter I want 75 cents worth of ground steak. P. H. Bell, Mt. Gainer," and then hang up.

• J. N. Rippy recalls a time when he and brother Glenn were a part of a crew that herded several thousand head of sheep and goats on foot from Florence, Texas, to Wimberley for Clay Gay. This was in the late '30s and at that time you could only cross the Colorado River over the Congress Avenue bridge in Austin or at Marble Falls. Permission could not be obtained for the Austin route, so it was Marble Falls. J. N. and Glenn were going over the proposed route from Dripping Springs to Florence in an old Model T. The clutch played out and they abandoned the vehicle, leaving behind all their camping equipment and supplies and made their way to Florence. This left them without these necessary things on the way back. They followed the roads as they went through Bertram, Liberty Hill, Leander, Lago Vista, Smithwick, Marble Falls, Cypress Mills, Hamilton Pool, and Dripping Springs. One of the problems was trying to keep the animals together while on foot because not much of the area had fences. Meals consisted of mainly cheese, crackers, and sardines they were able to buy along the way on the two-week journey. Upon reaching Dripping Springs, the animals were penned at the old gin yard and it was at this time J. N. decided he had had enough and left the drive.

• While attending flight mechanics school at Ft. Worth in 1940, J. N. fell victim to an old trick. He and a buddy were walking to school when they met a black man who wanted to know where the jewelry store was. All the while he was flashing a big diamond-looking ring. His story was a married couple got to fighting and one of them threw it out a window and he picked it up. More talking and he decided he would rather sell it to them than the store. They could not afford the $500 price but after more conversation, he accepted their five dollar offer. They hurried to a nearby jewelry store. As they entered the store, the jeweler flipped up his examiners glass and asked. "Well, how much did you boys pay for your ring?" They answered "five dollars." He said, "Why didn't you boys go down to the store and buy one for ten cents like he did." Seems like J. N. hadn't been his only customer.

• Joy Jernigan Harmon, the wife of O. C. Harmon at the time, tells this story about his grandfather, P. A. Glosson. As far as anyone knew, Mr. Glosson had not been to a church in his life. In 1954, when O. C. and Joy were married at the Dripping Springs Baptist Church, he broke that streak when he was a surprise witness to the ceremony. Two years later, after spending most of the year bedridden in which Joy spent much of her time tending to him, and on a day when she was not around, he got out of bed, dressed and walked the block to the Baptist Church where he was found dead. This was supposedly his second visit. He was 91.

• Grady Moore tells about the first house he lived in that had electricity. It was when he moved to Dripping Springs with his family in 1942. He was eight at the time and the only house he had seen with electricity had the lights hang down from the ceiling. You turned them off and on with a string that hung down where you could reach it. The house they moved into had a switch on the wall. He and his older brother went into the room and Grady eyed the lights. They were on but there was no string hanging down. He asked his brother how they were going to turn the light off with no string. His brother told him he would have to blow real hard and the light would go out just like the old lanterns had. He made Grady blow harder and harder several times before finally turning the switch off.

• There was a time when feed sacks were made with many different prints of cloth and most ended up as clothing. I can remember well wearing shirts made by my mother from these feed sacks.

• Prior to modern media, the circus advertised by pasting giant posters on prominent buildings in the surrounding small communities. The owners of these buildings would receive free tickets to the circus.

• According to Charlie Haydon, Mrs. Minnie Horner did more than sell ice. She also had a milk cow herd she let graze all over town. Complaints about the cows fell on deaf ears. The Baptist Church had to build a fence to prevent the cows from doing their business around the entrance of the church. The enterprise came to an end when one cow was killed when hit by a car.

• One thing that may surprise many who live around Dripping Springs is the history of the cedar tree. They have not always been native to this area. Mr. Bradley Davis says he can recall when there were few trees around. They were mostly oaks and the rest could be found along the streams. The few cedar "brakes" were located back in the hills. It was not until the farming and ranching habits of the area ceased that the cedars started their spread through the area. Mr. Davis says they have only been around maybe the last 50 or 60 years.

• Roy Breed tells of a time when a Hohman boy rode his black horse to the old hotel, which was also the post office, to pick up his mail. He tied his horse to the fence. The hotel was pretty rundown by this time. Roy rode up about this time. He took the horse upstairs and locked it in a room. The boy was able to find the horse when it made a sound. When someone spilled the beans on Roy the next day, the Hohman boy let Roy know how he felt about the trick.

• Roy Breed tells of the day that he thought was to be his last here on earth. It was the day he met up with Bonnie and Clyde on the backroads of his place. As he and his wife were having breakfast, they heard a report over the radio that there had been a shootout in Fredericksburg with Bonnie and Clyde. They surmised that Bonnie and Clyde would stay away from the main highways and use the backroads. Later in the morning as Roy was on his horse herding cattle along Martin Road, he saw this yellow car coming down the road and he immediately knew who it was but he had no place to go. They pulled up and Clyde got out of the car and summmoned Roy over. Even though he knew who they were, he did not let on. He felt like he was not going to get out of this situation alive. He said they were both dressed up like millionaires. As he rode closer to the car, he could see Bonnie in the front seat. On the floorboard he could also see the machine gun she carried. Clyde wanted directions to the next main road and Roy gave them to him and was able to breathe with a big sigh of relief as they drove off. It was only a short time later that they were killed by officers of the law.

• Dr. A.V. Duncan, whose office was in the old hotel, had a dun colored horse named Nellie. People reported he would talk to that horse as if it was his wife.

• On December 4, 1876, according to the *Austin American* newspaper report, B. F. Fairchilds, acting constable, Ed Riley, Bunyan Daniels, and William Wallace started out early to arrest three men camped on Barton Creek who had stolen a hog and butchered it and were suspected of being horse thieves. After exchanging the usual "good morning," Mr. Fairchilds told them to consider themselves under arrest. One of the thieves pulled a six-shooter and began firing as he asked, "What for?" When the short battle was over, three men lay dead and two more were wounded. Two of the thieves named Williams were killed outright and the third, G. W. Baker, who had not drawn a gun, was shot and probably died several days later. Ed Riley was killed on the spot and Fairchilds was wounded but recovered. The other two escaped injury.

• In the 1930s when Charles Haydon was the County Commissioner, his work crew dug up a body while doing repair work on the Fitzhugh Road at Barton Creek. One of the men brought the skull to town but Mr. Haydon made them carry it back and bury it. It is assumed to have been one of the two horse thieves of the 1876 incident.

• In the 1950s, a keymaker by the name of Bob Fulton lived in the building off Mercer Street that previously was used for embalming by W. S. Garnett. Charlie Haydon remembers him as an elderly gentleman with a long white beard. He had to use a cane in each hand in order to walk. Since the building had no water, he would pay Charlie and others a nickel a bucket to bring him drinking water.

• One of the pastimes for the young people of Dripping Springs at night was to tie a string to a purse and toss it in the middle of the highway. Vehicles would stop to pick up the purse. While the driver descended from the vehicle, the purse was pulled back out of sight. The fun was in watching the reactions and listening to the comments of the people getting out of the car and not being able to find the purse. Jack Lyle recalls one particular night when it was James Kelley's time to man the purse. He was located near the culvert at the Lions field. All the others were watching the proceedings from the Sinclair Station (located where the drive-in bank is now). This time an 18-wheeler threw on its brakes and came to a screeching halt. Instead of already pulling the purse to safety, James waited until the truck driver was reaching down to pick it up. Being the butt of a joke made the driver mad and he began to chase James. They went through the culvert and out the other side. James headed through the pastures toward Wallace Mountain with the driver in hot pursuit. Jack said they all got out in the road to watch the proceedings. Only James' youth and speed saved him from the angry driver.

Granddaughter Katherine Berkley Cannon tells of a favorite public relations habit her grandfather, Dr. C. H. Berkley, would like to use when making house calls. She said after entering the house, he would put his hat on a table. If there were kids in the house, he would ask them to get his hat for him when he was ready to leave. Upon lifting the hat up, the kids would find candy hidden under the hat.

Part Two

—Photo by Mark Myers

History of Land Ownership

In the beginning, it did not occur to me to find out about the history of the land ownership. After trying to find out information on the different owners of the buildings and businesses, I decided it would be fun to find out who all the owners of the land in the P.A. Smith survey were. Not only was it fun, but interesting as well. However, in my limited experience and knowledge concerning deeds, there were instances that gave me consternation during the research. Ownership did not appear to fit my beliefs. I assumed that if you built a building on property, you would first own that property or if you paid taxes on it, then likewise, you had a deed to the land. There were times when I would find an article in the newspaper that would report that someone had bought property or built a building on property. A study of the tax records would indicate they were, indeed, paying taxes on this property, sometimes for quite a few years. When I looked diligently for the exchange of deed, I would find futility. In the end, the person with the last property deed would be the one who made the next exchange of the property. I just assumed the person in the middle must have been trying to buy the property and at some point, just let it go back without the owner ever having transferred the deed, or possibly, there was some other type of deal made. I try to mention this whenever it happened.

It was very interesting to see the number of people who had their hands on a piece of property over the years. The real estate agent has to be one of the world's original professions. From the beginning, people seemed to buy property in the P. A. Smith survey for the purpose of resell and that tradition continues to the very present. It also became obvious why in every deed description, the phrase "more or less" is given after the size of the property. Too many times, the parts did not equal the whole. Another thing I discovered was that in some cases, today's property lines do not match the orginal deed description. Some of that has to do with putting up fences and including land that was not in the original deed. After years of it being this way, the property was considered to be owned by the person with the fence. Some have suggested it could also take place by having a surveyor who was a buddy. It also could be that the early descriptions of property included landmarks such as a tree, pile of rocks, or some other marking that did not last through the years. And since deed descriptions were not always easy to read, making interpretations of such may have been difficult for the surveyor. Iron stakes driven into the ground lasted the longest and therefore were the best way of marking property. Bradley Davis commented one time that he saw three different surveyors survey the same area of the Academy Block and each put down a stake in a different place. It is common to see people at the County Records building searching through the deed stacks trying to determine the official description of property, so they could get some legal matter resolved and ownership determined.

Sometimes finding deeds to the land was not easy and determining the actual date of sale was difficult as well. Sometimes the deed index at the Courthouse Annex gave those dates, but it, of course, was always the date the deed was filed with them. Sometimes a deal was completed before the deed was filed. This was backed up by newspaper articles that described the completion of houses about the same time as the deed shows the land was bought. So the deed dates given here could be off by a few months but they were the only dates that I had to go on.

The other problem was that people kept deeds for many years without ever filing them. Of course, they made a big problem for their heirs by doing that, as anyone wanting to buy the property would have to obtain all the heirs' signatures first. Randy Garnett found this out in 1976 when he bought parts of several blocks in Dripping Springs. It had been in a family's possession since 1901 and there were many, many heirs that he had to contact to accomplish the sale.

There have been a few parcels of land with gaps in ownership, because I was unable to take the time to find the missing links. This is especially true in the last fifteen years when there was so much economic turmoil, causing owners to lose their property, putting banks and federal government in the land business before things turned around in the early '90s and new owners were put in place.

I also have a problem with visualizing things. First of all, the league runs north and south, which puts it at an angle to my way of thinking, in terms of roads, etc. I put everything down on a sheet of paper as the paper runs, instead of the correct angle, so I had problems visualizing the actual acreage as it was, as opposed to what I was reading. In some cases, the boundaries were not as cut and dried as my drawings made them look. I'm also not sure all of the deeds had the correct directions on them when giving distance. At least, it did not seen so as I was trying to put the pieces of the puzzle together to make a correct map. Especially in the northwest quarter, I was unable to locate how some of the plots of land fit into the acreage the deeds stated and the overall picture. I plodded on as best I could.

Just like other parts of this history, I found that deeds did not always tell the correct story, nor mapmakers. Once something was put down on the deed, no one seemed to find out if the facts were right. The next person would just keep writing the same information down and perpetuating the problem. As I went through the deed hunt, I also drew a map to put all of these land purchases in their correct place. When studying some of the recent maps, they just did not have the right properties or owners in the right places. If I had not kept my own map, then I would have been guilty of perpetuating the same mistakes.

What all of this means is I'm not very good at reading deeds and knowing what all of the wording means. So, while going through this history, my interpretations might not be entirely correct, but hopefully close. There will be those who will know for sure. If you need gospel, then do the research to be sure.

PHILLIP A. SMITH LEAGUE

My research did not turn up much about Phillip A Smith. For a person to receive a league of land, they had to be living in Texas prior to March 2, 1836. The Texas Con-

stitution stated that the head of a family (headright) was to receive a league of land, if living in Texas prior to that time. Research at the State Archives showed a Phillip A. Smith lived in Sabine, Texas, in the 1832 census, but none lived in Texas for the 1840 census.

We know Mr. Smith received his league of land by virtue of Certificate No. 56, issued to him by the Board of Land Commissioners of Jasper County, on March 3, 1838. It was not unusual for someone to purchase these certificates from the recipients. The certificates gave the owners the ability to stake claim to any state lands that were not already claimed. George W. Glasscock obtained Mr. Smith's, as well as other certificates, and claimed land around the Austin area. By Patent No. 443, Volume 8, dated April 27, 1850, Mr. Glasscock was named the assignee of the Phillip A. Smith survey, No. 26, by The State of Texas, represented by Governor P. H. Bell and attested by George W. Smith, Commissioner General Land Office. The deed is recorded on page 394 of Volume D at the Hays County Deed Records. Below is a description of the P. A. Smith survey:

"Beginning at a mound on north side of and in the north line of survey #31, which an elm marked X bears 30 north 50 varas. Thence east 1860 varas to Archers fork 4450 varas to southwest corner of B. F. Mims one-quarter league No. 8 from which a live oak marked G bears south 31 north 47 varas and then bears 110 west 23 varas marked X. Thence north 5100 varas to spring branch 5681 varas to a mound from which a liveoak marked W bears south 39 west 20 varas, another marked I bears south 55 east 25 varas. Thence west at 100 varas crosses said spring branch 4450 varas a mound from which a liveoak marked II bears south 31 east 15 varas, another marked A bears west 50 varas. Thence south with east line of Ben Hanna survey No. 28 at 2827 varas crossed Archer's fork 5681 varas to the beginning."

This approximately two-square mile area is mostly rugged picturesque land with the north border being the highest ground, sloping toward the south. The drop is probably a couple hundred feet from the northern border to the southern one. Therefore, most of the watershed of the league flows south to the north fork of Onion Creek. Just a small amount of water finds its way into Barton Creek on the north. This becomes obvious when the area has heavy rains. Before Onion Creek became the name of choice, the north fork was known as Archer's Fork. There are five main waterways that drain the P. A. Smith league and three have known names. Starting on the west boundary is Cave Springs Branch. It begins in the back of the Meadow Oaks subdivision and winds its way southward through the Hidden Springs Ranches subdivision and then crosses under both the old 290 and new 290 highways. It is this stretch of land that produced its name, as it runs through some deep ravines that resembles caverns. It continues on until it drains into Onion Creek.

The next stream originates up in the southwest corner of Springlake and meanders through the Teddy Draper place down through the DSYSA-Middle School property and in front of the library and on down beside Sportsplex Road and under 290. This water then ends up flooding down to cross the Creek Road at Will Crow's rock house and then cascades over the bluff into the Milkhouse Branch. It was this tributary that caused Mr. Crow to build a rock fence to divert the water away from his yard. To my knowledge, this tributary has no name, although it could logically be called the Milkhouse Branch.

Next comes the watershed waterway which is the namesake of the town. The Dripping Springs Branch begins just behind the DS Butane building but collects all the watershed from the Old Fitzhugh Road and much of the land north of this point. It then heads under Loop 64 (Mercer Street) and 290 and picks up the water from the Milkhouse Branch and heads to Onion Creek. The next waterway takes most of the water that comes from the Pound and Wallace properties. It flows from behind the Pound house and any other way that it can to meet near the entrance to Founders Park and flows south, crossing under Loop 64 and 290 and then winds among a channel at the Promenade Center and finally under RR 12 south and into another channel that takes it down to Onion Creek. No name has been found for this waterway either.

The final waterway is Walnut Springs. Although the headwaters of it is next to the Anton Allen house on RR12 south, it also takes in the watershed of all the land east of the road and up to Wallace Mountain. This is obvious when heavy rains flood the roadway, trying to find an outlet to Onion Creek. There are a couple of other small streams that take runoff from the P. A. Smith league. They flow under RR150 and head south to Onion Creek outside the boundary of P. A. Smith.

NORTHWEST QUARTER

The ownership trail for the northwest quarter of the P.. A. Smith league starts with Glasscock and then Fielding S. Roy, who bought it from Glasscock on 9-19-1853. Roy sold the 1,107-acre tract to John L. Moss on 1-23-1854 for $1,350. Moss sold it to Phillip H. Raiford for $3,000 on 5-1-1860. In turn, Raiford sold the property to Josephine Steiner for $4,500 on 11-12-1861. Possibly the Civil War had something to do with this sell. The Steiners were already living in Wisconsin when they sold the acreage to Burrell J. Marshall for $2,500 on 1-19-1870. On 12-18-1871, he sold 193-acre tracts to A.. K Daniel and Edward J. Riley. Marshall died in February of 1872, leaving a widow, Martha Ann, and five minor children to divide the estate. Mrs. Marshall, who had already married W. T. Chapman, filed for the estate of B. J. Marshall on 10-19-1872. Each year, she had to file a report with the probate court. Finally on 5-17-1880, her eldest son, George W., asked for partition of the property. John L. Wallace, Jake Roberts, and J. W. Phillips were appointed as commissioners to partition the 457 acres among the five children. Their report was approved 9-23-1880. Jefferson Davis received 91 acres, Jasper Newton 70, Robert Lee 93, George Washington 80, and Fannie Marie 131 acres. Mrs. Chapman retained the other 260 acres. The reality of what they received, at least, when they sold their property, was the following: Jefferson D. 85, Jasper N. 73, Robert L. 93, George W. 81, Fannie M. 150, and Mrs. Chapman 239, which is in line with the quarter league total.

The first order of business will be to look at the ownership of the town of Dripping Springs as laid out by W. T. Chapman over the years. It fell entirely within the northwest quarter of the P. A. Smith league. After that, we will fill in the rest of the northwest quarter and do the same for the other quarters of the league. Actually, the land was not Chapman's, so he had to get a power of attorney from his wife to make the sales of all this land that was hers by inheritance from her previous husband.

NORTHWEST QUARTER

Original Plat

The original plat was filed on September 24, 1881. It consisted of twelve blocks. The first ten were 200x300 feet and the other two not quite that size, due to the Dripping Springs Branch. Each block was separated by roads of fifty feet in width. The main road bordered on the north boundary and was 75 feet wide. Each of the first nine blocks were divided into twelve lots, each 50x100 feet. It is interesting to note that all of the lots of each block were numbered in the same sequence, except three and four. Their number one lot started with the northeast corner, instead of the usual northwest. Even though this first filed plat did not show the lots on it, no doubt they had been done because W. T. Chapman began selling lots almost immediately.

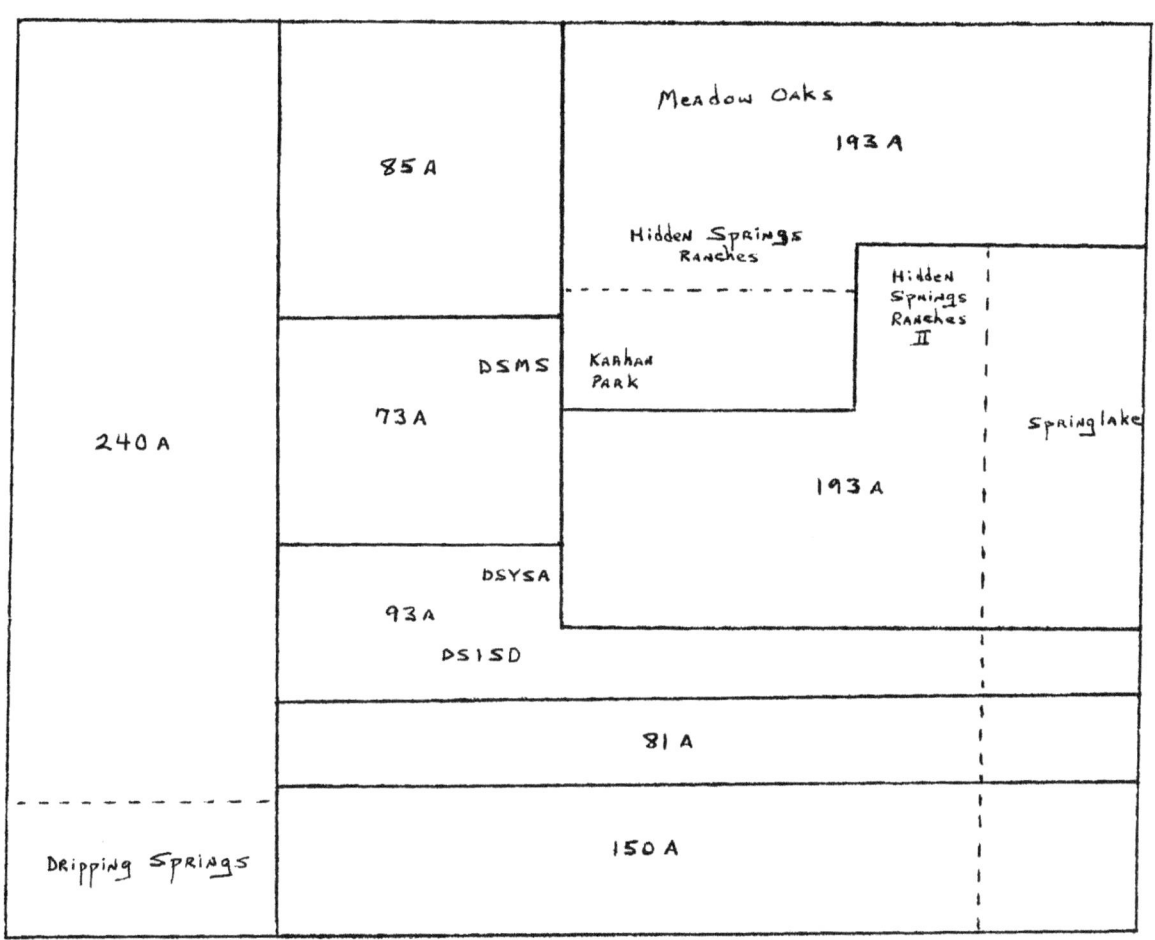

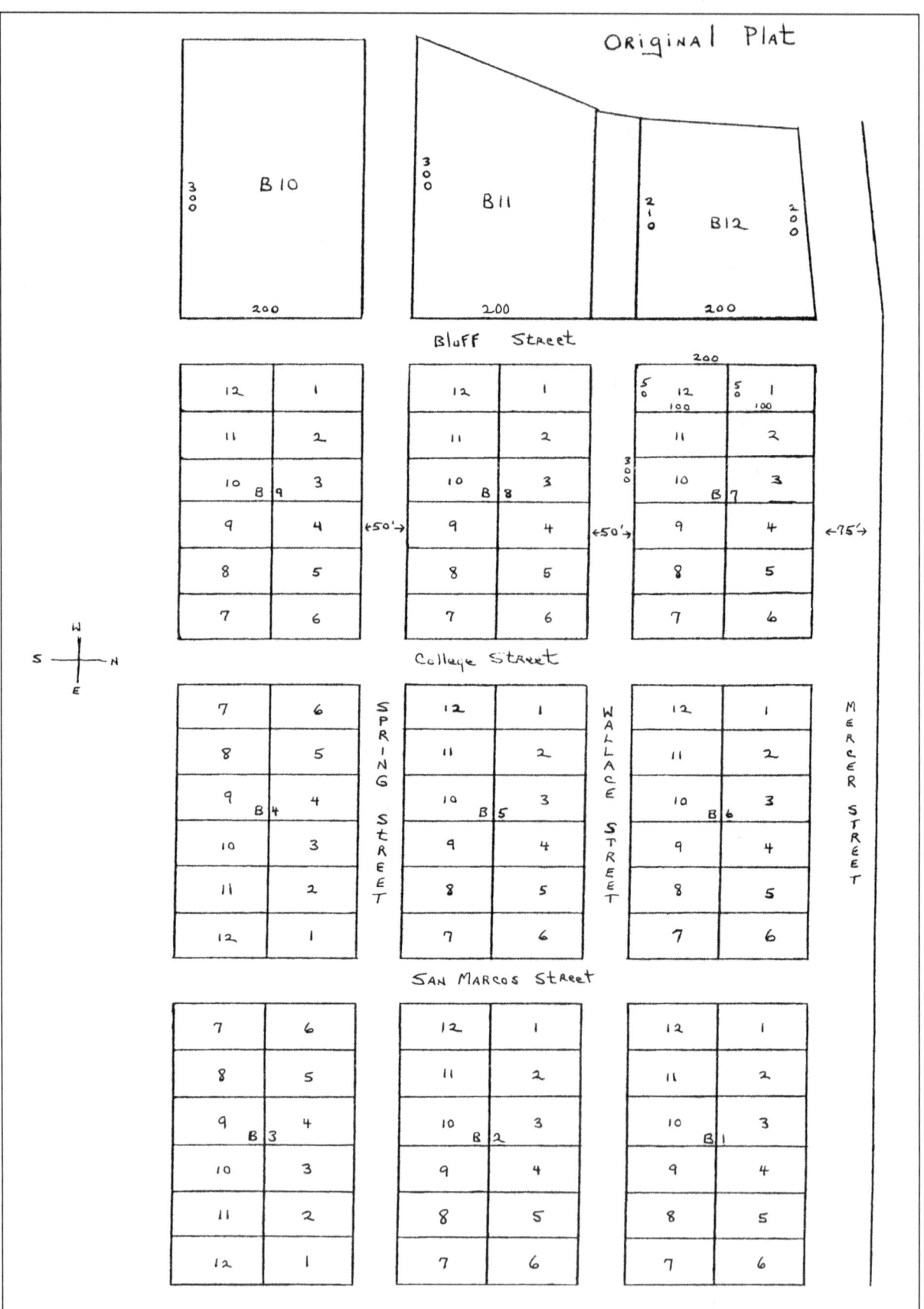

NORTHWEST QUARTER

Original Plat, Block One

Lot 1: Lot 1, to my knowledge, never had a building on it. Chapman never sold it to anyone. Bankers Edgar and W. B. Smith had some type of financial deal with Chapman dating back to 1905. Upon Mrs. Chapman's death in 1924, the lot became the property of the Smiths. A part of the lot was deeded to the State Highway Department on 9-18-1934 as right-of-way for the new Highway 290 that was coming through Dripping Springs. On 6-20-1939, W. S. McLendon purchased this lot, as well as the rest of their holdings, from the Smith estate. McLendon died in 1940 and his daughter, Erlene McLendon Davis, inherited his holdings. J. H. Howard purchased the lot on 3-9-1944 from Mrs. Davis. Virgil Conn bought it from Mr. Howard on 12-24-1945. He would hold onto it until 8-1-1961 when he sold it to O. B. McKown, Sr. It was 4-7-1969, when the company of Jones & Jones became its owners. Daniel Jones bought it from the Porta Craft company on 6-12-1971. King Feed Company bought it from Daniel Jones on 2-22-1974. James Hurlbut paid King Feed for it on 6-8-1977. He, in turn, sold it to the Dripping Springs National Bank on 9-17-1981. The bank has since changed ownership three times, from Texas Bank to Norwest to Wells Fargo, but the lot remains in their hands.

Lot 2: The Hays County Commissioners' Court ordered that Dripping Springs should have a Justice of the Peace building, if a suitable site could be found. On 6-6-1907, Chapman sold this lot to Hays County for $25, for that purpose. The building known as the Courthouse was built on this site and used until torn down around 1925. It, too, had to give up part of its northern boundary to the road right-of-way. This was done on 1-22-1935. Virgil Conn paid Hays County $35 for the lot on 6-22-1946. Virgil Conn sold it to O. B. McKown, Sr., on 8-1-1961. Jones & Jones bought it from McKown 4-7-1969. Then Daniel Jones bought it from Porta Craft on 6-12-1971. King Feed Company bought it from Jones on 2-22-1974. James Hurlbut bought it from King Feed on 6-8-1977, and sold it to the Dripping Springs National Bank on 9-17-1981. It is still a part of the bank property.

Lot 3: On 3-14-1924, the Smith brothers came into the property. The right-of-way was given on 9-18-1934. W. S. McLendon purchased it on 6-20-1939 and his daughter, Erlene McLendon Davis, inherited it upon his death in 1940. She sold it to the Dripping Springs school on 3-6-1942. The school sold it to James/Flemmie Felps on 6-27-1947. On 1-31-1967, Edward/Zelma Jones bought the east 25x80. On 7-11-1978, James Hurlbut bought the west 25x80 from Mrs. Felps. Next, Hurlbut bought the east 25x80 from Mrs. Zelma Faye Jones on 6-14-1979, giving him the entire lot. Hurlbut put it under the name of Wrangler Properties on 9-10-1980. On 9-17-1981, it became the property of the Dripping Springs National Bank and is still part of the bank property.

Lots 4, 5: The Smith brothers got it on 3-14-1924. The right-of-way was deeded on 9-18-1934. W. S. McLendon got it on 6-20-1939 and in turn, his daughter, Erlene McLendon Davis, inherited it in 1940. She sold it to the Dripping Springs school on 3-6-1942. James/Flemmie Felps bought it from the school on 6-27-1947. Edward/Zelma Faye Jones took possession from the Felps on 1-31-1967. James Hurlbut bought it from Mrs. Jones on 6-14-1979. He put it under Wrangler Properties on 9-10-1980. Wrangler Properties sold it to the Dripping Springs National Bank as part of their drive-in bank facility in 1984. It is still a part of the bank property.

Lot 6: Had the same owners as Lots 3, 4, and 5 down to the Felps in 1947. It was only 50x56 feet due to the right-of-way loss to the highway. Oscar G. Seal paid the Felpses $450 for it on 10-25-1952. He put a little BBQ place on it and later built a cafe. Will P. Crow bought it from Mr. Seal on 9-14-

1954. He did a little remodeling on the cafe building and later sold it to George/Lorena Wiest on 1-6-1955 for $6,500. Crow bought it back on 8-14-1957. He deeded it over to his grandson Mack Crow on 7-1-1969. However, his uncle, A. B. "Pete" Crow, made an agreement with his brother Will to live in this house until his death. Mack Crow sold the property to the Dripping Springs National Bank in 1984, after Pete Crow's death. It is still bank property.

Lot 7: Had the same owners as the above lots through 1947. On 10-25-1952, Oscar G. Seal bought the northern 12x50 foot section to go with Lot 6. In turn, Will Crow bought it from Mr. Seal, then sold it to George Wiest. Wiest bought the rest of the lot from James/Flemmie Felps on 4-30-1955. On 8-14-1957, Will Crow bought the 12x50 foot section back from Wiests. S. J. Moore bought the 50x88 foot section from Wiest on 8-25-1961. Mack Crow was deeded the 12x50 foot section by Will Crow on 7-1-1969. Robert Terry bought the 50x88 foot section from Mr. Moore on 10-15-1966. Both Terry and Crow sold their property to the Dripping Springs National Bank in 1984.

Lots 8, 9: Again, this lot had the same owners as the others through the Felpses in 1947. On 1-31-1967, Edward/Zelma Jones bought the lot from James/Flemmie Felps. James Hurlbut bought the lot from Mrs. Jones on 6-14-1979. He put it under Wrangler Properties on 9-10-1980 before selling it to the Dripping Springs National Bank in 1984. It is still bank property.

Lot 10: This lot had a little variation, although the same people were involved in ownership. After the Felpses in 1947. Edward/Zelma Jones bought the east 25x100 feet on 1-31-1967, and James Hurlbut the west 25x100 feet from the Felpses on 7-11-1978. Hurlbut purchased the east 25x100 feet from Mrs. Jones on 6-14-1979. The lot was under Wrangler Properties beginning 9-10-1980, and then sold it to the Dripping Springs National Bank on 9-17-1981. It is still a part of the bank property.

Lot 11: Ditto for lot eleven down through the Felps's purchase in 1947. O. B. McKown, Sr,. bought it on 6-26-1962. Jones & Jones bought it from McKown on 4-7-1969. Daniel Jones bought it from Porta Craft on 6-12-1971, and sold it to King Feed on 2-22-1974. James Hurlbut bought it on 6-8-1977 from King Feed and then sold it to the Dripping Springs National Bank on 9-17-1981. It is still bank property.

Lot 12: This lot produced much history over its lifespan. Its first sale occurred on 12-15-1900 when Thomas Robbins paid W. T. Chapman $17.50 for it. He quickly turned around and sold it to R. L. Raines on 12-31-1900 for $35, doubling his investment. On 12-28-1901, R. H. Raines paid R. L. Raines $300 for the property. Mr. Raines was a blacksmith and to have property value jump that much, we have to assume this included a blacksmith shop as part of the improvements. Four years to the day, Raines sold the lot and business to H. B. Harmon for $300. On 1-17-1907, McCreary Crow paid Harmon $480 and on the same day, sold it to W. A. Chesher for $500. On 10-31-1907, Sam Byars became a partner in the Chesher & Byars blacksmith shop by buying a one-half interest for $450. Chesher sold his interest to W. M. McElyea for $272 on 9-7-1908. McElyea wanted the whole business and bought out Byars's interest on 9-14-1908 for $340. We can only wonder what made the Byars' half more expensive than the Chesher's? McElyea sold the property to M. A. George on 9-21-1908 for $640, and on 10-24-1908, L. T. Guttery bought it for $620. P. A. Glosson paid Guttery $500 on 8-19-1912. J. W. Champion bought out Glosson for $550 on 9-9-1913 and did business as the Champion Brothers. At some point, the old blacksmith shop was torn down, some say around 1918. D. W. Crenshaw and James Ferrell bought the property from Champion on 2-11-1937 for $200. They built the present building there for the purpose of showing movies. The endeavor was not successful and they went bankrupt. On 1-7-1941,

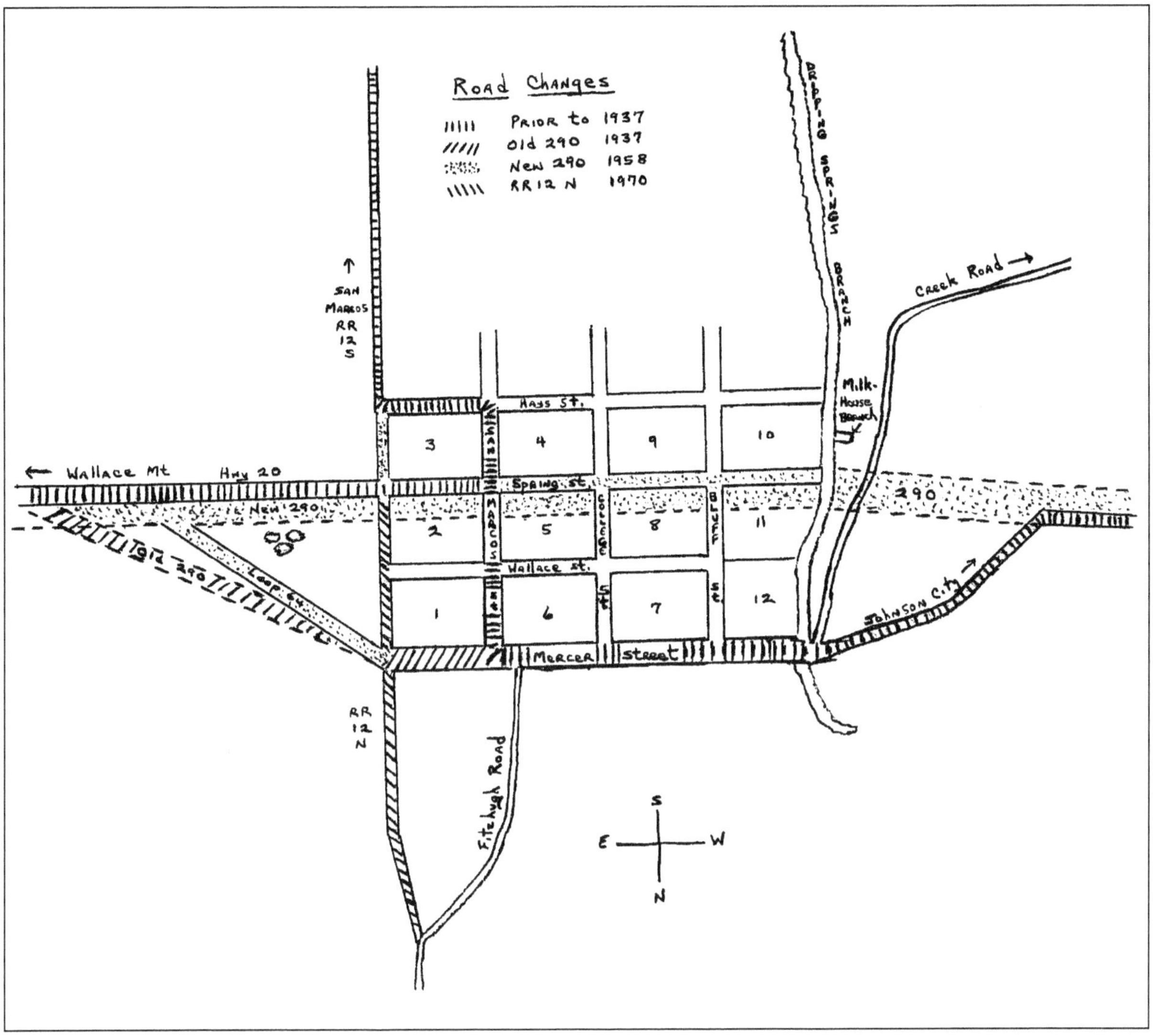

[Map of Dripping Springs showing road changes, streets including Hays St., Spring St., Wallace St., Mercer Street, and numbered blocks 1-12. Legend shows Road Changes: Prior to 1937, Old 290 1937, New 290 1958, RR 12 N 1970.]

Kuntz-Sternenberg Lumber Company bought the property in a sheriff's sale to protect their investment in it. Lomis Slaughter bought it from them on 12-24-1943 for $1,250. Joe K. O'Bryant, a movie theater owner in Austin, paid Mr. Slaughter $1,450 on 8-4-1945 and proceeded to resurrect the movie theater in Dripping Springs. It was not to be. M. Z. Piland and James J. Lumpkin bought the property from O'Bryant on 5-5-1948. They sold the property to O. B. McKown, Sr., on 7-19-1962. Jones & Jones purchased it from McKown on 4-7-1969. Daniel Jones bought it from Porta Craft on 6-12-1971, and sold it to King Feed on 2-22-1974. James Hurlbut became the owner on 6-8-1977, and sold it to the Dripping Springs National Bank on 9-17-1981. It is still bank property.

NORTHWEST QUARTER

Original Plat, Block Two

Block two has some mysteries associated with it, from my standpoint. Although no deed was found, tax records show that Peter Toombs paid taxes on this block for several years in the late 1890s. It ended up back in Chapman's hands and became one of those properties that did not sell during the time of Chapman ownership and went to the Smith brothers on 3-14-1924. It listed their acquisition as being Lots 1, 2, 3, 4, 5, and 6

and one-half interest in Lots 7, 8, 9, 10, 11, and 12. This one-half interest bothered me because I never could find who owned the other half interest. The way other deeds read concerning property in block three, I believe what happened was that Spring Street did not extend from one end to the other in a straight line as the plat was drawn. Instead, as the road came down Wallace Mountain and connected with San Marcos Street, it actually took 50 feet off the block two lots and not where it should have. This would have been easier to prove had Highway 290 not cut its swath through the town in the late '50s. It took a hundred-foot path that included Spring Street and half of the southside lots on blocks two, five, eight and eleven. This would then take in what should have been the land designated for Spring Street between blocks two and three. Anyway, that is my theory. As was the case in block one, the ownership was the same. On 6-20-1939, W. S. McLendon bought the property from the Smith estate and Erlene McLendon Davis inherited it in 1940. She sold it to the Dripping Springs school on 3-6-1942. The school sold it to James/Flemmie Felps on 6-27-1947. From that point, ownership spread out.

Lots 1, 2, 3, and 10, 11, 12: These lots have stayed together throughout. It is a 150x150 foot block of land. On 1-14-1948, M. Z. Piland and James J. Lumpkin paid the Felpses $800 for the property. They built an insulation plant on the land and on 2-19-1959, Alva Haydon paid $4,000 for the lots and later moved Central Garage there. Ben Metcalf bought the property from Haydon on 11-9-1976.

Lots 4, 9: The Felpses built a building that started out as a grocery store on the property. On 9-10-1974, they sold the building and the property to Morris Smith for $14,200. It is still owned by the Smith family. Gary Lee Smith took possession on 12-11-1995.

Lots 5, 6, 7, 8. The Felpses built a service station on these lots. Different people ran the station for years until it no longer served the purpose. Mrs. Flemmie Felps sold the old service station and property to James H. McCrocklin for $25,000 on 12-16-1975. He converted it to office space for his real estate business. James T. McCrocklin bought the property from his father on 1-21-1982 and it has remained in the business.

NORTHWEST QUARTER

Original Plat, Block Three

Chapman sold the land and at some point down the road, he sold it again to someone else. I could not find a deed to see how the land got back to him. Probably, they did like many sellers had to do over the years, they bought it back from the courts to prevent losing their investment. Many people, especially in the early days, were able to purchase land just by paying the back taxes at a public auction. This was one of the two blocks that had the opposite numbering system.

Lots 1, 2, 3, 10, 11, 12. On 4-10-1883, W. T. Chapman sold the six lots to W. H. Williams. Eighteen years later, the Dripping Springs Methodist Church purchased these six lots from A. L. Davis/W. T. Chapman on 3-21-1901 for five dollars. On 8-10-1939, W. S. McLendon purchased Lot 1 from the Chapman heirs. This lot was supposedly bought by the Methodists years earlier. John E. Spaw bought the lot from McLendon on 3-29-1940 and then sold it to the Methodists for one dollar on 1-15-1948. To continue the mystery, the Methodists paid the Williams heirs one dollar to quitclaim the six lots. This occurred on 12-22-1952. When the property got too small for the growing Methodist Church, they sold it to the Harrell Funeral Home in 1985. A few years later, they defaulted on the loan and gave up the property to the Texas Methodist Foundation in 1990. Better interest rates allowed Harrell Funeral Home to repurchase the property on 4-11-1994.

Lots 4, 5, 6, 7, 8, 9. On 8-24-1883, G. B. Phelps bought all six lots from W. T.

Chapman. David McNaughton bought the six lots from Phelps on 12-20-1887. On 7-23-1894, Richard Cruse paid McNaughton $600 dollars for the lots which included a house. On 11-20-1894, Richard Cruse bought what was called the north half of lots 4, 5, and 6, which was a 50x150 foot strip, from W. T. Chapman for $50. I think possibly this was what should have been Spring Street instead of being a part of the actual lots of 4, 5, and 6. Mrs. N. L. Middlebrook paid Richard Cruse $275 for his property on 2-12-1900. Mrs. Middlebrook sold the property to W. P. Hudson for $300 on 10-12-1901. Richard H. Raines took the property off Hudson's hands for $350 on 12-4-1902. Charles and Della Seal bought the property from R. H. Raines, Jr., for $375 on 2-17-1905. On 4-8-1957, the State of Texas paid the Seal heirs $47.50 for right-of-way for the new highway 290. On 1-19-1959, Oscar G. Seal paid the Seal heirs for lots 4, 7, 8, and 9. Then on 10-3-1959, Travis Garnett/J. F. Glosson, Jr., bought a portion of lots 5 and 6 that was approximately 38x100 feet off the north end from the Seal heirs. On 4-2-1975, J. F. Glosson bought out Travis Garnett's share of the property, which was a 70x100 foot portion of lots 5 and 6. On 10-9-1975, J. F. bought Charlie Mae Seal Bowers' share of lots 5, 6, 7, and 8. On 7-19-1976, J. F. bought the front part of lots 4, 5, and 6 from the state, which was a part of Spring Street. Wilma Seal Lowe bought Edyth Seal Hudson's share of lots 4, 8, and 9 on 4-15-1978. Glosson brought all six lots under one ownership on 2-28-1983 when he bought Lowe's share of 4, 9, 7, and 8. All of this property is now under the umbrella of Glosson Exxon, Inc.

NORTHWEST QUARTER

Original Plat, Block Four

This block eventually totally became the property of the First Baptist Church of Dripping Springs.

Lots 1, 2, 3, 10, 11, 12. Following closely on the heels of the Methodist Church, the Baptists purchased these six lots from W. T. Chapman for $85 on 5-2-1901. It has been their property since.

Lots 4, 9. On 1-25-1937, the Baptist church purchased these two lots from George Marshall. He was Chapman's stepson and I found no deed of sale to Marshall. It could be that Chapman gave him the property or he could have bought it from Chapman.

Lots 5, 6. On 9-23-1901, J. W. Garrett paid $30 to Chapman for these two lots. Garrett sold the lots to Mrs. N. J. Davis for $100 on 11-3-1903. On 8-24-1944, the First Baptist Church paid $100 to Mrs. Ethel May Davis for the lots.

Lots 7, 8. On 3-14-1924, the Smith brothers took over ownership when Mrs. Chapman died. The two lots went to W. S. McLendon on 6-20-1939 when he bought them from the Smith estate. Mrs. Erlene McLendon Davis inherited them from her father in 1940 and sold them to the First Baptist Church on 5-16-1944. The parsonage was built on these two lots.

NORTHWEST QUARTER

Original Plat, Block Five

Lot 1. J. T. Wortham bought this lot from Chapman on 12-8-1883. Lucy Wortham sold it to J. T. Roberts on 1-6-1888. W. C. McKellar bought it from Roberts on 2-12-1901. McKellar sold it to A. B. Egger on 6-12-1905. J. L. Patterson took possession of it on 5-20-1908. Miles H. Cook bought it from Patterson on 7-5-1913. Peter A. Huey then bought it from Cook on 3-24-1914. L. U. Huey took over on 9-4-1919 and Charles Haydon purchased it from P. A. Huey on 5-5-1924. Sons Alva and Charlie N. Haydon bought it from their mother, Mrs. Beulah Haydon Malott, on 11-1-1957.

Lot 2. Thomas Williams purchased the lot from Chapman on 6-17-1884. W. B. Estill bought it from Williams on 7-29-

1884. J. T. Wortham bought it on 9-11-1884 from Estill. J. T. Roberts purchased it from Lucy Wortham on 1-6-1888. From that point, W. C. McKellar bought it from Roberts on 2-12-1901. A. B. Egger bought it from McKellar on 6-12-1905. The rest of the possessions were the same as Lot 1.

Lot 3. Lot three followed the same ownership trail as did Lot 2.

Lots 4, 9. C. C. Patton bought these lots from Chapman on 9-5-1882. He sold them to A. L. Davis, Jr., on 9-30-1885. Davis sold them to Thomas F. Voight on 3-19-1892. Voight then sold them to W. C. McKellar on 7-29-1893. The rest of the ownership trail was the same as Lots 1, 2, 3. The only variation occurred on 2-21-1957 when the State of Texas paid Mrs. Beulah Haydon Malott for the right-of-way for Highway 290, which took much of Lot 9.

Lots 5, 8. Sam Herring bought these two lots from Chapman on 11-5-1882. From that point, the lots took the same ownership history as did Lots 4 and 9. Eight took a big hit from the right-of-way, too. These two lots went to U First LLC, Jim Powers' purchase of the old Texaco station in 1998.

Lots 6, 7. These lots are shrouded in early mystery. In the deed describing the lots that Sam Herring bought, it said that the two lots east of them were owned by George Womack. This was in 1882. However, I was never able to find a deed where Chapman sold the lots to Womack but he did pay taxes on them for several years. However, the 1891 tax records has Chapman paying the taxes on these two lots. This means that Thomas Voight must have bought the two lots from Chapman to build his gin on. The next time I find them mentioned is when Thomas Voight sold his gin property to W. C. McKellar on 7-29-1893. Voight built his gin in June 1891 on this property, which means he owned the land at the time. He moved back to Dripping Springs in March 1889. After selling to McKellar, these two lots followed the same trail as the above ones. Lot 7 lost out to right-of-way. Jim Powers bought these two lots from the Haydon brothers under the name of U First LLC in 1998 and converted the old station to a Popeye's Fried Chicken/Texaco station.

Lot 10. Thomas Williams bought the lot from Chapman on 6-17-1884. It followed the same ownership link as Lots 2 and 3, until it was sold to Miles H. Cook by J. L. Patterson. According to deed transfer, Patterson only sold the east three-fourths to Cook. Although it did not say so, Charles Haydon had to have bought the other one-fourth when he bought lots 11 and 12 from Joel Patterson on 11-26-1924. Again, much of Lot 10 was given to the right-of-way of 290 in 1957, before Alva and Charlie N. Haydon bought it from their mother on 11-1-1957.

Lot 11. Thomas Williams bought this lot from Chapman on 6-17-1884. It went the same route as Lot 10 up to the purchase by J. L. Patterson on 5-20-1908. It stayed in the Patterson family until Charles Haydon bought it from Joel M. Patterson on 11-26-1924. It has stayed with the Haydons since, although most of it went to the 290 right-of-way in 1957.

Lot 12. J. T. Wortham was the initial owner when he bought the lot from Chapman on 12-8-1883. It followed the path of Lot 1 until it reached the Patterson ownership in 1908 and then it followed Lot 11.

NORTHWEST QUARTER

Original Plat, Block Six

Lots 1, 2, 11, 12. The history of these lots are intertwined throughout. J. T. Wortham purchased these four lots from W. T. Chapman on 9-4-1882. He built the Wortham Business House on the northern part of Lots 1 and 2. He sold his business and the four lots to Hollis, Milam & Company for $1,200 on 9-20-1886. H. W. Cook paid $500 to the partners for the part of Lots 1 and 2 that included the business on 12-1-1887. E. H. Wallace paid Mary Cook

$600 for the business on 9-7-1888. Lewis Bartley Milam paid his partners, C. B. Hollis and Ed Womack, $466.11 for their shares of Lots 11, 12 and parts of 1 and 2 on 3-1-1889. S. D. Gilpin, a druggist, and David G. Jones, a merchant, paid Wallace $575 for the business lots on 2-23-1890. Less than two years later, they went bankrupt and H. C. Pearcy was named trustee for it on 1-5-1892. Nelson Davis Company, a major creditor, paid $1,638.05 for everything, including the furniture, goods, and fixtures on 6-29-1892.

Nannie M. Jones paid the Nelson Davis Co. $1,898.70 for the business on 7-2-1892. Meanwhile, D. C. Dunn purchased the rest of the lots from L. B. Milam on 10-14-1892 for $250. On 11-5-1894, J. M. Livingston paid D. C. Dunn $400 for his property. Jones put the four lots back under one owner when she bought the rest from Livingston on 11-19-1894. H. W./M. E. Griffin paid Nannie Jones $625 for the lots on 10-6-1896. The Griffins turned it over to David/M. E. Hughes for $500 on 1-14-1899. W. P. Hudson and W. H. Crenshaw bought out the Hugheses on 11-12-1901 for $725. Son W. M. Hudson bought out Crenshaw's share for $362.50 on 2-28-1905. On 2-7-1906, W. P. Hudson & Son sold out to I. T. Applewhite for $2,000. Applewhite sold the south half of Lot 12 on 6-17-1919 to Solon B. Glosson for $30. W. A./Ila Horner bought it from Glosson on 10-1-1921. Virgil Stubbs paid the Horners $400 for this half lot on 11-1-1923. This jump in price usually meant some type of improvement on the property. Charles Haydon paid I. T. Applewhite $200 for the rest of the four lots on 1-1-1925. The old Wortham Business House had been torn down by this time. Haydon brought the four lots together again when he purchased the half lot owned by Stubbs on 3-13-1925 for $381. It has been in the Haydon family since.

Lot 3. Charles Haydon paid the Chapman heirs for this lot on 10-9-1936 and it has remained in the Haydon family since.

Lot 4. J. C. Breed paid W. T. Chapman $50 for the lot on 4-11-1914 and built his meat market. J. W. Champion paid J. C. Breed $300 for a share of the lot on 5-2-1921. W. P. Crow paid Champion and the J. C. Breed heirs $1,000 for the lot on 12-20-1943. O. B. McKown, Sr., bought it from Crow on 8-2-1961 and he, in turn, sold it to Jones & Jones on 4-7-1969. Daniel O. Jones bought it from Porta Craft on 6-12-1971. Jones sold it to King Feed on 2-22-1974. The Senior Citizens Center purchased the property from King Feed on 3-28-1994 to build their new Thrift Shop.

Lot 5. George McCuistion, a druggist, paid W. T. Chapman $25 for the lot on 12-27-1900 to build a drugstore on the site. McCuistion sold his property to W. H. Crenshaw on 12-23-1905. D. W. Crenshaw purchased the lot on 4-22-1919. Clell Basket bought the property from Crenshaw on 6-1-1929. This was during the beginning of tough times and he had to let the property go back to Crenshaw on 11-1-1930. W. C. Goslin bought it on 3-5-1934. He replaced the wooden building with a rock one in 1941. Edith Goslin Cauthen inherited the property on 4-15-1976. Joy Purcell bought the property from the Cauthens on March 3, 1997.

Lot 6. C. Waite Crenshaw paid W. T. Chapman heirs $75 for this lot on 11-7-1924. He built a garage on it. On 4-3-1934, D. W. Crenshaw bought the property from C. W. Crenshaw. When D. W. decided to build a movie theater across the street, he put up his property as collateral and John McClaferty held the deed of trust note. When the theater property went into bankruptcy a couple of years later, John McClaferty became the owner on 10-9-1940. The property has remained in the McClaferty family from that point.

Lots 7, 8, 9. Charles Haydon bought the three lots from the Chapman heirs on 10-9-1936. Lewis B. Jennings bought Lots 7 and 8 from Mrs. Beulah Haydon Malott on 7-11-1959. O. B. McKown, Sr., bought Lots 7 and 8 from L. B. Jennings on 8-1-1961 and then Lot 9 from Mrs. Malott on 8-2-1961.

He built a lumber yard on the property. McKown sold the three lots to Jones & Jones on 4-7-1969. Then Daniel O. Jones bought them from Porta Craft on 6-12-1971, and King Feed Co. gained ownership on 2-22-1974. Joy Purcell purchased the property on July 11, 1995.

Lot 10. W. M. Hudson paid W. T. Chapman $20 for it on 7-15-1905. I. T. Applewhite bought it for $15 on 3-24-1906. Charles Haydon bought it from Applewhite on 1-1-1925, and it is still in the Haydon family.

NORTHWEST QUARTER

Original Plat, Block Seven

Lots 1, 12. These two lots stayed together throughout their history. A. L. Davis, Sr., bought the two lots from W. T. Chapman on 2-9-1882. He sold them to George Dickey for $45 on 3-18-1885. On 9-1-1889, J. C. Rowe paid $125 to George Dickey for the lots. Pedernales Leinneweber bought the property from Rowe on 9-12-1894 for $200. This included the building and blacksmith tools. W. S. Garnett, Sr., purchased the lots from Leinneweber on 5-9-1904. Billie Calvin Garnett paid W. S. Garnett $100 for the lots on 5-21-1945, and has owned them since.

Lot 2. W. P. Hamilton bought the lot for $20 from W. T. Chapman on 10-12-1883. George Dickey paid $350 to Hamilton for it on 9-15-1884. This means the store had been erected on this site by then. Nannie M. Jones purchased the property on 10-12-1896. David G. Jones bought it from her on 12-13-1901. G. W. Daniel bought the property from D. G. Jones on 10-29-1909. E. H. Purtle gained possession of the $2,500 note on 11-10-1909. It became the property of Robert J. Hammond, and Stark Washington bought it from him on 12-23-1912. Washington sold two-thirds of his interest to J. L. Costley on 1-22-1916 and the other third to Mrs. M. A. Johnson on 4-15-1916. Her daughter, Connie Richards, bought Mrs. Johnson's interest on 5-11-1918. Costley paid Richards $300 for her interest, giving him total control of the lot. He sold it to Louis Scheh on 12-4-1919. Louis Scheh moved a building from Buda to the site in 1936. Addie Tschoepe bought the property from Scheh on 6-12-1934. Carl M. Scheh bought the property from Addie Tschoepe Scheh on 9-6-1951. P. A. Glosson bought it from Scheh on 8-22-1952. J. N. Rippy bought the property from the P. A. Glosson heirs on 12-16-1963 and sold it to Oran Hill/Janet Rippy on 4-25-1985.

Lot 3. In late 1883, W. T. Chapman built a two-story building on this lot—the first for business and the top story for the meeting place of the Masonic Lodge, which would move from the Friendship Baptist Church building. On 1-1-1884, Chapman sold one-half interest in the building to the Masons (the top story). On 7-25-1905, J. W. Glosson and W .G. McKellar bought the lot from Chapman. After McKellar's death, Glosson paid his widow, Mrs. Florence McKellar, $390 on 5-11-1907 for her share. On 11-25-1907, the Masonic Lodge paid Glosson $115 for the 20x26 foot upstairs addition. Tax records indicate that sometime around 1913, George Houchin purchased the property from Glosson. The next deed I found had J. W. Carter paying George Houchin $800 for his interest in the property. This was 2-23-1915. This would be the last deed transaction I found until 1936. In the meantime, the Rambo Masonic Lodge sold their interest in the building to the Mountain Camp #243 Woodmen of the World for $400 on 9-4-1920. Tax records indicate that J. A. Patton became the owner about that time as well. The next deed was on 12-2-1936 when W. P. Crow paid J. A. Patton $100 for one-half interest. The next day, Crow purchased the Woodmen of the World's interest for $300, making him the sole owner of the property. He would later sell this property to J. N. Rippy on 1-10-1962. Oran Hill/Janet Rippy bought it from his uncle on 4-25-1985.

Lot 4. This lot had a split personality for most of its history. Although no deed showing ownership was found, this was the lot on which J. C. Rowe had his woodworking shop in the late 1880s and paid taxes on from 1885-89. Chapman paid taxes on it beginning 1890. For whatever reason (maybe the building was still there) J. W. Glosson and W. G. McKellar only bought the western three-fourths of the lot from Chapman when they bought Lot 3 on 7-25-1905. The ownership of this portion followed that of Lot 3. Glosson bought Mrs. McKellar's 3/8 interest on 5-11-1907. It was not until W. P. Crow purchased it on 12-2-1936 that changes were made. After losing his other location, Johnny Spaw looked for a place to build a new barbershop. On 1-21-1937, he bought the remaining eastern one-quarter of the lot from the Chapman heirs for $25. It was a 12½x100 foot strip—not really enough to put much of a building on. So he made a deal with Crow on 12-11-1937. Spaw traded the southern half of his strip for one the same size on the west side. This gave him a 25x50 foot lot and gave Crow's portion an L look. Crow's portion went with the dealings of Lot 3 to the Rippys. On 1-1-1964, Spaw sold his lot to Ira Ruston. Ruston sold it to John Bender on 5-13-1978, Bender sold it to W. B. Howell on 3-17-1979, and on 11-16-1979 Peggy Jamison bought the property from Howell for $8,000. Joy Purcell bought the property on 5-11-1994.

Lots 5, 6, 7, 8. These lots have stayed together for most of their history. Galen Crow bought them from Chapman on 9-4-1882. He erected a wooden business building on the site and ran it for a few years until it burned down in 1887. He did not rebuild, but instead sold it to A. L. Davis, Jr., on 5-30-1891. Mr. Davis built a two-story rock general merchandise building that same year. The W. T. Chapman firm, which included his son and son-in-law, bought it from Davis on 11-1-1901. They got into some financial straits and sold the property to W. B. Smith, a banker, for $3,000 on 4-26-1905. They reserved the right to buy it back within the year. They did not, but did continue to lease the business for the next fifteen years. On 6-14-1920, the Rambo Masonic Lodge purchased the property from Smith and they moved their meeting quarters to the second story. David G. Jones bought one-half interest in Lot 6, which was the first floor of the building. Will P. Crow bought Jones' interest for $2,500 on 4-11-1934. Crow bought Lot 5 from the Masons for $1,000 on 10-5-1946. After the building burned down on November 19, 1951, Crow bought the Masons' interest in Lot 6 for $200. On 9-6-1952, the Masonic Lodge sold Lots 7 and 8 to D. C. Hall for $300. W. E. McNair, a longtime employee of Crow, bought the two lots from Mr. Crow on 2-1-1962 for $12,000. The Masonic Lodge bought back Lots 7 and 8 from D. C. Hall on 4-15-1963. W. E. McNair paid the Masons $1,050 for the two lots on 12-14-1963. McNair sold the lots to O. C. Harmon on 3-31-1976. Mack Crow became the third of the Crow family to own these lots when he bought them from Harmon on 7-13-1982. In 1991, Pedernales Electric Coop bought the property from Crow and on 10-28-1994, they sold it to the Todd Purcell Co.

Lot 9. Mrs. A. M. Sorrell paid W. T. Chapman $15 for this lot on 1-20-1897. Flora F. Sorrell Cavett inherited it from the A. M. Sorrell estate in 1917 and her daughter, Aletha Cavett Cobb, inherited it in 1936. Aletha's son, Clarence Cobb, received it on 2-14-1969. Barbara Johnson bought it from Cobb on 9-22-1979. Mack Crow purchased it from Johnson on 12-14-1983. Oran Hill/Janet Rippy bought the lot on 6-19-1989.

Lot 10. Jane Caldwell bought the lot from W. T. Chapman on 2-25-1884, and on the same day sold it to Ella G. O'Pry. She built a house on it, and then sold it to Mrs. A. M. Sorrell on 10-2-1894. From that point, the ownership history was the same as Lot 9.

Lot 11. George Dickey purchased this lot

for $20 from W. T. Chapman on 3-18-1885. He sold it to Ella O'Pry on 7-9-1888 for $15. It, too, would follow the same ownership history as for Lot 9.

NORTHWEST QUARTER

Original Plat, Block Eight

Although this block was surveyed off in the same 50x100 foot lot format as the others, it was bought and sold as a block or half block instead. A. K. Daniel got the ball moving when he paid W. T. Chapman $40 for the entire block on 11-9-1881. W. C. McKellar bought it from Daniel for $100 on 9-29-1899. Since the price was not out of hand for a block of land, it is believed that it was McKellar who built the house known as "Short Mamas" around 1900.

East one-half. On 6-12-1905, A. B. Egger purchased it from McKellar. Egger sold it to Joel M. Patterson for $1000 on 5-20-1908. Patterson was able to sell it to W. M. Perry for $650 on 2-24-1919. Lou Breed purchased it from Perry on 3-17-1923 for $700. Charles Haydon bought it from Breed for his family on 11-5-1934 for $1,500. On 2-21-1957, the State of Texas paid Mrs. Beulah Haydon Malott for most of Lots 7, 8, and 9 for the 290 right-of-way. Mrs. Malott lived in the house until her death in 1989 at the age of 97. The Haydon heirs sold the property to Mrs. Wanda Graham on 11-1-1993. She remodeled it into a bed and breakfast house known as "Short Mama's." In early 2000, the bed and breakfast was closed and it was leased for a coffee shop, antique shop, and business offices. Mrs. Graham turned the property over to her three daughters.

West one-half. Jacob F. Roberts bought this part of the block on 2-12-1901 from Mr. McKellar. On 2-21-1957, they gave up most of Lots 10, 11, and 12 to Hwy. 290 right-of-way. This land stayed in the Roberts family until Randy Garnett went to the trouble to look up all of the heirs and get them to sign off on the sale that took place on 2-12-1976. Upon Randy's death in the early '90s, the property was inherited by his parents, Billie and Alma Garnett. On 12-28-2000, they sold the property to Whit Hanks.

NORTHWEST QUARTER

Original Plat, Block Nine

Lots 1, 2, 11, 12. It is not known who bought these four lots first. I found no original deed. They had to have been bought from W. T. Chapman from the start. Tax records in 1884 showed the taxes being paid on the lots by J. B. Smith with a value of $300. This possibly means a house was on the property.

In July 1885, a newspaper reported that the State of Texas paid $7.40 for the lots with the owner being unknown. This means the state bought it for delinquent taxes. Then the partnership of Chapman/A. L. Davis, Sr., bought the lots from the state. They paid taxes for the property with a value of $250 on the 1886 tax roll. They sold the property to Indiana Weber on 6-15-1886 for $290. Harold C. Durar bought the property from Weber on 12-4-1888 for $175. M. H. Howard bought it from Durar on 11-15-1897 and sold it to Mary Foster on 9-28-1901. J. T. Roberts bought it from Foster on 9-9-1902.

Mercer Chapman purchased the property from Roberts on 5-10-1905. On 10-10-1923, Tom Puryear took it off Chapman's hands. Ten years later, on 8-26-1933, Jesse Ragland bought it from Puryear. Ragland sold it to Mrs. S. E. Lyle on 12-16-1941. She sold the property to her son, William A./Lura Lyle on 1-27-1949. Upon their deaths, their children, Jack and Dean, inherited the property. On 11-16-1973, Jack Lyle bought the half interest of the property from his sister, Dean Lyle Kumlacky, and has owned the property since.

Lots 3, 10. J. C. Linderman bought these two lots from W. T. Chapman on 8-16-1882. No records have been found but, at some point, F. W. Capt came into their pos-

session but failed to pay taxes on them. They came up for public auction and on 4-7-1891, H. C. Durar paid the county $5.19 for the lots. He included these lots in his sale to M. H. Howard on 11-15-1897. From this point on, the ownership trail stayed the same as for Lots 1, 2, 11, and 12, until Jack Lyle sold all but the west 24 feet to Mike Poston in the '80s.

Lots 4, 9. T. W. Saverance bought these two lots from W. T. Chapman on 8-16-1882 at the same time that Linderman bought his. I found no paper trail for them until M. H. Howard sold them to Mary Foster at the same time as Lots 1, 2, 3, 10, 11, and 12. Perhaps Howard bought them for back taxes, much like Durar did. Anyway, after Mary Foster bought them, they were owned by the same individuals as the above lots, until Jack Lyle sold them to Mike Poston in the '80s.

Lots 5, 8. The early history of these two lots are shrouded in mystery. The first time they are mentioned in a deed filing is 5-15-1895 when Anna Fischer sold them to W. C. McKellar. Most likely, she got them for back taxes. On 4-4-1901, W. S. McLendon bought them from McKellar. McLendon then sold them to W. H. Crenshaw on 11-12-1901. McKellar bought them back on 12-2-1905 and sold them to A. L. Davis, Jr., on 7-2-1924. W. S. McLendon came into the property again when he bought it from the Davis heirs on 5-9-1938. He must have still owed on it when he died because John/Erah Killen bought it on 5-31-1940 and the grantor was listed as the Davis heirs.

The Killens sold it to P. A. Glosson on 3-19-1946. Frank/Lura Womack bought them on 7-1-1946 from the Glossons. Vira Haster bought the lots from the Womacks on 1-18-1949. Virgil Conn bought Lot 5 from Haster on 6-13-1958 and Lot 8 on 10-13-1969. Jack Lyle bought them from Virgil Conn on 5-15-1970. He would later sell them to Jesse "Mike" Poston in the early '80s.

Lots 6, 7. T. F. Keesee bought these two lots from W. T. Chapman on 8-24-1883. A. K. Daniel purchased the property on 1-5-1884. The State of Texas claimed it for taxes in 1886. Anna Fischer later paid the state for the property. She sold these two lots, along with Lots 5 and 8, to W. C. McKellar on 5-15-1895 for $250. Most likely, a house was on this property by this time. The ownership trail stayed the same as for Lots 5 and 8 until Virgil Conn bought Lot 6 on 6-13-1958 and Lot 7 on 10-13-1969. Jack Lyle bought the two lots from Conn on 5-15-1970.

These two lots were sold to Jesse "Mike" Poston in the early '80s. He built a restaurant on Lot 6.

NORTHWEST QUARTER

Original Plat, Block Ten

A. L. Davis, Sr., bought this block from W. T. Chapman on 9-14-1882 and built a home on the property. A. L. Davis, Jr., sold the property to J. W. Phillips on 7-1-1903 for $750. Phillips sold it to W. R. Yancey for $1,200 on 4-16-1909. I. T. Applewhite paid Yancey $1,000 for the property on 12-12-1910. Mrs. Mayme B. Roberts paid that same $1,000 to Applewhite on 2-19-1921. C. W. Crenshaw and W. S. Garnett, Jr., paid Mrs. Roberts $1,200 for the place on 3-10-1923. J. M. Earls bought it from them for $800 on 10-28-1925. J. M. Earls sold it to C. H. Gustafson on 10-14-1929. Gustafson turned around and sold it to L. W. McClintock on 12-23-1929. J. W. McClintock bought all of the block from L. W., except a lot 50x150 feet in the southeast corner of the block on 12-29-1930. Charles Haydon bought J. W. McClintock's part on 11-22-1933. The grantor on the deed was Thomas Hamby, who probably held the note. Haydon bought the lot from L. W. McClintock on 12-14-1935 to now own the entire block. After his dad's death, Alva Haydon bought the block from his mother, Mrs. Beulah Haydon, for $500 on 10-11-1938. He built his house on the property

in 1943. On 3-22-1965, he sold a 75x100 foot lot out of the southeast corner to J. E. Murrah for $1,000. They sold the lot to the church of Christ in the mid-'80s for a parsonage. Later, Matthew Walker bought the lot from the church on 12-27-1990.

NORTHWEST QUARTER————

Original Plat, Block Eleven

South One-Half. M. M. Caperton bought the entire block from W. T. Chapman on 11-10-1881. On 1-1-1884, C. J. Hamilton paid Caperton $800 for this half block. Evidently, Caperton had some type of building on this property, possibly his house. A. K. Daniel paid Hamilton $300 for that same property on 4-13-1889. Something had to happen to the improvements because A. L. Davis, Jr., bought it from Daniel for only $60 on 4-10-1892. Davis sold it to J. F. Roberts for $80 on 11-1-1901. On 2-21-1957, the State of Texas paid the Roberts heirs for the 290 right-of-way which wiped out the entire half block.

North One-Half. On 8-18-1898, J. F. Roberts paid M. M. Caperton $350 for this half of the block. There was a house on this property as well. It burned to the ground on 3-19-1922. Randy Garnett made the effort to get all the Roberts heirs to sign the bill of sale for this property and took ownership on 2-12-1976. He built the Bluff Business Center on this property in the 1980s. Upon his death in the early '90s, his parents, Billie and Alma Garnett inherited the property. They sold the property to Whit Hanks on 12-28-2000.

NORTHWEST QUARTER————

Original Plat, Block Twelve

We know that Sam D. Gilpin bought the entire block from W. T. Chapman but I have not found the actual deed. He ran a drugstore on the property—first in a wooden building that burned down and then in a rock building. At some point, probably in 1885, J. H./F. A. Wilson bought the block from Gilpin. The Wilsons sold the block to Z. I. Williams for $300 on 10-26-1886. H. W. Cook paid Williams $79.59 for a 50x60 foot lot out of the northeast corner. This piece of property had the business building on it. On 11-16-1891, J. E. Pritchett paid Williams $200 for the rest of the block. P. M Massey paid Pritchett $65 for his property on 8-31-1892. J. F. Roberts paid P. M. Massey $25 for his property on 10-3-1898. Billie Garnett bought the 50x60 foot lot from Mrs. Maudine McMain on 1-6-1976. Randy Garnett bought the rest from the Roberts heirs on 2-12-1976. Billie and Alma Garnett inherited the property upon Randy's death in the early '90s. They sold the entire block to Whit Hanks on 12-28-2000.

NORTHWEST QUARTER————

First Addition

It did not take long for W. T. Chapman to add to his township. He finished surveying the first addition on May 19, 1882, and filed it on June 22, 1882. This addition flanked the Academy Block, bordering on the north side of Mercer Street. Like some of the other surveys to follow, the figures did not always add up and would have to be adjusted later. I'm not sure the block one lots are as they should be. It is hard to tell if there is enough land for all the measurements given.

NORTHWEST QUARTER————

First Addition, Block One

Lots 1, 10. On 8-5-1882, J.R.B. Fairchild bought these lots from W. T. Chapman. He built a house and store on the site before selling them to J. T. Wortham for $300 on 2-20-1883. H. C. Pearcy bought them on 8-29-1883. Pedernales Lienneweber purchased the lots on 7-17-1890. Lienneweber held onto the property until 1904 when he

sold them to W. S. Garnett on 5-9-1904. On this property he built his blacksmith business. Oran/J. N. Rippy purchased these lots on 2-8-1955 from the Garnett heirs. They, in turn, sold them to J. Spurgeon Breed on 8-26-1963 and he built a feed store on the property. On 2-6-1968, Mr. Breed deeded it over to Breed Milling and Feed Company. Breed Milling sold it to Viron G. Sims and the feed business continued. Wayne Mathewson and Raymond Whisenant bought the property from Sims in the late '70s. On 3-25-1983, Mathewson bought out Whisenant's half interest in the property. The hard times of the late '80s caught up with the Mathewsons, as well, and they ended up going through bankruptcy and losing the property, which was bought by Kevin Bogan on 8-30-1991.

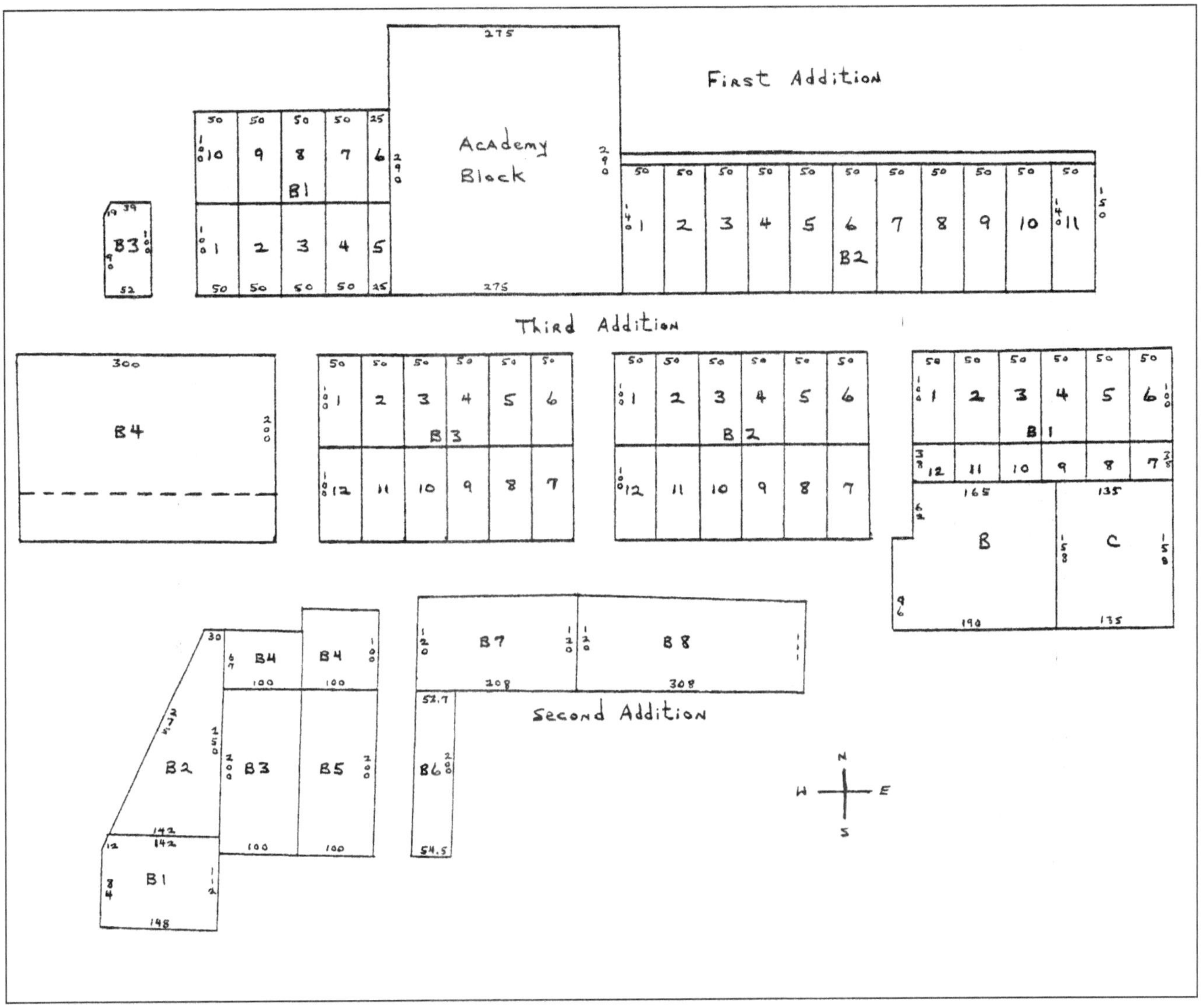

Lot 2. Chapman never sold this lot. Part of it had the hotel located on it. So, on the Chapmans' deaths, this lot became a part of the holdings that went over to the Smith brothers on 3-14-1924. W. S. McLendon bought this lot from the Smith heirs on 6-20-1939. Even though there was no record found that transferred Lot 2 to the Garnetts, when the Rippys bought the Garnett holdings in this block, this lot was included. Its trail of ownership followed Lots 1 and 10.

Lot 3. This lot was also never sold by Chapman, so went the route of Smith to McLendon. It, too, had the hotel on the property. It had been torn down before

Virgil B. Conn bought the lot from McLendon on 10-14-1939. F. W. Miller, Sr., bought the lot from Conn on 1-17-1940 and build a little Texaco station on the premises. Mrs. Ella Miller sold the lot to M. Z. Piland on 6-23-1964. He sold it to Mrs. Zadie Brown Lumpkin on 6-1-1965. Mrs. Lumpkin sold it to Dr. Allen Neighbors on 2-7-1973. Clem Best bought it on 3-29-1973. It has remained in the Best family since that time.

Lot 4. This lot followed the ownership trail of Lot 3. Miller built the Rock Cafe on this lot. It stayed in the Lumpkin family until Ned Wilson bought it. Joy Purcell purchased the lot on 8-5-1994. The lot includes only the eastern 41 feet of Lot 4. The other 9 feet went with Clem Best when he purchased Lot 3.

Lot 5. According to the original plat, Lot 5 was only twenty-five feet wide. I think it may have gotten swallowed up by the Academy Block and not survived, although the deeds include it. There is a probability it became a part of the Patterson store lot. Certainly the tape and the deeds do not work out the mathematics. On 3-6-1940, F. W. Miller, Sr., bought the lot from McLendon for $200. Someone did not get their fair share. Lot 5 then follows Lot 4 in the ownership trail.

Lots 6, 7, 8, 9. These lots should be a 100x175 feet strip of land. They ended up being divided into a north half and a south half for a while. No deed date was found but, at some point, W. A. Hogan bought the northern half (50x175 feet) from Chapman and had a blacksmith shop on the property. Chapman paid him $350 for the lots on 4-15-1889. Chapman sold them to W. H. Robbins on 7-25-1893. James Walter Glosson bought them from the Robbins heirs on 2-18-1907. Glosson sold them to W. S. Garnett on 4-6-1907. The southern half, which was included in the hotel property, went to the Smith brothers in 1924 and onto W. S. McLendon in 1939. Once again, even though no deed was found recorded that transferred the property, when the Rippys bought the property from the Garnetts, the transaction was for the complete lots. This was possibly by the rule that if one used it as their own long enough, it became theirs. Part of the property was used for school playground purposes before the school moved in 1949. These lots followed the ownership trail of Lots 1 and 10.

NORTHWEST QUARTER

First Addition, Block Two

This block was another example of figures not adding up. The original plat showed ten lots and a later one showed eleven lots of 50x140 feet. The problem was the block was only 462 feet in length and fifty into that does not make eleven lots or actually, even ten lots, as later transactions will show. Adjustments would have to be made for this to work out to everyone's satisfaction.

Lots 1, 2. C. S. Graham bought the two lots from W. T. Chapman on 1-30-1884, and he built a house on the lot. Although one deed claimed that the property was already owned by a W. J. Collins, deeds do not bear this out. Sam D. Gilpin, a druggist, bought the property from Graham on 2-19-1885. George McCuistion, another druggist, bought the property from Gilpin on 12-25-1895. W. H. Crenshaw bought it from McCuistion on 12-23-1905. W. H. Crenshaw sold it to his son D. W. Crenshaw on 4-22-1919. Clell Basket bought it from D. W. Crenshaw on 6-1-1929 but was unable to pay for the purchase and had to let it go back on 11-1-1930. The Crenshaws finally found a buyer in the form of W. C. Goslin on 3-5-1934. It would stay in the family. Johnny Chase, a grandson, bought the property from the Goslin heirs on 4-15-1976 and he still owns the property.

Lots 3, 4. John Short bought these lots from Chapman on 2-6-1885. Lot 4 was given as a partial only. This was probably only a twelve-foot wide strip. Every deed gave Lot 4 as a partial and never was the

rest of the lot ever a part of another deed, so it is my belief that to balance the inequity of lots, Lot 4 just became a 12x140 foot lot. John Short moved and sold the lots to John Hamilton on 8-26-1886. Hamilton sold them to McCuistion on 11-18-1898 and then the ownership trail would stay the same as Lots 1 and 2, except Wilma Goslin Chase Patterson would keep ownership of these two. The Goslins built the rock house on this property in 1940. The heirs of Mrs. Patterson still own it.

Lots 5, 6, 7, 8, 9. A deed of 2-6-1885 had John Short paying W. T. Chapman $35 for the lots but when the John Short block was added to the Dripping Springs plat, it did not show Short owning those particular lots. When the Chapmans died in 1924, this was a part of the property that the Smith brothers attained from the heirs. W. S. McLendon bought the Smith holdings on 6-20-1939. Mrs. Erlene McLendon Davis inherited them on her father's death in 1940. She sold them to J. H. Howard on 1-25-1944. In all probability, Mr. Howard built a house on the property because R. S./Johnsie Shelley paid him $2,000 for the lots on 3-27-1947. Dayton Roberts paid the Shelleys $2,700 for the lots on 2-28-1949 and it has been in the Roberts family since. Mr. Roberts built the Veranda business complex in the mid-'80s. On 4-19-1984, Dayton had to quitclaim Lot 9. The reason was the length never did support eleven lots and not even ten full lots. So to get the two lots designated 10 and 11 correct, they had to drop eleven and make them nine and ten. Grandsons Marty and Tommy Roberts now own the property.

Lots 10, 11. These two lots were the last two on the block and measured 100x140 feet. P. T. Littlefield bought the two lots from W. T. Chapman for $75.85 on 12-12-1884. J. W. Hamilton paid Littlefield $125 for them on 4-10-1888. Hamilton sold the property to Ann Evart for $65 on 12-29-1898. On 10-

C. S. Graham House. L-R: William Hill Crenshaw, Anna Crenshaw, Dora P. Crenshaw, Ann McQueen Smith, Cecilia Jane McQueen Crenshaw, Caudential Waite Crenshaw, and Dave Wesley Crenshaw.

—Courtesy George Bruce Mading

27-1900, J. G. Pursley bought them from Ann Evart. Pursley sold the lots to R. E. Spaw on 12-1-1908. W. P. King bought the lots from Spaw on 8-1-1912. The house that was on these lots was torn down and another built in its place in 1958 for the Harvey Kings, who owned the property and lived on it until 4-19-1984, when daughter, Hazel Bell King Myers sold the property to James Hurlbut. It was at this time that Dayton Roberts had to quitclaim Lot 9 and these two lots became nine and ten. Hurlbut converted the house into a business complex called Mercer One in the mid-'80s. Hurlbut sold it in 1988 to Greg Tom. Mary McFadin, under Gateway Graphics, bought the property on 5-20-1994.

NORTHWEST QUARTER

First Addition, Block Three

This block was located on the west side of block one and separated by the fifty-foot North Street. It began at the juncture of Mercer and North streets, then north 100 feet, then west 39 feet until it hit the rock fence, then at an angle with the rock fence, southwest fourteen feet, and from that point, ninety feet south to Mercer, then along Mercer, east fifty-three feet. When the first deeds were made, it described the property as beginning at the southwest corner of the Caperton blacksmith shop. This means that at some point, the blacksmith shop must have been located where North Street was. Today, North Street is just a small road between the buildings and not fifty feet wide. So once again, usage overruns surveys. O. C. Barton bought the block from W. T. Chapman on 11-19-1883 for $25. He established a livery stable there and then sold the business to Galen Crow on 4-4-1884. A little later, David G. Jones paid Crow for the property on 11-18-1884. William Herndon took it off Jones's hands on 1-14-1885. C. S. Graham bought the block from Herndon on 2-8-1886. J. W. Hamilton bought the property from Graham on 2-19-1887. He ran a mail route between Dripping Springs and Blanco. Pedernales Leinneweber bought it on 2-27-1897. Leinneweber sold it to W. S. Garnett, Sr., on 5-9-1904. The Garnetts built a garage on the lot around 1925 and retired the livery stable. On 12-27-1935, W. S. Garnett, Jr., bought the property from his dad. Travis Garnett bought Billie Garnett's interest in the block on 12-14-1958 and on 11-29-1967, Fred Garnett bought the block when he converted the old Garnett garage and service station into the headquarters for his DS Butane business and he still owns the property.

NORTHWEST QUARTER

Second Addition

The second addition was located on the north boundary line of block one, in the first addition, the Academy block, and John Short block. The survey was completed on 10-12-1883 and filed on 10-27-1883. Due to property owner constraints, the blocks had some different configurations. Also, this addition was surveyed off in blocks only and did not have individual lots.

NORTHWEST QUARTER

Second Addition, Block One

In the survey, it labeled this as the M. G. Caperton block. Just like the blacksmith shop, there is no deed showing Caperton as the owner of this property, just the notation on the survey filed. The first deed found showed that H. C. Pearcy paid W. T. Chapman $38 for this block on 8-29-1883. Pearcy was once a partner to Chapman in his grocery store. Pearcy built a house on this property. Pedernales Leinneweber bought the property from Pearcy on 7-17-1890. Leinneweber sold it to W. S. Garnett, Sr., on 5-9-1904. The Garnett family made it their home for the rest of their lives. On 3-29-1951, Mary Lou Garnett Haster inherited the block. On 9-15-1972, she deeded it over

to her children, Walter D. Haster and Mary Madeline Haster Jones, with the stipulation that she could stay there for the rest of her life. In the late '80s the Hasters sold the property to Richard Garza and he still owns the property.

NORTHWEST QUARTER

Second Addition, Block Two

Again, when the survey was filed, block two was designated as the Fairchild block. No deed was found to corroborate this. However, the first deed found was on 2-11-1889 when J. W. Hamilton paid J.R.B. Fairchild $45 for it. Hamilton sold it to Pedernales "Pete" Leinneweber on 2-27-1897. He sold it to W. S. Garnett, Sr., on 5-9-1904. It became the property of Mary Lou Garnett Haster on 3-29-1951 and she deeded it over to her children with the same stipulation as block one. The Hasters sold it to Richard Garza in the late '80s and he still owns it.

NORTHWEST QUARTER

Second Addition, Block Three

James Glosson bought this block from W. T. Chapman on 4-28-1883. James A. Smith paid Glosson $300 for the property on 12-5-1884. This price usually means some type of improvement, most likely, a house was on the property. J. W. Graham paid Smith $200 for it on 9-11-1889. Graham sold it to C. F. Davis for $365 on 12-2-1890. Davis defaulted on his note and since J. A. Smith held the note and had the most to lose, got the property back in a sheriff's sale on 12-6-1892 for $65. Smith resold the property, this time on 12-30-1895 to Mrs. B. Pursley for $125. Pedernales Leinneweber was some kin to Mrs. Pursley and therefore inherited the property on 10-18-1899. He sold it to Walter Glosson on 1-28-1905. A. L. Davis, Jr., bought the property from Glosson on 6-13-1907 for $350.

Davis sold the block to the Dripping Springs District #20 for $150 on 3-7-1931 and it has stayed the school's property since.

NORTHWEST QUARTER

Second Addition, Block Four

This block was chopped up because it was on the edge of ownership problems. Chapman did not own all of this land at the time. His stepchildren had some ownership rights but probably had his blessings on the survey. Most of the sale activity occurred on the west one-half of the block. The first thing we know was that Neeley Jane Ross bought a section approximately 50x100 feet from W. T. Chapman on 8-14-1884. Now it becomes a little fuzzy. No deed was found where Ross sold the lot. From other sources, it gave W. B. Harmon as an owner and, at some point, H. C. Harris had to become an owner because Pedernales Leinneweber paid him $10 for it on 6-8-1901. The next record of exchange was on 11-23-1926 when A. L. Davis, Jr., bought the lot from L. R. and Bessie Lackey. Davis sold the lot to the Dripping Springs school on 3-7-1931. Bradley Davis bought this lot from DSISD in the early '90s. There was a 33x100 foot strip on the top of the 50x100 foot lot. I think it might have been a part of North Street at one time. J. W. Glosson bought it from W. T. Chapman on 6-3-1905. On 4-21-1906, I. V. Davis, Jr., bought the lot from Glosson for $10. The eastern half of the block was a full 100x100 feet. W. H. Robbins bought this lot from George Marshall on 7-25-1893. Robbins built his house on it, and when I. V. Davis, Jr., bought the lot from Mrs. M. J. Martin, the widow of Robbins, on 6-3-1904, they moved into the five-room house. Tax records had the Davises paying taxes on this property for 1902 and 1903, so they must have been occupying the property then as well. Bradley Davis sold block four to Bo Murphy Davis in the mid-'90s. He sold it to Carole Howard on 7-8-1997.

NORTHWEST QUARTER

Second Addition, Block Five

Maggie Caldwell bought this block from W. T. Chapman on 1-30-1884. She sold the block in two parcels to Sallie McLendon. On 2-22-1892, it was the north 50x100 feet for $10 and on 9-18-1893, the other 150x100 feet for $30. W. S. McLendon inherited the block on 10-23-1915. He sold it to Oscar V. Stubbs on 12-1-1921. Stubbs sold it to John E. Spaw on 4-6-1925. I. D. Hedges bought the property from Spaw on 4-4-1934 and, in turn, sold it to D. W. Crenshaw on 6-23-1936. Crenshaw sold it to the Dripping Springs school for $300 on 11-14-1938 and it is still part of the school's property. A teacherage was moved to the northeast corner in the mid-'40s. The bus shed that was built around 1946, was torn down after the school moved to another campus in 1949. The teacherage was finally razed in the mid-'90s.

NORTHWEST QUARTER

Second Addition, Block Six

This block ended up being divided early on and has remained that way since. One of the first things that Chapman did after donating the Academy block and beginning this town, was to build a two-story boarding house on the southern end of this block in the fall of 1881. The house was within fifteen feet of the south property line that abutted the north boundary line of the Academy block. On 1-8-1885, Chapman sold the property to R. G. Horsley, the school principal, for $700. He sold it to Mrs. A. C. Scroggins for $610 on 1-1-1887. Mrs. Scroggins sold the lot to R. E. Spaw on 2-13-1902. Tax records show that W. A. McMillan paid taxes on the property the entire time that Mrs. Scroggins owned the property. W. T. Chapman would again come into the property when he bought it from Spaw on 5-11-1903. McCreary Crow took it off Chapman's hands on 2-9-1907 and on that same day, sold it to Mrs. O. V. Ward and Mrs. M. M. Horton for $525. Mrs. Ward paid Mrs. Horton $200 for her share of the lot on 9-27-1909. George W. Nuckols paid Mrs. Ward $500 for it on 8-15-1912. He and his sister lived in the house until both died in the early '30s. The property was left to his niece and nephew, Mrs. Sloss and Mr. Kettler. They sold it to Allen Stephenson on 1-9-1933 for $400. Stephenson sold the lot to Leroy Roberts for $400 on 11-1-1936. It stayed in the Roberts family until 5-20-1969, when Mrs. Katherine Roberts sold it to Paul J. Allen, the school principal. Mr. Allen renovated the house with rockwork and other indoor improvements before selling it to Galen and Jerry Lou Dodson on 6-12-1973. It has remained in their hands and as their residence for most of the years since.

The northern part of the block got its start when W. T. Chapman sold it to I.C.P. McLendon on 9-17-1884. He built his house on the northern end and it remains there today. Upon Mr. McLendon's death, his wife, Sallie, had to pay the trustee, J. R. Wilhelm, $400 for the lot. This was on 3-13-1914. Upon her death, W. S. McLendon inherited the property on 10-23-1915. He sold it to O. V. Stubbs for $600 on 12-1-1921. Stubbs sold it to J. E. Spaw on 4-6-1925. He sold it to I. D. Hedges on 4-4-1934 and Hedges sold it to D. W. Crenshaw on 6-23-1936. On 11-24-1937, O. J. Bean paid Crenshaw $650 for the lot. John W. Ireland bought the property from the Beans on 6-24-1957. Bessie Ireland Scott bought the share of Ewall Scott Ireland on 12-30-1971 and still owns the property.

NORTHWEST QUARTER

Second Addition, Block Seven

J. A. Smith bought the block from W. T. Chapman on 11-9-1883 for $50. He immediately built his house on the property. On 11-3-1888, Smith sold the property to G. H./M. A. Cook for $630. A newspaper

article had Mr. Stapleton, a blacksmith, buying the property in 1889 and then putting it up for sale in 1890. On 5-23-1890, Mrs. A. M. Sorrell paid Mary Cook $300. Maybe it was a promissory note from Mrs. Sorrell. G. H. Cook then sold the property to Dr. E. P. Shelton for $400 on 8-23-1898. On 6-26-1954, Edgar Vaughn Shelton bought the property from the Shelton heirs. On 10-3-1962, John Edgar Shelton got the property from Edgar V. Shelton. On 8-7-1968, Clarence Shelton, the last surviving child of Dr. Shelton, would get the property from the Shelton heirs. The Shelton house was torn down in 1998 and a grandson, Jack Huey, bought the property from Clarence Shelton on 9-9-1998. He built a house on it in early 1999.

NORTHWEST QUARTER

Second Addition, Block Eight

Block eight was never sold in the Chapmans' lifetimes and therefore became the property of the Smith brothers in 1924. It then went to W. S. McLendon in 1939 and was inherited by Erlene McLendon Davis in 1940. She sold it to J. E. Spaw for $50 on 6-8-1943. Clarence Shelton bought the block from Mr. Spaw on 5-11-1970 and built his house on the eastern end of the block. He died in the spring of 2002 and his heirs still own the property

NORTHWEST QUARTER

Third Addition

This addition was first filed, along with the second addition, on October 27, 1883. At this time, land had been divided into eight blocks, mostly splitting the 200x300 foot sections in half. Previous purchases had caused some surveying problems as well and the far eastern block of land never did really materialize as correctly as the map shows because of the land purchases. This addition was south of the original Dripping Springs plat divided by the newly installed Hays Street. Later, in a more completely surveyed plat filed on July 25, 1885, this addition was reduced to four blocks and the blocks surveyed in 50x100 foot lots. Because of this, some of the early deeds reflected the eight-block system and later, the four-block system. The numbering of the four block system were in reverse of the previous. Number one block was now on the east and worked its way west, whereas, previously, it began on the west and worked its way east.

NORTHWEST QUARTER

Third Addition, Block One

This block ended up being a little messed up from the beginning because of previous purchases and ended up really being three separate sections of land and therefore, I treated it as three separate sections when lining up the owners of each. Because of circumstances, this block of land ended up being larger than the other 200x300 foot ones. Block one was nestled in the southeast corner of the northwest quarter of the P. A. Smith league. The first transaction concerning this tract of land was on 7-28-1874, when W. T. Chapman sold a strip of land to the Dripping Springs Baptists for three dollars that bordered on the two acres of land that John Wallace had sold to the Baptists. It is not known which of these two tracts the first Baptist church was built on, probably the Wallace tract, but we do know the church burned to the ground in 1879 and although, at this time, no deed has been found, that sent the property back to Chapman. It was back in his hands before he had this addition filed.

Section A. At some time before this addition was surveyed, this 158x135 foot tract of land was sold by Chapman to others and because of this, the block did not sell exactly in the smooth lots that other blocks were able to do, regardless of how it looked on the surveys. At the present, no deed has been found, but we do know by other documents that J. R. Brown purchased this tract from W. T. Chapman probably on 5-22-1874. Tax records reveal that W. L. Armstrong paid taxes on this property from 1877-79. However, it was Brown who sold it to D. J. Meers in 1880. Meers was a veternarian who was also starting up a mule-raising business about this time. It could have been he or Brown who first built the house on the northern end of this tract that is now hidden by dense growth. We know that Meers sold the tract to W. M. Jordan, a Baptist preacher, on 1-2-1883. A deed was not found but again other reports in the county records tells us that J. D. Walker, a Baptist minister, had possession of the property, probably buying it soon after Jordan left in the summer of 1883. On 12-9-1885, Walker's successor, G. W. Wood bought the property from him. W. N. Albright bought the property from Wood on 2-27-1899. R. E. Spaw bought the property on 3-14-1899 and part of the price paid was a dun horse. Next, W. M. Collenback paid Spaw $45 for the tract on 3-28-1899. The $45 was a used wagon and $20 on credit. A. L. James, a Baptist minister, bought the property from Collenback on 10-23-1903, paying him $275 for two tracts he bought that day. On 5-20-1905, James sold the property to W. T. Chapman & Son and they sold it to the next Baptist minister, Henry T. Peal, on 6-1-1905. Thomas B. Barnette bought the tract from the H. T. Peal heirs on 10-19-1940 and William C. "Bill" Bassett bought it from Mrs. Vivian Peal Barnette on 11-20-1979. On 7-12-1994, the Bassetts deeded the land over to their daughters, Bren, Romi, and Leasa.

Section B. Because a section about 158x135 feet was sold out of the southeast corner, the twelve-lot division as surveyed, really never did develop as a tract of land. Instead, this section became a tract of land 135x300 feet, that included all of Lots 1, 2, 3, 4, 5, 6 and part of Lots 7, 8, 9, 10, 11, and 12. Throughout the history of this block, this section remained intact when being transacted. It lost a little off the eastern end when RR12 right-of-way took a few feet. Richard Cruse was the first to purchase this tract from W. T. Chapman on 11-20-1894. He sold it to O. G. Shockley for $75 on 1-10-1901. Shockley sold it to C. B. Smith on 10-8-1901 for $200. A jump in price like that usually meant a building on the property. We know that the little Walnut Springs Methodist church was moved onto that site and made into a dwelling. The Methodists had already bought property across the street by this time, so it may have been that Shockley bought the building and moved it there during his ownership. C. B. Smith sold the property to Hattie Goslin Byers on 4-27-1908. Foster and Susan Harmon paid Mrs. Byers $150 for it on 1-25-1940. Nine months later, on 10-26-1940, the Harmons sold it to P. A. and Annie Glosson for the same amount. W. J. Sheppard bought the property from the Glosson heirs on 8-31-1966. He hung onto it until Betty Garnett bought it from him on 4-28-1980. Because James Hurlbut had some land in block one that the bank needed for expansion purposes, a deal was made for the bank to purchase the property from Mrs. Garnett and then swap it to Hurlbut for his land in block one in 1984. Hurlbut proceeded to clear the lot and built the Pioneer Plaza office complex on the site. The financial bust of the late '80s caught up with him and he lost the building. Elry A. "Skeeter" Hudson bought the property on 8-25-1992.

Section C. This section covers approximately a 158x165 foot tract of land carved out of the southwest corner of this block. W. M. Collenback was the first to buy the property from W. T. Chapman. He paid $30 for it on 11-18-1901. A. L. James, the Baptist minister, bought the property from Collenback in conjunction with section A on 10-23-1903. After he left, W. T. Chapman & Son bought the tract from him on 5-20-1905. They sold it to another Baptist minister, Henry T. Peal, on 6-1-1905. Thomas B. Barnette bought it from the H. T. Peal heirs on 8-8-1940. William C. "Bill" Bassett bought the property from Mrs. Vivian Peal

Barnette on 11-20-1979. On 7-12-1994, the Bassetts deeded the property over to their daughters, Bren, Romi, and Leasa.

NORTHWEST QUARTER

Third Addition, Block Two

Lots 1, 12. We found no record but know that A. E. Heep must have bought these two lots from W. T. Chapman because he sold them to George W. Marshall on 7-2-1889. J. W. Wood bought them from Mrs. Millie Alexander Marshall on 9-24-1942. Billie R. and Jo G. Rippy bought the lots from Wood on 4-17-1957. The Wood's house, which at one time had been the Millseat school, had already burned at this time. A couple of years later, Felix Rippy took over the property. After his death, J. N. Rippy assumed the debts of the Rippy heirs on 4-12-1968. These lots were sold to the Dripping Springs First Baptist Church in the 1970s.

Lots 2, 11. George W. Marshall bought these lots from W. T. Chapman on 7-10-1889. His widow, Mrs. Millie Alexander Marshall, sold them to J. W. Wood on 9-24-1942 and the ownership trail stays the same as for Lots 1 and 12.

Lots 3, 10. At this time, I have found no evidence that these lots were ever sold to anyone. I don't know if they were absorbed within the other four out of use or what. They are now listed as being owned by the Baptist Church in part of the Rippy acquisition.

Lots 4, 5, 6, 7, 8, 9. These lots were first bought when the survey was a part of the eight-block plat and they were listed as being bought as a block. W. J. Hall bought them from W. T. Chapman on 10-12-1883. J. W. Daniel bought it from him for $325 on 8-11-1884. S. T. Walters bought it from Daniel on 9-15-1884 for the same $325. George Dickey paid Walters $300 for the lots on 7-23-1889. The DS Methodist Church paid Dickey $300 on 10-8-1892, for a parsonage. J. N. Rippy paid the Methodist Church $1,750 for the lots on 2-19-1948. He sold it to the First Baptist Church in the 1970s.

NORTHWEST QUARTER

Third Addition, Block Three

This block eventually disdained the lot system that it had been surveyed into and different sections were sold from it as the years went by that had no lot designations. The block itself was a 200x300 foot tract of land. Block three was one of those parcels of land that was never sold while the Chapmans were around and therefore, was transferred to the Smith brothers on 3-14-1924 and then on to W. S. McLendon on 6-20-1939. John and Erah Killen paid Erlene McLendon Davis $150 for the block on 6-8-1943. From this point, the carving took place. First, on 4-19-1945, Virgil Conn paid the Killens $30 for a 30x200 foot strip off the eastern end of the block, so that he would have some land running to his house at the end of the block. This represented a portion of Lots 6 and 7. Next the Killens sold Mrs. Dosia Hohman an 87x270 foot strip off the south side of the block for $300 on 3-19-1951. This was the southern part of Lots 7, 8, 9, 10, 11, and 12. She built her house there. After her death in 1988, her heirs sold the property. It is now owned by Steven Osborn who bought it on 7-28-1995. On 1-19-1956, James W. and Tula Glosson paid Erah Killen $4,000 for the rest of the block which was a strip 113x270 feet which represented all of Lots 1, 2, 3, 4, and 5 and parts of Lots 6, 7, 8, 9, 10, 11, and 12 and the rock house on the northeast corner of the tract. The Mt. Gainer Baptist church was moved to the northwest corner of this tract and converted to a dwelling place for their mother. On 2-28-1959, Lou Glosson purchased the 113x270 foot tract from James W./Tula Glosson. Jerry "Woody" Glosson then bought the northeast 113x152 foot section from Lou Glosson for $2,700 on 3-17-1959. On 11-15-1963, O. B. McKown bought the 113x152 foot tract from Woody Glosson. Evidently Woody Glosson got title to the other 113x118 foot section because a deed showed James W. Glosson buying it from Woody on 4-20-1964, but on the other hand, on 1-27-1965, Floyd and Lorena Walker paid the Glosson heirs $9,500 for this tract of land. Virgil Conn bought the 113x152 foot tract from O. B. McKown on 4-29-1968. Vira Haster bought a half-interest in the property from Virgil on 10-13-1969. Bob Purcell bought the property from Virgil Conn for $15,000 on 9-23-1978. They sold it to Betty Barton Christianson. It changed hands a couple of times and Jeff Coffman bought the property on 6-13-2001. Wayne Smith purchased the 113x118 foot tract from Walker heirs on 1-1-1995. After doing a great job of remodeling and landscaping, the Smiths moved out and their kin, Shawn and Ann Connolly, moved there in September 1997.

NORTHWEST QUARTER

Third Addition, Block Four

This block was divided into two under the eight block system mainly because Dr. J. W. Harrison had already bought the northern 150x300 foot section of what would become the 200x300 foot block. He bought this from W. T. Chapman for $25 on 8-9-1883. On this land he built the two-story showplace now owned by Joanie Crosswell. On 6-27-1888, Dr. Harrison completed the block by purchasing the final 50x300 foot strip off the southside for $25 from Chapman. Dr. Harrison sold the block to Dr. S. G. Shaw for $475 on 1-2-1891. Dr. E. P. Shelton paid $500 for the property on 10-29-1892. Possibly, Dr. Shelton decided to let the property go back or maybe Dr. Shaw wanted it back, but on 9-1-1894, Dr. Shaw paid Dr. Shelton $414.50 for the property. David G. Jones paid $450 to Dr. Shaw on 5-1-1895 and added the porches and columns on the house in 1905. Mr. Jones sold the property to G. W. Daniel on 10-29-1909. Then there were several ownership transfers that I suspect had to do with holding the note to the place. On 11-10-1909, E. H. Purtle paid G. W. Daniel $2,500. At some point, Robert J. Hammond held title to it because he sold it to Stark Washington on 12-23-1912. On 1-22-1916, J. L. Costley bought two-thirds interest in the place from Washington and on 4-15-1916, Mrs. M. A. Johnson bought the other one-third from Washington. On 5-11-1918, Mrs. Johnson's daughter, Connie Richards, bought her third interest. J. L. Costley proceeded to buy Connie F. Richards' interest for $300 on 3-15-1919, which gave him full control of the block. Louis P. Scheh bought the property from Costley on 12-4-1919. Addie Tschoepe got the property from Scheh on 6-12-1934. She became Addie Scheh and sold the property to Carl M. Scheh on 9-6-1951. Carl Scheh sold the property to Annie Francis Gibson on 4-10-1952. Richard Clay Gibson sold the block to John Elbert and Lillian I. Shelton for $4,000 on 4-2-1963. Mr. Shelton was born in this house in 1893. He passed away in 1967. Mrs. Shelton sold a 100x150 foot lot from the southeast corner of the block to I. A. Applewhite on 11-20-1968. The Applewhite heirs sold the property to Raymond Jenkins in the '90s. After Jenkins' death, Chris Boldt bought it on 4-3-2000. Robert Shelton, the only child, sold the rest of the block to Joan J. Crosswell on 11-9-1977. She has since made major improvements to the lot to make it a showplace in these times and still lives in the house.

NORTHWEST QUARTER

Fourth Addition

The fourth addition plat was filed on April 8, 1886. It was called the John Short Block because Mr. Short was the owner of the property when it was added to the town plat. The block originally covered three acres. It was bordered on the south by block two of the first addition, on the east by John Wallace's property, on the north by blocks

214

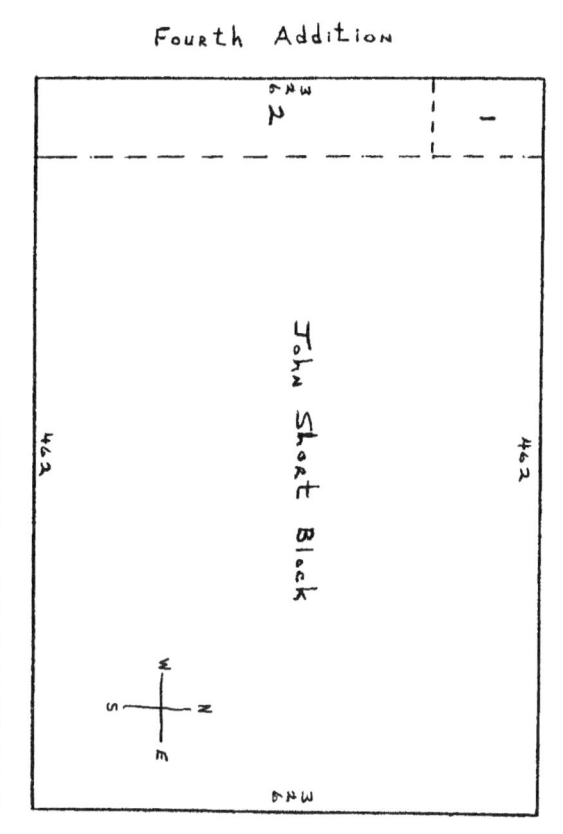

seven and eight of the second addition and on the west by block six of the second addition and the Academy Block. When the plat was surveyed, it made some changes in the John Short block, as well as block two in the first addition. This block was practically landlocked because there was only a small 20x50 foot lane in front of block six of the second addition that connected with Eve Street, although Eve Street was also a deadend. I believe the reason the owners of the block bought Lots 3 and 4 of block two of the first addition, was to have a way in and out. Anyway, the plat took ten feet off the northern ends of the block two lots, which were originally 150 feet in length, and ten feet off the southern border of the Short block, to give the property a twenty-foot alley.

Actually this block had its beginning in November of 1881 when W. M. Jordan paid W. T. Chapman $10 for the southern two acres. Jordan completed the package on 4-11-1883, when he paid $50 for the northern one acre. W. C. Roy purchased the block from W. M. Jordan on 11-10-1883. O. C. Barton bought it from W. C. Roy on 11-10-1883 and he turned it over to Galen Crow on 4-4-1884. David G. Jones purchased it from Crow on 11-18-1884 and then sold it to John Short on 1-31-1885. On 2-6-1885, R. G. Horsley, the school principal who owned block six of the second addition, paid $35 to Short for a 50x270 foot strip of land off the west side of the block. I.C.P. McLendon, who owned the northern half of block six of the second addition, paid Short $10 for the 50x71½ foot strip of land on his eastern border.

When Short decided to set up a new business on Barton Creek, he sold the remaining property to John W. Hamilton on 8-26-1886. Hamilton sold it to R. H. Raines for $150 on 8-12-1899. Raines turned it over to J. B. Middlebrooks on 11-24-1906 for $500. Mary J. Cavendar paid the Middlebrooks $500 for the property on 4-12-1912. W. L. Dye purchased the property from Mary Cavendar for $475 on 3-23-1916. D. W. Crenshaw paid $600 to Mr. Dye for the property on 10-14-1925. They proceeded to tear down the old two-story house and built the house that is on the property today. They sold it to Cecilia Jane Crenshaw on 4-16-1931 for $2,550. On 7-7-1939, Quinton C. Taylor paid $1,000 to the Cecilia Crenshaw estate for the property. He sold it to John E. Spaw for $1,500 on 4-28-1941. It is still in the Spaw family, as it was deeded over to their daughter Marie and husband, J. O. Eckols, on 9-1-1982. They still live there today.

NORTHWEST QUARTER

Fifth Addition

On February 3, 1911, W. T. Chapman filed his final plat for Dripping Springs. It filled in the land between the Dripping Springs branch and already platted blocks, plus the land area between the south boundary line of the northwest quarter and the third addition. Most of it went unsold and

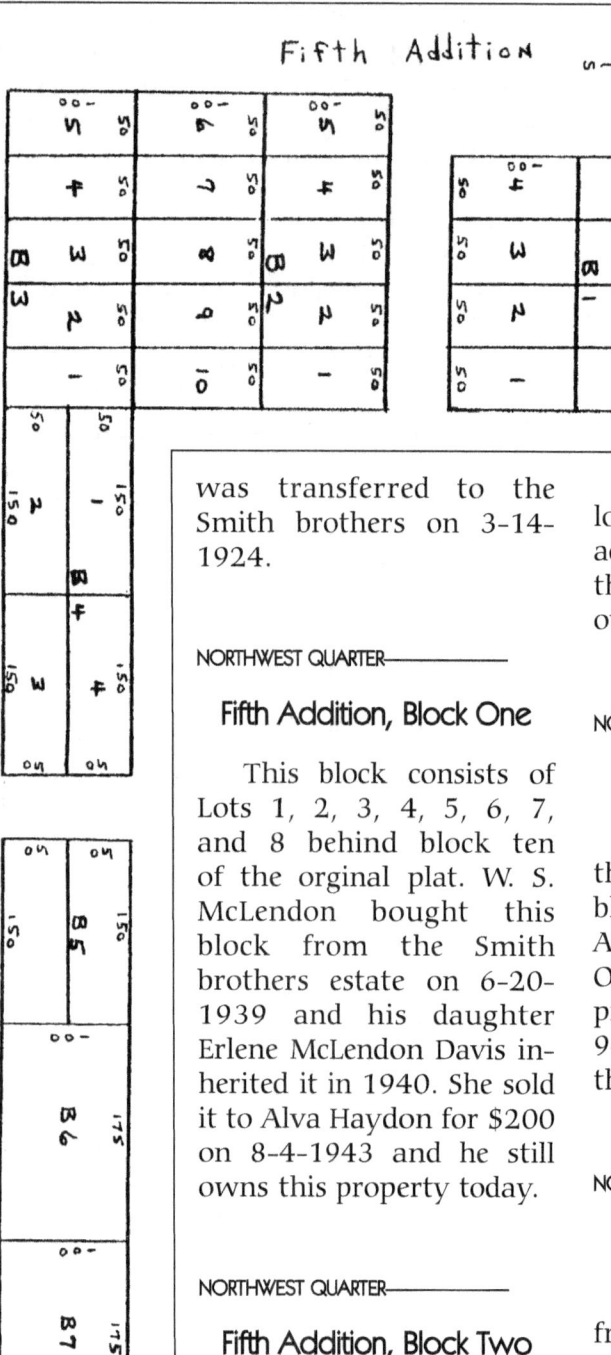

also sold Lots 8 and 9 to Ennis Follis on 3-19-1966, and then on 4-16-1969, Miss Follis also bought Lots 2 and 3. After Miss Follis's death, Craig Carr got possession of the lots on 12-28-1995. Alva Haydon continues to own the rest.

NORTHWEST QUARTER

Fifth Addition, Block Three

This block consists of five lots on the south side of block two of this addition. The ownership trail is the same as that of block one, with Alva Haydon still owning the property.

NORTHWEST QUARTER

Fifth Addition, Block Four

This block has four lots. This block went through the same ownership trail as did block three in the first three transactions. Alva Haydon then sold the block to Wesley O. Malott on 1-20-1950. He deeded the property over to his son, W. E. Malott on 4-9-1967 and W. E. still retains ownership of the block.

NORTHWEST QUARTER

Fifth Addition, Block Five

This block was divided in half. It passed from Chapman to Smith to McLendon to Davis. She sold the block to John and Erah Killen for $35 on 8-4-1943. Erah Killen then sold it to Virgil B. Conn for $100 on 8-8-1947. Virgil Conn sold it to Mae Watson on 4-17-1965 for $400. She built a brick home on the lot that year. Upon her death, on 7-1-1992 under the Jones Family Trust, the property went to her daughter, Mrs. Norma Watson Jones, and she and her family still reside there.

was transferred to the Smith brothers on 3-14-1924.

NORTHWEST QUARTER

Fifth Addition, Block One

This block consists of Lots 1, 2, 3, 4, 5, 6, 7, and 8 behind block ten of the orginal plat. W. S. McLendon bought this block from the Smith brothers estate on 6-20-1939 and his daughter Erlene McLendon Davis inherited it in 1940. She sold it to Alva Haydon for $200 on 8-4-1943 and he still owns this property today.

NORTHWEST QUARTER

Fifth Addition, Block Two

This block has ten lots and is located on the west side of block four of the third addition. It went through the same first three owners as block one. On 1-24-1964, Alva Haydon sold Lots 4 and 5 to Ernest Williamson. He

NORTHWEST QUARTER

Fifth Addition, Block Six

W. L. Dye paid W. T. Chapman $25 for this block on 12-12-1900. Dye sold it to R. E. Spaw for $200 on 5-6-1907. There was probably a house on the property at that time. R. E. "Bob" Spaw sold it to P. L. Turner on 9-25-1912 for $375. Lou Breed paid Turner $700 on 11-25-1918. She sold it to Gibb A. Searight for $801 on 3-14-1923. W. P. Crow bought the property from Searight for $800 on 10-9-1935. Virgil B. Conn paid Crow $800 for the property on 3-1-1937. He built the present house in 1947 and Mrs. Conn still lives there today.

NORTHWEST QUARTER

Fifth Addition, Block Seven

This block passed through the hands of Chapman to Smith brothers to McLendon to Davis. Mrs. Davis sold it to E. M. Strahan on 6-8-1943 for $25. On 3-6-1945, Ray and Emma Kelley bought it from Strahan for $30. Alva Haydon bought it from the Kelleys on 6-18-1969. He then sold the property to Minnie Lea Posey Rogers in 1977 but retained a 40x140 foot right-of-way to his property in the back. She built her house on the lot. After her death, the First Baptist Church purchased the property and still owns it today.

NORTHWEST QUARTER

Fifth Addition, Block Eight

I.C.P. McLendon paid W. T. Chapman $25 for this block on 5-2-1903. He evidently built a small wooden frame house on the property and then sold it to Jane Nicholson for $200 on 12-14-1903. She sold it to T. W. Evans on 7-29-1905 for $250. Evans sold the property to T. L. Sansom on 3-20-1911 for $200. J. W. Champion paid $300 on 9-16-1912 to Sansom for the property. Champion sold it to Granville Huey on 2-4-1920 for $250. On 11-24-1920, I. T. Applewhite bought it for $250 from Huey. One year later, on 12-24-1921, Applewhite sold it to J. E. Spaw for $200. Albert Owens paid Spaw $250 for it on 7-21-1925. W. H. Crenshaw paid the same $250 to Owens on 7-29-1929. On 10-18-1939, E. M. Strahan bought the property from the Crenshaw heirs for $700. The Strahans deeded it over to their daughter Doris Strahan Palmer on 3-4-1943. She sold the property to Ray Kelley on 3-13-1945. He was responsible for building the rock house that now stands there. He rocked over the old house to produce the one that survives today. Jack Lyle purchased the property from the Kelleys and he still owns the house and property today.

NORTHWEST QUARTER

Academy Block

This block makes you think about the old question, "Which came first, the chicken or the egg?" W. T. Chapman made this block of land available to build the Dripping Springs Academy. He retained the ownership. This building was begun in August of 1881 and the plat was filed in September. Still one has to wonder, which came first, the thought for the school or the plan for having a town? Probably the idea was hatched at about the same time when W. M. Jordan started to make his spiel. Who knows, maybe this was one of the selling points that Jordan made to Chapman or vice versa.

The block plat showed that the block was 275x290 feet. I really think it actually took in an additional 25 feet of the 25-foot lots of block one of the first addition. Otherwise, some of the figures do not add up for me. When Jordan left the school and the Baptists were in control of the curriculum, Chapman deeded the property to the Pedernales Baptist Association on 1-13-1884, with the stipulation that if they no longer taught religion as part of the curriculum, the property would revert to the Dripping Springs First Baptist Church. This it did in 1889. Although the church thought they had turned the property over to the public school system in 1905, the title was not actually transferred until March of 1921. After the school left the campus in 1949, the block began to see some ownership transfers.

Patterson store—Lot 1. This was a 50x100 foot lot that was carved out of the southwest corner of the Academy block. W. T. Chapman bought it back from the Dripping Springs Baptists on 8-15-1905. He sold it to J. L. Patterson for $50 on 8-6-1906. Patterson erected the 26x80 foot stone building on the lot that still survives today. Patterson sold the property to P. A. Glosson on 12-29-1914 for $3,000. G. A. Searight bought it for $3,500 on 5-21-1921. G. A. Searight sold it to W. E. Searight for $3,000 on 6-8-1925. W. S. McLendon bought the property from the Searights on 10-18-1938 and then sold it to Sybil Brumley on 4-24-1940. Mrs. Brumley sold it to W. P. Crow on 2-27-1942. W. P. Crow deeded the property over to his grandson and wife, Mack and Betty Crow, on 9-6-1968. Hilton and Jeannine Lewis purchased the property from the Crows on 12-20-1973. The Lewises sold it to the Allen-Crosswell-McFarland group on 6-1-1977 and it still remains in their hands. In actuality, Anton Allen thinks his lot is only a few feet wider than the building and that looks about right, although taxes are on a 50x100 foot lot.

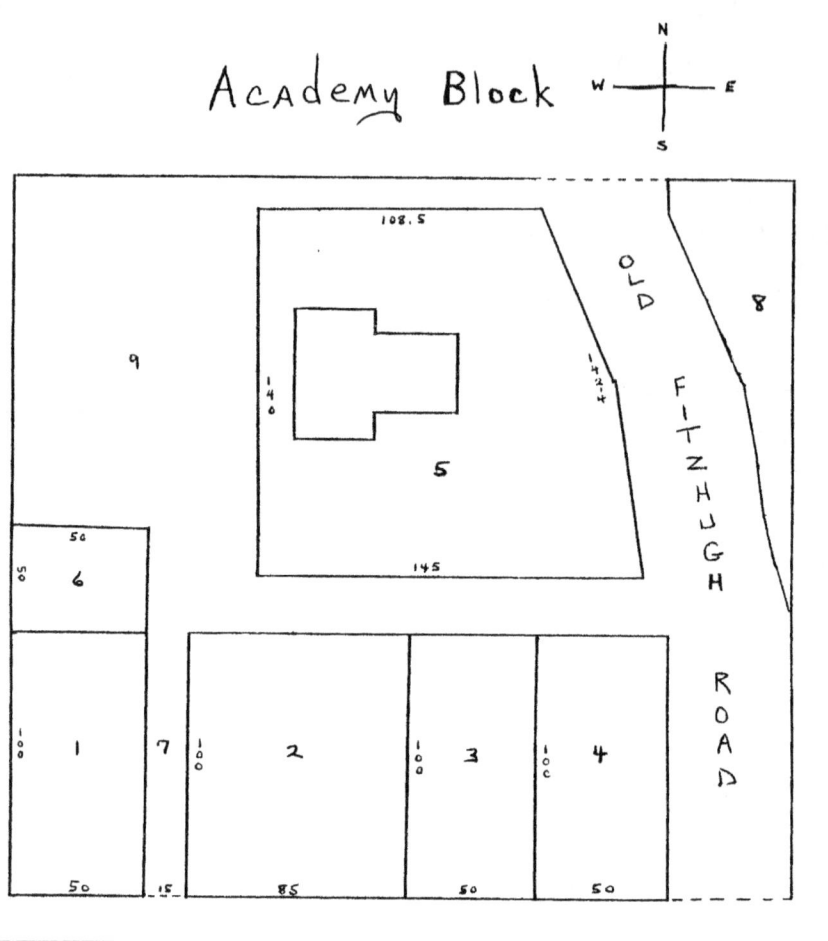

Glosson store—Lot 2. On 3-7-1950, Solon B. Glosson purchased an 85x100 foot lot from DSISD for $1,062.50. The lot ran parallel but fifteen feet away from the Patterson lot. He ended up building a grocery store on the property in 1952. Father and son, James W. "Jimmy" and Jerry "Woody" Glosson, bought the store from Lou, the widow of Solon Glosson, on 5-12-1961. Jimmy and Judy, Woody's widow, sold the lot to Hilton and Jeannine Lewis on 5-1-1970. On 12-31-1975, the Lewises sold the property to Larry Brown but he defaulted on the payments and the Lewises had to buy it back in a public auction. In 1986, a deal was worked out by Roger Hanks to purchase the property, remodel it, and then lease it to the government to use as the Dripping Springs Post Office. This was done and the Hanks family still retains ownership of the property under the Roger/Lucy Hanks Residuary Trust.

Lots 3, 4. These were two 50x100 foot lots that were adjacent to the east side of the Glosson lot. Lester Brenizer purchased these two lots from DSISD for $2,000 on March 14, 1950. After Brenizer's death, Slayton Phelps got the lots from Brenizer's heirs on 12-22-1956. Jimmy Glosson bought the lots off Phelps on 2-8-1961. Jimmy built the small red brick building on Lot 3 and leased it to the U.S. Post Office. Woody Glosson purchased the other lot from Jimmy on 2-20-1963. Judy Glosson sold Lot 2 to the Lewises and it went with Lot 1 the rest of the time. Lot 3 ended up being part of the deal when the Post Office took over the old store in 1987. It is now under the Roger/Lucy Hanks Residuary.

Academy building—Lot 5. The Rambo Masonic Lodge lost their meeting place in a fire and were looking for another. Their tradition was to meet in the second story of a building. That did not leave much choice in Dripping Springs. The only building available was the vacated DS Academy building. DSISD sold it to the Masons for $3,000 on 7-19-1952. The lot was S 142.4x W 145x N 140x E 108.5. The Masons have been the owners of the lot since that time.

Lot 6. L. B. Jennings ran a feed store and lumber company out of the Patterson lot and decided he needed a little more room. He bought a 40x50 foot lot that matched up and elongated the north end of the Patterson lot from DSISD for $275 on 11-21-1952. He sold the lot to the Lewises for $725 on 10-8-1973. From that point, it has followed the same ownership trail as Lot 2.

Lot 7. Lot 6 is the fifteen-foot alley between the Patterson lot and Lot 2. The Lewises purchased this parcel of land from Hays County on 7-14-1975. From then on, it followed the same ownership trail as Lot 2.

Lot 8. This small sliver of land was marooned from the rest of the block when Old Fitzhugh Road was carved out to connect Eve Street with Mercer Street. It had always matched up with the block six, second addition land. The people who owned block six always wondered whose land it was. Galen Dodson inquired and found that it was still part of DSISD property, and in the 1980s the property was sold to Mr. Dodson.

Lot 9—High School building. This is the block of land that the rock high school building sits on. This property was the only portion of the Academy block that DSISD retained. They still own it today.

NORTHWEST QUARTER

E. P. Shelton Subdivision

This 5.38 acre tract of land was part of the purchase that W. H. Robbins made in 1893. W. H. Robbins died shortly after acquiring the property and R. E. Spaw paid the Robbins heirs $120 for this tract of land on 9-5-1904. This stretch of land lay on the east side of the Old Fitzhugh Road and bordered on blocks seven and eight of the second addition. The survey directions covered a long slender section of land toward the north that was given as 515 feet east along blocks seven and eight, then north 1,544 feet, then west 30 feet and then along Old Fitzhugh Road south 1,642 feet to the beginning. As the years went by, the small tract of land above the Wallace boundary was ignored and it later, by use, became a part of the James Hall acquisition that was supposed to be a part of the Stephenson one hundred acres. On 9-24-1904, Spaw sold the tract of land to his brother-in-law, Dr. E. P. Shelton. Dr. Shelton had already bought block seven. From this point, he began selling off most of it.

Lot A. Dr. Shelton always kept this strip of land between block seven and the tracts he was selling. After the Sheltons' deaths, one of the sons, Edgar Vaughn Shelton, bought the property on 6-26-1954. Another son, John Edgar Shelton, got it from E. V. Shelton on 10-3-1962. The surviving son, Clarence Shelton, got it from the Shelton heirs on 8-7-1968. He sold this strip of land to his grandson, Corby and Misty Shelton, on 1-27-1996 and they built a house on the property.

Lot B. On 1-17-1911, W. S. McLendon bought this lot and two more from Dr. Shelton. He built a house on this lot that year, designed so that the front room would serve as the telephone office. McLendon, at this time, owned the Dripping Springs Rural Telephone Company. He sold the house and property to Arthur Patton for $2,000 on 9-25-1918. It included taking over the telephone business as well.

Patton decided to take over the Buda Telephone Company and McLendon bought back the property and business from him for $2,000 on 1-1-1922. McLendon sold the lot to I. D. Hedges on 2-20-1934. J. E. Spaw paid Hedges $2,000 for the property on 4-4-1934. I. T. Applewhite bought the lot off J. E. Spaw on 1-3-1940. Mrs. I. T. Applewhite sold it to the high school principal, Quinn Schlortt, on 3-12-1953. Elmo Hall bought the property from Mr. Schlortt on 7-20-1957. The house and property stayed in the Hall family. During their ownership they gave .25 acres to their daughter, Earlene Hall McNair, and her daughter, Sherry Richey, now owns it. On May 3, 1995, Charlie Haydon bought the rest of the property and remodeled the house for rental property.

Lot C. This is part of the property that McLendon bought from Shelton in 1911. It went to Patton in 1918 and returned to McLendon in 1922.

Lot C1—1 acre. McLendon built a small house for a telephone office and its operators around 1923. Finally, on 5-1-1928, McLendon sold the telephone company to Mid-Continental Telephone Company and sold this one acre to them. This property stayed in the hands of the different telephone companies until 1961. By this time, dial telephones were in and there was no need for operators.

The Southwestern Telephone Company, who owned the property, sold a section of the acre that included the telephone building to C. N. Hambrick on 9-21-1961. Mr. Hambrick sold it to J. E. Ragland on 1-2-1962. James Ollie Roberts bought the property from the Raglands on 6-8-1962. He rocked up the little building for their residence and run their cedar post business from there. It is still in the Roberts family. The rest of the property, .168 acres, is still owned by the telephone company, which today is Verizon.

Meanwhile, the rest of this lot stayed with Lot B. McLendon sold it to I. D. Hedges on 2-20-1934 and Hedges sold it to J. E. Spaw on 4-4-1934. I. T. Applewhite bought it from Spaw on 1-3-1940. The Applewhites sold their portion of this lot to Nellie Rae Owens on 8-11-1941. Mrs. Nellie Rae Owens Moran sold her property to W. E. Spaw for $100 on 4-3-1951. This property was bought by Dennis and Katherine Cannon in 1968 and became part of the Cannon West Estates subdivision. It went to

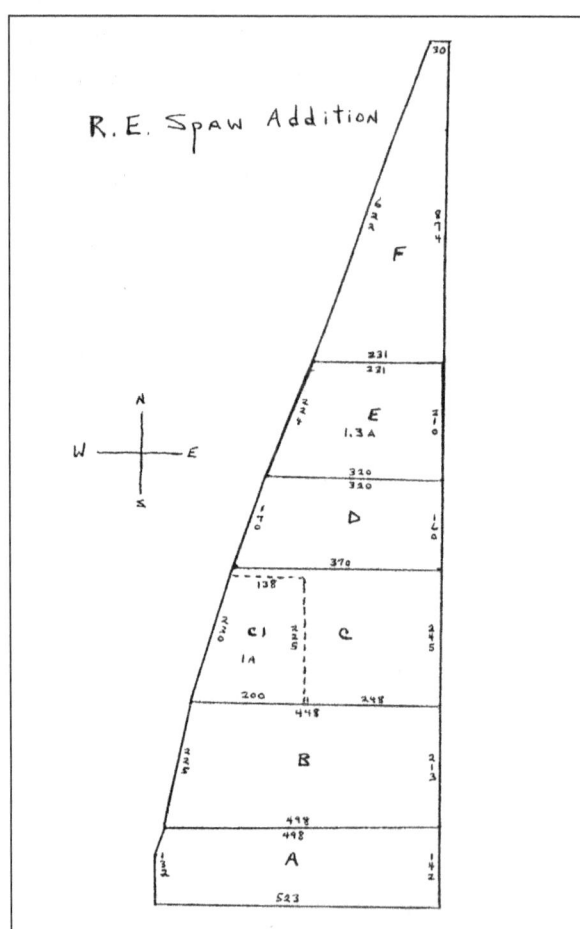

Dripping springs telephone office and house, 1923
312 Old Fitzhugh Road

James Stewart when he purchased his lot on 11-19-1975. He continues to own it.

Lot D. W. S. McLendon sold this lot to J. T. Spaw on 12-17-1912 for $75. He built his house on this property in 1913. Ellie Spaw got the property from the Spaw heirs on 4-26-1941. Mrs. Nellie Rae Owens would get the property from Mrs. Spaw on 8-1-1941. On 4-3-1951, W. E. Spaw bought the property from Mrs. Nellie Rae Owens Moran. The property was sold by the Spaw heirs in late 2002.

Lot E—1.3 acres. On 2-29-1908, Dr. Shelton sold this tract of land to W. A. Chesher for $25. M. E. Peal bought the property from Chesher on 5-20-1908. P. A. Glosson took ownership of the property from Mr. Peal on 11-1-1919. G. W. Houchin paid Glosson $800 for the property on 4-22-1921. On 7-31-1928, O. V. Stubbs paid Houchin $900 for the lot. Addie Scheh paid Stubbs $1,200 for the lot on 5-23-1934 and then sold it back to them on 12-26-1936 for $1,000. Stubbs then sold it to S. W. Byars for $1,250 on 12-23-1939. On 12-31-1985, W. E. "Bill" and Clarene McNair bought the lot, which had now shrunk to .949 acres, from the Byars estate. They first sold it to Benny De los Santos in 1994, but he had to default on it. It was then sold to Pam Maynor in October of 1996.

NORTHWEST QUARTER

P. L. Turner Subdivision

This 171 acres, located in the northeast corner of the northwest quarter, got its start on 7-25-1893 when W. H. Robbins bought a huge block of land from the Marshall heirs. One hundred and fifty acres of this belonged to Frances (Fannie) Mary, who by this time had married D. W. Burkett. Shortly after purchasing the land, Robbins died, leaving behind a widow and fifteen children. Walter Glosson purchased 171 acres from the W. H. Robbins heirs on 2-18-1907 and then sold it to Mrs. Florence McKellar on 4-6-1907. Mr. J. L. Patterson bought the acreage from Mrs. McKellar on 11-25-1907. There is some question in my mind as to how much acreage was involved in those transactions. Probably, more like 146 acres. Patterson owned much land on the north end of the P. A. Smith survey and his sale to Mr. Turner probably included some of this when it was given as 171 acres. Mr. Turner paid Mr. Patterson $4,750 for it on 3-6-1920.

Lot A—4.0 acres. Mr. I. V. Davis, Jr., purchased this tract of land, located on the northern boundary of the second addition to Dripping Springs. He bought it from Mrs. M. J. Robbins Martin on 6-3-1904. Mrs. Robbins had since married Mr. Martin. As you can see, this tract was actually started before Mr. Turner had bought and sold the rest of the tract, but I'm treating it as part of the Turner subdivision.

Prior to buying these four acres, the Davises had already bought a portion of block four of the second addition. It was this tract that had the house on it and where the Davises lived. They added two rooms, which are the only two that remain at this time. Mr. Davis died in 1911. Mrs. Davis lived in the house until 1935, when she moved to

Austin. She used the lumber from the old house to build another house on part of the four acres in 1941.

A1—1.19 acres. This was the property with the house built in 1941 on it. Mrs. Katie May Davis sold it to J. W. Butler on 3-7-1949 for $3,000. The Butler heirs sold it to Edwin and Dora Meek for $5,700 on 10-8-1966. Howard and Willie Meek came into the property on 4-23-1970. James L. Clowdus bought the property in the 1980s and then sold it to Bo Murphy Davis in the 1990s. Carole Howard purchased the property from Bo Davis on 7-8-1997.

A2—.37 acres. Mrs. Davis sold this lot to Walter and Gertrude Clayton for $2,500 on 7-30-1951. They built a house on the property that year. James and Martha Flaherty bought the property on 8-5-1985 from the Gertrude Clayton estate. They sold it to Richard and Katherine Wright in the late 1980s and they, in turn, sold the property to their son, Tim, in the 1990s. Tim and his wife, Jamie, sold the house to Maureen Cassedy Shankling on 8-5-1994.

A3, A4—1.65 acres. Son Bradley Davis bought the remaining two sections of the property from Mrs. Davis on 3-16-1953. He moved back to his old hometown to continue his teaching career in 1962 and build his house on the site in 1964. He lived there until he moved to an assisted living facility in 2000, but returned in 2002. He sold the property to a nephew with the right to live out his days there.

Lot B—1 acre. Jesse E. Ragland paid Mr. Turner $50 for this lot on 10-15-1929. On 8-10-1933, W. A. and Ila Mae Horner paid Jesse Ragland $75 for the lot. They built a house on the property in 1950. V. E. "Bill" and Louise Prescott bought the southeast .36-acre tract, that included the house, for $7,000 on 8-1-1972 from the Horners. On 2-1-1973, the Prescotts bought the .12-acre tract that was adjacent to their west boundary. The other half-acre of the lot became a part of Lot C. Mrs. Prescott still owns the property.

Lot C—1 acre. W. A. and Ila Mae Horner bought this acre of land from P. L Turner on 3-11-1930. They sold the north quarter of the lot (C1) to J. E. Ragland on 11-18-1941 for $55. He had a house built on this lot by the end of 1941. Mr. Ragland sold C1 to Robert H. McIntyre on 12-15-1969. Mr. McIntyre would end up going bankrupt in his business and had to let this property go back to the Ragland family (J. E. and R. J.). They would later sell this property to Eddie Needham in the early '70s. He sold this property to Mrs. Sherri Lynn Bennett in 1993 and she established an upholstery business in a building next to her house. She became sole owner on 7-18-1996. The Horners moved a house on the northern part of what they had left in the 1940s. The partial lots of B and C went with Lot E in property transactions.

Lot E—5.61 acres. W. A. and Ila Mae Horner paid P. L Turner $420.75 for this acreage on 9-10-1943. On 1-1-1946, the Horners bought another .7-acre sliver on the western edge of the property, to give them a straight border on that side. Ila Mae Horner sold the entire 7.38-acre tract, which includes part of Lots B and C, to Johnny Gonzales on 3-5-1979. Don Ray George purchased the property from Gonzales on 11-28-1983. He sold it the next day to Wanda Greer and Rose Wallace Glass. They had to let the property go back to Olivia Gonzales. Later on, she sold it to A. M. Kindred in late 1990.

Lot D—1 acre. J. H. Howard bought this lot from P. L. Turner for $100 on 9-1-1936. Mr. Howard sold it off in two sections.

D1—.25 acres. On 11-18-1941, J. E. Ragland paid Howard $50 for the south quarter of the lot. This coupled with the north quarter of Lot C gave Mr. Ragland a half acre lot. On 12-15-1969, Robert H. McIntyre bought this lot from Mr. Ragland. The rest of its history goes with Lot C1.

D2—.75 acres. Nora Bryant bought the rest of the lot from Mr. Howard on 9-9-1943. W. E. and Clarene McNair bought the lot from Nora Bryant on 7-12-1949. Charlie "Buck" Haydon bought the property from

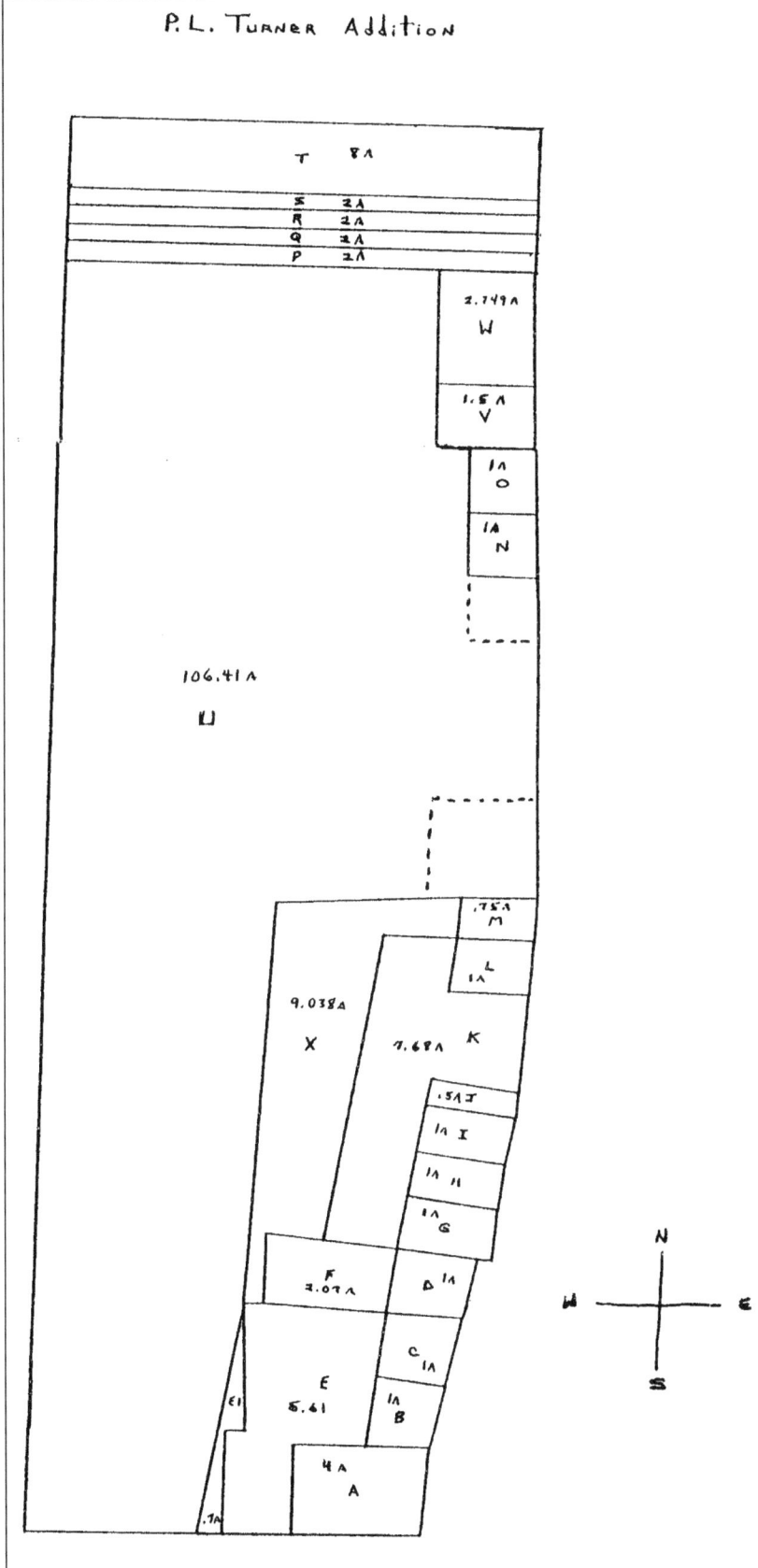

the McNairs on 7-30-1959. They continue to own this property.

Lot F—2.07 acres. Nora Bryant bought this tract from P. L. Turner on 9-9-1943. She, in turn, sold the lot to the McNairs on 7-12-1949 and they sold it to the Haydons. The property still remains with the Haydons.

Lot G—1 acre. T. W. Ragland paid P. L. Turner $100 for this lot on 12-21-1938. It was divided into two tracts later on.

G1—.50 acres. On 8-24-1940, J. D. Ragland paid $50 for this half acre to T. W. Ragland. They built a house on the property in 1941 and sold their lot to C.H.A. Wallace on 9-9-1946 for $1900. T. W. Ragland bought the property back from Wallace on 1-11-1950. At some point, James L. Eastwood got the property because on 10-12-1952, Melvin Williamson paid him $3,000 for the lot. Austin Frances Glass paid Williamson $3,900 for the lot on 9-18-1967. Austin Glass sold it to Alvin and Virginia Thomas on 1-14-1969. Rosemary Kay Baen bought the property from Virginia Glass on 3-29-1974. She sold it to Fred Garnett on 4-30-1993 and he still owns it.

G2—.50 acres. Materials used in the house on this property by T. W. Ragland came from the old hotel on Mercer Street that

Mr. Ragland tore down in 1938. The house was completed by November 1939. The Ragland heirs sold this lot to M. T. and Abby Jones for $3,000 on 8-27-1963. It is still in the Jones family. Billie Jones Tracy gained possession on 7-1-1987. It was up for sale at the end of 2002.

Lot H—1 acre. Mrs. Lula J. Fairley paid P. L. Turner $150 for this acre on 11-15-1939. After that, it gets a little confusing. A deed on 8-24-1964 had Wilson Fairley buying the property from H. J. Fairley. Then the next deed had Joseph B. Townsend buying the property from Mrs. Lula J. Fairley Smith on 12-21-1966. Mr. Townsend died in 2002 and his heirs now own the property. The house is no longer on the property.

Lot I—1 acre. Della Cockrell paid P. L. Turner $100 for this lot on 3-29-1941. A house was completed later in the year. Again, it gets confusing. On 8-13-1960, a deed had the Wilson heirs buying this property from Della Cockrell. Then on 1-27-1961, a deed had Joseph B. Townsend buying the property from the Cockrell heirs. He lived in the Cockrell house until his death in 2002. His heirs still own it.

Lot J—.5 acre. Vanda Volmering paid P. L. Turner $50 for this half acre on 8-12-1941. A house was built on it in 1941. On 2-26-1970, Armando Garcia paid the Volmering heirs $1,800 for the property. They tore down the house. Armando Garcia sold the property to George and Cherry Fry on 12-18-1975. They built a house there and they still own the property.

Lot K—7.68 acres. This property included the homesite of Mr. Turner, who died in 1956. The first transaction was on 3-23-1959. Noah Edwards paid E. O. Wiley $6,000 for the property. Wiley was probably a realtor. From that point, it was subdivided into four different tracts.

K1—.32 acre. On 10-6-1960, Lupe Lerma paid Noah Edwards $1,600 for the lot which had a small house on it. On 1-18-1978, Benito F. Garza paid Ramon Lerma $3,700 for the property. Mr. Garza's son, Ramiro "Ramsey" bought it from his dad on 5-15-1997.

K2—2.6 acres. Benito Falcon Garza paid Noah Edwards $650 for this tract of land on 10-6-1960. They built their house on this property and continue to live there today.

K3—2.6 acres. On 10-6-1960, Antanacio Boconegra paid Noah Edwards $650 for this tract of land. Boconegra sold this tract of land to Joseph B. Townsend on 9-29-1961. Townsend heirs own it.

K4—2.16 acres. Noah Edwards sold his final tract of land to Thurman T. Sewell on 4-25-1963 for $6,500. Sewell sold it to Elvin W. Glass on 5-4-1964. Raymond Whisenant bought the property from Glass on 10-11-1966. This lot includes the home of P. L. Turner. The Whisenants still own this property.

Lot L—1 acre. William A. Roberts paid P. L. Turner $100 for this acre on 5-29-1945. They built a house on the property that year and it has stayed in the family since.

Lot M—.75 acre. T. L. Maxey bought this lot from P. L. Turner on 10-4-1943. Mrs. Mabel Herwig paid the Maxey heirs $500 for the lot on 7-5-1957. Sometime soon after that, Jesse Langston came into the property because on 7-15-1960, D. R. Mulhollen bought the property from Langston and built a house on the lot that year. It is now owned by Thea Marie Jensen, who bought it on 9-3-1992.

Lot X—9.038 acres. W. L. Bushwar paid Nelson Davidson, Sr., $10,076 for this tract of land on 8-26-1977. Ramiro "Ramsey" Garza and Sandra Blaney bought the property on 12-26-1996.

Lot U—119.7 acres. C. W. Spillar paid P. L. Turner $5,500 for this acreage on 1-1-1946. On 6-23-1952, Nelson Davidson, Sr., paid Spillar $3,000 for the remaining acreage. They built a home in the southeast corner of this property on the Old Fitzhugh Road in 1954 (U1). It burned in the early '70s and they rebuilt. They sold an acre of land to son, Nelson Davidson, Jr., in the early '80s to build his residence on (U2).

The property is still in the hands of the Davidson heirs.

Lot N—1 acre. On 1-1-1946, Thomas L. Turner bought this acre of land from P. L. Turner. On 2-27-1971, C. W. Spillar, Jr., bought it from the T. L. Turner heirs. His daughter, Audrey Spillar Baldi, bought the tract from Spillar on 2-19-1975. She sold it to Charlie N. Haydon on 5-13-1975 for $3,500. The Haydons still own the property.

Lot O—1 acre. Wade Turner bought this acre of land from his father, P. L. Turner, on 1-1-1946. They built their house on the property and lived in it until their deaths. The Turner heirs sold it to John and Carolyn Schilthuis in 1994. He died in an automobile accident and Carolyn inherited the property on 12-14-2001. The Turner house was rented out and another building has been moved onto the property for business rental purposes.

Lot V—1.5 acres. Thomas Blaine Fine paid C. W. Spillar $600 for this acreage on 4-11-1957. Mr. Fine sold it to Charlie N. Haydon on 7-20-1965. The Haydons built their home there and still reside in it today.

Lot W—2.749 acres. J. F. Glosson, Jr., purchased this block of land that bordered on the southern border of the Garza property and the northern property line of the Haydon property. He bought it from C. W. Spillar, Jr., on 4-30-1982. It included the Spillar house. Glosson still owns the property today.

Lot P—2 acres. S. M. Garza bought this two-acre tract from P. L. Turner for $100 on 7-3-1944. The land stayed in the Garza family with a tax problem hanging over it. On 4-13-2000, Richard and Eduardo Garza gained title to it.

Lot Q—2 acres. Remedius F. Garza bought this two-acre tract from P. L. Turner for $100 on 7-3-1944. On 1-10-1958, Felipe F. Garza bought the tract from Remedius and it has been in the family since. It is a part of the Felipe F. Garza Estate today.

Lot R—2 acres. Felipe F. Garza completed the two-acre tract buyouts by the Garzas when he, too, paid P. L. Turner $100 for his tract on 7-3-1944. It is a part of the Felipe F. Garza Estate.

Lot S—2 acres. This two-acre tract was first sold to Cleto Q. Duran by Mr. Turner for $100 on 8-12-1941. On 1-5-1946, Mr. Duran sold the land to G. H. Ferrell for $130. After her husband died, Mrs. Inthaberry Lyle Ferrell sold the property to B. E. Hudson on 9-18-1961. Mr. Hudson sold the land to Robert A. Reed, Jr., on 6-16-1965. They still own this property.

Lot T—8 acres. I. D. Hedges bought this tract of land from P. L. Turner on 4-12-1934. Valentin Duran bought the land from Hedges on 8-12-1941. G. H. Ferrell paid Mr. Duran $400 for the acreage on 9-29-1944. This was part of the land that B. E. Hudson bought from Inthaberry Lyle Ferrell on 9-18-1961. Then it would become a part of the package that Robert A. Reed, Jr., bought from Mr. Hudson on 6-16-1965. The Reeds still own the property today.

NORTHWEST QUARTER

J. L. Smith Subdivision

J. L. Smith purchased 140.45 acres from the Marshall heirs, Jasper Newton Marshall being the one who signed the deed, on 6-30-1942. This was a part of the Chapman homestead land located in the southern portion of the quarter league. The land is bordered on the south by Creek Road.

Smith sold his lots in two major areas. One was the western parcel and the other, the eastern portion. The western parcel will be the one that we explore first. When I came here in 1965, I heard it referred to as Little Mexico, because many of our local Mexican-American citizens bought plots of land in this sector. Most of those purchases have stayed in the families. A small sliver of this subdivision was actually bought from R. J. Ragland. It includes the 30-foot roadway, now known as Ramirez Lane. It was a part of a 66.1-acre tract that Ragland purchased from Smith on 3-23-1951, which included all of the western portion of the 140.45 acres that had not already been sold. Ragland sold 50.02 adjacent acres to the L. O. Jackson Land Company, 39 coming from the 66.1, which would become the Dripping Springs Heights subdivision, on 3-13-1973. Ragland sold the rest of the 66.1 acres to Roger Hanks in March of 1996.

Lot A—4 acres. Barney Castor bought these four acres, located in the southwest corner of the league from Smith on 4-28-1943. On 2-13-1960, Barney Castor deeded the property over to his wife, Santos Castor. Upon Mrs. Castor's death, the estate was divided in half on 11-24-1984. Augustin Castor received the eastern two acres and Guadalupe Castor, the western two acres. On 10-10-1989, Bonnie Castor Salazar and husband, Geraldo "Harry," received a deed for the northwest half acre of Augustin's two acres. On 5-4-1991, Belinda Castor Carmona Zapata received the northeast half acre of Augustin's two acres, leaving Augustin the southern one acre. On 12-8-2000, Hancock/Hanks Investments bought Guadalupe's two acres and called it the Creek Road Villas.

Lot B—2 acres. Gilbert Nevarez purchased this two-acre tract on 7-30-1943 from Smith for $100. The Nevarez heirs deeded the land to Gilbert's wife, Casimira Garza Nevarez, on 8-12-1971. On 10-16-1974, Maximillino Zepeda bought a 100x146 foot portion of the lot from Mrs. Nevarez. On 9-24-1976, Gilbert Nevarez, Jr., received the rest of the property from Mrs. Nevarez. After his death, Angela Marie Nevarez received the 1.66 acres as a gift on 4-14-2000.

Lot C—4 acres. Felix Cruz bought this tract of land from Smith on 3-2-1944. On 3-19-1970, the tract of land was divided equally among the four Cruz sons by Felix Cruz. Edward received C1, Juan C2, Concepcion C3, and Antonio C4. On 9-24-1990, Antonio and Adelia Cruz were deeded C4 by Antonio Cruz. On 10-10-1994, Adelia S. Cruz received .3857 acres from Edward's part of C1. Johnny Cruz, Jr., received Juan Cruz, Sr.'s, C2 on 6-17-1998.

Lot D—1 acre. Cleofas and Gregoria Garza Ramirez bought this lot on 9-28-1944. It has remained in the family since. Son Jose Ysmael bought .5 acres on 2-7-1993. Daughter Carmen lived in the family home until her death and her children, Fatima and Gabriel, received that .5 acre on 6-1-1996.

Lot E—4.76 acres. J. C. Harmon bought this tract from Smith on 1-9-1945. A later 1973 deed said Mr. Harmon sold an acre of land (E1) to Frank Castor. No deed has been found. Epifanio and Francisca Garza bought the acre in 1955, possibly from Castor, and built their home and raised a family there. Mr. Harmon built his house on this property in 1957. On 3-16-1973, Joe and Betty Lindsey, Jr., paid the Harmon heirs $15,200 for the remaining 3.75 acres. Larry Straley purchased the property from the Lindseys on 3-31-1976 and has owned it since. Francisca Riza Garza inherited the acre on 5-11-2001, after her husband's death.

Lot F—1 acre. Y. L. Lawrence paid Smith $50 for this lot on 4-27-1943. It stayed in the family until 11-18-1971, when his heirs, daughters Beulah Lawrence Needham and Thelma Lawrence Penna, sold the lot to John and Susan Steele for $3,000. They are still the owners.

Lot G—.5 acre. F. A. Sprouse bought this property from Smith on 11-14-1944. Mrs. Ada Brainard bought the property from Mr. Sprouse on 12-16-1946. Her daughter, Allene Norrell, inherited the property and sold it to J. W. Massey on 2-20-1955. Mr. Massey sold the lot to Elmer D. and Nelawyn Dalley for $3,500 on 10-8-1960. They still make their home there.

Lot H—1.92 acres. J. C. Harmon purchased this tract on 1-15-1949 from Smith for $110. His heirs sold it to Joe and Betty Lindsey, Jr., on 3-16-1973 and they sold it to Larry Straley on 3-31-1976. The Straleys still own the property.

Lot I—5 acres. Tom Lang would take this tract of land off Smith's hands on 7-13-

1946 for $300. On 1-10-1958, Remedios F. Garza paid Mrs. Leila L. Lang $1,000 for the property. Later on, the property was further subdivided among the children. On 8-30-1969, Adolph and Julie Garza received one acre (I1) and Alfred and Margie Garza another acre (I2). On 1-9-1976, three more portions were deeded. Remedios and Jane Garza, Jr., 1.49 (I3), Ernest and Angie Garza Cordova .54 (I4), and Alfred Garza .32 (I6). Daughter Amy Garza inherited the .62 acre tract (I5) that included her parents' house. Ernest Cordova purchased I1 from Aldolph Garza on 6-26-1990. Sesario Garza bought I2 from Alfred Garza on 4-28-1995. Amy and her husband, Dan Cisneros, bought Alfred Garza's (I6) on 12-30-96 to expand their lot to .94 acres. Ida Angelina (Angie) Cordova Sell received title to I4 in a divorce settlement on 5-21-1990.

Lot J—1.43 acres. This tract of land came together under the ownership of Ramon Beltran in two purchases. On 7-15-1964, Beltran paid R. J. Ragland $10 for a 75x90 foot strip (.15 acre) that appears to be on the northern end because it butted up to the 30-foot road that ran along the northern border of this subdivision. On 3-7-1967, V. S. Magee purchased the southern strip of land, beginning at Creek Road, from R. J. Ragland. Magee eventually defaulted on his payment and H. L. Joseph bought the property from the trustee, James Clark II, on 3-7-1978. Soon after, Ramon Beltran bought the property and built a small house on the southern end. Much of the strip became part of Ramirez Lane.

Lot K—2.6 acres. Joe M. Picasio paid R. J. Ragland $600 for this tract of land on 4-6-1965. Joe sold it to Guadalupe Picasio, Sr., on 4-18-1980. Guadalupe sold it to Conise and Michael Green in 1993. They in turn, sold it to Mark Lundeen on 4-22-1998.

Lot L—1 acre. Andrez Beltran paid Smith $10 for one acre on 12-1-1945. Ramon Beltran inherited this acre and it became a part of the 2.25-acre tract he now owns.

Lot M—2 acres. No deed was found but it is known that Eddie Needham bought this tract from Smith, probably about the same time that Lawrence bought his, which was in 1943. Enoch Needham got the property from Eddie Needham on 2-19-1951. On 11-18-1952, Tamaso Alarcon and Sanfilo Casarez paid Enoch Needham $100 for the property. Sanfilo Casarez paid Tamaso

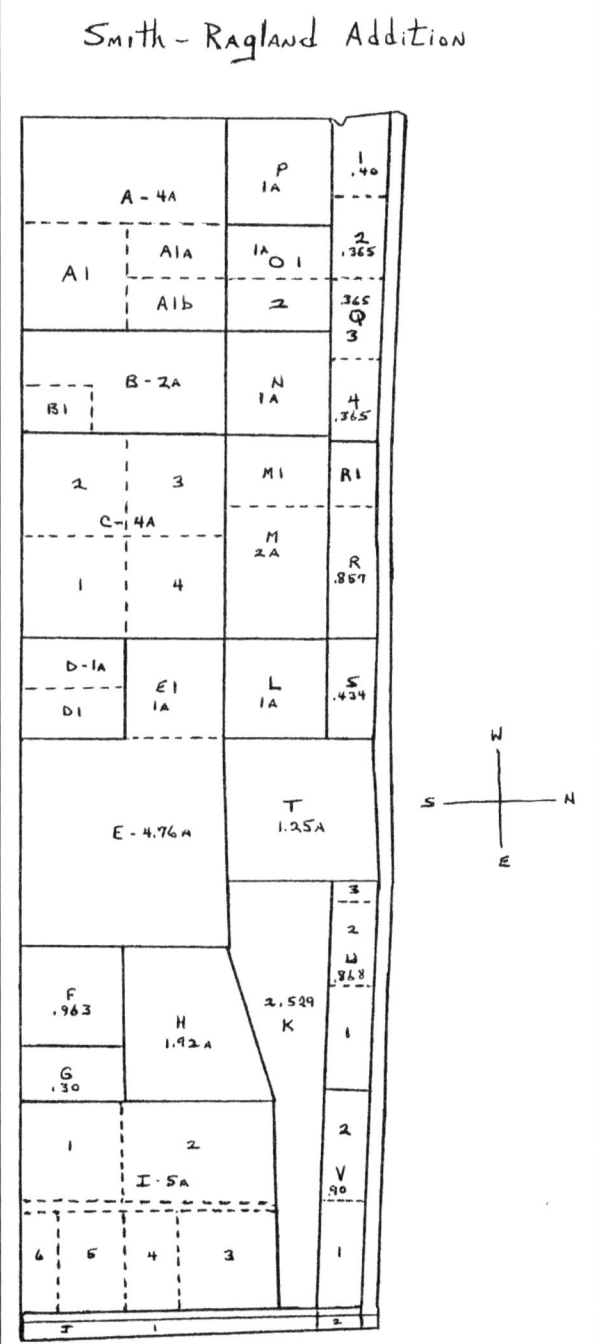

Alarcon $150 for his share of the property on 2-16-1953. Concepcion Sanchez paid Casarez $600 for the property on 6-15-1962. On 4-25-1981, Concepcion Sanchez deeded the property over to the kids, Dominga, Louisa, Valentin, and Julian Sanchez. Julian is on the tax rolls as owning the property. The two acres now have been configured a little differently. It is the eastern two acres of the two combined parcels (Lot R) that Concepcion bought. The western one-third of this lot was combined with part of Lot R to make the acre that Jesus Velasquez bought on 5-15-1971.

Lot N—1 acre. Antonio G. Nevarez bought this lot from Smith on 5-25-1946. Barney Castor paid Nevarez $65 for the lot on 3-24-1954. Barney Castor deeded the property over to his wife, Santos Castor, on 2-13-1960. It is now owned by Amanda Aguilar and Angela Castor Camacho.

Lot O—1 acre. Jesse Castor paid Smith $60 for this lot on 3-16-1946. Augustin and Dora Castor got the property from Jesse Castor on 4-26-1985. Bonnie and Geraldo Salazar received the western half acre on 10-10-1989 and Belinda Carmona Zapata received her half acre on 5-4-1991. This, along with the division in Lot A, gave each an acre of land.

Lot P—1 acre. Frances Garza paid Smith $55 for this lot on 11-27-1944. This is possibly a mistake. Francisca Garza said they never owned this land. Maybe it should have been Frank Castor. A later deed in 1967, concerning land on the northern border, said this was land owned by Barney Castor. If so, it was probably given to Guadalupe Castor as part of his inheritance from Santos Castor. This lot ended up being landlocked and could not be reached by a road. One of the Castors tried to get right-of-way but to no avail and on 2-17-2001, Hancock/Hanks Investments bought the property.

Lot Q—.817 acre. V. S. Magee bought this tract from R. J. Ragland on 3-7-1967. He defaulted on payments and H. L. Joseph bought the property from the trustee, James Clark, II, on 3-7-1978. On 8-13-1981, Alfredo and Rosemary Salazar bought a .365 acre lot (Q2) from Joseph. Frank and Nora Salazar bought a .365 acre lot (Q4) from Joseph on 1-6-1982. Raymond Beltran, Jr., bought a .40 acre lot (Q1) from Joseph on 4-13-1982, and David Lee Beltran the other .365 acre lot (Q3) on 4-23-1982. David sold his lot to Armando Prouty on 9-12-1991.

Lot R—.857 acre. Concepcion Sanchez paid R. J. Ragland $330 for this tract of land on 3-5-1965. Jesus Velasquez bought an acre from Sanchez on 5-15-1971 which included part of this lot and part of Lot M.

Lot S—.434 acre. Leslie H. Juliano bought this section of land from R. J. Ragland on 11-30-1985.

Lot T—1.25 acres. No deed has been found for this purchase, but most likely, Ramon Beltran bought this adjoining tract to Andrez Beltran in the early 1950s from R. J. Ragland. Ramon now owns the entire 2.25 acres.

Lot U—.868 acre. Ernest Nevarez bought this tract of land from R. J. Ragland on 7-6-1967. John Frank Salazar bought the S1 tract (.43 acres) from Nevarez on 6-8-1970. On 5-2-1977 Manuel Salazar bought .33 acres of the S1 tract from John Salazar. John retained the rest.

Lot V—.90 acre. Lewis C. Cruz bought this tract of land from R. J. Ragland on 4-23-1970. On 5-13-1981, Lewis Cruz sold the property to Antonio Cruz (V1) and Concepcion Cruz (V2), each getting .45 acres. Joe and Teresa Salazar bought Lot V1 from Antonio Cruz on 11-21-1995.

NORTHWEST QUARTER

Smith/W. P. Crow Subdivision

The eastern section of the J. L. Smith section was combined with the W. P. Crow property to make this addition. When the school was contemplating moving their campus to larger surroundings, the school purchased 34 acres from the Marshall heirs on 12-20-1935. The school eventually

changed its mind and sold the land in two tracts to W. P. Crow. On 3-18-1938, he bought a 9.8 acre tract and then on 5-23-1940, he bought the final 24 acres. Mr. Crow sold about seven acres from the northwest corner of the old school tract to J. L. Smith on 3-13-1943.

Lot A—2.96 acres. E. B. "Pete" Glosson bought this lot from Mr. Smith on 4-7-1945 and built a rock house on it that same year. He and Naoma have lived in that house since. He sold a half-acre lot, just west of his house, to his daughter, Patricia, on 4-7-1976.

Lot B—.83 acres. Doyle J. Moore, Pete's brother-in-law, bought this tract of land from Smith on 4-7-1945 and likewise built a rock house on the lot that year. Andrew Herwig bought the property from Moore on 4-29-1946. He turned ownership over to S. J. "Jay" Spillar, Jr., on 12-19-1952 for $9,500. J. E. Spaw bought the property from Spillar on 2-9-1959. Hillary Canon purchased the property from Spaw on 5-26-1960 but had to let it go back to Mr. Spaw on 2-3-1967. Mrs. Aletha Cobb paid Mr. Spaw $10,000 for the property on 5-30-1969. She deeded it over to her sons, Joe and Clarence, on 6-18-1971. On 5-20-1880 Clarence bought his brother's share.

Lot C—2.88 acres. Mr. T. F. Warren bought this parcel of land from Smith on 4-

E. B. "Pete" Glosson House, 1945

Doyle J. Moore House, 1945

7-1945. Mr. Warren sold the acreage off in two tracts.

C1—1.41 acres. P. L. Turner paid Mr. Warren $10 for this lot on 6-26-1945. No doubt, Mr. Turner built the cinderblock house on it and sold it to Allie Mae Malott on 3-8-1946 for $750. Mrs. Malott sold it to Oma Fulton for $7,000 on 8-16-1956. Joy Purcell purchased the property from the Fulton heirs on 12-23-1991. The house has been converted to house businesses.

C2—1.47 acres. On 2-4-1946, K. C. Whisenant bought this lot from Warren for $200. He must have built the house that is on it because he sold it on 12-9-1947 to Oran Rippy for $2,500. Carroll Glosson bought the property from the Rippys on 12-8-1962. Glosson sold it to Robert L. Terry on 4-9-1966. Robert Terry sold it to Diana Terry Bonham for $8,800 on 3-28-1967. She sold it back to Robert Terry on 9-27-1973. Terry would then sell the property to James B. Tucker, Sr., for $13,000 on 2-20-1974. Ray Vollette bought the property from the Tucker heirs on 8-30-1996.

Lot D—1 acre. Olen Lowell Hudson bought this lot from Smith on 5-15-1946. He ended up selling it in two tracts as well.

D1—.47 acres. The Hudsons built a house on this part of the lot and Charles Burton Morris bought it from them on 11-13-1950 for $3,500. James W. and Tula

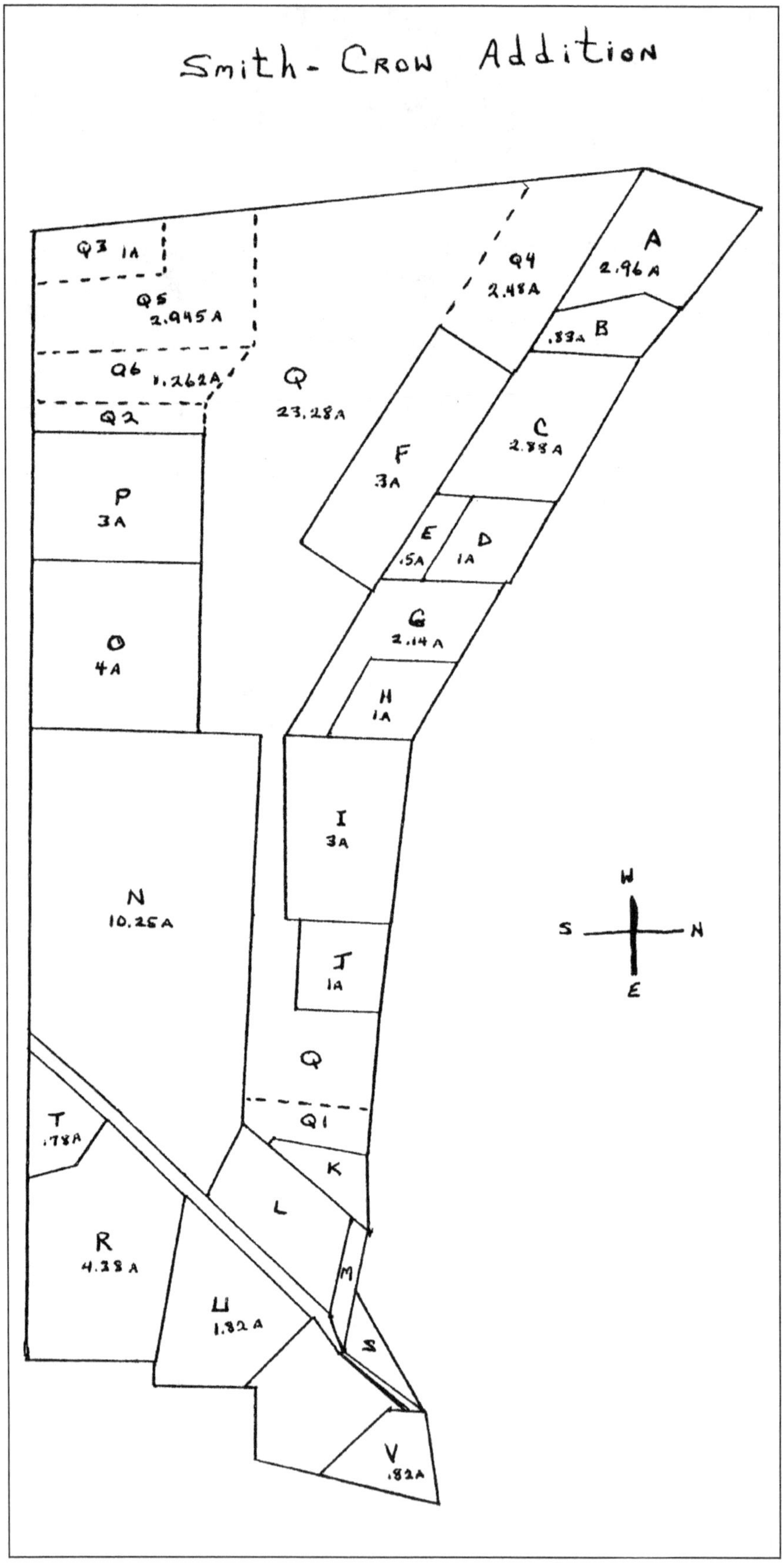

Smith-Crow Addition

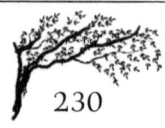

Glosson purchased it from Mr. Morris for $6,500 on 5-29-1964 to bring the entire lot under one ownership. Fred Garnett purchased this property from the Glosson heirs on 3-17-1993.

D2—.53 acres. Eugene Rauch paid Hudson $100 for this lot on 4-24-1948. James W. and Tula Glosson bought the property from Rauch on 1-18-1949 for $880. They moved a house there in May 1949. Fred Garnett bought this property from the Glosson heirs on 3-17-1993 as well.

Lot E—.50 acres. K. C. Whisenant bought this lot from Smith for $50 on 1-19-1946. Oran Rippy bought it from Whisenant on 12-9-1947. Carroll Glosson bought it from Rippy on 12-8-1962 and sold it to Robert L. Terry on 4-9-1966. Robert Terry sold it to Diana Terry Bonham on 3-28-1967 and got it back from her on 9-27-1973. Mr. Terry then sold it to James B. Tucker, Sr., on 2-20-1974. Carroll Glosson purchased the property from Tucker on 3-3-1975. Fred Garnett bought this property on 3-17-1993.

Lot F—3 acres. Dripping Springs had an active roping club in the 1940s and on 7-13-

1946, the Dripping Springs Roping Club purchased this tract of land from Smith for $300. As the roping club became inactive, the taxes on the land began to be in arrears. When Alfard Hohman heard about it, he began paying the taxes on the land. Later, Carroll Glosson heard what Alfard was doing and went on halves on the taxes. On October 31, 1998, Jim Spencer culminated going through the proper procedures to buy the property with Alfard and Carroll's widow signing off on the property. He still owns it.

Lot G—2.14 acres. Lewis Jennings bought this lot from Smith on 4-12-1945. He later sold two tracts from it. The other .81 acres stayed in the Jennings family until they sold it in 2002.

G1—.69 acres. On 2-8-1968, James and Tula Glosson bought this lot from Jennings and moved a house onto the property. Carroll Glosson bought the lot from his father on 4-19-1972 for $15,000. At some point, Larry Bishop became the owner and he sold the property to J. P. Tate on 3-16-1981 for $32,512.61. It then fell under the J. P. Tate Co., Inc. on 3-23-1982. Dave Edwards was a part of the property beginning 10-11-1983. Tate went into bankruptcy and lost all this property to First Texas Savings Association on 2-2-1988. R. C. Voight obtained the front half (.37 acres) of the property in 1993, which included the house, through the auction process. At the same time, Fred Garnett got the back portion (.37 acres) that included the rental buildings, through the auction. Jim Spencer bought the rental buildings from Fred Garnett on 4-8-1998. Joe Miller bought the property from Voight on 8-31-2001, and has turned the house into his dental office.

G2—.64 acres. The J. P. Tate Co., Inc., bought this tract of land from Lewis Jennings on 7-6-1981 and built the Plaza, Too business building, plus another metal business building on the back portion. It, too, came under Dave Edwards and the bank on 10-11-1983. It fell under bankruptcy proceedings and McCrocklin Development, Inc., took over on 9-1-1987. R. C. Voight purchased the property through the R.T.C. auction process in 1993. This property was bought by Joe Miller on 8-31-2001.

Lot H—1 acre. Lewis Jennings paid Smith $10 for this tract on 10-6-1944. Mr. Jennings built a rock home on the property in 1945. The family continued to live in this house and on the property until March 2002, when the heirs sold the property to Robert Chaffee.

Lot I—3 acres. Samuel M. Strong purchased this tract of land from Smith, who had purchased it from Crow, on 12-11-1947 for $625. He built a house on the property. John Glass paid Strong $1,000 for it on 1-3-1950. Eventually he sold this off in three tracts.

I1—1.48 acres. This lot includes the house. John Burke, Jr., bought this tract of land from John Glass on 1-26-1984. Mack Crow bought the property from Burke but later returned it to Burke on 8-5-1985. On 9-17-1986, Burke sold it to Nancy Frasher and she still owns the property.

I2—.76 acres. John Glass deeded over this tract to his son, John L. Glass, on 12-3-1976. He sold this tract to Clem Best on 6-1-1979. The Best heirs sold it to Mason Bass in the late 1990s and he sold it to Lisa Gilliam on 4-20-1999. She built Sophia's Garden business there.

I3—.76 acres. John Glass deeded this tract of land to his daughter, Laura Glass Hunnicutt, on 12-3-1976. She sold it to John Burke, Jr., who sold it to Rex Miller on 3-31-1984. Miller moved the Alamo-like building on the property to make office space. Miller sold the property to Bill Wheat in 1994. Wheat sold the property to Pedernales Electric Coop on 10-1-1998. They intended to remodel the building for their area office but were forced to raze the building. They built a new limestone rock building on the site instead. This was completed in 2000, with the open house being held in November.

Lot J—1 acre. Hydro Gas & Supply Co. paid Smith, who had bought it from Crow, $275 for this tract on 11-24-1947. John

Lewis B. Jennings House, 1945

Glass bought the property from Hydro Gas on 1-17-1951 for $325. He went into business with James Tucker in 1966. The property came under the ownership of Glass & Tucker, Inc. on 2-29-1972. The building was constructed on the lot in 1970. In 1984, John Glass retired and the property became that of Tucker Drilling, Inc., on 11-13-1985.

Lot K—.646 acres. This small tract of land was a part of the tract that Smith bought from Crow. He built a rent house on this property. W. W. "Buddy" Williamson paid Smith $3,500 for this lot on 8-13-1951. It had a four-room house on it. Frank Hall, who had married Williamson's daughter, Clara, came into the property on Williamson's death. He sold it to M. T. and Abbie Jones on 8-21-1955. The Joneses sold the property to R. J. Ragland on 6-24-1961. The Raglands built Village Center and incorporated the house into the business structure. Ragland sold the business to Charles G. Stigall on 7-16-1964. Stigall turned it over to Guy Dietcher on 8-29-1966 for $15,000. Bill Tracy became the owner on 9-7-1967 for $19,900. Mack Crow bought the property from Tracy in 1981 but let it go back in 1985. Tracy sold it to James and Billy Peters on 5-24-1985 for $100,000. They sold it to Jim Powers in the 1990s and he passed it on to Jeff Harris and Keith Askew in August 1993. They sold it in 1994. The Arab group who owned it sold it to Elsan, Inc., on 9-15-2001.

Lot L—1.71 acres. Roy Volmering purchased this property from W. P. Crow on 2-9-1942. He built a house on the property. Felix Lindsey bought the property from Volmering on 9-30-1954 and then sold it to his son, P. D., and Emma Maude, on 10-30-1954. P. D. Lindsey sold a .153-acre parcel to Bill Tracy to go with his store property and it has stayed with the ownership trail of Lot K since.

Lot M—.137 acres. Roy Volmering bought this little sliver of land from Crow on 10-20-1949. Felix Lindsey bought this property from Volmering on 9-30-1954. He then sold it to P. D. Lindsey on 10-30-1954. The Lindseys lost part of this to the 290 right-of-way in the late '50s.

Lot N—10.25 acres. Will Crow deeded this tract of land to his grandson, Mack Crow, on 12-26-1973. Mack sold seven acres to O. C. Harmon (N1) on 7-13-1984. O. C. Harmon sold a five-acre tract to Pedernales Electric Coop (N1a) on 1-27-1986. O. C. also built a couple of duplexes on the other two acres (N1b) and then later sold the property to Sarah Bolton and her mother in 1993. On 10-8-1997, they sold the southern portion to W. F. "Dub" Smith and he put a rental house on that property. Sara Bolton received full title to her property on 10-15-1999. Mack Crow deeded the final 3.25 acres to his two sons,

Travis and Morgan, on 7-5-1994. Travis recently completely a house on his share.

Lot O—4 acres. James W. and Tula Glosson paid Smith $300 for this tract of land on 4-4-1947. Joe Delbert Malott took it off their hands for $600 on 8-21-1953. He built a house on the property. Petreta Mae Malott, his wife, got a 1.75 acre tract (O1) on 10-21-1968, which included the house. On 4-17-1996, son Ronald Joe Malott, bought the 1.75 acre tract from his mother. The adjacent two acres were deeded to daughter Nikki Malott McVey and granddaughter Anicia Holweger on 5-5-1999 by Joe Delbert Malott. The other .25 acre was part of the two-acre tract deeded to Ronald Joe Malott on 5-4-1999.

Lot P—3 acres. J. L. Glosson paid Smith $225 for this tract of land on 4-4-1947. Joe Delbert Malott paid him $300 for the acreage on 8-20-1953. On 10-14-1974, Virginia Malott Holcomb bought a .75 acre lot (P1) from Malott. She deeded the tract to her daughter, Tonya C. Gray on 11-3-1998. Grace Strackbein bought a half acre lot (P2) next to Holcomb's on 3-27-1986 and still owns it. The remaining 1.75 acre was deeded to Ronald Joe Malott on 5-4-1999 as part of the two-acre inheritance.

Lot Q—23.28 acres. On 8-22-1950, J. B. Whisenant bought this tract from J. L. Smith. He sold it to L. F. Rader on 5-8-1952. Rader and Oran Rippy sold it to the Veterans Land Board for $11,500 on 5-16-1956. On that same day, Samuel Langston bought it from VLB for the same $11,500. On 10-24-1959, Oran Rippy bought .877 acres (Q1) from Langston and built a house on the property. Oran Rippy bought another .993 acre (Q2) from Langston on 1-8-1963 and the Smith house was moved to this property. Charles Schandua purchased one acre (Q3) of land from Langston on 4-29-1972 and built his house on the property. Carroll Glosson bought another 2.48 acre tract (Q4) from Langston on 10-2-1975. Oran Hill Rippy purchased a 2.995 acre lot (Q5) from Vida Rippy on 5-4-1977 and built a house on it. Charles Schandua sold his lot (Q3) to Delphine Chance in 1979. Chance then sold it to Carter Investments for $43,000 on 7-22-1980. Rip Gravell bought 1.262 acres of land (Q6) from Vida Rippy on 8-22-1994 and built his home on the lot. Oran H. Rippy sold his lot (Q2) to his daughter, Robin, on 6-27-2000. Enoch "Buzzy" Needham bought Q4 from the Carroll Glosson heirs on 11-15-1995. Dosia Mae Rippy Langston, the widow of Samuel Langston, owns the remaining 13.567 acres, getting title to it on 12-29-1994.

Lot R—4.38 acres. This was part of the property that W. P. Crow bought from the Dripping Springs schools on 3-18-1938. He built a rock house on this property in that same year. He later deeded the property to his grandson, Mack Crow, on 12-26-1978. Mr. Crow continued to live in the house until his death. Mack Crow sold the property to Joe Miller for $85,000 on 10-19-1983. Mr. Miller sold it to Tom Arons and Anne Morris on 8-6-2001.

Lot S—? acres. Again, this was part of the school property. W. P. Crow sold this triangle of land between highway 20 and the creek road to the church of Christ for $50 on 11-8-1940. They built a church building on this property. They lost part of it to Hwy 290 but gained some back in Creek Road right-of-way.

Lot T—.78 acre. Still more of the school property. W. P. Crow sold this parcel of land to W. E. McNair on 7-23-1959 and Mr. McNair built a brick home on it in early 1960. He sold it to Mike Hemingway in 1994 and he, in turn, sold it to Thomas Miller and Peggy Farley on 6-9-2000.

Lot U—1.82 acres. W. P. Crow sold this tract of land to John A. and Lou McNair on 9-19-1961 and they built their brick home on the property in 1962. They sold .04 acre to Ernest Williamson on 3-4-1985.

Lot V—.82 acre. W. P. Crow sold this strip of land surrounding the Dripping Springs Branch to Dave Fowler for $300 on 10-16-1967 and he built his house on the ledge. His heirs sold this property to Hancock/Hanks Investments in 2001.

NORTHWEST QUARTER

J. W. Wilson, Sr., Subdivision

Mr. Wilson purchased 76.78 acres from the Marshall heirs on 4-7-1942. This property included the Marshall-Chapman house. Almost immediately, Mr. Wilson began selling off portions of this property.

Lot A—22.77 acres. When the Dripping Springs school decided to expand and build on a new campus, it was this property they chose. It actually came in four purchases. The first purchase was made on 7-19-1947 and it was an 11-acre tract (A1). The school was erected on this site. On 9-23-1952, the school just about doubled their property with two purchases (A2, A3). A2 was a 682x600 lot, matching up with the north side of A1. A3 was a 50x550 strip beginning at the northeast corner of A1 and running south. The final parcel was purchased on 5-25-1957 (A4) to make room for the baseball field. It was a lot 150x330½x129x293 that bordered the southwest corner of A1.

Lot B—1 acre. On 10-23-1942, L. J. Sorrell bought this lot from Mr. Wilson and eventually it was divided into two tracts. The Sorrells moved their house on the western half in 1943 and built a cafe building on the eastern half in 1949.

B1—.256 acres. O. B. McKown, Sr., bought the eastern part of the lot from Mr. Sorrell on 2-6-1963. McKown would then sell the property to S. J. Moore for $4,000 on 5-31-1968. The Moore heirs sold the property to O. C. Harmon on 6-21-1971. Harmon later sold the property to Larry Jackson and Karen Crenwelge. Lynette Ritter paid them $16,500 for the property on 6-1-1979, and sold the property to Mrs. Pam Maynor on 1-1-1996.

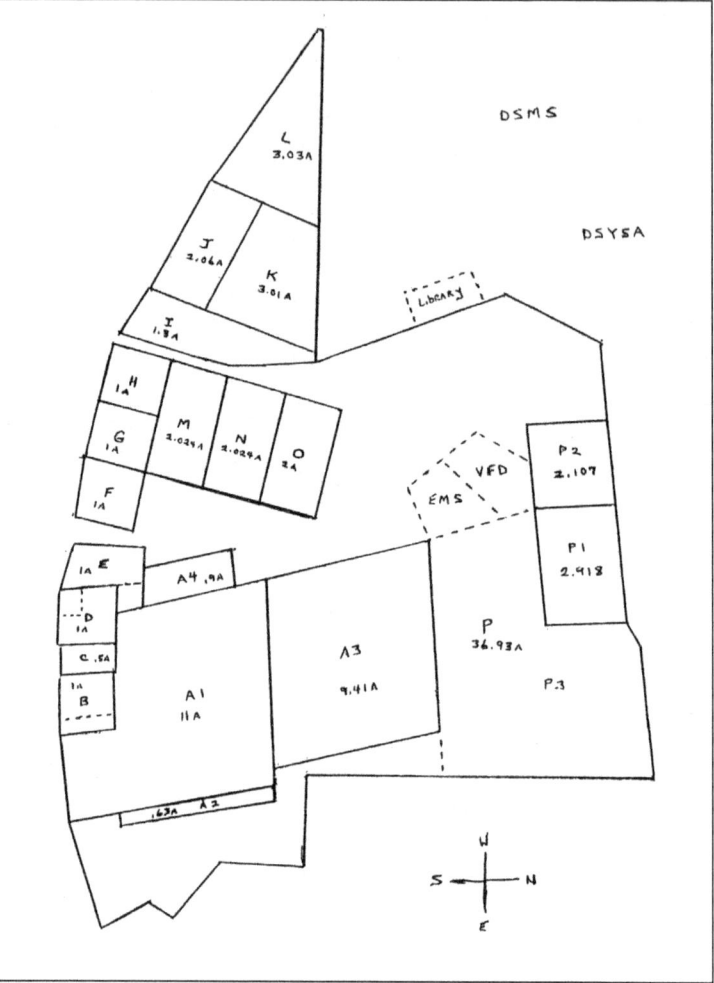

B2—.75 acres. Lloyd D. Pate bought the remaining .75 acre tract from Mr. Sorrell on 11-6-1974. Marvin Crumley bought the property from Pate on 3-24-1982.

Lot C—.5 acres. Lloyd D. Pate bought this tract of land from Wilson on 4-15-1944 and built a house on it that year. W. W. "Buddy" Williamson bought it from Pate on 9-20-1945. For a while in the late '40s, it served as the office for Dr. A.E.C. Pope. Alfard Hohman bought it from Williamson on 7-23-1951 and still owns the property.

Lot D—1 acre. W. W. Williamson bought this lot from Wilson on 10-16-1945. It ended up being split into two tracts.

D1—.27 acres. Williamson sold a tract of land from the southwest corner to Dovie Beauchamp on 4-3-1947. She built a rock home on the site in 1948. She also bought a

12-foot strip on her north boundary line from Alfard Hohman on 8-18-1955. Mrs. Beauchamp sold her property to O. B. McKown, Sr., on 7-25-1968. McKown sold it to Grady Moore for $7,900 on 8-29-1970. Jack Sedwick paid Grady Moore $37,800 for it on 8-14-1978. Sedwick sold it to Richard Thompson on 7-6-1993.

D2—.73 acres. Alfard Hohman bought the remaining tract from Williamson on 7-23-1951. As mentioned before, Hohman sold Mrs. Beauchamp a 12-foot strip on her north boundary line on 8-18-1955. The Hohmans built their house on this tract of land in 1963 and have lived there ever since.

Lot E—1 acre. Wallace Garrett purchased this tract of land from J. W. Wilson, Sr., on 7-14-1956. Mr. and Mrs. Garrett built a small frame house on the front portion of the lot nearer Highway 290 that year. After Mr. Garrett's death, O. B. McKown married the widow Garrett. They built a brick home on the north side of the lot by 1963. They sold some parts of the tract. On 4-22-1963, Alfard Hohman bought a small tract of land about 75x80 feet that bordered on the back of Hohman's lot. The McKowns sold the property to Willie G. Bohot for $38,000 on 6-1-1971. On 4-22-1975, Curtis Quisenberry purchased the property from Bohot. At some point, the partnership of Roger Hanks/Joe Gillman purchased the property under the name of Austex Acres. On 8-31-1998, Danny Turner bought the property from Roger Hanks. It now covers 1.179 acres.

Lot F—1 acre. This tract of land was sold to Robert Kumlacky on 10-4-1947. Eventually, with the building of several houses on the property to the east and the property north, a right-of-way was carved out alongside the eastern edge to have access to Highway 290. On 1-13-1951, W. B. Rhodes paid Kumlacky $850 for the lot. J. W. Wilson, Jr., bought the property from Rhodes on 12-24-1951. On 2-2-1974, there was some type of land swap between J. W. Wilson and Alva Haydon, presumably having to do with a right-of-way situation. On 9-12-1985, the partnership of Roger Hanks/Joe Gillman purchased the tract of land from J. W. as part of a land swap. Bill/Judy Schlueter bought the land on 9-29-1994 and erected Hamburger Hill Plus Restaurant on the premises in December 1994. In April 2001, they sold the property to Steve Axelrod and Melanie Stanford and their 13-year stay in Dripping Springs, running the Hamburger Hill Plus Restaurant, seemed to end. After remodeling, Axelrod reopened it as Que Pasta. By April 2002, Axelrod leased it to another group that opened it as The Great Dane. That failed as well, and by June 2002, the Schlueters ended up with the property again and began remodeling to operate Hamburger Hill Plus Restaurant again. It reopened on July 9. It now has a total of 1.14 acres.

Lot G—1 acre. Walter Haster bought this tract of land on 7-4-1947 from J. W. Wilson, Sr. At some point, H. F. Hohmann bought the property from Haster and on 8-20-1965, J. W., Jr., and his wife, Lurline Hohmann Wilson, inherited the property from the Hohmanns. They later built their new and enlarged appliance business on this lot in 1987.

Lot H—1 acre. J. W. Wilson, Jr., bought this acre of land from his dad on 7-4-1947. They built their home on the northern portion of the property in 1948. In 1953 they built their first appliance store on the southern section fronting Highway 290. It burned down in 1963 and was promptly rebuilt. The property is still in the Wilson family.

Lot I—1.8 acres. On 9-23-1960, James F. Hoard bought this tract of land from the Wilson family and build a brick home on the property fronting Highway 290 in July 1961. On 3-13-1973, Jimmy P. Moore paid Mr. Hoard $2,500 for the back 1.09 acre portion of the tract. Mr. Moore located two houses on the property. He, in turn, sold William P. Crisp .52 acres (IB), that included the two houses, for $30,000 on 5-19-1978. Son Paul Crisp purchased the lot on 6-16-1997. Steven Stroud paid Mr. Moore $3,500 for the remaining .57 acres (IA) on 8-15-1979. J. W. Wilson, Jr., bought the remaining .71 acre of the lot that included the house from Mr. Hoard when the Hoards decided to retire to another area on 8-19-1983. Around 1983, Robert M./Flora Townsend bought IA from Stroud. They sold it to Charles/Linda Levingston on 11-22-1985. In early 1986, Ben Steele got the property from the Levingstons. On 8-12-1986, Stephen Pasquini bought it from Steele. Ferris Clements bought it from Pasquini on 12-4-1987. On 5-20-1997, Jack Townsend bought the property from the Clements estate. They continue to own the property.

Lot J—2.06 acres. On 10-12-1946, John D. Ragland bought this two-acre tract and built a rock house on the property in 1947 and made his home there until he sold it to Petrick & Beaman Interests on 7-30-1985 for $470,470, which included the land in Lot K. The Raglands were forced to take the property back when the previous owners defaulted on the deal. I am not sure how many times it changed hands after that before Rex Baker/Jim Powers bought the property on 12-8-1999, razed it, and built the Arbor Center, an office complex that includes five buildings.

Lot K—3.01 acres. John D. Ragland added to his land holdings on 9-15-1956 when he purchased this tract of land from the Wilson family. This was included in the sale to Petrick & Beaman Interests on 7-30-1985. It went through the same ownership trail as Lot J.

Lot L—3.03 acres. L. B. Wootton bought this tract of land from the Wilson family on 8-27-1956. He built a small house on the property in 1958. Fred and Ruth Trimble purchased the property from Mr. Wootton on 1-30-1965 for $11,330. On 4-28-1994 Gary Groce, who had been leasing the metal warehouse for his welding business since 1988, bought the western half .68 acre of the property, which included his business. He added a small BBQ stand in the western corner of it. The other 2.37 acres, including the house, were sold to Gamal F. Said on 10-25-1996.

Lot M—2.024 acres. Mr. H. F. Hohmann purchased this tract of land from J. W. Wilson, Sr., on 3-31-1948. They built their house on this property and stayed there until their deaths when J. W. and Lurline Hohmann Wilson, Jr., inherited it on 8-20-1965.

Lot N—2.024 acres. H. F. Hohmann added to his land holdings when he purchased the adjoining acreage from J. W. Wilson, Sr. for $400 on 3-31-1949. J. W./Lurline Wilson inherited the land on 8-20-1965.

Lot O—2.0 acres. H. F. Hohmann added the next tract of land on 11-30-1953 when he purchased it for $400 from the Wilson family. J. W./Lurline Wilson inherited it on 8-20-1965.

Lot P—36.93 acres. Alva Haydon purchased the final 36.93 acres of the Wilson family acreage on 2-29-1972. It included the Marshall-Chapman house. Alva Haydon still owns the house property but has sold most of the rest. He sold off the property to Richard Youngblood in the 1970s but Youngblood had to let all go back except for the five acres where he had built his house, and when he sold another tract above the school property to James Burrows. Alva Haydon had to buy it back in auction to keep from losing it. He sold a 10.08-acre tract to James Burrows and the rest of the land became the property of Roger Hanks, who donated the land along Sportsplex Road that now houses the EMS and the Volunteer Fire Department. The Hanks family still owns 9.649 acres in small strips of land along Sportsplex Road. Alva Haydon still owns 3.58 acres, which includes the house.

NORTHWEST QUARTER

Remainder of Transactions

The rest of the transactions are a little mixed and not easy to break down into nice packages. I will try to start out with the

original tract of land and try to trace it to the present. What happens is that people bought portions of several tracts, so their totals will not be reflected in each tract. You may have to search through several tracts and take notes to get their total holdings. It is a little difficult to follow at times.

As mentioned before, Burrell J. Marshall sold two 193-acre tracts before his death to Edward and Martha Jane Daniel Riley, and brother-in-law, Aaron K. and Manerva Daniel.

Edward J. Riley Tract A—193 acres. This tract of land was located in the northwest corner of the league. Mr. Riley purchased the land on 12-18-1871. Mr. Riley was involved in the arrest of three thieves in 1876 and was killed in the gunfight. Mrs. Riley was remarried by 1880 to Warren J. Collins, a young man fourteen years her junior. On 12-30-1885, she bought the eighth shares of her sons, W. E. and W. P. The Collins and Daniel families took their herd of cattle and reestablished themselves in New Mexico in the fall of 1887. Mrs. Collins held onto her land until 1-1-1901 when she sold it to H. L. Moore. Mr. Moore sold a 40-acre tract to J. L. Puckett on 10-19-1901. Mr. Puckett gave it to his son J. A., as part of his inheritance on 7-17-1924. I. T. Applewhite purchased the land from Mr. Puckett on 8-19-1929. Allen L. Pearson bought the tract from Mrs. Applewhite on 3-27-1942, a part of a 198.74 acre tract. F. O. Haug bought it from Pearson on 10-9-1943 and he sold it to C. F. Blinka on 8-29-1946. From there, Edward Killer bought it from Blinka on 8-4-1950. J. V. Gregg became the owner when he purchased it from Killer on 1-17-1962. C. B. "Chuck" Draper bought it from Gregg on 6-1-1966. Draper sold the tract to the Jackson Land Company on 10-8-1984. It was meant to be subdivided into home lots but the crash of the '80s put the land into bankruptcy proceedings. The bank ended up with the property and, consequently, Jim Karhan purchased the land in 1992. His thought was to also sell lots and build houses. He donated a little over 14 acres to the City of Dripping Springs in 1999 to establish the Karhan Park. He decided he did not want to build a subdivision and sold the other 25 plus acres as part of a 95-acre tract to Bruce Jones on 11-11-1999 and it became part of Jones' Hidden Springs Ranch II.

Mrs. Maggie Moore had gotten in poor health and her property was turned over to kin, in order to sell it. J.E. Spaw bought the 153-acre tract on 4-17-1939. J. H. Musick bought it from Spaw on 2-24-1942. Fred Bremer took it off Musick's hands on 9-8-1942. Joe Bradford bought it from Bremer on 11-2-1943 and then sold it to C. A. Hart on 2-28-1944. William C. Green bought it from Hart on 4-25-1946 and sold it to Elbert E. Fine on 3-16-1951. Ernest Morgan bought the property on 7-1-1955 from Mr. Fine. The Morgans sold this tract to the Jackson Land Company in 1984. The Jacksons had it all platted and began to develop Meadow Oaks subdivision when bankruptcy proceedings began and they lost it all. The Vitolich brothers ended up acquiring the unowned lots in Meadow Oaks and are working toward completion there. Around 76 acres went back to the Morgans. Bruce Jones bought this tract in 1998 and is completing the plat under the Hidden Springs Ranch subdivision.

Aaron K. Daniel Tract B—193 acres. This tract of land matched the eastern border of the Riley tract, making a square tract of the two. Mr. Daniel bought the property on the same day that the Rileys did, 12-18-1971. The note was entertwined somehow. Aaron K. Daniel paid his brother J. W. and sister Martha Jane Collins for their share of the acreage on 9-1-1886. He sold the tract to W. E. Daniel on 3-27-1893. A. K. would already be in New Mexico with the others. Albert L. Davis, Jr., was the first one to break away a portion of the tract. He bought 68.8 acres off the northern side on 6-3-1897. Mr. Davis sold the land to T. J. Watts on 1-1-1901 and then Watts sold it to E. W. Herndon on 8-21-1901. Along came J. L. Patterson and he bought all of

Herndon's property, including this acreage on 6-10-1903. It stayed in the Patterson family for many years. Barbara Patterson Wood was deeded 812 acres that included this acreage by her sister, Mattie McKellar, on 6-13-1928. She later married Ben Everett and in 1971, this acreage was part of the 714-acre purchase by Gary and Brian Beach. On 10-12-1973, Lee Blocker purchased the total package from the Beaches and this was developed as part of the Springlake subdivision.

James O. Rowland bought the remaining 124.2 acres from W. E. Daniel on 11-6-1899. Rowland sold it to Annie O. Breed on 10-17-1922. Annie Breed sold it back to James O. Rowland on 1-14-1928 and he promptly sold it to Earl and Elbert Shelton on 2-15-1928. I. T. Applewhite acquired it from the Sheltons on 1-24-1929. Mrs. Applewhite sold it to Allen L. Pearson on 3-27-1942, a part of a 198.74 acre tract. Mr. Pearson sold it to F. O. Haug on 10-9-1943, then to C. F. Blinka on 8-29-1946, then to Edward Killer on 8-4-1950. Next, J. V. Gregg bought it from Killer on 1-17-1962 and he sold it to C. B. Draper. The Jackson Land Company bought the land from Draper on 10-8-1984. This section was to be made into a subdivision too, but the crash of the '80s put this land into bankruptcy proceedings. As a part of the agreement, Mr. Draper received 49.6075 acres back and the rest was bought by Jim Karhan in 1992 as part of Brown-Karhan. He had it tagged as part of a subdivision but changed his mind and sold it to Bruce Jones, as part of a 95-acre tract, on 11-11-1999. It is slated to be a part of the Hidden Springs Ranch II subdivision. Teddy Draper bought his dad's acreage on 7-1-1992.

Jasper N. Marshall Tract C, 73 acres. Originally his inheritance was listed as 70 acres but the first transaction was for 73 acres. W. H. Robbins bought the total acreage on 7-24-1893. W. R. Baird bought 73 acres from Mrs. M. J. Robbins Martin on 2-18-1907. Willie Edna Baird Crow received an acre of land from the southwest corner of the tract to build their house on in 1956. On 5-9-1978, Mrs. Crow inherited the rest of this acreage. A. H. Benny bought 31.51 acres from the Crows on 9-30-1982 and another 42.52 on 5-8-1984. Roger Hanks bought 60.56 acres from A. H. Benny on 5-8-1984. He gave 20.518 acres to the Dripping Springs Youth Sports Association, in memory of his daughter, Hope, on 5-15-1989. On 6-27-1994, DSISD purchased the other 40.0514 acres from Hanks to build a middle school on. The other 13 acres owned by the Bennys is being developed into the Benny subdivision by Mrs. Benny. This began in 2002. Donald Crow inherited the 1.269-acre lot of his mother on 9-14-2000.

Robert L. Marshall Tract D—98 acres. This was another of those problems of numbers. The inheritance called for 93 acres but in the two tracts sold by Robert, the total comes to either 95 or 98. On 7-25-1893, W. H. Robbins bought a 68-acre tract from Robert. W. R. Baird bought this acreage from Mrs. M. J. Robbins Martin on 2-18-1907. W. T. Chapman bought 35 acres from the southern end of this tract from Mr. Baird on 4-20-1907. The rest would stay in the Baird family. John Marcus Baird inherited this tract from the estate on 5-9-78. Mr. Baird sold the rest to Richard Schmidt on 5-1-1984 as part of a 34.29-acre deal, but it would fall through and Mr. Baird retained it. He donated three acres to the Drippings Springs Library as a site for their new facility on 3-30-1995. On 7-26-1893, W. R. Baird bought a 30-acre tract from R. L. Marshall. In a description found later, the same dimensions were given as 27, so I am not sure of total acreage. On 1-1-1901, A. L. Davis, Jr., bought 12 acres of a 27-acre purchase from Baird on the northern end of this acreage. Davis sold those 12 acres to T. J. Watts on 1-1-1901 and then it went to E. W. Herndon on 8-21-1901. J. L. Patterson bought it on 6-10-1903. It became a part of the Patterson estate that was divided among his children. On 6-13-1928, it was a part of an 812-acre tract deeded to Barbara Patterson Wood from Mattie McKellar. This was a part of the 714-acre sale to Gary and Brian Beach in 1971 by Ben and Barbara Wood Everett. Lee Blocker purchased the block of land from the Beaches on 10-12-1973 and it became a part of Springlake subdivision. On 6-29-1935, Baird sold a 12-acre tract, bordering on the 27-acre tract, to I. D. Hedges. Hedges sold to J. C. Stinson on 4-14-1939. Stinson sold to Ben and Barbara Wood Everett on 1-20-1940. It went to the Beach brothers in 1971 and then onto Lee Blocker on 10-12-1973 and then to become a part of the Springlake subdivision. On 1-20-1937, Baird sold another 11.75 acres, from the northern end of his property, that bordered on the 12-acre tract, to G. H. Ferrell. Part of it came from this acreage. Inthaberry Ferrell sold it to B. E. Hudson on 4-18-1961 and then he sold it to Robert A. Reed, Jr., on 6-16-1965 and it remains in his hands. J. M. Baird sold 6.6 acres, which included the house, to William Henry Taylor II on 2-15-1985. On 7-4-1995, the Taylors moved away and let the property go back to Mr. Baird.

George W. Marshall Tract E—81 acres. This was his inheritance and he ended up selling it to his stepfather, W. T. Chapman, in two tracts. He sold a 65-acre tract to him on 4-3-1883. Lewis B. Milam bought it from Chapman on 4-26-1884. The north 32.5 acres were sold to J.A.H. Thurman on 1-19-1885. Mr. W. R. Baird then bought the southern 32.5 acres (but claimed 35) from Milam on 10-23-1888. H. G. Thurman, Sr., bought the J.A.H. Thurman acreage on 11-23-1897 and then T. S. Wilhite bought it from Thurman 8-19-1899. Mr. Baird unified the strip again when he bought Mr. Wilhite's 32.5 acres on 3-27-1900. It did not stay unified very long because Mr. Baird sold the northern 15 acres, as a part of a 27-acre purchase by A. L. Davis, Jr., on 1-1-1901, and, in turn, he sold it as a part of a 135.8 acre tract, to T. J. Watts on the same day. Mr. Watts sold the package to E. W. Herndon on 8-21-1901 and J. L. Patterson bought the entire tract from Herndon on 6-10-1903. It was part of the Patterson inheritance package that stayed in the family. It was a part of the 812 acre deed transfer from Mattie Patterson McKellar to her sister, Barbara Patterson Wood, on 6-13-1928. This was a part of the 714-acres that Barbara Wood Everett sold to Gary and Brian Beach in 1971. Lee Blocker purchased this acreage from the Beaches on 10-12-1973 and developed it into the Springlake subdivision. Baird sold off a couple of more tracts that included the northern acreage of this tract. On 6-29-1935, he sold a 12-acre tract bordering on the 27-acre tract, which included part of this tract, to I. D. Hedges. He sold it to J. C. Stinson on 4-14-1939. Stinson sold it to Ben and Barbara Wood Everett on 1-20-1940. It went to the Beach brothers in 1971 and finally to Lee Blocker on 10-12-1973 to become a part of Springlake. On 1-20-1937, Baird sold 11.75 acres, which bordered on the 12-acre tract, to G. H. Ferrell. Inthaberry Ferrell sold it to B. E. Hudson on 4-18-1961 and then he sold it to Robert A. Reed, Jr., on 6-16-1965. Son John Marcus Baird inherited this acreage on 5-9-1978. On 5-1-1984, he sold 34.29 acres to Richard Schmidt, which came from a part of this tract, but this deal fell through and he got the land back.

W. T. Chapman got the other 16 acres shortly after acquiring the other 65. He sold it to W. H. Robbins on 7-25-1893. I'm not sure how it fit into present acreage but I never did find it came out anywhere else, so I assume it was a part of the Patterson purchase and therefore a part of the P. L. Turner subdivision history. The deed description history does not make the map look like it does today.

Fannie Marie Marshall Tract G—150 acres. Actually, her inheritance called for 131 acres but by the time she sold this property to W. H. Robbins on 7-25-1893, she had married D. W. Burkett and it was given as 150 acres. I am not sure where the added acreage came from. Mr. Robbins died in 1895 and his wife, Mary J. Robbins, had possession of the land. On 6-3-1899, Albert L. Davis, Jr., bought 40 acres from the northern section of this tract. In 1897, Mr. Davis purchased 68.8 acres from Mr. Daniel and that is why he had to purchase the 27-acre tract from Mr. Baird in 1901. That tract connected the two land holdings and he was then able to sell the total package to T. J. Watts on 1-1-1901. Mr. Watts then sold the tract that included the 40 acres to E. W. Herndon on 8-21-1901. Mr. Herndon then sold the property to J. L. Patterson on 6-10-1903.

I. V. Davis, Jr., purchased a four-acre tract that bordered on the northern edge of block four of the second addition to Dripping Springs. This purchase was made on 6-3-1904 from Mrs. Robbins and is covered under the P. L. Turner subdivision history. On 9-5-1904, Robert E. Spaw purchased approximately five acres from Mrs. Robbins. The land bordered on blocks seven and eight of the second addition. It is covered in the E. P. Shelton subdivision history. The remaining 101 acres were sold to James Walter Glosson by Mrs. Robbins on 2-18-1907. Mr. Glosson sold it to Florence McKellar on 4-6-1907. She sold it to J. L. Patterson on 11-25-1907. P. L. Turner bought it as a part of a 171-acre tract from Mr. Patterson on 3-6-1920. In the 1930s, I. D. Hedges bought the northern 30 acres from Turner. J. C. Stinson bought it from Hedges on 4-14-1939 and he sold it to Ben and Barbara Everett on 1-20-1940. Antonio Nevarez bought two acres from the Everetts on 12-21-1950. The rest went to the Beaches in 1971, then to Lee Blocker in 1973. The rest of Turner land is covered in the P. L. Turner subdivision history. The Nevarez property is in the hands of two of the children. Rudy Nevarez got the two acres on 4-12-1986 and sold .5 acres to Olivia Nevarez on 12-30-1998.

Jefferson D. Marshall Tract H—85 acres. This was Jefferson Davis Marshall's inheritance. Actually, in the original deal, he was given 91 acres. There was some dispute about its boundaries. He married Laura Bailey and they wanted to sell the property. They had to go to court and settled the claim with Harold Durar for $55 on 12-11-1882. In the settlement, the Marshalls agreed upon the boundary line connecting with Cave Spring Branch and following it to the Riley line. Actually, there was still a part of the P. A. Smith league on the west side of the branch that went with other property from that time on. On 12-13-1882, they sold the 85 acres to Ernst/Bertha Kubens for $450. The Kubenses sold the property to J. L. Puckett on 9-12-1883. On 7-17-1924, Mr. Puckett divided his property among his two sons. J. A. Puckett received 35 acres and E. E. Puckett, the other 50. I. T. Applewhite bought 35 acres from J. A. Puckett on 8-19-1929. Mrs. Applewhite sold the 35 acres, which became a part of a 198.74 acre tract, to Allen L. Pearson on 3-27-1942. As it has been recorded in other sections above, Pearson sold it to F. O. Haug on 10-9-1943, then Haug to C. F. Blinka on 8-29-1946, then Blinka to Edward Killer on 8-4-1950, then to J. V. Gregg on 1-17-1962. C. B. Draper bought the property from Gregg on 6-1-1966. Draper sold it to Jackson Land Company on 10-8-1984. It went through bankruptcy and Jim Karhan acquired the property. The Draper house was built on this tract in 1967 and Karhan has remodeled it to become the Brown-Karhan administrative building. In the spring of 2001, another Brown-Karhan facility was started and opened in early 2002.

Lewis B. and Alice Milam bought the 50-acre tract from E. E. Puckett on 5-12-1927 for $2,500. Mr. Milam died and the family could not or did not pay the mortgage. The property was put on the auction block by the sheriff, G. M. Allen. Mrs. Sophia Wendlandt bought the property on 4-1-1930 for $100. She sold the property to A. W. Wusterhausen and he sold the property to A. B. Wusterhausen on 6-30-1930 for $1,500. On 10-27-1930, Mr. Wusterhausen sold the 50 acres to M. C. and Virtice Sloan for $1,600. The old Highway 290 was making its way through Dripping Springs and on 7-16-1934, the Sloans received $61 for 3.1 acres of right-of-way for the road.

This left them with 46.9 acres. B. C. Leifeste paid the Sloans $1,000 for the acreage on 6-24-1935. C. C. Graves bought the property from Mr. Leifeste on 5-20-1941. On 9-27-1944, Marvin Puryear purchased the acreage from Graves. Puryear sold the property to the Veteran's Land Board for $6,500 on 1-18-1950. On that same day, J. F. Murray bought the land from VLB. R. J. "Skeet" Ragland begin leasing the property in March 1951, living in the Puckett house. A couple of years later, Murray let it go back and Ragland bought all of it; deeds would be filed over a period of years. In the meantime, the new Highway 290 came through Dripping Springs in 1958 and took a swipe out of the middle of this property. Mr. Ragland, at first, received deeds on three sections. The first was a 10-acre tract in the late '50s, then on 5-20-1961, the second was the 7.68 acres between old 290 and the new 290 and divided it into lots known as the Ragland subdivision. He sold the most eastern lots to Woody Glosson and he built his house there in 1963. The western end lots went to the Jernigans, Bradshaws and Simpsons, who built their houses there soon after Woody did. Foster Harmon owned much of the rest and all of this part of the property is taken for the Hill Country Senior Citizens building and the Hill Country Cottages. The Raglands lived in the old Puckett house until they built their house on the 10-acre tract. They moved into their new home in February 1960. Cecil Whinery later bought the lot that included the Ragland home. On 6-16-1961, Mr. Ragland bought a 5.125 acre tract, which included the Puckett house. He sold 3.498 of this to M. T. Jones on 6-24-1961. Mr. Jones sold a 50x75 foot section to Sidney Cook, Jr., on 10-6-1961. On 8-17-1963, O. B. McKown, Sr., bought the remaining 2.937 acres from M. T. Jones. Ragland bought back the lot from Sidney Cook. On 4-6-1965, the Texas Quail Farm bought McKown's property. On 3-1-1972, E. C. Jancik bought the acreage from Texas Quail Farm. On 12-9-1983, Greg Tom and Mark McManus bought the property from Jancik. They, in turn, sold the property to Dennis Green and partners on 11-13-1998 and they built a Diamond Shamrock complex on the property under the name of Hays City Corp.

Mr. Ragland got the deed for the rest of the 60.45 acre tract of land from VLB on 5-4-1970. He built another house on a section of land on the west side of Cave Spring in 1970. They sold this house in 1992 to Mark Hester. Randall Kirchoff bought the 2.48-acre lot from Hester on 7-30-1999. In late 2002, Kirchoff sold it to Hancock/Hanks Investments. On 3-13-1973, Ragland sold 11 acres to Jackson Land Company as part of the Dripping Springs Heights subdivision. It would include the 1960 house that Cecil Whinery bought. Raymond Whisenant purchased a .75 acre lot on 290 for his well-drilling business on 3-15-1983 and then expanded it on 1-16-1985 with another .34 acres under the name of Turkey Track Investments. Roger Hanks bought the remaining 43.03 acres, which included a part of the 66.1 tract bought from Smith, from the Raglands in March 1996. On 12-29-2000 it was put under the Hanks R. S. Reserve Tract and it is now under the control of Whit Hanks. On 5-1-2001, Hancock/Hanks Investments bought Lots 8 and 9 of the Ragland subdivision from Joy Jernigan Stephenson.

As mentioned previously, there was still land west of Cave Spring Branch that was in the P. A. Smith survey. All of that land was first a part of a 200-acre tract bordering on the western boundary line of J. D. Marshall's property. There is a 6.34-acre tract of land between the two 290s, west of Cave Spring, that has 5.75 acres in the PAS. It was first a part of a 200-acre tract that the Riley brothers bought from their parents around 1885. On 1-14-1887, W. P. Riley bought W. E. Riley's share and then sold it to W. T. Chapman on 9-29-1887. Chapman sold 140 of it to Mary E. Foster on 3-20-1900. She sold off 8.35 acres to Samuel W. Adams and then sold the other 131.65 acres to M. Herbert Howard on 9-28-1901. He sold it to W. R. Lyle on 9-29-1905. It is believed it was probably Lyle who built the house on this property. W. R. sold it to S. E. Lyle on 12-1-1925. C. C. Graves bought it from Mrs. S. E. Lyle on 7-16-1941. Graves sold it to J. Watson Wolf on 11-29-1944, and he, in turn, to Jim Boardman on 8-6-1945. Boardman sold it to Oscar Hermes on 3-15-1947. Hermes sold it to E. W. Mahler on 3-15-1948. Pearl Brannan bought it from Mahler on 8-30-1950. P. K. Odiorne bought it from Brannan on 7-1-1952 and then sold it to H. R. Harrison on 8-14-1952. As part of the divorce settlement, Mary Alice Harrison deeded her part over to H. R. on 2-2-1957. By the time Mr. Harrison sold the property to Elmer Griffin on 10-1-1960, the new Highway 290 had gone through and formed the six acre tract of land between the roads. Mr. Griffin sold this tract to Guy Powell on 5-20-1966. Aubrey Spence bought it from Powell 9-8-1970. The Spences sold it to Billy F. Hyde on 7-19-1974. They sold it to James Cross on 6-25-1976. Cross sold it to Hudson Hill on 7-26-1883. It stayed in the Hill family until 6-20-2000 when it sold to Security State Bank & Trust. They built their new bank facility on the west end, Lot 1 of Security Plaza, and sold the eastern 3.237 acres (Lot 2), with the house on it, to Security Plaza LTD under Whit Hanks.

Elmer Griffin sold 98.5 acres of his land to H. A. Beaver on 7-5-1963. Texas Quail Farm purchased the acreage from H. A. Beaver on 9-4-1963 and built a house for the Worth Kingsbery family. The Quail Farm sold it to E. C. Jancik on 4-10-1972. On 11-2-1981, Sam C. Roberto bought a 14.749-acre strip from Jancik, which was mostly in the PAS. He sold five acres to Eugene Reimers on 4-6-1982 and he sold it to Hill Country Care, Inc., on 6-27-1983 for the purpose of building the nursing home. Netalie Russell Bateman bought the other ten acres from Roberto on 4-6-1982. Mrs. Bateman sold .896 acre to Kimberly Allison Roper Flannery on 3-5-1984 and she built a Montessouri school on the site. The Antiochian Church (St. Sophia) bought this property on 5-2-2000. Rita Worthy bought another 6.9717 acres from Mrs. Bateman on 8-20-1987 and part of that is probably in PAS. There is another strip of land between the creek and Hill Country Care. Woody Butler bought this strip of land from E. C. Jancik in 1974. He sold the land to Stan Booth, against his better judgment, under a second lien arrangement in 1984. Mr. Booth's financial world crashed and burned the next year and before Mr. Butler even knew about it, the bank had taken over with a courthouse bid and Mr. Butler lost the property without a chance to get it back. Mr. Wachel bought the strip of land in 1985 and built a metal building to house his garage business. It did not go over and he left after a year, leaving the property in the hands of his lenders. The property was sold to Don Chapman in 1986. He had in mind to build a small subdivision on all the acres he had bought but met opposition and finally gave up on the project. He sold about four acres in front to Jimmy Skipton on 7-17-1996 and the house to David Trejo on 12-19-1996. Skipton leased out the building to Johnny and Eddie Garza for their Garza Automotive business until he decided to use it himself. The Highway 290 frontage acreage (1.14) was bought from Mr. Skipton by Mark and Barbara Tholen on 11-1-2000 and they erected a building for their optometrist business known as Eyecare Associates.

NORTHEAST QUARTER

This quarter of the P. A. Smith league had the same beginnings as the others. Glasscock received the whole league and Fielding S. Roy bought it from him. On 11-13-1853, Willis Fawcett paid F. S. Roy $1,387.50 for this quarter. He sold it off in two sections. The first section of 377.5 acres went to John L. Wallace. The exact date of sale has not been found. A deed of trust dated 12-21-1854 for Dr. Joseph M. Pound's purchase of the final 700 acres of this quarter, stated this was the final section of the

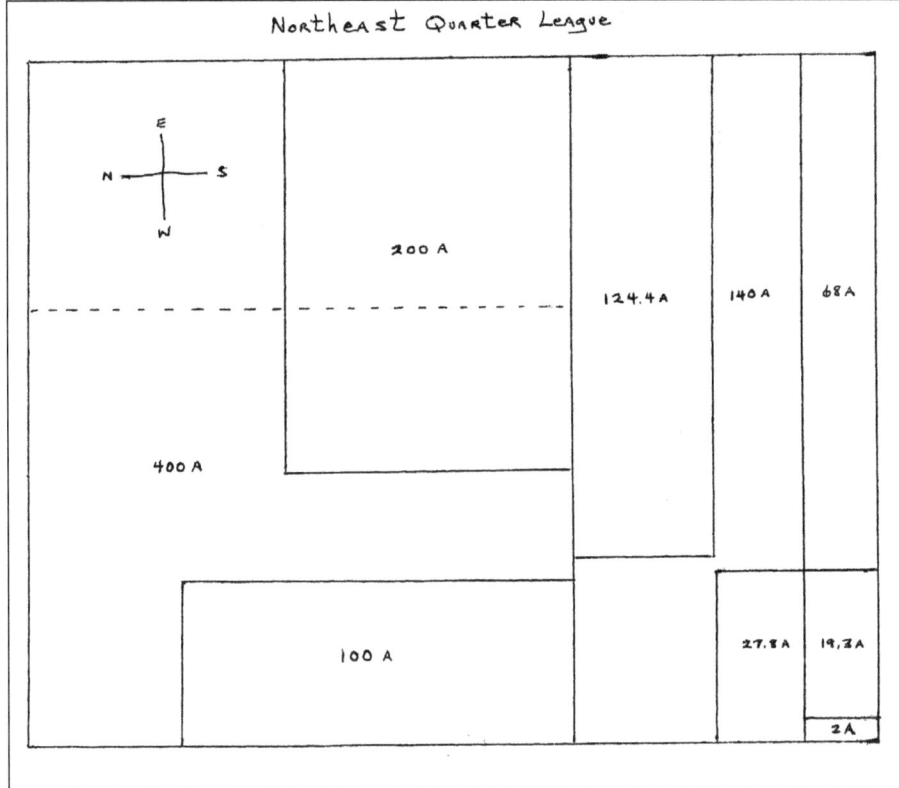

quarter and that Wallace had already purchased the rest. The deed for Wallace is dated 6-28-1855 and says he paid $755 for it. The deed for Pound is dated 12-15-1855, almost a year later than the deed of trust, when he paid $900 for his acreage. With this in mind, it is my opinion that Wallace probably bought his property from Fawcett in June 1854. The fly in the ointment is the lore that all three families came together and we know the other two bought their property in January 1854.

Dr. J. M. Pound—700 acres. Dr. Pound would eventually sell off two parcels of this land but would end up keeping 400 acres in the family until the early 1990s when the family was forced to sell the property to pay off the taxes.

300 acres. This section of land was taken from the eastern part of the acreage. On 4-10-1860, Mary Gates paid Dr. Pound $600 for this tract. Mrs. Gates died and Dr. Pound had to buy it back at an auction rather than lose it. On 9-27-1869, Dr. Pound sold it again, this time to N. H. Izard. Mr. Izard sold it to W. H. Howard on 11-5-1870. No deed was found for the transaction, but Mr. Howard sold the land to T. N. Nance. Jake Sorrell bought it from Mr. Nance on 1-27-1880 for $300. E. H. Wallace bought it from Jake Sorrell for $300 on 1-1-1881. Wallace sold it to his brother-in-law, Thomas F. Voight for $350 on 8-8-1882. For the third time, this property came back to Dr. Pound when he paid Voight $450 on 2-9-1883. This ended the odyssey of the three hundred acres but not the sale of the top 200 acres.

200 acres. The next time Dr. Pound sold the eastern portion of this acreage, he would lop off one hundred acres and sell the most southeastern 200 acres. On 1-8-1884, Nannie J. Jones paid Dr. Pound $800 for the tract. She sold it to R. S. Cavett on 9-13-1884 for $1,500. Frank R. Calvert bought the property from the Cavetts sometime in the early 1900s. Mr. Calvert sold it to Fletcher Randerson on 11-10-1904 for $1,500. Randerson sold it to John Ireland on 11-12-1942. It would then be bought by W. R. and Bessie Ireland Scott on 6-11-1957. The Scotts have owned it since.

400 acres. This section was the one that included the Pound House. After the Pounds' deaths, Mrs. Georgia Pound Cavett paid her sister, Mary Pound Hunt, $800 for her share of the property and became the owner. Upon Mrs. Cavett's death in 1968, her daughter, Marguerite Cavett Hammack inherited the property. Just prior to her death in 1985, she deeded five acres over to the Dripping

Springs United Methodist Church on 12-1-1984. On 2-17-1987, the Hammack estate deeded three acres, that included the house and other buildings, to the City of Dripping Springs to be dedicated for a museum. Later, the city turned this project over to a non-profit group known as the Friends of the Pound House. Also in conjunction with this, the city bought two parcels of land to be used as a community park with the aid of a Parks and Recreation grant. The first was 13.39 acres and was bought on 4-23-1988. The other was 11.61 acres, which was bought on 5-14-1988. By this time, the Hammack estate was in financial problems with the IRS over inheritance tax. John Hill purchased about 161 acres on 7-3-1990 and J. F. Glosson, Jr., the other approximately 208 acres on 6-12-1992. Charles Hammack purchased a 1.9 acre parcel from Glosson. In 2000, he donated this acreage to the Pound House Museum to expand their acreage to nearly five acres. The necessary arrangements were made to swap land within the park to accomplish this. It occurred on 8-31-2000. Later, H. C. Carter Investments bought 100 acres from Glosson to develop a subdivision. He sold 17.185 acres to the Dripping Springs Water Corporation for purposes of establishing a sewage plant. It was met with opposition and at the end of 2002, this project appeared dead. Carter sold 3.571 acres to the Methodist Church from his subdivision on 10-21-1998.

100 acres. Dr. Pound sold this one hundred acre tract to his daughter, Indiana Adelia Pound Stephenson on 8-5-1874. The Stephenson family owned this property until 1-2-1957, when Nelson Davidson bought the property from the heirs. Mr. Davidson sold off this tract completely in various parcels.

Parcel A—40 acres. On 12-11-1959, James Hall bought the southern 40 acres from Davidson. From that point, Mr. Hall began selling lots. This 40 acres also included the small sliver of land that had originally been deeded to R. E. Spaw in 1904.

A1—2.02 acres. Originally, James Hall had set this aside as the Hall Reserve. On 6-3-1963, he sold this lot to John Mang. John Mang sold the lot to Sunrise Gardens, Inc., owned by Randy Rogers, on 7-13-1973. William P. Johnson bought this lot from Rogers on 2-11-1981.

A2—2 acres. John Mang bought this lot from Hall on 2-27-1962 and built an A-frame house on it. On 5-23-1968, Mang sold .529 acres to the state for right-of-way for RR12 north. Sunrise Gardens, Inc., purchased the property from Mang on 7-13-1973. Randy Rogers, the owner, then sold the lot to William P. Johnson on 2-11-1981.

A3—.57 acre. John Mang bought this lot from Mr. Hall on 6-3-1963. John L. Barnes paid Mang $2,300 for this lot on 1-13-1970. On 4-9-1975, Barnes defaulted on his debt and the property was taken over by the Federal Housing Authority (FHA). H. Alyne Rodgers bought this lot from FHA on 11-25-1975 and sold it to Mac Belk on 9-7-1976.

A4—.43 acre. John L. Barnes bought this lot from James Hall on 1-14-1971. Like his other lot, Mr. Barnes defaulted on his debt. The FHA took over the lot on 4-1-1975. H. Alyne Rodgers bought this lot, too, on 11-25-1975 and Mac Belk bought it from her on 9-7-1976.

A5—.46 acre. William R. Scott bought this lot from James Hall on 6-7-1973, moved a house on the lot, and his son Jon and family have lived there since.

A6—.46 acre. T. B. Porter paid James Hall $4,000 for this lot on 4-17-1973. It had a house on the property. The Porters, T. B. and Aileen, sold the lot to Alfred and Carol Chance on 11-2-1973. The United Methodist Church, needing a parsonage, paid the Chances $22,008.51 for the lot on 5-23-1975. After the house was damaged by fire, the Methodists sold the property to Daisy Russell Binkley for $8,080 on 1-9-1979. Mrs. Binkley sold the lot to Doug and Nita Jernigan in 1980. Doug Jernigan sold the property to Joe and Carol Felkel on 9-22-1993.

A7—.443 acre. Fred Garnett bought this

lot from James Hall on 5-8-1969. Lewis C. Cruz bought the property from Fred Garnett on 10-26-1971. Calvin Knauth bought the property from Lewis Cruz on 8-24-1973. James Hurlbut bought the property from Mr. Knauth on 3-31-1978, moved a house on the lot and then traded it to Zelma Faye Jones for block one property on 6-14-1979.

A8—.47 acre. Jonathan Clower bought this lot from James Hall on 5-18-1962. He built a house on the property, but had to let the lot go back to Mr. Hall on 12-10-1963 when he took a job somewhere else. John Greiner bought the property from Hall in 1965. He sold it to Calvin Knauth on 11-23-1966. L. D. and Mary Beth Spears paid the Knauths $32,000 for the lot on 2-23-1980. On 1-11-1985. Aileen Gillis bought the property from the Spears and converted the house into the Fun Factory day care center.

A9—.54 acre. Shortly after buying this tract of land from Nelson Davidson, James Hall moved a small house onto this lot for his mother to live in. After her death, Mr. Hall sold the lot to Calvin Knauth for $9,325 on 11-10-1972. Alice F. Benny bought the lot from the Knauths on 8-24-1979. She sold to Aileen Gillis on 10-24-1986 for $51,183.

A10—.30 acre. George L. Johnson paid James Hall $2,500 for this lot on 11-12-1971 and he built a brick home on the lot. Jean Parker bought the property from the Johnson heirs in 1998 and Cheryl Elizondo bought it from her on 6-23-2000. She turned the house into the Ole Hen House eatery and it lasted in that capacity until early 2002. A second house was moved on the western part of the property facing Old Fitzhugh Road.

A11—.35 acre. C. B. Blowers bought this lot from James Hall on 8-25-1971. His heirs still own the property.

A12—.28 acre. John Steger paid James Hall $3,600 for this lot on 8-3-1973. He moved a mobile home onto the property. Mr. Steger sold it to Clem Best for the same price on 4-26-1976. The Best heirs still own the property.

A13—.29 acre. L. E. "Shorty" DuPuy bought this lot from James Hall on 3-28-1972. He built a house on the lot. On 5-23-1980, Don DuPuy bought the lot from his father. Lowie E. Walker paid Don DuPuy $31,900 for the lot on 7-7-1980. The Walkers sold the property to Steve and Kay Carter for $73,150 on 6-28-1984. They sold it to Marie Moody on 3-19-2001.

A14—.28 acre. Dan O'Hara paid James Hall $3,600 for this lot on 9-14-1973. William K. O'Day bought the property from O'Hara on 3-14-1979. On 4-8-1985, James and Elise Hudson bought the lot from the O'Days. They put their veterinary business on this lot. Later, he built a new vet place on

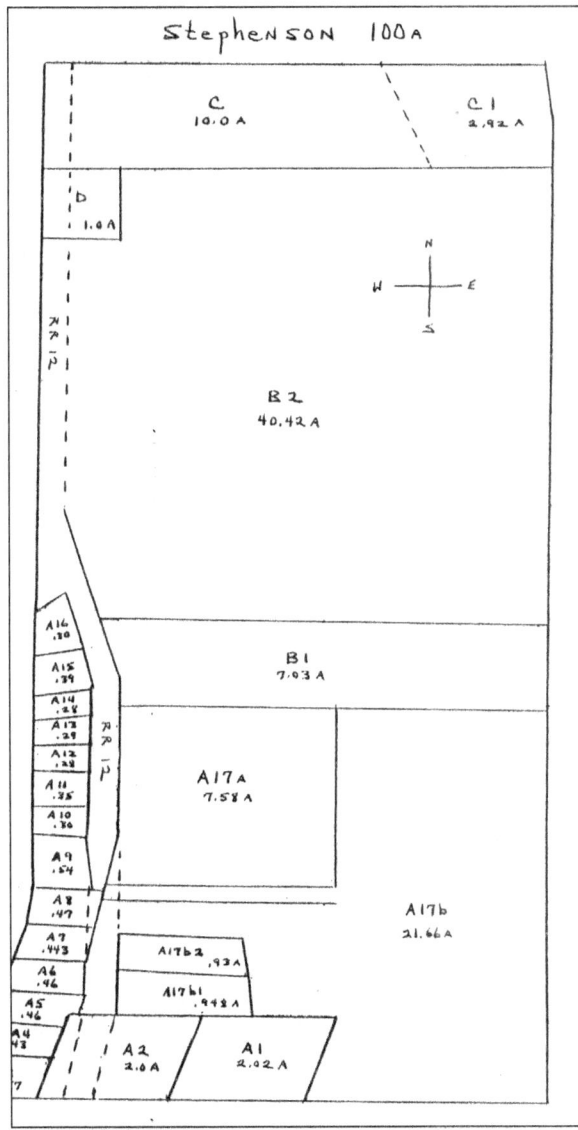

Hwy. 290 and has since turned the property back into his residence after his divorce.

A15—.39 acre. Jerry Jenkins bought this lot from James Hall on 9-1-1972. Jenkins would default on his payment and James Hall had to pay $3,168.21 to get it back. Dan O'Hara paid James Hall $542.76 for .0525 acre from the south side of the lot. William K. O'Day bought this small portion from Dan O'Hara on 3-14-1979. Billy F. Hyde bought the remaining .3372 acres of the lot from James Hall on 12-23-1981. On 4-8-1985, James and Elise Hudson bought the small lot from the O'Days. Ricky Lindholm bought the Hyde's portion in June 1983. As part of their divorce settlement, Jill Lindholm received the property on 10-13-2000.

A16—.377 acre. This is a little portion of land that was formed by the creation of RR12 N, where it meets Old Fitzhugh Road. It was actually a part of the Davidson land and not Hall's. Jack and Mickey Davidson Kroll bought it from the Davidsons on 5-9-1980. Rick and Jill Lindholm bought it from them on 10-19-1991. They sold the lot to Whit Hanks in September 2002.

A17—30 acres. James Hall sold the remaining 30 acres of his purchase to the Veterans Land Board for $5,700 on 11-19-1962. On 4-5-1965, C. L. Harris bought the acreage from VLB for $5,700 and then on the same day, sold the property to John Greiner. He sold the land in two tracts.

A17a—7.58 acres. Thomas G. Edwards paid John Greiner $3,000 for this tract on 4-6-1966. Edwards sold this tract to the Garnett brothers, Travis 1/2, Fred 1/4, Billie 1/4, for $14,000 on 6-22-1979. Travis and Fred bought Billie's share of the property on 3-7-1983. On 4-17-1985, Fred Garnett bought 1.730 acres from Travis and Travis bought 1.729 from Fred. Fred built the DS Hardware building on this property and Travis built three rent houses on the north side.

A17b—21.66 acres. James E. Felps paid John Greiner $4,500 for this tract on 7-20-1965. O. E. Longuet bought the property from Felps on 3-9-1968 for $9,500. The right of way for RR12 north took a portion of the property and on 10-13-1972, Longuet sold the remaining 20.877 acres to Hill Country Land Company for $21,000. Edward R. Fetty bought the property from the Hill Country Land Company on 2-19-1977. Fetty sold the property to Bobbe R. Grace for $45,280 on 7-17-1981. Grace sold the property to William Hines on 4-26-1982. William Hines built his house on a .945 acre lot bordering the William P. Johnson property. He sold this lot to Robert Lewis Pewitt II on 5-24-1995. Clarence Buckelew bought a .93 acre lot next to Hines on 3-29-1984. He sold it to Wayne E. Smith on 9-2-1999. Smith bought the adjoining property and sold both to Calvin and Faye Edmonds in the spring 2002 and they established the Gateway Landscaping Materials and Grass business. The rest of this property was developed into the Grand Prairie subdivision.

Parcel B—47.45 acres. J. F. Glosson, Jr., paid Nelson Davidson $18,500 for this tract on 3-28-1969. He sold it off in two separate tracts.

B1—7.03 acres. Chester Davis bought the property on 12-8-1970. After Mr. Davis's death, Mrs. Daisy Davis sold the tract to Charles R. Pilcher for $15,000 on 8-10-1976. On 11-15-1983, Mike Rose and Lee Blocker paid Charles Pilcher $57,000 for the tract and still own it.

B2—40.42 acres. A deed on 5-25-1971 had Buddy White paying Glosson $23,000 for this tract. However, on 2-14-1973, a deed shows that Glosson sold the property to William H. Bingham as Bison Incorporated. Bison, Inc. sold the tract to the Zent Development Corporation for $66,000 on 3-10-1975. This tract of land was developed as the North Forty subdivision.

Parcel C—10 acres. On 1-28-1961, Fred Garnett bought this tract of land from Nelson Davidson. The RR12 north right of way took a small portion off the west end. He built his house on the west side of his property. On 4-13-1984, Fred sold 2.922 acres of this tract to his son, Terry.

Parcel D—1 acre. Calvin Knauth bought this one acre tract from Nelson Davidson on 5-4-1966. The RR12 north right of way took a good portion of this lot. The next record found was when George M. Jones bought .33 acre of this tract from H. H. Rothell, Jr., on 5-17-1979. The J. P. Tate Company, Inc., bought this tract from Jones on 1-6-1982. Tate lost the property when he defaulted on debts. It went to the First Federal Savings & Loan of New Braunfels, where McCrocklin Development purchased the property on 1-6-1988. James Lee purchased this lot on 12-22-1995.

John L. Wallace—377.5 acres. As we have already mentioned, John Lee Wallace paid $755 for this acreage. He lived in the house he built on this land until his death in 1893, although he sold off some of it before then.

A—124.4 acres. This was the first section of land to be sold and it was done on 5-15-1874. It was actually kept in the family. Wallace's eldest daughter Carrie married Thomas F. Voight, a carpenter by trade. Wallace sold this tract, located between him and the Pound's, to them for $5. Voight built his gin on the western three acres of it and built their home on the eastern end of it. On 9-1-1882, Voight sold the three acres that included the gin and all the accompanying equipment to F. D. Henry for $1,400. The other 121.4 acres were sold to Thomas F. Martin for $1,000 on 1-19-1883. F. M. Granger came into the 121.4 acres. No deed has been found to date and possibly, he held the note on it. He sold the acreage to Z. I. Williams on 11-18-1884. Williams purchased the other three acres from F. D. Henry on 10-10-1885. No mention of the gin. A. L. Davis, Jr., bought the 121.4 acre tract from Williams for $1,200 on 2-19-1891. On 6-1-1894, Davis purchased the other three acres for $25. J. W. Glosson paid Davis $1,400 for the entire 124.4 acres on 8-13-1894. In 1897 Pedernales Lienneweber bought the property from Glosson. C. H. Berkley paid Lienneweber $1,650 for the acreage on 12-9-1909. Katherine Berkley Cannon, a granddaughter, bought the property.

B—27.8 acres. J. A. Kelly paid $550 to John L. Wallace on 8-26-1885. Tax records show that R. J. Delaune bought the property in 1899. On 12-16-1908, W. A. McMackin paid Mrs. M. E. Delaune $800 for it. T. D. Walker bought it from McMackin on 5-10-1913. Mr. Walker sold two tracts of land, 1.65 and .68 acres, to Hays County on 5-29-1926. This is today's triangle, which holds the county barn, as well as the first fire station. From this point, there is a lot of selling among the Walker heirs and all of this may not be entirely correct. On 4-17-1972, the Dripping Springs Water Supply Corporation bought a 100x100 foot lot (.23 acre) from Hays County for their offices. On 9-18-1980, Carl Bible purchased 1.23 acres from the northwest corner of the tract from Veda Walker Baker. On 9-20-1980, J. W. Walker received 15.96 acres from the northeast side of the property from the Walker heirs. Knox Williams paid J. W. Walker $7,000 for a .995 acre tract on 9-21-1981. On this property, he built his real estate building that later become an eating place before being returned to a real estate business again, before returning to an eating place by the end of 2002. Then Knox Williams bought the 1.23 acre tract from Carl Bible on 2-15-1982 for $3,750. Rainwash, Inc. bought this property from Williams on 12-28-2001. Williams bought another acre from Walker on 4-2-1982 for $8,000. On 8-8-1984, Williams sold 1.28 acres to John R. Knippa. On 12-31-1991, the DS Noon Lions bought the property. In 2002, a deal was made with the Lions to put a Chamber of Commerce Visitors Center on this property. On 1-18-1985, Williams, in partnership with John Burke, Mark McManus, and Bob Peerman, formed the Loop 64 Venture that would develop one acre and another 4,535 square feet into the Drippin' Office Center. Carter Investments purchased the Office Center on 3-24-2000. On 8-23-1985, Dan McMahon bought six acres from J. W. Walker and this became the

Commons. On 9-9-1987, McMahon sold back two acres to Walker. The complex went into bankruptcy and Jim Powers led a group that bought it from FDIC. A short while later, the Powers group sold it to a Korean group, headed up by Ruth Shu. This past year, it was sold to Commons Retail LTD, with Skip Reissig as the managing partner. On 3-24-2000, Carter Investments purchased the .949 acres, which included the little real estate building, from Knox Williams and built his office building between the Lions acreage and the Drippin' Office Center.

C—19.3 acres. This tract of land was bought from Wallace by Moses C. Cavett on 9-22-1884 for $386. Cavett added other acreage from the southeast quarter and the ownership trail of this 19.3 acre tract can be found in the I. D. Roberts 83.3 acre tract discussed in the southeast quarter.

D—68 acres. Carrie Wallace Voight got title to this tract of land from John L. Wallace on 7-12-1892, a few months before Wallace's death. They had moved back from Blanco and probably built the house now on the property. The Voights sold it to W. J. Norwood for $750 on 12-28-1896 and moved to San Marcos. Mrs. M. R. Hudson paid $800 to W. J. Norwood on 8-12-1902. W. P. Hudson got the property from Mrs. Hudson and sold it to T. L. Sansom for $2,500 on 9-12-1912. On 7-12-1927, Robert Sansom bought his sister, Arrilla Carson's share of the place for $400. R. R. Sansom came into the property on 2-1-1938, getting it from George Sansom. On 9-18-1944, Tinnie G. Sansom inherited the tract from her husband, Robert Sansom, upon his death. On 9-16-1948, Frank Reeder bought the acreage from J. R. Wilhelm, the trustee for the property. Robert F. Shelton bought the property from Reeder on 1-6-1949 and it has stayed in the Shelton family since.

E—140 acres. This tract of land was the homestead and had the Wallace home on it. Mr. Wallace died in 1893 and it stayed in the family until 8-30-1899 when they sold it to H. D. Kelly for $800. W. A. Stone paid the Kellys $1,200 for it on 12-31-1903. John L. Tinney paid the same $1,200 for the acreage to W. A. Stone on 11-18-1905. On 6-6-1934, the State of Texas paid the Tinneys for 5.08 acres for right-of-way for Highway 290. On 6-7-1943, Dr. A. G. Garcia paid J. L. Tinney $4,000 for the remaining 134.92 acres. Dr. Garcia sold the acreage to the Veterans Land Board for $7,500 on 8-24-1955. Charles Henry Berkley purchased the acreage from the VLB on 10-12-1955 for $7,500. On 3-15-1960, Dennis and Katherine Berkley Cannon purchased the land from Berkley. The Cannons sold 5.12 acres to the City of Dripping Springs on 4-26-1988 as an addition and entrance to the future Founders Park. Also, they set up a Texas Heritage subdivision along Hwy. 290. They sold one lot to Dairy Queen in 1986 and then in 1995, Cattleman's National Bank bought a lot next to the Dairy Queen to put their bank on.

NORTHEAST QUARTER

Cannon Estates West

When Ranch Road 12 was extended north from Highway 290 in the early 1970s, it cut off part of the Cannon's acreage. When given lemons, you make lemonade. The Cannons simply subdivided this tract of land into eight lots and sold them.

Lot 1. On 12-28-1977, this lot was sold to Jessie R. West. James L. Clowdus bought the lot from West and then on 2-16-1983, sold it to Peggy Florence McDonald. At this time, Paul Roten is in the process of buying it from his aunt.

Lot 2. On 12-28-1977, Jessie R. West bought this lot from the Cannons. Bunny Toepler bought the property in the 1980s and Pamela Ann Miller purchased the property from the Toepler heirs on 6-5-1995. Bunny had a sewing supplies business while she was alive and Miller's husband, Chet Simmons, opened a half-price books store by the name of Another Roadside Attraction in the building.

Lot 3. Alice L. Roten paid $4,200 for this lot on 2-23-1978 and built her house on it and is still living there.

Lot 4. James Stewart bought this lot from the Cannons on 7-19-1979. Still owns it.

Lot 5. Robert F. Isaacs purchased this lot for $3,000 from the Cannons on 2-21-1976. The Isaacses are the parents of James Stewart's wife, Jewel. Jewel Isaacs Stewart got the property from the Isaacses on 4-2-1983.

Lot 6. On 11-19-1975, James Stewart bought this lot from the Cannons. This is the lot on which they built their home and still live in.

Lot 7. James Stewart bought this lot from the Cannons on 4-23-1977 and still owns it.

Lot 8. This was the first lot sold. Clarence/Merle Shelton came back to Dripping Springs to make their retirement home. He bought block eight of the second addition and built his home. This lot gave him access to RR12. He bought the lot on 6-8-1972.

F—2 acres. This tract of land, located in the southwest corner of the quarter, was mostly overlooked in its history. It was bounded on the east by the 19.3 acre tract. On 7-25-1874, John L. Wallace sold this tract of land to the Dripping Springs Baptists for $3. It is possible the first Baptist church was built on this tract of land. The Baptist church was burned to the ground in 1879. Wallace ended up buying the property back from the Baptists on 1-1-1882 for $2. Then it appears to have been forgotten until W. J. Sheppard discovered it on 3-28-1963. He paid Arthur Patton, who had married Wallace's granddaughter, Pauline Seal, $150. He built an A-frame house on the property. On 4-3-1980, Fred Garnett bought the .292 acre tract that included the house from Sheppard. On 3-26-1981, Fred Garnett purchased the remaining 1.158 acres from Sheppard. On 9-2-1982, J. P. Tate Co., Inc., bought the acreage from Fred Garnett and built the Promenade Center on the property. He went through bankruptcy proceedings in the late 1980s and lost the property. Butch Wooten bought the property in the mid-'90s. After keeping it for a year or so, Lisa and Kevin Glass bought it. They owned it for two years and then sold It to David Edelman under DS Retail LTD on 5-28-1999.

SOUTHEAST QUARTER

George Glasscock got the ball rolling when he was assigned the P. A. Smith league by the State of Texas on 4-27-1850. He sold it to Fielding S. Roy on 9-19-1853 and Mr. Roy began to sell it off to different owners. Dr. William H. Howard bought this complete quarter from F. S. Roy on 10-3-1853. Over the years, the Howards sold portions of this quarter and we will examine the different portions.

300 acres. This was the first parcel of land sold. It consisted of the southern end of the quarter league. Ed Womack purchased it from Dr. Howard on 11-28-1874. He sold it in two equal portions.

150E. Mitchell Putnam bought the eastern half for $400.20 on 3-1-1875. On the same day, he turned the acreage over to Lucy Gibson. On 1-17-1902, J. M. Gibson bought M. C. Gibson's share of the property. He then bought his mother, Lucy Gibson's share on 5-18-1912, with the stipulation that she could live out the rest of her days on the property. Annie F. Gibson sold it to F. L. Bishop on 6-15-1945. D. R. Mulhollen bought the tract of land from Bishop on 8-27-1946. On 6-9-1960, Floyd Ray Owens bought it from Mulhollen. Owens sold it to Jack Stuessy on 2-15-1974. Stuessy ran into financial difficulties and James H. McCrocklin took the land off his hands on 2-1-1977 and began to develop what is now part of the Springwood subdivision. Springwood, Too purchased 62.837 acres from J. H. McCrocklin on 4-1-1981 and then defaulted on the payments and lost the property on 9-4-1990. Edmund Kunz, Jr.,

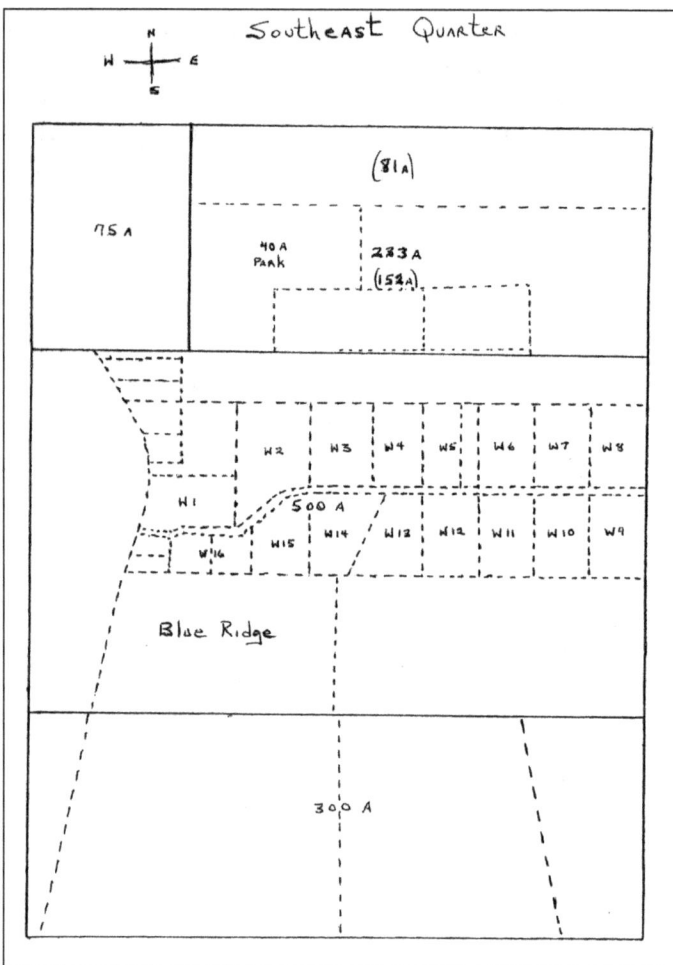

bought 43 acres, about eleven of which are in the southeast corner of this acreage, on 3-31-1994. He sold a one acre lot to William Gilbert on 12-29-1997. He is calling this the Crooked Oaks subdivision. Bruce Development LLC took possession of the 62.837 acres on 4-27-2001.

150W. On 3-25-1882, Ed Womack sold about half an acre to Hays County, along with a parcel from J. W. Phillips, to establish a community cemetery. J. M. Mading bought this property from Ed Womack on 4-15-1901. He sold it to A. A. Elsner on 10-4-1915 and he and his heirs dispensed of it in smaller parcels over the years. Elsner sold another half acre to the cemetery on 3-8-1922. The next parcel was a 13.2 acre tract to J. T. Southwell on 7-20-1940. Marion E. Summers bought a 40-acre tract from the Elsner heirs on 3-22-1960. The Elsner heirs bought .3 of an acre from Jesse Langston on 11-13-1962. Jack Stuessy bought the 40 acres from Summers on 10-18-1972. Then on 2-23-1973, Stuessy purchased 13.2 acres from the Southwell heirs. Stuessy purchased another 104.67 acres from the Elsner heirs, part of which was not in the P. A. Smith league, but abutted it on the south. Mrs. Alice Elsner gave another .53 acres to the Phillips Cemetery on 5-2-1975. On 10-31-1976, Stuessy turned 25 acres into part of the Springwood subdivision. At this point, Stuessy started getting into financial difficulties and James H. McCrocklin began buying property from him. On 2-1-1977, McCrocklin bought the 25-acre tract. On 2-18-1977, Stuessy sold a 1.28 acre parcel from the 13.2 acres to Eluterio Falcon and the other 11.38 to McCrocklin. McCrocklin bought the 40 acres from Stuessy on 4-1-1977. The Allen/Crosswell/McFarland group purchased 11.38 acres from McCrocklin on 3-10-1978. On 9-23-1981, J. B. and Ethylene Marsh bought 40 acres. Joy Purcell bought 1.28 acres from Falcon on 8-20-1982. The discrepancy in the total for the 13.2 acres is due to land taken for RR 12 right-of-way. The 11.38 acre tract had a house built in 1921 and a log cabin type built by the A/C/M group in 1978. They traded this acreage to the Coyote Crew Corporation that is developing a 600-acre subdivision for similar acreage next to the Anton Allen place. The St. Martin de Porres Catholic Church purchased 40 acres to establish their church. It came in several purchases. They sold off part of the property that had the house on it. The rest of the 150 acres has become a part of Springwood subdivision.

500 acres. The first three owners are the same, Glasscock, Roy and Howard. On 1-28-1878, this 500 acre tract was purchased jointly by Bascom C. Sorrell, his mother,

A. M. Sorrell and his brother-in-law, W. J. Norwood. Bascom Sorrell died on 3-13-1880. On 11-23-1880, the property was divided among the three families. A. M. Sorrell received 243.4 acres, Nancy Sorrell, widow of Bascom, 175 acres, and W. J. Norwood 81.6 acres. R. J. Cavett bought W. J. Norwood's acreage on 11-20-1882. On 11-28-1882, W. H. Banks, who had married Nancy Sorrell by this time, bought 199.4 acres from Mrs. A. M. Sorrell. R. S. Cavett bought the remaining 44.6 acres owned by Mrs. Sorrell on 12-15-1882. W. A. Mayne bought 43 acres from W. H. Banks on 11-20-1883. George Dickey bought the two tracts of land totalling 126.2 acres from R. S. Cavett on 9-12-1884. H. E. Carey and George Dickey bought 43 acres from Mayne on 11-19-1886. They sold it to W. H. Banks on 12-20-1888. E. W. Herndon began to purchase parcels of this property. On 10-20-1898, he bought 126.2 acres from George Dickey and another six from the 175-acre tract of W. H. Banks. On 10-28-1898, W. H. and Nancy Banks bought the shares of the five Bascom Sorrell's children on the 175 acre-tract. On 11-1-1898, Herndon purchased 199.4 acres from Banks. Banks bought back the six acres from Herndon on 3-10-1899. J. L. Patterson came to Dripping Springs and bought 126.2 and 199.4 acre-tracts from Herndon on 6-10-1903. Patterson bought the rest of the 500 acres from S. A. Goslin on 12-24-1904. After Mr. and Mrs. Patterson died in 1921, the estate was divided among the four children. Patterson had expanded his land empire quite a bit beyond the 500 acres of the Sorrell purchase, which also included the C. H. Malott survey east of the 500 and more from the P. A. Smith survey. The 500 acre part of the estate was divided among three of their children on 2-16-1925. Edith Patterson Butler received a total of 439.81 acres but 391.01 acres were in PAS. Barbara Patterson Wood would receive 69.58 acres, but six came from the 75-acre tract. Mattie Patterson McKellar received a total of 280 acres but only 217.58 came from PAS and only 65.58 came from the 500. This section will deal with 500 acres only.

69.58 acres. This tract of land was situated west of RR12 and included the George Dickey house. All but six are within the 500 acre tract. Lester Brenizer purchased the property from Barbara Wood on 10-5-1935. He sold 3.06 acres to the State of Texas for RR12 right-of-way on 10-7-1946. After his death in 1954, his sister, Vivian Brenizer Caswell, would inherit the 66.52 acres. This was 1-2-1957. On 1-28-1958, O. B. McKown, Sr., bought the property from Mrs. Caswell. His ex-wife, Bernice Henderson McKown, got the property as part of their divorce settlement and she sold it to Curtis Quisenberry on 6-15-1966. On 11-14-1966, Quisenberry sold Eluterio Falcon one acre from the southeast corner of the property on RR12. On 4-12-1968, Jack Wiggins bought the four acres next to Falcon. Clyde Weathersby bought 25 acres from Quisenberry on 9-9-1968 and then on the same day, sold it to Burl Eastup. On 10-28-1969, Burl Eastup bought two parcels of land from Quisenberry, one for 8.1 acres and the other for 14.27. On 4-14-1975, Anton Allen purchased the final 14.131 acres of the original tract that included the Dickey house. Steve Spillar bought four acres from Jack Wiggins on 2-9-1976 and built his home on it. Spillar lost the property and in the process, Canyon Springs Joint Venture came to own it. Bobby Needham bought it from them on 3-30-1984 and the Needham family still owns the property. Susan Eastup King would inherit 8.1 and 14.27 acre tracts on 4-19-1988 and later that year, sell the two parcels to M. K. Hage. The 14.27 acre tract was traded for the 11.38 acre tract owned by the Allen/Crosswell/McFarland group near the cemetery on 5-1-2000. The 8.1 acres, which included the six acres of the 75-acre tract, was sold to John Simmons. He began to build apartments on this segment. He built two on about 2.02 acres before selling them to Steve Vandigriff on 9-7-1999. The rest was sold to H. C. Carter. Carter Investments built apartments, called Chestnut Ridge, on most of the rest but sold a parcel to Anton Allen that abutted his place.

391.01 acres. This was the southernmost section of the 500 acres. By the time the Butler family began selling off the property, that total had shrunk by nearly ten acres, possibly from RR12 right-of-way. Marvin Burrier bought a five-acre tract from the northwest corner on RR12 from Edith Butler on 8-5-1953 and built their home. Burrier sold Elmer Russell 1.66 acres on his south side on 8-22-1957 and the Russells built their house on the property. Malcolm Burchard bought ten acres, that encompassed the Burrier five on two sides, from Edith Butler on 6-4-1966. Burchard sold the acreage to Robert Burke on 1-16-1969. John E. Crabb made the first major purchase by buying 100 acres from the Edith Butler heirs on 5-17-1978. 75.43 acres of this became Section One of the Blue Ridge subdivision. The group of David Baldry, Nancy Becker, and Robert Whiting bought 182.64 acres from the Butler heirs on 5-26-1978. Sometime about then, Virginia Wesson bought the other 83.08 acres from the heirs. She sold it to John Crabb on 11-12-1981. Mr. Crabb then sold 106.642 acres to H. C. Carter, Jr., on 6-15-1983. This included 83.08 acres and the rest of his 100 acre purchase. Carter defaulted on the purchase and John Crabb regained possession on 12-8-1988. A court battle ensued on this acreage after John Crabb's death. It was determined Lydia Crabb should inherit this acreage. She sold it to Lanny Counts on 3-26-1990. Elmer Russell bought an additional .294 acre from Betty Burrier Cobb on 3-16-1979, who inherited her mother's property. James P. Towers bought the 3.212 acre tract from Betty Cobb on 10-12-1979. Wayne Mathewson would eventually end up with the property and after going through bankruptcy, the property became part of the Friar Commercial Reserve. Todd Purcell purchased the property on 5-1-1992. Mrs. Russell sold her lot to Janie Rios in the early

'90s and Mrs. Rios sold it to Reed Smith on 3-23-1998.

Western Woods, Inc. purchased the 182.64 acre tract from the Baldry group on 5-30-1979. This set off a flurry of land sale action. Rodney Whitley was the first to buy a 10-acre tract (Lot 4) in 1980. Walter A. Skornjak bought two ten-acre tracts (Lots 5, 6) on 10-24-1980 and Lanny Counts bought two parcels of land (Lots 12, 13), totalling 19.87 acres on 12-10-1980. ABR Investments bought a 10.1 acre tract (Lot 15) on 5-20-1981. Hallie M. Pinson bought a two-acre tract on 8-15-1981, which included the Willie Sam Butler house. J. P. Tate bought 10.03 acres (Lot 16) at about the same time. On 8-31-1981, George Bracken bought a 10-acre tract (Lot 9). Lanny Counts added another 11.53 (Lot 14) on 9-15-1981. Leonard Holloway bought 11.57 acres (Lot 3) on 10-22-1981. On 2-16-1982, Greg and Joyce Tom purchased 10.01 acres (Lot 1) from Western Woods. They would have to let it go back to the bank and then to FDIC. From that point, Joy and Bob Purcell bought the acreage from the FDIC on 3-16-1992. Paul Kay bought 15.64 acres (Lot 2) from Western Woods on 8-5-1982. J. P. and Helen Tate formed the J&J Tate Partnership for five of their acres on 7-23-1982. Dave Edwards bought Hallie Pinson's two acres on 12-20-1983. Edwards went in with Tate. J. B. Marsh bought six acres from W. A. Skornjak on 5-8-1985 and another acre on 6-11-1985, all from Lot 5. The 12 South Business Park Joint Venture formed on a .349 acre tract by Dave Edwards and J. P. Tate Co. on 7-19-1985. Edwards' share would later be bought by Tate. Jane Skornjak received 13 acres (Lot 6 and part of Lot 5) from W. A. Skornjak on 6-25-1986. The bank foreclosed on 1.642 and 2.926 acre tracts of J. P. Tate, which were part of Lot 16. All of Tate's property in Lot 16 was lost to creditors. Alan M. Tomlin purchased 4.72 acres (part of Lot 16) from the Dripping Springs National Bank on 11-1-1989. Charles Sellers purchased the 10-acre tract (Lot 11) on 12-4-1989. Frank Pennington (Lot 8), Miles Kaltenbaugh (Lot 7), and William Brown (Lot 10) all bought ten acre tracts from Western Woods in the '80s. Western Woods also sold three 10-acre lots on the eastern end of their total acreage, most of which was in the C. H. Malott survey. Larry Jacobson had Lot 17, Dale Walston had Lot 18, and Jack Garison Lot 19. Only lots 17 and 19 had any P. A. Smith acreage in them. Terry Henninger bought seven acres from J. B. Marsh on 11-25-1991. On 11-19-1993, Efford Johnson purchased Lot 3 from Holloway. On 12-22-1993, Stephen Cox purchased Allan Tomlin's part of Lot 16. On 4-4-1994, Melvin Wolf bought Lot 9 from Bracken. On 4-22-1994, Stephen Venski purchased Lot 10 from Brown. On 1-21-1995, Thomas Robert Toms purchased Lot 7 from Kaltenbaugh. He, in turn, sold a four-acre tract of his property to James Carroza on 2-26-1997. On 1-25-1996, Virgil Flathouse bought Lot 15 from the ABR Investors. Donald Doyle bought Lot 8 from Pennington on 3-2-2000. On 6-14-1996, Rosemary Foster bought the front five acres of Garison's Lot 19, which had some P. A. Smith acreage. Wayne Ziegler bought Jacobson's Lot 17 on 2-26-1997. The rest of Tate's Lot 16 changed hands after the bankruptcy years. Robin Parsley bought the 1.642 acre tract that included the rental storage buildings, the 2.926 acre tract that included the fourplexes from FDIC in the early 1990s. Parsley added two acres, which included the Oakwood Plaza, in two parcels of 1.301 and .669 acres soon after. He divided part of the property into two partitions. He sold Lot 2, a 2.196 acre tract, which includes the fourplexes, to Vern and Renne Waldo on 5-23-1994. Lot 1, which was the two acres, came under the control of Best Storage Dripping Springs LP, which is owned by Parsley. This transaction took place on 2-5-1997. One partial lot is a 1.301 acre tract that has Oakwood Plaza on it, and the other was .699 acre, on which he added more storage buildings.

65.58 acres. Mattie McKellar inherited more property but because we are working with the 500 acre tract at this time, we will deal with that first. The rest of the property will be found in the next section. Mrs. McKellar sold the entire property to Mrs. Ellen Wiedebusch on 11-29-1946. She built her house on a three-acre tract fronting RR 12 S. On 11-13-1952, she sold the rest to George Wiest. Mr. Wiest sold a 3.67-acre tract on RR12 to Raymond Whisenant. Mr. Wiest sold the rest to Charles Dahlstrom on 8-25-1961. On 6-29-1963, Bernice Burrier sold the three acres that included her mother's, Mrs. Wiedebusch, home to her daughter, Betty Cobb. Clarence Cobb bought the 3.67 acre tract from Raymond Whisenant in the early '60s. Virginia Wesson bought the property from Dahlstrom on 10-31-1967. Bill and Pat Thurman bought the 3.67 acres from the Cobbs on 2-7-1970 and put a beauty shop and later a day care facility on the frontage property with Minnie Jenkins. On 5-30-1975, Wayne Mathewson purchased the three acre tract from the Cobbs. In 1978 Minnie Jenkins bought the front acre from the Thurmans with the nursery and Gary Pennington bought the other 2.67 acres on 3-28-1980. Both still own the property. Virginia Wesson sold her acreage to Lawrence E. & Gay Crabb Karger on 2-25-1981. The Mathewsons had financial difficulties in the late '80s and lost their three acre tract. David Wallace acquired the property on 8-8-1991 in a sheriff's auction. Viktor Kopponen purchased the rest from Karger on 8-30-1996. Part of Kopponen's acreage included land in the 152-acre tract discussed later.

308 acres. The final acreage of the southeast quarter was bought from the Howard heirs on 10-13-1881 by the real estate team of A. L. Davis, Sr., and W. T. Chapman. This acreage finally split into three distinct tracts. Davis & Chapman sold 75 acres to J. M. Wallace in 1882 and then the other 233 to James Lincoln on 5-16-1883. One acre of the Lincoln tract was designated by Chapman & Davis to be a community cemetery. Lincoln sold it in two tracts, one for 81 acres and the other 152 later on.

81 acres. This acreage bordered the south line of the northeast quarter and included the Wallace Mountain crest where the cemetery is located, because it was designated in the deed. W. J. Lyle bought this tract of land from Lincoln on 11-10-1883. Z. I. Williams bought it from Lyle two days later. On 12-1-1883, W. G. Castellow bought the land from Williams. James E. Bell bought it from Castellow on 3-18-1885. David Hughes took possession from Bell on 8-16-1893. Hughes sold it to H. W. Griffin on 1-14-1899. W. P. Hudson bought it on 10-25-1902 and sold it to W. H. Crenshaw on 2-28-1905. W. C. Clayton bought it from Crenshaw on 10-25-1905. Clayton held onto the land until 2-21-1931, then sold it to Robert R. Sansom. Tinnie G. Sansom inherited the property on 9-18-1944 and sold it to Frank Reeder on 9-16-1948. Robert F. Shelton bought the property from Reeder on 1-6-1949 and the Shelton family still owns it. In 1995, the Shelton acreage, including this 81 acres was divided among the five children. Each received 22 acres and the rest was put in a reserve.

152 acres. This acreage gets mixed up with the rest of the J. L. Patterson holdings, but basically stayed with the same throughout most of the years. James Lincoln sold the land to H. M. Lincoln on 4-30-1890 and he sold it to F. M. Kirk on 7-19-1890. E. W. Herndon bought it from Kirk on 10-13-1899. A little later (a deed was not found), W. H. Banks purchased it from Herndon because S. A. Goslin bought it from Banks on 10-14-1901. On 12-24-1904, Goslin sold it to J. L. Patterson and it became a part of Mattie McKellar's inheritance on 2-16-1925. Ellen Wiedebusch bought it as part of the total package from McKellar on 11-29-1946. She sold it to her son-in-law, Marvin Burrier, on 4-11-1947. Mr. Burrier sold it to the Veterans Land Board on 7-31-1953. Earl Ross Curry bought it from the VLB on the same day. On 8-27-1956, W. P. Crow bought it from Curry. George Wiest bought the property from Crow on 5-19-1959 and he sold it to Virgil Conn on 2-27-1960. Conn sold it to Robert Lee Thompson on 8-29-1960. J. H. McDaniel bought it from Thompson on 8-1-1963. Jack Howell got the property from McDaniel on 3-25-1968. Stan Booth bought the acreage from Howell on 10-2-1985. He sold 40 acres to Dripping Springs ISD for $360,000 on 12-30-1986. DSISD deeded the 40 acres to the city in 1998, so they could get matching grants from the State Parks and Recreation to build a Sports Park. The great landfall of the late '80s got Booth and Jack Howell ended up with the rest of his property again. On 6-2-1989, Main Pass Partners, Ltd., purchased 102.3275 acres from Jack Howell. On 8-15-1989, Howell sold Gary J. Doucet 10 acres. On 8-30-1989, Jean-Claude Cardwell purchased 17.0518 acres from Main Pass. Tracey Schlatter purchased Doucet's acreage on 9-7-1993 and later added the five acres between them and Cardwell. Robert Mokhtarian, of Farias, Jett & Co. CPA, bought 61.949 acres from Main Pass on 1-21-1995. The rest of the 152 acres is a part of the land now owned by Viktor Kopponen.

75 acres. This was the last section of the southeast quarter, but, for most of its early history, it was combined with a 19.3 acre tract from the northeast quarter that bordered it. It was later subdivided by I. D. Roberts and his heirs. The total of their property was 83.3 acres. No deed could be found on the first transaction but it is my belief that Davis-Chapman sold the 75 acres to J. M./Roslee Wallace, probably in 1882. On 12-8-1884, the Wallaces sold the property to C. B. Hollis. They built a two-story house on the property that the Norwoods and Needhams lived in until the late 1970s. George Dickey purchased 6.6 acres from the southwest corner of the property. C. B. Hollis sold another 1.75 acre tract, next to the Dickey purchase, for $900, which included the house. John A. Bowles purchased the remaining 67 acres from Hollis on 12-21-1888. The Hollises had already moved to Louisiana. Moses C. Cavett bought the 67 acres from Bowles on 10-10-1891. Cavett's purchase brought the 83.3 acre tract under one owner for the first time. He had purchased the 19.3 acres from John Wallace for $386 on 9-22-1884. Cavett sold the property to J. H. Gary on 8-2-1907. Mrs. J. H. Gary sold the acreage to I. D. Roberts on 11-25-1916. In the 1940s, Mr. Roberts began to sell off his land.

A—10.25 acres. S. J. Moore bought this tract from Mr. Roberts on 6-20-1944. He built his house on the property in October 1947 and began selling off the rest.

A1—3.2 acres. Pulaski A. Glosson bought this tract from Moore on 5-9-1945. Ivy Roberts bought the property from Mr. Glosson on 8-28-1950. Douglas "Weebud" Cauthen bought it from Mr. Roberts on 5-16-1959 and he owned it until he sold it to Butch Wooten in 1995. Michael Alexander went in with Wooten as Point 5 International. Kevin Glass and partner, Jimmy French, bought out Wooten's share under GAF Development Co. Glass and French bought out Alexander under F & G Partners on 11-30-2000 and built a Taco Bell-Mobil-Grocery complex on the 290 frontage. They sold the complex to the Smiths (Ford, Allan, Ford Jr.) under the name of Triple S TETCO and retained the rest of the property for development.

A2. P. A. Glosson bought this tract on 8-28-1946. He sold it to Wilson Fairley for $900 on 7-10-1948. Marvin Odell bought it for $5,000 on 10-2-1956. He sold it to Johnny B. Galloway for $4,500 in 1963. His daughter, Tera Mae Galloway Glass, got the property from Galloway on 6-19-1973. She sold it to Robert Terry on 1-20-1976. Mr. Terry sold the property to Joseph R. DeAnda on 9-18-1996.

A3. George Wiest bought this tract from Moore on 8-25-1961. Robert Terry bought the tract on 2-10-1969 and sold it to Joseph R. DeAnda on 9-18-1996.

A4. Robert Terry bought this tract from Moore on 10-15-1966. Mike Rose bought it from Terry on 9-20-1991. He moved his real estate office to this location.

A5. Robert Terry bought this tract, that included the house, from Mr. Moore on 5-10-1967. Mr. Terry sold it to Mike Rose on 9-20-1991. They moved into the house. The house had a mold problem in late 2001 and had to be torn down. Rose built a new real estate office building on the spot.

A6. E. E. "Nookie" Myers bought this tract from Mr. Moore on 3-25-1955. He built their home on this property and lived in it until his death in 1998. His wife, Hazel Bell, continued to live in the house until her health began to fail in the fall of 2001. After her death in late March 2002, her daughter, Ginger Tipton, inherited the property. Craig Koenig bought the property in October and converted the building to hold his offices.

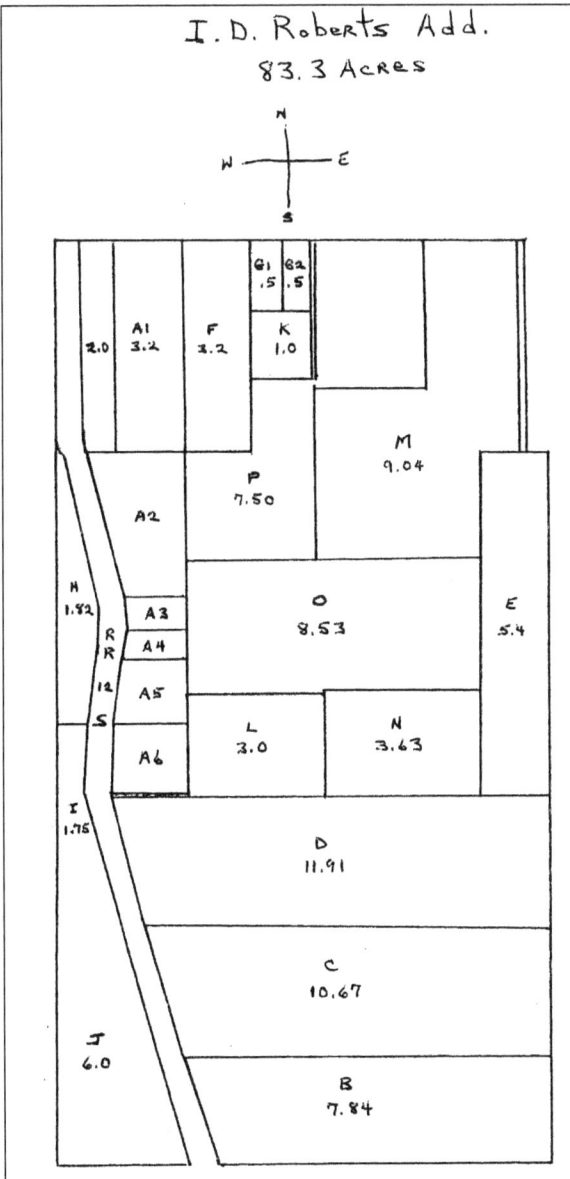

A7. When the property behind the Moore acreage was bought by James "Jim" Montague, a 20-foot right-of-way was allowed to access the property. On 9-10-1977, Mr. Montague bought the road from the Moore heirs. It would go with the property when John Hudson bought the acreage from the Montague heirs on 7-2-1993.

B—7.84 acres. O. M. Williamson bought this tract from Mr. Roberts on 10-16-1943. He sold it to W. A. Breed for $6,500 on 1-8-1951. Oscar L. C. Woodward paid the same amount for it on 12-13-1961. Robert L. Terry bought it from Woodward on 4-5-1966. He converted the property to the Terry's Mobile Home Park. Diana Lynn Terry Bonham purchased the back 2.5 acres on 7-1-1981 and made her home there. She bought the remaining 5.34 acres from Terry on 3-7-1988.

C—10.67 acres. William Tinney paid Mr. Roberts $533.50 for this tract on 10-16-1943. Gracie Griffin, acting in behalf of Dovie Stephenson, sold the tract to James Hoard and Chester Brewer for $7,000. Neville B. Hutto paid the Brewer heirs $14,000 for the tract on 3-24-1972. Randy Hutto got the property from his father on 4-11-1983. He sold it to Frank D. Walker, Jr., for $72,780 on 8-20-1983. Walker, in turn, sold it to Stan Booth on 8-15-1985 for $200,000. After selling the school district 40 acres above the tract, Mr. Booth used 1.6015 acres of this tract for a 50-foot right-of-way that split the property and then divided the remaining land into six lots, three on each side. He sold the remaining 8.7778 acres to DS 12 Investors on 9-6-1988. The road was deeded to the city on 1-7-2000.

D—11.91 acres. James E. Felps paid Mr. Roberts $595 for this tract on 10-16-1943. Mr. Felps sold it to Fred DeGraaf on 12-3-1945. Enoch Needham paid Mr. DeGraaf $1,800 for the tract on 5-2-1947. Bobby J. Zirkle paid $6,000 on 11-1-1968 to Mr. Needham. He built a house on the property before selling the property to Neville B. Hutto for $34,000 on 6-5-1972. He sold it to the Perrymans and they split up before putting their plans into action and Mr. Hutto got it back. Randy Hutto recalls that J. B. Marsh owned it for a while, followed by Brown, Westbank Properties, Upfront, Inc. and finally Stephen Hurd bought the property on 8-23-1999 under the name of DSHESEDLLC and opened up The Springs Fitness Center.

E—5.4 acres. The first transaction or transactions for this tract of land is unknown. The first deed found was on 5-21-1958 when J. N. Rippy paid W. A. Smith $1,200 for it. A. L. Wells bought the property from Mr. Rippy on 12-8-1971. Mr. Wells sold the property to Bobbie Roper Cameron on 1-24-1975. The Camerons sold it to the Episcopal Church on 8-9-1985 and they built church buildings on it. The City of Dripping Springs bought the property from the Episcopal Church on 10-5-2000 and moved in around September 2001.

F—3.2 acres. Harvey Killen bought this parcel of land from Mr. Roberts on 4-5-1946. Ivy Roberts bought it from Mr. Killen on 7-29-1948. He sold it to Douglas "Weebud" Cauthen on 5-16-1959. Weebud built a house on the property and lived there until he sold the property to Butch Wooten in 1995. The Jack Brown family purchased 1.104 acres on 2-14-1996 and built a Jack Brown Cleaners on the Hwy. 290 frontage, where the house once stood. The rest of this lot's history follows the A1 history in the section, except this was not a part of the Smith's transaction.

G—1 acre. Walter Clayton paid $200 to Mr. Roberts for this on 4-5-1946. He sold it to Mrs. Katie Davis on 8-17-1951. On 4-18-1953, Mrs. Davis split the property down the middle and sold the western half to Mrs. Ola Butler and the eastern half to Mrs. Rena Tetley. The Butler heirs inherited the property on 4-16-2000 and the Tetley heirs inherited her property in 2001.

H—1.82 acres. Mr. S. J. Moore bought this tract of land from Mr. Roberts on 6-20-1944. Raymond Whisenant paid Mr. Moore $300 for the property on 3-25-1955 and built a house on it. In February 1972, he sold the property to his dad, K. C.

Whisenant. On 5-10-1985, the group of Roger Hanks/Joe Gillman/Harriet Rutland bought the property from K. C. Whisenant. The acreage now only totals 1.515 acres due to right of way expansion of RR12. After Mr. Gillman's death, the property went to the other two partners. The house was expanded in late 1997 or early 1998. Mr. Hanks' share was put under an estate plan.

I—1.75 acres. This tract was not part of the Roberts' 83.3 acre property, but was a part of the original 75 acre tract. J. H. Morrow paid C. B. Hollis $900 for this tract and it included the house. At some point, A. L. Davis, Sr., came into this property. No deed has been found; it might have been a tax situation. Upon Mr. Davis's death, his son, Addison R. Davis, inherited this parcel of land. He sold it to W. A. Mayne on 11-1-1900. W. J. Norwood bought the property from the Maynes on 8-22-1902. On 1-11-1949, Mr. Norwood's daughter, Vina Norwood, bought the rights from her other two siblings. She then deeded it over to her niece, Beulah Lawrence, and her husband, Enoch Needham, on 6-21-1967. The land has now been subdivided among the Needham children and this acreage now belongs to Eddie Needham.

J—6 acres. This was the second tract of land that was not a part of the Roberts' 83.3 acres, but was a part of the original 75 acres in the southeast quarter. George Dickey bought the tract from C. B. Hollis on 2-27-1885. He sold the tract to E. W. Herndon on 10-20-1898. Herndon sold it to J. L. Patterson on 6-10-1903. After the Pattersons' deaths in 1921, the estate was divided up and their daughter, Barbara Wood, inherited this tract of land. She sold it to Lester Brenizer on 10-5-1935. After his death, his sister, Vivian Brenizer Caswell, inherited the property. She sold it to O. B. McKown, Sr., on 1-28-1958. As a part of the divorce settlement, his ex-wife, Bernice Henderson McKown received the property. She sold it to Curtis Quisenberry on 6-15-1966. He sold this tract to Burl Eastup on 10-28-1969. On 4-19-1988, Mrs. Susan Eastup King inherited the property from the Eastup estate. She sold it to M. K. Hage on 7-24-1988. He sold it to John Simmons in the mid-'90s. He built a couple of duplexes on 2.02 acres and sold it to Steve Vandigriff on 9-7-1999. The rest he sold to H. C. Carter, who built more apartments on the rest of the six acres, called Chestnut Ridge, plus a little more from the rest of the 8.1 acres in this tract.

K—1 acre. On 2-26-1947, John Ferrell paid Mr. Roberts $200 for this acre. D. W. Cauthen paid the Ferrell heirs $500 for this tract on 7-30-1970. He sold it, along with the rest of his property, to Butch Wooten in 1995. The rest of the history follows that of F in this section.

L—3 acres. James "Jim" Montague paid I. D. Roberts $300 for the acreage on 11-5-1945. He built his house on the front part of the property. His son, Carroll Montague, bought the back 1.37 acres on 3-25-1977 and built a house on it. John Hudson purchased the front acreage from the Montague heirs on 7-2-1993. John England purchased Carroll's property on 9-10-1999.

M—9.04 acres. Cecil and Minnie Jenkins paid the I. D. Roberts heirs $9,500 for this tract of land on 8-27-1971. It included the Roberts' house and surrounding buildings. They have owned it since.

N—3.63 acres. W. F. Rippy bought this tract of land from I. D. Roberts on 6-27-1960. J. N. Rippy bought the acreage from the Rippy heirs on 8-14-1967. On 12-8-1971, A. L. Wells purchased the land from J. N. Rippy. Bobbie Roper Cameron bought it from Wells on 1-24-1975 and the Camerons sold it to the Episcopal Church on 8-9-1985. The City of Dripping Springs bought the property from the Episcopal Church on 10-5-2000. They moved in during September 2001.

O—8.53 acres. Robert Terry bought this land from the Roberts' heirs on 7-9-1971. Joseph R. DeAnda bought the property from Terry on 9-18-1996.

P—7.50 acres. On 7-26-1971, Enoch Norwood "Buzzy" Needham bought this tract from the I. D. Roberts' heirs. He sold the property to Butch Wooten in 1996.

Immediately, Sonic Development of Central bought 1.148 acres on the northeast corner of the property and built a Sonic Drive-In. This deal was sealed on 10-22-1996. The rest followed the Cauthen property until French and Glass broke from Michael Alexander and let him have this property. He sold it to the DS 290/RR12 LTD group, who bought the remaining 6.356 acres on 9-28-2000.

SOUTHWEST QUARTER

This quarter league has the same first three owners as the southeast quarter. Glasscock to Roy to Howard. Over the years, the Howards sold portions of this quarter and we will examine the different portions because most of them stayed in that form.

600 acres. This section, which represents the southern half of the quarter, was actually accumulated in two separate purchases from Dr. Howard. On 8-16-1873, Thomas M. Caldwell bought 400 acres and then added the other 200 on 7-21-1874. In Bob Barton's newspaper edition covering Hays County history until 1880, one article said that Mr. Caldwell was the wealthiest person in Hays County at the time. He sold the entire tract to John W. Phillips on 5-30-1876. It is not known for sure who built the house on this property. In an article written by one of the Marshall boys, who moved with his family to Dripping Springs in 1870, he related that Dr. Howard was one of three families who lived within two miles of them. If so, then I'm betting on the Howard family, but when is still a mystery. Mr. Phillips was a Methodist and on 1-10-1880, he sold 1.3 acres to the Methodists to build their church. On 3-25-1882, he sold .23 acre in conjunction with George Womack to Hays County for the purpose of establishing a community cemetery. The 4,000 square vara parcel shared the south boundary of the church property. J. D. Dillingham bought the property from Phillips on 7-22-1909. On 3-26-1912, Albert W. Berner bought it from Dillingham. Berner sold it to Thomas G. Buttery on 12-20-1912. After Buttery's death, his heirs sold the property to Mrs. Allie D. Heierman on 11-14-1916. Mrs. Heierman expanded the cemetery by deeding one-half acre on the south side on 3-8-1922. Hugo Tschoepe bought the property from Mrs. Heierman on 1-18-1923 and sold it to Felix Lindsey on 12-4-1924. On 8-27-1942, Mr. Lindsey donated 2.3 acres to the cemetery. This acreage bordered the western boundary line of the cemetery. James S. Phelps bought the property from the Lindsey heirs on 7-23-1968. Burl E. Eastup bought the property from Phelps on 3-8-1969. When he died, his daughter, Susan, was a minor and had to wait for her

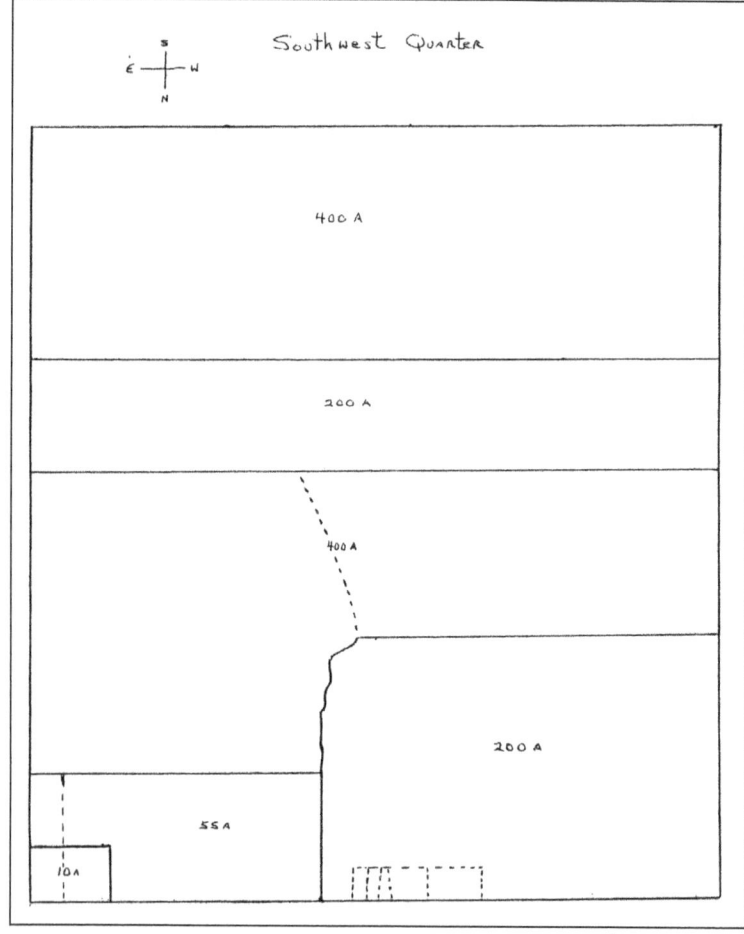

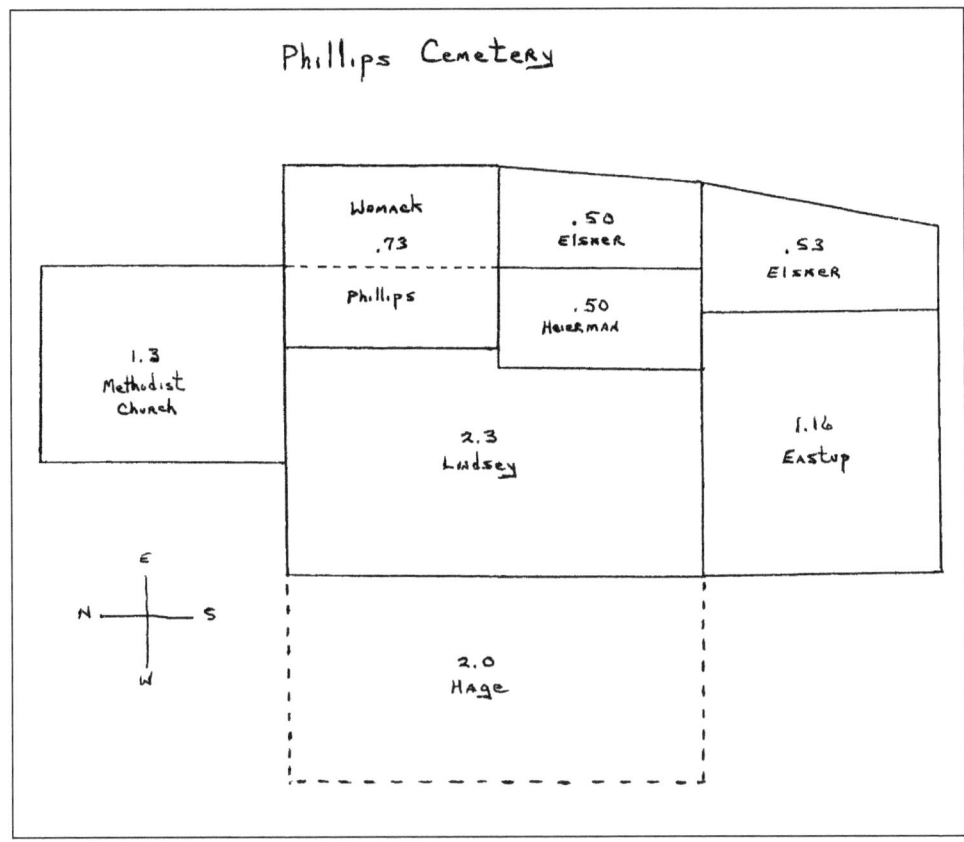

A—240 acres. This tract first went to W. A. Mayne. He sold it to W. J. and M. E. Norwood on 8-22-1902. It would stay in the Norwood family from then on. When the Norwoods died, the property was inherited by their three children. One of those was Vina Norwood. She bought the interest of the other two on 1-11-1949. Miss Norwood raised Beulah Marie Lawrence, her niece, for much of her life. Her mother, Miss Norwood's sister, died when Beulah was only three weeks old. Beulah married Enoch Needham and they lived with Miss Norwood. Miss Norwood deeded the property to the Needhams on 6-21-1967. The Needhams divided the property equally and then had their kids draw for the lots and it will continue to stay in the family for many years to come.

B—160 acres. O. S. Sorrell bought the 160 acres. He sold the tract to W. J. and Alice Roberts on 6-3-1902. Carl H. and Eleanor T. Richter bought the property from the Alice M. Roberts' heirs on 12-6-1940. Richter sold it to Ruby C. Piland on 3-30-1943. Mrs. Piland leased it to J. W. Crenwelge on 4-10-1943 and then sold the land to James J. and Zadie Brown Lumpkin on 8-15-1944. A. B. Tiner would take it off the Lumpkin's hands on 6-10-1949. H. A. Bardwell bought the property on 2-2-1950. He sold it to Lomis Slaughter on 4-23-1959. He deeded it to his daughter, Lois Elizabeth Slaughter, on 12-

inheritance. The estate gave 1.16 acres to the cemetery on 4-25-1981. Susan Eastup King got the property on 8-19-1981. She sold 25.856 acres to Max and Beverly Jo Eastup Welch on 4-19-1988 and the rest to M. K. Hage on 7-22-1988 and 7-23-1988. More land was donated to the cemetery and Hage sold the property on 8-20-1998 to Coyote Crew LTD. Their intention is to turn the acreage into a subdivision, convention center and golf course.

400 acres. This parcel of land bordered on the 600 acre tract on its south. Albert Lawson Davis, Sr., bought this tract of land in two purchases as well. He bought 398 acres of it on 3-5-1872. The final two acres were added on 6-17-1874. These two acres included the site of the mill and that is why it was not for sale at the first purchase. After Mr. Davis's death, one of his sons, Addison R. Davis, inherited the tract. He and his wife, Fannie, sold this tract in two portions on 11-1-1900. One was for 160 acres and the other being 240 acres.

28-1960. When Mrs. Slaughter died in 1998, her heirs inherited the property under the Slaughter Family Ranch LTD.

200 acres. This tract was on the western side of the quarter. J.W. E. Sampson bought this tract from Dr. Howard's heirs on 3-17-1882. On 1-15-1883, W. P. Hamilton bought the property from Sampson. B. A. Gower bought the property from Hamilton on 10-23-1884 and then Hamilton got it back on 2-3-1885. James W. Glosson bought it from Hamilton on 1-20-1886. J. F. Glosson, Sr., got the property from the Glosson heirs on 9-18-1940. On 2-6-1941, P. A. Glosson got four acres from the northeast corner of the property from J. F. Glosson, Sr. Lomis Slaughter bought the other 196 acres from S. B. Glosson on 2-5-1945. Mrs. Dovie Beauchamp bought the four-acre tract from P. A. Glosson on 5-15-1947. W. P. Crow bought the four acres from Mrs. Beauchamp on 12-3-1949 and gave it to his son's widow, Mrs. Agnes E. Crow. She remarried and as Mrs. Agnes E. Crow Dahlstrom, sold the property to Lomis Slaughter on 9-23-1953 to bring the 200 acre tract under one owner again. He would deed the entire tract to his daughter, Lois Elizabeth Slaughter, on 12-28-1960. Upon her death in 1998, her heirs inherited the property under the Slaughter Family Ranch LTD.

30 acres. This tract of land was located in the northwest corner of the quarter. J.W.E. Sampson bought it from the Howard heirs on 3-17-1882. He sold it to J. C. Rowe for $86 on 1-22-1883. James W. Glosson bought the property from Rowe on 1-2-1893. J. F. Glosson, Sr., bought the property from the James W. Glosson heirs on 9-18-1940. On 2-5-1945, Lomis Slaughter bought the property. The deed showed S. B. Glosson as owner. Lomis Slaughter deeded the land to his daughter, Lois Elizabeth Slaughter, on 12-28-1960. She died in 1998 and her heirs inherited the property under the Slaughter Family Ranch LTD.

4 acres. This small tract of land is nestled along the northern boundary along the Dripping Springs branch. J.W.E. Sampson also bought this property from the Howard heirs on 3-17-1882. He sold it to W. P. Hamilton on 1-15-1883. Hamilton sold it to F. D. Henry on 1-1-1884. Somewhere along in here, a house was built on the property. C. S. Graham bought the tract from Henry on 4-23-1887. Graham sold it to J. W. Phillips on 10-1-1889 and then got it back on 10-1-1891. There is a gap in the ownership trail at this point. Somewhere in between, S. W. Adams bought the property because on 11-6-1907, he sold it to Charles Robinson. Susan Glosson bought the property from Robinson on 9-22-1908. A daughter, Agatha Glosson, got the property from Mrs. Glosson on 2-11-1913. Again, no deed was found but P. A. Glosson ended up with the property, probably in 1941, and ended up selling it to Mrs. Dovie Beauchamp on 5-15-1947. She sold it to W. P. Crow on 12-3-1947 and he gave it to Mrs. Agnes E. Crow, his daughter-in-law, on 5-3-1949. She sold the property to Lomis Slaughter on 9-23-1953 and he deeded it to his daughter, Lois Elizabeth Slaughter, on 12-28-1960. After her death in 1998, her heirs inherited the property under the Slaughter Family Ranch LTD.

10 acres. This ten-acre tract is located in the northeast corner of the quarter. J. R. Brown purchased this tract from Dr. Howard on 5-22-1874 for $30. The deed was not recorded but, at some point, Brown sold the property to W. J. Meers. He went into the mule business on this property. W. M. Jordan paid Meers $250 for the tract on 1-2-1883. In July of the same year, the property went to J. D. Walker, the pastor of the Baptist Church. G. W. Wood bought it for $500 on 12-9-1885. Wood sold it to W. N. Albright on 2-27-1899. Less than one month later, on 3-14-1899, A. L. Davis, Jr., bought it from Albright. George W. Houchin paid Davis $315 for the acreage on 5-6-1913, with the stipulation that Houchin dig a well and build a three-room house by January 1st. Houchin met the requirements and later sold the property to J. W. Champion for $800 on 1-9-1918. O. S. Brumley bought the property on 4-12-1934. After his death,

Sybil Brumley sold it to Thomas Barnette on 1-29-1942. This was not the original ten acres. It was configured so that this ten-acre tract would be only 325 feet wide and stretched south to the Needham north property line, which was part of the original 55-acre tract. On 11-20-1979, William C. "Bill" Bassett bought it from Mrs. Vivian Peal Barnette. On 7-12-1994, the Bassetts deeded the property, sans their homestead, to their daughters Bren, Romi, and Leasa. The rest of the original ten acres went to Alva Haydon as part of the 55-acre tract he bought from the Brumley heirs in 1961.

55 acres. No deed was found to show the sell from the Howard heirs but other deeds keep relating how J. M. Hampton bought the property from the heirs and conveyed it to J. C. Rowe and then to J. D. Walker. On 12-9-1885, Walker sold 28 acres to A. L. Davis, Sr., and 27 to W. M. Miller. Davis bought Miller's acreage on 1-9-1886. A. L. Davis, Jr., bought the tract from his brother, Addison Davis, on 8-25-1890. J. W. Glosson bought the property from Davis on 5-27-1907. He, in turn, sold it to P. A. Glosson on 9-13-1912. Glosson put it in the hands of F. G. Bailey on 11-7-1914. J. W. Champion bought the tract from Bailey on 1-6-1922. On 4-11-1934, Mr. Champion deeded one acre at the end of Bluff Street to his mother, Mrs. G. W. Leneham. The next day, he sold the other 54 acres to O. S. Brumley. Cecil Breed bought the one acre from the Leneham heirs on 6-1-1960. Alva Haydon bought the 54 acres from the O. S. Brumley heirs on 11-15-1961. On 8-28-1976, Robert Bennett Worley bought the one acre tract from Cecil Breed. On 8-31-1984, Jack W. Lyle bought .54 acre of the one acre tract from Worley and the rest was divided by W. E. Malott and Bobby Watson.

15 acres. This tract of land rests along the northern boundary of the quarter between the four acre and 30 acre tracts. J.W.E. Sampson bought this strip from the Dr. Howard heirs on 3-17-1882. J. C. Rowe bought the tract on 1-22-1883. No record of what happened next could be found but it looks like Rowe, or someone else, lost it to a mortgage company. The next deed shows that M.H. Howard, Sr., bought the property from the W. C. Belcher Land Mortgage Company on 9-24-1902. On 9-11-1906, W. J. Roberts bought the property from Howard. At some point, Mrs. M. J. Martin came into the property, possibly buying it from Roberts. Her daughter, Della Cockrell, either bought or inherited the property and sold it to S. B. Glosson on 6-8-1936. His widow, Lou Glosson, sold the land to James S. "Shot" Glosson on 1-19-1959. The deed gave the acreage as 14.07 acres. Shot made his homestead on the easternmost 1.91 acres of the tract and then began to sell off the rest. Alvie L. Tucker bought the 4.03 acre tract that included the Glosson house on 5-10-1967. Robert Clayton Murphy bought the western 5.63 acres on 3-10-1970. On 4-17-1972, Bernice H. Pack bought the 1.69 acre tract next to Shot Glosson's. She sold the tract to Edward F. Martin on 9-1-1972. Alvie Tucker bought another 1.16 acres from Glosson on 1-16-1976 and then sold his acreage, totalling 5.19 acres to Kenneth Eaves that same day. On 11-11-1976, John G. and Minnie L. Lunsford bought the 5.63 acre tract from R. C. Murphy. Tom and Emily Hausler bought the 1.69 tract from E. F. Martin on 5-26-1977. Paul "Bud" McDaniel bought the 5.19 acre tract from Kenneth and Harriet Eaves on 6-28-1977 and added the 1.69 tract from the Hauslers on 10-29-1981. The McDaniels divorced and Sharon McDaniel Pike got the property on 12-5-1997. The 1.69 acres was separated again and on 3-30-2001, Terese Peabody and Douglas Scott Daves purchased the property. Charles Jones purchased the 5.63 acres from the Lunfords on 4-2-1984. The Joneses sold it off in three parcels. Robert F. Neal got it started with the purchase of 1.50 acres (Lot 1) on 12-31-1991. Gorman and Mary Lou Beeson bought 2.04 acres (Lot 2) on 4-16-1992. The Basurtos bought the other 2.03 acres (Lot 3) from the Joneses in the early '90s as well. Kenneth and Sheryl Brown bought the Basurto's property on 3-18-1996.

John Wallace stagecoach corrall

J. M. Pound Museum, 2003

Allie Mae Malott House, 1945

Founder's Park Pavillion/Swimming Pool, 1990.

L-R: John Wood, W. R. "Buddy" Baird, and Dr. E. P. Shelton, 1946
—Courtesy Travis Garnett

Part Three

Good People

Anytime you have a community that lasts over the years, then you know there had to be some quality people involved. Dripping Springs is one of those places. Many communities like to have a sign entering their towns extolling the fact that their town has Good Schools, Good Churches, and Good People. Most certainly, Dripping Springs is well justified in having such a sign.

The list given in the following pages includes only a few of those I know or have studied during my research. Foremost on that list are Dr. Pound and John Wallace. Many residents of our community can be added to the list as well.

William Thomas Chapman

When talking about the founders of Dripping Springs, one individual usually does not get the recognition that is his due. The true founder of the town of Dripping Springs is William Thomas Chapman (1835-1917). He was born in Coweta County, Georgia. Chapman came to Hays County and Dripping Springs in the early 1870s. He was not included on the 1870 census but was here by 1872. Prior to his excursion to Texas, W. T. Chapman enlisted in Company A, 12th Regiment Artillery and Infantry where he served from May 1862 to August 1864 when he was wounded and captured at Winchester, Virginia. He was released in 1865 from the famous Point Lookout in Maryland.

In a letter from W. T. Chapman to his stepson, Jasper Newton Marshall, written in 1915 and later included in Mr. Marshall's book, *Prophet of the Pedernales*, he told a little bit about his life after the Civil War. He said that after the close of the war he moved to Houston, Texas, from Georgia. His health began to give way after a few years and he began a search for a more healthy county. He finally located in Hays County and in Dripping Springs. He wrote "Here we established our home on the 15th day of March, 1872." It is hard to believe that he was talking about he and Mrs. Marshall but it is possible. Most likely, it was he and other family members.

We know that this land speculator received pay in 1872 from Hays County as a teacher. We also know that Burrell Jackson Marshall died in February 1872 and before 1872 had come to an end, Chapman married the recently widowed Martha Ann Box Marshall. The Marshalls purchased the original John Moss quarter league in 1870 and his death left Mrs. Marshall with five children to raise. Chapman moved into the Marshall residence and this marriage produced two children, Willie Pearl (1875-1949) and Mercer Ernest (1879-1945). Mr. Chapman also served as the postmaster from 1872-1889. The first story I heard had Mr. Chapman buying a league of land at Dripping Springs and that is why he came to Dripping Springs. It was not until 1875 that he bought a league of land for taxes.

Chapman was an industrious person, delving into many enterprises during his lifetime. The cause of education was always foremost with him, and that was understandable with teaching as part of his background. It is not clear as to where and when, but it is believed he built a building for the Dripping Springs school. We do know the county paid the Wallaces and Chapmans for their desks and etc. in 1874. It is my belief this building was built on what would become the northeast corner of the Academy Block. In 1876, the county put Dripping Springs in District #10 and it did not mention building another school. By the 1880 census, Chapman's occupation was listed as running a grocery store. For most of the '70s, his tax records showed that he rendered several hundred dollars in merchandise and goods. In 1880, the Marshall family divided what was left of the quarter league their dad had bought. His wife inherited her share, which meant Chapman shared with her.

The year 1881 was a glorious one for Chapman and Dripping Springs. Two things put Dripping Springs and Chapman on the map. The Dripping Springs Academy was started and so was the town of Dripping Springs. They were entertwined closely. When the Reverend W. M. Jordan came to town and talked up the possibility of building a private school here, it probably got Chapman to thinking about his other plan as well. After all, he was already running a store and the school should bring people to Dripping Springs and they would need a place to stay and do business. He donated the Academy Block and the groundbreaking took place in August. By September, he had already had County Surveyor, Professor Joe C. Eve, survey and file the plat that would be Dripping Springs. It consisted of twelve blocks, 200x300 feet each, and divided by six streets. The main street would be the 75 foot Mercer Street that ran in front of Academy Block.

Success was immediate as people began to buy lots and put businesses and residences on them. Chapman built a boarding house, hotel and general merchandise/ Masonic Lodge building in the next three years. During that time he also added four more additions to Dripping Springs. In the late 1880s, he and two of his companions took off to California for a look around to see if it would be worth moving there. They came to the conclusion that Dripping Springs was the place to be.

Chapman continued to be a strong influence in the community until his death in 1917. Have you ever wondered what the fate of Dripping Springs would have been had Mr. Marshall not passed away and Chapman not stepped in and developed the town from that land?

Albert Lawson Davis, Jr.

His father was a land speculator and business partner of W. T. Chapman until his death in 1888. A. L., Jr., followed in his father's footsteps in a lot of ways. The elder Davis owned over 450 acres in the southwest quarter of P. A. Smith's league, plus he lived on block ten of Dripping Springs. He inherited his share of the property. He was a partner with Chapman as well and ran the store on Lot 3 of block seven for much of the '80s. He acted as the postmaster in Chapman's stead. He bought the four lots on the east end of block seven and built the two-story merchandise store in 1891. He ran this store until 1901 when he sold it to Chapman and moved to San Marcos. Davis was a good baseball player and was the pitcher on a team he sponsored from 1884-96.

He married Willie Herndon on December 16, 1885, and they had five children. They were daughters Hallie, Ethel May, and Carol, and sons Howard Herndon and William Sherman. He went into the wholesale grocery business in San Marcos and was successful. Later on, he moved into the cotton industry and also owned a part of an insurance company. He served as mayor of San Marcos for eight years during the '20s. He died on January 23, 1938, and his wife ten months later.

George Dickey

George Dickey and his family came to Dripping Springs in the fall of 1884. He was a rockmason and businessman. He bought several lots in block seven and ran a store with his partner there for a while. Perhaps his most lasting accomplishment was the house he built at Walnut Springs. He began this house in 1886 and completed it in 1887. It is the two-story rock house on the sharp turn just south on RR12. It was said he built several other houses as well. Finally in 1898, he decided to leave Dripping Springs and find his fortune elsewhere. By this time his wife was in an asylum and he had to go to court to have the right to sign for her half of all the land and property that he sold, mostly to E. W. Herndon. Mr. Dickey gathered up his family and his belongings in a covered wagon and headed for Henrietta, Texas, in the winter of 1898.

His grandson, Dan Dickey, Jr., said it had been chronicled that this was one of the coldest winters on record in Texas. Mr. Dickey says that they believe one of their kin, Armanda Lee, is possibly buried in Dripping Springs. They have not been able to locate where she is buried.

Dr. Edgar Poe/Lula Shelton

The Shelton clan lived in parts of Travis and Hays counties. After finishing at the head of his class at Louisville Medical College in 1891, he decided to come to Dripping Springs. It was his intent to stay a year or two and then move on to the greener pastures of a larger town. He arrived on July 1, 1891, with little more than an education and a desire to help others. He bought a horse and saddle on credit and had a pair of secondhand saddlebags full of medicine bottles, the present of his uncle, W. A. Ellison, of Manchaca. Love has a way of changing the shade of green sometimes. He met Lula Spaw and they were married in 1892. They would raise thirteen children and four of their grandchildren. They ended up buying a house on block seven of the second addition in 1898. They lived in this house without modern conveniences until his death in 1946 and hers in 1950. He built an additional room on the front facing the road and that was his office.

According to Shelton history compiled by one of the family, Dr. Shelton delivered 3,888 babies, including all thirteen of his. The most amazing statistic of his practice was that he had only two mothers die at childbirth. In those days of more primitive medical facilities, that was an outstanding record. Besides medical services, Dr. Shelton served the community in many, many ways. He served on the County School Board and the Dripping Springs School Board for many years. He was elected to the state legislature for two terms and was also president of the County Medical Society. He was there to support many other worthwhile causes. After Dripping Springs took up football in 1938, he became the team doctor. You could tell when it was about time for football practice. Dr. Shelton would leave his house just above the school and slowly walk down to the practice field next to the theater. His career and service to Dripping Springs and the school system was honored in December of 1952 when Dripping Springs' first indoor gymnasium was dedicated to him.

Robert F. Shelton

One cannot think of education in

Dripping Springs without the name of Robert Shelton being in the forefront. Robert was the son of Dr. Shelton's oldest son, Elbert, and was born in Dripping Springs on August 3, 1917. His father had a career in the postal service and they lived in Fort Worth where he graduated from Ft. Worth Poly Tech.

He went to the University of Texas and graduated with honors. For much of that time, he comtemplated becoming a lawyer, which explains his way with words, like some of his kinfolk. He said that during his senior year he decided that he wanted to go into education, no doubt a direct influence of his uncles. He taught in Blanco and Austin a year, before deciding to give the postal service a try. This was interrupted by WWII.

He was being shipped to one of the hotspots in the war, when his ship was docked at a place. This place was in need of someone who could type and Mr. Shelton was the only one there who could. He was kept at this station while the rest of his buddies went on to fight a big battle. Very few of those in his group survived the battle.

After the war, he went back to the postal service for a total of seven years before the education bug hit him again. In 1947, he was named the first high school principal of Dripping Springs. While the principal, he is given credit for penning the school song for the high school. When the superintendent retired, he became superintendent of DSISD in 1951. He served at this position until 1963. During this time he pushed for and got the first gym and cafeteria and also helped coach several of the teams.

In 1963 he decided to make a move to Roma, Texas, to be with his uncle, Clarence Shelton, at that school. That experiment lasted only two years and he returned to his Dripping Springs home and took a job at the Gary Job Corps in San Marcos. In 1970 he became the first elementary principal in DSISD history and he held this job until his retirement in 1981.

He was a competitor in all that he did, even make-up games. I can remember playing volleyball on Monday night's in the gym for fun. The games were always competitive and lines were called on honor. Even though there was nothing at stake in the games, he would question someone's call of out of bounds.

Ima Lois Breed Shelton

Ima Lois Breed was born in Dripping Springs on April 4, 1920. She was the youngest daughter of James Carter Breed and was brought into this world by Dr. Shelton. Her mother died when she was quite young. She graduated from Dripping Springs and met Robert Shelton when he came back on visits to his grandfather. They married and quickly had three children, Robert F., Jr., Becky, and Jimmy during the war years. Later would come Poe and Lisa. All graduated from DSHS. She opened a Ready to Wear Dress Shop at the Billie Garnett building on Mercer Street in 1947 and then moved it to her father's store up the street in 1950. She then opened up the first dress shop in South Austin on Lamar Boulevard in 1953. She later moved her shop to the Lamar Plaza Shopping Center. She was quite proud of being the first in South Austin and the fact that in 1970 she was the first teacher's aide that Dripping Springs ever had. She held this position until she retired. Education careers were instilled in their children and Robert, Becky, and Poe made education their career. Jimmy tried it for a couple of years and left.

James L./Ellie Patterson

The Pattersons provide an interesting story as to how to end up in Dripping Springs. This couple was married in 1880 and set up in Rice's Crossing, near Hutto, Texas. Evidently they were very successful at their farming endeavor. However, a big storm blew up one time and destroyed their home. At this time Mr. Patterson started looking for a house that would withstand a

giant windstorm. Somehow they ended up in Dripping Springs and discovered what they thought was the perfect house. It was the house built by George Dickey in 1886. The walls on this two-story building were about 12-18 inches thick. He bought the house from E. W. Herndon in 1903. He brought his three daughters with him and left his son behind in Rice's Crossing.

Mr. Patterson bought all of Herndon's considerable acreage, as well. Before he was through, Mr. Patterson purchased 4,464 acres in and around the P. A. Smith survey. He did not stop there in his investments. In 1906 he purchased a 50x100 foot lot from the Academy Block and built a two-story merchandise store on Mercer Street. By 1908, they had convinced their son Joel and his family to come to Dripping Springs and run the store for them. The deal was, if they did not like Dripping Springs, they could return to Rice's Crossing. They toughed it out for six years, but in the end they left Dripping Springs about 1914.

One of the reasons they needed help with the store in 1908 was because the Pattersons bought the entire block five, which included a gin and grist mill. They ran this business until 1913, when they sold it. Sometime around 1917, the house burned and had to be rebuilt. Both of the Pattersons died in 1921 and their total estate was divided among their four children. Other than Joel, there was Mattie, who was married to Edwin McKellar, Edith L., who was married to Willie Sam Butler, and Barbara L., who was married to Earl Wood until his sudden death in June 1931. She later married Ben Everett.

William "Grampy" Stapleton / Emma Garnett

The Garnett clan is a large and prominent one in and around the area. Mr. Garnett came to Dripping Springs in 1904 and settled in with his family. He bought property from Pedernales Leinneweber. It included Lots 1 and 12 of block seven, Lots 1 and 12 and block three of the first addition, plus blocks one and two of the second addition. He acquired other property in the first addition later. His home was on block one. He is best known for his blacksmith shop on Lot 1 of the first addition but he managed to diversify as well. Blacksmiths were a do-it-all group of people because in many instances they had to improvise to fix a problem. He also was a funeral director, having a hearse and storing coffins in one of his other buildings. He kept his blacksmith shop open until just before his death in 1950.

William Sampson "Samp" McLendon

A native of Dripping Springs, "Samp," as he was best known, got involved in several enterprises in Dripping Springs during his lifetime. He is probably best noted for owning the telephone company for a while. He probably took over ownership of the telephone company in 1908 and ran it until 1918 when he sold it to Patton. He left Dripping Springs for a few years but re-inherited the telephone company in January 1922. It was his until he sold it for good to Mid-West Telephone Company in 1928. In 1939, he acquired all of the remaining Chapman properties that had passed into the Smith brothers hands upon Mrs. Chapman's death. He did not get to enjoy the purchase of these very long. In 1938 he became the Dripping Springs postmaster and held that post until his sudden death in 1940.

Eldridge B. "Pete"/Naoma Glosson

Pete, a 1932 graduate of Dripping Springs, is one of those diehard citizens of Dripping Springs. He let his future wife, Naoma Black, know right off the bat that if she did not want to live in Dripping Springs the rest of her life, then she had better not marry him because that is where he was going to stay. He has been true to his word. He and Naoma have done a little of everything to make that possible. They met where a lot of others met over the years, at the Camp Ben McCullough Reunion. This was before they had gotten out of high school. Naoma went to school at Darden Hill and Driftwood before graduating from San Marcos in 1933. They were married in 1939 and moved into the Lyle house on the corner of Bluff and Spring. They lived on the farm down Creek Road for four years before purchasing the land that he built his house on. He ran the Texaco station and she the Rock Cafe for a short while beginning in 1940. Pete was a good rockmason and built his house in 1945. He worked in his dad's grocery store, running the meat market for four years, ran a feed store for six years, was a mail carrier for over twenty years and drove the school bus for DSISD for twenty-eight years as well. Naoma worked for the post office for twenty-one years beginning in 1957. They have also been long-time members of the Methodist Church where he served over forty years in the choir. Their daughter, Merlene, was the pianist at the church for over twenty-five years. They have two other daughters, Minnie Lou was the oldest and Patricia the youngest. They still live in that same rock house.

E. E. "Nookie"/Hazel Bell Myers

Elbert Earl Myers was a 1939 graduate of Dripping Springs High School where he was an outstanding athlete in three sports. He played on the very first football team (1938) at Dripping Springs and led them to a 7-2 record and tri-championship. He was elected team captain and was the only Tiger to make first team all-district. He played basketball and was a member of the 1936-37 team that defeated San Marcos in the semi-finals of the Hays County tournament and the 1937-38 team that won the first county championship for Dripping Springs. His speed was legendary. He was county champion in the 100 and 220 dashes all four years with a best time of 10.0 in the 100, although it has been said he was clocked in 9.9 once. A second place finish in the long jump his senior year kept him from dominating that event all four years as well. He qualified for the state meet in the 100 in 1939 by placing fourth at regional, but sickness caused him to miss the meet.

E. E. "Nookie" Myers, running back, 1938
—Courtesy Hazel Bell Myers

After graduation he worked around Dripping Springs for a year or so before joining the army and serving in WWII. After the war, he returned to marry the girl who had waited for him, Hazel Bell King, a 1938 graduate. They wed on August 21, 1948, and moved to Austin where Nookie was a member of the Firestone Experimental driving team. In September 1951, he got the opportunity to take over the Central Mobil Station from Leroy Roberts. He ran the Mercer Street station until 1958 when he became the first business to relocate along the new Highway 290.

Nookie told his landlord, Alva Haydon, that when their daughter, Ginger, a 1969 DSHS graduate, graduated from college, then he was retiring from the business. Sure enough, when Ginger graduated from SWTU in December of 1972, he and Hazel packed everything in the store and locked the doors for the last time. After that, he did odd jobs like masonry work and kept an outstanding garden at the house that he and Hazel Bell had lived in since 1958 on RR12 S. He also was a member of the Masonic Lodge for over fifty years. He passed away in August 1998. She passed away in March 2002.

Travis/Lois Garnet

Travis is a 1943 graduate of DSHS. After graduation, he served in the army and served in WWII. He came back and married Lois Erlene Huey, a 1941 DSHS graduate and the granddaughter of Dr. E. P. Shelton. Travis worked with his dad at the Gulf station and garage on Mercer Street until his dad's untimely death in 1948. He and Lois lived with Mrs. Shelton and looked after her after Dr. Shelton passed away in 1946 and until she passed away in 1950.

He worked around the Gulf station but wanted to run a Humble station in its place. To do this he had to run the Humble station down the street. This he did beginning in 1952. In 1955, his dream came true as he moved the Humble station into his dad's old Gulf building. He asked J.F. Glosson, Jr., to be his partner and moved the business to the new Highway 290. They opened for business in the summer of 1960. In 1973 Travis sold his share of the station to J.F and opened the 5G garage at his home located just north of the Dripping Springs namesake. He served in the volunteer fire department for many, many years and when he retired, the members honored his service by naming the fire hall after him. He is now semi-retired. Travis and Lois have three sons, Gary Dale, Billie Carroll, and Danny. Gary and Danny are helping Travis carry on his business.

J. F./Cleo Glosson, Jr.

J.F. is a 1950 graduate of DSHS where his prowess as an athlete carved him a niche as one of the most outstanding athletes to come out of DSHS. In his senior season, J. F. led the Tigers to a perfect 12-0 season and regional championship in football, a zone championship in basketball, and a district championship in track. The class president was a standout performer in the 1950 six-man all-star game played at Bobcat stadium in San Marcos. Afterwards, he turned down the opportunity to play on that same field for the Southwest Texas State Bobcats.

After graduation, J.F. spent most of the next ten years working with his dad in the trucking business. In 1960, he accepted Travis Garnett's offer to join him in opening the Humble station on Hwy. 290. In 1973, he became the sole owner of the business when he took Travis up on the offer to buy his half.

J. F. married Cleo Lowden, a Buda graduate, and they had two children, Monte and Mitzi. Monte began working with his dad after his graduation in 1972. This put him in the position to take over the business when J. F. and Cleo decided to retire from the profession in June 1999.

Alfard/Ann Hohman

This pair have been public servants to the people of Dripping Springs for a long time.

Alfard was born in Mt. Gainer in 1922 and as he said, in those days that was a long ways from Dripping Springs, so he really did not know much about Dripping Springs as he was growing up. His family lived on several hundred acres where the rural life was not easy and it got tougher on the Hohman family when his father died in 1936. Alfard was only fourteen. He had an eleven-year old brother and six-year old sister to look after. Those were the final days of the Great Depression.

He attended the Mt. Gainer school through its ten grades. When he became seventeen in 1939, he joined the CCC and went to Albany, Texas, to work on the restoration of Fort Griffin for thirty dollars a month. He kept eight and sent twenty-two to his mother. After the bombing of Pearl Harbor in 1941, he came back to Mt. Gainer where he took a ranching job on the Henry Brooks ranch north of town. He worked for Leonard East and another fellow. There was a misunderstanding and Alfard moved over to the Dripping Springs ranch east of town. It was during this stay that wedding bells were heard for Alfard.

Ann Nite graduated from Flatonia High School. This was the nearest school. She actually lived nearer Muldoon in Fayette County. She attended Southwest Texas State Teachers College in San Marcos for two years and got an emergency teaching certificate for her first job at Dripping Springs in the fall of 1943. Her room was in the old Academy building. As many teachers in those days, Ann finished her degree by going to school in the summers and on Saturdays. In fact, she earned both her degrees this way. She was a mainstay on the teaching staff for 35 years. Those 35 years represented the longevity record among the hundreds of teachers to have served Dripping Springs, until Mrs. Marion Voudouris tied it in 2001.

She took two years off when she gave birth to son, Alfard Nite, and one for daughter, Charlotte Ann. She retired at the end of the 1981 school year but she was not through serving the school. In 1981 Dripping Springs and Lake Travis split the school district. Ann was asked to be on the Dripping Springs Board of Trustees to go through the transition period for Dripping Springs. She accepted and gave her input for the next couple of years and did not run for reelection. She was instrumental in making it possible for me to have a place to continue as a teacher at DSISD. She continued to substitute for a few years to wean herself of longtime habits. She continues to be active in church and senior citizen endeavors.

Wedding bells rang for the pair on December 27, 1944. Ann moved to the Dripping Springs ranch with Alfard. Several months later they moved to a house across the North Onion Creek to spend a very cold winter. This prompted them to move again. Alfard accepted a job with S. J. Moore, a contractor. Among their accomplishments was Virgil Conn's house and the Dripping Springs School. He said he was there from beginning to end, including getting the foundation prepared and poured. After gaining this experience, he went into private business for himself. One of his buildings was the Horner house on Old Fitzhugh Road that he built with the help of students Woody Glosson and Perry Roberts.

In January 1954, Alfard tried his hand at the grocery business. He bought out Dayton Roberts' Drug and Grocery. He - operated it for a year before selling it to Virgil Conn. He spent the next two or three years being a member of the Firestone Experimental Driving Team. For a few years after that, he worked for Jim Hall in the surveying business. He went back to his roots of ranching until May of 1964 when he began his career in law enforcement. He said a group of men came to him, gave him a pistol, and said get to work. He worked as a Hays County Deputy Sheriff for the next sixteen years. In the election of 1980, he won the job of Hays County Sheriff. He held this office until his retirement in 1989.

As we mentioned before, ranching has always been in Alfard's blood. Even when he was holding all these other jobs, he would still lease land and run cattle, sheep and goats. This meant working all day and then using part of his spare time doing his ranching business, especially before the time of eradication, the doctoring of the worms caused by blowflies.

In his younger days, he recalls entertainment was roping at the arena on Tuesdays and Saturdays and baseball games on Sunday afternoons. My favorite recollection of Alfard is seeing his old pickup loaded down with coon hounds, heading out to some area to sit around and listen to his hounds howl after prey all night long. And if he had the same experience of people in the area I grew up, he spent the next couple of days trying to find some of them. There might have been baseball games on Sunday afternoon, but you can be sure that on Sunday morning you could find Alfard and Ann, with children, attending the United Methodist Church. They have always been active members of the church and have served in every capacity possible. It was families like the Hohmans who kept the church moving forward when everything pointed to stubbornness in that direction. It was families like the Hohmans who made others glad they chose Dripping Springs for a place to call their home.

Charles C./Beulah Haydon

This couple was married in 1909 and moved into Hays County that year, but did not reside in Dripping Springs until 1923. Among the things they did for a living was own a gin in Driftwood. In May 1924, they decided to make a career move to Dripping Springs where they bought the ten lots of block five that included the gin. Beulah ran the gin in Driftwood while Charles ran the one in Dripping Springs. They decided to sell the Driftwood gin and purchase the other two lots in block five which included a house in which they could live. They did not stop there. They bought Lots 1, 2, 7, 8, 9, 10, 11, and 12 of block six and block ten. In 1934 they bought the eastern half of block eight which included a two-story house into which they moved.

Ginning is a very seasonal occupation but Mr. Haydon had a talent for every season. He moved the grist mill onto Lot 12 but later returned it to the gin lot. A small wooden frame building was on Lot 1 of block six and it was leased out for a barbershop and hamburger place. Ten years later he moved the building to Lot 12 and began building the rock Central Garage and Station on that site in 1935. He also spent time digging water wells for others. He and his wife had nine children but only seven survived infancy.

In March 1931, Charles Haydon installed a lighting system from his gin to light up the school house for gatherings. He served on the Dripping Springs school board and was elected as the County Commissioner from Pct. #4. This was a post he held until he died of a heart attack on May 2, 1938, at the age of 48. His wife, Beulah, was selected to finish out his term and thus became one of the few women to serve in that capacity at that time.

Mrs. Beulah Crumley Haydon, affectionately known as "Short Mama" because of her stature, was anything but short when it came to anything else. She married J. W. Malott on October 17, 1940, and remained his wife until his death 27 years later. She died at the age of 97 in 1989. The family eventually sold the home place in the mid-'90s. It was turned into a bed and breakfast known as "Short Mamas" to commemorate the lady who had made it her home for 55 years. In early 2000, it was converted to hold several businesses within.

Alva/Willie Mae Haydon

Alva Haydon was the eldest son of Charles C. Haydon and came with the family to Dripping Springs in 1923. He pretty well followed in his father's footsteps as an innovator and astute businessman. He helped with the gin and garage businesses. He was still a newlywed when his dad died on May 2, 1938. He had just married Willie Mae Wilson on January 1, 1938, and moved into Austin. He helped his dad build the rock Central Garage and Station on Mercer Street which opened in 1937, and returned to take over the job of running the gin and garage with his brother, Charlie Neal, in 1939. He never left Dripping Springs again.

When Central Garage was being built, the building on the old lot was moved down to the southwest corner of Lot 12 of block six. A couple of people used it for a residence and Mrs. Haydon set up her beauty shop in it until they were able to build their house on block ten in 1943. They built an addition to it where she set up shop for many years.

They have been active in community affairs for most of their lifetimes—she in the PTA, First Baptist Church choir for 50 years, and as a Sunday School teacher for nearly as many, to name a few. He helped found several much-needed organizations. The first was the volunteer fire department in 1958. The fire truck was stored in his mother's garage for a while and he required workers at the garage to be members of the department. He served as fire chief for the first seventeen years. Another need was met when he was a part of a group that got the necessary requirements together to set up the Dripping Springs Water Corporation that went on-line in 1965. He served as president of that organization for many years as well. He served on the school board for many years, was mayor of Dripping Springs and a deacon in the First Baptist Church. I wonder when he had time to carry on his other business duties.

When the new Highway 290 went through town in 1958, he and his brother were the first to move the service station business over there. They built the Mobil station on the site of the old gin and it opened in 1959. A year later they built a building that housed a local restaurant for many years—the Western Kitchen. A short while later they built another building on the same block that housed Nut's Hobby Shop. They closed the gap between the two buildings in 1984. All of these buildings are located on block five. He moved his Central Garage business to its present site and ran it until he sold it to Ben Metcalf in 1977.

The Alva Haydons raised two sons. The oldest is Charles. He graduated from Dripping Springs in 1961 and then married Sherry Graves. They had three children, Laura, Lea Anne, and Jason, all graduating from DSHS. Charles and Sherry have spent their adult lives in the field of education.

The second son is Robert, a 1965 graduate of DSHS. He married Martha Bledsoe, the daughter of the First Baptist minister, also a DS graduate of 1966. Robert entered the medical profession as a doctor. They have two children, Kerri and Chad.

Johnny/Mary Spaw

Johnny E. Spaw was a lifelong resident of Dripping Springs and his wife, Mary Applewhite, was almost. She was born in 1900 and moved with her parents to Dripping Springs in 1901. I am not quite sure when Johnny began cutting hair in Dripping Springs, only when he quit. He was barbering in a room at the old Haydon building during the years 1925-35. When it was moved, he had to find another place to ply his trade. He negotiated for the plot of land in block seven and built the little rock barber shop in late 1937. He worked there until his retirement on December 31, 1963. His daughter, Marie Spaw Eckols, said that he also had a small trucking business between barber shops and worked for the companies that were building the highway that came through in 1937.

Meanwhile, Mary embarked on a teaching career. Over the years she taught at Darden Hill, Driftwood, Dripping Springs, Fitzhugh, Glenn, and Millseat school districts. There may have been others. When W. S. McLendon, the postmaster, died suddenly in October 1940, she applied for the position and became the acting postmaster. She received a permanent appointment one year later in October 1941. The little barbershop of her husband served as her place of business as well. This was the post office until the little red brick post office was built in 1961. She retired in 1963.

They bought the Crenshaw house and moved there in 1941 and remained there until their deaths. They had two daughters, Clydene and Marie. Their daughter, Marie, and husband, Jones Eckols, now reside there. The Eckols have two daughters, Merrie Jean and Elizabeth Jo.

Solon Bell/Lou Glosson

Like many other couples in Dripping Springs, the Glossons ended up doing quite a few things over the years to make ends meet. Most notably was their involvement in the grocery business. They ran the Red and White Grocery in the first floor of the Davis building all through the 1940s until 1951 when the building burned. They moved temporarily to Billie Garnett's building until they could build their new store next to the Patterson building on the Academy Block. They were in charge of the store until his death in 1956.

O.S./Sybil Brumley

The Brumleys ran the Brumley Cash Grocery located in the Patterson building all of the '30s and even survived the fire that destroyed their store in 1938. Mr. Brumley died in 1940 and Mrs. Brumley continued to run the store for a couple more years.

Lewis/Pauline Jennings

In 1942, Lewis Jennings went into partnership with Andrew Herwig. They set up a feed store in the Patterson store. Also during the 1943-46 time span he served as County Commissioner. The Jennings-Herwig partnership added lumber to their business. In 1952, Mr. Herwig left the business and let Jennings go it alone. Finally in 1956, he sold his feed business and moved the lumber business across the street for five years. He then finished out his working days working on the county road crew.

Virgil/Delores (Pokey) Conn

Like most, Virgil was involved in many careers. When Central Garage opened in 1937, he ran the Magnolia station for a couple of years. He carried on a dual role for quite some time as well. He served as County Commissioner from 1947-62. During that time they ran Conn's Grocery and Drugstore located in the Goslin building for six years. After that they opened up a little specialty store on the site of the present Central Garage block and then moved up to block five and opened up another specialty store that he named Nut's Hobby Shop in 1961. He stayed in this business for eight years before retiring.

William "Bill"/Clarene McNair

Bill, an electrician, worked for Will Crow in his hardware business for about ten years. It was first housed in the building where the Rippy Ranch Supply now stands. After the two-story Davis building burned in 1951, Mr. Crow decided to move the hardware business to the rebuilt one-story building. Mr. Crow decided to get out of the business altogether and offered it to Bill, who accepted the offer in 1953. For the next twenty years it was known as McNair's Hardware. He sold the business and went into semi-retirement.

W.P."Will"/Faye Crow

Will was one who got into many businesses over his lifetime. One of his first endeavors was to run a grocery store/service station for Crenshaw in 1930. When Crenshaw moved back to his store a year later, Mr. Crow took over the business altogether. It was called Crow's Service Station. A few years later he bought the lot and tore down the two-story building. In its place he built a warehouse for his budding wool and mohair business. He stood alone in the business for over a decade. He also built a building back on Lot 3 and set up the first hardware store in Dripping Springs. After getting out of the two businesses, he got involved in acquiring much of the land around Dripping Springs and civic works. He worked at the PEC substation for many years and served as president of the Dripping Springs Water Corporation until his death.

Jimmy/Tula Glosson

After probably working in his father's grocery business for a few years, in 1942 the Glossons decided to take over the little Rock Cafe that had been open for the past two years. They renamed the cafe Bonnie's Cafe in honor of their daughter. They ran this business until 1956. It was at this time that Jimmy's dad died and he took over the family grocery business. He retired from this in 1971. He served on the DS Water Corporation Board from its conception in 1965 and was elected the first mayor of Dripping Springs in 1981. He died one week after being re-elected to that position in 1983.

Dr. Camillus Henry/Katherine Berkley

Dr. C. H. Berkley graduated from the Memphis Hospital Medical College on March 31, 1892. He had previously married Katherine Hayes Keeble on October 18, 1890. As had Dr. Pound in years past, Dr. Berkley had health problems and it was feared he might have tuberculosis. A drier climate was the remedy, and Texas became the answer. He and his family moved to Aledo, Texas, in the early 1900s, and in 1907 made the move to Wimberley when their only doctor died. He wanted to be a little closer to Austin, so that his sons would have the opportunity to go to the University of Texas.

A chance to buy acreage in Dripping Springs was accepted in December of 1909. He began his practice here and continued to do so until 1934 when he broke a hip working cattle and never regained the good health to continue his practice at his usual pace. Finally, in 1937, he had to give up his practice after 42 years in medicine. Like most doctors of the time, he made many home visits to rural families around Dripping Springs and his home was always open to anyone needing his help. He spent many nights with a patient when around-the-clock care was called for. He usually went on calls in a buggy pulled by his faithful horse "Charlie." Dr. Berkley bought a Model T Ford but never learned how to drive. Usually his son Lee drove him to his calls. People traded, bartered and even chopped cedar to help pay their bills. If a family had fallen upon hard times, it would not be unusual for Dr. Berkley to tear up the bill.

His wife died in 1931 and he on January 8, 1947. They are buried in Phillips Cemetery.

Dr. C. H. Berkley, his wife, and three sons

Good Churches

From the very beginning religion has been important to the citizens of Dripping Springs. In the beginning, circuit riders came by periodically, but as the population grew, so did the need for more organized worship. The first to form were the Methodists but not far behind were the Baptists. Some of the early publications mentioned that the three top churches were the Methodists, Baptists, and Christian.

I'm not sure when the Christian church ceased to exist in Dripping Springs, but the other churches struggled through the hard times of slow growth, and survived to enjoy the tremendous growth of the area beginning in the 1980s. There have been a few other churches that started up during this time but did not have staying power.

There are individuals and families who worship as they see fit in their own way. Either they meet in small groups in the area or go to other places to meet with people of like beliefs. That is the way that it should always be.

In this chapter we will explore the history of the churches that were formed in Dripping Springs and had staying power in the conventional manner. That is not to say this is a complete list because some possibly will be overlooked.

The Methodist Church

Anytime an area in the frontier had a few people in it, there would be a Methodist circuit rider coming around soon. In Dripping Springs the first Methodist services were held in the newly constructed one-room log cabin of Dr. Joseph Pound, possibly around 1855 or 1856. The large oaks outside provided an ideal place on nice days. This site continued to be used for the next couple of years. As his family began to expand, so did his house. He built a second room to the east with a traditional dogtrot in between. This is mentioned because it allowed children to be taken care of in the other room while the services were being conducted.

Supposedly a few years later, services were held in a log cabin located near the present Masonic Lodge site (the Old Academy). The building also doubled as a school as well. Afterall, with the large circuits, services were not held that often or regular, as circuit riders made it to a church only once or twice a month. Some newspapers I read held reports in which one group was disappointed when the preacher did not make it to the services. On another occasion, when the preacher arrived he found only two in attendance and he returned home without preaching a sermon. The preachers' mode of transportation was mostly by horseback and sometimes on foot, so they may have incurred many difficulties in getting to the assigned places on time.

In my research a bit of information came to light that I think disputes part of the history of the church. It was in the January 22, 1954, edition of the *San Marcos Record*. Mittie Pound Sorrell, the daughter of Dr. J. M. Pound, died on January 1, 1954, at the age of 90. She was born December 13, 1863. In the obituary particulars, it said she was the last charter member of the Dripping Springs Methodist Church. Miss Ennis Follis, in researching the history of the church, could not find a preacher assigned to Dripping Springs before 1866. It seems to me that the time table that had been given as to when events happened was probably compressed. The transition from Dr. Pound's house to the church did not occur as rapidly as first believed. It would make sense that the Dripping Springs Methodist Church was chartered around 1866. Mittie Pound would have been two or three at the time. The Civil War was over and things were beginning to return to some normalcy. The small school near the Academy site was probably built by 1869. Reconstruction was over and Texas had an education system in place. Carrie Wallace was listed as a teacher in the 1870 census. Combining school and church in the same building was the norm in those days.

By 1880, the area had grown enough that members saw the need for their own church building. On January 10, 1880, one and one-third acres were purchased from one of its members, John W. Phillips, for the sum of five dollars. By March 12, 1880, the little church had been completed on the site located about two miles south of Dripping Springs and adjacent to the present Phillips Cemetery. It was known as the Walnut Springs Methodist church and for a few years doubled as the Walnut Springs Academy. It was the only ten-month school in the area at the time.

This building lasted only eleven months. On February 2, 1881, someone deliberately set fire to it and completely destroyed the structure. Although saddened by their loss, the members, along with the help of conference donations, promptly rebuilt on the same spot. It continued to prosper for another two decades. Dripping Springs became a mission church in 1884. The significance of this designation meant this congregation could now receive financial assistance from the Conference.

By this time, the town of Dripping Springs had been platted by W. T. Chapman and was flourishing. However, the church did not make their move for a while. One of the first decisions they made was to have a live-in preacher. This meant they had to have a place for he and his family to stay. On September 10, 1892, the church purchased six lots in Dripping Springs from George Dickey for $300. By 1893, the parsonage was completed and A. G. Nolen became its first tenant. These lots were located in the third addition and south of the First Baptist Church just across Hays Street. Today they are owned by the Baptist Church.

Nine years later, the congregation brought its dream of a new church to a reality. They decided they wanted to locate their church in Dripping Springs. This was accomplished when they purchased the eastern half of block three from W. T. Chapman/ A. L. Davis on March 21, 1901, for five dollars. Before the year was out, the new wooden structure was completed.

Originally the church faced south toward Hays Street. At that time, the present RR12 did not exist to Highway 290. It was connected in October 1947. In March 1950 a new foundation was built and the church was moved so that the front now faced east. They even added a rock barbeque pit at the same time. It was repainted in September 1950. The old Walnut Springs church building was sold and it was later moved to the property south of Hays Street and directly across from the new church. It was used as a residence until the mid-'80s when it was torn down for the office building called Pioneer Plaza.

For many years, the Baptist and Methodist churches, built at about the same time and one block apart, had only two services a month. They cooperated by alternating their services so that after attending their respective Sunday School programs, the congregations could attend a church service each week.

In 1911, D. W. Waller's wife died of tuberculosis while living in the parsonage. The church decided the solution to this possible health hazard was to tear down the parsonage and rebuild on the site. Harold Goodenough received his first charge in 1912. It was at Dripping Springs. He and his wife had to stay with Dr. C. H. Berkley until the new parsonage was completed and they became its first occupants.

Changes continued for the next half century. In 1933, Bill Garnett built a shed to the north of the church and installed a 32 volt DC current Delco electric plant for their source of light. Mr. Garnett and Leroy Roberts were responsible for building a tabernacle on the grounds in 1936. It was located between the church and what is now RR12, running parallel to the road. Boilers from old gins were used to make the outside railing. Benches and tables were also made. The tabernacle had to be torn down when the church was moved in 1950. This caused some controversy because some did not want it torn down. The old parsonage was sold in 1948 and a new one erected just to the north of the church in April 1948. Preston Atkison had the honor of living in it first. In October of 1951, the parsonage was expanded by adding a garage and storage space. A foundation was poured and John Baird, along with volunteers, did the work.

Another addition to the church was a beautiful old piano given to the church by the Murphy family of San Antonio in June 1951. It gave them the luxury of moving the other piano to the Sunday School rooms. Miss Ennis Follis donated an organ to the church in 1975 to compliment the piano.

Growth called for more expansion and in January 1953, the rock education building was completed. It consisted of four classrooms, a nursery, two restrooms, and a kitchen. Three of the classrooms were divided with sliding doors to allow more room for dinners and meetings.

It was not growth that caused the next building program, but safety. The old wooden church was getting on the frail side. It had already received some extra bracing. One Sunday in 1962 convinced the congregation a new church was a necessity. Will King was occupying a back pew in the choir with his arm resting on the back of it. A strong wind was gusting outside. One good gust caused the wall to shift and trapped Mr. King's hand between the wall and the pew. This hula hula dance by the walls could not be tolerated any longer. It was feared the building was near collapse. The last service held in the old structure was in October 1962.

First Methodist Church, 1901-62
—Courtesy Hazel Bell Myers

The old church was bought by J.W. Wilson and moved behind his TV and Appliance store for additional storage. In the mid-'80s it burned to the ground. Until that time, all of the first three Methodist church buildings were still of value to the community. In the meantime, services were held in the educational building. The new rock sanctuary was completed in January 1963 and the formal opening was held on February 10. The cornerstone was laid for the new church. Charlie Oldham, the contractor, and Willie Lyle, who assisted with the rockwork, laid the stone. The breezeway connecting the church with the educational building was enclosed around 1975.

In the late '60s the parsonage started a period of off and on use. Due to the size of the congregation, many of the ministers appointed were retired or shared with other churches and were not live-in ministers. By 1975, it was determined a live-in minister was necessary for continued growth but the parsonage just was not suitable. It was decided to buy an existing home rather than build. The new parsonage was located on Old Fitzhugh Road with an outlet to RR12. The old parsonage continued to be used for much-needed classroom space until torn down when the property was sold in the mid-'80s. Chris Rodriguez became the first tenant in the new parsonage. Unfortunately, the parsonage situation would not be solved as a new crisis challenged the church.

In August 1978, while Theo Cox was the pastor, fire swept through the structure, destroying a portion of the house and much of the pastor's belongings. The pastor and his family were moved into a mobile home until decisions could be made.

The present site had not been ideal but the best available at the time. This disaster gave the congregation more choices to be made. Rather than rebuild the structure, it was decided to sell the property and use the insurance money to buy a lot in the Springwood subdivision south of Dripping Springs off RR12 and build a new parsonage. October 1979 was pride day for the Methodists. The new three bedroom, two bath, two-car garage home was ready for occupancy. So was the pastor. Grady and Tricia Roe had been living in a church-rented house since his appointment in January. In 1993, the garage area was converted into a room to provide more living space. The new church edict along about that time was the parsonage needed to have a garage and so the congregation went about the task of building a new garage.

The growth of the area also equated into the growth of the church. The problem lay in the site. It was not ideal for any expansion plans. Drainage was bad and space lacking. The Methodists were in a bind. A Future Planning Committee formed in 1983 determined the need for a new site. The Conference recommended a site of three to five acres. A search was started and a site was proposed. It was located on RR12 north. The committee approached Mrs. Marguerite Cavett Hammack about buying four acres of her land. After conferring with her children, Mrs. Hammack, the granddaughter of Dr. Joseph Pound, returned to give her answer. She had decided, rather than sell, that she wanted to give the church five acres.

The significance of this gesture was enormous. Not only was it generous due to the premium placed on acreage at the time but it brought the church full cycle. The early meetings of the Dripping Springs Methodists were held in Dr. Pound's house. Now the church would be built on his property. This was May 1983. Mrs. Hammack insisted she sign a contract of this agreement in case something happened to her. In August, she passed away. It was several years before the deed work was finished. The old property was sold in 1986 and construction begun on the new site. The congregation met at the new Dripping Springs High School cafeteria until Easter 1987 when the first service was held in the new church.

The church has continued to grow with the community. Very popular programs include the Day Care and After School Kare programs. The church is used by many community groups for meetings, most of which are held in the Marguerite Hammack Fellowship Hall. In the mid-'90s growth made it necessary to build the classrooms upstairs that had been put in the orginal plans for just this reason. Dripping Springs

United Methodist Church, 1987

growth patterns have done nothing but spiral upward. So much so that the Methodist Church outgrew its present space. In 1998 another building program got underway to build more additions to the present structure. Included in that is the purchase of more acreage (three acres) from the original Pound property. Ground breaking ceremonies took place on October 3, 1999, for the new expansion plans. These plans called for another wing of classrooms extended to the south of the original structure and expansion of the sanctuary by taking in the church offices and part of the fellowship hall.

While this construction was going on, it was decided to complete their future plans at this time by including a family center on the west side of the new addition. A three-tiered parking lot was completed on the east side and more parking was provided on the south side of the family center. Prior to the construction plans, a double-wide mobile home was already moved along the north edge of the property line to provide needed classroom space. The plan to sell it upon completion of the construction was scrapped when the advantage of more space was seen to be a plus.

In the Methodist church, pastors are assigned by the conference. This means they can serve a church for a year to several years and may be reassigned to that church after an absence of some years. Only since 1961 has the assignments been made in the summer. Previous to that, assignments were made in December and the move made in January. This really worked a hardship on the families by having to uproot in the middle of school years.

Although possibly some were assigned before 1866, in Miss Ennis Follis's research for the history of the Dripping Springs Methodist church, her list of pastors assigned to Dripping Springs began that year. The following list comes from her research and will be listed in the order they first served, although they may have served again.

J. S. Gillett	J. A. Garrison
Wm. J. Joyce	Thomas S. Ballard
T. A. Lancaster	A. G. Nolen
Wesley Smith	J. R. Barden
O. A. Fisher	H. F. Harris
C. M. Carpenter	Hiram Graham
Wm. M. Crow	Rex B. Wilkes
E. H. Holbrook	August S. Swanson
Joel W. Vest	J. S. Simmons
W. H. Killough	W. G. Whitehead
Thomas S. Garrett	J. A. Foster
B. Harris	C. F. McKinney
J. G. Walker	J. I. Kelly
M. A. Black	D. W. Waller
L. D. Coggin	Harold Goodenough

O. M. Cole
W. L. Hightower
R. S. Collier
E. J. Sloan
Hugh Revely
B. W. Allen
J. J. Shaw
R. K. Heacock
S. J. Franks
W. H. Birkner
A. F. Foerster
T. M. Mitchell
J. W. Griffin
A. Leonard Miller
L. D. Hardt
F. C. Harrell
F. A. Banks
H. G. Walton
F. L. Meadow
Preston Atkison
M. H. Jackson
Gilbert Nihart
Carl Israel

Jasper Snow
Windell Bell
Dennis Macune
B. J. Gossett
Glen Weimer
Cecil Carl Taylor
Robert Johnson
Mark E. Lett
C. Earl Lewis
Virgil Eicher
Sherwood S. Davis
Steve Ling
R. E. Newcomer
Walter Pilgrim
Ben McGee
Paul Lockey
Myron Ricketts
J. Chris Rodriguez
Theo Cox
Wm. Grady Roe
Clint Rabb
Andy Smith

First Baptist Church

Whereas the Methodist Church was not sure exactly when they started meeting, the First Baptist Church of Dripping Springs is. It was organized the fifth Sunday of June in the year 1872. They had twelve charter members on that date. They were Ed Womack, Virginia Womack, A. L. Davis, Sr., Nancy J. Davis, Missouri Runnels, S. S. Middlebrook, Mary Middlebrook, R. B. Fairchilds, Nancy Riley, Jane Riley, and Minerva Daniels. A. L. Davis, Sr., and S. S. Middlebrook were the deacons. The church's first sermon was preached by J. C. Tally and G. G. Rucker was called to be the church's first pastor.

In July 1872, the Dripping Springs Baptist Church voted to join the Austin Baptist Association. By 1873, they decided their lot would be better served by forming an association of hill country churches. Delegates were sent to Dripping Springs and the result was the Pedernales Baptist Association. It was made up of congregations from Bandera, Blanco, Gillespie, Hays, and Kerr counties. It was at this time that the fifth Sunday meetings were instituted. Every fifth Sunday of a month, members from all the congregations gathered at one of the churches and had a morning worship, dinner on grounds, and then an afternoon worship service.

The church began to grow almost immediately. In a camp meeting held jointly with Mount Zion Baptist Church on Onion Creek, twelve new members were added to the rolls. The Baptist organization is a democratic organization and takes the position that the Christian life of each member is the concern of all the members. Each month, usually on Saturday, the church conference met and determined the fate of some of their members who were not being good citizens. The record books for the church from the '70s, '80s and '90s have many accounts of members being excluded from fellowship of the church because of their misdeeds. Drinking, dancing, swearing, unchristian conduct, and even stubbornness were reasons given for exclusion. Other decisions were made by the church conference. It was decided in 1874 that the practice of admitting people into the watch care of the church was to be abolished because it was like accepting them on a trial basis. Also it was decided in 1875 that fasting was an ancient practice but was not a doctrine of the church. The matter of finances was a part of the conference as well. The deacons were authorized in the 1880s to see members about the matter of contributing to the church. In 1885, the Sabbath School was requested to collect funds for a new church organ.

Like most early churches, the Baptist Church probably met in someone's house or community gathering place. In 1874, they decided to build a church of their own. They bought two acres of land from John Lee Wallace on July 25, 1874, for three dollars and adjacent land on the west side from W. T. Chapman on July 28, 1874, for three dollars. Today that land is where the

Promenade Center is. The actual site of the church is thought to be on the Wallace land, which is the Promenade land. Although started in 1874, due to financial problems, the building was not completed until 1876. The church spent $274.71 on the building. The size of the building is unknown except they spent $21.75 for 216 feet of flooring.

The history of Dripping Springs is also the history of having some active arsonists. They spared no one. In 1879 they torched the Baptist Church. This left them without a church of their own until 1882.

In 1881 the Reverend W. M. Jordan convinced the community that it should have a private school. The cornerstone was laid on August 6, 1881, and by the middle of January, the $4,000 two-room school/church was completed. The Reverend Z. N. Morrell, a famed Baptist minister, whose daughter was one of the teachers, was present at the dedication of the chapel. After two years, Jordan left to start another school in Kyle and the leadership of running the school was turned over to the Pedernales Baptist Association when they paid W. T. Chapman $10 for the Academy Block. The stipulation was that if the school ever ceased being a denominational one, the property would revert to the Dripping Springs Baptist Church. A ruling in the late '80s made it illegal to use public school funds for attending a denominational school. The school was not able to operate without those funds and so these courses were dropped with the result that the Dripping Springs Baptist Church now had title to the Academy Block property which was also their church.

In 1901, the Baptists decided to follow in the footsteps of the Methodist church and build a separate church. They bought the east six lots of block three from W. T. Chapman on May 2, 1901, for $85. They hired a Mr. Rippstein from Guadalupe County to be the designer and builder. He built a typical Texas church, complete with a steeple, using native cedar and cypress timber. The pine lumber was hauled in from Austin. In August 1902, the church was dedicated with the Reverend Jasper Newton Marshall, whose dad once owned the land, presenting the sermon. The pastor at the time was Henry Peal.

First Baptist Church, 1901

Originally the little church faced north toward Spring Street with the pews facing south. A tabernacle was built in 1923. The church was reshingled in December 1941. In May 1948 the church remodeling was completed so that the entrance now faced east. A baptismal extension was added to the west end and the pews now faced west. The steeple was removed. The ceremony took place on Sunday, May 23, and Jasper Newton Marshall was again the main speaker. By 1944, the Baptist church acquired the entire block. The rock parsonage was completed in September 1944. An educational hall was added to the south side in the 1940s and as the church continued to grow by leaps and bounds, the educational hall was expanded even more in the 1970s and 1980s. In 1980, a complete new sanctuary wing was added to the north side of the old church with the entrance along the north side of the old church. The old church was converted into offices and classrooms. Even a church split in the mid-1990s did not slow the growth of the church and remove the need for more room. The church has purchased the entire block of land that is block two of the third addition and have added modules for rooms. Also, the sanctuary underwent another expansion program beginning in late 1997. The white limestone rock walls were removed and the building expanded eighteen feet on the east and west sides. The project was completed in early 1998.

Baptists select their pastors by calling them to preach. Their pastors may be there only a short time or they could be there for many years. Some pastors returned again. Since 1872, the following have been pastors of the Dripping Springs First Baptist Church.

G.G. Rucker	J.W. Reynolds
W.W. McCowen	H.E. Peters
M.H. Bell	H.M. Mohrmann, Jr.
W.M. Jordan	J.R. Davis
J.D. Walker	S.D. Lunsford
C.B. Hollis	Charlie Parker
J.E. Bell	H.R. Carroll
F.M. Walker	Theron Stevens
J.A. Parker	Jim Hoard
T.Y. Adams	C.R. Perrin
H.T. Peal	J.D. Benson
A.L. James	B.A. Bledsoe
A.L. Aulick	Dave Cannon
L.D. Hornburg	Ira Irvin
T.S. Baskin	Don Duvall
J.W. Thomas	George Magnor
Lee Pledger	David McNary
J.M. Earls	David Smith
W.L. Lockhart	Lanny Tanton
E.A. Franks	

Church of Christ

The Dripping Springs Church of Christ got its start much like the consolidation of schools. The communities of Driftwood, Henly, Millseat, and Teck had active congregations, but in the late 1930s, they decided to form a church in Dripping Springs also.

The third oldest established church in Dripping Springs began like all the others—without a permanent home. In the early years services were held in the Methodist tabernacle, a movie theater, or the school, among other places. On November 8, 1940, the congregation purchased a triangle of land from W. P. Crow for $50. It was bordered on the north by Highway 290 and to the east by Creek Road. Although December 7, 1941, might have been a "Day of Infamy" for Americans, it was a day of triumph for the Church of Christ in Dripping Springs. On that day Paul Sorrell, Wylie Haydon, and Glenn Key signed a $500 note with the Austin National Bank. The proceeds were to be used to build their very own church on the land they had purchased. The materials were bought at cost from Calcasieu Lumber Company of Austin with Bill Dewey and Pete Turner hired as carpenters, and many others donating their time and talents to the project. It was reported in the 8-1-1941 issue of the *San Marcos Record* that work was beginning on a new Church of Christ. The 1-2-1942 edition said the building was rapidly nearing completion.

The one-room building faced east toward Creek Road. Automobiles served as classrooms for the children during good weather while the adults met inside. Bad weather forced everyone to make do within the one room that was heated by two wood stoves. Later the situation was improved by the addition of two classrooms.

When the new Highway 290 came through in the '50s, the roadway took part of the church's property on the south side. Also, the new 290 severed the old Creek Road route that had veered off alongside the western edge of the Dripping Springs

Church of Christ building, 1942
—Courtesy Grady Moore

branch. To offset some of this loss, the Church of Christ was given that portion of land on their eastern edge by the highway department that had previously been the old Creek Road. The highway department also paid to have the building moved, so that the church now faced north toward the old 290 route, now Loop 64. At this time, the "preacher's house" was attached to the church.

Another problem was brought about by change occurring in the 1950s. Prior to this time, it was normal for youngsters to stay where they were born and follow in their parents' footsteps. Since farms and ranches called for fewer and fewer workers, the young people left to go to the larger cities to make their fortunes. Worship attendance dropped, causing some lean times.

There were other turning points for the church during this span. When it was time to appoint elders and deacons, Brothers Hudson, Glenn Key, and S. J. Moore were named the first elders of the church, while Wylie Haydon, Lloyd Sorrell, and Frank Toungate became the first deacons.

Soon, though, the church experienced the same growing pains as all the other churches. Their original building was just not big enough to hold all their members comfortably. In 1968, they had a metal building constructed in the western point of their property. The old building was moved to J. N. Rippy's place on RR12 South. A brief lull in growth occurred in the 1970s when the "gasoline crisis" scared people into moving closer to their jobs. That scare was over after just a few years.

The metal building did its job for 24 years but once again it became necessary to make room for an increasing number. A decision was made to tear down the metal building, expand the existing foundation and build a much larger structure on the same site. The church set up temporary quarters in the Promenade Center and held services there until December 13, 1992. At this time the congregation came back home to new surroundings with a limestone rock edifice.

Church of Christ in Dripping Springs, 1992

Their site has become very valuable by its location, but a growing problem has been the limiting confinement of the triangle-shaped property. It is bounded on the south by Hwy. 290, the north by Loop 64 and on the east by the Dripping Springs branch ravine. With this in mind, the church has purchased property in the Meadow Oaks subdivision just west of town and plan to relocate to that spot in the future.

Preachers are chosen by the congregation. Since its early beginnings in the late 1930s, the following men have served as preachers for the Church of Christ in Dripping Springs. Some of the early first names are not remembered, but the title "Brother" goes before each name.

Boyd Hays	Showalter
R. C. Ledbetter	Westbrook
Noble	Smith
Bryant	Black
Hall	Crow
Fred Parker	Jerry Webb
Clifford Maxwell	Jim Moore
Dee Wheeler	Jim Taylor
Ernest Bradley	Kent Singleton
Norman Starling	Don Prather
Fay Starr	Carl Garner
Leathel Roberts	John Moore
Dick Still	

The Catholic Church

The Dripping Springs Catholic Church is a modern-day replica of all the other churches that have started before. They first formed and met in the available places until they could get on their feet and have their own special place to worship. It was not an easy journey but it was a persistent one. Prior to the 1950s, those of Catholic persuasion, mostly Hispanic, attended mass when they could by traveling to Austin. This was not a trip that could be made easily by the families who lived in the area.

In the late 1950s Wimberley established and built St. Mary's Catholic Church. It was built primarily to serve the needs of the many summer visitors who liked to spend time there. St. Mary's was a mission of St. Ferdinand's in Blanco. Since Wimberley was a great deal closer at 15 miles and more accessible than Austin, many of the families were active in building and maintaining St. Mary's. They were especially active with the cemetery, helping to clear the land and maintain it in return for credit toward their plots. The Garza, Picasio, Alba, Beltran, Ramirez and Salazar families were some of the early members of the parish. These families became the core of the Catholic community that has become the St. Martin de Porres parish of Dripping Springs.

In the 1960s the people gathered for an occasional home mass. The parish of record was still St. Ferdinand's in Blanco but many families traveled to Wimberley for mass. In December of 1973, a large crowd attended a mass at the home of Mr. and Mrs. Cleofas Ramirez to celebrate the feast of Our Lady of Guadalupe. Mrs. Ramirez asked the pastor, Fr. Edward Jordan, if he would come more often. Fr. Jordan agreed and for several months celebrated mass in private homes. It quickly became apparent that a larger meeting place was needed.

That first place was the old high school building located on Academy Block. The building was mostly in a period of disuse since the move to a new campus in the fall of 1949. Although the building was in serious need of repair, including many of the windows being broken out, the rental fee was just right—free. The condition was not overlooked by others. The Methodist Church which has a long history of sharing their facilities with other denominations stepped forth. Longtime members, Ennis Follis and Lorena Walker approached Mrs. Alberta Quisenberry and asked if the Catholics would like to use their small church on the corner for their meeting place. Fr. Lonnie Urban had replaced Fr. Jordan in August of 1974 and he accepted the generous offer. Each weekend the Catholics of the area gathered in the Methodist church to celebrate mass.

While the pastor from Blanco was willing to come and say mass, the Bishop had not approved Dripping Springs as a mission. In fact, Bishop Vincent Harris often chided Fr. Urban. The Bishop worried that Fr. Urban was needlessly wearing himself out with this project. He believed Dripping Springs would never have enough people for a mission church. His belief was strengthened when only eight to ten people attended mass at times. Although Fr. Urban was sometimes discouraged, he persevered.

Fr. Urban brought a mass kit with him from Blanco so the children of the parish learned quickly how to set it up. Following services, the smaller children raced to be the first to blow out the candles. In his haste, sometimes Fr. Urban forgot to check the kit supplies and ended up having to make a quick trip to the county line for wine and substituting Paula Valesquez' tortillas for communion.

Several early members of the parish deserve recognition. Raymond Garza, Sr., was the first Eucharistic minister commissioned in the parish. The gold chalice, ciborium, and patent that bear the Knights of Columbus crest were gifts by Penny Matthews in memory of her husband David. They were the last chalice and patent donated by the Knights in this area. Mrs. Matthews bought the ciborium to complete the set. When the hall was built, she paid for a three door confessional unit.

A religious education program began in 1974 with the children gathering after school at the Methodist church. Mary Anne Foster, Pat Gibson, Mary Shults, Zulema Cordova, and others picked up the children at school and delivered them to class. Paula Valesquez babysat for the preschoolers while the older children had class. There were never enough children to teach each grade separately so three or four grades had class together. The Missionary Catecists of Divine Providence from San Antonio assisted the program as often as possible. Sr. Mary Louise Barba, M.C.D.P., was a frequent member of the team and has remained a firm friend of the "persistent" Dripping Springs community. In the summer, the sisters came for two or three weeks, presenting summer programs in Dripping Springs, Blanco, and Wimberley. Often the children from Dripping Springs and Wimberley held classes together with the program alternating between the two communities.

Over the next few years, the schedule often changed with mass sometimes being conducted on Saturday evening and sometimes early Sunday morning before the Methodists needed the sanctuary. The joint use of the facility led to several ecumenical services such as Ash Wednesday, Christmas Posada, and Thanksgiving. The Catholics also helped with fundraisers and workdays to maintain the building.

Even with all this activity, Dripping Springs had still not been approved as a mission by Bishop Harris. When the Dripping Springs congregation could not afford to pay a visiting priest, mass was discontinued, as Wimberley needed the priest's attention for summer visitors. The Wimberley congregation had grown so large it was necessary to hold two services. Fr. Eugene Shepard replaced Fr. Urban on June 8, 1980, and those from Dripping Springs who were attending services at St. Mary's continued requesting that he conduct services in Dripping Springs. Fr. Shepard agreed to return as long as the attendance for mass was consistently high. The ushers diligently made the count each Sunday evening. After a few months it was evident the Catholic community was growing.

In the early 1980s membership had grown to the point that the small Methodist church could not comfortably seat all the members. Fr. Shepard saw the need for a building of their own. This meant raising money. In 1982 the first Jamaica event was held. It was renamed Fall Festival in 1998. It was held in front of John Burke's law offices which have since been replaced by the new PEC building on Hwy. 290. It was very successful. In 1983 it was moved to a vacant lot across from Mike's Restaurant. In 1982 the church purchased four acres of land in the Springwood subdivision as a church location. Mass continued to be held at the Methodist church on Sunday mornings.

In 1984 a metal building was bought and erected on the land to serve as the church hall. Original plans were to just finish the shell and do the interior as they were able to raise the funds. However, energetic members forged ahead and had the interior completed by the summer. Donations of materials and labor kept the cost low. Dan Riestenberg installed the floor tile and Leon Hernandez, the son-in-law of E. F. and Frances Garza, and his sons hung the suspended ceiling. An anonymous donor gave $10,000 that was used to buy and put up the exterior stone. Leonard Tanalski was one of the leaders in getting the building constructed. A retired Marine, he worked tirelessly on the building and bargained for low prices or donations on everything he arranged. He developed a rare liver cancer shortly after the congregation moved into the building and his funeral was the first held in the new hall.

The year 1984 was a cornerstone year in many ways. Bishop Harris finally agreed to recognize Dripping Springs as a mission church. Thanks to Fr. Shepard's devotion to St. Martin, he requested and received from the Bishop the name for the church as St. Martin de Porres Catholic Mission. The 1984 Jamaica event was held on the church grounds. Fr. Shepard designed a gazebo on wheels to hold the altar. Henry Boesl built the gazebo and it was called "Gene's Bird Cage" by Fr. Neal Wise, O.P., when he assisted at the blessing of the building on December 8, 1984. It was dismantled when Fr. Shepard left the parish. In 1984 the Missionaries of the Sacred Heart approached Bishop Harris and volunteered to take over St. Ferdinand's parish in Blanco and assume the responsibility for Wimberley, Johnson City, and Dripping Springs. In 1985 Fr. Frank Neland, MSC, became the pastor at Blanco. Wimberley became a full parish with St. Martin's as its responsibility. Fr. Neland was from Ireland as was Fr. Jeremiah Murphy, who took over in 1986 and Fr. William Barrow in 1987. The Missionaries returned the responsibility for the two parishes to the Diocese of Austin in 1990. Fr. George Tzankas became the pastor and remained so until June 1993.

Church attendance grew to the point that two masses were held each Sunday. The Religious Education program also grew from two to three children in each grade to several classes for each grade. These classes were held between masses, the younger children around tables at the Hall and the older in the DSISD Middle School. In May 1993, Bishop John McCarthy gave permission for St. Martin de Porres to become a full-fledged parish. He named Fr. George Henninger pastor. The first official parish mass was held June 12, 1993. To mark the first mass as a parish, Fr. Henninger requested bread baked by Bob Bentley, a retired member of the parish whose bread is legendary, and homemade Mustang grape wine made by Vince Taylor.

The stay of Fr. Henninger was expected to last a long time. The parish purchased a house in Sunset Canyon subdivision for his stay. Instead he received a serious neck injury on one of the rides on a youth trip to AstroWorld. The surgery plus other health ailments and the stress of a new parish caused him serious problems. This coupled with major health problems incurred by his parents, who were from Indiana, caused him to resign and move back to Indiana to take care of his parents. This left the parish without a pastor for several months. Fr. Oliver Johnson and Fr. Jerry Smith of St. Catherine's parish in Oak Hill celebrated mass each Sunday at St. Martin's until one could be assigned by the Bishop. In early 1994 Fr. James L. Evans became the pastor. Fr. Evans was an Anglican priest, converted to Roman Catholicism, and ordained a Roman Catholic priest in May 1994. He was the first Anglican rite priest serving a Roman rite parish in the world. He and his wife Mary had two grown children.

In 1989, the parish bought 24 acres between their Hall and RR12 S which included a large house with outbuildings. In 1989 they were able to sell seven acres that included the house that allowed them to pay off most of their debts. They sold the parish home in Sunset Canyon in 1994 which paid off the remaining debt and now they were ready to begin planning for a true church building. Ground was broken for the new

St. Martin de Porres Catholic Church, 1996

church on August 20, 1995. The first mass was celebrated in the new church on May 25, 1996, by Pastor Evans. On May 26, Pentecost Sunday, Fr. Evans officiated as a large class of young people received the sacrament of Confirmation.

The new sanctuary is graced with a beautiful altar and lectern hand built by long time parishioner Joseph Syring. The altar was patterned after the altar at St. Mary's Cathedral in Austin and the lectern after the one at the Episcopal seminary where Fr. Evans was first ordained. Custom designed stained glass windows were installed in the wall above the entrance to the church in September. These windows were donated by Colleen and Bob Moreau. The small window at the top is in the memory of their mothers, Helen Phelan and Grace Moreau. The lower window was their gift to each other. The larger than life, Italian hand-carved crucifix above the altar was donated by Jim Phelan in memory of his wife Helen. The white stone building with dark green trim was dedicated on November 2, 1996. Bishop McCarthy officiated and allowed the feast of the parish partron, St. Martin de Porres to be celebrated early.

The St. Martin de Porres Catholic Parish has continued to experience great growth. It now holds four masses each weekend, three in English and one in Spanish. A Knights of Columbus chapter has been founded and the church is very active in community affairs.

Pat Gibson graciously supplied the above information.

The Episcopal Church

The Episcopal Church of the Holy Spirit of Dripping Springs got its start on April 29, 1984, when it was organized by thirteen adults and three children. This meeting took place at 3:00 P.M. in the snack bar of the high school (now the DSISD Administrative building). After hearing of this meeting, two Methodist women, Lorena Walker and Jerry Lou Dodson, suggested they consider meeting in the Methodist church for their services. The congregation, led by Hunter Morris, held their services at the Methodist Church on Sundays at 3:00 P.M. until August 1985, when they bought property just off Hwy. 290, with an entrance beside the Cecil Jenkins house. They constructed several buildings over the years as their congregation grew. They purchased acreage a couple of miles east on Hwy. 290 and began the process of getting their building program started at the new site. Ground was broken on September 20, 2000. The architect for the project was Jim Polkinghorn and the main building contractor was Craig Simecheck. Their old site was purchased by the City of Dripping Springs. The city moved into part of the facility in September 2001 and shared the facilities with the church until May 19, 2002, when they held their final services at the site. Their first worship service in the new facility was May 26, 2002, and the dedication and consecration of the Episcopal Church of the Holy Spirit was held at 6:00 P.M. on Sunday, June 2, 2002. Nancy Coon is now leading the services.

Grace Worship Center

This church, behind the pastorate of Bob Milby, has remained small but steadfast in their faith since its beginning in 1984. They initially began to meet in a room at the Oakwood Plaza, located a mile south of Highway 290 on RR12 South. They met at this place until 1992 when they moved into the old Methodist church building on the corner of Hwy. 290 and RR12. The sale of this building in 1994 prompted another move, this time across the street and into a room in the Promenade Center. The rental of this room put them on the move again when they moved less than 100 yards south into another room in the Promenade Center. It was the meeting room of the Dripping Springs *Century-News* offices. In October 2002 they began meeting in one of the buildings in the City Hall complex.

Community Fellowship

The youngest of the churches, but perhaps the fastest growing has been the Dripping Springs Community Fellowship. It was established in January 1995 with Steve Smothers as its pastor. It was the result of the vision of winning all of Hays County for Christ by the Cypress Creek Church of Wimberley and its pastor Rob Campbell.

Their first place of worship was the old lumber company property located on the corner of San Marcos and Wallace streets. Growth forced the church to look for larger facilities, and in December 1997, the move was made. The A. L. Davis building, owned by the Purcell family, became available and the church leased the old hardware portion. The building is located on the corner of Mercer and College streets. Growth demanded more space again and in late 2000, the church made another move. This time they moved out of town and out of the P. A. Smith league when they chose the Stone Mountain Center, west of town on Highway 290. Recently they bought land and will build. Until then they are meeting at the Springs Fitness Center.

In 1996, DSCF joined with Cypress Creek Church to plant their first church together. It was the San Marcos Community Church, pastored by Bob Maas. In 1997 DSCF joined Cypress Creek and San Marcos Community to begin the University Church on the campus of Southwest Texas University in San Marcos. It was 1999 when DSCF established the Apostolic Advisory Team consisting of Robert Mearns, Rob Campbell, and Bob Maas. It was also in 1999 that DSCF ordained Overseers (Elders). In July 1999 DSCF established the mission church of Castillo Del Rey in Monterrey, Mexico, under the leadership of Enrique Porras. In September DSCF helped pastor Michael Meek establish Grace Community Fellowship in San Antonio.

First Baptist Church, 2003

Dripping Springs Methodist Church, 1963

Good Schools

Good schools have always been the pride of Dripping Springs as long as they have had education in the community. Today's school system had nothing on the past endeavors. It is no wonder that education stood at the forefront from the very beginning. After all, Dr. Pound was a college graduate and John Wallace was from a long line of learned educational kin. They knew the value of a good education and did their best to instill this in their families and the community. At every opportunity they were leaders in seeing that the community had an educational system. From its humble beginnings in 1860-61, the process would stumble forward, inconsistently, through no fault of the Dripping Springs people until 1880, when education began to blossom all over and Dripping Springs became the hub and envy of education people everywhere. One has to understand the history of education in Texas to understand some of the struggles the community had to go through before righting itself.

Education in Texas traveled a bumpy road in the early days of its existence. It would really not head down the right path until the 1900s. Most of the early attempts at education, with good reason, were limited to hiring private tutors, sending the students off to out-of-state schools, or to private schools within the state that were usually church-related. Because of the financial situation of the state, very few public schools were in existence.

When Texas gained its independence from Mexico, President of Texas, Mirabeau B. Lamar, gave Texas its first push into education, although it was more symbolic than real. He persuaded the Legislature to designate much of the public lands to education. His vision was to sell this land and the proceeds put into a permanent school fund for the purpose of using it to set up a public education system. Unfortunately, the price of land at the time was so low that not enough money could be generated to even get the system off the ground. However, just the thought and effort earned Lamar the title of "Father of Texas Education."

When Texas became a state in 1845, the Constitution committed at least ten percent of all state taxes to the permanent school fund. Even this did not generate enough revenue to start up the system. It would take the settlement of an old border dispute to give Texas the jumpstart it needed.

After Texas gained its independence from Mexico, it declared its borders to be the Rio Grande River to its source, which took in much of New Mexico and Oklahoma. Mexico did not agree to this. After the United States defeated Mexico in 1848, a war that Dr. Pound had fought in, Mexico agreed to the Rio Grande boundary. However, those living in the New Mexico territory did not want to be a part of Texas and protested. Finally, the Compromise of 1850 solved the problem. Texas would give up its claim to that area for ten million dollars. Five million of that went to paying off debts incurred while a Republic. Another 1.25 million went to paying off the state's debts. This left 3.75 million in the coffers. Elisha M. Pease ran for governor in 1853 and campaigned heavily on improving the educational system in Texas. After winning, he convinced the Legislature they should put two million of the reserve into the permanent school fund. The Public School program in Texas officially began January 31, 1854. The interest from the fund gave Texas its first significant amount of money for education. Governor Pease also supported the law that divided the counties into school districts and the process to select the school boards. Although Dripping Springs had no schools at the time, it fell into the confines of District #8. In 1856, the only child of school age listed for Dripping Springs was Joseph Moss, the son of John and Indiana Moss.

In the meantime, the counties received a blessing from the compromise. Because the state government was out of debt and did not need the money, it was decided to return ninety percent of the county's taxes back to the county for a period of six years. The counties, in turn, used part of this windfall to further the cause of education. Due to the scarcity of public schools, the parents were usually paid an allotment to pay the tuition to a private school for their children.

In 1860-61, several Dripping Springs children, including Carrie Wallace and Indiana Pound, became of school age. It is said that Dr. Pound hired a tutor to teach the children at his place. This educational process was interrupted when the Civil War erupted in 1861. Texas joined the Confederacy and Dr. Pound joined the Confederate Army. Many adults signed up and the others left behind, both young and old, had to put their minds to supporting the cause and taking care of business on the homefront, so education had to take a hiatus.

After the war ended in 1865, the southern states thought things would get back to normal and return to pre-war days, sans slavery. And it might well have if the Confederate states had accepted their situation. The Texas Legislature met and amended the 1845 Constitution to receive acceptance by the federal government. In August of 1866, President Johnson declared Reconstruction ended. The elected Texas legislators refused to ratify the 13th, 14th, and 15th amendments to the U.S. Constitution which abolished slavery and made them citizens. They proceeded to pass "labor laws" with the purpose of keeping the freed Negroes enslaved.

These actions by Texas and the other southern states infuriated the northern legislators who had already thought the punishment was too light. After the November elections, supporters of a harsher policy were elected throughout the northern states and they came to Congress loaded with venom. They refused to allow southern legislators to be seated and set up a Reconstruction Plan that would have the army as the basic unit of control. General Philip Sheridan was in charge of District five, which included Texas and Louisiana. At first they tried to leave the elected officials in place to carry out day-to-day activities. When this did not work out, General Sheridan dismissed all the government officials and appointed others in their place to serve until a new constitution could be written and ratified.

Meanwhile, back to Dripping Springs education. There was still the possibility that private tutors were brought in. There were reports that what formal education was taking place was administered by the military. School terms, in those days, seldom lasted more than four months and many times less. Children were needed to help on the farms from March to November. So mostly you went to school during the winter months and the weather dictated how much.

The new constitution was ratified in 1869 and on April 16, 1870, Reconstruction was declared over. Again. This constitution treated education quite favorably. It set up a system of free public education with compulsory attendance and a state superintendent to set minimum standards and norms. It also included the first adequate financial backing for schools for all races.

One article I read claimed the people of Dripping Springs purchased land in 1869 and built a school. I found no deed to verify this claim. However, in the 1870 census, taken in August, it listed the occupation of Carrie Wallace, 16, as teaching school. This would seem to indicate that some type of school was taking place. Also, in a deed dated August 12, 1874, Hays County paid John L. Wallace, W. T. and Martha Ann Chapman $42.49 for benches and desks for the school, which probably indicates the year it was built. It was given as District #2 and the trustees were J. R. Brown, Jacob Roberts, and John J. Chapman.

On another occasion while visiting Galen Dodson, I noticed a couple of big flat rocks under the oak tree that was a part of the Academy block. I asked him about them and he said that Mary Spaw had answered his same query by saying it was once the site of an old school. It might explain how W. T. Chapman chose the Academy block for the new school—because one was already on the property. More proof of that theory came in an article written by Robert Lee Marshall and published in the July 4, 1947, edition of the *San Marcos Record*. In it he said that while the Dripping Springs Academy was being built, classes were held in the one-room school and the school president's living room.

The article claimed the school was built by W. T. Chapman next to his store. If the school was built in 1874, then it is probably true. Given the location of the school, I'm not so sure about the store part. Robert Lee Marshall's article pointed out that Chapman taught school in Dripping Springs and other evidence verifies that Chapman taught in the early '70s. He married the Marshall widow in 1872 and did not open up a store until the mid '70s. He was not included in the 1870 census. I'm not sure where that store was located, maybe across from his house where the Church of Christ now stands.

Although the Constitution of 1869 was a step in the right direction for education, the reality was not. Governor Davis, a Republican, was opposed strongly because he pushed for the law to be extended equally to all races as the Constitution called for. He was elected for four years but in the 1872 elections he lost his Republican majority in the legislature and his last two years were tough, to say the least.

Democrat Richard Coke defeated Davis in 1874 and that sounded the death knell for financial support for education for years to come. Many believed the state could not afford it and did not believe in the state providing education. To top it all off, the Democrats did not like the 1869 Constitution because of the powers put in there by Republicans. The result was another constitutional convention and the Constitution of 1876, which placed limitations on state aid for education. Compulsory attendance and a central control of standards were left out completely. It did provide for local school districts but did not give them the power to tax, which meant having no money to finance the districts. Most of the money came from county school funds. In 1878, Governor O. M. Roberts even vetoed a small appropriations bill for education on the grounds that the state could not afford it. Due to the uncertainty of finances in this 1878 decision, many schools were encouraged to delay the start of their school until January when they would know for sure how much money they would have to operate on. It is little wonder that communities turned to private schools, again mostly church-related, for their educational needs.

The Constitution of 1876 did set up the Free Public School System in Texas. Under this system, Dripping Springs established a school on December 12, 1876, with 29 pupils. This was Hays County School District #10. The trustees were J. L. Wallace, A. L. Davis, Sr., and W. T. Chapman. In an 1876-77 financial record book for Hays County listing drafts approved for teaching, there was an entry that W. L. Armstrong was paid $30 on 2-10-1877 and $33.80 on 4-3-1877 for District #10. Since there was no record of a school being built, it is assumed the school that was already in operation continued to serve the purpose. In the fall of 1879, Dripping Springs received $121.50 from the county school fund.

Another turning point in education for Dripping Springs occurred in 1880. The Methodists built a church adjacent to what is now the Phillips Cemetery. In September they opened the Walnut Springs Academy and had the first ten-month school in the area. Horace Rowe was the teacher. Even though someone burned it to the ground in February 1881, it was quickly rebuilt and education continued. In the meantime, W. M. Jordan came to Dripping Springs to visit with some of his relatives. He was an educator and evangelist. He had been a student at Howard College, Alabama, and then presided over the Baptist College at Emminence, Kentucky. He was also a great organizer. Upon seeing the opportunities for having a private school in Dripping Springs, he talked with the community leaders and got them excited about establishing the Dripping Springs Academy. Plans were made in 1881 to do just that.

The Academy was to be basically a Baptist enterprise. Their church was burned to the ground in 1879 and they did not have a new church building. This new building to be erected was also to serve as their chapel. Others in the community were equally interested in having a good school. It would mean the end to the little Dripping Springs public school. It had survived an arsonist's attempt in 1880, but could not withstand competition. W. T. Chapman, a local merchant and land owner, got the ball rolling by donating a tract of land 275x290 feet and designating it the Academy Block. It was decided to build a three-room stone edifice that would cost approximately $4,000. Many locals were active in its construction by donating their time and talents. Dr. J. M Pound allowed some of his patients to pay off their debts to him by working on the project. The main room was to be 30x50 and to double as the chapel. Two wings on the east and west sides were to be 30x30, which gave it the form of a cross. According to an article written by Robert Lee Marshall, when the money and volunteer help was slow to come around as fast as expected, it was decided to build only the east wing. There was supposed to be a music room attached but nowhere have I found that another room was attached to the school for that purpose. Possibly the little school in the northeast corner sufficed because the Academy, indeed, was noted for its music programs.

The celebration associated with the laying of the cornerstone was the talk of the county. Four Masonic Lodges were called on to perform the task on August 6, 1881. The four were San Marcos, Mountain City, Onion Creek, and Rambo Lodge, then of Friendship Church, but later to be in Dripping Springs. Felix E. Smith of Onion Creek was appointed as acting Grand Master, Ed J. L. Green as the Grand Marshall. After laying the cornerstone, Judge Ed R. Kone introduced the orator of the day, Judge G. W. Walters of San Marcos. Then dinner was served with a grand barbeque that included roasted pigs, mutton, kids (baby goats), and beef. The reporter estimated the crowd to be 700 while another letter writer guessed 500. It was a large crowd for a happening in Dripping Springs. Elder W. M. Jordan was the after dinner speaker. Some of the more active people there were Dr. Pound, W. T. Chapman, John

L. Wallace, Jesse McLendon, Captain McLendon, Ed Womack, Davis Gibson, and county commissioner Peter Schmidt.

I always thought that the cornerstone was the first stone to be laid in a new building. An article I read had the cornerstone ceremony after the building was completed. This confused me, so I went to John Hudson for an answer. John is a longtime member of the Masons. He explained that particularly in the days when the Masons were in charge of constructing the buildings, the cornerstone was indeed the first stone laid. Today that is not always the case. He said that any time Masons are in charge of laying the cornerstone, it will be positioned in the northeast corner of the building. We were at the Academy building at the time and he took me around to the northeast corner. Sure enough, there was the stone with the Masonic emblem and several dates that he explained would be on each stone. The wear and tear of the weather on the 120 year old building has worn away a clear picture of how it was when first laid by the Masons that August day, but clearly it is the cornerstone.

The building was completed sometime around the middle of January. The first session for the Dripping Springs Academy began in January for Professor Jordan and his assistant, Miss Lizzie Morrell, the daughter of the famous Baptist preacher, R. N. Morrell, who attended the dedication of the chapel. Until the building was completed, the high school department held classes in the living room of Jordan's two-story house located where the John Spaw house now stands just east of the campus. That first session sixty-four students attended the Academy. Along with students from Dripping Springs, others came from Blanco and Gillespie counties and some from Waco University.

That very first session closed on May 31, 1882. The finals were thus. On Monday, the 29th, the morning session covered geography. One at a time, in the form of a lecture, the students exhausted a topic and then closed with a critical class exam. Monday evening was devoted to elocution. There were three lectures on the topics of posture, gesture, and rudiments followed by select readings. Tuesday was spent examining arithmetic, in the same manner as the previous day. Wednesday morning was devoted to English grammar. In the evening, there were lectures on Latin and Greek followed by a test on German to end the exams.

The next school year, the Walnut Springs Academy received $94.60 as their apportionment from the school fund and the Dripping Springs Academy $262.30. Mr. Rowe was still the teacher at Walnut Springs and Mr. Jordan and Miss Morrell at the Academy. Mrs. Jordan was the music teacher. The Academy had 99 students attend the first session with about sixty of those from Dripping Springs. One hundred and thirty attended the second session. A reporter attending the commencement exercises estimated that 700 people could be seated in the two-room Academy. That seems to be an overexaggeration to me.

Several changes to education and Dripping Springs took place in 1883. Because of the constant clamor by pro-education people, an amendment to the Texas constitution was offered and passed by the voters. It allowed local school districts to tax and an increase in the state's school appropriations was made. Another change was the resignation of W. M Jordan in August. He took a job teaching in Kyle. This left the Academy without a teacher less than a month before school was to begin.

The Academy was first organized with a military curriculum as part of its offerings. In the summer of 1883, Mr. Jordan's 19-year old son was accidentally killed in a mock battle. Some say this was the reason he left and it may well have been. However, he may have been one of those strong-willed individuals who liked to start things but not hang around long after getting it off the ground. He got crossways with the school in Kyle and moved on to Lockhart after a two-year stint to found the Jordan Institute there. However, he did return in the late 1890s where he would found a school to teach high school subjects according to a newspaper report with Chapman and A. L. Davis, his trustees. His school is believed to be in the second story of the A. L. Davis store.

Marshall's article put much credence to the dispondence theory over his son's death. However, he mentioned that Jordan had met opposition from the beginning on this project and this weighed on him as well. One article I read had said the failure of the Methodists to buy in on the plan was a problem. The Methodists continued to operate their school at Walnut Springs.

The military curriculum was dropped from the school and religious classes were added in its place. Also, W. T. Chapman deeded the Academy Block over to the Pedernales Baptist Association in late 1883. The stipulation was that if the school were to stop its religious curriculum, then the property would revert to the Dripping Springs First Baptist Church. The decision was made to have Professor Martin, a young man who had served on the faculty the previous year, take over the Academy until a corp of teachers could be hired. The first was Miss Etta Dibblee from the eastern part of Texas. There is a little confusion. In another article, a teacher named Miss Eddie Callahan of Mineola, Texas was listed as one of the teachers, who came aboard in October. Whether these are the same people and the writers misspelled names is possible. However, in another article down the line, a Miss Etta Dibble was said as returning. It is known that in January 1884, Mr. R. G. Horsley took over the reins as the principal of the Academy. His wife became the music teacher.

Walnut Springs Academy received $102.60 for their 19 students while the Dripping Springs Academy received $367.20 for its 68. The Academy enrolled seventy students to begin with and they expected another fifteen in October. This was probably the last year the Walnut Springs Academy held classes.

The Academy was growing and plans to meet that growth were being made. A third room was being planned so that the school could accommodate up to 200 students. That would not take place for another year. A third teacher, Mrs. Graves, had been hired. Over 130 students were enrolled in the fall session of 1884. Professor Lincoln was the music teacher. Present day teachers, with good reason, complain when their classes reach twenty students. It appears by the figures we have seen in the first few years that the early teachers were over burdened with students and we wonder how they did it. I'm pretty sure they made use of student assistants to alleviate part of this burden. Mostly, I suspect, they had good discipline and controlled the numbers by teaching one group a lesson while another was doing an assignment.

Professor Horsley was ably assisted by Mr. Bell and Miss Branch for the 1885-86 school year. The school had more than 150 pupils enrolled for the first session. By the end of 1885, the wooden wing attached to the west wall of the Academy had been completed. It was expected to hold an additional eighty pupils. In the fall of 1886, Drippings Springs was listed as District #10 and had received $664.20 as their apportionment. This was all a part of the reorganization act of 1884. It re-established the state central office for minimum standards, set up districts, and election of trustees. This was the beginning of a modern public free school system in Texas, although it did not take hold until later in the twentieth century.

Mr. Horsley remained as the principal for the 1886-87 school year. The apportionment remained at $664.20. A Miss Dunn was his assistant and probably Mr. Bell. Their combined salaries were $150 a month. The school term lasted from November through February. B. R. Wilhite was paid $20 for wood. The school had 130 enrolled in the first session. After this year, Mr. Horsley and family moved to Queen City. Professor J. E. Cook took the reins for the 1887-88 school year. Miss Minnie C. Cook and Mrs. Caperton were teachers, too. Appropiation by the county was $674.40. Cook and Caperton received a total of $105 a month. The school year lasted from November through March. Approximately 100 students attended the fall term. B. R. Wilhite was paid $11.50 for wood and J. E. Bell another $7.50 for wood.

Cook stayed another year. This time he was assisted by a Miss Hamilton for a month or two. The county appropriation was $387 for 86 students. Cook was paid $75 a month for November through March. J. E. Bell was paid $12.50 for wood.

The year 1889-90 had Dripping Springs receiving $432.45 for 73 students. J. P. Collier was now in charge and received $75 a month while his assistant, Florence Ligon, took home $30 a month. School was in session November through February. The wood bill was $22.95 and paid to A. L. Davis. It was a year that narrowly escaped major disaster for the school. In early November, the stove pipe coming out of the tin roof caught fire and if not for the quick action of two students, would have probably burned down or been severely damaged. Wayne Weaver and Chester Harrison were able to get the fire out without incident. It was reported the tin was red hot for several feet around. It helped that it was also drizzling outside that day.

A. L. Stubbs took over the head job for the 1890-91 school year for $65 a month. Miss Branch L. Phillips was paid $35 and later Mrs. Sallie McLendon finished up the last two months at $30 per. The county's appropriation was $500. This was the last year that Dripping Springs was school District #10.

Although the law allowing for school districts and the right to tax for revenue had been on the books since 1883, the Dripping Springs Academy had not used it. One reason was that they were a boarding school and had access to some funds, plus the county appropriated funds to each school based on local students. The issue of church and state was broached as to state money going to church schools. The Academy was owned and operated by the Baptists. A judge ruled that it violated the principal of church and state to give schools appropriations that taught religion as part of their curriculum.

Actually, a newspaper article written in 1887 had said that the Academy was a part of the Free Public School system. The Academy, like other tuition schools, used the county's funds for running a public school. Although the Academy's year ran from September through May, the free-for-local-students classes were usually from November to February or March, depending on appropriations. The rest of the year had to be paid for by the parents. Evidently, many parents did not go beyond the free classes. One newspaper article bemoaned the fact that parents were not paying for their kids to go the full term.

As early as June 1889, the district school system was discussed after the election of trustees for the coming year. On May 15, 1891, Dripping Springs had met the requirements and was designated District #20 in the Hays County school system. In December, S. D. Gilpin, the local druggist, petitioned the Hays Commissioners' Court to set an election to determine whether or not the people of School District #20 were for levying a 20-cent tax on each $100 evaluation for school purposes. The request was granted and the election set for January 4, 1892. The issue passed 33-10.

Mr. Stubbs got a $10 a month raise for the 1891-92 school year. His teaching partner, R. L. Marshall received $50 a month. The salaries covered the months of November, December, and January. The county appropriated $433.30. The county's ante was up to $646.19 for 1892-93. The school year stretched from November to March. It was a new faculty headed up by J. H. Bishop. His assistant was Dorothy Folts and together they were paid $112.50 a month with Bishop probably taking $65-75 of that. Annie Cavett entered the picture in January at $25 a month. A. Z. Oldham was paid $8.45 for his assistance in November.

The total appropriation for the school year 1893-94 was up to $667.88. This included some repair work and wood. Again, the school year ran from November through early April. H. P. Tidd was now in charge. He and an assistant, possibly Annie Cavett, received a total of $110 per month. C. S. Graham received a total of $39.03 for repairs and A. L. Davis was paid $18.85 for wood.

According to an article written by Lucy Black Martin, the teachers for the 1897-98 school year were Professor Oscar Stubbs, Miss Nannie Dorroh, and Annie Cavett. Mr. Jordan returned to Dripping Springs in 1897. At that time, the school system was not graded. Jordan set up a private high school with A. L. Davis, Jr., and W. T. Chapman acting as his trustees, and began advertising for students. He taught at least two years, possibly more. It is not known where he held his classes. It could have been in the upper story of the Davis merchantile building.

For the 1905-06 school year, Dripping Springs became a graded school. They published a pamphlet extolling the greatness of the school and all the rules and expectations. A. B. Corder was the principal and handled the high school classes. Mrs. Georgia Cavett was in charge of the intermediate grades and Miss Madie Sorrell, the primary. The Baptist church said this was the year they turned the property over to the county public school system. There was no deed transfer recorded to substantiate the claim, and the transfer did not take place until March 28, 1921.

For the 1910-11 school year, the Dripping Springs Public School published their first annual catalog. In it they mentioned that the school system dropped the high school grades in the past five years for lack of interest in school affairs. They vowed that this next year would be the best in history. Mrs. Georgia Cavett remained with the system and was in charge of the Primary department. They hired Miss Lizzie Garrett to head up the Intermediate department.

Sidney R. Saunders was hired as the superintendent and taught English, science, Latin, general history, and higher mathematics. The outlined curriculum provided for only seven grades. They must have carried through with their promise. In the County Board minutes of October 2, 1911, Dripping Springs was classified as a high school of the third class. On November 29, 1920, the County Board decided to classify all schools in the county as either elementary or grammar, depending on the number of grades taught. There were a few exceptions. Among them was Dripping Springs. It was credited with three years of high school work. Each year after that, the County Board classified Dripping Springs as a high school with three grades. However, that usually meant that if one wanted to go on to college, they had to attend another school for an extra year to qualify for entrance.

Dripping Springs #20 had been established for 1891-92 school year. In 1911, the 34th Texas Legislature passed Article 2817, Revised Statutes of Texas, and in accordance with Chapter 36. This legislation set up the procedure for re-establishing and redefining school district boundaries. On April 10, 1916, the Hays County School Trustees met and approved the district. At that time District #20 covered $30^{17}/_{32}$ square miles. The district would not meet that definition for much longer. On March 3, 1917, the County Board ordered all of John Gibson's land to be transferred from Dripping Springs #20 to District #31, Darden Hill. This was the beginning of changes in the boundaries of the Dripping Springs school district.

By the time the school district had bought the Academy property in 1921, the old original two-room rock building with the wooden room attached on the west was in need of repairs. Throughout the history of this building, there were articles in the paper reporting community fundraisers for the purpose of repairing the school house. These were in the form of ice cream socials, suppers, contests, etc. In 1906, they were raising funds for a dual purpose. Not only did the building need repairs but the community was raising money to build a big rock water tank, a windmill and a trough for watering horses. This was built in the southwest corner of the campus and used until the mid-'20s. It was decided to tear down the wooden portion of the school and add a second story. This was done beginning in the summer of 1921.

While the school building was being renovated during the school year of 1921-22, the students attended classes in the old Applewhite store and the courthouse building, plus possibly some others. To help pay for this, a bond issue needed to be passed. The bond issue was for $3,000 and the election was held in June 1921. It was defeated 50-42. The County Commissioners were asked to set another election date. This time the bond was for $4,000. This time the election was held on November 21, 1921. It was defeated 46-43. Undaunted, the school went back to the commissioners for another $4,000 bond election. They set the date for February 11, 1922. They must have worked a little harder because they certainly got more voters out as it passed 75-62. Now the second story, which had been completed by this time, could be paid for and this district would be out of debt. This included the stairs on the west side. Another set of stairs was on the northeast corner of the building for emergency exits.

History would be repeated during the school term of 2001-02. The Primary School was closed down for extensive renovations due to the discovery of mold. The students in grades K-3 were farmed out to four different locations around Dripping Springs, including the First Baptist Church and the First United Methodist Church.

The school population in the 1920s mostly hovered just above the century mark The high mark was 115 in 1921-22 and the low mark was 82 in 1923-24. In those days, it was not uncommon for students to transfer to and from any of the common school districts. In most years, Dripping Springs would receive more transfers in than out. Some of the growth in the 1930s was the result of increasing the school district by consolidation but mostly it came from a ruling in 1929. On August 5, 1929, the County Board decided to divide the Common School Districts of the County into three high school units and Dripping Springs was one of those. That meant the schools designated in the Dripping Springs unit would send their students to Dripping Springs after going as far as their school taught. Bell Springs, Darden Hill, Driftwood, Henly, Millseat, Mt. Gainer, Salem, and Union (Fitzhugh) were assigned to Dripping Springs. Until 1929, the required entry age for a student was seven years of age. Beginning in 1929, the Texas school system lowered the required school entry age from seven to six. Any student who attained the age of six prior to the first of September must enroll in school. This made easing into the twelve-grade system a little easier a few years later.

Most schools in the county were classified as Common School Districts. This meant they were under the control of a County Superintendent and County School Trustees. Each school was under the charge of Common School Trustees as well. In 1934, the first of fourteen districts, Glenn Common School District #13, agreed to consolidate with Dripping Springs. This occurred by the County Board's action on May 12, 1934. Because it met the requirements of the 1925 law passed by the State Legislature, the consolidation gave Dripping Springs the designation of a Rural High School District.

By 1935, the trustees were trying to figure out what they needed to do to accomodate the growth. They decided to purchase 35 acres from the Chapman heirs on December 20, 1935, with the idea of moving the school to the new site. Had this plan reached fruition, the new school would have been built on land bordered on the east by the Dripping Springs Branch, on the south by Creek Road, on the north by the old

Johnson City Road up to the Lewis Jennings acreage and the west line was from JC Road straight across to the Creek Road. There must have been some discussion about moving and a change of heart. The new school site was not used. It was later sold in two parcels to W. P. Crow in 1938 and 1940.

The decision was made to build a high school addition just west of the Academy building, still on Academy Block. They bought block three of the second addition in 1931 and then purchased block five, second addition in 1938 to add space to the campus. A $4,000 bond election for the purpose of constructing a stone building was held. It passed 34-5. The work on the building was under the auspices of the Works Progress Administration (WPA). It began about October 25, 1938, and was completed in time to open the 1939-40 school year.

The 46x88 foot rock building had four classrooms and included an auditorium with a stage. Wallace and Young Lumber of Kyle got the contract. Work was done by season laborers and was superintended by Mr. Gengston of Round Rock and W. R. Robbins of Dripping Springs. The present building was remodeled as well. The total cost was $10,380. The new school was dedicated to the memory of Allen Stephenson, a 15-year-old student, who died on May 2, 1938, from complications from a broken leg received in a baseball game.

The 1940s really brought a lot of changes to the school system. The first was in the school structure. Dripping Springs started thinking about going to the four-grade high school. At the County Board meeting held on May 27, 1939, the Deputy State Superintendent, M. B. Brown explained what it would take: (1) It must have 60 students; (2) It must have seven teachers; and (3) Have $500,000 in taxable property. In the August 6, 1940, County Board meeting, the Deputy State Superintendent, Alex Dickie, discussed the possibilities of a Rural High School in Dripping Springs.

Dripping Springs reached its goal in 1941. At the County Board meeting on May 16, 1941, Dripping Springs was classified a 12-grade school. In fact, all schools in the county went to 12 grades, but so slim was the margin for going to 12 for Dripping Springs, the County Board had to rescind its approval for the three Stubbs children to transfer to Buda. It was found that the loss of these three students would cripple Dripping Springs' chance to get the extra teacher they needed for affiliation.

They opened the 1941-42 school year with over 150 students. To do this they contracted with Mt. Gainer to send their high school students and teacher, G. C. Herring, to Dripping Springs. This gave them the seventh teacher they needed to qualify. As part of the affiliation the school had to put a new pump on the well and plans were made and met to raise the necessary funds. They got what they wanted when they brought their application before the County Board for classification and affiliation. It was adopted on January 31, 1942. By April 16, 1943, the school received notice that it had been given full affiliation and credit for 19 subjects carried by the high school.

Consolidation was the next big movement in the 1940s. On April 17, 1943, an election was held to consolidate the common school districts of Darden Hill, Union, Millseat and Mt. Gainer with Dripping Springs. The total vote was 131-25 for. Each school district had to approve before it was official. Darden Hill, Union, and Millseat approved but Mt. Gainer's vote was 23-23, so they did not make it on this vote. The County Board made it official at their meeting April 30, 1943. This meant a new school board had to be appointed for the newly formed Dripping Springs District #20. The Board appointed Lewis E. Gage, C. W. Spillar, F. C. Thielepape (DS), B. T. Crumley (Union), Jesse Langston (Darden Hill), and Roy Breed (Millseat). A couple of months later, R. T. Hadley was appointed to fill out the board. The district voted 52-0 on April 1, 1944, to increase the school tax to 62 cents and 54-1 to assume the $4,900 bonded indebtedness of the districts.

Land transfers to the Dripping Springs district were taking place even before the above consolidation vote. On September 13, 1941, the Board granted the following lands to be transferred to Dripping Springs. The Glenn Key Ranch and E. E. Townes Ranch were to be transferred from the Union and Salem districts. J. L. Smith's 267.5 acres and Willie Tschoepe's 192 were approved. All the lands of the T. R. Jackson survey belonging to McCarty, Duval, Garrett Black Estate, Eppler and 245 acres belonging to William Glosson on west side of Gatlin Creek were transferred from Driftwood to Dripping Springs.

On March 3, 1942, Dripping Springs added to its property when it bought all but Lots 1, 2, and 12 in block one and all of block two from Mrs. Erlene McLendon Davis. This property was just southeast of the campus and became the location of the football field for the Tiger football team that was inaugurated in 1938. This land had always been the location of the community sports field.

On August 14, 1943, the Board approved the transfer of Neal McNair's 305 acres and Tom Beauchamp's 740 acres from the Henly district. On October 29, the Puryear land from Bell Springs and the D. C. Foster land from Salem were transferred. They all wanted the advantages afforded by the quality Dripping Springs school system.

Consolidation continued. Another election with Mt. Gainer #28 was held on August 19, 1944. Dripping Springs agreed 53-0 and this time so did Mt. Gainer, 19-3. On August 26, 1944, Dripping Springs voted 66-0 to accept Hamilton Pool #69 into the fold. Hamilton Pool was in Travis County, making Dripping Springs a County Line District. On March 3, 1945, the County School Board was authorized to form the Dripping Springs Rural High School District by grouping Dripping Springs, Salem, and Bell Springs together. In the election Dripping Springs approved 78-0, while Salem and Bell Springs disapproved by 11-0 and 10-0 votes. Since all the votes were counted in the overall total, the DS vote gave the majority to designation.

Earlier in the 1930s, a well was dug just north of the northeast corner of the building. Now a rock pumphouse shelters the well. At first, the drinking water was gotten from an old prime pump that took two people to operate to get a cool drink of water. One had to pump while the other drank. Later in the 1940s, a rock water fountain was built just west of the Academy between the two buildings. This was a much better arrangement. A lot of horseplay took place around it as well. Until the last paving job between the buildings, the base of this water fountain could still be seen.

After Hamilton Pool was annexed, the school building was torn down and the materials used to build the first cafeteria at the school. Previously, the cafeteria was located in the southeast corner of the bottom floor of the Academy but the space was needed for classrooms. In 1946, a bus shed was built

Water fountain

Dosia Hohman, Lillian Whisenant, and Opal Hadley in the Dripping Springs Cafeteria, 1942

Ola Butler, Ottie Langston, and Dosia Hohman in the Dripping Springs Cafeteria, 1946

just north of the well and a shower room was added for the athletes. The materials to do so came from two rooms of the Mt. Gainer school. The old slab is still there today.

Another addition to the campus occurred in March of 1941. Until that time the campus was unprotected and the improvement of Mercer Street to become part of the main highway and the faster traffic that traveled it made it a dangerous situation for the students. The citizens of Dripping Springs began to raise funds to erect a seven-foot ornamental fence between the campus and the main highway. It was expected to be completed in a short while and would add much to the appearance of the school ground. The basketball court was removed and two volleyball and two tennis courts added. The equipment was donated by the PTA. The State Highway Department donated enough wire to enclose the entire grounds.

With all the consolidation came continued growth. Growth that left the campus sadly lacking in space. Once again the school began to look for property to build a new campus. They found the property they wanted just across the Dripping Springs Branch. On June 27, 1947, the school district sold their land holdings in blocks one and two to James and Flemmie Felps, and used this money to purchase an eleven-acre tract from J. W. Wilson, Sr. This transaction took place on July 19, 1947. The football team used the old field for the 1947 season and then played the 1948 season on the new campus, even before any other buildings were erected. Also in late June 1947, Dripping Springs had contracted to take the Bee Caves students into the school system. This affected 50 students and gave Dripping Springs 310 students and 11 teachers.

Dripping Springs began proposing the formation of a rural high school district that included the Johnson Common School District #52 of Travis County. An election was called for on 4-1-1948 and passed. On 4-5-1948, the County School Board approved the County Line school district and named new trustees for the newly formed district. They included F. C. Thielepape, S. J. Moore, M. Z. Piland, T. C. Anderson, B. J. Reimers, Glenn Key, and Douglas C. Foster.

A bond election was held on May 18, 1948, and passed. A new plant on the new site would be built. It included nine classrooms, a library, and indoor restrooms on both ends. John Lynn Scott would be the architect and S. J. Moore, the foreman. The cornerstone to the new school was laid with appropriate ceremony on November 1. It was expected to be finished in late January. Again, local labor was utilized to construct the cinder block, flat-roofed structure. In the fall of 1949, the school was ready for occupancy and classes were held in the new

Dripping Springs School, 1939

school for the first time. In May 1949, Deputy State Superintendent of Schools, W. T. Leftland visited the school and approved more high school credits. Commercial law, first year homemaking, health, and P.E. were the additions. He praised the community for their modern school plant and the P.E. upgrade.

Changes took place on the old Academy campus as well. The school district sold an 85x100 foot lot located in the southwest corner to S. B. Glosson on March 7, 1950, for $1,062.50 and the 100x100 feet from the southeast corner to Lester Brenizer for $2,000. Glosson's purchase, whether he already had plans or not, was a good one. In November 1951, the two-story A. L. Davis building, where he had his grocery store, was burned to the ground. He built a cinder block building to house his grocery store. It was ready for business one year later.

Glosson was not the only one who had to make changes after the fire. The second story was the meeting place for the Rambo Masonic Lodge. When it was decided to not rebuild the second story, the Masons had to find another meeting place. To keep their history of meeting in a second story building, they turned their eyes to the old Academy building. A deal was cut on July 19, 1952. They paid the school district $3,000 for it and it has been their home ever since. The school kept the old high school building and blocks three and five of the second addition. Since the new campus did not have a gym or auditorium, the old building served the district for graduation exercises and other school functions for the next few years. After that, for most of the next twenty years, the building was mostly unused for school purposes, although it was used by the community for meetings and elections.

On September 23, 1952, the district purchased two more tracts of land from J. W. Wilson. The bigger block butted up against the northern boundary of the 11-acre tract and stretched 600 feet to the north. The east-west line matched the 682 feet of the original. The second tract was a 50x550 foot strip along the east line of the original purchase, beginning at the northeast corner. This added an additional 10.03 acres to the campus.

Additions to the new campus started almost immediately. Lights to the football field were added in 1949, but no bleachers. The community sold bonds and had other fundraisers to finance the installation of the lights. Since the new school did not include a cafeteria, the wooden building from the old campus was moved over for that purpose. It was located just off the northeast corner of the school. It later sufficed as a first grade room, a music room, and then even later, it was moved up to the northern end of the campus and converted into living quarters for school custodians. After serving as a storage building, it was torn down. In 1950, an army barracks was moved onto the campus and placed on the north side of the school. It served as the vocational agriculture building until 1970, when it was used as a band hall until 1972. It was torn down to make room for the library, science and homemaking wing in 1972. Only the slab remains.

Another milestone for the school system occurred in 1950. The 51st Texas Legislature passed House Bill 439 that set out rules for schools converting from rural high school districts to independent school districts. On February 18, 1950, the voters of the district were asked to determine what they wanted to do. The vote was 73-58 in favor of converting. The Commissioners' Court of Hays County considered the results and formally declared that Dripping Springs would now become the Dripping Springs Independent School District and defined the boundaries. It meant DSISD would now be accredited and its graduates could now enter college without having to take entrance exams or more classes elsewhere. This designation had another effect. On September 1, 1951, the Bee Cave District, which also included the former districts of Johnson, Teck, and Haynie Flat in Travis County, voted to consolidate with Dripping Springs. This completed the fourteen-district consolidation and enlarged the DSISD district to 360 square miles.

In 1952, two needed additions were completed—a cafeteria and auditorium-gymnasium. In April of that year, the Dripping Springs voters passed a $67,000 bond election for that purpose by 104-10. These two were attached to the northwest portion of the main building. Dripping Springs had played basketball over three decades but never had an indoor gym of its own. The gym was dedicated to Dr. E. P. Shelton on December 23, 1952. The County Attorney of Travis County, Les Procter, was the principal speaker. Major Horace Shelton, brother of Dr. Shelton, was in attendance as well as the County Treasurer of Travis County, Steve Heffington, a lifelong friend. A future U.S. president, then U.S. Senator, Lyndon B. Johnson jumped up on the stage and made an impromptu speech.

A boys' basketball tourney was held in the Dripping Springs gym in early January and the Tiger boys were triumphant. In 1955, permanent bleachers were built on the east side of the football field.

The baseball team played their games on a field located at the north end of the campus. On May 25, 1957, the school district purchased another small strip of land along the west boundary where the football field was located. This strip became the backstop and infield for the baseball field. The football field served as the outfield. Lights were put up and baseball was played there beginning with the 1958 season. It later served as a girls softball field until it was razed in the summer of 1998 to make room for a new Intermediate School on that campus. Also in 1958, a classroom, girls dressing room, an equipment storage room, and coaches offices were built onto the west end of the gym.

Previously, the girls had used the dressing room on the northeast corner of the gym. The boys dressed in a cellar room under the stage area, nicknamed "The Dungeon," with the shower room on the northwest corner of the gym. A classroom and administrative offices were added to the south side of the gym entrance, giving the school a covered lobby entrance to the gym, cafeteria, offices, and restrooms.

The school board voted on August 4, 1961, to build a science room that would attach to the north side of the

Dripping Springs High School, 1953

original science room. L. B. Jennings was given the contract and forty-five days to build it.

Next it was determined that a new elementary wing needed to be added. A $140,000 bond election was held on May 18, 1963. It passed 87-57. The result was a brick wing that included a much larger cafeteria, restrooms, and six classrooms. It was completed in April 1964. In 1966, four more classrooms and restrooms were added to the east end of the elementary wing. In 1967, Mr. Bradley Davis and the Student Council decided their school project would be to construct a victory bell tower at the entrance to the campus. The bell came from the old Academy building. (Its story will be told later.) The idea was to ring the bell whenever Dripping Springs won a game or some other important event. It also served as a memorial to two Dripping Springs students who were killed in the Vietnam War. The tower was dismantled in 1997. It was expected the bell and memorial plaque would end up at the high school but there was a change of plans. Instead, a new bell tower was constructed about thirty yards south of the old one at the old high school site. The old high school site became the district administrative office building in the fall of 2000.

Metal buildings became the vogue beginning in 1970 when the new agricultural building was erected, running parallel to the east side of the football field. The building included three classrooms and the shop area. In 1971, the old football bleachers were made portable and became the bleachers for the visitors on the west side during the season and then moved to the rodeo pens for the FFA rodeo. New 800-seat capacity stands for the home team Tiger fans, complete with a new pressbox, replaced them. In an ironic twist of fate, the home stands were moved to the new campus football field in 1985 and became visitors' seating. Meanwhile, the old original bleachers were brought back to life. In 1987, when the decision was made to move the middle school games back to their campus and the old football field, this set of bleachers was made permanent again on the home team side. Finally, they were torn down for good in 1997 when the new Middle School field was completed.

The year 1972 witnessed the construction of a library, science, and homemaking building on the site of the old tennis courts. A fieldhouse-band hall building was built at the same time on the north side of the agriculture building. A new elementary school, Lake Travis Elementary, opened its doors that year as well. It was located on RR 620, about four miles south of the Lake Travis Mansfield Dam. New tennis courts, which accommodated two courts, were added in 1974. A metal Industrial Arts building was completed in 1976. It was later used as the Transportation Department until torn down in 1998 for the new school. New football lights were installed in time for the 1978 season. They, too, would be dismantled in 1998.

The population explosion in DSISD in the 1970s caused an epidemic of portable buildings on the campus to accommodate the students. The first four rooms were built on the east end of the high school wing in 1971. Others soon followed on the northeast corner of the library building, between the library and agricultural building, and between the high school and elementary

Bell Tower, 1967

wings. A big six-room building was built on the northeast corner of the elementary wing. An elementary music room was built on the southeast corner of the six-room building. The old high school building on the Academy campus was even brought out of retirement. After a couple of years of use by a Project Search staff, the building was renovated in 1977 to house the kindergarten classes.

Finding buildings was not the only problem caused by the student enrollment surge of the '70s. It became obvious the 21-acre campus was inadequate and a new high school building was needed. The site of the high school became a bone of contention. The far-flung DSISD split into two factions over the issue. Once a low-populated area, the old Bee Caves district, with the development of Lakeway, soon outnumbered the voters of the more rural Dripping Springs section and began to hold a majority of the board positions. Quite naturally, the Lake Travis people wanted the school in or around their area. Just as naturally, the Dripping Springs people wanted to keep their school.

During the 1975-76 school year, the Lake Travis faction presented a petition to the Travis County Board of School Trustees for a split of the district. This was something new in the State of Texas. Part of the deal was that another district would have to give up part of their area to the splitting district. Lake Travis was able to get Marble Falls to turn over some property they were not getting taxes on anyway to fulfill the rule. It was approved by the Travis County Board, but when the decision reached the office of the Education Commissioner, it was overturned. The reason given was that since the Dripping Springs district included land in Hays County as well as Travis County, the petition should have been presented to Hays County as well. Several elections for sites around the district were defeated by the people in the county where the site wasn't located. The district was in a serious stalemate and going nowhere fast.

The next tactic was to have both sides sign petitions showing support for the proposed split. This time it was approved by the appropriate legal parties on December 13, 1978. Several of the Dripping Springs citizens, including Bert Hurlbut and Henry Brooks, Jr., fearing a rise in their taxes, filed suit and put the issue in the courts. This put a halt to the split decision as the trial dragged through the courts. Relations became more and more strained as the Lake Travis side took complete control of the Board. Long-time superintendent Calvin Knauth resigned in the Spring of 1979. The next two years were very tense in the district. Finally on June 12, 1981, the court allowed the split. After settling the division of debts and property, Lake Travis took about 80% of the taxable property and 20% of the student population of DSISD and set up the new Lake Travis ISD in the Fall of 1981. They had originally toyed with the idea of continuing to send their high school students to Dripping Springs until they could build a high school. At the last minute, they decided it best to put the entire campus on the Lake Travis Elementary School site. The old Bee Cave District that had asked to be a part of the Dripping Springs school system in 1951 changed direction and was back on its own again.

Part of the settlement was the renovation of the original plant on the Dripping Springs campus to make it more efficient. This included enclosing all the large windows, lowering the ceilings, and putting in air conditioning units for each room. The John Preslar Company was contracted to cover the old cinder block building with lathing to give it a fresh new look.

The split temporarily solved the bulging student population of the district but not for very long. Subdivisions popped up all around Dripping Springs during the boom of the early 1980s to repopulate the overworked campus. The fieldhouse was expanded to enclose the area between the fieldhouse and the agriculture building. In 1982, a large metal building was erected just north of the six-room building. It first served as an activity gym for the elementary students and then for middle school. Also a metal slanted roof was added to the west end of the gym.

It had been obvious for a long time that the 21-acre site was just not adequate for a twelve-grade campus. As soon as things could be arranged, a bond election was passed by the residents of the district and by Fall 1985, the high school students of DSISD moved into a new facility. It was located on a site about a mile west just off Hwy. 290, on the old 290 route. The frontage road became Tiger Lane. The 800-student capacity school included two academic wings, and a third wing that included a band hall, cafeteria, gym, and dressing rooms. A four-court tennis facility, a football field with cinder track and baseball field completed the athletic complex. The track was later upgraded to an all-weather facility. More seating capacity was added to the home side bleachers. The school was dedicated to the fourteen Common School Districts that had originally formed the district.

The kindergarten classes that had been housed in the old high school rock building were moved to the 21-acre campus with the other eight grades. The rock building was renovated and converted into office space for the district's administrative staff and tax personnel. More office space was provided in another renovation project in 1990. In this move, the superintendent's office was moved to the southwest corner of the building and an outside door added. A window to the north end was added in 1994.

A huge portion of the new families who were moving in had small children which were filling up the elementary grades, and space was running out on the campus. Even as the high school was being completed, the school board bit the bullet and took the chance of holding another bond election for the purpose of constructing a 1,200-student capacity structure. Whereas the previous high school bond had little trouble passing, this one, even though really needed, passed by a small margin. The board looked for a site to put the Elementary Campus, and before they had to pay out money to purchase the needed acreage, John Hill came to the rescue. He donated 21 acres from his ranch on RR12 North, about two miles from Hwy. 290. The school would house grades K-5. It was ready in the 1987-88 year.

In 1990, another important addition was added to the elementary campus. The space shuttle, *Challenger*, blew up just after takeoff with a teacher, Christie McAuliffe, aboard. To honor her, a foundation was set up to hand out grants each year in her memory. Dripping Springs had a very active Young Astronauts Club under the leadership of teacher/sponsor, Paula Formby. She applied for one of those grants and qualified. With the grant money, contractors Paul Snider and Richard Mach followed the plans and constructed a replica of *Challenger*. It was a classroom with the capability to do science projects with computers.

Now the old campus was left to house grades six, seven, and eight to be called a Middle School. The school district continued to grow and changes in the law caused another facility problem. The law stated that grades K-4 were limited to 22 students per teacher. This caused the surplus classroom situation to turn into a shortage, and portables were moved in. The Middle School had the same problem. It got to the point where the campus had more students on it than when all twelve grades were located there. On top of that, the elementary division had classes of two hundred plus getting ready to move up. Something had to be done. The answer was a new middle school.

Once again, the patrons of the district were asked to pass a bond package. It was to include a middle school campus, improvements at the Elementary and more classrooms at the High School. In 1986, the School Board purchased forty acres just off RR12 South for the purpose of investment and possibly a future school site. After the bond election passed, the site was considered for the Middle School but it was determined it would be too expensive to make it campus ready. One of the major problems was access to the acreage. The right-of-way road from RR12 did not meet specifications and would be very costly to fix, and there was no outlet to Hwy. 290. Acreage was bought from Roger Hanks, scarcely a half-mile west of the old campus. The move to the new quarters was made in the summer of 1995 and classes began in August. Its design had each grade with a wing of its own. It included two gyms and a four-court tennis facility. In 1997, a football field was added.

The building of the Middle School caused problems for the bond issue. By the time the building was started, the price of construction had gone up. The figures used in the bond issue were no longer valid. In the end, the projects at the Elementary and High School were sacrificed as the entire bond issue was used for the Middle School. However, the projects at both schools were much needed as overcrowding on both campuses was working a hardship. The High School had to build several portable buildings to house the overflow of students. The district purchased about seven acres on the east side of their High School property that included a house. The house is currently being used to house the Alternative Education Program (AEP). The next solution was to move the fourth and fifth grades over to the old middle school campus and make it an Intermediate School. The third was still another bond election.

The district decided to put forth a $24.7 million bond issue before the voters. The first phase would build the needed buildings at the high school. One wing on the east side would house the library and two floors of classrooms. Two of the old wings were extended south and another wing on the west side duplicated the old band hall, cafeteria, gym complex, but on a grander scale. Later, an intermediate school would be built on the old high school campus. Taxes were already weighing the populous down, so passing the bond issue was not easy. The district used creative voting by having early voting booths at important school functions to attract those most likely to be for it. On February 10, 1996, when the election was held, most voted against it. However, the bond passed 709-609.

The projects at the high school were supposed to be ready by mid-July 1998. The contractor began dragging his heels and with the school pushing, the academic wings were finished just days before the opening of school. The west side wing wasn't ready. The school board fired the contractor and the project carried on under new management. It was ready to move into on January 1, 1999.

The school board decided to move up the schedule for starting the Intermediate school. Groundwork began in June 1998. To do this, the old ag building, fieldhouse/bandhall, transportation building, tennis courts, football/baseball field all bit the dust in the name of progress. Land was purchased just west of the High School on 290 to house the evicted Transportation Department. The materials from the fieldhouse/bandhall and ag building were reconstructed on the transportation campus, plus the main building had to be built from scratch. Although not completely ready for occupancy when the 1998 school year began, the transportation site served its purpose anyway. The new Intermediate School was slated to be open for occupancy in September 1999. The move took place September 13. To cut the costs of the Intermediate school, the gymnasium was nixed in favor of using the E. P. Shelton gym at the old school site. The proposed gym was not close to a regular size court anyway. There was still a clamor for a gym at a site much closer to the Intermediate school. A grant of half a million dollars from Coke that was pursued by then basketball coach, Poe Shelton, became the savior for this project. The Board used a portion of that grant to finance the construction of a gym on the southeast corner of the school plant. This project began in the year 2000 and should have been completed sometime during the year 2001. Unfortunately, money became an issue and the interior work was halted and at press time, the gym was unusable for classes. Part of the old football field was brought back to P.E. activities and a small walking/running track was completed in the summer of 2001 around the football field.

Other changes to the athletic facilities took place as well. To make room for football practice fields at the high school, the baseball field was dismantled and the area behind the baseball field was filled in and sodded. This was prior to the 1997 football season. This meant the baseball team needed a field in a hurry. The site was part of the plan for the 40-acre park in which the school and city were partners. It was rushed through and was barely ready for action by the 1998 season. The girls softball team lost its field after its 1998 season and their new field was also located at the 40-acre park. It made the deadline for readiness by the 1999 season.

Another four-court tennis complex was completed by the 2000 school year. Also ready for the 2000 school year was another ten-row addition to the homeside bleachers and a much-needed new and larger pressbox. The athletic booster club was mostly responsible for the erection of a much larger concession/restroom facility on the north end of the football field. They were asked to come up with the funds when bond money had been depleted before this much-needed facility could get off the drawing board.

Mold became the dreaded word in the 21st century and the school was unable to escape it. First, the new Intermediate School was hit during the summer of 2001 and the situation was taken care of before the beginning of school. Unfortunately, the next case was at the Primary School where grades K-3 were housed. A week before the 2001 Thanksgiving holidays were to take place, the Primary students were given early holidays because of the presence of mold in the classrooms. They stayed out of school until December 1, when the Kindergarten classes were moved to the First United Methodist Church, the first grade went to the First Baptist Church, the second grade to the administrative complex, and the third grade took over a portion of the Intermediate School. It was hoped the students could return to their school on January 7 but that did not happen as the mold was more extensive than thought. The Baptist Church needed their facility and the administrative campus was completely renovated in time to house them along with the second grade. All grades are due to be back at the Primary school by the start of the 2002 school year. Continued growth has spawned the recommendation of more schools and expansions in the near future for the district.

School Programs

School Yearbook: The first yearbook for the Dripping Springs school system was published in 1945. The Annual Staff for that first addition was: Editor: Lila Faye Smith; Asst. Editors: Danna Foster, Margaret Glosson; Advertising Manager: Glynn Key; Typists: Ruthie Mae Crumley, Minnie Ferrell; Publicity Managers: Margaret Glosson, John Lee Gillespie; Treasurer: Gale Puryear; Sponsors: Mrs. Lura Lyle and Supt. G. C. Herring. It was dedicated to the men of the Dripping Springs school district who were serving in the Armed Service of our Country. They were named in the Annual.

In the early years, it was usually the responsibility of the senior class to be in charge of producing and publishing the yearbook. For many years, the staff did not have a class period in which to work on the project. They might be given some time within a class but mostly had to find time on their own. Much of the final preparations and deadlines came after school was out and the sponsors and a few dependable students had to take their summer time to get it ready for the publisher so the students could have it at the beginning of the next school year. That has all changed with technology and classes specifically for that purpose. The early editions were quite simple but effective in covering the essentials of the school year. Improvement in size and quality took place over the years. Even the focus of the yearbook in the last couple of decades has changed. Today, many record the history of the world as well as what is going on around the campus. The purpose of the yearbook is to record the history and happenings of everyday life for the students of the school year and in such a way that one can come back to it years from now and still understand and know the people involved. One of the shortcomings of late is the lack of acknowledgement and detail so that generations later a reader knows who they are looking at and why.

Only two graduating classes since 1945 were not honored with a visual history of their senior year. There were administrative problems in 1946-47 that resulted in not having a 1947 yearbook. Financial problems hit the school in 1950-51 and it was not possible to finance the yearbook that year. Yearbooks are not necessarily a moneymaking or a break-even deal in most years. Ads are sold in yearbooks to help defray the cost, but the school still has to subsidize the program.

Librarians: The Dripping Springs school board voted to equip a library during their January 27, 1938, meeting. Most schools had libraries of some sort but seldom had librarians to run the program. Most of the time a teacher assigned a class period or student aides to help out. The library was usually housed with the study hall room. In the 1950-51 school year two members of the faculty were designated as part-time librarians. They were Mrs. Helen David and Mrs. I. A. Ebough. Quite possibly they were needed because the previous May, Lester Brenizer donated over one thousand volumes of books, magazines, etc., to the school library. The first person hired at Dripping Springs with a librarian's degree was Norma Crawford in 1966. She stayed until 1970. Following her was Glenda Haeberlin from 1971 until 1976. She oversaw the move from the library room in the old high school wing to the new site in the metal building that also housed the science and homemaking departments. Barbara Knippa Hopson did the same thing during her stay of 1976-91 when the new high school was completed in 1985. She turned over the reins to Kay Coleman, who stayed only two years. Jenny Dailey accepted the assignment in 1993 and is still serving in that capacity. She moved into new quarters at the beginning of the 1998 school year.

Jill Gathright became the first elementary librarian in 1977. She retired in 1994. Kay Coleman returned for one year (1994-95). Barbara Davidson took over beginning in 1995. With the addition of the intermediate school in 1995, a librarian was needed there. Victoria Crawford was hired in that position. Jan Campbell became the middle school librarian in 1990 and retired in 1998. Brenda Crawford took over in 1998.

Vocational Agriculture: It was a needed department for a rural school but it depended on a growing school to be able to set it up. Dripping Springs asked for and received a Future Farmers of America (FFA) charter in October 1950. The school bought an old barracks building from the army and located it just north of the main building. It served in that capacity until 1970. To help them get their start, Dripping Springs appealed to the Hays County Vocational School, which had a satellite school located in the Billie Garnett building, to allow them to share some of their equipment. After much discussion, the Hays County Board decided there were too many obstacles involved in sharing. Instead, they agreed to donate $200 from the soda and cigarette machines of the Vocational School for the purchase of equipment for the Dripping Springs Public School agriculture shop.

H. G. Haby was the first agricultural teacher, serving through the 1952 school year. The next teacher did not have such a short term. Elmer Russell was fresh out of college and he soon made Dripping Springs his permanent home. He held that position until 1980, when cancer forced him to retire. Bill Tom Burch taught from 1980-83. The school wanted to hire Tom Ayres for the job when the position became vacant. He still needed one more semester of work. Mr. Russell agreed to come back and teach the first semester of 1983-84. Tom then stepped in and held the job until 1990. Next, Galen Dodson took over. He was a former Dripping Springs High School principal who had gotten out of teaching for a few years to go into ranching and then returned as a science teacher. Mr. Dodson retired in 1993 and Rip Gravell was hired and has served until the present.

In the past, many students worked their parents' places after graduating. The purpose of FFA was to teach students skills needed to work on a farm or ranch—such things as welding, handling and tending stock animals, showing animals, the study of leadership through contests, conducting meetings through Roberts Rules of Order, and carrying on the duties of farming and ranching.

Field trips to various ranches to get personal experience by working livestock were always a favorite among the students. These field trips were also filled with many memorable events. Over the years, the art of farming and ranching has changed. It has become more mechanized with fewer of the problems from the past.

The emphasis of FFA has changed over the years. The change was needed because of the shift from a rural to an urban population. For a time, ag classes struggled to have enough enrollees to justify keeping the program. The changes have revived the program and the classes are becoming popular again.

One of the first fundraisers was the most popular for many years—the FFA Rodeo. The first rodeo was held in the spring of 1951 and annual events were held until the mid-'80s when finding an arena and the logistics of putting one on became too difficult. During the early years the rodeo was held in the DS Roping Club arena located just south of Highway 290 and the storage buildings owned by Jim Spencer. He now owns the arena site as well. Later, in the summer of 1961, an arena was built with the help of members of the Civic Club on the campus just north of the football field. It was torn down to make room for the bus yard in the mid-'80s.

One of Mr. Russell's FFA projects with interesting results was the building of birdhouses. He gave each student the plans and they were expected to follow them. As you might expect, some were magnificent for their good work as well as magnificent for their lack of good work. Sometimes it was a monumental task for some birds to actually get to use the houses. Mr. Russell's favorite for show and tell was one created by Gaither Wilder.

A major honor bestowed upon one of the ladies of the school was that of being named the FFA Sweetheart. Her duties included representing the school against other chapters in the region and at school functions. The FFA banquet was always a big deal at the school I attended. The first FFA sweetheart selected at Dripping Springs was Mae Francis Sansom, later the wife of Carroll Glosson. This time-honored tradition was dropped in the 1990s.

Homemaking. On the other side of the coin, while the boys were expected to learn skills related to rural life on a farm or ranch, the girls were expected to learn skills needed around the house. This would include cooking, sewing and housekeeping. Their organization was known as the Future Homemakers of America (FHA). Most of these skills were first expected to be taught in the home by the mothers, but eventually they became a part of the school curriculum. In the 1871 school law, it was required that girls be taught how to sew for a certain amount of time each day. Miss Margaret Stewart was listed as teaching home economics, along with her fifth and sixth grades in 1934-35. She left before the second semester was over. The first teacher designated in a school yearbook at Dripping

Springs as a homemaking teacher was Mabel Kretzmeier in 1948. First year homemaking was approved for credit by the Deputy State Superintendent of Schools, W. T. Leftland, in a visit in May 1949. It is not known how long she served in this capacity but probably until 1954. She taught until 1956 and in a *Tiger Cry* interview in 1951 said she liked teaching homemaking best of all the subjects she taught. Next, Patricia Pierson and Beatrice Hindman taught the course in 1954-55. It was at this time that the Dripping Springs Future Homemakers of America chapter was organized. The Kyle FHA chapter was given the honor of being in charge of installing the first slate of officers in November 1954. Kathryn Stokes took over in the fall of 1955 and stayed through the first semester of the 1956-57 school year. JoAnn Beauford finished the second semester of that year. Novelle Daugherty taught from 1957-60. At that point Elizabeth Williamson stepped in to teach from 1960-65. Bertha Hill arrived in the fall of 1965 and stayed until 1981, when she retired.

Since boys could use the skills of etiquette, etc., just as much as girls, they were enrolled in Home and Family Living classes. Necia Hildreth Kinnison, a DSHS graduate, came back home to teach in 1970 and stayed until 1980 when she moved away to try her hand in another type of business. The curriculum has continued to evolve. Seeing most of that change has been Sherry Haydon, who took Mrs. Hill's place in 1981 and stayed until her retirement in May 2001.

Student Council: On January 19, 1951, the student body voted to form the first Student Council. The next week it was organized with fifteen students voted as class representatives. The first officers elected were: President Harvey Goslin; Vice-President Buddy White; Secretary Betty Lois Pope; and Treasurer Mae Frances Sansom. They had two faculty sponsors. The Council chose the Principal, Quinn Schlortt, as the first, and the Superintendent, Robert Shelton, appointed Lura Lyle as the other. Over the years, the Student Council, which gives the students a shot at a working governmental organization from a student's standpoint, has varied from taking a strong political stance to a more mundane one. The fact is they never had much power to get things done in the school system. The most they can do is plead their case and hope to get the administration and school board to listen. They do, however, serve to lead the student body in worthwhile projects. While Bradley Davis was the sponsor in the 1960s, the Student Council had one project to improve the campus each year. Among those projects was the bell tower and the trophy case and bench at the entrance to the building at the gym.

Honor Society: The first organization formed at Dripping Springs to honor academic achievement was called the Beta Club. It was started in 1959-60 with Louise Gravenor, the high school English teacher, as the sponsor. The first set of officers were: President Mickey Davidson, Vice-President Cecil Jenkins, Secretary Billie Ferrell, Treasurer Patricia Puryear, Reporter Becky Shelton, Historian Jean Turner. The Beta Club continued in existence until replaced by the National Honor Society in 1977-78. Marilyn Stefka Wright was the Beta Club sponsor who led the movement to the more prestigious NHS.

Other Organizations. Throughout the history of the school there have always been different clubs, many of which had to do with class subjects. There have been History, French, Spanish, Drama, Debate, and Rodeo clubs. Whenever an enthusiastic person wants to sponsor a club, they usually have a go at it.

Band. As outstanding as the Dripping Springs band program is, it might surprise some that it is relatively young when compared to the age of the school. Usually the band program is thought of as going hand-in-hand with the football teams. Dripping Springs first organized football season was in 1938. For many years, the equivalent of the band was the pep squad. It had a couple of members who would play the drums and the majorette and twirlers went along with the cheerleaders. They did routines on the field at halftime. This format continued until 1963.

During the 1963-64 school year, E. W. Tampke was given the responsibility of forming the school's first band program. Mr. Tampke was very experienced in starting up band programs. In 1930, he formed San Marcos' first band and taught it for years.

Dripping Springs had a school song since 1947 but no band to play it at the games. Russell Omeis took charge in 1964 and guided the infant band for the next three years. In April 1966, the band wore their first official uniforms and got to show them off in the Spring Concert. After Mr. Omeis left, Gene Lewis gave the program his leadership for the years of 1967-69 before moving from Dripping Springs. A slight bump in the program occurred for the 1969-70 year. Joyce Felts was hired but did not pan out for the betterment of the program. He did make the district aware that a person with ability and enthusiasm was needed.

Their next choice, Charles Schandua, could not have been a better choice. He brought the program to a new level. The next eight years brought much pleasure to everyone as the band reached new plateaus, including the first Sweepstakes Award by achieving all one's in the UIL contest. Mr. Schandua formed a stage band and toured the area schools to perform. Assemblies that featured the band were the most popular and there were always surprises in the well-attended concerts, including people getting to be "guest conductor."

One of the better ones was Jonathan Hole in his white tuxedo with tails. His was still in the era when bands had a different show for each game, complete with twirlers. When he decided to step down at the end of the 1978 school year, he had the program on the edge of greatness.

Greatness was left up to Linda McDavitt and she did not disappoint. She not only extended the string of Sweepstakes Awards but she took the program to the next level, which was competing in the state contest. She stayed until 1984, and moved on to the college ranks. From 1979 to 1984, the band qualified for the state contest and the Tiger band finished either fifth or fourth in each. McDavitt was the first to introduce the flags section to the band and phase out the twirlers.

Bill Peace came in for a stint from 1984-86. It was the ultimate stint as the Tiger Band reigned as State Class AA Champions for both years. His successor was Don Hopkins, who led the band from 1986 to 1993 and made it back to the big show twice. Jeff Rudy, who had worked with the DS band under Hopkins a few years before, was asked to return, serving from 1993-98. Keith Lancaster was hired to lead the band into the world of Class 4A competition in the fall of 1998. The Sweepstakes string is still alive and well.

In the early days, the high school band included the seventh and eighth grade students. In the fall of 1992 the high school decided to go it alone and the middle school had their own band. The band program was so small that the band director had to direct both bands alone. One of the earlier middle school band directors was Trey Wilson (1982-83). Cheryl Spooner Hopkins served from 1985-93. Daniel Smith (1993-98), Melissa Vauk (1994-99), Paul Schlichting (1998-00), Jeff Murphy (1999-) and Adam Cartwright (2000-).

Pep Squad. As soon as football became a sport at Dripping Springs, there was a pep squad and cheerleaders to make plenty of spirit. Without a band, the pep squad was the main attraction. There were usually two or three drums. Later, majorettes were added. Everyone had similar, if not the same uniforms. In the early years it was not hard to spot the football sweetheart because she had a big heart on the front of her blouse.

The pep squad and cheerleaders made their debut in the 1940 football season.

They even got the school board to approve making one trip with the football team that year.

Sometimes the pep squad was the entertainment at halftime. When the band began in 1963-64, it gave the pep squad a little help with the cheering. In the early '70s, a drill team was formed and the pep squads began to be phased out. There was still a pep squad in 1974-75; it was called a Pep Club in 1980-81, and a Spirit Club was formed for 1986-87. Not having a pep squad has hurt organized cheering at the games. The cheerleaders are faced with having to try and get a mostly disinterested group of fans that are intent on watching the game and know few of the cheers, to follow their leadership. They have been relegated to a mostly unnoticed group that do cheers without crowd participation and perform acrobatics and other skill events to get attention. With a pep squad, they always had a group who knew the cheers and were enthusiastic throughout the game.

Drill Team: Drill teams became the vogue in the early '70s as some young teachers just out of college were eager to start a new type of spirit and entertainment group to follow in the footsteps of the likes of the Kilgore Rangerettes. Michelle Rohrer came to Dripping Springs in 1971 and formed the Tiger Paws. She stayed for two years. Barbara Ernst took it for the next two years and then turned it over to Anne Weisman. They had a few problems with numbers in the early '80s and finally dropped the program after the 1982-83 school year. It did not stay down long. In 1987-88 Peggy Howell reincarnated the program and renamed the group The High-Steppers. She was an elementary teacher who had a daughter entering high school. She worked the group out before school each morning. This was a time-consuming adventure and the next year Mrs. Howell did not want to be the sponsor, as her daughter had enrolled in an Austin school. However, when a replacement did not work out, she returned for another year. She was assisted by Mary Blanck and was able to turn the activity over to her the next year. Mrs. Blanck put much energy into the program and brought it to a very high level of quality before turning it over to Tracy Neef in 1994. She has maintained its excellence.

The Basics

Counselors: Like so many other phases of the school programs, in the early times, the art of counseling was usually practiced by individuals who were respected by the students or, at least, in positions of authority. This was usually the principal, sometimes the coach or other designated teachers. Mostly, this counseling usually had to do with the student getting into trouble. The scope of education began to change to the point that many students needed to have questions answered about phases of their education. What classes to take? College requirements? Job opportunities? Scholarship opportunities? It was obvious that as the school was growing there was a need for an individual who could handle those questions full-time. The decision to do so was made in 1970.

In high school that person was Eldon K. Shipp. His most recent job was as an employee of the Gary Job Corps in San Marcos. He was an excellent counselor. The students received very expert advice—after wading through numerous war stories and name-dropping. He was able to namedrop because he had no fear of going up and meeting those people he needed to get the job done. He was most adept at finding and getting scholarship opportunities for his students. He retired at the end of the 1983 school year. Keith Burnett was hired to take Mr. Shipp's place and stayed in that position until 1985 when he became the first DS Middle School principal. Don Phillips served from 1985-91. Next was Daymun White (91-93) and Sylvia Evans (93-95), Julie Jones (94-00), Viki Fuller (95-99), Rhonda Duke (99-), Bonnie Dunn (00- 02), Joe Burns (01-) and Julie McDonald (02-).

The middle school counselor, Mary Lee Lenshke, worked with the Junior High in 1980 and Mrs. Bridget Cave has held the Middle School position since its inception in 1985. Mrs. Cave began getting some help in 1995 when she shared Kelly Spain Coffey with the Intermediate students. In 1996 she began fulltime at the middle school and Ann Dodson became the full time counselor at the Intermediate school.

In 1990 Alicia Blythe was the first counselor for the elementary school. She stayed a year. Nannette Newbern served from 1991-98, Anita Kelly from 1993-, and Traci Henze from 1998-.

Mrs. Cynthia Snider came to Dripping Springs for the school year 1972-73 as a special education counselor. She headed up the Talent Research and Development Program. Its purpose was to find those students who were not performing to their abilities and find ways to get them to do so. The next year she was the Coordinator for the Special Services Department and had a Resource Room to help her with her duties. The object was to help students obtain diplomas by substituting on-the-job or vocational training as part of their academic electives. All of this was the forerunner of the Special Education program that had to be met when the Federal government determined that all children had the right to an education, no matter their lot in life. She moved up to Curriculum Director in 1975-76 and became a strong advocate of special education rights.

Early Special Ed classes were self-contained units with students spending most or all of their day in one class with one teacher. The government decided there was a stigma to children being isolated from the rest of the school population and decided they should no longer be given preferential treatment, but must be mainstreamed. All students were to be placed in the same classroom. This proved to be a problem with the special ed student keeping apace of the class. A compromise was found when a program called Content Mastery was instituted by Malyna Miller at the Middle School in 1989. This allowed the students to be assigned to the same classroom but allowed to go to the content mastery room for more specialized study and modified tests as needed.

School Nurse: Another program that was deemed necessary as the population grew was to provide the students with medical attention, plus someone to see to it that all the medical records were kept in proper order. The first person to be hired as the school nurse was Mary Carson in 1975-76. She did not return the next year. Kathy Nichols took the job in 1976 and still holds the senior position. Not only does she keep up with the records but for many years she had to stretch herself very thin to be at all campuses during the week. She now has help at the various campuses.

High School Principals: All through the history of the Dripping Springs school system, the school had principals as the head of the school. Even so, the principals were teachers foremost but paid a higher salary for the position. As a part of the Common School District system, the person heading up the school was a principal because the superintendent for all the CSDs was the County School Superintendent. This leaves this list a little in the gray area because of this. It was not until 1941-42 that Dripping Springs qualified for all twelve grades and was actually approved as a four year high school in March 1942.

The first person hired to be the high school principal was Robert F. Shelton in 1947. He served in that position until 1951, when he became superintendent. The high school principals since that time are: Quinn Schlortt (51-57); Marvin Hill (57-60); Jerry Garnett (60-63); J. F. Holt (63-65); Roy Worley (65-68); Paul Allen (68-72); Charles Whatley (72-73); Alfred Chance (73-74); Galen Dodson (74-79); Jeffrey K. Lindzey (79); Carol Cunningham (79-81); Joe Searcy (81-82); Mike Caplinger (82-83); Nolan Raney (83-87); Ronnie Bourland (87-88); Don Forrestor (88-Jan. 95); Jim Rosebrock (Jan. 95-97); David Shanley (97-99). Greg

Jung took over the position at the beginning of the 1999 school year.

In the early 1980s when the school population was beginning to grow, assistant principals were employees assigned a couple of periods of the school day to mostly take care of discipline problems while the principal kept up with growing paperwork and responsibilities. In 1980-81, the year before the Lake Travis-Dripping Springs split, Aggie Painton handled duties of assistant principal. Tom Jackson spent one year as a part-time intern while working on his administrative certificate. Carl Waits spent a couple of classes a day performing the discipline assignments until the new high school was built in 1985. Don Forrester was moved to the high school from the elementary school, where he had spent the previous year, 1988, to become the assistant principal but was moved up to principal when the previous principal resigned before school began. The first bonified assistant high school principal hired was June Coleman (90-97). She was joined by David Shanley (96-97). Then came Dean Blair (97-98), Jane Miller (97-Jan. 99), Mike Garrison (98-99), Joe Burns (99-01), Athena Caroselli (99-01), Stuart Foreman (01-), and Darlene Billman (01-)

Elementary School Principals: As the school system continued to grow through consolidation, it became necessary to add elementary school principals to go along with the high school principals. In the beginning, the position was that of teacher mostly. The first was Claude Goode (1949-50). Next came Joe B. Cox (1950-51 1st sem.), L.U.C. Kaufman (1951-52), Joe Reichert (1952-55) and Tom Jones (1955-70). At this point there was a change in the grade alignments at the school. Although generally called junior high, grades seven and eight were grouped with the elementary. In 1970, seven and eight came under the wing of the high school and the other six became the elementary. The first true elementary principal was Robert F. Shelton. He was the first high school principal hired and he was also the first elementary. After serving as superintendent, he moved to Roma in 1963, returned to Dripping Springs two years later and went to work for Camp Gary Job Corps in San Marcos. He served as elementary principal until his retirement in 1980. Richard Stark took over and held the position until his retirement in 1995.

Another realignment of grade took place in 1985. With the high school moving to another campus and the elementary within two years of having their own campus, it was decided to include grade six with seven and eight to make a middle school and the elementary consist of K-5. Don Forrester was hired to be Richard Stark's assistant principal in 1987-88. The next year Mr. Forrester moved to the high school and Mike Cave took his place at the elementary school. With the new school rules about class size in the elementary grades and the growth that had the 1,200 capacity elementary school bursting at the seams, it became too great for one person to control. In 1991 the elementary was split into K-3 and 4-5. Mr. Stark was principal of K-3 and Mike Cave the principal of 4-5.

Several things happened in 1995, beginning with Mr. Stark's retirement. A new middle school campus was completed and to help alleviate the overcrowding of the elementary campus, grades 4-5 were moved over to the old middle school campus as an intermediate school with the promise of a new intermediate school building in the next couple of years. Mike Cave took the reins of the primary campus of K-3 in 1995. In 1996 it was decided Mr. Cave needed additional help and Tresa Anderson was named as his assistant principal. She retired in December 2001 and Rhonda Whitman took her place. Delores Covington was named the Intermedate school principal and in 1997 Lestant Flake became the assistant principal. Mrs. Covington left after the 1999-2000 school year and Donna Janssen took her place.

The Dripping Springs elementary school was not the only elementary school in the district. In 1972, the Lake Travis elementary school opened. Paul J. Allen, who had served as the high school principal the previous four years, took the appointment for that position and served in that post for Dripping Springs until the split became a fact at the end of 1981. Then it became a part of the Lake Travis ISD beginning in the fall of 1981.

Middle School Principals: As mentioned before, when the high school was moved to another campus, grade six was added to seven and eight to make a middle school. Keith Burnett, who was the high school counselor, became the first principal of the Middle School. He served in that capacity until he accepted another position in the district at the end of the 1993 school year. Lynn McDonald was selected to succeed Burnett and served for four years. Then Tyler Damron, who came to Dripping Springs in 1991 and had served as assistant principal under Burnett and McDonald, was named the principal beginning in 1997. Donna Janssen became assistant principal for (97-00), Paula Finnessey (98-00), and Kim Gravell and Paula Sternberg took over in 2000.

Superintendents: Although Dripping Springs had been classified as a high school since 1920, they did not officially have a twelve-grade system until 1942 and the county superintendent was put in charge. It is believed that Merlin Bright Tilley (1941-43) was the official first superintendent of Dripping Springs, even though the school was still under the auspices of the County Board. G. C. Herring served the post from 1943-46. The others in order are: S. P. Conn (46-47), Ross Columbo Donaho (47-51), Robert F. Shelton (51-63), Calvin Knauth (63-79), Jeffrey K. Lindzey (79-81), Cynthia Snider (81-82), Joe Searcy (81-83), Mike Caplinger (83-86), Julian Shaddix (86-89), Bob Denton (89-93), Tony Riehl (Feb. 94-98), Mike Owens (98-99), and Mary Ward (Jan. 00-)

Cafeteria: For many years in the education system of Dripping Springs, there were no lunchrooms where meals were served to the students. The first lunchroom opened on Monday, January 6, 1941. It was known as a WPA lunchroom and many schools began serving lunches at this time. This was brought about with the aid of Surplus Commodities Corporation and Works Progress Administration (WPA). Certain foods were made available by SCC and the labor was furnished by WPA. The equipment was supplied by the PTA and donations from others.

John McClaferty was said to have donated the money and some of the work toward installing the sinks in the room. Students were asked to contribute a nickel for the meal, or if they could not do this, then they could contribute eggs, butter, or other commodities that could be used in the program. If they could do neither, they would still be served. The cafeteria averaged 500 meals a week and everyone was contributing after the first two months.

In the beginning, the cafeteria was located in the southeast corner of the Academy building. The first staff was headed up by a Mrs. Jungers. When the WPA removed themselves from the program, Dosia Hohman, Lillian Whisenant and Opal Hadley became the staff. J. F. Glosson said he can still remember the smell of brown beans cooking as he would come down the stairs from the second story. My memories of the lunchroom at the two-room, seven-grade school I attended were those of it being much like home. After eating the meal prepared, we were allowed to take our spoons and scrape the dessert bowls and icing pans, just like at home. In the early days, the students were responsible for bringing their own eating utensils. One could purchase a tin plate complete with a collapsible cup, plus the spoon, fork, and knife.

Needing the room for the increased enrollment, a new building was constructed on the campus and the cafeteria was moved to it. There is a little confusion as to the origin of the building. In her research, Cynthia Snider claims the lunchroom was the old Bell Springs school they had moved there.

Grady Moore claims that he and his father, S. J. Moore, tore down the old Hamilton Pool school and used the lumber to build the lunchroom. Others substantiate the Hamilton Pool building as well.

When the new campus was built across the Springs, it did not include a cafeteria. The old cafeteria building was moved over to continue its profession. It would do so until 1952-53, when the cafeteria/gymnasium was added. From that point, it was used for a first grade room, then music room before being moved to the north end of the campus after 1958 and converted to living quarters for janitors' families and later storage before being razed in the 1990s in a campus cleanup campaign.

It is amazing to visit old facilities and compare them with the facilities of today. That first cafeteria at the high school site had only about a 20x30 area for eating purposes. Over the years it served as part of the homemaking department, classrooms, and finally back to a snack bar/concession facility for school and games before being converted to a workroom for the Intermediate school. Remember that the number of students was much smaller in the '50s and the high school students could run over to the small cafe next to the campus.

In 1964, a new cafeteria was built in the elementary wing. It was somewhat larger but as the school grew, the space was fully utilized. The snack bar was used to alleviate part of the problem and later during Middle School days, an outside covered area was added to give the students a place to eat lunch. As the other schools were built, large cafeterias were a part of the plan. Even so, the high school's turned out to be too small in a few years and a new and improved one went on line January 1, 1999.

Ottie Langston and Ola Butler joined Mrs. Hohman as cooks and this combination worked until Mrs. Hohman retired on December 22, 1963, after 18½ years of service. Mrs. Langston and Mrs. Butler did likewise after the 1970 school year. Many other cafeteria workers have stayed with the Dripping Springs system for many years, including Zulema Cordova.

District Growth: A state law passed in 1884 allowing schools to form districts and set tax rates. It was not until 1891 that Dripping Springs asked to have a district. The Hays County Commissioners' Court approved Dripping Springs District #20 on May 15, 1891. The boundaries of the district began at the northwest corner of the George Harvey survey, then south with the west line of said survey and west line of B. F. Hanna survey to the southwest corner of B. F. Hanna. Then due south to the south line of Jesse Massey. Then west to the northwest corner of the southwest Yeager No. 35. Then south to the southwest corner of same. Then east with the south line of same. Then east to the southeast corner of Joseph Mix survey. Then north to the northwest corner of the William Cockburn No. 33. Then east to the northeast corner of William Cockburn No. 32. Then north to the northwest corner of the Thomas R. Jackson survey. Then east to the northeast corner of same. Then north with the east line of B. F. Mims survey. Then north across

DSISD Cooks Ola Butler, Ottie Langston, Mrs. Thomas, and Abbie Jones, 1969.

the William Walker survey to the corner of survey No. 1160. Then northeast to the corner of same. Then northwest to the north corner of the William Wood survey. Then northeast to the Marcus Roper survey. Then northwest to west corner of same. Then north to northeast corner of A. G. Davy survey. Then northwest to northeast corner of Jean Darrigeant survey. Then to the northwest corner of same. Then to southwest corner of same. Then east to the north corner of George W. Lindsey. Then to the southeast corner of P. H. Rice survey. Then to the southwest corner of same. Then west with the north line of the George A. Harvey survey to the place of beginning. $30^{17}/_{32}$ square miles.

Another state law passed by the legislature in 1911 called for all districts to be reestablished and redefined. The County School Board approved the survey for Dripping Springs #20 in their meeting of April 10, 1916. This survey was correct for most of the next year. After that, especially in the 1940s, the district went through much change, mostly through consolidation with many of the common school districts surrounding it. On March 3, 1917, all of John Gibson's land was transferred from Dripping Springs #20 to Darden Hill #31. In 1934, the first of many consolidations took place. On May 12, 1934, Glenn CSD #13 joined Dripping Springs.

The 1940s was a busy time for Dripping Springs. The end was clearly in sight for common school districts all over the state. As the state was getting more and more involved in the finances of the public education, they began to realize fewer was better when it came to school systems and encouraged consolidation as a means to that end. Being the only large community in the area, Dripping Springs was on the receiving end of consolidation. The first land received was through individual requests and not by districts. Later on, many districts became a part of the system anyway.

The County School Board meeting of September 13, 1941, was productive for Dripping Springs. The Glynn Key Ranch (Union) and E. E. Townes Ranch (Salem) were transferred to Dripping Springs. J. L. Smith's 267.5 acres in #19 and 192 acres of Willie Tschoepe (Darden Hill) went to Dripping Springs. All lands of Thomas R. Jackson survey belonging to McCarty, Duval, Garrett Black Estate, Eppler, and 245 acres belonging to William Glosson on the west side of Gatlin Creek transferred from Driftwood to Dripping Springs.

It was not a bad year in 1943 either. Millseat #21, Union #22, and Darden Hill #31 were consolidated with Dripping Springs on April 30, 1943. On August 14, 1943, Neal McNair's 305 acres and Tom Beauchamp's 740 acres (the old W. J. Davis land) were transferred from Henly #26 to Dripping Springs. Puryear's land in Bell Springs and D. C. Foster's land in Salem were transferred to Dripping Springs on October 29, 1943.

The consolidation business slowed for a year. Mt. Gainer #28 and Hamilton Pool #69 of Travis County were consolidated on February 5, 1945. Salem #12 and Bell Springs consolidated on March 12, 1945. The Johnson CSD #52 (Travis County) became a part of the system on April 5, 1948. O. T. Hodge's 230 acres were transferred from the Buda district to Dripping Springs. The final consolidation took place on September 1, 1951, when the Bee Cave district agreed to consolidation with Dripping Springs. This district was made up of the former Travis County CSD's of Teck, Johnson, and Haynie Flat. This would bring DSISD to an area of approximately 313 square miles. Thirty years later, this same district was allowed to sever its relationship with Dripping Springs and form a separate school district again.

Transportation: In the early days of school, small school districts were formed. Part of the reason was transportation. The school needed to be located where the students could easily reach the school on foot or horseback. The common school districts, as they were called, were governed by a County School Board and led by a County

Superintendent. Each district would elect their own school trustees to run the daily operations but any decisions over and beyond had to be approved by the County School Board.

The first mention of provided transportation for the Dripping Springs district was in the County School Board minutes of November 1, 1933. A contract for a Dripping Springs bus driver was approved. It did not name the driver and that might be because one was not needed at the time. On May 12, 1934, Enoch Needham received the first bus contract. This coincided with the consolidation of Glenn CSD #13 and thus expanded the Dripping Springs district.

Unlike today, a school could not just order up a bus and get one. Sometimes ingenuity had to prevail. That is what took place for Dripping Springs to get its very first bus for the 1934-35 school year. The men most responsible for the conversion of the 1930 Chevrolet truck described below were Charles Haydon, Carter Breed, Neal McNair, and Alva Haster.

On September 2, 1935, the County Board directed that bus drivers were to report total mileage on their buses, and on each bus, a sign must be made on back and each side designating they were school buses.

Bradley Davis took over Needham's route in the Spring of 1935. He described that first bus. He said it was a Chevrolet truck. A wooden frame box, covered with sheetmetal, was attached to the bed of the truck. It had benches nailed along each side and one down the middle. Slots were cut in the side to suffice for windows and a cloth hung down to protect the openings from the elements when needed. The back of the cab was cut out and half of the front seat. The students entered the bus from the passenger side of the cab and walked back to get a seat. The vehicle was painted yellow. Mr. Davis said that when he first started to drive the bus, it had no muffler. The exhaust came straight out of the manifold and could be heard for several miles around. He said many of his passengers used this noise to start their trek to the pickup spot. Finally, he got Bill Garnett to remedy the situation. With a combination of pipes and angles, Garnett ran the pipes down the middle of the bus and out. This allowed the back to have a heater system the year round and it also muffled the noise to the point that the students could not use the noise factor as an alert for the bus's arrival.

P. D. Lindsey received a bus contract on 9-2-1936 for $25 a month and drove it until he resigned 11-2-1937. Possibly Will King took over the route then as he received the contract 9-8-1938. By 1942, the old bus had seen its days. The County School Board, at their meeting of 6-20-1942, gave Dripping Springs permission to sell the old school bus for $75 dollars and put the money in the maintenance fund. Charlie Haydon remembers playing in the metal frame box on his dad's property while growing up.

As districts started to consolidate with Dripping Springs, more bus routes had to be approved by the County Board. In 1943-44, the bus drivers were Norville Henslee, Mrs. Malcolm Naumann and Mrs. R. M. Robinson. For the 44-45 year, drivers were K. C. Whisenant, Susie Danforth, James Henslee, Mrs. Roy Volmering, and Theron Stephens. When Mr. and Mrs. R. M. Robinson resigned as bus drivers 1-3-1949, Jesse Langston was hired as a driver and mechanic for $150 a month. His wife, Ottie Langston, was hired as the other bus driver. In August 1950, Mrs. Roy Volmering, Ola Butler, Ottie Langston, G. A. Pringle, Mrs. G. A. Pringle, and Joe B. Cox were drivers. Their salaries ranged from $35-55 a month. Mr. Cox resigned in January 1951 and E. B. "Pete" Glosson was hired on. Jimmie Hoard joined Glosson, Butler, Langston, and Volmering to start the 1951-52 year. Volmering resigned in November and Ollie Sorrell took her place. Glosson, Butler, and Langston drove the buses for over two decades each.

The transportation department was basically run by the superintendent and school

E. B. "Pete" Glosson, longtime DSISD bus driver.

board for many years. When I came on in 1965, it was Travis Garnett and J. F. Glosson in charge of keeping up the buses. They were owners of the Garnett & Glosson Humble station. They also drove bus routes. The situation was not bad because there were only about five buses to keep up with. The first new bus purchased after I began working at DSISD was in 1968. It was still in the fleet of buses until 1998. David Fields was the first person outside the administration who was given some authority in looking after the scheduling of buses for trips, etc. Usually some individual would earn extra money by fueling the buses and general maintenance. The buses were just parked out front of the school.

As the school population grew, so did the need for more buses. Finally in 1984, it was decided to establish a transportation department and hire a director to run it. That person was Elmer D. Dalley. A bus yard to protect the buses was later constructed at the north end of the football field. When the high school moved down the road, the old Industrial Arts building was converted into the transportation department. Under Mr. Dalley's guidance, the drivers' wages were raised and such things as insurance, etc., were made possible. Also, the drivers were now in charge of driving to extracurricular activities, which allowed them to make some extra money as well.

In the early '90s, the bus yard had to be expanded and took in the old rodeo arena. In 1991, the problem of bus maintenance increased greatly. The local businesses were unable to keep up with all the work and it was expensive to boot. At this time Mr. Dalley convinced the School Board they could save money by hiring a school mechanic. They heeded the advice and hired Steve Malone. Brett Holder was added in 1995 and Chris Carter was added in 1998 after Steve Malone left for private business. Brett Holder left for other employment in the spring of 2002 and so did Chris at the end of the school year.

Mr. Dalley retired in 1996 and Chester Sparks was hired. The IA building was remodeled to be used only for the transportation department and garage area. This was short-lived. When it was decided to build the new Intermediate school on that end of the campus, the transportation department had to go. Ten acres of land were found on Highway 290 West, just north of the high school. In June 1998 the Ag. building, Fieldhouse/bandhall and IA building were razed to make room for the next school. The material from the Ag. building and fieldhouse/band hall was used to rebuild at the new site. Since the IA building could not be rebuilt from the old materials, the main office/storage/garage complex at the new site had to be built from scratch. Pushed to the limit, the transportation department was up and running by August 1998. For the 2000-01 school year, the transportation department had 29 regular routes, not to mention six special education buses that travel everywhere to pick up handicapped students and take them to school and return them later in the day. The increase in the school population has put a strain on the transportation department to supply sufficient drivers and buses to do the job. Once again there has been talk that it may be necessary to do tier busing to alleviate some of the problems, especially the shortage of drivers. Much of the extra pay for the drivers through field trips was taken away in the fall of 2000 when their biggest opportunity, athletic trips, was taken away. To meet budget restraints, the athletic department decided to require the coaches to drive the buses as part of their contracts. This was a fallback to the old days.

Shortly after hiring on as the transportation director, Mr. Sparks was given extra duties, such as head of maintenance, custodians, etc. He had help in the transportation department with longtime bus driver, Patsy Weiershausen, being elevated to bus coordinator in 1995. She resigned the position in the summer of 2001 and the school board decided to split the duties of Mr. Sparks. He was given the job of head of maintenance and Larry McGilvray was hired in October 2001 to take over the transportation department.

PTA: All through the history of the Dripping Springs school system, the people have been instrumental in helping out with the expenses of the school. In 1919, the Dripping Springs Baptist women formed a club for the express purpose of working for the school. They called it the Women's Earnest Workers Club. They had contributed several hundred dollars to the school for furnishings and had helped on the building as well. The February 3, 1922, edition of the *San Marcos Record* said their present project was to put the floor in the second story auditorium that was in the process of being completed.

This group changed their name to the Parent and Teacher Association (PTA) so they could be affiliated with other PTA groups in the area, and because the state doled out money to the PTAs. Even before the name change they had received $915 from the state.

The PTA has always been a strong booster club for the betterment of the Dripping Springs schools. Fundraising is just one of the important functions they have always capably handled. For a time the name changed to the PTSA to include students in its membership. Nowadays, it is known as PTO for Parent-Teachers Organization.

Interesting Transactions: With the consolidations, the Dripping Springs school system became the owner of property it would not have need of, mainly in the form of buildings, but also land as well. At the July 3, 1943, meeting the Dripping Springs school board asked the Hays County Board for permission to sell the Millseat and Union school houses. In April 1944, the board voted to sell the Millseat building to John Woods for $526 and the Union building to R. L. Hadley for $300. Mr. Woods moved the building to a lot just south of the First Baptist Church for his residence. It burned in 1958.

On June 23, 1944, several transactions were made. First of all, the Hays County Board approved the sale of the two acres of land that once was the Union school campus to Mr. and Mrs. S. L. Langston for $25. The Langstons deeded the property to the school in 1936, with the stipulation that when it was through serving as a school, it would revert to them.

Next, they approved the sale of the Darden Hill building to the First Baptist Church of Dripping Springs for $300. Jesse Langston purchased the Darden Hill toilet for $20. It was approved on May 21, 1945, to allow Dripping Springs to use two rooms of the Mt. Gainer school for material to build a bus shed and athletic shower room at the Dripping Springs campus. Mr. Sam Strong was hired to construct that building. Also in 1945, board member S. J. Moore sold scrap lumber, doors, and windows in exchange for the construction of the water fountain that was located between the Academy and High School buildings. The school also purchased the seesaws and swings from the old Henly school from Mrs. Warren Harris for $25.

At the 9-10-1936 Board meeting, the Board agreed to purchase four typewriters, so that typing could be taught at the school. Ten had been proposed. The Board agreed to purchase ten typewriters at their 6-1-1937 meeting, five of which would be on option, according to need.

At the 10-14-1940 Board meeting Bill Garnett was given permission to overhaul the bus (new rings, valves, etc.) as long as it did not cost over $20.

In 1946 the board approved the building of a rock house over the water pump. It still remains.

Fred Alba paid $100 for the three-acre Millseat site on January 3, 1949.

School Spirit

School Bell: There is one symbol of Dripping Springs education still around that has a history almost as long as the education system itself. It has pulled periodic disappearing acts but always reappears in a prominent role. It may seem insignificant to some but it has played an important role throughout the ages. We are speaking of our school bell.

Early on, it was my belief the bell was the original one installed when the Academy was completed in 1882. Everything I had found out led to that conclusion. That conclusion had to be changed when evidence came to light that disproved the theory. As I was gleening the *San Marcos Free Press* issue of October 29, 1885, the answer was in black and white. In the column giving all the news about the community of Dripping Springs was mention of the bell. It seems the previous bell had broken the winter before and the community had purchased a new one for the upcoming 1885-86 school year.

The bell was housed under a little cupola roof structure on the front of the one-story rock structure. Mr. Bradley Davis recalls the bell could be heard a great distance around when rung. Various articles in papers mentioned the bell and its ringing reminding them that school was in session. The bell maintained its place of prominence until 1921. At this time, the wooden wing located on the west side was torn down and the rock second story added to the Academy. While this construction was taking place the bell was removed and placed in a protected place within the rock walls of the Garnett stables. After the building was completed, the bell was brought back but now occupied another site. It was moved inside, this time to near the southwest corner of the second floor. Mr. Davis said it was rather loud inside the building but it could not be heard as far from school as before. It would continue to be used by the school until 1949, when the building closed its doors and school moved to the new campus. The bell was left behind in silence.

The Masonic Lodge purchased the building from DSISD in 1952. This left the bell outside the realm of education for the first time in its life. It stayed that way until the 1966-67 school year. Enter Bradley Davis. He was the science teacher at the school, but, more important to this story, he was the sponsor for the Student Council. They had the rule of doing at least one service project each year for the school. Mr. Davis had the idea to construct a bell tower at the entrance to the campus and bring the grand old bell out of retirement. They built an attractive tower with a roof and the bell was installed. Instead of being used to call students to class, it called them to recognize achievements of the school. It was designated as the victory bell. Anytime a team won a game or for other accomplishments, the bell was lustily rung in recognition of this. The community was made aware by this ringing that something important at school had happened. It was not uncommon for someone to jump off the bus after returning from a victory and ring the bell, even though it may be late at night.

The bell tower even served as a memorial to a couple of students who lost their lives in the Viet Nam War, Bobby Roberts and Kenny

DSISD Bell Tower
1885 Bell in a 2000 Tower

McLendon. A plaque was placed on one of the columns to their memory.

The bell witnessed the growth changes of Dripping Springs education. In 1985, the high school moved down the road and in 1987, grades K-5 moved north on RR12, leaving just the middle school to look after. When the new middle school was being built, the Middle School Principal Lynn McDonald wanted to incorporate the bell into a prominent new bell tower there. Money considerations caused this plan to be scrapped, but, even then, there was the thought by many of us that the bell should be a part of the high school lore. Finally in 1997, the bell tower was dismantled, for reasons that I do not understand because it was certainly still an attractive addition to the campus. The bell was put in storage until plans could be completed to make it a prominent addition to the high school campus—a place it has always held in the history of Dripping Springs education.

Plans for the bell changed. Instead of being placed at the high school, it was decided to give it a prominent place of honor at the entrance to the 1949 school site on Loop 64. This school became the headquarters for the school administration in the summer of 2000. It was to be located in the same isle of land that it had previously occupied prior to 1997. This time the bell tower was constructed in the front portion of the strip of land and visible to all entering. The roof is made of sheetmetal. Geronimo Garza did the limestone rock support columns and the memorial rock altar underneath the bell that will display the memorial plaque to Roberts and McLendon. The project was begun in November of 1999 and was completed in February 2000.

School Song: Dripping Springs has had a school song since 1947. The words were written by Robert Shelton, the principal for the school and later to become the superintendent. He asked Mrs. Pauline Stephens, the Baptist church pianist, to put the words to music. This collaboration gave the Dripping Springs High School their school song in today's version. In an article written in the October 2, 1947, issue of *Tiger Cry*, Mrs. Theron (Pauline) Stephens was thanked for writing the school song. Mr. Stephens was the First Baptist Church's pastor. It is my belief that she was being thanked for her contribution to the effort and not solely responsible. It was a cooperative effort by the two. She used a tune that was very popular among schools doing the same thing. This becomes obvious when attending football games and listening to the various school songs. The tune is the same, only the words change. The tune comes from an old college song entitled "Far Above Cayuga's Water."

Through the years someone has unknowingly changed the wording of the school song and others continue to follow the erroneous suit. It is obvious that a person cannot be a victory. This is the way that the school song should be worded:

> *Dear Old High School,*
> *Far Famed High School,*
> *Thou Shall Never Fail,*
> *Round Thy Name There Cling the*
>   *Tendrils of Traditions Trail,*
> *Thou Art Victor,*
> *Fame Has Followed,*
> *Clad in Dignity,*
> *May Thy Name to All Be Hallowed,*
> *By Our Love For Thee.*

School Mascot/Colors: While Dripping Springs was fielding athletic teams in basketball in the '20s and early '30s, according to E. E. Myers and confirmed by Sid Hall, they were called Cardinals, although none of the paper accounts ever mentioned a mascot. Their colors were red and white. When they fielded their first football team in 1938, they were called Tigers and their colors were maroon and gold. The story I was told said that the team got a real good deal on some maroon and gold uniforms that someone else had ordered but later changed their minds about. With the color change came the mascot change. Joel Thielepape seems to remember a campaign to name the mascot. A good guess would be September 1938. One article I read concerned the first Southwest Texas State football team. They were nicknamed the Tigers and were really, really bad, taking some pretty severe lickings. After the season, they decided they were not tough enough to be called Tigers, instead, they decided upon a smaller cat and adopted the Bobcat as their mascot. I just wonder if Dripping Springs decided the Cardinal was not a tough enough symbol for a football team and changed to something more ferocious.

The girls' teams did not have mentioned names either. Finally when they were using nicknames, the girls were called Tigerettes, which literally means female Tigers, which seems appropriate. They remained this until the mid-1980s when Bob Scott was the coach. It was the time when the UT girls' basketball team became known as the Lady Longhorns and many decided to mimic them by putting the word "Lady" in front of the school mascot. Coach Scott made the change, probably without any official permission, and ordered uniforms accordingly. This was 1985-86. It seems to me that Tigerettes comes a lot closer to being an appropriate name than Lady Tigers. I just don't see female Tigers as ladies. Coach Jerry English had in mind to change the name back to Tigerettes when he arrived in 1987 but found out that there might be some dissension in this decision and backed away. Too bad, as we were both from the traditional mold of history.

Becky Boone was the first person to dress up as the Tiger Mascot for the 1966-67 year. For whatever reason, this tradition stopped after the 1978-79 school year. It again became a prominent part of the cheerleader group beginning with the 1987-88 school year and continues to be an important plus to the program.

For one bright shining moment, Dripping Springs had a real live Bengal Tiger to go along with their own Tiger mascot. George Turner, a school maintenance man at the time, really got into the school spirit thing and purchased a real tiger in time for the 1975 homecoming parade. Unfortunately for everyone, the tiger had an unknown heart problem and died a few weeks later.

Athletic Programs

Football. Football was one of the newest sports to come to the Dripping Springs school system. It was not that Dripping Springs didn't want to be a part of the football world. Football took at least eleven players and Dripping Springs just was not large enough to have that many players. That chance finally came in 1938. Not because they had enough people to play eleven-man football but because the rules were changed. Other states with the same

First Dripping Springs Football Team, 1938
Left to right, bottom row: Cecil Maxey, J.W.T. Goslin, J. L. Glosson, E. E. Myers, T. K. Cauthen, Damon Hollingsworth; top row: J. P. Butler, Robert Glosson, Curly Glosson, Worth Spillar, Ed McIntyre, Jay Spillar. Not pictured: Coach W. R. Robbins.

problem of small rural schools came up with rules for a football game played by six people. Texas decided to instigate this brand of football for the smaller schools in the fall of 1938.

W. R. Robbins, the school principal, was given permission by the school board to promote a six-man football team, provided there was no expense to the school district. Dripping Springs joined 48 schools in this inaugural season. Nine districts were formed and Dripping Springs was placed in District 3 along with Prairie Lea, Martindale, Kyle, Dale, Wimberley, Lytton Springs, and Uhland. The plan was to have district champions but not have any playoff system. Dripping Springs lost a one-sided game to Prairie Lea in their first game ever and then behind the talented back, E. E. Myers, the Tigers rebounded for seven straight wins and ended up being Tri-champions with Prairie Lea and Martindale. The Tigers tried to get a rematch with Prairie Lea to avenge their only loss but Prairie Lea declined. Instead, they traveled to Victoria to match up with St. Joseph. The game was played in a downpour on the Wednesday night prior to Thanksgiving. The Tigers dropped the contest 24-6 to end their initial season at 7-2.

The next year was just as great. The marquee name this year was QB Damon Hollingsworth. Their only district loss was to Prairie Lea in a 7-2 season. That second loss was to Van Horn. This game was played in San Angelo and the paper made it out to be a state championship game but it was not. First of all, six-man did not play beyond district. What really happened was that the people playing six-man were anxious to show their game to others. So Coach Robbins of Dripping Springs and the coach of Van Horn got together and decided to play a match game as an exhibition for the people of San Angelo. The game was played on a Tuesday. The Tigers had played a game the previous Friday and were scheduled to play another the next Friday. Coach Robbins even brought his star RB of the previous season, E. E. Myers, along for the game. The Tigers lost the game 23-22.

Beginning with the 1941 season, district champions got to play a bi-district game as well. This format continued through the 1948 season. It did not help the Tigers for the next few years. These were the war years and many prospective players joined the war effort. One year the graduating class was composed of all girls. After the war, things got much better for the Tigers as a string of very good athletes made their appearance. They hired a bonified coach in 1946, G. A. Pringle, Jr. The Tigers won the championship in 1947 and then lost in bi-district. A close loss to Blanco knocked them out of the running in 1948 but 1949 was different. The format was changed to allow the schools to play to the regional level. Spearheaded by J. F. Glosson with a very good cast of players, the Tigers went through the entire year undefeated with a 12-0 record and a regional championship.

After the 1950 season, Dripping Springs had another major decision to make. Many of the schools of the area were getting large enough to go eleven-man or were deciding to drop football altogether. A vote was taken at Dripping Springs as to whether they wanted to remain in six-man or make the jump to eleven-man. The final decision was made to advance. The first two years, the Tigers had enough talent to break even in the win-loss column but the rest of the '50s were not very good ones. The student population was still not very large and it was difficult to have enough players. The Tigers played an inelgible player in 1957 and the UIL kicked Dripping Springs out of football for the 1958 season. They would play only five non-UIL schools that year. The 1961 team was one of the best as they finished 6-4. The 1964 team finished the season with only twelve players. Finally Dripping Springs began to grow and the number of players increased as well. The 1968 team won the first district championship in eleven-man football and lost at the regional level, still the highest level for Class B schools. Dripping Springs moved up to Class A in 1970 and won district championships in 1970 (lost bi-district), 73 (lost regional) and a tri-championship in 1975 (lost a flip). By 1976 the school had grown to the point it was classified a Class AA school and some lean years followed. The district would have moved up another notch if it had not been for the split with Lake Travis. Dripping Springs dropped to Class 2A (Class B had been dropped as a classification and the As moved up to 5A) until 1986. The 1985 team was a co-champion and got to go to the playoffs as the format allowed runnerups to gain playoff status as well. They lost the bi-district game. In 1988 the Tigers were the runnerup and advanced to the area game. The 1995 team placed second and lost bi-district and the 1997 team became the first to win an outright championship since the 1973 team and lost out in the area game. District growth moved Dripping Springs to 4A classification in 1998. We will never return to the days of yore when numbers were a problem.

Boys' Basketball. Even though it is well documented when Dripping Springs started playing football, the same could not be said for basketball. The first newspaper acknowledged game that I have been able to find at present was in February 1922 against Driftwood in which the boys won 13-3. No doubt basketball was around a few years prior to this.

Basketball was invented in 1891 as something to do inside during the winter months between the football and baseball seasons. For Dripping Springs and other small schools, there were no gyms and outdoor courts were the norm. There were a few gyms of various sizes in the area but Dripping Springs would not get their first

1937-38 Basketball Team
Left to right: E. E. "Nookie" Myers, O. S. Brumley, Tommy Turner, Dudley Lindsey, Leroy Johnson, Damon Hollingsworth. Not pictured: Coach Ralph Shelton.

one until 1953, although W. R. Robbins was allowed to solicit funds for a gymnasium at the January 27, 1938, board meeting. The UIL began sponsoring boys' basketball in 1915 and until 1920 only county champions were declared. Beginning in the 1920-21 season the boys played to a state championship. Until 1942 as many teams as wanted would gather at a site to declare a county champion. There were no classifications. Everyone was thrown into the same pot. The winners of a designated number of counties (maybe 14 or 15) was elgible to compete for a district title. There was a regional tourney for a certain number of district tourneys and those winners went to the state tourney to declare one state champion.

Many of the early games were low-scoring and it wasn't necessarily because there were poor shooters. It was a matter of time. One of the articles I read said they had 15-minute halves. The clock did not stop except for timeouts, fouls, and jump balls. On top of that, after each point was made, either field goal or free throw, the ball would be returned to midcourt for a jumpball by the centers. There were times when the coaches had to referee half of the game. One person was designated the free throw shooter for all fouls. Four fouls and you were out of the game. Eventually, there were eight-minute quarters but the clock still did not stop except for timeouts, fouls, and jump balls. The center jump was dropped after points. Today the clock stops at each whistle and there is only a jump ball to start the game.

At the present, no information has been found as to whether Dripping Springs entered any of the county tournaments in the '20s. They did start to enter regularly in the '30s. They had some very fine teams but were unable to get past the much larger San Marcos, losing to them in several county finals. Finally in 1938, they were able to come away with the county championship. Usually the teams competing were Buda, Kyle, Wimberley, Mt. Gainer, Henly, Dripping Springs, San Marcos High School, and San Marcos Junior High. When only five or six entered, a round robin format was played, but as more entered it became a regular type tourney format. Early tourneys were played in San Marcos because the college had a gym and then the site was moved from time to time to Kyle when they built their gym.

In 1942 the UIL decided to form districts just as football did and the classifications were B, A, AA, and later the city division was added. They played to state championships. In 1949-50 and 1950-51, the Tigers won their district zone but were defeated in the district championship game. All through the '50s they had good teams but had the misfortune of being in the same district as Kyle, a basketball powerhouse. The Tiger teams of 1957-58 and 1958-59, led by Bobby Shelton, were poised to upset Kyle but still could not get over the hump. It took a little luck and the skills of Poe Shelton to bring Dripping Springs its first district title in 1968-69. The Tigers returned to the throne in 1970-71. Poe Shelton returned to Dripping Springs as its head coach in 1978. During his tenure his teams won district titles in 1983-84, 1985-86, 1987-88, 1994-95, and had eight other playoff teams. His 1985-86 team made it to the state finals in Class AA. He won 441 games in his 22-year career at Dripping Springs.

Girls' Basketball. Girls basketball had to endure many ups and downs in its early days and did not really start getting some consistency until 1950 when the UIL decided to sponsor it again. Mostly it was an image thing. People had problems thinking of the female as being capable of being an athlete, and the early rules reflected this. Until 1978, girls basketball in Texas had six players on each team instead of the five that boys did. Because of the belief that girls could not and should not exert themselves in strenuous exercises, the rules were modified. The court was divided into three sections. The two forwards played in the third that was under their goal. The two centers played in the middle third and the two guards were in the third that included their opponent's goal. Only the forwards could score. After each basket the ball was brought to the center circle and given to one of the other team's centers. No player could dribble more than twice before having to pass it. Later the court was divided in half and each half had three players, guards and forwards. The forwards again were the only ones to score and the ball was returned to midcourt after each basket. This practice was dropped in the mid-'50s and put more importance on the ballhandling skills of the guards and forwards and speeded up the pace of the game but did cause much congestion at the half-court line at times. In 1978 the decision was made to make the girls' game a full court affair with only five players and have the same rules as the boys.

It is not known when the Dripping Springs girls began to play basketball. There is a picture of a girls' team that claims to be a 1912 photo. Could be. An article in the February edition of the *San Marcos Record* mentioned the girls' basketball team defeated Driftwood 11-0 on a Saturday in 1922. We know that the UIL did not begin to sponsor the sport until 1918 and the girls would play only to the county level. By 1928, the UIL was pressured into dropping the sponsorship for girls' basketball because of the stigma about it being unhealthy for girls to compete in athletics. This did not put an end to girls' basketball, however. They simply found other sponsors for the next 22 years. Girls' basketball was mostly a rural sport as most large schools did not field girls' teams until the 1970s.

Even so, the Dripping Springs girls did not play that much basketball during the '20s and '30s. They played more volleyball than basketball, although there are articles with them playing some of the schools around. They began playing more in the '40s and then joined the UIL in 1950 to start a full-time participation in the sport. Their first district championship came in 1959-60 with Becky Shelton leading the scoring. Donna Pittman, the school's all-time leading scorer, started a string of titles under DSHS grad Oran Rippy. In 1967-68, they were co-champs, losing in a playoff, then becoming the champions the next year. The Tigerettes would go on to win titles for the next three years and then a drought began. Five-girl basketball took place in 1978-79 and the Tigerettes continued to struggle until Coach Jerry English came on board in 1987-88. He had a record that exuded winning. He took the Lady Tigers to the Big Show five times and won it all in 1993-94 before retiring in 2000. Pecos McDaniel led them back to the state tourney in 2001-02

Boys' Track and Field. Track was the sport that got the UIL started in 1911. Of course track had always been a natural sport. There was always the race to see who was the fastest, who could jump the longest or highest, or throw the fartherest. The University of Texas began having an invitational track meet in 1905 and by 1911 the UIL held a state meet. That first meet had about 20 schools represented by 100 participants. In the early days scoring was 5-3-2-1 for four places and relays counted the same, so many teams did not waste good athletes on relays because they could score more as individuals. Today the points are 10-8-6-4-2-1 for the top six places for individuals and relays double the points. Again the track format was like that of basketball. You had a county meet and the people placing in that meet participated in a district meet made up of several counties and then a regional meet with a certain number of county-meet qualifiers. The top four finishers qualified for the state meet.

Dripping Springs usually participated in the county meet. San Marcos did not participate in this meet because they were considered a Class A team. Kyle and Buda were the top teams that Dripping Springs had to compete against. They had only a few participants, did not score that many points, and usually finished no higher than third until 1940 when the Tigers won their first county championship.

The most dominant trackster for the Tigers was Elbert Earl Myers. He won the 100 and 220 all four years at the county meet and a second in the broad jump his senior year kept him from doing the same in that event. In his sophomore year he was the high point individual in the meet with 22 points when he won the 100, 220, broad jump, and javelin throw, and was third in the shot put. Prorated under today's scoring that would have him scoring 46 points out of a possible 50. It has been said he ran a 9.9 100 yard dash and he ran a 10.0 twice in those four years, so it is certainly possible. In his senior year he placed fourth at the regional meet in the 100 to qualify for the state meet. However, he got sick and was unable to go to Austin for that meet.

Dripping Springs won their first district championships in 1946-47-50 with a few good individuals. One of those was Raymond Whisenant who scored 46 points in '46 and 33 in '47. Dripping Springs won district championships in 1971-72-73-74 and second in 1975 with numbers over talent, although their mile relay team went to state in 1975 and an 880 man in 1976. Since that time Dripping Springs has not had the numbers to compete for the title but have had some outstanding individuals who have made it to the state. In 1997 Travis Couey won the 800 meter dash to be the only boys' state champion to date.

Girls' Track and Field. The stigma of girls participating in athletics was never stronger than in track. Finally in the late 1960s an association was formed and the girls began to participate in track outside the UIL umbrella. Dripping Springs got involved then and had some girls and relays compete in the state meet. Finally in the 1971-72 school year, the UIL began sponsoring the sport and the records just kept toppling, nullifying the myth about females not being able to compete. Like the boys, the girls have not had the numbers to really compete for the title but one year did come up with a strong effort that netted them a second place. Just like the boys, they have sent some outstanding individuals to the state meet with the most notable being Kirsten Diltz.

Volleyball. Volleyball has been a favorite among the girls for a long time. While basketball was not being sponsored by the UIL, volleyball was played. Several articles in the newspaper had the boys playing a basketball game and the girls playing that same team in volleyball. Volleyball was an event at the county meet and the Tigerettes won the county meet in 1941 and qualified for the district meet in Georgetown where they made it to the quarter finals. When the school decided to build a fence around the campus, they removed the dirt basketball court and replaced it with volleyball and tennis courts. In those days the boys also played volleyball at the county level. The Tigerettes won a couple more titles in the '40s and the boys one. The boys still competed at the county meet until 1964-65.

The UIL began to sponsor girls' volleyball in 1967. The season moved around in the early days. It started out being a spring sport but it seemed to conflict with too many spring sports and finally it was decided to put it in the fall slot where it remains to this day. This put it opposite the football season where no girls' sports were being played. However, it was not, and in many cases, still is not accepted by the basketball coaches because it interferes with basketball practice time and takes some of the athletes away from this early practice. Many schools did not even offer volleyball because basketball's influence rules, but volleyball has caught on and most school programs today include it.

Paul Allen came to Dripping Springs as the high school principal in the fall of 1968. He decided that Dripping Springs should have a volleyball team and he started one in 1969-70. Dripping Springs was still a Class B school and not many teams were playing. The playoffs had only two classifications. The early years saw the team play each team once and then have a district tournament. Volleyball stuttered for a few years until Barbara Nixon Ernst was hired to coach the volleyball team and the program began to get on its feet in 1972. Rhonda Havins took over and steered them to a co-championship in 1976-77. The Tigerettes had a string of district titles, made easier, in some cases, by being the only team in their district. This was certainly not the fault of the Tigerettes. The titles kept coming even when they had opponents. They were led to the state championship in 1994-95 by the play of Jinni Touchstone and coached by Melissa Koopman. The district titles came in 1948, 1950, 1957, 1976, 1978-81, 1988-94, 1996-97.

Baseball. Baseball was the national pastime for the longest. Every community and school had a baseball team. There were no district or county tournaments. Each school fielded a team, if they could, and matched other common school districts. Dripping Springs played Fitzhugh, Mt. Gainer, Driftwood, Wimberley, and others around. School terms ended so early that most of the baseball was played as a community team more than a school team. All the games played in Dripping Springs were on the field located on blocks one and two where the bank complex and Central Garage now stand. Early players recall how the backstop was in the southwest corner and faced northeast toward the county barn with the raised road down the rightfield line. As the years progressed and buildings and roads became a part of the area, the playing field was squeezed down. Before the school was moved across the Dripping Springs branch, the baseball field shared the space with the football field. However, it is said that after Allen Stephenson's death in 1938, as a result of an injury in a baseball game, school baseball was discontinued for over a decade.

The UIL began sponsoring baseball in 1948 where all play stopped at the district level. The next year the AA division played to a state championship while the others played to bi-district. Dripping Springs started fielding a team in 1951. They won the district championship in 1957-58-59. Another string was put together in 1966-67-68.

Baseball was dropped for lack of participation in 1975 and was not picked up until 1980. Dennis Seale started up the new program and guided it for 14 years, the big season being 1986 when the Tigers made it to the state finals. They repeated that lofty perch in 1998 under Tom Hancock.

The first baseball field for the Tigers was located on the north end of the campus, where the new intermediate school now stands. In 1957, the district purchased a small sliver of land on the west side of the football field and this became the backstop and infield while the football field served as the outfield. Lights were added at the same time. This field served as the baseball field until the new high school was completed in 1985-86. This was one of the better fields in the district but growth dictated that it be torn down to make room for other things. The new field was built in time for the 1998 season at the 40-acre park on RR12 S.

Tennis. Tennis was the second sport added by the UIL. Boys' doubles came in 1914 and finally singles and doubles for girls by 1920. Dripping Springs, if they played, were in the county meets in the spring along with track and field and the other activities. The first winning tennis team was in 1941 when Wilma and Edith Goslin won the county championship by beating a San Marcos team. They placed third in the district meet. Dripping Springs has played tennis ever since then and has had some good tennis players along the way, winning at the district level in singles and doubles and finishing high in the regional tourney. Today, they are competing in team tennis as well.

The early teams had to practice and play on a dirt court in the front playground of the old Academy school. When I arrived at Dripping Springs in 1965, there was an old asphalt court with a wire net and that was it. The gym was used for most practices. Finally in 1976, a two-court facility was built on the campus. Many times the kids had to go to peoples' houses with private courts to practice. The players who lived in the Lakeway area have added courts over there. Even when the four courts were a part of the new high school built in 1985, there was a shortage of courts and private ones were still used when necessary. The new middle school opened in 1995 with four additional courts. There was a drive by some to build a tennis complex on the east side of the high school campus but it was dropped when what enthusiasm there was was not met by an equal financial fervor. The court shortage was eased for a while when four courts on the north side of the high school courts were completed in 2000.

Golf. Golf was made available for all classifications in 1951. To the best of my knowledge, the first time a Dripping Springs golf team entered a district competion was in 1966 but they have fielded teams ever since. The first girl, Kathy Glosson, played in the early '70s. Seldom have the girls had enough players to fill a team which takes at least four to compete. The usual team is five with the best four scores counting. District titles were taken by the boys in 1966, 1971-72, 1976, 1979, 1983-84, 1986, 1988. The 1986-88 teams earned trips to the state tourney.

Cross Country Running. This is another sport that got its start before the UIL began sponsoring it in 1972. Prior to that time, San Marcos Academy hosted what they called the state cross country meet. In the early years the sport was seen as a way to keep track people interested in the off season. The district meet consisted of getting a group of people not playing the sport in season and have them run. The cross country season is in the fall now and the people running in this sport are those who want to run and train for that purpose. In the last decade, the Tigers have been fortunate to have some very dedicated and talented people taking part in this sport. Kirsten Diltz placed high in the state meet several years and Erik Hernandez and Shawn Sultemeier come to mind in the boys' division.

Soccer. Soccer had a stuttering start at Dripping Springs. In 1979-80, Dripping Springs had a superintendent who was a big soccer fan and played the sport himself. Jeffrey K. Lindzey pushed for and got a school team started under the eye of Larry LeCompte. Soccer was not a UIL sport but they played teams around Austin, playing some of their games at Zilker Park. They did not win a game that first year but the next year they finished with a 6-2 record. Lindzey left when the school split with Lake Travis, and so did soccer.

Soccer came under the auspices of the

UIL in the early '80s but only for 4A and 5A schools. If you wanted to play the sport, a school had to get in with the larger districts to do so. Thinking that soccer was a good conditioning sport during the off-season, school teams were formed again. An outside person coached the teams that played in 1987-89. Again the sport did not take off, mainly because Dripping Springs was a 3A school and there were few 3A schools playing soccer.

As Dripping Springs kept growing and it became obvious that they would soon be joining the 4A ranks, plans were made to get the program going again. In the 1997 season Coach Steve Krupp oversaw an intramural program. The next year a team was formed that played outside competition. In 1999, the Tigers were in 4A and they finally competed in the UIL as a member of 25-4A. This time the sport of soccer took at Dripping Springs.

Powerlifting. As athletics got more and more involved in weightlifting for off-season and all sports, it was only a matter of time when schools wanted to compete in that area as well. Randy Rockhold came to Dripping Springs in 1987 as the volleyball coach and trainer. He began the program and it continues to prosper.

There are different weight divisions, usually in about nine-pound increments, which allows more competitive divisions. Girls and boys alike compete for the right to make it to the state meet. Dripping Springs has had several of its athletes make it to the state meet and finish high. Coach Brian Parker has taken the sport to another level as he has a good group of boys and girls compete every year.

Girls' Fastpitch Softball. Softball has been around for a long time in Dripping Springs history. It was usually called playground ball. Teams matched up with other schools around, just as the baseball team did, sometimes playing as part of a doubleheader.

A couple of championships were won in the late '40s and the sport was played into the early '60s before being discontinued. Title IX, which basically says that girls had to be offered the same opportunities or alternatives as the boys, had a lot to do with many additions to girls' sports. There was not an alternate sport for baseball and some girls played on the high school baseball teams, but could not compete in numbers. The colleges began to offer fastpitch and where there is a college sport you can bet high schools will follow. So fastpitch softball was offered. Dripping Springs had their first team in the spring of 1994 under the tutelage of Dennis Seale. They won district the first three years and made it to the state tourney in 1995. They won district and made it to the regional finals in 1998. Other district titles came in 2002-03.

Things Read or Heard

The *San Marcos Free Press* issue of June 15, 1882, described Commencement Day for the first class of the Dripping Springs Academy. It occurred on a Thursday after three days of exams. The writer said it was the largest assembly that had ever been held in Dripping Springs. After having eaten a good dinner, as many as could get in, assembled in the chapel to witness the primary department. It consisted of dialogues, speeches, and music, both vocal and instrumental. At 7:00 P.M., high school commencement began with a song of welcome by the school. It continued with orations and essays, intermixed with music, both vocal and instrumental. About 11:00 P.M., the exercises were closed with a comical song by Mr. Isom Good.

The Nutshell, a paper published in Kyle, covered the first closing ceremonies of the Academy, too. The paper came out on June 10, 1882, and the information was published in the March 4, 1938 edition of the *San Marcos Record*. Someone had found the *Nutshell* and brought it in to them. It gave the participants in both the Primary and High School ceremonies.

The participants in the Primary closing were Alpha Caperton, Frank W. Jordan,

Willie Meers, Mamie Jordan, Lola Busch, Cynthia Crow, Millie Jordan, Charles Jordan, Bertie Boardman, Robert and Herbert Meers, Mark Polk, Samuel Fairchilds, Lillie Jordan, Genie Bush, Willie Chapman, Eddie Loralls (sp), Bedford Caperton, and Ruth Wallace. An oration on the evils of temperances was given by H. L. Morrell. A Mr. Bell of Blanco gave a speech complementing Miss Morrell's ability and gave her a present in behalf of the children.

Participants of the high school program were listed as Mamie Jordan, Milton B. James, Millie and Lillie Jordan, oration by James M. Hubbs of Blanco, music by Mr. Riley and Miss Jordan, Lou Womack, Charlie Jordan, John Baldwin, Daniel Gibson, Thomas Womack, Newton Marshall, Millie Jordan, A. L. Davis, Jr., Richard Hare, Robert Marshall, Lillie Jordan, W. B. Harmon, W. P. Riley, Dannie Crow, Lee J. Good, and John Bell.

The August 17, 1882, issue of SMFP mentions that the young men of the Academy had been preaching and holding revivals. There will be five young ministers in school next year. The following students did not miss a single question in any recitation during last session. They were Solon Bell, William Harmon, James Hubb, Newton Marshall, Henry Morrell, and Annie McCowen.

Music was a big thing in those days. During the summer a normal vocal music school was now in session with about 80 pupils. Professor Shook and others were teaching it. (SMFP 8-16-1883)

Our school getting along fine. Patrons believe children learning under Horsley and Callahan. Yesterday was picnic day. Had good music. Morning spent crowning the May Queen. Some maids nervous before they finished their parts. Marshall won't be scared anymore when doing his part. Next was dinner. There was a bunch of tables with pies and cakes. Attended by an estimated 300. Mr. Preyham and Alex Smith stood in the middle and called all to come. Mrs. Dunn, who was sick and could not be there, was sent food on a buggy. By this time, yellow and blue jackets were on the ground with bats and balls. Ground was quite wet. (SMFP 5-8-1884)

Alphonzo writes about Academy's commencement exercises. Tuesday night, two societies composed of little girls and young ladies gave an entertainment. He did not have a program to name names. Young ladies opened with a president's address by Miss Dellie Graham saying her society named after "Enterpe," goddess of music. The closing ceremonies were held Wednesday night. Roll of Honor—Boys: D. W. Burkett, F. N. Conover, W. H. Milam, D. P. Hollis, R. G. Richardson, T. J. Womack, S. B. Caperton. Girls: Lelia Bush, Cora Hollis, Fannie Marshall, Jennie Williams, Lina Hamilton, F. R. Williams. Gold medals went to Miss Georgia Pound and Mr. Bedford Caperton. Thirty singers gave a concert. D. W. Burkett had a solo "The Laziest Man in Town." Another solo by Cora Hollis. Quartet of R. L. Marshall, W. R. Lincoln, D. W. Burkett and T. J. Womack sang "Jolly Jonathan." *Profundo Basso* was sung by H. N. Lincoln, D. H. Womack, Della Wortham and Fannie Marshall. Misses Carrie Bell and Lou Womack sang "Shun the Broad Road." "The Crown of Love" sung by six little girls and Miss Alice Lincoln was deemed best by the writer. Dellie Graham presented to our school the motto "God Bless Our School." (SMFP 6-18-1885)

On Saturday, June 12, 1886, everyone invited to grand entertainment to be held at Walnut Springs. Ice cream, lemonade, etc. will be sold for the benefit of the Academy. At 5:00 P.M. musical entertainment will take place at the Academy. Included will be vocal and instrumental and string band. There will be candidate speeches and social conversation. (SMFP 6-10-1886)

School closed on Wednesday for Thanksgiving and reopened on Monday. Ladies are planning a Christmas dinner to raise funds for the damage done to the school. Tickets are 50 cents. (SMFP 12-2-1886). Christmas dinner for the school netted $53. (SMFP 1-6-1887)

Dripping Springs Academy closes for the summer vacation with an exhibition on Wednesday night. Academy exhibition showed lack of rehearsal but individually done well. The prologue by Chester Harrison was good. The juveniles in "When I'm a Man" ranked high and the Four Seasons were carried out with better stage effects than other pieces. Willie Chapman as "Summer Queen" was a success as was Love Pound as Folly. Miss A. Greer was cut out for an old maid. The parting salutation by Alpha Caperton was very good. Professor Cook's airs on the violin were enjoyed by the boys. (SMFP 6-28-1888)

Daily bell reminds us that school is in session. More than half the students that should be in school are missing due to picking cotton. They are earning money for needed articles. (SMFP 11-17-1889)

People getting ready for Christmas. Had concerts on Thursday and Friday nights to raise money to improve condition of the school house. Thursday night was given by the younger members: Walter Garrett "Don't Want to be Good." Pauline Seal—"Flirt," Walter Etheridge "A Solemn Face," Sallie Rowe "What a Girl Thinks of a Boy," Floyd O'Pry "What a Boy Thinks of a Girl," Maud Harrison played military music. Lizzie Bell, Callie Rowe, Sampie McLendon gave speeches. Music by Carrie Stephenson, also "Family Matters." Music by Ivanhoe Grand and closed with the "Stage Struck Darky." Friday night's agenda included: Willie Chapman, Deck and Stella Roberts plus Herbert Howard, John Garrett, Tom Walker, Tom Womack, and Chester Harrison played the "Little Brown Jug" showing the evils of drink. Showed that Professor Collier had done a good job. "How He Popped the Question" by Katie Howard and Tom Womack, Mr. Toddy Marshall was a "Thorn Among the Roses" played by Misses Chapman, McMillan, Weaver, Alpha Caperton, Carrie Stephenson and Lulla Deck. Music rendered by Stella Roberts, Birdie McLendon, Willie Chapman, Katie Howard, Georgia Pound, and Alpha Caperton. Ended with a darky farce with boys being blacked almost beyond recognition. (SMFP 12-26-1889)

School opened September 7 and after a two months' successful private term, began November 2 with 90 students. During private term all students received good grades in written and oral work in recitations and examinations. (*Hays County Times* and *Farm Journal* 11-5-1891)

The influence of the Dripping Springs education system can be seen in the number of students who later became teachers around the area. Some that were listed in county records during the 1891-94 school years were: R. L. Marshall (Rock Springs, Bluff Springs), G. W. Marshall (Rock Springs, Cherry Springs, Mt. Sharp), Aquilla Deck (Mt. Gainer), Alice Rowe (Bell Springs, Rock Springs), Lovonia Pound (Liberty Hill which is now Driftwood), Flora Sorrell (Mt. Gainer), Ada Sorrell (River Side), Alpha Caperton (Pounds Chapel), and Annie Cavett (Henly). Teachers tended to not stay at the same school very long.

There was an ice cream supper at Mr. Madings' hotel last Saturday night. Proceeds went to fixing up the school. It was in bad need of repairs. (HCTFJ 9-28-1894)

In the *Driftwood Heritage* book, there was an excerpt from Lucy Black Martin's diary dated 4-7-1898. Her comments were: "Went to Dripping Springs to concert, carried our supper and ate at Walnut Springs. Driftwood, Gatlin and Wildwood crowd had a jolly time. Concert given by Public School of Dripping Springs. Professor Oscar Stubbs, Miss Nannie Dorroh and Annie Cavett being teachers."

The community held a fundraiser for the school and windmill projects. Bad weather held down the expected crowd. Dr. E. P. Shelton emceed a spelling bee which was won by 76-year old Mrs. M. H. Howard, Sr. A cake was put up for penny a vote for the prettiest girl. Miss Emma McCuistion won over Miss Lou Spillar 6060-5238. There was an ugliest man cake. Ed McKellar won over Dr. Shelton 85-58. Professor Corder was a distant third with 17. It was McKellar's birthday. He cut the cake and found that it was made of cornbread, covered with icing and coconut. This event raised $136. Part went to buy desks and some to the windmill fund. The people raised $480 for the two projects. (*Kyle News* 11-17-1905)

Ennis Follis recalls her days at the Academy while a student. It had a very high ceiling. Rooms were separated by dividers that would only go up maybe eight feet high. One of the pastimes of the students was to toss paper wads back and forth over the dividers while the classes were going.

Ennis Follis remembers the day Rosa Lyle left school to get married to W. E. Spaw. She was only about fourteen at the time. She was in the room where they had blackboards all around the walls so that quite a few students at a time could do lessons of the various subjects. Evidently Rosa just up and walked out of the room to meet Mr. Spaw. Miss Follis was not in the same room but remembers there to be quite a commotion at the time over the incident.

At the time in the early '20s after the second story was added to the Academy, as well as the outside stairs, Eva Glimp was one of the teachers. The outside stairs led to an auditorium. After one of the meetings, Mrs. Glimp slipped as she was coming down the stairs and slid the rest of the way down. A gentleman at the bottom, who helped her up asked " Did you miss a step, Mrs. Glimp?" To this she answered, "Hell no, I hit every one of them."

E. B. "Pete" Glosson recalls an incident that occurred at his 1932 graduation exercises. There were only four in the class. Pete was joined by Leland Lyle, Vivian Thielepape and Fannie Wilson. A part of the program was for the four to sing a song. Leland and Vivian began singing with gusto while Pete and Fannie spent the entire song laughing and giggling. After this, someone was heard to comment "That graduating class is made up of one gentleman, one lady, and two fools."

The School Board, at the 9-10-1936 meeting, decided to buy four typewriters so that typing could be offered at the school.

When Ed Thomasson resigned as teacher and coach before the school term had begun, Dr. E. P. Shelton had to resign from the school board, where he was president, so that his son Ralph could be considered for the position. Ralph Shelton was hired. This was at the 9-19-1935 meeting.

When the Board hired Irvin Nixon as the principal at the 9-1-1936 meeting, it was with the understanding that he would have to live in the district.

The School Board, in its meeting on 10-14-1940, gave Bill Garnett permission to overhaul the bus with new rings, valves and other necessary parts not to exceed $20.

In the days of wood stoves, kids had a favorite, if not dangerous, trick to pull. The stove was a big round pot-bellied type of stove with a little ledge. A piece of sheet metal was fashioned to make a barrier from the stove, so students would not get burned. After the teacher had the kids go to their seats, someone dropped some 22 shells on the little shelf. A few minutes later, as everyone was seated, they exploded and made a big noise as the casings rattled around the metal protector.

Louella Williamson McNair tells a couple of incidents that she was a part of when she went to school at Dripping Springs. She said one of her teachers, Rayma Dillingham, usually had papers piled all over her desk. Some of the boys found a dead mouse and put it under one of her piles of paper. They waited what seemed like forever for her to discover this mouse. She said the wait was worth the while when she discovered it and let out a blood-curdling scream and panicked.

On Halloween, the seniors had decided that they would make it skip day and go into Austin. Lou and another classmate went to their parents to clear it with them. They had their blessing to go on a bus to Austin that day. Unfortunately for Lou and her friend, the bus depot was just across the street from the school at the Goslin drugstore. As they were getting ready to board the bus, Superintendent M. B. Tilley, grabbed them by the shoulders and escorted them back to school. The only two with permission were the only two who had to attend school that day. The others got away.

The first cafeteria at the Academy was located in the northeast corner of the building. John McClaferty is said to have donated the money and some of the work in putting in the sinks. Opal Hadley, Dosia Hohman, and Lillian Whisenant were among the first cooks for the Dripping Springs school. J. F. Glosson says he can still remember smelling the beans cooking as he would come down the stairs. Later as more room was needed, the old Hamilton Pool school building was rebuilt on the campus and used as the cafeteria. In those days, each student had to bring a tin plate, cup, and utensils for their meal.

Grady Moore recalls an incident that happened while he, his dad, S. J. Moore, Bill Spillar, and A. B. Cauthen were tearing down the Hamilton Pool school in the summer of 1945 to make the new cafeteria. Luckily his dad was not there at the time. He says Bill was about 6'6" and had just returned from the Navy. Grady would not graduate for a few more years. It was a very hot day and Bill had his shirt off and was sweating profusely. After getting an ice cold drink of water, Grady proceeded to pour a cup of this cold water on Bill. Reaction was predictable. Bill chased and caught Grady. Bill pulled every stitch of clothing off Grady and tossed them high up into a nearby cedar tree. A naked Grady proceeded to try and climb the cedar tree to retrieve his clothes. Just as he was about to get near them, Bill would shout "Here comes a car," and Grady would scramble down to prevent someone from seeing him naked. After two or three times of this, Grady finally decided to get a long stick and get his clothes down. Suffice it to say, Grady did not toss cold water on Bill again.

R. L. Lyle remembers a rockpile at the Academy campus and his contribution to it. Seems when a kid got into trouble at school, the punishment was to go out on the playground and pick up a bucket of rocks and dump them on this pile. R. L. remembers dumping his share of rocks on the pile. (I did not know this history then, but when we moved to Dripping Springs in 1965 and lived on the property, there was a rock pile located in the northwest corner of the campus—maybe some of the residue from years before).

According to R. L. Lyle, when Robert Shelton was superintendent of DSISD, he had the school divided with a painted line in the hallway. It was necessary to solve a problem he had at school. In those days, all twelve grades were housed under the one roof. High school occupied the western part of the building and elementary the eastern part. He painted the line from the north entrance to the hallway officially dividing the building. If any student was caught crossing into the other's territory, they stood a good chance of getting a paddling. Mr. Shelton's office was at the southeast entrance to the building and on the wall outside his office was the manual fire alarm bell. Seems his painted line became necessary because high school students were forever running up, ringing the alarm, and then taking off. His line put the alarm in forbidden territory for high school students.

I believe a complete book could be written on the things Grady Moore did while a student at Dripping Springs. There never seems to be a shortage for this 1954 graduate. Here are a few he told me himself.

Grady was always trying to think up ways to get laughs from his fellow students. While he was a younger student attending classes in the second story of the Academy building, one of the stunts he liked to pull was to hang outside a window. This was to make the teacher think he had left the room. It would have been a dangerous fall if he had lost his grip.

In Lura Lyle's English class, Grady sat in one of the front row desks (I wonder why?). One of his favorite tricks was to catch Mrs.

Lyle not facing him and he would call out "Hey Moore," "Hey Moore." He would then turn around and tell one of the boys (calling them by name) to quit bothering him as he was trying to pay attention to the teacher. Mrs. Lyle would then admonish the other student for interfering with Grady's study habits.

Still another way he managed to get a laugh and disrupt the class at the same time occurred in his vocational agriculture class. He would act like a punch-drunk fighter. He had convinced the ag teacher that he had once been a boxer and he always reacted to a bell sound. In the ag room were metal light reflectors. Grady would throw a rock up and hit the reflector. When the rock would hit the metal and make the sound, Grady would jump up and start beating on one of the other boys and, of course, causing a disruption of the proceedings.

Katherine Berkley Cannon tells this story on her English teacher, Lura Lyle. She was described as being a very prim and proper person and a stern disciplinarian. She simply would not put up with foolishness and the students seldom saw any other side in the classroom. A slip of tongue during one class proved her to be human after all. On this day, Mrs. Lyle announced to the class that they would begin the study of the book "The Tale of Two Titties." When she realized what she had said, she put her head on her desk and began to laugh uncontrollably, showing a side of her that was unknown before.

Alva Haydon said that in the late '20s, he and another student had the responsibility of starting the wood stove fire each morning at the school. They noted this chore was made a little unpleasant because of the smell as they began the fire. Later they discovered why the fire smelled. It seemed the way the principal, Pop Stephens, chose to put the fire out at the end of the day was to urinate on it.

Both Alva Haydon and "Pete" Glosson had the same remembrance of Pop "Purple Head" Stephens. Their most vivid memory of him was his purple hair. Alva surmised that his hat must have gotten wet and faded on his hair. Pete wasn't sure that he didn't dye it on purpose. Sounds like Mr. Stephens was just ahead of his time. Certainly would not have been noticed in today's times.

Alva Haydon recalls that when H. L. Peavy was his principal, the school building did not have a phone. On April 1, a person came to school and told him he had a phone call in the store across the street. He went over to answer it, only to find it was an April Fool's joke. In the meantime, it was hailing outside and Alva had opened the window to get a hand full of hailstones to throw at classmates. Mr. Peavy grabbed him from behind and gave him a paddling, which was an embarrassing moment for Alva.

Alva also recalls another interesting event in the classroom. He and friend, U. S. McNair, sat in a double-seat desk together and there was a girl in front of them who sat in a single desk seat. U.S. drilled a hole in the back of her seat and put a nail in it. He would then, from time to time, push the nail with his foot, causing it to stick the girl. Fortunately, the girl did not tell on the two.

At the 10-14-1940 Board meeting, the pep squad was given permission to make one trip with the football team during the season.

The School Board met on 2-5-1942 to consider measures for War Time, since the United States had just declared war on Japan in December. Their first consideration was for students to attend school six days a week, so that it would shorten the school year. This was voted down by the Board. Their decision was to start classes at 10:00 A.M. until March 2, then 9:30 A.M. until March 30th. Thereafter, until the end of the school year, it would start up at 9:00 A.M. They would later consider ways to make up the lost time.

The 1942 graduating class at Dripping Springs consisted of seven girls. All the boys in the class who could have graduated with them had joined the armed forces to fight in WWII.

Poe Shelton, a student at DSHS, and later to become its all-time winning basketball coach, had a very embarrassing moment during his senior year. One of the teachers was partaking of a drink of water at the water fountain in the hall near the east entrance to the main building. He thought it was a student he knew and he patted her on the behind as he went by. When she raised up, he realized who it was and you have never seen the shades of red on a face before. He apologized profusely, but she did not want to drop it at that. She even brought in her husband before it was settled. No doubt he was more careful when walking by a water fountain after that.

Joyce Felts, the band and choir director provided a lasting memory for me and the others who attended the choir concert in the gymnasium that night. As he raised the baton to begin the first song, he spied one of the girls chewing gum. He immediately went to her place on the riser and grabbed her by the shoulders and shaking her while telling her in a loud voice he had told everyone "No gum." Then he turned around, as everyone watched in disbelief, and with a composed smile on his face, returned to his place to continue the concert as if nothing had transpired. Needless to say, he only lasted one year.

The strength of numbers was brought out by Paul Allen, the high school principal. It was the year that new football bleachers were installed at the football field. The old bleachers had to be removed first. Steel slides were welded to the supports so that they could become mobile and be used for the visitors side. Mr. Allen said we would just get a group of students and walk them across the field. I thought to myself, "Are you crazy?" Instead, he rounded up all the high school male students and coaches, had them grab a place along the steel girders, counted to three, and sure enough, the bleachers were lifted up as if they were made of match sticks and walked sixty yards across the field. I would have never believed, if I had not seen it.

All through the 1950s, Kyle had great basketball teams and kept the Tigers out of the throne room. Head-to-head had failed to produce victories so the Tigers tried another tactic in hope of getting a victory. In the January 31, 1956 match, Kyle jumped out to a 10-3 first quarter lead. From this point, Dripping Springs decided to play keep-away and Kyle went along, since they were leading anyway. Neither team scored in the second and third quarters. Kyle went on to a 19-3 victory.

In the early '50s, the Bastrop Bears were in the same district as the Tigers. In the season they were to play on the Tiger field, the Bastrop school wrote to Dripping Springs requesting half of the bleacher space for their school band, which was their right. It was all right with Dripping Springs. The football field had no bleachers at this time.

Today's athletic teams expect that the school will provide them with transportation, even to the extent of chartered buses. That has not always been the case in the history of Dripping Springs athletics. In the early days of sports, lasting into the late 1940s, athletic teams had to find their own transportation to the games. Many times it was someone's station wagon, pulling a trailer. Other times it might be someone who had a flatbed truck or parents providing cars. The students did not drive. They just piled on and enjoyed the ride. When the school finally started having buses, it still took a special game before the school provided a bus for the athletes.

Football might not have gotten its start at Dripping Springs in 1938 if it had not been for the benevolence of the principal and the future football coach, W. R. Robbins. When he went to the school board to ask them for permission to form a six-man football team, the board let him know they would not be liable for the expense of the sport. The Board president was heard to ask "Mr. Robbins, just how do you propose to pay for the expenses?" His reply was "Sir, you can take it out of my salary." And with that method of meeting expenses, Dripping Springs had a team in the fall of 1938.

When property was bought for the new high school in 1947, the football field was moved to that campus for games in 1948. As before, there were no lights for the field and home games had to be played in the afternoon. A drive was started to raise money for the installation of football lights. When the drive began to falter, W. P. "Will" Crow came to the rescue with a $1,000 donation. Without it, the likelihood of the Tigers playing their first game of the 1949 season under the lights, would probably not have occurred.

In 1968, Dripping Springs beat Florence for the first and only time in football. It meant the district championship. The Tigers won 12-6. After the game, the Florence fans jumped the cable barrier and grabbed the officials in protest. The players let the DS fans know of their displeasure with obscene gestures as they marched in front of the Tiger stands. This brought both schools before the UIL Board for explanation and subsequently, Florence was banned from the title chase the next year. To add to the situation, the two school superintendents were brothers. Calvin Knauth at Dripping Springs and Leroy Knauth at Florence. In his written report to the UIL, Leroy made the following comment. After the game, the Dripping Springs fans gave our team a standing ovation. It went like this. Boooooooo.

Pete Glosson recalls a classroom incident during his high school days concerning one of his teachers. Mrs. Klett was a red-headed teacher from Johnson City. When she came into the classroom, she found Vaughan Shelton reading a book. She told him to put up the book and get ready for class. He did put the book away, but then picked up another and began to read it. She marched back to where he was sitting and slapped the fire out of him for his impudence. That is certainly an effective way to deal with it but it would not fly in today's society. Bet the parents backed her, too.

Can remember an incident about Pete Glosson when he was driving a bus. Seems he had a couple of students who kept trying to get into it on his bus while on the way to school. He stopped the bus, ordered the two off the bus to settle their differences right then. They did, got back on the bus and rode peacefully to school. Those were the good old days.

Pete says he, Norman Breed, Vaughan Shelton, and Newt Cavett, skipped out of school all the time to go down to the Dripping Springs Branch and play marbles. Claims the principal never knew they were gone. Could it be the principal encouraged their absence by pretending not to miss them? Hard to believe four out of maybe twenty students wouldn't be missed.

One year we had a Downs Syndrome student nicknamed Chonga because he liked to imitate Tarzan. He became an ardent supporter of the football team. During the last pep rally, he asked to make a speech. Mrs. Snider, the special ed teacher wrote him one. He got on stage and said Mrs. Snider wrote me a speech but I'm not going to use it. Mrs. Snider started for the stage, not knowing what he would actually say. He made a very good speech from his heart.

School Faculties

I think that each of us have, at one time or another, tried to remember one of our teachers in a certain year and the name would not come to us. With this in mind and to help this memory, while researching the history of the schools, I started keeping tabs of the staffs for the Dripping Springs school for each year. The early faculties were not always available in the paper or documents that I was able to look through. Listed below are the faculties of the school beginning in the year 1869-70, which is the year I think Dripping Springs might have built a school and held classes for themselves. Prior to that there is some evidence that private tutors were hired and military personnel held the classes during the time of Reconstruction. For at least the first one hundred years of formal education in Dripping Springs, the faculties were small and will be easy to list. The list includes the administration and teaching faculty only and not the equally important people who help make the school day the success that it is—the cafeteria workers, custodians, maintenance personnel, secretaries, aides, volunteers, and bus drivers.

Throughout the years there have been many teachers who have stayed for long periods of time in the Dripping Springs system. Ann Nite Hohman spent a total of 35 years, beginning in 1943, but took out a couple of years to have children before retiring in 1981. Carl Waits was the first to teach 30 consecutive years beginning in 1965. He retired from teaching in 1995 but continued in the employment of the school as a bus driver and had 37 years of service with more to come. Marion Voudouris, who has over 50 years in the profession, started a year after Waits at DSISD and had reached 36 consecutive years as a teacher at the end of the 2002 year and was going for another. The next in line to challenge Mrs. Voudouris is Marilyn Stefka Wright, who has completed 29 years of teaching at the end of 2002. She still has the desire and energy to continue her career at DSISD.

1869-70: Carrie Wallace
1870-71: Carrie Wallace (just guessing)
1871-72: Carrie Wallace (just guessing)
1872-73: Possibly W.T. Chapman
1873-74: Possibly W. T. Chapman
1874-75: Possibly W. T. Chapman
1875-76: Possibly W. T. Chapman
1876-77: Became District #10 on 12-12-1876 with W.L. Armstrong teaching.
1877-78: Possibly W. L. Armstrong
1878-79: Possibly W. L. Armstrong
1879-80: Unknown
1880-81: Unknown
1881-82: W.M. Jordan (Prin.), Lizzie Morrell
1882-83: W.M. Jordan (Prin.), Lizzie Morrell, Mr. Martin
1883-84: R.G. Horsley (Prin.), Miss Eddie Callahan, Mr. Martin
1884-85: R.G. Horsley (Prin.), Miss Eddie Callahan, Mrs. Graves, Mr. Lincoln (music)
1885-86: R.G. Horsley (Prin.), Miss Branch, Mr. Bell
1886-87: R.G. Horsley (Prin.), Mr. Hendon, Miss Dunn
1887-88: J.E. Cook (Prin.), Mrs. Caperton, Minnie M. Cook (Asst. Teacher)
1888-89: J.E. Cook (Prin.), Miss Hamilton (Asst. Teacher)
1889-90: J.P. Collier (Prin.), Florence Ligon
1890-91: A. L. Stubbs (Prin.), Branch L. Phillips, Sallie McLendon
1891-92: A. L. Stubbs (Prin.), R.L. Marshall, School system became District # 20
1892-93: J.H. Bishop (Prin.), Dorothy Folts, Annie Cavett, A.Z. Oldham (Asst. Teacher)
1893-94: H.P. Tidd (Prin.), Assistants unknown
1894-95: H. P. Tidd (Prin.), Assistants unknown
1895-96: D.W. Burkett (Prin.), Assistants unknown
1896-97: D.W. Burkett (Prin.), Assistants unknown
1897-98: Oscar A. Stubbs (Prin.), Nannie Darroh, Annie Cavett
1898-99: Robert L. Marshall (Prin.), Assistants unknown
1899-00: Robert L. Marshall (Prin.), Assistants unknown
1900-01: John T. Parker (Prin.), Georgia Cavett, Others unknown
1901-02: W. A. Pile (Prin.), Georgia Cavett, Others unknown
1902-03: W. A. Pile (Prin.), Georgia Cavett, Others unknown
1903-04: R. A. Robertson (Prin.), Georgia Cavett, Others unknown
1904-05: P.S. Newberry (Prin.), Georgia Cavett, Others unknown
1905-06: A.B. Corder (Prin.), Georgia Cavett, Madie Sorrell
1906-07: Georgia Cavett (Prin.), Others unknown
1907-08: Byrdie Henry (Prin.), Georgia Cavett, Pauline Patton
1908-09: W.E. Parr (Prin.), Georgia Cavett, Viola Hage
1909-10: William Connally (Prin.), Georgia Cavett, Minnie Clark
1910-11: Sidney R. Sanders (Prin.), Lizzie Garrett, Georgia Cavett
1911-12: Mr. Hurff (Prin.), Georgia Cavett, Others unknown
1912-13: Georgia Cavett, Others unknown
1913-14: Georgia Cavett, Others unknown

1914-15: Georgia Cavett, Others unknown
1915-16: Unknown
1916-17: Vina Norwood, Others unknown
1917-18: J.L. Day (Prin.), Mayme Doyle, Louise Rascher
1918-19: Mary Dodgen (Prin.), Vina Norwood, Alma Davenport
1919-20: Martha E. Kelley (Prin.), Framie Smith, Inez Franklin
1920-21: J.C. Johnson (Prin.), Sarah H. Walker, Vina Norwood
1921-22: W.H. Holcombe (Prin.), Eva Glimp, Bessie Burns, Georgia Cavett (thru November), Myrtle Holland (rest of year)
1922-23: W.H. Holcombe (Prin.), Mrs. B. B. Thomas, Florence Pryor, Eva Glimp
1923-24: D.V. MacNaughton (Prin. 1st sem.), Earl H. Spencer (Prin. 2nd sem.), Ida A. Pearson (1st sem.), Lucille I. Bridges (2nd sem.), Eva Glimp, Lura Branum
1924-25: J.O. Banta (Prin.), Eva Glimp, Thelma Chessher (until Nov.), Agnes Elgin (a couple of months), Charley Mae Seal (finished school year), Mae Florida (until April), Mary Elsie Hancock (finished year).
1925-26: Guy Kidder (Prin.), Bertha Kennedy, Ruth Rackley, Elma Burleson
1926-27: Walter G. Miller (Prin.), Ruth Rackley, Ennis Follis, Bernice Elsner
1927-28: Walter G. Miller (Prin.), Ruth A. Fisher, Read S. Morgan, Thelma Coovert
1928-29: Walter G. Miller (Prin), Thelma Coovert, Others Unknown
1929-30: Pop Stephens (Prin), Thelma Coovert, Mrs. Klett, Other Unknown
1930-31: O.V. Stubbs (Prin.), Annie Follis, Williard Drumm, Mary Spaw
1931-32: O. V. Stubbs (Prin.), H.L. Peavey, Annie Follis, Virgil Giles
1932-33: O. V Stubbs (Prin.), Annie Follis, Elbert Davis, Champion Callihan, Cordia Stephenson (died 1-9-33), Erlene Keeney (2nd sem)
1933-34: O.V. Stubbs (Prin.), Champion Callihan, Zepha Lee Peters, Annie Follis, Erlene McLendon Keeney, Elbert H. Davis
1934-35: Elbert H. Davis (Prin.), Zepha Peters, Champion Callihan, Margaret Stewart (until March), Bradley Davis (rest of year), Opal Brumley
1935-36: Elbert H. Davis (Prin.), Opal Brumley, Zepha Peters, Ralph Shelton, Dorothy Richardson,, Lucille Callihan, (Ed Thomasson was hired as teacher/coach but resigned before school began), Ralph Shelton

1936-37: Irving Nixon (Prin.), Oleta Fletcher, Opal Brumley, Dorothy Richardson, Ralph Shelton
1937-38: W.R. Robbins (Prin.), Dorothy Richardson, Opal Brumley, Oleta Fletcher, Mrs. W.R. Robbins
1938-39: W.R. Robbins (Prin.), Mrs. W.R. Robbins, Oleta Fletcher, Opal Brumley, Dorothy Richardson
1939-40: W.R. Robbins (Prin.), Mrs. W.R. Robbins, Dorothy Richardson, Opal Brumley, Clarence T. Shelton
1940-41: M.B. Tilley (Prin.), Mrs. M.B. Tilley, Lura Branum Lyle, Rayma Dillingham, Henry D. Teas
1941-42: M.B. Tilley (Prin.), Mrs. M.B. Tilley, Eleanor Crate, Quinnetta Hahn, Rayma Dillingham, Lura Lyle
1942-43: M.B. Tilley (Prin.), G.C. Herring, Lorena Walker, Lura Lyle, Mrs. M.B. Tilley, Inez Harris, Ethel S. Grove, Hardie Arlington (one week)
1943-44: G.C. Herring (Supt.), Ann Nite, Lorena Walker, Mrs. G.C. Herring, Eva S. Owen, Lura Lyle, Mrs. Malcolm Naumann
1944-45: G.C. Herring (Supt), Lura Lyle, Lorena Walker, Mrs. Malcolm Naumann, Inez Harris, Ann Nite, Ramona Osburn
1945-46: G.C. Herring (Supt), Della Culpepper, Lura Lyle, Susie Danforth, Inez Harris, Estelle Walters, Ann Nite Hohman, Berta Barnes
1946-47: S.P. Conn (Supt), Susie Danforth, Lorena Walker, Berta Barnes, Lura Lyle, G.A. Pringle, Mrs. S.P. Conn, Marjorie M. Hall, Ann Hohman
1947-48: R.C. Donaho (Supt), Robert F. Shelton (Prin), G.A. Pringle, Lura Lyle, Mrs. Clint Swart, LaZelle Barber, Mabel Kretzmeier, L.A. Fritts, Jr., Nellie B. Kidd, Ann Hohman, Nell Huggins
1948-49: R.C. Donaho (Supt), Robert F. Shelton (Prin), G.A. Pringle, Mrs. Clint Swart, Lura Lyle, L.A. Fritts, Jr., Mabel Kretzmeier, Nellie B. Kidd, Naomi Donaldson, Ann Hohman
1949-50: R.C. Donaho (Supt), Robert F. Shelton (Prin), G.A. Pringle, Albert R. Scasta, Lura Lyle, Pearl Kuhns, Claude Goode, Mabel Kretzmeier, Naomi Donaldson, Ann Hohman, Nellie B. Kidd
1950-51: R.C. Donaho (Supt), Robert F. Shelton (Prin), Helen D. David, Quinn Schlortt, Ann Hohman, H.G. Haby, Nellie B. Kidd, Mabel Kretzmeier, G.A. Pringle, Lura Lyle, Mr. Cox (1st

sem), Mr. May (quit early Sept), Ernest O. Bethke (took May's place)

1951-52: Robert F. Shelton (Supt), Quinn Schlortt (Prin), Lura Lyle, John Malone, Mabel Kretzmeier, Hayden G. Haby, Ernest O. Bethke, Ina G. Kaufman, L.U.C. Kaufman, Nellie B. Kidd, Ann Hohman

1952-53: Robert F. Shelton (Supt), Quinn Schlortt (Prin), Lura Lyle, John Malone, Elmer Russell, Zelle Petmecky, Nellie B. Kidd, Mable Kretzmeier, Marvin Hill, Joseph Reichert, Della Culpepper, Wardine Broyles

1953-54: Robert F. Shelton (Supt), Quinn Schlortt (Prin), Marvin Hill, Lura Lyle, Lawrence Parker, Mabel Kretzmeier, Elmer Russell, Zelle Petmecky, Della Culpepper, Nellie B. Kidd, Joe Reichert, Wardine Broyles

1954-55: Robert F. Shelton (Supt), Quinn Schlortt (Prin), Patricia Pierson, Marvin Hill, Beatrice Hindman, Elmer Russell, Bailey Daugherty, Lura Lyle, Joe Reichert, Lillie Mitchell, Zelle Petmecky, Mable Kretzmeier, Wardine Broyles, Ann Hohman, Della Culpepper

1955-56: Robert F. Shelton (Supt), Quinn Schlortt (Prin), Marvin Hill, Katherine Stokes, Elmer Russell, Lura Lyle, Bailey Daugherty, Tom Jones, Lillie Mitchell, Billie Green, Mabel Kretzmeier, Willene Johnson, Ann Hohman, Della Culpepper

1956-57: Robert F. Shelton (Supt), Quinn Schlortt (Prin), JoAnn Beauford, Marvin Hill, Katherine Stokes, Elmer Russell, Bailey Daugherty, Lura Lyle, Tom Jones, Bette Mays, Elaine Crouch, Lillie Mitchell, Alice Upchurch, Della Culpepper, Harriet Pope

1957-58: Robert F. Shelton (Supt), Marvin Hill (Prin), Elmer Russell, Tom Jones, Bailey Daugherty, Della Culpepper, Lillie Mitchell, Novelle Daugherty, Lura Lyle, JoAnn Lange, Amboline Engle, Ann Hohman, JoAnn Beauford, Harriet Pope

1958-59: Robert F. Shelton (Supt), Marvin Hill (Prin), Elmer Russell, Tom Jones, Bailey Daugherty, Della Culpepper, Lillie Mitchell, Novelle Daugherty, Jodie Witte (1st sem), Patricia Fain, Amboline Engle, Ann Hohman, Hazel Rose, Robbin Borum, Nola Nelms, Lura Lyle, Waymon Hennessee (2nd sem)

1959-60: Robert F. Shelton (Supt), Marvin Hill (Prin), Tom Jones, Louise Gravenor, Bailey Daugherty, Novelle Daugherty, Amboline Engle, Ann Hohman, Lillie Mitchell, Nola Nelms, Mrs. Jessie Winans, Della Culpepper, Mrs. Kilpatrick, Elmer Russell, Bob Coker, Mr. Leissner

1960-61: Robert F. Shelton (Supt), Jerry Garnett (Prin), Bob Coker, Louise Gravenor, Jack Kroll, Elmer Russell, Twila Tate, Elizabeth Williamson, Tom Jones, Amboline Engle, Ann Hohman, Lillie Mitchell, Jessie Winans, Nola Nelms, Della Culpepper

1961-62: Robert F. Shelton (Supt), Jerry Garnett (Prin), Bob Coker, Louise Gravenor, Jack Kroll, Elmer Russell, Patricia Sims, Elizabeth Williamson, Tom Jones, Amboline Engle, Ann Hohman, Lillie Mitchell, Jessie Winans, Bessie Kirby, Della Culpepper, M.Z. Piland, Jr.

1962-63: Robert F. Shelton (Supt), Jerry Garnett (Prin), Patty Coleman, Bradley Davis, Louise Gravenor, Jack Kroll, Oran Rippy, Elmer Russell, Elizabeth Williamson, Tom Jones, Amboline Engle, Ann Hohman, Lillie Mitchell, Jessie Winans, Bessie Kirby Odell, Della Culpepper, M.Z. Piland, Jr.

1963-64: Calvin Knauth (Supt), J.F. Holt (Prin), Bradley Davis, Jack Kroll, Oran Rippy, Mr. E.W. Tampke, Elmer Russell, Myrtle Turner, Elizabeth Williamson, Tom Jones, Amboline Engle, Ann Hohman, Lillie Mitchell, Jessie Winans, Patsy Buckner, Chris Robbins, Zelle Petmecky

1964-65: Calvin Knauth (Supt), J.F. Holt (Prin), Bradley Davis, Louise Gravenor, Carolyn Holt, Mildred Lamb, Oran Rippy, Elmer Russell, Jack Stork, Elizabeth Williamson, Tom Jones, Russell Omeis, Amboline Engle, Ann Hohman, Lillie Mitchell, Jessie Winans, Zelle Petmecky, Anne Taylor Evans, Patsy Buckner

1965-66: Calvin Knauth (Supt), Roy D. Worley (Prin), Oran Rippy, Carl Waits, Louise Gravenor, Bradley Davis, Mildred Lamb, Elmer Russell, Bertha Hill, Lillian Ottinger, Tom Jones, Russell Omeis, Ann Hohman, Amboline Engle, Lillie Mitchell, Jessie Winans, Mrs. Novella Sorrell, Zelle Petmecky, Patsy Buckner, Polly Scott

1966-67: Calvin Knauth (Supt), Roy D. Worley (Prin), Elmer Russell, Bertha Hill, Mildred Lamb, Carl Waits, Bradley Davis, Louise Gravenor, Lillian Ottinger, Russell Omeis, Oran Rippy, Norma Crawford, Tom Jones, Amboline Engle, Ann Hohman, Zelle Petmecky, Ann Lewis, Jessie Winans, Marion Voudouris, Novella Sorrell, Martha Pearson, Patsy Buckner, Carolyn Boggs, Martha McCain

1967-68: Calvin Knauth (Supt), Roy D. Worley (Prin), Tom Jones, Lillian Ottinger, Louise Gravenor, Bertha Hill, Elmer Russell, Mike McGlothen (part of 1st sem), Billie Garnett (rest of 1st sem), Preston Densman (2nd sem), Carl Waits, Oran Rippy, Bradley Davis, Amboline Engle, Janet Rippy, Ann Hohman, Zelle Petmecky, Ann Lewis, Martha Pearson, Jessie Winans, Marion Voudouris, Novella Sorrell, Patsy Buckner, Carolyn Boggs, Gene Lewis, Martha McCain, Norma Crawford

1968-69: Calvin Knauth (Supt), Paul Allen (Prin), Bradley Davis, Galen Dodson, Harriet Eaves, Mary Fomby, Jack Livingston, Sarah Nichols, Lillian Ottinger, Oran Rippy, Elmer Russell, Gayle Stork, Carl Waits, Gene Lewis, Bertha Hill, Tom Jones, Janet Rippy, Amboline Engle, Ann Hohman, Zelle Petmecky, Ann Lewis, Martha Pearson, Jessie Winans, Marion Voudouris, Martha Owens, Jerry Lou Dodson, Novella Sorrell, Sharlene Frances Atkinson, Martha McCain, Norman Crawford

1969-70: Calvin Knauth (Supt), Paul Allen (Prin), Elmer Russell, Galen Dodson, Harriet Eaves, Joyce Felts, Wayne Grohman, Bertha Hill, Jack Livingston, Lillian Ottinger, Melinda Perrin, Oran Rippy, Gayle Stork, Carl Waits, Tom Jones, Novella Sorrell, Jerry Lou Dodson, Joann Griffin, Mary Fomby, Marion Voudouris, Jessie Winans, Patty Knauth, Norma Crawford, Lynn Hadley, Amboline Engle, Zelle Petmecky, Ann Hohman, Ann Lewis, Martha Owens, Sharlene Atkinson, Barbara Bridwell, Martha Pearson, Bradley Davis

1970-71: Calvin Knauth (Supt), Paul Allen (Prin), Eldon K. Shipp, Lillian Ottinger, Lynn Hadley, Harriet Eaves, Galen Dodson, Jack Livingston, Carl Waits, Necia Kinnison, Charles Schandua, Gayle Stork, Joanne Griffin, Melinda Perrin, Bob White, Oran Rippy, Wayne Grohman, Bertha Hill, Tom Jones, Elmer Russell, Carole Campbell, Novella Sorrell, Mary Fomby, Martha Owens, Jessie Winans, Marion Voudouris, Helen Byers, Martha Pearson, Zelle Petmecky, Ann Hohman, Amboline Engle, Patty Knauth, Susan Grohman, Barbara Bridwell, Robert F. Shelton

1971-72: Calvin Knauth (Supt), Paul Allen (Prin), Eldon K. Shipp, Lynn Hadley, Charles Schandua, Paul Fulkerson, Tom Jones, Sharon East, Michelle Rohrer, Mack Crow, Galen Dodson, Bertha Hill, Joanne Griffin, Gayle Stork, Wayne Grohman, Carl Waits, Authur Casey, Oran Rippy, Lillian Ottinger, Jenny Wilson, Elmer Russell, Necia Kinnison, Loraine Tiggeman, Jack Livingston, Martha Owens, Carole Campbell, Mary Fomby, Susan Grohman, Jessie Winans, Marion Voudouris, Martha Pearson, Helen Byers, Ann Hohman, Zelle Petmecky, Amboline Engle, Patty Knauth, Glenda Heaberlin, Barbara Bridwell, Robert F. Shelton

1972-73: Calvin Knauth (Supt), Charles Whatley (Prin), Eldon K. Shipp, Mack Crow, Galen Dodson, Sharon East, Gary Endsley, Paul Fulkerson, Joanne Griffin, Lynn Hadley, Bertha Hill, Tom Jones, Necia Kinnison, Jack Livingston, Lillian Ottinger, Barbara Nixon, Oran Rippy, Michelle Rohrer, Elmer Russell, Charles Schandua, Gayle Stork, Loraine Tiggeman, Carl Waits, Tom Wells, Jenny Wilson, Martha Owens, Carole Campbell, Mary Fomby, Jerry Lou Dodson, Alice Gryska, Helen Byers, Martha Pearson, Ann Hohman, Jessie Winans, Marion Voudouris, Dee Reiter, Joyce Mahoney, Zelle Petmecky, Carolyn McAninch, Patty Knauth, Frances Henderson, Verna Price, Barbara Bridwell, Glenda Heaberlin, Robert F. Shelton

1973-74: Calvin Knauth (Supt), Alfred Chance (Prin), Eldon K. Shipp, Tom Jones, Larry Sutton, Mack Crow, Lynn Hadley, Lillian Ottinger, Loraine Tiggeman, Harriett Eaves, Jenny Wilson, Tom Wells (1st sem), Ruth Sullivan, Paul Fulkerson, Jack Livingston, Pat Hauser, Cecilia Cope, Galen Dodson, Bertha Hill, Necia Kinnison, Elmer Russell, Charles Schandua, Jerry Nelson, Barbara Nixon Ernst, Marilyn Stefka, Carl Waits, Glenda Heaberlin, Carole Campbell, Helen Dodson, Carroll Fain, Carolyn McAninch, Martha Pearson, Verna Price, Dee Reiter, Helen Byers, Jerry Lou Dodson, Frances Henderson, Ann Hohman, Patty Knauth, Joyce Mahoney, Zelle Petmecky, Martha Owens, Marion Voudouris, Jessie Winans, Judy Shelton, Poe Shelton, Beverly Robbins, Robert F. Shelton

1974-75: Calvin Knauth (Supt), Galen Dodson (Prin), Eldon K. Shipp, Barbara Bertling, Mack Crow, Harriett Eaves, Barbara Ernst, David Fields, Lynn Hadley, Bertha Hill, Rebecca Huffman, Tom Jones, Necia Kinnison, James Lampley, Jerry Nelson, Sarah Nichols, Lillian Ottinger, Oran Rippy, Elmer Russell, Charles Schandua, Poe Shelton, Marilyn Stefka, Paul Steldt, Ruth Sullivan, Larry Sutton, Lorraine Tiggeman, Richard Vaughn, Carl Waits, Jenny Wilson, Sharon Wolbrecht, Kay Baen, Valerie Bernat, Glenda Heaberlin, Valarie Pruegle, Beverly Robbins, Helen Byers, Jerry Lou Dodson, Frances Henderson, Ann Hohman, Patty Knauth, Joyce Mahoney, Zelle Petmecky, Mary Pruett, Judy Shelton, Marion Voudouris, Jessie Winans, Carole Campbell, Helen Dodson, Carroll Fain, Isabelle Mollenhauer, Martha Pearson, Verna Price, Dee Reiter, Robert F. Shelton

1975-76: Calvin Knauth (Supt), Galen Dodson (Prin), Eldon K. Shipp, Mary Carson, Harriett Eaves, David Fields, Lynn Hadley, Glenda Heaberlin, Sarah Nichols, Bertha Hill, Larry Austin, Rebecca Huffman, Tom Jones, Necia Kinnison, James Lampley, Pam Lampley, Jerry Nelson, Lillian Ottinger, Oran Rippy, Elmer Russell, Charles Schandua, Mack Crow, Poe Shelton, Helen Sheffield, Marilyn Stefka, Ruth Sullivan, Larry Sutton, Lorraine Tiggeman, Diane Thomas, Richard Vaughn, Carl Waits, Sharon Wolbrecht, Georgeanne Weber, Anne Weisman, Frances Henderson, Ann Hohman, Patty Knauth, Zelle Petmecky, Marion Voudouris, Beverly Robbins, Helen Dodson, Joyce Mahoney, Essley, Martha Pearson, Dee Reiter, Jessie Winans, Mary Pruett, Kay Baen, Barbara Bertling, Valerie Bernat, Helen Byers, Carole Campbell, Carroll Fain, Peggy Powell, Verna Price, Sarah Schandua, Judy Shelton, Robert F. Shelton

1976-77: Calvin Knauth (Supt), Galen Dodson (Prin), Eldon K. Shipp, Larry Austin, Barbara Bertling, Don Clark, Mack Crow, Harriett Eaves, David Fields, Becky Harlow, Rhonda Havins, Bertha Hill, Carol Howie, Rebecca Huffman, Tom Jones, Necia Kinnison, Barbara Knippa, Margaret McClure, Kathy Nichols, Sarah Nichols, Oran Rippy, Patty Rowland, Elmer Russell, Charles Schandua, Helen Sheffield, Poe Shelton, Marilyn Stefka, Larry Sutton, Ruth Sullivan, Diane Thomas, Lorraine Tiggeman, Richard Vaughn, Carl Waits, Patricia Ward, Georgeanne Weber, Anne Weisman, Jimmy Wren, Jerry Nelson, Jerry Lou Dodson, Marion Voudouris, Ann Hohman, Beverly Robbins, Patty Knauth, Zelle Petmecky, Frances Henderson, Helen Dodson, Joyce Mahoney Essley, Martha Pearson, Dee Reiter, Jessie Winans, Mary Pruett, Kay Baen, Cathy Austin, Ruth Brinkman, Virginia Davies, Suzanne Heaney, Lyndon Knippa, Barbara Lawrence, Lou Miller, Isabelle Mollenhauer, Susan Morgan, Janean Pankhurst, Peggy Powell, Yvonne Prugel, Susan Roderick, Sarah Schandua, Robert F. Shelton

1977-78: Calvin Knauth (Supt), Galen Dodson (Prin), Eldon K. Shipp, Sue Adcock, Larry Akers, Don Clark, Mack Crow, Sharron Ervin, David Fields, Sara Gaetjens, Jack Grieder, Rhonda Havins, Charles Hensen, Bertha Hill, Carol Howie, Rebecca Huffman, Steve Huntsberger, Tom Jones, Necia Kinnison, Sandy Kyser, Paul McDaniel, Tim Miller, Roger Morey, Chad Murphy, Jerry Nelson, Sarah Nichols, David Pauley, Oran Rippy, Elmer Russell, Charles Schandua, Poe Shelton, Marilyn Stefka, Ruth Sullivan, Larry Sutton, Lorraine Tiggeman, Carl Waits, Ms. Hale, Georgeanne Weber, Jimmy Wren, Barbara Knippa Hopson, Marcia Shields, Kathy Nichols, Jerry Lou Dodson, Patty Knauth, Marion Voudouris, Beverly Robbins, Frances Henderson, Ann Hohman, Cathy Austin, Ruth Brinkman, Liz Charbonnet, Helen Dodson, Joyce Mahoney Essley, Jill Gathright, Peggy Ginn, Suzanne Heaney, Debbie Lentz, Lou Miller, Janean Pankhurst, Martha Pearson, Zelle Petmecky, Letha Phillips, Peggy Powell, Mary Pruett, Yvonne Prugel, Dee Reiter, Janet Rippy, Susan Roderick, Janie Rogers, Kathy Spaller, Janice Whitefield, Jessie Winans, Suzanne Morgan, Kay Baen, Robert F. Shelton.

1978-79: Calvin Knauth (Supt), Galen Dodson (Prin), Eldon K. Shipp, Sue Adcock, Larry Akers, Don Clark, Mack Crow, Sharron Ervin, David Fields, Jack Grieder, Charles Hensen, Bertha Hill, Carol Howie, Rebecca Huffman, Steve Huntsberger, Tom Jones, Roy Jones, Necia Kinnison, Sandy Kyser, Roger Morey, Chad Murphy, Paul McDaniel, Linda McDavitt, Jerry Nelson, Sarah Nichols, Oran Rippy, Elmer Russell, Charles Schandua, DennisSeale, Poe Shelton, Marcia Shields, Marilyn Stefka, Ruth Sullivan, Larry Sutton, Lorraine Tiggeman, Carl Waits, Georgeanne Weber, Jimmy Wren, Peggy Scott, Barbara Hopson, Kathy Nichols, Frances Henderson, Jerry Lou Dodson, Angela Murphy, Marion Voudouris, Beverly Robbins, Patty Knauth, Ann Hohman, Cathy Austin, Kay Baen, Ruth Brinkman, Liz Charbonnet, Helen Dodson, Joyce Essley, Carroll Fain, Peggy Ginn, Katherine Gist, Anita Kelly, Lou Miller, Isabelle Mollenhauer, Suzanne Morgan, Janean Pankhurst, Martha Pearson, Zelle Petmecky, Letha Phillips, Peggy Powell, Yvonne Prugel, Dee Reiter, Janet Rippy, Susan Roderick, Janie Rogers, Jo Ann Smith, Kathy Spaller, Janice Whitefield, Jessie Winans, Robert F. Shelton, Jill Gathright

1979-80: Jeffrey K. Lindzey (Supt), Carol Cunningham (Prin), Eldon K. Shipp, Lamarr Brack, Jim Brock, Don Clark, Teresa Copeland, Mack Crow, Sharron Ervin, David Fields, Sara Gaetjens, Charlotte Gelineau, Michelle Gordon, Frances Henderson, Bertha Hill, Barbara Hopson, Carol Howie, Rebecca Huffman, Tom Jackson, Steve Johnson, Shauna Kidd, Necia Kinnison, Sandy Kyser, Larry LeCompte, Liew Ledbetter, Paul McDaniel, Linda McDavitt, Denise Michele, Roger Morey, Sarah Nichols, Karen Perez, Janice

Rhodes, Tommy Riggs, Oran Rippy, Elmer Russell, Peggy Scott, Dennis Seale, Poe Shelton, Marcia Shields, Eric Shultz, Marilyn Stefka, Ruth Sullivan, Lorraine Tiggeman, Vicky Thompson, Carl Waits, Cary Weinheimer, Jimmy Wren, Kristi Shelton, Kathy Nichols, Jerry Lou Dodson, Ann Hohman, Marion Voudouris, Angela Murphy, Beverly Robbins, Frances Henderson, Susan Roderick, Glenda Eaves, Marge Foster, Max Rumelhart, Lavon Acton, Rita Ogletree, Maggie Gable, Rochelle Payne, Beth Ingram, Barbara McManus, Jo Ann Smith, Terry Utley, Jessie Winans, Janie Rogers, Janet Rippy, Dee Reiter, Janice Whitefield, Joyce Essley, Barba Lu Hazard, Janice Morris, Janean Pankhurst Whitten, Ruth Brinkman, Liz Charbonnet, Lea Cresswell, Helen Dodson, Anita Kelly, Lou Miller, Kay Baen Brooks, Richard Stark, Letha Phillips, Katie Gist, Martha Pearson, Lynn Peterson, Peggy Ginn, Yvonne Prugel, Suzanne Morgan, Marsha Lowe, Judy Blair, Zelle Petmecky, Robert F. Shelton, Jill Gathright

1980-81: Jeffrey K. Lindzey (Supt), Carol Cunningham (Prin), Eldon K. Shipp, Mike Caplinger, Vicki Alberts, Cherie Bolton, Lamarr Brack, Jack Bradshaw, Bill Burch, Susan Burch, Don Clark, Ann Crawford, David Fields, Sara Gaetjens, Francie Hardwick, Mary Jane Harned, Bertha Hill, Carol Howie, Rebecca Huffman, Randy Hutto, Shauna Kidd, Larry LeCompte, Liew Ledbetter, Paul McDaniel, Linda McDavitt, Ken McIlvain, Roger Morey, Chad Murphy, Karen Perez, Kathryn Pfeffer, Marilyn Quinton, Tommy Riggs, Oran Rippy, LuAnn Rush, Peggy Scott, Poe Shelton, Sarah Nichols, Ruth Sullivan, Carl Waits, Jimmy Wren, Marilyn Stefka Wright, Barbara Hopson, Kathy Nichols, Angela Murphy, Frances Henderson, Jerry Lou Dodson, Marion Voudouris, Beverly Robbins, Ann Hohman, Tom Jackson, Jim Brock, Zelle Petmecky, Jean Horn, Peggy Ginn, Lea Cresswell, Judy Blair, Carolyn Caplinger, Anita Kelly, Janice Whitefield, Janice Morris, Jessie Winans, Janet Rippy, Martha Graves, Terry Utley, Barbara McManus, Paula Formby, Lou Miller Parks, Marge Foster, Ms. Hale, Jill Gathright, Nancy Pickens, Kay Brooks, Bob Scott, Martha Pearson, Richard Stark

1981-82: Joe Searcy (co-Supt), Cynthia Snider (co-Supt), Eldon K. Shipp, LuAnn Rush Belcheff, Jim Brock, Susan Burch, Bill Burch, Liew Ledbetter, Paul McDaniel, Linda McDavitt, Ruth Sullivan, Sarah Nichols Sparks, Carl Waits, Marilyn Wright, Roger Morey, Zelle Petmecky, Mary Jane Harned, Chad Murphy, Kathryn Pfeffer, Poe Shelton, Jack Bradshaw, Randy Hutto, Steele Fleming, Barbara Hopson, Peggy Scott, Sherry Haydon, Carol Howie, Don Clark, Oran Rippy, Dennis Seale, David Fields, Sara Gaetjens, Chris Timco, Bob Scott, Katherine Cannon, Kathy Nichols, Cherie Bolton, Marge Foster, Frances Henderson, Paula Formby, Jim O'Donnell, Terry Utley, Barbara McManus, Janice Morris, Martha Graves, Angela Murphy, Janice Whitefield, Janet Rippy, Jerry Lou Dodson, Marion Voudouris, Lea Cresswell, Anita Kelly, Kay Brooks, Nancy Pickens, Bettie Cagle, Jill Gathright, Beverly Robbins, Judy Blair, Susan Stark, Zelle Petmecky, Richard Stark

1982-83: Joe Searcy (Supt), Mike Caplinger (Prin), Eldon K. Shipp, Rick Eickenloff, Barbara Hopson, Don Clark, Oran Rippy, Zelle Petmecky, Roger Morey, Linda McDavitt, Marilyn Wright, Carl Waits, Bob Scott, Virginia Woods, Jack Bradshaw, Trey Wilson, Gay Lynn Wilson, David Fields, Sara Gaetjens, Elyse Allbright, Dennis Seale, Vivian Conway, PoeShelton, Ruth Sullivan, Randy Hutto, Mary Jane Harned, Steele Fleming, Sherry Haydon, Peggy Scott, Susan Burch, Carol Howie, Liew Ledbetter, Bill Burch, Sarah Nichols Sparks, Marion Voudouris, Angela Murphy, Frances Henderson, Cherie Bolton, Beverly Robbins, Marge Foster, Paula Formby, Jim O'Donnell, Janice Morris, Jill Gathright, Anita Kelly, Susan Stark, Richard Stark, Janice Whitefield, Bettie Cagle, Lea Cresswell, Janet Rippy, Carolyn Caplinger, Nancy Pickens, Barbara McManus, Kay Brooks, Jerry Lou Dodson, Joni Henderson, Judy Blair, Joyce Essley,

1983-84: Mike Caplinger (Supt), Nolan Raney (Prin), Elmer Russell (1st sem), Tom Ayres (2nd sem), Vivian Conway (1st sem), Debbie Nedbalek (2nd sem), Susan Burch, Elyse Allbright, Sara Gaetjens, Mr. Wolfe (1st sem), Larry Deal (2nd sem), Jack Bradshaw, Don Clark, Rick Eickenloff, Martin Earley, David Fields, Steele Fleming, Darlene Heckman, Barbara Hopson, Liew Ledbetter, Linda McDavitt, Roger Morey, Chad Murphy, Kathy Nichols, Zelle Petmecky, Peggy Scott, Dennis Seale, Poe Shelton, Ruth Sullivan, Carl Waits, Gay Lynn Wilson, Marilyn Wright, Vicki Harris, Virginia Woods, Mary Jane Harned, Frances Henderson, Marion Voudouris, Beverly Robbins, Cherie Bolton, Angela Murphy, Bob Scott, Bettie Cagle, Lea Cresswell, Anita Kelly, Jerry Lou Dodson, Rae McCartney, Janet Rippy, Janice Whitefield, Susan Stark, Richard Stark, Janice Morris,

Carolyn Caplinger, Sheila Harmon, Joni Henderson, Jim O'Donnell, Marge Foster, Joyce Essley, Paula Formby, Jill Gathright, Beth Puckett, Carol Howie, Keith Burnett

1984-85: Mike Caplinger (Supt), Nolan Raney (Prin), Keith Burnett, Tom Ayres, Jack Bradshaw, Susan Burch, Don Clark, Larry Deal, Martin Earley, Rick Eickenloff, Nancy Faust, David Fields, Steele Fleming, Sara Gaetjens, Mary Jane Harned, Barbara Hopson, Carol Howie, Liew Ledbetter, Roger Morey, Tim Oliver, Bill Peace, Zelle Petmecky, Peggy Scott, Dennis Seale, Poe Shelton, Ellis Smith, Ruth Sullivan, Carl Waits, Terry Wicke, Marilyn Wright, Vicki Harris, Virginia Woods, Elyse Allbright, Kathy Nichols, Marion Voudouris, Frances Henderson, Beverly Robbins, Gay Lynn Wilson (1st sem), Lee Ann Wilkins (2nd sem), Sherry Haydon, Bob Scott, Bettie Cagle Frost, Anita Kelly, Jerry Lou Dodson, Rae McCartney, Janice Whitefield, Susan Stark, Richard Stark, Janice Morris, Sheila Harmon, Joni Henderson, Jim O'Donnell, Marge Foster, Mary Ayres, Beth Puckett, Jill Gathright, Angela Murphy, Carolyn Caplinger, Lea Cresswell, Amy Kadlecek, Laura Taylor, Susan Myers, Kathy Warren, Malinda Holt, Paula Formby

1985-86: Mike Caplinger (Supt), Nolan Raney (Prin), Don Phillips, Keith Burnett, Elyse Allbright, Tom Ayres, Susan Burch, Jane Canales, Don Clark, Carol Cummings, Rick Eickenloff, Mark Engeling, Nancy Faust, David Fields, Mary Jane Harned, Sherry Haydon, Barbara Hopson, Liew Ledbetter, Nancy McCarley, Roger Morey, Kathy Nichols, Ed Palmer, Bob Scott, Dennis Seale, Poe Shelton, Terry Wicke, Virginia Woods, Marilyn Wright, Ellis Smith, Bill Peace, Peggy Scott, Carl Waits, Ruth Sullivan, Bridget Cave, Carol Howie, Steele Fleming, Martin Earley, Lee Ann Wilkins, Marion Voudouris, Angela Murphy, Frances Henderson, Carolyn Caplinger, Scott Dean, Karen Deaver, Paula Dimmitt, Mary Clare Dodson, Sheila Harmon, Donna Hightower, Cheryl Spooner, Susan Troppy, Jim Whites, Polly Harlan, Beth Puckett, Joni Henderson, Jim O'Donnell, Paula Formby, Janice Morris, Mary Ayres, Cherie Bolton, Mrs. Jackie Jonas, Susan Stark, Richard Stark, Malinda Holt, Kathy Stienke, Janice Whitefield, Kathy Warren, Rae McCartney, Max Hardee, Roberta Carnes, Jerry Lou Dodson, Peggy Howell, Mrs. Linney, Mrs. Dana Ware, Amy Kadlecek, Barbara Krause, April Alford, Anita Kelly, Mrs. Janice Hudnall, Bettie Frost, Judy Kelley, Jill Gathright

1986-87: Julian Shaddix (Supt), Nolan Raney (Prin), Don Phillips, Keith Burnett, Kathy Nichols, Jane Canales, Barbara Lewis, Nancy McCarley, Peggy Scott, Don Clark, Carol Cummings, Tom Ayres, Sherry Haydon, Debbie Hazard, Paula King, Susan Burch, Mary Jane Harned, Roger Morey, David Fields, Ed Palmer, Terry Wicke, Liew Ledbetter, Rick Eickenloff, Mark Engeling, Nancy Faust, Poe Shelton, Dennis Seale, Virginia Woods, Marilyn Wright, Carl Waits, Martin Earley, Bridget Cave, Carol Howie, Ruth Sullivan, Steele Fleming, Lee Ann Wilkins, Marion Voudouris, Frances Henderson, Angela Murphy, Ellis Smith, Bob Scott, Don Hopkins, Cheryl Spooner, Barbara Hopson, Jane Click, Scott Dean, Karen Deaver, Sheila Harmon, Donna Hightower, Shirley Johnson, Deb Palmer, Susan Troppy, Gay Lynn Wilson, Anita Kelly, Polly Harlan, Joni Henderson, Jim O'Donnell, Janice Morris, Paula Formby, Mary Ayres, Cherie Bolton, Susan Stark, Richard Stark, Kathy Stienke, Janice Whitefield, Kathy Warren, Rae McCartney, Max Hardee, Roberta Carnes, Jerry Lou Dodson, Peggy Howell, Dana Ware, Amy Kadlecek, Barbara Krause, April Alford, Bettie Frost, Judy Kelley, Mary Clare Dodson, Jill Gathright, Beth Puckett

1987-88: Julian Shaddix (Supt), Ronnie Bourland (Prin), Don Phillips, Keith Burnett, Bridget Cave, Susan Burch, Liew Ledbetter, Ellis Smith, Elyse Allbright, Tom Ayres, Jane Canales, Don Clark, Carl Covington, Carol Cummings, Colleen Davis, Glen Davis, Rick Eickenloff, Jerry English, Barbara English, David Fields, Peggy Scott Grooms, Mary Jane Harned, Sherry Haydon, Don Hopkins, Cheryl Spooner Hopkins, Barbara Hopson, Glen Jones, Leslie Jones, Paula King, Debbie Hazard Klein, Liew Ledbetter, Barbara Lewis, Nancy McCarley, Roger Morey, Kathy Nichols, Ed Palmer, Randy Rockhold, Dennis Seale, Poe Shelton, Jim Whites, Terry Wicke, Virginia Woods, Marilyn Wright, Carl Waits, Ruth Sullivan, Carol Howie, Steele Fleming, Jane Click, Scott Dean, Karen Deaver, Galen Dodson, Martin Earley, Sheila Harmon, Donna Hightower, Shirley Johnson, Deb Palmer, Susan Troppy, Lee Ann Wilkins, Gay Lynn Wilson, Mrs. Nancy Boddeker, Lori Blythe, Beth Puckett, Polly Harlan, Bob Scott, Judy Kelley, Connie Burrus, Jill Gathright, Bettie Frost, Grace Dormont, April Alford, Mary Clare Dodson, Anita Kelly, Barbara Krause, Janey Russell, Amy Kadlecek, Roberta Carnes, Jerry Lou Dodson, Jeanie Fuelberg, Deanna Rees, Marion Voudouris,

Dana Ware, Barbara English, Max Hardee, Peggy Howell, Angela Murphy, Kathy Warren, Janice Whitefield, Marge Foster, Malinda Holt, Rae McCartney, Susan Stark, Richard Stark, Kathy Stienke, Mary Ayres, Cherie Bolton, Tommie Sue Bourland, Mike Cave, Paula Formby, Frances Henderson, Joni Henderson, Jim O'Donnell, Janice Morris, Don Forrester

1988-89: Julian Shaddix (Supt), Don Forrester (Prin), Don Phillips, Keith Burnett, Tom Ayres, Susan Burch, Jane Canales, Don Clark, Julie Colston, Carl Covington, Glen Davis, Rick Eickenloff, Jerry English, Barbara English, David Fields, Mary Jane Harned, Don Hopkins, Cheryl Hopkins, Glen Jones, Leslie Jones, Shauna Kidd, Debbie Hazard Klein, Liew Ledbetter, Barbara Lewis, Roger Morey, Ed Palmer, Randy Rockhold, Dennis Seale, Terry Wicke, Jim Whites, Virginia Woods, Marilyn Wright, Kathy Nichols, Bob Scott, Carl Waits, Ruth Sullivan, Carol Howie, Steele Fleming, Lee Ann Wilkins, Carol Cummings, Paula King, Sherry Haydon, Jane Click, Colleen Davis, Barbara Hopson, Peggy Grooms, Galen Dodson, Jerry Lou Dodson, Marion Voudouris, Frances Henderson, Angela Murphy, Ellis Smith, Sheila Harmon, Joni Henderson, Scott Dean, Donna Hightower Earley, Martin Earley, Nancy Boddeker, Shirley Johnson, Malyna Miller, Deb Palmer, Mark Schlicke, Susan Troppy, Gay Lynn Wilson, Janice Wycoff, Lori Blythe, Polly Harlan, Beth Puckett, Jill Gathright, Judy Kelley, Connie Burrus, Bettie Frost, Nancy Witwiski, Anita Kelly, Barbara Krause, Janey Russell, Mrs. Tracy, Bridget Williams, April Alford, Roberta Carnes, Jeanie Fuelberg, Kathy Jernigan, Deanna Rees, Max Hardee, Peggy Howell, Kathy Warren, Janice Whitefield, Amy Kadlecek, Sharon Fleming, Marge Foster, Rae McCartney, Susan Stark, Richard Stark, Kathy Stienke, Mrs. Susan Webber, Mary Ayres, Cherie Bolton, Tommie Sue Bourland, Pat Hennessee, Paula Formby, Jim O'Donnell, Mike Cave.

1989-90: Bob Denton (Supt), Don Forrester (Prin), Don Phillips, Keith Burnett, Barbara Hopson, Jane Botkin, Julie Colston, Jane Canales, Carol Cummings, Peggy Grooms, Barbara Lewis, David Fields, Ed Palmer, David Shaw, Susan Burch, Carl Covington, Don Clark, Mary Jane Harned, Roger Morey, Dennis Seale, Glenn Davis, Glen Jones, Leslie Jones, Rick Eickenloff, Shauna Kidd, Karen Stripling, Terry Wicke, Debbie Hazard Klein, Ellis Smith, Tom Ayres, Jerry English, Barbara English, Sheila Harmon, Sherry Haydon, Don Hopkins, Cheryl Hopkins, Paula King, Jim Whites, Marilyn Wright, Carl Waits, Jane Click, Ruth Sullivan, Carol Howie, Gay Lynn Wilson, Bridget Cave, Galen Dodson, Becky Denton, Steele Fleming, Lee Ann Wilkins, Marion Voudouris, Jerry Lou Dodson, Frances Henderson, Angela Murphy, Susan Stark, Richard Stark, Joni Henderson, Melissa Koopman, Poe Shelton, Jessica Allen, Scott Dean, Donna Earley, Martin Earley, Effie Eastham, Nancy Faust, Shirley Johnson, Kathy Leopold, Robert Martinez, Deb Palmer, Sandy Southwell, Susan Troppy, Mike Cave, Jill Gathright, Polly Harlan, Janice Wycoff, Lori Blythe, Beth Puckett, Connie Burrus, Judy Kelley, Nancy Witwiski, Janey Russell, Bridget Williams, Barbara Krause, Jeanie Fuelberg, Anita Kelly, Deanna Rees, Kathy Jernigan, Roberta Carnes, Peggy Howell, Kathy Warren, Janice Whitefield, Sharon Fleming, Marge Foster, Amy Kadlecek, Rae McCartney, Mary Ayres, Cherie Bolton, Tommie Sue Bourland, Max Hardee, Pat Hennessee, Janice Morris, Paula Formby, Jim O'Donnell, Kathy Stienke

1990-91: Bob Denton (Supt), Don Forrester (Prin), Don Phillips, Keith Burnett, Bridget Cave, Howard Ballard, Jane Botkin, Jane Canales, Colleen Davis, Glenn Davis, Peggy Grooms, Shauna Kidd, Barbara Lewis, Georgia Tomlin, Terry Wicke, Carol Cummings, Susan Burch, David Fields, Mary Jane Harned, Roger Morey, Ed Palmer, Deb Palmer, Dennis Seale, Melissa Koopman, Don Clark, Glen Jones, Leslie Jones, Rick Eickenloff, Susan Lundin, Marilyn Wright, Poe Shelton, Galen Dodson, Sheila Harmon, Sherry Haydon, Don Hopkins, Cheryl Hopkins, Paula King, Sonja Vandivier, Jim Whites, Virginia Woods, Mary Alice Webster, Ruth Sullivan, Lee Ann Wilkins, Carl Waits, Pecos McDaniel, Gay Lynn Wilson, Becky Denton, Carol Howie, Steele Fleming, Jane Click, Jerry English, Barbara English, David Shaw, Barbara Hopson, Mark Engeling, John Merz, Cheryl Calame, Jessica Allen Dean, Scott Dean, Effie Eastham, Nancy Faust, Marsha Hurlbut, Shirley Johnson, Kathy Leopold, Kay McCrary, Malyna Miller, Sandy Southwell, Susan Troppy, Richard Stark, Susan Stark, Mike Cave, Alicia Blythe, Jill Gathright, Polly Harlan, Janice Wycoff, Lori Blythe, Beth Puckett, Barbara Davidson, Connie Burrus, Barbara Staelens, Holly Miller, Judy Kelley, Stacy Hurwitz, Nancy Witwiski, Linda Garza, Rebecca Harvey, Cheryl Hayden, Yvonne Paulsgrove, Janey Russell, Laurinda Schaertl, Bridget Williams, Barbara Krause, Jerry Lou Dodson, Jeanie Fuelberg, Anita

Kelly, Marion Voudouris, Roberta Carnes, Peggy Howell, Angela Murphy, Kathy Warren, Janice Whitefield, Sharon Fleming, Marge Foster, Amy Kadlecek, Rae McCartney, Mary Ayres, Cherie Bolton, Tommie Sue Bourland, Max Hardee, Pat Hennessee, Janice Morris, Janet Rippy, Paula Formby, Frances Henderson, Joni Henderson, Jim O'Donnell, Barbara Schwartz, Cassie Smith, Cathy Thornhill

1991-92: Bob Denton (Supt), Don Forrester (Prin), Daymun White, Keith Burnett, Bridget Cave, Jane Botkin, Jane Canales, Roger Morey, Ed Palmer, Anne Cook, Shauna Kidd, Mary Jane Harned, Susan Burch, Colleen Davis, Glenn Davis, Jerry English, Barbara English, David Fields, Ellis Smith, Terry Wicke, Randy Meek, Poe Shelton, Rick Eickenloff, Dennis Seale, Kelly Broussard, Howard Ballard, Melissa Koopman, Carol Cummings, Georgia Tomlin, Susan Lundin, Kay Coleman, Sherry Haydon, Galen Dodson, Paula King, Sheila Harmon, Marilyn Wright, David Shaw, Jim Whites, Ruth Sullivan, Jane Click, Carl Waits, Becky Denton, Steele Fleming, Pecos McDaniel, Lee Ann Wilkins, Virginia Woods, Mark Engeling, John Merz, Effie Eastham, Nancy Faust, Stuart Foreman (1st sem), Debbie Gray, Bobbette Hewgley, Cliff Holubec, Don Hopkins, Cheryl Hopkins, Malyna Miller, Diane Howe, Marsha Hurlbut, Betsi Johnson, Shirley Johnson, Kathy Leopold, Kay McCrary, Deanne Miller, Kathy Nichols, Deb Palmer Sandy Southwell, Brenda Strahan, Susan Troppy, Sonja Vandivier, Steve Vinson, Mary Alice Webster, Richard Stark, Mike Cave, Marion Voudouris, Joni Henderson, Susan Stark, Nannette Newburn, Connie Burrus, Amy McDonald, Janice Wycoff, Lori Blythe, Beth Puckett, Barbara Davidson, Polly Harlan, Judy Kelley, Jill Gathright, Stacy Hurwitz, Nancy Witwiski, Linda Garza, Rebecca Harvey, Cheryl Hayden, Susan Kollaja, Yvonne Paulsgrove, Laurinda Schaertl, Bridget Williams, Jerry Lou Dodson, Jeanie Fuelberg, Kathy Jernigan, Anita Kelly, Barbara Krause, Patty Low, Deanna Rees, Rhonda Whitman, Kathy Warren Clark, Becky Davis, Deborah Ericson, Peggy Howell, Janey Russell, Janice Whitefield, Sharon Fleming, Marge Foster, Amy Kadlecek, Rae McCartney, Carolyn Soltau, Kathy Stienke, Mary Ayres, Cherie Bolton, Tommie Sue Bourland, Max Hardee, Pat Hennessee, Janice Morris, Janet Rippy, Paula Formby, Frances Henderson, Barbara McManus, Jim O'Donnell, Barbara Schwartz, Cassie Smith, Cathy Thornhill

1992-93: Bob Denton (Supt), Don Forrester (Prin), Daymun White, Keith Burnett, Bridget Cave, Evelyn Coffman, Beth Rawlings, Jim Whites, Pearl Horner, Sonja Vandivier, Barbara Lewis, Shauna Kidd, Melissa Koopman, Jane Canales, EllisSmith, Dennis Seale, Ed Palmer, Susan Burch, Roger Morey, Mary Jane Harned, Sherry Haydon, Anne Cook, Colleen Davis, Glenn Davis, Galen Dodson, Lisa Gregory, Nancy White, Natalie Davis, Randy Meek, Marilyn Wright, Kelly Broussard, David Shaw, Susan Lundin, Jerry English, Rick Eickenloff, Georgia Tomlin, Don Hopkins, Paula King, Becky Denton, Howard Ballard, Kaye Coleman, Jane Botkin, Poe Shelton, Susan Warwick, Linda Bohrer, Jan Campbell, Jane Click, Nancy Faust, Steele Fleming, Deborah Fredrickson, Debra Gray, Lydia Hewett, Bobbette Hewgley, Cliff Holubec, Cheryl Hopkins, Diane Howe, Marsha Hurlbut, Betsi Johnson, Shirley Johnson, Scott Kvapil, Kathy Leopold, John Merz, Deanne Miller, Malyna Miller, Kathy Nichols, Deb Palmer, Dan Pollard, Diane Pollard, Carla Quijano, Sandy Southwell, Brenda Strahan, Ruth Sullivan, Susan Troppy, Carl Waits, Mary Alice Webster, Lee Ann Wilkins, Mark Hester (part of 1st sem), Anita Kelly, Nannette Newburn, Janice Wycoff, Lori Blythe, Beth Puckett, Barbara Davidson, Polly Harlan, Judy Kelley, Vickie Harris, Holly Miller, Amy McDonald, Barbara Rutherford, Nancy Witwiski, Jill Gathright, Stacy Hurwitz, Sandy Broussard, Linda Garza, Cheryl Hayden, Diane Jasinski, Susan Kollaja, Yvonne Paulsgrove, Rebecca Weiser, Marilyn Chalmers, Jerry Lou Dodson, Jeanie Fuelberg, Kathy Jernigan, Barbara Krause, Deanna Rees, Marion Voudouris, Rhonda Whitman, Kathy Clark, Becky Davis, Barbara English, Deborah Ericson, Fran Hoggard, Peggy Howell, Kim Morrow, Janey Russell, Janice Whitefield, Mimi Boelter, Rae McCartney, Sharon Fleming, Marge Foster, Amy Kadlecek, Patty Low, Carolyn Soltau, Susan Stark, Richard Stark, Mike Cave, Kathy Stienke, Mary Ayres, Cherie Bolton, Tommie Sue Bourland, Max Hardee, Pat Hennessee, Janice Morris, Janet Rippy, Connie Burrus, Paula Formby, Joni Henderson, Jim O'Donnell, Barbara Schwartz, Cassie Smith, Cathy Thornhill

1993-94: Tony Riehl (Supt), Don Forrester (Prin), June Coleman, Mrs. Lynn McDonald, Bridget Cave, Jim Whites, Sonja Vandivier, Barbara Lewis, Shauna Kidd, Melissa Koopman, Jane Canales, Ellis Smith, Dennis Seale, Ed Palmer, Susan Burch, Roger Morey, Mary Jane

Harned, Sherry Haydon, Anne Cook, Colleen Davis, Glenn Davis, Randy Meek, Marilyn Wright, Kelly Broussard, David Shaw, Jerry English, Rick Eickenloff, Paula King, Howard Ballard, Jane Botkin, Poe Shelton, Susan Warwick, Cole Reynolds, Monte Cain, Rip Gravell, Karen Thompson, Oswaldo Sanchez, Gary Jarosz, Jeff Rudy, Evelyn Coffman, Sylvia Evans, Lisa Gregory, Pearl Horner, Steve Krupp, Diana Boehm, Kristi Steger, Sue Wendel, Doug Agnew, Jan Campbell, Nancy Faust, Steele Fleming, Deborah Fredrickson, Debra Gray, Lydia Hewett, Lou Jean Milford, Cliff Holubec, Daniel Schmidt, Diane Howe, Marsha Hurlbut, Betsi Johnson, Shirley Johnson, Scott Kvapil, Kim Gravell, Kathy Leopold, Deanne Miller, Malyna Miller, Kathy Nichols, Deb Palmer, Dan Pollard, Diane Pollard, Irma Lewis, Carla Quijano, Sandy Southwell, Brenda Strahan, Ruth Sullivan, Carl Waits, Mary Alice Webster, Dennis Schommer, Lee Ann Wilkins, Randy Parks, Cheryl Patton, Jayne Edwards, Nona Michaelson, Beth Rawlings, Barbara Scroggie, Letty Vasquez, Irene Wooten, Mary Black, Effie Eastham, Stacy Hurwitz, Ginger Berdoll, Sandy Broussard, Linda Garza, Diane Jasinski, Pam McFaddin, Yvonne Paulsgrove, Rebecca Weiser, Bridget Williams, Marcie Danzeiser, Jeanie Fuelberg, Kathy Jernigan, Barbara Krause, Deanna Rees, Marion Voudouris, Rhonda Whitman, Kathy Clark, Becky Davis, Barbara English, Barbara Flake, Fran Hoggard, Peggy Howell, Kim Morrow, Sandra Tuck, Janice Whitefield, Charlene Arnold, Mimi Boelter, Sharon Fleming, Marge Foster, Amy Kadlecek, Patty Low, Rae McCartney, Carolyn Soltau, Susan Stark, Kathy Stienke, Carol Taylor, Mary Ayres, Cherie Bolton, Tommie Sue Bourland, Marilyn Chalmers, Max Hardee, Pat Hennessee, Denise Kelly, Janet Rippy, Elizabeth Wallin, Connie Burrus, Vickie Harris, Joni Henderson, Jim O'Donnell, Barbara Schwartz, Cassie Smith Ikels, Cathy Thornhill, Lori Blythe, Janice Wycoff, Judy Kelley, Jill Gathright, Donald Massey, Beth Puckett, Polly Harlan, Mark Engeling Janey Russell, Susan Troppy, Holly Miller, Cindy Frazer, Barbara Rutherford, Nancy Witwiski, Karon Brown, Janice Morris, Nannette Newburn, Anita Kelly, Richard Stark, Mike Cave

1994-95: Tony Riehl (Supt), Don Forrester (Prin-1st sem), Jim Rosebrock (Prin-2nd sem), June Coleman, Sylvia Evans, Julie Jones, Jenny Dailey, Howard Ballard, Jane Botkin, Kelly Broussard, Brooke Burton Parks, Susan Burch, Monte Cain, Jane Canales, Evelyn Coffman, Kelly Coleman, Colleen Davis, Glenn Davis, Rick Eickenloff, Jerry English, Dan George, Rip Gravell, Phyliss Gregory, Mary Jane Harned, Sherry Haydon, Shauna Kidd, Paula King, Melissa Koopman, Steve Krupp, Barbara Lewis, Randy Meek, Peggy McCabe, Roger Morey, Tracy Neef, Ed Palmer, Beth Rawlings, Jeff Rudy, Barbara Scroggie, Dennis Seale, David Shaw, Poe Shelton, Ellis Smith, Lisa Gregory Terrill, Karen Thompson, Sonja Vandivier, Melissa Weiss, Susan Warwick, Jim Whites, Irene Wooten, Marilyn Wright, Nona Michaelson, Doug Agnew, Mary Black, Diana Boehm, Jan Campbell, Bridget Cave, Lynn McDonald, Tyler Damron, Pamela Dieringer, Effie Eastham, Nancy Faust, Steele Fleming, Deborah Fredrickson, Kim Gravell, Debra Gray, Lydia Hewett, Cliff Holubec, Marsha Hurlbut, Lora Johnson, Shirley Johnson, Jayne Edwards Kenesson (1st sem), Nancy Nixon (2nd sem), Scott Kvapil, Kathy Leopold, Irma Lewis, Lou Jean Milford, Deanne Miller, Malyna Miller, Kathy Nichols, Deb Palmer, Dan Pollard, Diane Pollard, Carla Quijano, Daniel Schmidt, Shelley Seaver, Sandy Southwell, Anne Spacht, Kristi Steger, Diane Howe Stolte, Brenda Strahan, Ruth Sullivan, Melissa Vauk, Diane Wagner, Carl Waits, Mary Alice Webster, Sue Wendel, Lee Ann Wilkins, Stacy Hurwitz, Sandy Broussard, Tonna Evans, Linda Garza, Diane Jasinski, Pam McFaddin, Yvonne Paulsgrove, Rebecca Weiser, Rhonda Whitman, Bridget Williams, Ginger Berdoll, Marcie Danzeiser, Jeanie Fuelberg, Carolyn Jackson, Kathy Jernigan, Barbara Krause, Deanna Rees, Tammy Stellato, Mary Steinberg, Marion Voudouris, Kathy Clark, Becky Davis, Barbara English, Barbara Flake, Fran Hoggard, Peggy Howell, Sandra Tuck, Janice Whitefield, Charlene Arnold, Mimi Boelter, Sharon Fleming, Marge Foster, Laura Goodwin, Amy Kadlecek, Patty Low, Carolyn Soltau, Susan Stark, Kathy Stienke, Mary Ayers, Cherie Bolton, Tommie Sue Bourland, Marilyn Chalmers Max Hardee, Pat Hennessee, Denise Kelly, Janet Rippy, Carol Taylor, Elizabeth Wallin, Connie Burrus, Vickie Harris, Joni Henderson, Cassie Ikels, Joe Moore, Kristin Needham, Jim O'Donnell, Barbara Schwartz, Cathy Thornhill, Janice Wycoff, Carol Pringle, Beth Puckett, Kim Townsend, Kay Mangrum, Mark Engeling, Judy Kelley, Kaye Coleman, Janey Russell, Susan Troppy, Karon Brown, Cindy Frazer, Holly Miller, Barbara Rutherford, Nancy Witwiski, Janice Morris, Mike Cave, Anita Kelly, Richard Stark, Nannette Newburn

1995-96: Tony Riehl (Supt), Jim Rosebrock (Prin), June Coleman, Julie Jones, Howard Ballard, Jane Botkin, Kelly Broussard, Susan Burch, Monte Cain, Jane Canales, Evelyn Coffman, Kelly Coleman, Glenn Davis, Rick Eickenloff, Jerry English Dan George, Rip Gravell, Mary Jane Harned, Sherry Haydon, Lora Johnson, Shauna Kidd, Paula King, Melissa Koopman, Steve Krupp, Skipper Lay, Barbara Lewis, Peggy McCabe, Pecos McDaniel, Randy Meek, Nona Michaelson, Roger Morey, Tracy Neef, Margaret Nudo, Ed Palmer, Brooke Parks, Beth Rawlings, Jeff Rudy, Dennis Seale, Darren Shaw, David Shaw, Poe Shelton, Ellis Smith, Lisa Terrill, Karen Thompson, Tara Tower, Patty Uffman, Melissa Vauk, Susan Warwick, Jim Whites, Irene Wooten, Marilyn Wright, Oran Rippy, Doug Agnew, Mary Black, Jan Campbell, Bridget Cave, Tyler Damron, Pamela Deiringer Jackson, Effie Eastham, Nancy Faust Sutherland, Steele Fleming, Deborah Fredrickson, Kim Gravell, Debra Gray, Cliff Holubec, Marsha Hurlbut, Shirley Johnson, Scott Kvapil, Kathy Leopold, Irma Lewis, Lynn McDonald, Lou Jean Milford, Deanne Miller, Malyna Miller, Nancy Nixon, Deb Palmer, Dan Pollard, Diane Pollard, Carla Quijano, Daniel Schmidt, Shelley Seaver, Sandy Southwell, Anne Spacht, Kristi Steger, Diane Stolte, Brenda Strahan, Ruth Sullivan, Diane Wagner, Mary Alice Webster, Sue Wendel, Lee Ann Wilkins, John Russell, Tom Alholm, Stuart Fyall, Cherie Bolton, Tommie Sue Bourland, Marilyn Chalmers, Max Hardee, Pat Hennessee, Denise Kelly, Kari Phillips, Janet Rippy, Elizabeth Wallin, Sheila Bosworth, Connie Burrus, Vickie Harris, Joni Henderson, Cassie Ikels, Joe Moore, Kristin Needham, Jim O'Donnell, Barbara Schwartz, Lisa Schormann, Janice Wycoff, Carol Pringle, Beth Puckett, Sonya Vandiview, Kay Mangrum, Mark Engeling, Judy Kelley, Laurinda Schaertl, Barbara Davidson, Victoria Crawford, Janey Russell, Cheryl Hayden, Susan Troppy, Pam Phillips, Cindy Frazer, Holly Miller, Shelley Morgan, Barbara Rutherford, Myra Sutherland, Kathy Hernandez, Nancy Witwiski, Janice Morris, Kathy Nichols, Mike Cave, Anita Kelly, Delores Covington Nannette Newbern, Kelly Spain, Carolyn Jackson, Pam Blanchette, Sandy Broussard, Tonna Evans, Linda Garza, Diane Jasinski, Yvonne Paulsgrove, Rebecca Weiser, Rhonda Whitman, Ginger Berdoll, Marcie Danzeiser, Jeanie Fuelberg, Kathy Jernigan, Barbara Krause, Deanna Rees, Tammy Stellato, Mary Steinberg, Marion Voudouris, Kathy Clark, Barbara English, Barbara Flake, Marge Foster, Laura Goodwin, Peggy Howell, Carol Taylor, Sandra Tuck, Janice Whitefield, Charlene Arnold, Mimi Boelter, Sharon Fleming, Amy Kadlecek, Patty Low, Carolyn Soltau, Susan Stark, Kathy Stienke, Mary Ayres

1996-97: Tony Riehl (Supt), Jim Rosebrock (Prin), June Coleman, Doug Agnew, Carolyn Bailey, Jorey Berry, Howard Ballard, Jane Botkin, Kelly Broussard, Susan Burch, Jane Canales, Kelly Coleman, Pat Daigle, Jenny Dailey, Tom Davis, Rick Eickenloff, Jerry English, Viki Fuller, Judy Gardner, Bryan Grabman, Rip Gravell, Mary Jane Harned, Sherry Haydon, Howard Herrera, Greg Howard, Lora Johnson, Julie Jones, Shauna Kidd, Paula King, Pecos McDaniel, Nona Michaelson, Roger Morey, Tracy Neef, Kelly Nolan, Beth Rawlings, Bethany Rosebrock, Jeff Rudy, Barbara Scroggie, David Shanley, Darren Shaw, Poe Shelton, Brian Parks, Stacy Smith, Mary Jo Tykoski, Irene Wooten, Steve Krupp, Susan Warwick, Marilyn Wright Debra Zupancic, Dan George, Evelyn Coffman, Darleen Ramos, Brian Eggleston, Barbara Lewis, Ed Palmer, Dennis Seale, David Shaw, Ellis Smith, Karen Stout, Jim Whites, Lynn McDonald, Tyler Damron, Bridget Cave, Tom Alholm, Erica Bacon, Mary Black, Jan Campbell, Effie Eastham, Steele Fleming, Paula Fletcher, Shelley Seaver Franklin, Deborah Fredrickson, Stuart Fyall, Carolyn Giannone, Kim Gravell, Debra Gray, Marsha Hurlbut, Pamela Jackson, Shirley Johnson, Scott Kvapil, Kathy Leopold, Irma Lewis, Trent Lyle, Lawrence Mikulak, Lou Jean Milford, Deanne Miller, Malyna Miller, Nancy Nixon, Cammie Ockman, Deb Palmer, Shirley Phillips, Dan Pollard, Diane Pollard, Carla Quijano, Oran Rippy, John Russell, Daniel Schmidt, Deborah Simpson, Sandy Southwell, Anne Spacht, Diane Stolte, Brenda Strahan, Ruth Sullivan, Nancy Sutherland, Karen Thompson, Tara Tower, Helena Tselos, Kristine Urbanovsky, Melissa Vauk, Diane Wagner, Elizabeth Wallin, Ann Walsh, Mary Alice Webster, Sue Wendel, Lee Ann Wilkins, Mary Ayres, Denise Kelly, Kari Phillips Dodson, Pat Hennessee, Lisa Woodland, Janet Rippy, Marilyn Chalmers, Tommie Sue Bourland, Cherie Bolton, Max Hardee, Jim O'Donnell, Delores Covington, Anne Dodson, Barbara Schwartz, Myra Sutherland, Vickie Harris, Joni Henderson, Susan Troppy, Sheila Bosworth, Mark Engeling, Cassie Ikels, Connie Burrus, Janice Morris, Joe Moore Sonja Vandivier, Carol

Pringle, Sandy Broussard, Diane Jasinski, Rhonda Whitman, Yvonne Paulsgrove, Pam Blanchette, Tonna Evans, Becky Weiser, Linda Garza, Ginger Berdoll, Laura Brown, Tammy Stellato, Deanna Rees, Marion Voudouris, Marcie Danzeiser, Barbara Krause, Rita Cochran, Kathy Jernigan, Mary Steinberg, Kathy Clark, Barbara English, Barbara Flake, Marge Foster, Peggy Howell, Diane Massey, Carol Taylor, Sandra Tuck, Janice Whitefield, Patty Low, Laura Goodwin, Carolyn Soltau, Stephanie Love, Sharon Fleming, Mimi Boelter, Phyliss Woods, Felice McCreary, Amy Kadlecek, Charlene Arnold, Cheryl Hayden, Janey Russell, Barbara Rutherford, Kay Mangrum, Mary Kniffen, Beth Puckett Shuman, Anne McDonald, Laurinda Schaertl, Holly Miller, Cindy Frazer, Kathleen Marko, Dabney Kowis, Kathy Stienke (1st sem), Nancy Witwiski (until April), Anita Kelly, Nannette Newbern, Tresa Anderson, Barbara Davidson, Martha Clements, Janice Wycoff, Judy Kelley, Mike Cave, Brian Eggleston, Mary Hughes

1997-98: Tony Riehl (Supt), David Shanley (Prin), Dean Blair, Jane Miller, Viki Fuller, Howard Ballard, Jane Botkin, Susan Burch, Jane Canales, Kelly Coleman, Rick Eickenloff, Jerry English, Mary Jane Harned, Sherry Haydon, Howard Herrera (1st sem), Tom Hancock (2nd sem), Lora Johnson, Julie Jones, Shauna Kidd, Steve Krupp, Barbara Lewis, Pecos McDaniel, Dennis Seale, Poe Shelton, Brian Parks, Mike Segleski, Ellis Smith, Irene Wooten, Marilyn Wright, Dan George, Doug Agnew, Debra Zupancic, Paula King, Jenny Dailey, Susan Warwick, Roger Morey, Ed Palmer, Derrl Ohnheiser, George Hamilton, Rip Gravell, Jim Whites, Jeff Rudy, Greg Howard, Karen Stout, Mary J. Tykoski, Tracy Neef, David Shaw, Nona Michaelson, Evelyn Coffman, Jan Lindsey, Lawrence Mikulak, Bryan Grabman, Tom Alholm, Erika Bacon, Mary Black, Barbara Blair, Jan Campbell, Bridget Cave, Carol Culp, Tyler Damron, Larry DeLacretaz, Melissa Denis, Leslie Dunn, Joseph Felkel, Steele Fleming, Susan Flynn, Shelley Franklin, Deborah Fredrickson, Stuart Fyall, Carolyn Giannone, Kim Gravell, Lee Hipp, Marsha Hurlbut, Pamela Jackson, Donna Janssen, Shirley Johnson, Kendra Kahn, Scott Kvapil, Kathy Leopold, Irma Lewis, Trent Lyle, Lou Jean Milford, Deanne Miller, Malyna Miller, Angela Moore, Kathy Nichols, Nancy Nixon, Cammie Ockman, Deb Palmer, Shirley Phillips, Dan Pollard, Diane Pollard, Carla Quijano, Oran Rippy, Daniel Schmidt, Mark Schroeder, Deborah Simpson, Sandy Southwell, Anne Spacht, Kelly Spain, Diane Stolte, Brenda Strahan, Nancy Sutherland, Karen Thompson, Tara Tower, Kristine Urbanovsky, Melissa Vauk, Diane Wagner, Elizabeth Wallin, Ann Walsh, Mary Alice Webster, Sue Wendel, Lee Ann Wilkins, Carolyn Jackson, Ginger Berdoll, Pam Blanchette, Tonna Evans, Linda Garza, Jennifer Hampton, Diane Jasinski, Shannon Kelly, Rebecca Weiser, Rhonda Whitman, Rita Cochran, Marcie Danzeiser, Gloria Dunlap, Kathy Jernigan, Laura Brown Kirk, Barbara Krause, Jodi Meixelsperger, Mary Steinberg, Tammy Stellato, Marion Voudouris, Kathy Clark, Barbara English, Barbara Flake, Susan Stark, Marge Foster, Peggy Howell, Mary Ledbetter, Deanna Rees, Carol Taylor, Vickie Smith, Janice Whitefield, Charlene Arnold, Mimi Boelter, Sharon Fleming, Lois Neumeyer, Amy Kadlecek, Stephanie Love, Patty Low, Felice McCreary, Carolyn Soltau, Phyliss Woods, Martha Clements, Janice Wycoff, Catherine Hovey, Dabney Kowis, Laurinda Schaertl, Barbara Davidson, Beth Shuman, Anne McDonald, Kay Mangrum, Mary Kniffen, Janey Russell, Anna Finley, Cheryl Hayden, Susan Troppy, Holly Miller, Cindy Frazer, Priscilla Martinez, Kathleen Marko Alley, Mike Cave, Tresa Anderson, Anita Kelly, Nannette Newbern, Delores Covington, Lestant Flake, Mary Ayres, Cherie Bolton, Tommie Sue Bourland, Marilyn Chalmers, Susan Counts, Kari Dodson, Max Hardee, Pat Hennessee, Denise Kelly, Kristen Needham, Janet Rippy, Lisa Woodland, Sheila Bosworth, Connie Burrus, Vickie Harris, Joni Henderson, Cassie Ikels, Joe Moore, Janice Morris Jim O'Donnell, Lisa Schormann, Barbara Schwartz, Victoria Crawford, Mark Engeling, Judy Kelley, Carol Pringle, Sonja Vandivier, Mary Hughes, Tanyo Lyons, Myra Sutherland, LaJean Warren, Sharon Watkins, Anne Dodson

1998-99: Mike Owens (Supt), David Shanley (Prin), Mike Garrison, Jane Miller, Julie Jones, Viki Fuller, Howard Ballard, Mindy Beatty, John Bombach, Jane Botkin, Diane Bray, Linda Brown, Susan Burch, Jane Canales, Sherron Cherry, Evelyn Coffman, Kelly Coleman, Lisa Cappolette (1st sem), Yvonne Kaatz (2nd sem), Pat Daigle, Tom Davis, Cheryl DeLacretaz, Rick Eickenloff, David England, Jerry English, Ed Fasanella, Tracy Garcia, Robert Gier, Bryan Grabman, Rip Gravell, George Hamilton, Tom Hancock, Mary Jane Harned, Sherry Hayden,

Fran Herron, Greg Howard, Katie Jones, Shauna Kidd, Paula King, Steve Krupp, Keith Lancaster, Barbara Lewis, Jan Lindsey, Pecos McDaniel, Nono Michaelson, Larry Mikulak, Ann Miller, Roger Morey, Tracy Neef, Kelly Nolan, Brian Parks, Eddie Porter, Beth Rawlings, Dennis Seale, Mike Segleski, Kelly Jo Sexton, David Shaw, Poe Shelton, EllisSmith, Stacey Smith, Joyce Sommerfield, Diane Stolte, Peggy Till, Mary Jo Tykoski, Derek Tyler, Virginia Volpe, Susan Warwick, Irene Wooten, Marilyn Wright, Debra Zupancic, Tom Alholm, Erika Bacon, Mary Black, Bryan Branch, Carol Culp Brandt, Bridget Cave, Kelly Spain Coffey, Brenda Crawford, Tyler Damron, Larry DeLacretaz, Leslie Dunn, Joseph Felkel, Paula Finnessey, Steele Fleming, Susan Flynn, Deborah Fredrickson, Stuart Fyall, Carolyn Giannone, Christopher Godwin, Kim Gravell, Lee Hipp, Marsha Hurlbut, Donna Janssen, Shirley Johnson, Kendra Kahn, Frances Kaiser, Landa Leavy, Allyson Lee, Irma Lewis, Trrent Lyle, Judy Mears, Lou Jean Milford, Deanne Miller, Malyna Miller, Angela Moore, Kathy Nichols, Nancy Nixon, Cammie Ockman, Deb Palmer, William Person, Shirley Phillips, Dan Pollard, Diane Pollard, Carla Quijano, Susan Raybuck, Oran Rippy, Lela Sadler, Paul Schlichting, Mark Schroeder, Deborah Simpson, John Smith, Sandy Southwell, Anne Spacht, Brenda Strahan, Nancy Sutherland, Karen Thompson, Tara Tower, Dawn Turk, Kristine Urbanovsky, Melissa Vauk, Diane Wagner, Elizabeth Wallin, Ann Walsh, Sue Wendel, Lee Ann Wilkins, Mary Ayres, Cherie Bolton, Sheila Bosworth, Tommie Sue Bourland, Connie Burrus, Marilyn Chalmers, Susan Counts, Delores Covington, Victoria Crawford, Anne Dodson, Kari Dodson, Mark Engeling, Lestant Flake, Max Hardee, Vickie Harris, Joni Henderson, Pat Hennessee, Mary Hughes, Cassie Ikels, Judy Kelley, Denise Kelly, Kathy Latteo, Vicki Lynch, Joe Moore, Janice Morris, Kristen Needham, Jim O'Donnell, Carol Pringle, Janet Rippy, Lisa Schormann, Susan Troppy, Sonja Vandivier, Sharon Watkins, LaJean Warren, Ramona Welch, Lisa Woodland, Debra Bradford, Mary Buchanan, Amy Dalland, Carolyn Jackson, Ginger Berdoll, Pam Blanchette, Diane Jasinski, Shannon Kelly, Susan Knape, Patricia Lawrence, Jennifer Hampton Miller, Chandra Moore, Rebecca Weiser, Rhonda Whitman, Dene Burttschell, Rita Cochran, Marcie Danzeiser, Kathy Jernigan Jenkins, Laura Kirk, Barbara Krause McClure, Kari Schroeder, Tammy Stellato, Marion Voudouris, Jodi Witt, Kathy Clark, Gloria Dunlap, Barbara English, Barbara Flake, Micaela Gutierrez, Peggy Howell, Deanna Rees, Jan Rice, Susan Stark, Marge Foster, Vickey Smith, Carol Taylor, Charlene Arnold, Mimi Boelter, Sharon Fleming, Amy Kadlecek, Melania Miller, Mary Ledbetter, Stephanie Love, Patty Low, Felice McCreary, Lois Neumeyer, Carolyn Soltau, Phyliss Woods, Martha Clements, Janice Wycoff, Maggie Southard, Laurinda Schaertl, Barbara Davidson, Beth Shuman, Anne McDonald, Kay Mangrum, Mary Kniffen, Janey Russell, Anna Finley, Cheryl Hayden, Mary Steinberg, Holly Miller, Cindy Frazer, Priscilla Martinez, Kathleen Alley, Mike Cave, Tresa Anderson, Anita Kelly, Traci Henze

1999-00: Mary Ward (Supt), Greg Jung (Prin), Rip Gravell, Sherry Haydon, Ann Miller, Marilyn Wright, Katie del Hierro, Paula King, Keith Lancaster, Virginia Volpe, Mindy Beatty, Jane Canales, Jennifer Foreman, Judy Gardner, Shauna Kidd, Jane Botkin, Linda Brown, Cheryl DeLacretaz, Vanessa DeLacretaz, Tracy Garcia, Katie Jones, Yvonne Kaatz, Barbara Lewis, Sandy Schneider, Lea Anne Schroeder, Debra Zupancic, David England, Bryan Grabman, David Hall, Fran Herron, Lewis Jenkins, Kendra Kahn (1st sem), Kathy Romero (2nd sem), Sarah Wayne Kight, David Shaw, Cindy Sultemeier, Susan Warwick, Jerry English, Tom Hancock, Lawrence Mikulak, Derryl Ohnheiser, Brian Parks, Kelly Jo Sexton, Howard Ballard, Susan Burch, Mary Jane Harned, Steve Krupp, Roger Morey, Dennis Seale, Rachel Skinner, Diane Stolte, Mary Jo Tykoski, Robb Wilgoren, Kelly Coleman, Rick Eickenloff, George Hamilton, Greg Howard, Jan Lindsey, Pecos McDaniel, Mike Segleski, Ellis Smith, Peggy Till, Amy Thompson, Evelyn Coffman, Tamara Crowley, Tracy Neef, Beth Rawlings, Joyce Sommerfield, Myra Sutherland, Athena Caroselli, Joe Burns, Jenny Dailey, Julie Jones, Rhonda Duke, Oran Rippy, Tyler Damron, Donna Janssen, Paula Stiernberg, Bridget Cave, Kelly Coffey, Erika Bacon, Tandy Betak, Mary Black, Bryan Branch, Vonnie Brizendine, Margaret Brock, Brenda Crawford, Larry DeLacretaz, Patricia Dickerson, Andrea Dove, Edie Dunn, Leslie Dunn, David Ellis, Joseph Felkel, Steele Fleming, Susan Flynn, Deborah Fredrickson, Stuart Fyall, Carolyn Giannone, Christopher Godwin, Kim Gravell, Marsha Hurlbut, Shirley Johnson, Sandra Joyner, Frances Kaiser, Landa Leavy, Ann Leffingwell, Irma Lewis, Trenton Lyle, Michelle Marenco,

Judy Mears, Lou Jean Milford, Malyna Miller, Angela Moore, Carla Morton, Jeff Murphy, Cammie Ockman, Deb Palmer, Will Person, Shirley Phillips, John Pineda, Dan Pollard, Carla Quijano, Lela Sadler, Paul Schlichting, Deborah Simpson, Anne Spacht, Brenda Strahan, Nancy Sutherland, Karen Thompson, Tara Tower, Kristine Urbanovsky, Julie Wade, Diane Wagner, Elizabeth Wallin, Ann Walsh, Sue Wendel, Lee Ann Wilkins, Leslie Wittenburg, Ginger Berdoll, Chandra Moore Betak, Pam Blanchette, Donna Eshelman, Diane Jasinski, Shannon Kelly, Patricia Lawrence, Jennifer Miller, Rebecca Weiser, Rhonda Whitman, Lori Anderson, Dene Burttschell, Rita Cochran, Laura Kirk, Barbara McClure, Tracy McDaniel, Kathy Jenkins Murray, Janey Russell, Vicky Shoopman, Tammy Stellato, Marion Voudouris, Kathy Clark, Barbara English, Barbara Flake, Micaela Gutierrez, Martha Lockard, Gwen Portie, Jan Rice, Kathy Simmons, Vickey Smith, Carol Taylor, Lisa Wilson, Charlene Arnold, Mimi Boelter, Traci Bounds, Peggy Howell, Stephanie Love, Patty Low, Felice McCreary, Melania Miller, Lois Neumeyer, Carolyn Soltau, Phyliss Woods, Kathleen Alley, Martha Clements, Barbara Davidson, Anna Finley, Cindy Frazer, Cheryl Hayden, Judy Holmes, Susan Knape, Mary Ledbetter, Anne McDonald, Kay Mangrum, Priscilla Martinez, Holly Miller, Amy Kadlecek, Laurinda Schaertl, Beth Shuman, Maggie Southard, Janice Wycoff, Mike Cave, Tresa Anderson, Traci Henze, Anita Kelly, Mary Ayres, Cherie Bolton, Tommie Sue Bourland, Marilyn Chalmers, Susan Counts, Pat Hennessee, Denise Kelly, Jan McGowan, Kristen Needham, Janet Rippy, Barbara Schwartz, Lisa Woodland, Sheila Bosworth, Connie Burrus, Vickie Harris, Joni Henderson, Cassie Ikels, Kathy Latteo, Vicki Lynch, Joe Moore, Janice Morris, Jim O'Donnell, Lisa Schormann, Mark Engeling, Judy Kelley, Gwen McCloud, Carol Pringle, Susan Troppy, Sonja Vandivier, Mary Buchanan, Mary Hughes, LaJean Warren, Leslie Wallace, Sharon Watkins, Ramona Welch, Anne Dodson, Delores Covington, Lestant Flake.

2000-01: Mary Ward (Supt), Mary Bob Kosub, Greg Jung (Prin), Joe Burns (A. Prin), Athena Caroselli (A.Prin), Howard Ballard, Sherilyn Beard, Mindy Beatty, Jane Botkin, Linda Brown, Bryan Bryant, Susan Burch, Jane Canales, Lori Chester, Llewellyn Colborne, Kelly Coleman, Jeff Coward, Jenny Dailey, Kathy del Hierro, Cheryl DeLa Cratez, Tamara DeLaCratez, Vannessa DeLaCratez, Rhonda Duke, Bonnie Dunn, Rick Eickenloff, Jennifer Foreman, Mary Gardner, Christy Goodney, Bryan Grabman, Rip Gravell, David Hall, Tom Hancock, Mary Jane Harned, Sharon Hause, Sherry Haydon, Flynt Huey, Lewis Jenkins, Evelyn Jent-Coffman, Katie Jones, Yvonne Kaatz, Shauna Kidd, Sarah Kight, Paula King, Steve Krupp, Keith Lancaster, Barbara Lewis, JanLindsey, Tammy Lusinger, Toni McClish, Pecos McDaniel, Lawrence Mikulak, Ann Miller, Roger Morey, Tracy Neef, Kathy Nichols, Brian Parks, Karan Parrack, Ed Porter, Her-bert Rainbird, Beth Rawlings, Aimee Reese, Amy Ruede, LaDonna Rushing, Ronald Saylor, Sandra Schneider, Lea Ann Schroeder, Dennis Seale, Shauna Seaman, Mike Segleski, Mark Shackleford, David Shaw, Janet Shropshire, Ellis Smith, Joyce Sommerfield, Diane Stolte, Myra Sutherland, Peggy Till, Virginia Volpe, Robb Wilgoren, Marilyn Wright, Debra Zupancic, Tyler Damron (Prin), Kim Gravell (A. Prin), Paula Stiernberg (A. Prin), Erika Brown, Tandy Betak, Mary Black, Vonnie Brizendine, Margaret Brock, Tina Buitron, Adam Cartwright, Aimee Clement, Bridget Cave, Kelly Coffey, Brenda Crawford, Larry DeLa-Cretaz, Patricia Dickerson, Edie Dunn, Leslie Dunn, Annelise Eckhardt, David Ellis, Joe Felkel, Steele Fleming, Susan Flynn, Deborah Fredrickson, Paige Frontera, Stuart Fyall, Carolyn Giannone, Chris God-win, Richard Ivy, Shirley Johnson, Sandra Joyner, Frances Kaiser, Landa Leavy, Irma Lewis, Todd Long, Joanne MacIntyre, Michelle Marenco, Judy Mears, Lou Milford, Malyna Miller, Carla Morton, Jeff Murphy, Cammie Ockman, William Peace, William Person, John Pineda, Dan Pollard, Carla Quijano, John Russell, Lela Sadler, Jacqulyn Sallis, Deborah Simpson, Anne Spacht, Brenda Strahan, Nancy Sutherland, Robin Thurmond, Tara Tower, Kristine Urbanovsky, Julie Wade, Diane Wagner, Elizabeth Wallin, Ann Walsh, Sue Wendel, Leslie Wittenburg, Donna Janssen (Prin), Lestant Flake (A. Prin), Mary Ayres, Carla Bell, Cherie Bolton, Sheila Bosworth, Tommie Sue Bourland, Laura Breeden, Mary Buchanan, Connie Burrus, Marilyn Chalmers, Susan Counts, Anita Coy, Carol Crozier, Anne Dodson, Mark Engeling, Vickie Harris, Pat Hennessee, Mary Hughes, Cassie Ikels, Judy Kelley, Kathy Latteo, Jan McGowan, Gwen McLeod, Joe Moore, Janice Morris, Kristin Needham, Jim O'Donnell, Janet Rippy, Lisa Schormann, Barbara Schwartz, Susan Troppy, Sonja Vandivier, Leslie Wallace,

LaJean Warren, Sharon Watkins, Ramona Welch, Lisa Woodland, Mike Cave (Prin), Tressa Anderson (A.Prin), Cindy Frazer, Kathy Alley, Lori Ander-son, Charlene Arnold, Ginger Berdoll, Chandra Betak, Pam Blanchette, Mimi Boelter, Traci Bounds, Linda Bruce, Dene Burttschell, Kathy Clark, Martha Clements, Rita Cochran, Robbie Cripe, Amy Dalland, Marcie Danzeiser, Barbara Davidson, Donna Eschelman, Anna Finley, Barbara Flake, Kelly Garner, Micaela Gutierrez, Cheryl Hayden, Rosemary Hearn, Traci Henze, Glenda Hjornevik, Judy Holmes, Peggy Howell, Carolyn Jackson, Nicole Jaeckle, Diane Jasinski, Amy Kadlecek, Diane Kainer, Anita Kelly, Shannon Kelly, Laura Kirk, Susan Knape, Patricia Lawrence, Martha Lockard, Patty Low, Natalie Mahany, Kay Mangrum, Barbara McClure, Felice McCreary, Anne McDonald, Holly Miller Kathy Murray, Lois Neumeyer, Gwen Por-tie, Janice Rice, Debra Roberts, Janey Russell, Laurinda Schaertl, Beth Shuman, Kathy Simmons, Vickey Smith, Carolyn Soltau, Margaret Southard, Mary Steinberg, Tammy Stellato, Carol Taylor, Marion Voudou-ris, Rebecca Weiser, Rhonda Whitman, Lisa Wilson, Phyllis Woods, Janice Wycoff.

2001-02. Mary Ward (Supt), Mary Bob Kosub, Greg Jung (Prin), Stuart Foreman (A. Prin), Darlene Billman (A. Prin), Howard Ballard, Jay Bates, Sherilyn Beard, Steven Beasley, Melinda Beatty, Tandy Betak, Eric Blume, Heather Boss, Jane Botkin, Jane Canales, Llewellyn Colborne, Jeff Coward, Richard Cronshey, Brenda Cullison, Matthew Darroh, Cheryl DeLaCretaz, Davis Ellis, Jennifer Foreman, Mary Gardner, Rebecca Garrison, Abby Gode, Bryan Grabman, Lewis "Rip" Gravell, Laura Grice, David Hall, John Hall, Joyce Hancock, Tom Hancock, Mary Jane Harned, Christina Hector, Lewis Jenkins, Evelyn Jent-Coffman, Katie Jones, Yvonne Kaatz, Thomas Kane, Shauna Kidd, Jerri Lynn Kihl, Paul King, Steven Krupp, Keith Lancaster, Barbara Lewis, Jan Lindsey, Regina Mabry, Pecos McDaniel, Lawrence Mikulak, Roger Morey, Tracy Neef, Brian Ormande, Walter Page, Brian Parks, Susan Powell, Todd Raimond, Herbert Rainbird, Beth Rawlings, Aimee Reese, Kathy Romero, LaDonna Rushing, Ronald Saylor, Sandra Schneider, Lea Anne Schroeder, Dennis Seale, Shauna Seaman, Michael Segleski, Jill Shelton, Janet Shropshire, Ellis Smith, Joyce Sommerfield, Myra Sutherland, Nancy Trapp, Virginia Volpe, Susan Warwick, Toni West, Robb Wilgoren, Marilyn Wright, Debra Zupancic, Tyler Damron (MS Prin), Kim Gravell (MS A. Prin), Paula Stiernberg (MS A. Prin), DeeAnn Arterburn, Erika Bacon, Mary Black, Vonnie Branch, Margaret Brock, Tina Buitron, Heather Campbell, Adam Cartwright, Bridget Cave, Aimee Clement, James DeLaCretaz, Edith Dunn, Leslie Dunn, Steele Fleming, Susan Flynn, Paige Frontera, Stuart Fyall, Chris Godwin, Richard Ivy, Shirley Johnson, Patricia Kilpatrick-Ayers, Irma Lewis, Joann MacIntyre, Michelle Marenco, Jeff Mayes, Nicole McCleary, Judith Mears, Edye Melton, Lou Milford, Malyna Miller, Jeff Murphy, Chris Payne, Bill Peace, William Person, John Pineda, Dan Pollard, Carla Quijano, Debra Raimond, John Russell, Lela Sadler, Jacqulyn Sallis, Deborah Simpson, Anne Spacht, Brenda Strahan, Nancy Sutherland, Robin Thurmond, Peggy Till, Tara Tower, Kristine Urbanovsky, Julie Wade, Diane Wagner, Elizabeth Wallin, Ann Walsh, Sue Wendel, Annelise White, Leslie Wittenburg, Donna Janssen (IS Prin), Lestant Flake (IS A. Prin), Mary Ayers, Carla Bell, Rebecca Berdoll, Cherie Bolton, Sheila Bosworth, Tommie Bourland, Mary Buchanan, Connie Burrus, Marilyn Chalmers, Susan Counts, Anita Coy, Carol Crozier, Mark Engeling, Joseph Felkel, Vickie Harris, Pat Hennessee, Mary Hughes, Cassie Ikels, Judy Kelley, Kathleen Latteo, Jan McGowan, Janice Morris, Kristin Needham, Jim O'Donnell, Janet Rippy, Barbara Schwartz, Julie Spector, Susan Troppy, Sonja Vandivier, Leslie Wallace, LaJean Warren, Sharon Watkins, Ramona Welch, Lisa Woodland, Mike Cave (PS Prin), Tressa Anderson (PS A. Prin), Lori Anderson, Ginger Berdoll, Chandra Betak, Pamela Blanchette, Mimi Boelter, Traci Bounds, Linda Bruce, Dene Burttschell, Carrie Chism, Kathy Clark, Martha Clements, Nicole Cmerek, Rita Cochran, Robbie Cripe, Amy Dalland, Marcie Danzeiser, Donna Eshelman, Barbara Flake, Stacy Frithiof, Kelly Garner, Micaela Guitierrez, Cheryl Hayden, Traci Henze, Glenda Hjornevik, Judy Holmes, Peggy Howell, Carolyn Jackson, Diane Jasinski, Amy Kadlecek, Diane Kainer, Anita Kelly, Laura Kirk, Susan Knape, Patricia Lawrence, Martha Lockard, Patty Low, Natalie Mahany, Kathy Mangrum, Priscilla Martinez, Barbara McClure, Felice McCreary, Anne McDonald, Holly Miller, Kathy Murray, Lois Neumeyer, Gwen Portie, Janice Rice, Debra Roberts, Janey Russell, Laurinda Schaertl, Elizabeth Shuman, Kathy Simmons, Vickey Smith, Carolyn Soltau, Mary Steinberg, Tammy

Stellato, Kathy Stienke, Carol Taylor, Marion Voudouris, Julie Walker, Rebecca Weiser, Jacquelyn Whalen, Rhonda Whitman, Lisa Wilson, Phyllis Woods, Janice Wycoff.

2002-03. Mary Ward (Supt), Mary Kosub, Greg Jung (HS Prin), Darlene Billman (A. Prin), Stuart Foreman (A. Prin), Howard Ballard, Jay Bates, Sherilyn Beard, Mindy Beatty, Tandy Betak, Eric Blume, Jane Botkin, Jane Canales, Lew Colborne, Jeff Coward, Richard Cronshey, Matthew Darroh, Cheryl DeLa-Cretaz, Alissa Dyson, Davis Ellis, Jennifer Foreman, Mary Gardner, Rebecca Garrison, Abby Gode, Chris Godwin, Marcus Gonzales, Bryan Grabman, Rip Gravell, Laura Grice, David Hall, Randy Hall, Tom Hancock, Christina Hector, Donna Hood, Laura Jenkins, Lewis Jenkins, Evelyn Coffman-Jent, Katie Jones, Yvonne Kaatz, Shauna Kidd, Jerri Lyne Kihl, Paula King, Steve Krupp, Keith Lancaster, Barbara Lewis, Jane Lindsey, Marisa Maher, Pecos McDaniel, Lawrence Mikulak, Jason Myers, Tracy Neef, Kathy Nichols (Nurse), Derrl Ohnheiser, Brian Ormonde, Ed Palmer, Brian Parks, Susan Powell, Todd Raimond, Herbert Rainbird, Beth Rawlings, LaDonna Rushing, Erin Samuels, Ronald Saylor, Sandra Schneider, Lea Anne Schroeder, Dennis Seale, Mike Segleski, Jill Shelton, Janet Shropshire, Ellis Smith, Joyce Sommerfield, Myra Sutherland, Nancy Trapp, Virginia Volpe, Susan Warwick, Toni West, Robb Wilgoren, Marilyn Wright, Diane Wrinkle, Debra Zupancic, Tyler Damron (MS Prin), Kim Gravell (A. Prin), Paula Stiernberg (A. Prin), Erika Bacon, Mary Black, Vonnie Branch, Courtney Brown, Tina Buitron, Heather Campbell, Bridget Cave, Aimee Clement, Kelly Coffey, Brenda Crawford, James DeLaCretaz, Edith Dunn, Steele Fleming, Susan Flynn, Paige Frontera, Stuart Fyall, Richard Ivy, Shirley Johnson, Brenda Johnston, Frances Kaiser, Patti Kilpatrick-Ayers, Jay Larson, Kathy Leopold, Irma Lewis, Joanne MacIntyre, Michelle Marenco, Amy McCarty, Nicole McCleary, Judith Mears, Edye Melton, Wendy Middleton, Lou Milford, Malyna Miller, Jeff Murphy, Cammie Ockman, Chris Payne, Bill Peace, William Person, Dan Pollard, Carla Quijano, Debra Raimond, Adam Robinson, John Russell, Lela Sadler, Jacqulyn Sallis, Deborah Simpson, Anne Spacht, Brenda Strahan, Nancy Sutherland, Nelson Terroba, Robin Thurmond Brady, Tara Tower, Kristine Urbanovsky, Julie Wade, Diane Wagner, Elizabeth Wallin, Ann Walsh, Sue Wendel, Leslie Wittenburg, Donna Janssen (IS Prin), Lestant Flake (IS A. Prin), Mary Ayers, Carla Bell, Becky Berdoll, Cherie Bolton, Sheila Bosworth, Mary Buchanan, Connie Burrus, Marilyn Chalmers, Anita Coy, Carol Crozier, Anne Dodson, Mark Engeling, Joe Felkel, Mary Ellen Fernandez, Pat Hennessee, Susan Horton, Mary Hughes, Cassie Ikels, Judy Kelley, Kathleen Latteo, Jan McGowan, Gwen McLeod, Vickie Michaels, Janice Morris, Kristin Needham, Jim O'Donnell, Janet Rippy, Barbara Schwartz, Julie Spector, Susan Troppy, Sonja Vandivier, Leslie Wallace, LaJean Warren, Ramona Welch, Lisa Woodland, Mike Cave (PS Prin), Lori Anderson, Laura Aulenbacher, Ginger Berdoll, Becky Bergfeld, Chandra Betak, Pamela Blanchette, Amy Bram, Natalie Brewer, Linda Bruce, Sarah Burns, Shirlene Burroughs, Dene Burttschell, Kathy Clark, Martha Clements, Nicole Cmerek, Robbie Cripe, Amy Dalland, Marcie Danzeiser, Barbara Davidson, Barbara Flake, Stacy Frithiof, Kelly Garner, Cheryl Hayden, Traci Henze, Glenda Hjornevik, Judy Holmes, Peggy Howell, Misty Humphrey, Carolyn Jackson, Jamie Jordan, Amy Kadlecek, Diane Kainer, Anita Kelly, Susan Knape, Amy Larson, Martha Lockard, Patty Low, Natalie Mahany, Kathy Mangrum, Nancy Marfin, Barbara McClure, Felice McCreary, Anne McDonald, Leslie Meadows, Holly Miller, Kathy Murray, Lois Neumeyer, Janice Rice, Debra Roberts, Janey Russell, Laurinda Schaertl, Victoria Shoopman, Elizabeth Shuman, Vickey Smith, Kimberly Smolen, Carolyn Soltau, Mary Steinberg, Tammy Stellato, Kathy Stienke, Carol Taylor, Marion Voudouris, Julie Walker, Jharon Ward, Rebecca Weiser, Jacquelyn Whalen, Rhonda Whitman (PS A.Prin), Lisa Wilson, Phyllis Woods, Janice Wycoff.

Teaching Careers

Although there are maybe another two dozen individuals who taught at Dripping Springs, this list is as complete as I could compile from the records and newspaper articles that I was able to come across. I would have liked to have gotten it to be 100% to honor all who have served in the education of the Dripping Springs youth, but, it was just not possible at this time. This is a list of all the teachers that I could find and maybe this will help you with cross references.

Between this and the list of faculties, the subject should pretty well be covered.

Teacher	Grades	Total Years	Years Taught
Acton, Lavon	K-6	1.0	1979-80
Adcock, Sue	9-12	2.0	1977-79
Agnew, Doug	6-9	5.0	1993-98
Akers, Larry	9-12	2.0	1977-79
Alberts, Vicky Thompson	9-12	2.0	1979-81
Albright, Elyse	9-12	6.0	1982-88
Alford, April	K-5	5.0	1985-90
Alholm, Tom	6-8	4.0	1995-99
Allen, Paul	Prin.	13.0	1968-81
Alley, Kathleen Marko	K-3	4.2	1996-00
Anderson, Lori	K-3	4.0	1999-
Anderson, Tressa	K-3	5.5	1996-02 (1st Sem)
Arlington, Hardie	8-11	0.1	1942-43
Armstrong, W. L.	All	1.0	1876-77
Arnold, Charlene	K-5	8.0	1993-01
Arterburn, DeeAnn	6-8	1.0	2001-02
Atkinson, Sharlene	1-6	2.0	1968-70
Aulenbacher, Laura	K-3	1.0	2002-
Austin, Cathy	K-5	3.0	1976-79
Austin, Larry	9-12	2.0	1975-77
Ayers, Mary	K-5	20.0	1983-
Ayers, Tom	9-12	6.5	1983-90
Bacon, Erika	6-8	7.0	1996-
Bailey, Carolyn	9-12	1.0	1996-97
Ballard, Howard	9-12	13.0	1990-
Banta, J. O.,	Prin	1.0	1924-25
Barber, LaZelle	1-6	1.0	1947-48
Barnes, Berta	9-12	2.0	1945-47
Bates, Jay	9-12	2.0	2001-
Beard, Sherilyn	9-12	3.0	2000-
Beasley, Steven	9-12	1.0	2001-02
Beatty, Mindy	9-12	6.0	1997-
Beauford, Jo Ann	9-12	1.5	1956-58
Belcheff, Lu Ann Rush	K-6	2.0	1980-82
Bell, Carla	4-5	3.0	2000-
Bell, Mr.	All	1.0	1885-86
Benson, Sue	9-12	1.0	1997-98
Berdoll, Ginger	K-5	10.0	1993-
Berdoll, Rebecca	4-5	2.0	2001-
Bergfeld, Becky	K-3	1.0	2002-
Bernat, Valerie	1-6	2.0	1974-76
Berry, Jorey	9-12	1.0	1996-97
Bertling, Barbara	9-12	3.0	1974-77
Betak, Chandra Moore	K-3	5.2	1997-
Betak, Tandy	6-12	4.0	1999-
Bethke, Ernest O.	9-12	2.0	1950-52
Billman, Darlene	9-12	2.0	2001-
Bishop, J. H.	Prin	1.0	1892-93
Black, Mary	6-8	10.0	1993-
Blair, Barbara	6-8	1.0	1997-98
Blair, Judy	K-6	4.0	1979-83
Blanchette, Pamela McFaddin	K-3	10.0	1993-
Blume, Eric	9-12	2.0	2001-
Blythe, Alicia	K-5	2.0	1989-91
Blythe, Lori	K-5	7.0	1987-94
Boddeker, Nancy	K-6	2.0	1987-89
Boehm, Diana	6-8	2.0	1993-95
Boelter, Mimi	K-3	10.0	1992-02
Boggs, Carolyn	1-6	2.0	1966-68
Bohrer, Linda	6-8	1.0	1992-93
Bolton, Cherie	1-6	23.0	1980-
Bombach, John	9-12	1.0	1998-99
Borum, Robbin	1-6	1.0	1958-59
Boss, Heather	9-12	2.0	2000-02
Bosworth, Sheila	4-5	8.0	1995-
Botkin, Jane	9-12	14.0	1989-
Bounds, Traci	K-3	3.0	1999-
Bourland, Tommie Sue	K-3	15.0	1987-02
Brack, Lamarr	9-12	2.0	1979-81
Bradshaw, Jack	9-12	5.0	1980-85
Brady, Robin Thurmond	6-8	3.0	2000-
Bram, Amy	K-3	1.0	2002-
Branch, Bryan	6-8	1.0	1999-00
Branch, Miss	All	1.0	1885-86
Branch, Vonnie Brizendine	6-8	4.0	1999-
Brandt, Carol Culp	6-8	2.0	1997-99
Bray, Diane	9-12	1.7	1998-99
Breeden, Laura	4-5	1.0	2000-01
Brewer, Natalie	K-3	1.0	2002-
Bridges, Lucille I.		0.5	1923-24
Bridwell, Barbara	K-3	4.0	1969-73
Brinkman, Ruth	K-6	5.0	1976-81
Brock, Jim	7-12	3.0	1979-82
Brock, Margaret	6-8	3.0	1999-02
Brooks, Kay Baen	1-6	9.0	1974-83
Broussard, Kelly	9-12	6.0	1991-97
Broussard, Sandy	K-5	5.0	1992-97
Brown, Courtney	6-8	1.0	2002-
Brown, Karon	K-5	2.0	1993-95
Brown, Linda	9-12	2.1	1998-00
Broyles, Wardine	1-8	3.0	1952-55
Bruce, Linda	K-3	3.0	2000-
Brumley, Opal		5.0	1935-40
Bryant, Bryan	9-12	1.0	2000-01
Buchanan, Mary	4-5	5.6	1997-
Buckner, Patsy	1-6	5.0	1963-68
Buitron, Tina	6-8	3.0	2000-
Burch, Bill	9-12	3.0	1980-83
Burch, Susan	9-12	21.0	1980-01

Name	Grade	Years	Dates
Burkett, D. W.	Prin	2.0	1895-97
Burleson, Elma		1.0	1925-26
Burns, Bessie		1.0	1921-22
Burns, Joe	9-12	4.0	1999-
Burns, Sarah	K-3	1.0	2002-
Burroughs, Shirlene	K-3	1.0	2002-
Burrus, Connie	K-5	16.6	1987-
Burttschell, Dene	K-3	5.0	1998-
Byers, Helen	1-6	6.0	1970-76
Cain, Monte	9-12	3.0	1993-96
Calame, Cheryl	6-8	1.0	1990-91
Callahan, Edie	All	2.0	1883-85
Callihan, Champion	8-11	3.0	1932-35
Callihan, Lucille	1-6	1.0	1935-36
Campbell, Carol	1-6	6.0	1970-76
Campbell, Heather	6-8	2.0	2001-
Campbell, Jan	6-8	6.0	1992-98
Canales, Jane	9-12	18.0	1985-
Cannon, Katherine	9-12	1.0	1981-82
Caperton, Mrs.	All	1.0	1887-88
Caplinger, Carolyn	1-5	5.0	1980-81; 1982-86
Cappolette, Lisa	9-12	0.5	1998-99
Carnes, Roberta	1-5	6.0	1985-91
Caroselli, Athena	9-12	1.0	1999-00
Carrell, Kimberley	K-5	1.0	1989-90
Carson, Mary	Nurse	1.0	1975-76
Cartwright, Adam	6-8	2.0	2000-02
Casey, Arthur (Skip)	7-12	1.0	1971-72
Cave, Bridget	6-8	18.0	1985-
Cave, Mike	K-3	16.0	1987-
Cavett, Annie		1.3	1892-93; 1897-98
Cavett, Georgia Pound	1-4	15.2	1900-15; 1921-22
Chalmers, Marilyn	4-5	11.0	1992-
Chance, Al	Prin	1.0	1973-74
Chapman, W.T.	All	1.+	1872-?
Charbonnet, Liz	K-6	4.0	1977-81
Cherry, Sherron	9-12	1.0	1998-99
Chessher, Thelma		0.2	1924-25
Chester, Lori	9-12	1.0	2000-01
Chism, Carrie	K-3	1.0	2001-02
Clark, Don	9-12	15.0	1976-91
Clark, Kathy Warren	K-3	19.0	1984-
Clark, Minnie		1.0	1909-10
Clement, Aimee	6-8	3.0	2000-
Clements, Martha	K-3	7.0	1996-
Click, Jane	6-8	7.0	1986-93
Cmerek, Nicole Jaeckle	K-3	3.0	2000-
Cochran, Rita	K-3	6.0	1996-02
Coffey, Kelly Spain	6-8	8.0	1995-
Coker, Bob	9-12	3.0	1959-62
Colborne, Llewellyn	9-12	3.0	2000-
Coleman, June	9-12	8.0	1989-97
Coleman, Kay	Lib	3.0	1991-93; 1994-95
Coleman, Kelly	9-12	7.0	1994-01
Coleman, Patty	9-12	1.0	1962-63
Collier, J. P.	Prin	1.0	1889-90
Colston, Julie	9-12	2.0	1988-90
Conn, Mrs. S. P.	9-12	1.0	1946-47
Conn, S. P.	Supt	1.0	1946-47
Connally, William	Prin	1.0	1909-10
Conway, Vivian	7-8	1.5	1982-84
Cook, Anne	9-12	4.0	1991-95
Cook, J. E.	Prin	2.0	1887-89
Cook, Minnie M.	All	1.0	1887-88
Coovert, Thelma	1-3	3.0	1927-30
Cope, Cecilia	9-12	1.0	1973-74
Copeland, Teresa	9-12	1.0	1979-80
Corder, A. B.	Prin	1.0	1905-06
Counts, Susan	4-5	5.0	1997-
Covington, Carl	9-12	3.0	1987-90
Covington, Delores	Prin	5.0	1995-00
Coward, Jeff	9-12	3.0	2000-
Cox, Joe B.	Prin	0.5	1950-51
Coy, Anita	4-5	3.0	2000-
Crate, Eleanor	1-7	1.0	1941-42
Crawford, Ann	9-12	1.0	1980-81
Crawford, Norma	Lib	4.0	1966-70
Crawford, Victoria	4-5	7.0	1995-
Cresswell, Lea	K-6	6.0	1979-85
Cripe, Robbie	K-3	3.0	2000-
Cronshey, Richard	9-12	2.0	2001-
Crouch, Elaine	4-5	1.0	1956-57
Crow, Mack	9-12	9.0	1971-80
Crozier, Carol Pringle	4-5	9.0	1994-
Cullison, Brenda	9-12	1.0	2001-02
Culpepper, Della	1-6	12.0	1945-46; 1952-63
Cummings, Carol	9-12	7.0	1985-92
Daigle, Pat	9-12	3.0	1996-99
Dailey, Jenny	Lib	10.0	1993-
Dalland, Amy	K-3	5.0	1998-
Damron, Tyler	Prin	12.0	1991-
Danforth, Susie	7-12	2.0	1945-47
Danzeiser, Marcie	K-3	9.0	1993-99; 2000-
Darroh, Matthew	9-12	2.0	2001-
Darroh, Nannie	All	1.0	1897-98
Daugherty, Bailey	9-12	6.0	1954-60
Daugherty, Novelle	9-12	3.0	1957-60
Davenport, Alma		1.0	1918-19
David, Helen D.	6-12	1.0	1950-51
Davidson, Barbara	K-3	11.0	1990-93; 1995-
Davies, Virginia	K-6	1.0	1976-77

Name	Grades	Years	Dates	Name	Grades	Years	Dates
Davis, Becky	K-5	4.0	1991-95	Ebough, Mrs. I. A.	9-12	1.0	1950-51
Davis, Bradley	7-12	8.2	1934-35; 1962-70	Eggleston, Brian	9-12	1.0	1996-97
				Eickenloff, Rick	9-12	19.0	1982-01
Davis, Colleen	9-12	8.0	1987-95	Elgin, Agnes		0.3	1924-25
Davis, Elbert H.	Prin	4.0	1932-36	Ellis, David	6-8	4.0	1999-
Davis, Glenn	9-12	8.5	1987-96	Elsner, Bernice	1-3	1.0	1926-27
Davis, Natalie	9-12	1.0	1992-93	Endsley, Gary	7-12	1.0	1972-73
Davis, Tom	9-12	2.5	1996-99	Engeling, Mark	4-5	15.0	1985-87; 1990-
Dawkins, Effie Eastham	6-8	7.0	1989-92; 1993-97	England, David	9-12	2.0	1998-00
Day, J. L.	Prin	1.0	1917-18	Engle, Emboline	1-6	15.0	1957-72
Deal, Larry	9-12	1.5	1983-85	English, Barbara	1-5	13.0	1987-00
Dean, Jessica Allen	6-8	2.0	1989-91	English, Jerry	9-12	13.0	1987-00
Dean, Scott	6-8	6.0	1985-91	Ericson, Deborah	K-5	3.0	1990-93
Deaver, Karen	6-8	3.0	1985-88	Ernst, Barbara Nixon	7-12	3.0	1972-75
DeLaCretaz, Cheryl	9-12	6.0	1997-	Ervin, Sharron	9-12	3.0	1977-80
DeLaCretaz, Larry	6-8	6.0	1997-	Eshelman, Donna	K-3	3.0	1999-02
DeLaCretaz, Tamara Crowley	9-12	2.0	1999-01	Essley, Joyce Mahoney	1-6	8.0	1972-81; 1982-83
DeLaCretaz, Vannessa	9-12	2.0	1999-01	Evans, Anne Taylor	1-6	1.0	1964-65
Denis, Melissa	6-8	1.0	1997-98	Evans, Sylvia	9-12	2.0	1993-95
Densman, Preston	9-12	0.5	1967-68	Evans, Tonna	K-5	4.0	1994-98
Denton, Becky	6-12	4.0	1989-93	Fain, Carroll	1-6	4.0	1973-76; 1978-79
Dibblee, Etta	All	1.0	1883-84				
Dickerson, Patricia	6-8	2.0	1999-01	Fain, Patricia	9-12	1.0	1958-59
Dillingham, Rayma	7-11	2.0	1940-42	Fasanella, Ed	9-12	1.0	1998-99
Dimmitt, Paula	9-12	1.0	1985-86	Felkel, Joseph	6-8	6.0	1997-
Dodgen, Mary	Prin	1.0	1918-19	Felts, Mr. Joyce	7-12	1.0	1969-70
Dodson, Anne	4-5	7.0	1996-	Fernandez, Ellen	4-5	1.0	2002-
Dodson, Galen	7-12	17.0	1968-79; 1987-93	Fields, David	9-12	18.0	1974-92
				Finley, Anna	K-3	4.0	1997-01
Dodson, Helen	1-6	8.0	1973-81	Finnessey, Paula	6-8	1.0	1998-99
Dodson, Jerry Lou	1-6	22.0	1968-70; 1972-75; 1976-93	Fisher, Ruth A.		1.0	1927-28
				Flake, Barbara	K-3	10.0	1993-
Dodson, Kari Phillips	4-5	3.5	1995-99	Flake, Lestant	4-5	6.0	1997-
Dodson, Mary Clare	1-6	3.0	1985-88	Fleming, Sharon	K-3	11.0	1988-99
Donaho, Ross C.	Supt	4.0	1947-51	Fleming, Steele	6-8	22.0	1981-
Donaldson, Naomi	9-12	2.0	1948-50	Fletcher, Oleta		3.0	1936-39
Dove, Andrea	6-8	1.0	1999-00	Fletcher, Paula	6-8	1.0	1996-97
Doyle, Mayme		1.0	1917-18	Florida, Mae		0.6	1924-25
Drumm, Williard	7-11	1.0	1930-31	Flynn, Susan	6-8	6.0	1997-
Duke, Rhonda	9-12	4.0	1999-	Follis, Annie	8-11	4.0	1930-34
Dunlap, Gloria	K-3	2.0	1997-99	Follis, Ennis		1.0	1926-27
Dunn, Bonnie	9-12	2.0	2000-02	Folts, Dorothy		0.2	1892-93
Dunn, Edie	6-8	4.0	1999-	Fomby, Mary	1-6	5.0	1968-73
Dunn, Leslie	6-8	5.0	1997-02	Foreman, Jennifer	9-12	4.0	1999-
Dunn, Miss	All	1.0	1886-87	Foreman, Stuart	6-12	2.5	1991-92; 2001-
Dyson, Alissa	9-12	1.0	2002-				
Earley, Donna Hightower	6-8	5.0	1985-90	Formby, Paula	K-5	13.0	1980-93
				Foster, Marge	K-3	18.0	1979-85; 1987-99
Earley, Martin	7-12	7.0	1983-90				
East, Sharon	9-12	2.0	1971-73	Franklin, Inez		1.0	1919-20
Eaves, Glenda	K-6	2.0	1979-81	Franklin, Shelley Seaver	6-8	4.0	1994-98
Eaves, Harriet	9-12	7.0	1968-71; 1973-77				
				Frazer, Cindy	K-5	8.0	1993-01

Name	Grade	Years	Dates
Fredrickson, Deborah	6-8	9.0	1992-01
Frithiof, Stacy	K-3	2.0	2001-
Fritts, L. A. Jr.	1-6	2.0	1947-49
Frontera, Paige	6-8	3.0	2000-
Frost, Bettie Cagle	K-5	8.0	1981-89
Fuelberg, Jeanie	K-5	9.0	1987-96
Fulkerson, Paul	9-12	3.0	1971-74
Fuller, Viki	9-12	1.0	1996-97
Fyall, Stuart	6-8	8.0	1995-
Gable, Maggie	K-5	2.0	1979-81
Gaetjens, Sara	9-12	8.0	1977-85
Garcia, Tracy	9-12	2.0	1998-00
Gardner, Judy	9-12	7.0	1996-
Garner, Kelly Nolan	9-12	6.0	1996-99; 00-
Garnett, Billie	9-12	0.3	1967-68
Garnett, Jerry	Prin	3.0	1960-63
Garrett, Lizzie	1-6		1910-?
Garrison, Rebecca	9-12	2.0	2001-
Garza, Linda	K-5	8.0	1990-98
Gathright, Jill	K-5	17.0	1977-94
Gelineau, Charlotte	K-6	1.0	1979-80
George, Dan	9-12	4.0	1994-98
Giannone, Carolyn	6-8	6.0	1995-01
Gier, Robert	9-12	1.0	1998-99
Giles, Virgil		1.0	1931-32
Ginn, Peggy	K-5	4.0	1977-81
Gist, Katherine	K-6	2.0	1978-80
Glimp, Eva		4.0	1921-25
Gode, Abby	9-12	2.0	2001-
Godwin, Christopher	6-8	5.0	1998-
Gonzales, Marcus	9-12	1.0	2002-
Goode, Claude	Prin	1.0	1949-50
Goodney, Christy	9-12	0.5	2000-01
Goodwin, Laura	K-5	2.0	1994-96
Gordon, Michelle	9-12	1.0	1979-80
Grabman, Bryan	9-12	7.0	1996-
Gravell, Kim	6-8	10.0	1993-
Gravell, Rip	9-12	10.0	1993-
Gravenor, Louise	9-12	9.0	1959-68
Graves, Martha	K-6	2.0	1980-82
Graves, Mrs.		1.0	1884-85
Gray, Debbie	6-8	6.0	1991-97
Green, Billie	4-5	1.0	1955-56
Gregory, Phyliss	9-12	1.0	1994-95
Grice, Laura	9-12	1.0	2002-
Grieder, Jack	9-12	2.0	1977-79
Griffin, Joanne	9-12	4.0	1969-73
Grohman, Susan	1-6	2.0	1970-72
Grohman, Wayne	7-12	3.0	1969-72
Grooms, Peggy Scott	9-12	13.0	1978-91
Grove, Ethel S.		1.0	1942-43
Gryska, Alice	1-6	1.0	1972-73
Gutierrez, Micaela	K-3	4.0	1998-02
Haby, Hayden G.	9-12	2.0	1950-52
Hadley, Lynn	9-12	7.0	1969-76
Hage, Miss Viola		1.0	1908-09
Hahn, Quinnetta	1-6	1.0	1941-42
Hale, Mrs.	K-6	1.0	1977-78
Hall, David	9-12	4.0	1999-
Hall, Marjorie M.	9-12	1.0	1946-47
Hall, Randy	9-12	2.0	2001-
Hamilton, George	9-12	3.0	1997-00
Hamilton, Miss		1.0	1888-89
Hancock, Joyce	9-12	1.0	2001-02
Hancock, Mary Elsie		0.2	1924-25
Hancock, Tom	9-12	5.5	1997-
Hardee, Max	K-5	14.0	1985-99
Hardwick, Francie	9-12	2.0	1979-81
Harlan, Polly	K-5	8.5	1985-94
Harlow, Becky	9-12	1.0	1976-77
Harmon, Sheila	7-12	9.0	1983-92
Harned, Mary Jane	9-12	22.0	1980-02
Harris, Inez	3-6	3.0	1942-43; 1944-46
Harvey, Rebecca	K-5	3.0	1989-92
Hause, Sharon	9-12	1.0	2000-01
Hauser, Pat	9-12	1.0	1973-74
Havins, Rhonda	7-12	2.0	1976-78
Hayden, Cheryl	K-5	11.0	1990-93; 1995-
Haydon, Sherry	9-12	20.0	1981-01
Hazard, Barba Lu	9-12	1.0	1979-80
Haeberlin, Glenda	Lib	5.0	1971-76
Heaney, Suzanne	K-6	2.0	1976-78
Hearn, Rosemary	Nurse	4.5	1997-02
Heckman, Darlene	9-12	1.0	1983-84
Hector, Christina	9-12	2.0	2001-
Henderson, Frances	1-6	20.0	1972-92
Henderson, Joni	K-5	18.0	1982-00
Hendon, Mr.		1.0	1886-87
Hennessee, Pat	K-5	15.0	1988-
Henry, Byrdie	Prin	1.0	1907-08
Hensen, Charlie	9-12	2.0	1977-79
Henze, Traci	K-3	5.0	1998-
Hernandez, Kathy	K-3	1.0	1995-96
Herrera, Howard	9-12	1.5	1996-98
Herring, G.C.	Supt	4.0	1942-46
Herring, Mrs. G.C.	9-12	1.0	1943-44
Herron, Fran	9-12	2.0	1998-00
Hester, Mark	6-8	0.3	1992-93
Hewett, Lydia	6-8	2.8	1992-95
Hewgley, Bobbette	6-8	2.0	1991-93
Hierro, Katie del	9-12	2.0	1999-01
Hill, Bertha	9-12	16.0	1965-81
Hill, Marvin	9-12	8.0	1952-60
Hindman, Beatrice	9-12	1.0	1954-55
Hipp, Lee	6-8	2.0	1997-99
Hjornevik, Glenda	K-3	2.7	2000-
Hoggard, Fran	K-5	3.0	1992-95

Name	Grades	Years	Dates
Hohman, Ann Nite	1-6	35.0	1943-52; 1954-56; 1957-81
Holcombe, W. H.	Prin	2.0	1921-23
Holland, Myrtle		0.4	1921-22
Holmes, Judy	K-3	4.0	1999-
Holt, Carolyn	9-12	1.0	1964-65
Holt, J. F.	Prin	2.0	1963-65
Holt, Malinda	K-6	2.0	1984-86
Holubec, Cliff	6-8	5.0	1991-96
Hood, Donna	9-12	1.0	2002-
Hopkins, Cheryl Spooner	7-12	8.0	1985-93
Hopkins, Don	7-12	7.0	1986-93
Hopson, Barbara Knippa	Lib	15.0	1976-91
Horn, Jean	7-12	1.0	1980-81
Horner, Pearl	9-12	2.0	1992-94
Horsley, R. G.	Prin	4.0	1883-87
Horton, Susan	4-5	1.0	2002-
Hovey, Catherine	K-3	1.0	1997-98
Howard, Greg	9-12	4.0	1996-00
Howell, Peggy	K-5	17.5	1985-
Howie, Carol	7-12	15.0	1976-91
Hudnall, Janice	K-6	1.0	1985-86
Huey, Flynt	9-12	2.0	1999-01
Huffman, Rebecca	9-12	7.0	1974-81
Huggins, Nell	9-12	1.0	1947-48
Hughes, Mary	4-5	7.0	1996-
Humphrey, Tressie	K-3	1.0	2002-
Huntsberger, Steve	7-12	2.0	1977-79
Hurff, Mr.	Prin	1.0	1911-12
Hurlbut, Marsha	6-8	10.0	1990-00
Hurwitz, Stacy	K-5	5.0	1989-94
Hutto, Randy	7-12	3.0	1980-83
Ikels, Cassie Smith	4-5	13.0	1990-
Ingram, Beth	K-6	1.0	1979-80
Ivy, Richard	6-8	3.0	2000-
Jackson, Carolyn	K-3	9.0	1994-
Jackson, Pamela Dieringer	6-8	4.0	1994-98
Jackson, Tom	9-12	2.0	1979-81
Janssen, Donna	4-8	6.0	1997-
Jarosz, Gary	9-12	1.0	1993-94
Jasinski, Diane	K-3	10.0	1992-02
Jenkins, Laura	9-12	1.0	2002-
Jenkins, Lewis	9-12	4.0	1999-
Jent-Coffman, Evelyn	9-12	11.0	1992-
Johnson, Betsi	6-8	3.0	1991-94
Johnson, J. C.	Prin	1.0	1920-21
Johnson, Lora	6-8	4.0	1994-98
Johnson, Scott	9-12	1.0	1979-80
Johnson, Shirley	6-8	17.0	1986-
Johnson, Steve	9-12	1.0	1979-80
Johnson, Willene	1-8	1.0	1955-56
Johnston, Brenda	6-8	1.0	2002-
Jonas, Jackie	K-6	1.0	1985-86
Jones, Glen	9-12	4.0	1987-91
Jones, Katie	9-12	6.0	1994-00
Jones, Leslie	9-12	4.0	1987-91
Jones, Roy	9-12	1.0	1978-79
Jones, Tom	6-8	24.0	1955-79
Jordan, Jamie	K-3	1.0	2002-
Jordan, W. M.	Prin	2.0	1881-83
Joyner, Sandra	6-8	1.1	1999-01
Jung, Greg	9-12	4.0	1999-
Kaatz, Yvonne	9-12	4.5	1998-
Kadlecek, Amy	K-5	19.0	1984-
Kahn, Kendra	9-12	2.5	1997-00
Kainer, Diane	K-3	3.0	2000-
Kaiser, Frances	6-8	5.0	1998-
Kane, Thomas	9-12	1.0	2001-02
Kaufman, Ina G.	3-4	1.0	1951-52
Kaufman, L.U.C.	Prin	1.0	1951-52
Keeney, Erlene McLendon		1.5	1932-34
Kelley, Judy	K-5	18.0	1985-
Kelley, Martha E.	Prin	1.0	1919-20
Kelly, Anita	K-5	25.0	1978-
Kelly, Denise	K-5	7.0	1993-00
Kelly, Shannon	K-3	4.0	1997-01
Kennesson, Jayne Edwards	6-8	1.5	1993-95
Kennedy, Bertha		1.0	1925-26
Kidd, Nellie B.	1-6	7.0	1947-54
Kidd, Shauna	9-12	17.0	1979-81; 88-
Kidder, Guy	Prin	1.0	1925-26
Kight, Sarah	9-12	2.0	1999-01
Kihl, Jerri Lynn	9-12	2.0	2001-
Kilpatrick, Mrs.	1-6	1.0	1959-60
Kilpatrick-Ayers, Patricia	6-8	2.0	2001-
King, Paula	9-12	16.0	1987-
Kinnison, Necia	9-12	10.0	1970-80
Kirk, Laura Brown	K-3	6.0	1996-02
Klein, Debbie Hazard	9-12	4.0	1986-90
Klett, Mrs.	9-11	1.0	1928-29
Knaggs, Barbara Scroggie	9-12	5.0	1993-98
Knape, Susan	K-3	5.0	1998-
Knauth, Patty	1-6	10.0	1969-79
Kniffen, Mary	K-3	3.0	1996-99
Knippa, Lyndon	K-6	1.0	1976-77
Kollaja, Susan	K-5	2.0	1991-93
Koopman, Melissa	9-12	7.0	1989-96
Kowis, Dabney	K-3	2.0	1996-98
Kretzmeier, Mabel	7-12	9.0	1947-56
Kroll, Jack	7-12	4.0	1960-64
Krupp, Steve	9-12	10.0	1993-
Kuhns, Pearl	1-6	1.0	1949-50

Name	Grades	Years	Dates	Name	Grades	Years	Dates
Kvapil, Scott	6-8	6.0	1992-98				2001-02
Kyser, Sandra	7-12	3.0	1977-80	Martinez, Robert	6-8	1.0	1989-90
Lamb, Mildred	9-12	3.0	1964-67	Massey, Diane	K-3	1.0	1996-97
Lampley, James	7-12	2.0	1974-76	Massey, Donald	K-5	1.0	1993-94
Lampley, Pam	7-12	1.0	1975-76	May, Mr.	6-8	0.1	1950-51
Lancaster, Keith	9-12	5.0	1998-	Mayes, Jeff	6-8	1.0	2001-02
Lange, Jo Ann	9-12	1.0	1957-58	Mays, Bette	6-7	1.0	1956-57
Larson, Amy	K-3	1.0	2002-	McAninch, Carolyn	1-6	2.0	1972-74
Larson, Jay	6-8	1.0	2002-	McCabe, Peggy	9-12	2.0	1994-96
Latteo, Kathy	4-5	5.0	1998-	McCain, Martha	1-6	4.0	1966-70
Lawrence, Barbara	K-6	1.0	1976-77	McCarley, Nancy	9-12	3.0	1985-88
Lawrence, Patricia	K-3	4.0	1998-02	McCartney, Rae	K-5	10.0	1983-93
Lay, Skipper	7-12	3.0	1995-98	McCarty, Amy	6-8	1.0	2002-
Leavy, Landa	6-8	3.0	1998-01	McCleary, Nicole	6-8	2.0	2001-
LeCompte, Larry	9-12	2.0	1979-81	McCleod, Gwen	Lib	3.0	1999-
Ledbetter, Liew	9-12	10.0	1979-89	McClure, Barbara Krause	K-3	18.0	1985-
Ledbetter, Mary	K-3	3.0	1997-00				
Lee, Allyson	6-8	1.0	1998-99	McClure, Margaret	9-12	1.0	1976-77
Leffingwell, Ann	6-8	1.0	1999-00	McCrary, Kay	6-8	2.0	1990-92
Leissner, Mr.	9-12	1.0	1959-60	McCreary, Felice	K-3	6.5	1996-
Lentz, Debbie	K-6	1.0	1977-78	McDaniel, Paul	9-12	5.0	1977-82
Leopold, Kathy	6-8	14.0	1989-	McDaniel, Pecos	6-12	10.0	1990-92; 1995-
Lewis, Ann	1-6	3.0	1966-69				
Lewis, Barbara	9-12	18.0	1985-	McDaniel, Tracy	K-3	1.0	1999-00
Lewis, Gene	7-12	2.0	1967-69	McDavitt, Linda	7-12	6.0	1978-84
Lewis, Irma	6-8	10.0	1993-	McDonald, Amy	K-5	2.0	1991-93
Ligon, Florence	All	1.0	1889-90	McDonald, Anne	K-3	7.0	1996-
Lindsey, Jan	9-12	7.0	1996-	McDonald, Julie	9-12	1.0	2002-
Linney, Mrs.	K-6	1.0	1985-86	McDonald, Lynn	6-8	4.0	1994-98
Livingston, Jack	9-12	6.0	1968-74	McGlothen, Mike	9-12	0.2	1967-68
Lockard, Martha	K-3	4.0	1999-	McGowan, Jan	4-5	4.0	1999-
Long, Todd	6-8	1.0	2000-01	McIlvain, Ken	9-12	1.0	1980-81
Love, Stephanie	K-3	4.0	1996-00	McLendon, Sallie	1-6	1.0	1890-91
Low, Patty	K-3	12.0	1991-	McLeod, Gwen	Lib	1.0	2002-
Lowe, Marsha	K-6	1.0	1979-80	McManus, Barbara	K-6	4.0	1979-83
Lundin, Susan	9-12	3.0	1990-93	Meadows, Leslie	K-3	1.0	2002-
Lusinger, Tammy	9-12	1.0	2000-01	Mears, Judy	6-8	5.0	1998-
Lyle, Lura Branum	9-12	20.0	1923-24; 40-59	Meek, Randy	9-12	5.0	1991-96
				Melton, Edye	6-8	2.0	2001-
Lyle, Trenton	6-8	4.0	1996-00	Merz, John	6-8	3.0	1990-93
Lynch, Vicki	4-5	2.0	1998-00	Michaels, Vickie Harris	1-8	13.0	1983-85; 1992-
Lyons, Tanya	4-5	1.0	1997-98				
Mabry, Regina	9-12	1.0	2001-02	Michaelson, Nona	9-12	6.0	1993-99
MacIntyre, JoAnn	6-8	3.0	2000-	Michele, Denise	9-12	1.0	1979-80
MacNaughton, D. V.	Prin	0.5	1923-24	Middleton, Wendy	6-8	1.0	2002-
Mahany, Natalie	K-3	3.0	2000-	Mikulak, Lawrence	6-12	7.0	1996-
Maher, Marisa	9-12	1.0	2002-	Milford, Lou Jean	6-8	9.7	1993-
Malone, John	9-12	2.0	1951-53	Miller, Deanne	6-8	7.5	1991-99
Mangrum, Kay	K-3	8.5	1994-	Miller, Deborah Ann	9-12	3.0	1998-01
Marenco, Michelle	6-8	4.0	1999-	Miller, Holly	K-3	14.0	1989-
Marfin, Nancy	Nurse	1.0	2002-	Miller, Jennifer Hampton	K-3	4.0	1997-01
Marshall, Robert Lee	Prin	3.0	1891-92; 1898-1900				
				Miller, Malyna	6-8	14.4	1988-
Martin, Mr.	All	2.0	1882-84	Miller, Melania	K-3	3.0	1998-01
Martinez, Priscilla	K-3	4.0	1997-00;	Miller, Sharon	9-12	1.0	1996-97

Name	Grade	Years	Period
Miller, Tim	9-12	1.0	1977-78
Miller, Walter G.	Prin	3.0	1926-29
Mitchell, Lillie	1-6	12.0	1954-66
Mollenhauer, Isabelle	1-6	5.0	1974-79
Moore, Angela	6-8	3.0	1997-00
Moore, Joe	K-5	7.0	1994-01
Morey, Roger	9-12	24.2	1977-02
Morgan, Read S.	8-11	1.0	1927-28
Morgan, Shelley	K-3	1.0	1995-96
Morgan, Suzanne	K-6	3.0	1977-80
Morrell, Lizzie	All	2.0	1881-83
Morris, Janice	K-5	24.0	1979-
Morrow, Kim	K-5	2.0	1992-94
Morton, Carla	6-8	2.6	1998-01
Murphy, Angela	K-5	13.0	1978-91
Murphy, Chad	9-12	2.0	1977-79
Murphy, Jeff	6-8	4.0	1999-
Murray, Kathy Jernigan	K-3	15.0	1988-
Myers, Jason	9-12	1.0	2002-
Myers, Susan	K-6	1.0	1984-85
Naumann, Mrs. Malcolm	9-12	2.0	1943-45
Nedbalek, Debbie	7-12	0.5	1983-84
Needham, Kristin	K-3	8.0	1994-96; 1997-
Neef, Tracy	9-12	9.0	1994-
Nelms, Nola	1-6	3.0	1958-61
Nelson, Jerry	6-8	6.0	1973-79
Neumeyer, Lois	K-3	6.0	1997-
Newbern, Nannette	K-3	7.0	1991-98
Newberry, P. S.	Prin	1.0	1904-05
Nichols, Kathy	Nurse	27.0	1976-
Nichols, Mindy	Nurse	1.5	1996-98
Nixon, Irving	Prin	1.0	1936-37
Nixon, Nancy	6-8	5.5	1994-00
Norwood, Vina	1-6	3.0	1916-17; 1918-19; 1920-21
Nudo, Margaret	9-12	1.0	1995-96
O'Donnell, Jim	K-3	22.0	1981-
Ockman, Cammie	6-8	6.0	1996-01
Odell, Bessie Kirby	1-3	2.0	1961-63
Ogletree, Rita	K-6	1.0	1979-80
Ohnheiser, Derrl	9-12	6.0	1997-
Oliver, Tim	9-12	1.0	1984-85
Omeis, Russell	7-12	3.0	1964-67
Ormonde, Brian	9-12	2.0	2001-
Osburn, Ramona	7-8	1.0	1944-45
Ottinger, Lillian	9-12	11.0	1965-76
Owen, Eva S.		1.0	1943-44
Owens, Martha	1-6	6.0	1968-74
Page, Walter	9-12	1.0	2001-02
Palmer, Deb	6-8	14.0	1986-00
Palmer, Ed	9-12	18.0	1985-
Parker, John T.	Prin	1.0	1900-01
Parker, Lawrence	9-12	1.0	1953-54
Parks, Brian	9-12	7.0	1996-
Parks, Brooke Burton	9-12	2.0	1994-96
Parks, Lou Miller	K-5	5.0	1976-81
Parks, Randy	6-8	1.0	1993-94
Parr, W. E.	Prin	1.0	1993-94
Parrack, Karan	9-12	0.8	2000-01
Patton, Cheryl	6-8	1.0	1993-94
Patton, Mrs. Pauline		1.0	1907-08
Patty, June	K-5	2.5	1989-92
Pauley, David	7-8	1.0	1977-78
Paulsgrove, Yvonne	K-5	7.0	1990-97
Payne, Chris	6-8	2.0	2001-
Payne, Rochelle	K-6	2.0	1979-81
Peace, William	6-12	5.0	1984-86; 2000-
Pearson, Ida A.		0.5	1923-24
Pearson, Martha	1-6	15.0	1966-81
Peavey, H. L.	7-11	1.0	1931-32
Perez, Karen	9-12	2.0	1979-81
Perrin, Melinda	7-12	2.0	1969-71
Person, William	6-8	5.0	1998-
Peters, Zepha Lee		3.0	1933-36
Peterson, Lynn	K-6	2.0	1979-81
Petmecky, Zelle	1-12	25.0	1952-55; 1963-85
Pfeffer, Kathryn	K-6	2.0	1980-82
Phillips, Letha	K-6	4.0	1977-81
Phillips, Miss Branch L.	All	1.0	1890-91
Phillips, Pam	K-3	1.0	1995-96
Phillips, Shirley	6-8	4.0	1996-00
Pickens, Nancy	K-6	3.0	1980-83
Pierson, Patricia	9-12	1.0	1954-55
Piland, M.Z. Jr.	9-12	2.0	1961-63
Pile, W. A.	Prin	2.0	1901-03
Pineda, John	6-8	3.0	1999-02
Pollard, Dan	6-8	10.5	1992-
Pollard, Diane	6-8	7.0	1992-99
Pope, Harriet	1-8	2.0	1956-58
Porter, Ed	9-12	4.0	1997-01
Portie, Gwen	K-3	3.0	1999-02
Powell, Peggy	K-6	4.0	1975-79
Powell, Susan	9-12	2.0	2001-
Price, Verna	1-6	4.0	1972-76
Pringle, G. A. Jr.	9-12	5.0	1946-51
Pruegle, Valarie	1-6	1.0	1974-75
Pruett, Mary	1-6	4.0	1974-78
Prugel, Yvonne	K-6	4.0	1976-80
Pryor, Florence		1.0	1922-23
Quijano, Carla	6-8	11.0	1992-
Quinton, Marilyn	6-12	1.0	1980-81
Rackley, Ruth		2.0	1925-27
Raimond, Todd	9-12	2.0	2001-

Name	Grades	Years	Term
Rainbird, Herbert	9-12	3.0	2000-
Ramos, Darleen	9-12	1.0	1996-97
Rascher, Louise		1.0	1917-18
Rawlings, Beth	9-12	11.0	1992-
Raybuck, Susan	6-8	1.0	1998-99
Rees, Deanna	K-5	12.0	1987-99
Reese, Aimee	9-12	2.0	2000-02
Reichert, Joseph	Prin	3.0	1952-55
Reiter, Dee	1-6	9.0	1972-81
Reynolds, Cole	9-12	1.0	1993-94
Rhodes, Janice	7-12	1.0	1979-80
Rice, Jan	K-3	5.0	1998-
Richardson, Dorothy	7-11	5.0	1935-40
Riggs, Tommy	7-12	2.0	1979-81
Rippy, Janet	1-6	22.0	1967-69; 1977-84; 90-
Rippy, Oran	7-12	25.5	1962-83; 1995-00
Robbins, Beverly	1-6	12.0	1973-85
Robbins, Chris	1-3	1.0	1963-64
Robbins, Mrs. W. R.	1-6	3.0	1937-40
Robbins, W. R.	Prin	3.0	1937-40
Roberts, Debra	K-3	3.0	2000-
Robertson, R. A.	Prin	1.0	1903-04
Robinson, Adam	6-8	1.0	2002-
Rockhold, Randy	9-12	2.0	1987-89
Roderick, Susan	K-6	5.0	1976-81
Rogers, Janie	K-6	4.0	1977-81
Rohrer, Michelle	9-12	2.0	1971-73
Romeo, Kathy	9-12	0.5	1999-00
Romero, Kathy	9-12	1.0	2001-02
Rose, Hazel	1-3	1.0	1958-59
Rosebrock, Bethany	9-12	1.0	1996-97
Rowland, Patty	9-12	1.0	1976-77
Rudy, Jeff	9-12	5.0	1993-98
Ruede, Amy Thompson	9-12	2.0	1999-01
Rumelhart, Max	K-6	1.0	1976-77
Rushing, LaDonna	9-12	3.0	2000-
Russell, Elmer L.	9-12	28.5	1952-80; 1983-84
Russell, Janey	K-5	16.0	1987-
Russell, John	6-8	5.0	1995-97; 2000-
Rutherford, Barbara	K-5	5.0	1992-97
Sadler, Lela	6-8	4.5	1998-
Sallis, Jacqulyn	6-8	3.0	2000-
Samuels, Erin	9-12	1.0	2002-
Sanchez, Oswaldo	9-12	1.0	1993-94
Saunders, Sidney R.	Prin	?	1910-?
Saylor, Ronald	9-12	3.0	2000-
Scasta, Albert R.	9-12	1.0	1949-50
Schaertl, Laurinda	K-5	11.0	1990-92; 1994-
Schandua, Charles	7-12	9.0	1970-79
Schandua, Sarah	K-6	4.0	1975-79
Schlichting, Paul	6-8	2.0	1998-00
Schlicke, Mark	6-8	1.0	1988-89
Schlortt, Quinn	9-12	7.0	1950-57
Schmidt, Daniel	6-8	5.0	1993-98
Schneider, Sandra	9-12	4.0	1999-
Schommer, Dennis	6-8	1.0	1993-94
Schroeder, Kari	K-3	1.0	1998-99
Schroeder, Lea Anne	9-12	4.0	1999-
Schroeder, Mark	6-8	2.0	1997-99
Schulte, Constance	6-8	1.0	1997-98
Schwartz, Barbara	K-5	12.0	1990-98; 1999-
Scott, Bob	1-12	9.0	1980-89
Scott, Polly	K-6	1.0	1965-66
Seal, Charley Mae	1-6	0.3	1924-25
Seale, Dennis	9-12	25.0	1978-
Seaman, Shauna	9-12	2.0	2000-02
Segleski, Mike	9-12	6.0	1997-
Sexton, Kelly Jo	9-12	3.0	1997-00
Shackleford, Mark	9-12	0.5	2000-01
Shanley, David	9-12	3.0	1996-99
Shaw, Darren	9-12	2.0	1995-97
Shaw, David	9-12	13.0	1988-01
Sheffield, Helen	7-12	2.0	1975-77
Shelton, Clarence T.	7-12	1.0	1939-40
Shelton, Jill	9-12	2.0	2001-
Shelton, Judy	1-6	3.0	1973-76
Shelton, Kristi	K-6	1.0	1979-80
Shelton, Poe	7-12	26.0	1973-99
Shelton, Ralph	8-11	2.0	1935-37
Shelton, Robert F.	K-12	26.0	1947-63; 1970-80
Shields, Marcia	7-12	3.0	1977-80
Shoopman, Vicky	K-3	2.0	1999-00; 2002-
Shropshire, Janet	9-12	2.5	2000-
Shultz, Eric	9-12	1.0	1979-80
Shuman, Beth Puckett	K-5	20.0	1983-
Simmons, Kathy	K-3	3.0	1999-02
Simpson, Deborah	6-8	7.0	1996-
Sims, Patricia	9-12	1.0	1961-62
Skinner, Rachel	9-12	1.0	1999-00
Smith, Ellis	9-12	18.0	1984-90; 1991-
Smith, Framie		1.0	1919-20
Smith, JoAnn	K-6	3.0	1978-81
Smith, John	6-8	1.0	1998-99
Smith, Stacy	9-12	2.0	1996-97; 1998-99
Smith, Vickey	K-3	6.0	1997-
Smolen, Kimberley	K-3	1.0	2002-
Soltau, Carolyn	K-5	11.5	1991-
Sommerfield, Joyce	9-12	8.0	1995-
Sorrell, Miss Madie	1-6	1.0?	1905-?
Sorrell, Novella	1-6	6.0	1965-71

Name	Grade	Years	Period
Southard, Margaret	K-3	3.0	1998-01
Southwell, Sandy	6-8	10.0	1989-99
Spacht, Anne	6-8	9.0	1994-
Spaller, Kathy	K-6	2.0	1977-79
Sparks, Sarah Nichols	9-12	10.0	1968-69; 1974-83
Spaw, Mary	1-6	1.0	1930-31
Spector, Julie	4-5	2.0	2001-
Spencer, Earl H.	Prin	0.5	1923-24
Staelens, Barbara	K-6	1.0	1990-91
Stark, Richard	K-5	16.0	1979-95
Stark, Susan	K-3	17.0	1981-97; 1998-99
Steger, Kristi	6-8	3.0	1993-96
Steinberg, Mary	K-5	8.0	1994-99; 2000-
Steldt, Paul	9-12	1.0	1974-75
Stellato, Tammy	K-3	9.0	1994-
Stephenson, Cordia M.	1-6	0.5	1932-33
Stewart, Margaret	6-7	0.6	1934-35
Stienke, Kathy	K-5	13.5	1985-97; 2001-
Stokes, Katherine	7-12	1.5	1955-57
Stolte, Diane Howe	6-8	10.0	1991-01
Stork, Gayle	9-12	5.0	1968-73
Stork, Jack	7-12	1.0	1964-65
Stout, Karen	9-12	2.0	1996-98
Strahan, Brenda	6-8	12.0	1991-
Stripling, Karen	K-6	1.0	1989-90
Stubbs, A. L.	Prin	2.0	1890-92
Stubbs, Oscar A.	Prin	1.0	1897-98
Stubbs, Oscar V.	Prin	4.0	1930-34
Sullivan, Ruth	6-8	24.0	1973-97
Sultemeier, Cindy	9-12	1.0	1999-00
Sutherland, Myra	9-12	8.0	1995-
Sutherland, Nancy Faust	7-12	16.0	1984-87; 1990-
Sutton, Larry	9-12	6.0	1973-79
Swart, Mrs. Clint	9-12	2.0	1947-49
Tampke, E. W.	7-12	1.0	1963-64
Tate, Twila	9-12	1.0	1960-61
Taylor, Carol	K-3	10.0	1993-
Taylor, Laura	K-6	1.0	1984-85
Teas, Henry D.	7-11	1.0	1940-41
Terrell, Lisa Gregory	9-12	4.0	1992-96
Terroba, Nelson	6-8	1.0	2002-
Thomas, Diane	9-12	2.0	1975-77
Thomas, Mrs. B. B.		1.0	1922-23
Thompson, Karen	7-12	7.0	1993-00
Thornhill, Cathy	K-3	11.0	1989-00
Tidd, H. P.	Prin	2.0	1993-95
Tiggeman, Cherry L.	9-12	9.0	1971-80
Till, Peggy	9-12	4.0	1998-02
Tilley, Merlin B.	Prin	3.0	1940-43
Tilley, Mrs. M. B.	1-6	3.0	1940-43
Timco, Chris	7-12	1.0	1981-82
Tomlin, Georgia	9-12	3.0	1990-93
Tower, Tara	7-12	8.0	1995-
Townsend, Kim	K-3	1.0	1994-95
Tracy, Pamela	K-6	1.0	1988-89
Trapp, Nancy	9-12	2.0	2001-
Troppy, Susan	1-8	18.0	1985-
Tselos, Helena	6-8	1.0	1996-97
Tuck, Sandra	K-5	4.0	1993-97
Turk, Dawn	6-8	1.0	1998-99
Turner, Myrtle	9-12	1.0	1963-64
Tykoski, Mary J.	9-12	4.0	1996-00
Tyler, Derek	9-12	1.0	1998-99
Uffman, Patty	9-12	1.0	1995-96
Upchurch, Alice	2-3	1.0	1956-57
Urbanovsky, Kristine	6-8	7.0	1996-
Utley, Terry	K-6	3.0	1979-82
Vandivier, Sonja	4-12	13.0	1990-
Vasquez, Letty	9-12	1.0	1993-94
Vaughn, Richard	7-12	3.0	1974-77
Vauk, Melissa	6-8	5.0	1994-99
Vinson, Steve	6-8	1.0	1991-92
Volpe, Virginia	9-12	5.0	1998-
Voudouris, Marion	K-3	37.0	1966-
Wade, Julie	6-8	4.0	1999-
Wagner, Diane	6-8	9.0	1994-
Waits, Carl	K-12	30.0	1965-95
Walker, Julie	K-3	2.0	2001-
Walker, Lorena	1-8	4.0	1942-45; 1946-47
Walker, Sarah H.		1.0	1920-21
Wallace, Carrie	All	?	1869-?
Wallace, Leslie	4-5	4.0	1999-
Wallin, Elizabeth	K-5	10.0	1993-
Walsh, Ann	6-8	7.0	1996-
Walter, Estelle	5-6	1.0	1945-46
Ward, Jharon	K-3	1.0	2002-
Ward, Patricia	9-12	1.0	1976-77
Ware, Dana	K-5	4.0	1985-89
Warren, LaJean	4-5	6.0	1997-
Warwick, Susan	9-12	10.0	1992-00; 2001-
Watkins, Sharon	4-5	6.0	1997-
Webber, Ms.	K-6	1.0	1988-89
Weber, Georgeanne	9-12	4.0	1975-79
Webster, Mary Alice	6-8	8.0	1990-98
Weinheimer, Cary	9-12	1.0	1979-80
Weiser, Rebecca	K-3	11.0	1992-
Weisman, Anne	7-12	2.0	1975-77
Weiss, Melissa	9-12	1.0	1994-95
Welch, Ramona	4-5	5.0	1998-
Wells, Tom	7-12	1.5	1972-74
Wendel, Sue	6-8	10.0	1993-
West, Toni McClish	9-12	3.0	2000-
Whalen, Jacquelyn	K-3	2.0	2001-

Name	Grades	Years	Dates
White, Annelise Eckhardt	6-8	2.0	2000-02
White, Bob	7-12	1.0	1970-71
White, Daymun	9-12	2.0	1991-93
White, Nancy	9-12	1.0	1992-93
Whitefield, Janice	K-5	21.0	1977-98
Whites, Jim	9-12	13.0	1985-98
Whitman, Rhonda	K-5	12.0	1991-
Whitten, Jeanine Pankhurst	K-6	5.0	1976-81
Wicke, Terry	9-12	8.0	1984-92
Wilgoren, Rob	9-12	4.0	1999-
Wilkins, LeeAnn	6-8	15.5	1984-00
Williams, Bridget	K-3	6.0	1988-92; 1993-95
Williamson, Elizabeth	9-12	5.0	1960-65
Wilson, Gay Lynn	7-12	7.5	1982-85; 1986-91
Wilson, Jenny	9-12	4.0	1971-75
Wilson, John W. III (Trey)	7-12	1.0	1982-83
Wilson, Lisa	K-3	3.5	1999-
Winans, Jessie	1-6	22.0	1959-81
Witt, Jodi Meixelsperger	K-3	3.0	1997-00
Witte, Jodie	7-12	0.5	1958-59
Wittenburg, Leslie	6-8	4.0	1999-
Witwiski, Nancy	K-3	8.7	1988-97
Wolbrecht, Sharon	9-12	2.0	1974-76
Wolfe, Mr.	9-12	0.5	1983-84
Woodland, Lisa	4-5	7.0	1996-
Woods, Phyliss	K-3	7.0	1996-
Woods, Virginia	9-12	8.5	1982-89; 1990-92
Wooten, Irene	9-12	6.0	1993-99
Wren, Jimmy	7-12	5.0	1976-81
Wright, Marilyn Stefka	9-12	30.0	1973-
Wrinkle, Diane	9-12	1.0	2002-
Wycoff, Janice	K-3	13.0	1990-
Zupancic, Debra	9-12	7.0	1996-

School Trustees

From the beginning, schools had a group of people in charge of making the decisions that would affect the property and the educational changes that would be made. Their main duty was to set the tax rate, hire the person in charge of the educational staff and approve the selection of teachers for each year. We are not sure exactly when the first formal school for Dripping Springs was actually established but it looks like one must have been taking place in 1870-71 with Carrie Wallace as the teacher. Most likely, her father, John L. Wallace, was one of the trustees, along with someone like Dr. Pound or A. L. Davis, Sr. For certain, beginning in 1876-77, a county school system was set up and a school established at Dripping Springs. From that point, trustees were named and elected for the school. Especially in the early days, trustees served for long periods of time. Not much information has been found naming the trustees of the school and when their names were mentioned, one can figure they had been serving a few years on either side of that date. One article, in giving school information, simply said the same trustees were elected to serve the next year, but, did not name who they were. In the early days, there were only three trustees elected to serve the school. Beginning in the early '30s, when Dripping Springs began to consolidate and grow, the board membership grew to seven and has remained so. Every time schools consolidated with Dripping Springs, a new set of trustees were appointed to the board, sometimes in the middle of the year. Below is as complete a list as I could find of those serving on the Board of Trustees for Dripping Springs Schools.

1876-77: W.T. Chapman, A. L. Davis, Sr., John L. Wallace
1877-78: W.T. Chapman, A. L. Davis, Sr., John L. Wallace
1878-79: W.T. Chapman, A. L. Davis, Sr., John L. Wallace
1879-86: Not Available
1886-87: C. S. Graham, J. W. Phillips, B. R. Wilhite
1887-88: Not Available
1888-89: Not Available
1889-90: Last Year's Trustees were re-elected
1890-91: Not Available
1891-92: Not Available
1892-93: Not Available
1893-94: Not Available
1894-95: Not Available
1895-96: Not Available
1896-97: W. G. McKellar, E. P. Shelton, B. R. Wilhite

1897-98: W. G. McKellar, E. P. Shelton, B. R. Wilhite

1898-99: Pedernales Leinneweber, George McCuistion, B. R. Wilhite

1899-00: Pedernales Leinneweber, George McCuistion, B. R. Wilhite

1900-01: Pedernales Leinneweber, George McCuistion, J. P. Sorrell

1901-02: George McCuistion, E. P. Shelton, J. P. Sorrell

1902-03: George McCuistion, E. P. Shelton, J. P. Sorrell

1903-04: I. T. Applewhite, George McCuistion, E. P. Shelton

1904-05: I. T. Applewhite, George McCuistion, E. P. Shelton

1905-06: I. T. Applewhite, I. V. Davis, Jr., J. L. Patterson

1906-07: I. V. Davis, Jr., J. L. Patterson, E. P. Shelton

1907-08: I. V. Davis, Jr., J. L. Patterson, E. P. Shelton

1908-09: McCreary Crow, Frank Randerson, E. P. Shelton

1909-10: McCreary Crow, Frank Randerson, E. P. Shelton

1910-11: McCreary Crow, J. L. Patterson, Frank Randerson

1911-12: McCreary Crow, J. L. Patterson, E. P. Shelton

1912-13: A. A. Elsner, J. L. Patterson, E. P. Shelton

1913-14: W. H. Crenshaw, A. A. Elsner, E. P. Shelton

1914-15: W. H. Crenshaw, A. A. Elsner, Unknown

1915-16: W. H. Crenshaw, A. A. Elsner, Unknown

1916-17: Not Available

1917-18: McCreary Crow, W. S. McLendon, Unknown

1918-19: McCreary Crow, W. S. McLendon, Unknown

1919-20: D. A. Brack, McCreary Crow, W. S. McLendon

1920-21: D. A. Brack, S. B. Glosson, W. S. McLendon

1921-22: D. A. Brack, A. A. Elsner, S. B. Glosson

1922-23: D. A. Brack, A. A. Elsner, P. L. Turner

1923-24: J. C. Breed, A. A. Elsner, P. L. Turner

1924-25: J. C. Breed, A. A. Elsner, S. B. Glosson

1925-26: J. C. Breed, A. A. Elsner, S. B. Glosson

1926-27: J. C. Breed, C. W. Crenshaw, W. S. McLendon

1927-28: J. C. Breed, C. W. Crenshaw, W. S. McLendon

1928-29: J. C. Breed, C. W. Crenshaw, W. S. McLendon

1929-30: J. C. Breed, Charles C. Haydon, Unknown

1930-31: J. C. Breed, O. S. Brumley, Charles C. Haydon

1931-32: J. C. Breed, O. S. Brumley, Charles C. Haydon

1932-33: J. C. Breed, O. S. Brumley, Charles C. Haydon

1933-34: H. H. King, E. P. Shelton, P. L. Turner

1934-35: H. H. King, E. P. Shelton, P. L. Turner

1935-36: J. G. Eastland, L. E. Gage, H. H. King, E. P. Shelton, C. W. Spillar, P. L. Turner, W. W. Williamson, Felix Lindsey for E. P. Shelton

1936-37: J. G. Eastland, L. E. Gage, H. H. King, Felix Lindsey, Lee Roberts, C. W. Spillar, P. L. Turner, S. J. Spillar for J. G. Eastland

1937-38: L. E. Gage, Herman Gold, H. H. King, Felix Lindsey, Lee Roberts, S. J. Spillar, P. L. Turner

1938-39: L. E. Gage, Herman Gold, H. H. King, Lee Roberts, C. W. Spillar, S. J. Spillar, P. L. Turner, James Ferrell for Lee Roberts, W. C. Goslin for P. L. Turner, F. C. Thielepape for H. H. King

1939-40: James Ferrell, L. E. Gage, Herman Gold, W. C. Goslin, C. W. Spillar, S. J. Spillar, F. C. Thielepape, W. A. Lyle for F. C. Thielepape, E. T. Mading for W.C. Goslin

1940-41: Truman Breed, James Ferrell, L. E. Gage, W. A. Lyle, E. T. Mading, C. W. Spillar, S. J. Spillar, J.W. Wilson, Sr. for James Ferrell, Foster Harmon for W. A. Lyle

1941-42: Truman Breed, L. E. Gage, E. T. Mading, C. W. Spillar, S. J. Spillar, F. C. Thielepape, J. W. Wilson, Sr., T. E. Gillespie for S. J. Spillar, William Glosson for J. W. Wilson, Sr.

1942-43: Truman Breed, L. E. Gage, William Glosson, R. T. Hadley, Glenn Key, C. W. Spillar, F. C. Thielepape

1943-44: Roy Breed, B. T. Crumley, L. E. Gage, R. T. Hadley, Jesse Langston, C. W. Spillar, F. C. Thielepape

1944-45: T. C. Anderson, Roy Breed, R. T. Hadley, Jesse Langston, B. J. Reimers, C. W. Spillar, F. C. Thielepape

2-5-45: T. C. Anderson, Roy Breed, R. T. Hadley, Gerald Moore, B. J. Reimers, C. W. Spillar, F. C. Thielepape

3-12-45: T.C. Anderson, Roy Breed, R. T.

Hadley, Mrs, C.N. Hambrick, George Ireland, B. J. Reimers, F. C. Thielepape

1945-46: T. C. Anderson, Roy Breed, R. T. Hadley, Mrs. George Ireland, S. J. Moore, B. J. Reimers, F. C. Thielepape

1946-47: T. C. Anderson, Roy Breed, George Ireland, Glynn Key, S. J. Moore, B. J. Reimers, F. C. Thielepape

1947-48: T. C. Anderson, D. C. Foster, George Ireland, Glynn Key, S. J. Moore, B. J. Reimers, F. C. Thielepape

1948-49: T. C. Anderson, D. C. Foster, Glynn Key, S. J. Moore, M. Z. Piland, B. J. Reimers, F. C. Thielepape, O. H. Cobb for S. J. Moore

1949-50: T. C. Anderson, O. H. Cobb, D. C. Foster, Glynn Key, M. Z. Piland, B. J. Reimers, F. C. Thielepape

1950-51: T. C. Anderson, Arno Brill, O. H. Cobb, Glynn Key, M. Z. Piland, B. J. Reimers, Dayton Roberts

1951-52: T. C. Anderson, Arno Brill, O. H. Cobb, Glynn Key, M. Z. Piland, B. J. Reimers, Dayton Roberts

1952-53: T. C. Anderson, Arno Brill, O. H. Cobb, Glynn Key, M. Z. Piland, Henry Reimers, Dayton Roberts

1953-54: T. C. Anderson, O. H. Cobb, Glynn Key, A. E. Maul, M. Z. Piland, Henry Reimers, Dayton Roberts

1954-55: T. C. Anderson, Foster Harmon, Alva Haydon, Glynn Key, A. E. Maul, A.E.C. Pope, Henry Reimers

1955-56: Foster Harmon, Alva Haydon, Glynn Key, A. E. Maul, A.E.C. Pope, Henry Reimers, Henry Spillman

1956-57: Foster Harmon, Bob Hatch, Glynn Key, Marvin Odell, A.E.C. Pope, Henry Reimers, Henry Spillman

1957-58: Foster Harmon, Bob Hatch, Glynn Key, Marvin Odell, A.E.C. Pope, Henry Reimers, Henry Spillman

1958-59: John Farley, Bob Hatch, Foster Harmon, Marvin Odell, A.E.C. Pope, Henry Reimers, Henry Spillman

1959-60: John Farley, James Hall, Foster Harmon, A.E.C. Pope, Henry Reimers, Henry Spillman, Alvin Walker

1960-61: Bob Baker, John Farley, James Hall, Foster Harmon, Henry Reimers, Henry Spillman, Alvin Walker

1961-62: Bob Baker, John Farley, James Hall, Foster Harmon, Alva Haydon, O. B. McKown, Henry Spillman

1962-63: Bob Baker, John Farley, James Hall, Foster Harmon, Alva Haydon, O. B. McKown, Steve Spillar

1963-64: John Farley, Willard Grumbles, James Hall, Foster Harmon, Alva Haydon, O. B. McKown, Steve Spillar

1964-65: John Farley, Willard Grumbles, James Hall, Foster Harmon, Alva Haydon, O. B. McKown, Steve Spillar

1965-66: John Farley, Willard Grumbles, James Hall, Foster Harmon, Alva Haydon, O. B. McKown, Steve Spillar

1966-67: John Farley, Willard Grumbles, James Hall, Foster Harmon, Alva Haydon, O. B. McKown, Steve Spillar

1967-68: Chuck Draper, L. E. "Shorty " DuPuy, James Hall, Foster Harmon, Steve Spillar, Fred Trimble, J. W. Wilson, Jr.

1968-69: Chuck Draper, L. E. DuPuy, James Hall, Milton Reimers, Steve Spillar, Fred Trimble, J. W. Wilson, Jr.

1969-70: Dana Cashion, Bob Crowder, L. E. DuPuy, Foster Harmon, Milton Reimers, Fred Trimble, L. L. Turnipseed

1970-71: Dana Cashion, Bob Crowder, L. E. DuPuy, Foster Harmon, Milton Reimers, Fred Trimble, L. L. Turnipseed

1971-72: Arthur Anderson, Dana Cashion, Bob Crowder, L. E. DuPuy, Milton Reimers, Fred Trimble, L. L. Turnipseed

1972-73: Arthur Anderson, D. W. "Weebud" Cauthen, L. E. DuPuy, Oscar James, Milton Reimers, L. L. Turnipseed, Ernest Williamson

1973-74: Arthur Anderson, D. W. Cauthen, L. E. DuPuy, Oscar James, Milton Reimers, L. L. Turnipseed, Ernest Williamson

1974-75: Arthur Anderson, D. W. Cauthen, L. E. DuPuy, Oscar James, Milton Reimers, L. L. Turnipseed, Ernest Williamson

1975-76: Arthur Anderson, D. W. Cauthen, L. E. DuPuy, D. B. Houle, Jack Pelton, Milton Reimers, Ernest Williamson

1976-77: Arthur Anderson, Clarence Cobb, Bob Crowder, D. B. Houle, Jack Pelton, Milton Reimers, Jack Stuessy

1977-78: Arthur Anderson, Clarence Cobb, Alva Haydon, D. B. Houle, Jack Pelton, Milton Reimers, Jack Stuessy

1978-79: Clarence Cobb, Alva Haydon, D. B. Houle, Merlin Jung, Pat Muennink, Milton Reimers, Jack Stuessy

1979-80: Alva Haydon, Merlin Jung, Pat Muennink, John Pate, Thomas Pollock, Milton Reimers, Jack Reynolds

1980-81: Dick Allison, Merlin Jung, Pat

Muennink, John Pate, Thomas Pollock, Jack Reynolds, Betty Stewart

1981-82: D. W. Cauthen, Clarence Cobb, Ann Hohman, Ray Nelson, Clarence Shelton, Vince Taylor, Ray Whisenant

1982-83: D. W. Cauthen, Clarence Cobb, Bill Crisp, Charles Dildine, Ray Nelson, Vince Taylor, Ray Whisenant

1983-84: D. W. Cauthen, Bill Crisp, Charles Dildine, Grady Moore, Terry Palmer, Vince Taylor, Ray Whisenant

1984-85: D. W. Cauthen, Mike Davidson, Jr., Charles Dildine, Grady Moore, Terry Palmer, Lynette Ritter, Ray Whisenant

1985-86: Mike Davidson, Jr., Charles Dildine, Grady Moore, Terry Palmer, Lynette Ritter, Don Spraggins, Ray Whisenant

1986-87: Mike Davidson, Jr., Charles Dildine, Vickie Harris, Grady Moore, Lynette Ritter, Don Spraggins, Ray Whisenant

1987-88: Mike Davidson, Jr., Charles Dildine, Vickie Harris, Grady Moore, Lynette Ritter, Don Spraggins, Ray Whisenant

1988-89: Mike Davidson, Jr., Vickie Harris, Jerry Martin, Grady Moore, Lynette Ritter, Don Spraggins, Ray Whisenant

1989-90: Mike Davidson, Jr., Vickie Harris, Jerry Martin, Grady Moore, Lynette Ritter, Don Spraggins, Ray Whisenant

1990-91: Vickie Harris, Jerry Martin, Grady Moore, Roger Noack, Debra Rhodes-Miller, Kent Snodgrass, Don Spraggins

1991-92: Vickie Harris, Guy Henderson, Jerry Martin, Grady Moore, Roger Noack, Debra Rhodes-Miller, Kent Snodgrass

1992-93: Guy Henderson, Glenn Heckmann, Bill Hubbard, Jerry Martin, Roger Noack, Debra Rhodes-Miller, Paul Watkins

1993-94: Guy Henderson, Bill Hubbard, Jerry Martin, Roger Noack, Pam Peterson, Debra Rhodes-Miller, Paul Watkins

1994-95: Glenn Heckmann, Guy Henderson, Bill Hubbard, Pam Peterson, Debra Rhodes-Miller, Pat Seiders, Paul Watkins

1995-96: Mike Figer, Glenn Heckmann, Guy Henderson, Pam Peterson, Debra Rhodes-Miller, Pat Seiders, Paul Watkins

1996-97: Mike Figer, Glenn Heckmann, Lenny Jasinski, Pam Peterson, Debra Rhodes-Miller, Pat Seiders, Paul Watkins

1997-98: Mike Figer, Glenn Heckmann, Lenny Jasinski, Pam Peterson, Debra Rhodes-Miller, Pat Seiders, Paul Watkins

1998-99: Mike Figer, Glenn Heckmann, Lenny Jasinski, Pam Peterson, Debra Rhodes-Miller, Pat Seiders, Olivia Weekley

1999-00: Mike Figer, Glenn Heckmann, John Moore, Lenny Olsen, Debra Rhodes-Miller, Pat Seiders, Olivia Weekley

2000-01: Susie Dudley, Mike Figer, John Moore, Eddie Oliver, Lenny Olsen, Richard Stark, Olivia Weekley

2001-02: Bill Brock, Susie Dudley, Mike Figer, John Moore, Eddie Oliver, Lenny Olsen, Richard Stark

2002-03: Bill Brock, Susie Dudley, Mike Figer, John Moore, Eddie Oliver, Lenny Olsen, Richard Stark

Student Honors

Graduating Honor Students: Although there is always a top student in each graduating class, the earliest class that I could determine to name those students was in 1934. I'm not sure how many people were in each but do know there were only four students in the 1931-32 class, so naming top students prior to 1934 might not be a formal thing. We had too close to call valedictorians in 1941, 1942, 1978, and 1986. The valedictorian and salutatorian of each graduating class from Dripping Springs is listed below.

1933-34: Merle Glosson, Doris Reeder
1934-35: Willie Edna Baird, Ruth Champion
1935-36: Maxine Hill, Willie Mae Wilson
1936-37: George Adamson, Erlene Hall
1937-38: Hazel Bell King, Eloise Butler
1938-39: Willie Edna Puryear, Robin Stephenson
1939-40: Damon Hollingsworth, Gladene Crenshaw
1940-41: Irene Combs, Wilma Goslin, Louella Williamson
1941-42: Clarene Williamson, Edith Goslin, Dean Lyle
1942-43: Norma Champion, Lula Saunders
1943-44: Lula V. Key, Maxine Garnett
1944-45: Margaret Glosson, Lila Faye Smith
1945-46: Minnie Ferrell, Ruthie Mae Crumley
1946-47: Danna Foster, Gene Garnett
1947-48: Betty Jean Gourley, Fred Garnett
1948-49: Elbert L. Spaw, Virginia Weaver
1949-50: Erma Dean Bean, Louise Wallace

1950-51: Bill Tharp, Mary Stewart
1951-52: Norwood Needham, Zilman Piland
1952-53: Clarence Cobb, Jack Lyle
1953-54: Wallace Spillar, Woody Glosson
1954-55: Bernice Ellis, Linda Chapin
1955-56: Judy Hoard, Patsy Harber
1956-57: Melvin Lindsey, Joy Willie
1957-58: Beth Garnett, Mary Ellen Key
1958-59: Lorena Phillips, Bobby Shelton
1959-60: Becky Shelton, Sandra Foster
1960-61: Billie Ferrell, Sue Ann Thompson
1961-62: Hillery Canon, Jimmie Shelton
1962-63: Vicki Farley, Sandra Cauthen
1963-64: Ann Ella Harmon, Cathy Werth
1964-65: Robert Haydon, Janiece Hyatt
1965-66: Mike Davidson, Judy Wilson
1966-67: Linda Brizendine, Lucia Garza
1967-68: Bill Kingsbery, Lynn Weihrauch
1968-69: Brenda McNair, Randy Garnett
1969-70: Mike Hall, Nancy Irvin
1970-71: Al Hohman, Jay Lindsey
1971-72: Peggy Gravenor, Lore Canion
1972-73: Teddy Draper, Sandy Gravenor
1973-74: Beverly Brown, Marcus Murphy
1974-75: Glenda Rutter, Judy Anderson
1975-76: Sandra Miller, Daryll Keeling
1976-77: Marian Seitz, Gary Crowder
1977-78: Lorinda Reimers/Craig Olson, Mike Scott
1978-79: Jim Lumpkin, Eric Jerome
1979-80: Darrell Danielson, Sheryl Bagley
1980-81: Stuart Johnson, Geraldine Prochnow
1981-82: Marsha Riley, Stephanie Shepperd
1982-83: Eric Schule, Shantell Morgan
1983-84: Pecos McDaniel, Kathryn Hawkins
1984-85: Sarah Stark, Carlotta Carothers
1985-86: Shelly Sedwick/Robert Robbins, Lisa Pankratz
1986-87: Pat Fogarty, Melvyn Foster
1987-88: J. Chris George, Cooper Vertz
1988-89: Sandra Fletcher, Jennifer Hodgkins
1989-90: Corey Pennington, Lori Smith
1990-91: Daniel Smith, Lewis Jenkins
1991-92: Kris Stienke, Samantha Harlan
1992-93: Brian Wood, Sarah Kenton
1993-94: Joanna Kopponen, Kelly Wouters
1994-95: Cynthia Tom, Clay Forister
1995-96: Allison Hutto, Brannon Hyde
1996-97: Joey Gray, Daniel Vaughan
1997-98: Robert Lindsey, Sarah Jandle
1998-99: Shannon Kidd, Laura Lindsey
1999-00: Llewyn Paine, David Woodland
2000-01: Rex Baker IV, Brittany Cunningham
2001-02: Julie Lindsey, Nicole Laird
2002-03: Rachel Wofford, Willa Kramer

Senior Class Presidents:
1940-41: Gaylon Harber
1941-42: Clarene Williamson
1942-43: Norma Champion
1943-44: Lula V. Key
1944-45: John Lee Gillespie
1945-46: Annie Mae Spillar
1946-47: Douglas Foster
1947-48: Billie Breed
1948-49: Gennieve Cure
1949-50: J. F. Glosson
1950-51: Buddy White
1951-52: Norwood "Buzzy" Needham
1952-53: Hudson Hill
1953-54: Wallace Spillar
1954-55: C.B. Montague
1955-56: Vernene Lawson
1956-57: Pat Burke
1957-58: Lee Jones
1958-59: Wesley Ruston
1959-60: Jean Turner
1960-61: Cecil Jenkins
1961-62: Roy Ruston
1962-63: Pat Baker
1963-64: Bobby Baker
1964-65: Robert Haydon
1965-66: Mike Davidson
1966-67: Myles Kingsbery
1967-68: Bill Kingsbery
1968-69: Ray Whisenant
1969-70: Mike Arnold
1970-71: Pat Lyle
1971-72: Chad Murphy
1972-73: Teddy Draper
1973-74: Johnny Preslar
1974-75: Glenda Rutter
1975-76: David Freitag
1976-77: Gary Preslar
1977-78: Gerald Reid
1978-79: Jimmy Lumpkin
1979-80: Lori Holm
1980-81: Terry Pearson
1981-82: Ramsey Garza
1982-83: Diron Keeling
1983-84: Michelle Haldeman
1984-85: Dawn Orem
1985-86: Kelly Howell
1986-87: Jeff Dodd
1987-88: Chris M. George
1988-89: Todd Reimers
1989-90: Chad Hudson
1990-91: Jacob Tingle
1991-92: Jason George
1992-93: Sarah Kenton

1993-94: Bryan Linder
1994-95: Thomas Flemons
1995-96: Sean Hubbard
1996-97: Craig Tondre
1997-98: Christi Leopold
1998-99: Ashley Figer
1999-00: Marie White
2000-01: Rex Baker IV
2001-02: Mandy Francis
2002-03: Kingsley DeSpain

Senior Class Favorites: Like several other favorite categories, class favorites mysteriously disappeared after the 1994-95 school year. Like other honors, being a class favorite was a nice honor because it was your classmates who selected you for the honor. No doubt it was a yearbook-generated category, but it was one of those honors that should have been continued when others became passe in the politically correct society of today. Here are the students so honored.

1951-52: Dosia Mae Rippy Langston, Norwood "Buzzy" Needham
1952-53: Nancy Spillar, Hudson Hill
1953-54: Nancy Hendrickson, Delton Glass
1954-55: Linda Chapin, Gilman Hall
1955-56: Vernene Lawson, Lowell Johnson
1956-57: Joy Willie, Pat Burke
1957-58: Beth Garnett, James Gourley
1958-59: Peggy Needham, Wesley Ruston
1959-60: Becky Shelton, Joe Spillman
1960-61: Jackie Shackleford, Cecil Jenkins
1961-62: Martha Collier, Roy Ruston
1962-63: Vicki Farley, Dixie Smith
1963-64: Ann Ella Harmon, Malcolm Key
1964-65: Lynn Kingsbery, Jimmy Lyle
1965-66: Beatrice Herrera, Bob Worley
1966-67: Linda Brizendine, Myles Kingsbery
1967-68: Donna Cauthen, Bill Kingsbery
1968-69: Cherry Boone, Paul Freitag
1969-70: Diane White, Donnie Stigler
1970-71: Cathy Gravenor, Pat Lyle
1971-72: Audel Whisenant, Chad Murphy
1972-73: Eva Breed, Craig Grayum
1973-74: Theresa Garnett, Johnny Preslar
1974-75: Vicki Bess, Barry McNair
1975-76: Gail Anglin, Daryll Keeling
1976-77: Karen Woodcock, Larry Ray
1977-78: Gay Lynn Dodson, Tim Fitzharris
1978-79: Joy Davis, Ronny Burke
1979-80: Keli Luedecke, Chris Harvill
1980-81: Roberta Hoyer, Terry Pearson
1981-82: Debbie Sheffield, Ramsey Garza
1982-83: Paige Crisp, Diron Keeling
1983-84: Kathryn Hawkins, Pecos McDaniel
1984-85: Jill Reimers, Justin Chandler
1985-86: Lisa Counts, Pat Leonard
1986-87: Kim Ross, Michael Escobar
1987-88: Bobbi Hohmann, J. Chris George
1988-89: Keri Shults, David Jarvis
1989-90: Lissie Crosswell, Chad Hudson
1990-91: Alison Stegall, Danny Smith
1991-92: Bridgette Hurlbut, Jason George
1992-93: Brandi Read, Brandt Whisenant
1993-94: Missy Russell, Bryan Linder
1994-95: Brandi Smith, Thomas Flemons

Homecoming Royalty: Dripping Springs fell in line like most other schools in having school royalty. Early on it was the culmination of the Halloween event held at the school. Early in the '50s, it became a part of the homecoming football game and has stayed that way. It is one of those early traditions that has continued to flourish. Below is the list of the queens and kings who have held reign for Dripping Springs High School.

1946-47: Danna Foster, Raymond Whisenant
1947-48: Betty Jean Gourley, Jimmy Moore
1948-49: Gennieve Cure, Homer Cearley
1949-50: Louise Wallace, Gerald Brumley
1950-51: Betty Lois Pope, Robert Sansom
1951-52: Billie Barbara Butler, Billy Arnold
1952-53: Loretta McClaferty, Douglas Johnson
1953-54: Eleanor Anderson, John McClaferty
1954-55: Patsy Harber, R. L. Lyle
1955-56: Judy Hoard, Alvin Crumley
1956-57: Irene Phillips, Jack Millner
1957-58: Patricia Puryear, Larry DuPuy
1958-59: Becky Shelton, Larry DuPuy
1959-60: Gussie Myers, Joe Spillman
1960-61: Brenda Zuercher, Roy Ruston
1961-62: Patsy Whitley, Tommy Driska
1962-63: Carol Anschultz, Jimmy Lyle
1963-64: Lynn Kingsbery, Phillip Cook
1964-65: Merlene Glosson, Alford Hill
1965-66: Martha Bledsoe, Marvin Myers
1966-67: Becky Schenck, Ricky Schieffer
1967-68: Debbie Belvin, Bill Kingsbery
1968-69: Pat Corns, Randy Garnett
1969-70: Vicki Brotherton, Donnie Stigler

1970-71: Cathy Gravenor, Cecil McIntyre
1971-72: Kathy Pittman, Ronnie Wright
1972-73: Janet White, Ricky Mauck
1973-74: Theresa Garnett, Jay Pittman
1974-75: Dana Simon, Barry McNair
1975-76: Kelly Gable, Joe McNair
1976-77: Karen Woodcock, Gary Preslar
1977-78: Gay Lee Guyn, Bart Johnson
1978-79: Leslie Williams, Vern McCarty
1979-80: Carol Bankston, Mark Watson
1980-81: Kim Fries, Ramsey Garza
1981-82: Lorrie Nevarez, Todd Beasley
1982-83: Brenda Woodcock, Louis Alvarez
1983-84: Kathryn Hawkins, Steve Young
1984-85: Jill Reimers, Barry Haydon
1985-86: Suzy Shepperd, Matt Walker
1986-87: Kim Ross, Jeff Dodd
1987-88: Julie Henderson, Brian Hastings
1988-89: Laura Haydon, Marc Tinsley
1989-90: Lee Appelt, Brett Boydston
1990-91: Jennifer Hart, Chris Campbell
1991-92: Meredith Johnson, Morgan Crow
1992-93: Carrie Stewart, Brian Wood
1993-94: Lea Anne Haydon, Brad Schroeder
1994-95: Laura Edwards, Ray Herrera
1995-96: Thea Delamater, Daryl Dikes
1996-97: Colie Edmondson, Craig Tondre
1997-98: Julie Hurlbut, Eric Blandford
1998-99: Ashley Figer, Mark Bomar
1999-00: Leanna Jensen, Cole Peabody
2000-01: Sarah Lindsey, Rex Baker IV
2001-02: Julie Lindsey, Nathaniel Cox
2002-03: Rachel Wofford, Scott Briscoe

Mr. & Miss DSHS: In the first couple of yearbooks this honor was listed as the most popular students and then it evolved into the Mr./Miss title. This was a title bestowed on a couple of students until it was decided to forego this honor. Again, it seems a shame to have cut out a category like this that just seems to indicate popularity and nothing else. Below are those individuals who were selected for the honor over the years.

1944-45: Glynn Key, Margaret Glosson
1945-46: Jack Huey, Ruthie Mae Crumley
1946-47: Charles Haydon, Betty Butler
1947-48: Billie Breed, Mary Traylor
1948-49: Homer Cearley, Gennieve Cure
1949-50: J. F. Glosson, Louise Wallace
1950-51: Buddy White, Betty Lois Pope
1951-52: Hudson Hill, Mae Francis Sansom
1952-53: Hudson Hill, Nancy Spillar
1953-54: Woody Glosson, Merle Walker
1954-55: Gilman Hall, Merle Walker
1955-56: R. L. Lyle, Nancy Pope
1956-57: Pat Burke, Irene Phillips
1957-58: Lee Jones, Becky Shelton
1958-59: Harrell Robinson, Jean Turner
1959-60: Larry DuPuy, Mickey Davidson
1960-61: Sam Garnett, Martha Collier
1961-62: Pat Baker, Sandra Rippy
1962-63: Dixie Smith, Sandra Rippy
1963-64: Malcolm Key, Ann Ella Harmon
1964-65: Lupe Alarcon, Lynn Kingsbery
1965-66: Marvin Myers, Merlene Glosson
1966-67: Myles Kingsbery, Linda Brizendine
1967-68: Bill Kingsbery, Debbie Belvin
1968-69: Ray Whisenant, Brenda McNair
1969-70: Ricky Schieffer, Diane White
1970-71: Cecil McIntyre, Cathy Gravenor
1971-72: Ronnie Wright, Kathy Pittman
1972-73: Teddy Draper, Sandy Gravenor
1973-74: Jay Pittman, Theresa Garnett
1974-75: Barry McNair, Annette Gravenor
1975-76: Tem McCutchen, Gail Anglin
1976-77: Kerry Prescott, Cindy Reid
1977-78: Gerald Reid, Gay Lynn Dodson
1978-79: Ronny Burke, Melony Chandler
1979-80: Mark Watson, Carol Bankston
1980-81: Alec Gould, Beth Scantland
1981-82: Billy Ligon, Kim Fries
1982-83: Diron Keeling, Paige Crisp
1983-84: Steve Young, Tracy Archer
1984-85: Troy Burklund, Jill Reimers/ Katherine Crosswell
1985-86: Pat Leonard, Lisa Counts
1986-87: Matt Walker, Kim Ross
1987-88: Chris M. George, Julie Henderson
1988-89: Todd Reimers, Laura Haydon
1989-90: Michael Myers, Lee Appelt
1990-91: Chris Campbell, Paula Fletcher
1991-92: Kevin Dydalewicz, Meredith Johnson
1992-93: Tommy Fry, Rinda Rippy/Carrie Stewart
1993-94: Greg Dydalewicz, Missy Russell/Lea Anne Haydon
1994-95: Thomas Flemons, Katie Stienke

High School Drum Majors: It was not until the 1963-64 school year that Dripping Springs organized a band. From that point, band had a student leader called a Drum Major to lead the band. Below are those who have been selected since that time.

1963-64: Ann Ella Harmon
1964-65: Nikki Malott
1965-66: Lynn King
1966-67: Lynn King
1967-68: Lynn King
1968-69: Ginger Myers
1969-70: Shelley King
1970-71: Cindy Irvin
1971-72: Alice Hall
1972-73: Alice Hall
1973-74: Roy Taylor
1974-75: Lisa Shelton
1975-76: Lisa Shelton
1976-77: Lisa Shelton
1977-78: Tama Lumpkin
1978-79: Tama Lumpkin
1979-80: Tama Lumpkin
1980-81: Kim Hohmann
1981-82: Terri Turner
1982-83: Billy Simpson
1983-84: Paul Gerdes
1984-85: Sarah Stark
1985-86: Jewel Gray
1986-87: Michael Reagan
1987-88: Peter Gerdes
1988-89: Jeff Howell
1989-90: Corey Pennington
1990-91: Denise Edwards
1991-92: Oscar Tovar
1992-93: Jennifer Jones
1993-94: Sarah Davidson
1994-95: Lucas Horton
1995-96: Julie Karnes
1996-97: Matthew Hilgers
1997-98: Amanda Summers
1998-99: Ashley Figer
1999-00: Rex Baker IV
2000-01: Rex Baker IV
2001-02: Sarah Bingham
2002-03: Evan Webb

High School Majorettes: It was in the 1953-54 school year that Dripping Springs added majorettes (twirlers) to the program. The majorettes led the pep squad and the head majorette acted as the drum major as the pep squad performed. By 1980, majorettes had been replaced in the band by a flag corps. Below are the students selected to be the majorettes for Dripping Springs.

1953-54: Pat Forbes, Merle Walker, Betty Dean Burrier
1954-55: Joy Jernigan, Merle Walker, Betty Dean Burrier
1955-56: Nancy Pope, Patsy Harber, Ethel Spillar
1956-57: Penny Jo Forbes, Loyce Hoard, Myrene Phillips
1957-58: Lorena Phillips, Mickey Davidson, Wanda Glass
1958-59: Mickey Davidson, Patricia Puryear, Minnie Lou Glosson
1959-60: Mickey Davidson, Sandra Cauthen, Nisha Hildreth
1960-61: Nisha Hildreth, Sandra Cauthen, Mary Marshall
1961-62: Nisha Hildreth, Sandra Cauthen, Ann Ella Harmon
1962-63: Ann Ella Harmon, Mary Bonham, Vicki Farley
1963-64: Ann Ella Harmon, Darlene Brooks, Merlene Glosson
1964-65: Laura Glass, Merlene Glosson, Judy Wilson, Kathy Draper, Darlene Brooks
1965-66: Brenda McNair, Peggy Holton, Merlene Glosson
1966-67: Peggy Holton, Kathy Draper, Brenda McNair
1967-68: Brenda McNair, Becky Schenck, Shelley King
1968-69: Kathy Pittman, Donna Brotherton, Shelley King
1969-70: Kathy Pittman, Cindy Irvin, Letha Mae Phillips
1970-71: Charlotte Hohman, Alice Hall, Kathy Talbot
1971-72: Charlotte Hohman, Kathy Pittman, Tina Gillis
1972-73: Charlotte Hohman, Dorinda Moore, Tina Gillis
1973-74: Charlotte Hohman, Tina Gillis, Tammie Gillis
1974-75: LoAnne Lyle, Wanda Brotherton, Paula Smith
1975-76: LoAnne Lyle, Liz Winans, Paula Smith
1976-77: LoAnne Lyle, Liz Winans, Paula Smith
1977-78: Paula Smith, Dana Talbert, Janice Robinson, Sandra Woodcock (feature twirler)
1978-79: Dana Talbert, Janice Robinson, Kim Hohmann, Tracy Dempsey
1979-80: Janice Robinson (feature twirler)

Band Sweethearts/Beaus: Six years after being organized, the band began to

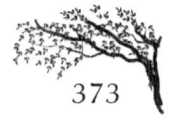

elect sweethearts and seven years later, the boys came in for equal rights as beaus. This tradition has continued to be a part of band history.

1968-69: Ginger Myers
1969-70: Shelley King
1970-71: Cindy Irvin
1971-72: Kathy Pittman
1972-73: Alice Hall
1973-74: Beverly Brown
1974-75: Lisa Shelton
1975-76: Sandra Miller, Trey Wilson
1976-77: Anita Moore, Trey Wilson
1977-78: Tammie Burrier, Holly Miller, Jay Johnson
1978-79: Tama Lumpkin, Tommy Gillis
1979-80: Tama Lumpkin, Scott Piland
1980-81: Kim Hohmann, Michael Kane
1981-82: Jana Syring, Steve Wegmiller
1982-83: Sarah Stark, Billy Simpson
1983-84: Lisa Biddle, Phillip Gerdes
1884-85: Kelly Howell, Phillip Gerdes,
1885-86: Julie Conrad, Jerry Simpson
1886-87: Julie Henderson, Mark Simpson
1887-88: Julie Henderson, Peter Gerdes
1988-89: Sandra Fletcher, Jeff Howell
1989-90: Denise Edwards, Craig Kunz
1990-91: Lance Whitefield
1991-92: Samantha Harlan, Nate Watkins
1992-93: Amanda Adams, Brad Schroeder
1993-94: Lea Anne Haydon, Brad Schroeder
1994-95: Sabrina Jones, Chris Glosson
1995-96: Christie Holloway, Daniel Payne
1996-97: Jennifer Boswell, Mike Lorber
1997-98: Kara Rees, Kris Riley
1998-99: Ashley Figer, Paul Frisinger
1999-00: Lisa Lehman, Patrick Hays
2000-01: Darcy Borella, Dan Gregory
2001-02: Lindsey Carter, Blake Wendel
2002-03: Nicole Parks, Kris Raven

Football Captains: In football circles, being named the captain of the team is the most prestigious honor a player can attain. That is because it is your teammates who give you that honor by electing you. It means they look up to you as someone they want to be led by. It can be one of the best players on the team but it does not have to be. Only a few ever get to attain this honor. Below is a list of those Tiger captains.

1938: E. E. "Nookie" Myers
1939: Damon Hollingsworth
1940: Truman "Red" Cauthen
1941: Travis Garnett
1942: Travis Garnett
1943: Jack Huey,
1944: Jack Huey
1945: D. W. "Weebud" Cauthen
1946: Raymond Whisenant
1947: Billy Breed, R. L. Harber
1948: J. F. Glosson, Harvey Goslin
1949: J. F. Glosson, Bobby Needham, Buddy White
1950: Buddy White, Harvey Goslin
1951: Weldon Johnson, Hudson Hill
1952: Hudson Hill, Perry Roberts
1953: Wallace Spillar, Woody Glosson, William Crumley
1954: Melvyn Foster, R. L. Lyle, Gilman Hall
1955: Oran Hill "Pug" Rippy, R. L. Lyle, Charles Stephenson
1956: Melvin Lindsey, Oran Hill "Pug" Rippy, Pat Burke
1957: Carroll Montague, Bobby Shelton, Lee Jones
1958: Bobby Shelton, Billy Cooper
1959: Larry DuPuy, Joe Spillman
1960: Jimmie Shelton, Hillery Canon
1961: Jimmie Shelton, Roy Ruston
1962: Pat Baker, Bill Smith
1963: Bobby Baker, Johnny McCarty
1964: Lupe Alarcon, Johnny McCarty, Phillip Cook
1965: Marvin Myers, Larry Tracy, Bill Crisp
1966: Myles Kingsbery, Sid Spillar, Gary Garnett
1967: Lynn "Rocky" Weihrauch, Dan Sansom, Albert Hudson
1968: Dennis Sansom, Ray Whisenant, Leon McIntyre
1969: Roy Gay, Mike Arnold, Ricky Schieffer
1970: Joe Williamson, Pat Lyle
1971: Terry Sansom, Teddy Draper
1972: Teddy Draper, Damon McIntyre
1973: Mike Sanders, Carroll Perkins, Johnny Preslar, Jay Pittman
1974: Ricky Lindholm, Barry McNair, Dale Bassford
1975: Tem McCutchen, Russell Burke
1976: Kerry Prescott, Harvey Bryant, Tommy Johnson, Gary Preslar
1977: Charles Tharp, Randy Burke, Tim Fitzharris
1978: James Godwin, Ronny Burke, Dewayne "Scooter" Sanders

1979: Chris Harvill, Mark Watson
1980: Walter Hudson, Andrew Muennink, Kelly Cauble
1981: Doug Jernigan, Billy Ligon, Ramsey Garza
1982: Diron Keeling, John Moore
1983: Ed Lumpkin, Greg Reid, Scott Daniels, Pecos McDaniel
1984: Eric Lambright, Troy Burklund, Mike Usery
1985: Kevin Glass, Steve Drane, Don Childs, Pat Leonard
1986: Kevin Spraggins, Doran Hole, Matt Walker, Chris M. George, Jeff Dodd
1987: Kevin Spraggins, Chris M. George, Shawn Bean
1988: Todd Reimers, Brett Boydston, Tate Puryear
1989: Brett Boydston, Travis Crow, Michael Myers, Mark Key
1990: Thomas Gil, Michael Lindemann, Danny Smith
1991: Ryan Street, Jason George, Kris Stienke
1992: Tommy Fry, Joey Case
1993: Greg Dydalewicz, Brock Stewart, Steve Alvarado, Ronnie Love
1994: Jeff Mayes, Jared Bray, Burt Dement, Micah Johnson
1995: Johnny "Trey" Preslar, Shane Whisenant, Travis Couey
1996: Cody Schmidt, Kevin Hemingway, Daniel Vaughn, Craig Tondre
1997: Zach Watkins, Narlen Baker, Jonathan Love, JoDan Minnink
1998: Britt Peterson, Tony Salazar, Mark Bomar
1999: Cole Peabody, Matt Preslar, Tony Salazar
2000: Joey Perrone, Blake Witwiski, Dustin Sageman, Brian Hendrickson, Alex Klein
2001: Justin Dredla, Matt Scarborough, Preston Jordan, Brad Stacey, Michael Purcell
2002: Cole Hayden, Sammy Martinez, Josh Wright

Most Athletic Boy/Girl: Although Dripping Springs had many good athletes prior to 1946, the tradition of naming the most athletic boy(s) and girl(s) began that year. No doubt, like many other similar honors, this was a yearbook generated honor. Nevertheless, it is a worthy honor to receive, much like being named a captain. This honor, like many others of long-standing tradition, was dropped in 1994-95. Below is a list of those who garnered the honor between 1946-95.

1945-46: Billie Breed, Ruthie Mae Crumley
1946-47: Raymond Whisenant, Mae Dell Crumley
1947-48: Billie Breed, Violet Rae Smith
1948-49: J. F. Glosson, Jr., Katherine Berkley, Louise Wallace,
1949-50: J. F. Glosson, Jr., Harvey Goslin, Katherine Berkley, Louise Wallace, Buddy White, Mae Francis Sansom
1950-51: Harvey Goslin, Mae Francis Sansom
1951-52: Lonnie Campbell, Norwood Needham, Billie Barbara Butler
1952-53: Lonnie Campbell, Martha Ann Stephenson
1953-54: Woody Glosson, Judy Hoard
1954-55: Gilman Hall, Merle Walker
1955-56: R. L. Lyle, Judy Hoard
1956-57: Melvin Lindsey, Oran Rippy, Irene Phillips
1957-58: Bobby Shelton, Mary Ellen Key
1958-59: Bobby Shelton, Lorena Phillips
1959-60: Larry DuPuy, Gussie Myers, Becky Shelton
1960-61: Dan Alvarado, Sue Thompson
1961-62: Roy Ruston, Vicki Farley
1962-63: Pat Baker, Vicki Farley
1963-64: Malcolm Key, Sandra Rippy
1964-65: Lupe Alarcon, Robin Brown
1965-66: Marvin Myers, Beatrice Herrera
1966-67: Thomas Combs, Kathy Draper
1967-68: Lynn Weihrauch, Dan Sansom, Donna Pittman
1968-69: Dennis Sansom, Donna Pittman
1969-70: Ricky Schieffer, Johnna Nichols
1970-71: Pat Lyle, Debra Spillar
1971-72: Teddy Draper, Kathy Pittman
1972-73: Teddy Draper, Tina Gillis, Melody Jones
1973-74: Jay Pittman, Luisa Sanchez
1974-75: Barry McNair, Kim Ferguson
1975-76: Tem McCutchen, Cindy Aulds
1976-77: Kerry Prescott, Cindy Reid
1977-78: Randy Burke, Gay Lynn Dodson
1978-79: Ronny Burke, Tami Purcell
1979-80: Chris Harvill, Mark Watson, Tracy Dempsey
1980-81: Andrew Muennink, Tracy Dempsey
1981-82: Richard Johnson, Sheryl Malott
1982-83: Diron Keeling, Janelle Gavlick

1983-84: Steve Young, Earlene Kemberling
1984-85: Pat Leonard, Lisa Counts
1985-86: Don Childs, Lisa Counts
1986-87: Michael Escobar, Codie Cobb
1987-88: Clinton Baty, Charlotte Carothers
1988-89: Michael Myers, Keri Shults
1989-90: Michael Myers, Paula Fletcher
1990-91: Jeff Hall, , Missy Odom, Carrie Stewart
1991-92: Kevin Dydalewicz, Carrie Stewart
1992-93: Greg Dydalewicz, Carrie Stewart
1993-94: Greg Dydalewicz, Melanie McMullin
1994-95: Jeff Mayes, Jinni Touchstone

Football Sweethearts: In the early days, the football sweetheart held a prominent place. They helped lead the pep squad and wore a heart on their uniform to let everyone know who they were. Later, at a banquet, they were presented flowers by the captains. The title changed to All-Sports Sweetheart in the final decade of the title's existence. For some unknown reason, tradition was stopped after the 1981 school year.

1945-46: Mary Ella Moore
1946-47: Betty Jean Gourley
1947-48: Betty Jean Gourley
1948-49: Betty Lois Pope
1949-50: Betty Lois Pope
1950-51: Betty Lois Pope
1951-52: Martha Jo Maul
1952-53: Nancy Spillar
1953-54: Nona Jane Volmering
1954-55: Nancy Pope
1955-56: Betty Dean Burrier
1956-57: Lorena Phillips
1957-58: Becky Shelton
1958-59: Jean Turner
1959-60: Patricia Puryear
1960-61: Ora Mae "Scooter" Montague
1961-62: Martha Collier
1962-63: Sandra Cauthen
1963-64: Linda Holweger
1964-65: Lynn Kingsbery
1965-66: Robin Brown
1966-67: Linda Brizendine
1967-68: Donna Pittman
1968-69: Donna Pittman
1969-70: Diane White
1970-71: Kathy Pittman
1971-72: Kathy Pittman
1972-73: Theresa Garnett

1973-74: Charlotte Hohman
1974-75: Mary Clare Dodson
1975-76: Cindy Reid
1976-77: Cindy Reid
1977-78: Melony Chandler
1978-79: Tami Purcell
1979-80: Carol Bankston
1980-81: Tracy Dempsey

Varsity Cheerleaders: With the advent of football in 1938, cheerleaders and pep squads were not far behind. From 1940 since, cheerleaders have been selected to lead the cheers for the football team and later on, for other sports as well. For many years, after tryouts, the cheerleaders were chosen by the student body. In the last decade or so, outside judges have been responsible for this selection. The number has also increased as the school population has grown. Many start as seventh grade cheerleaders and advance through the ranks to make it a career. In the late '40s, the school was represented with male cheerleaders but since then, it has been an all-female domain. Below are those who have served as cheerleaders.

1940-41: Cleo Nell Gage, Edith Goslin, Wilma Ruth Goslin
1941-42: Cleo Nell Gage, Vivian Henry, Lila Thielepape
1942-43: Lula Saunders, Lila Thielepape, Lila Faye Walker
1943-44: Maxine Garnett, Charlene Greer, Lila Faye Smith
1944-45: Ruthie Mae Crumley, Florene Foster, Lila Faye Smith
1945-46: Ruthie Mae Crumley, Merle Ragland, Violet Rae Smith
1946-47: May Dell Crumley, Nancy Haydon, Merle Ragland
1947-48: Doris Nell Arnold, Billy Glosson, Samuel Langston, Merle Ragland, Violet Rae Smith
1948-49: Gennieve Cure, Dosia Mae Rippy, Virginia Weaver
1949-50: JoAnn Glosson, Samuel Langston, Jean Montague, Zilman Piland, Louise Wallace
1950-51: Jerry Bond, LaVerne Grumbles, Mae Francis Sansom
1951-52: Lorinda Prewitt, Mae Francis Sansom, Nancy Spillar, Gay Wier

1952-53: Martha Jo Maul, Loretta McClaferty, Merle Walker, Gay Wier
1953-54: Bonnie Glosson, Judy Hoard, Loretta McClaferty
1954-55: Bonnie Glosson, Judy Hoard, Martha Ann Stephenson
1955-56: Shirley Combs, Bonnie Glosson, Judy Hoard
1956-57: Janice Combs, Irene Phillips, Clara Rippy
1957-58: Clara Rippy, Brenda Johnson, Jean Turner
1958-59: Lorena Phillips, Clara Rippy, Becky Shelton
1959-60: Clara Rippy, Becky Shelton, Jean Turner
1960-61: Billie Ferrell, Betty Ragland, Jackie Shackleford
1961-62: Betty Ragland, Sandra Rippy, Kay Roberts
1962-63: Sherry Canon, Betty Ragland,* Sandra Rippy (*) died in car accident prior to school year.
1963-64: Sherry Canon, Janiece Hyatt, Sandra Rippy
1964-65: Sherry Canon, Linda Holweger, Cherry Needham
1965-66: Linda Brizendine, Robin Brown, Cherry Needham
1966-67: Linda Brizendine, Cherry Needham, Mary Ellen Strong
1967-68: Vicki Brotherton, Peggy Holton, Donna Pittman
1968-69: Peggy Holton, Brenda McNair, Colleen Phelan, Becky Schenck
1969-70: Peggy Gravenor, Kathy Hutto, Colleen Phelan, Becky Schenck
1970-71: Theresa Garnett, Cathy Gravenor, Peggy Gravenor, Lynda McCarty
1971-72: Theresa Garnett, Annette Gravenor, Sandy Gravenor, Lynda McCarty, Janet White
1972-73: Theresa Garnett, Annette Gravenor, Carolyn Murphy, Margaret Murphy, Janet White
1973-74: Tonne Bonnett, Mary Clare Dodson, Theresa Garnett, Annette Gravenor, Donna Sandefur
1974-75: Billie Brotherton, Mary Clare Dodson, Sherry Glosson, Annette Gravenor, Tammy Shipp
1975-76: Gail Anglin, Gay Lynn Dodson, Mary Clare Dodson, Tammie Gillis, Tammy Shipp
1976-77: Mae Collier, Kim Ferguson, Yolanda Nevarez, Cindy Reid, Tammy Shipp
1977-78: Melony Chandler, Mae Collier, Joy Davis, Lynda Garza, Edye Tarbox
1978-79: Terri Anderson, Melony Chandler, Lynda Garza, Kim Jones, Tami Purcell
1979-80: Tracy Dempsey, Cindy Ilse, Lura Lyle, Dana Talbert, Adrienne Tarbox
1980-81: Sherri Danielson, Roberta Hoyer, Lura Lyle, Beth Scantland, Michelle Sisk, Adrienne Tarbox
1981-82: Sherri Danielson, Kim Fries, Janelle Gavlick, Heidi Noak, Dana Runnels
1982-83: Kim Anderson, Lisa Crumley, Jennifer McCartney, Heidi Noak, Misty Spencer, Darla Talbert
1983-84: Nadine Adams, Laura Butts, Jana Jordan, Dawn Orem, Misty Spencer, Terri Watts
1984-85: Lisa Counts, Kim Cox, Chawn Gibson, Robin Kelley, Bobbie Morgan, Jill Reimers
1985-86: Ella Dowling, DeAnne Formby, Becky Morgan, Bobbie Morgan, Kim Ross, Suzy Sheppard
1986-87: Kim Coleman, Ella Dowling, Shelley Hall, Julie Henderson, Kim Ross, Suzy Sheppard
1987-88: Charlotte Carothers, Kim Coleman, Carmen Donaghe, Shelley Hall, Laura Haydon, Julie Henderson, Kim Kelley, Kari Sorrels
1988-89: Lee Appelt, Tanya DeWind, Carmen Donaghe, Lorissa Dunk, Terri Gardner, Laura Haydon, Kim Kelley, Tricia Thomas
1989-90: Lee Appelt, Christy Bible, Tanya DeWind, Lorissa Dunk, Kristi Edwards, Jennifer Hart, Robin Puryear, Alison Stegall
1990-91: Christy Bible, Jennifer Hart, Christie Jones, Jill Montague, Robin Puryear, Tami Speir,* Alison Stegall, Lolly Thompson * (died in car accident prior to school year.)
1991-92: Elizabeth Archer, Gina Calderon, Rene Calhoun, Brandi Read, Rinda Rippy, Kristi Sorrells, Carrie Stewart, Lolly Thompson
1992-93: Elizabeth Archer, Gina Calderon, Amy Edwards, Lee Anne Haydon, Brandi Read, Rinda Rippy, Kristi Sorrells, Carrie Stewart

1993-94: Amy Edwards, Laura Edwards, Dusty Eickenloff, Jodi Harris, Lea Anne Haydon, Leah Koenig, Paige Low

1994-95: Laura Edwards, Dawn Franklin, Jodi Harris, Emily Heckman, Anna Jungman, Jessie McIlvain, Kelly McGraw, Shirl Rickman

1995-96: Stephanie Bonnell, Megan Costello, Dawn Franklin, Cheryl Jones, Anna Jungman, Jessie McIlvain, Shirl Rickman, Leah Schumann, Monika Seiders, Clair Short, Lynn Stacey, Krystal Stone

1996-97: Megan Costello, Colie Edmondson, Kelly Graham, Cheryl Jones, Cassie McGraw, Leah Schumann, Monika Seiders, Nicole Simmons, Sarah Smith, Krystal Stone

1997-98: Angela Anderson, Amber Bainum, Quincy DeSpain, Rachel Heckmann, Lissette Johnston, Emily Kinney, Stacey Sharp, Brooke Stacey, Ticer Stewart, Mindi Sultemeier

1998-99: Amber Bainum, Rachel Heckmann, Chase Jebousek, Tressa Kezar, Emily Kinney, Amy Larson, Stacey Sharp, Dennielle Singleton, Brooke Stacey, Lauren Sterling, Ticer Stewart, Jenny Sultemeier, Rebekah Wright

1999-00: Shanti Bosbach, Kaitlin Henslee, Chase Jebousek, Leanna Jensen, Amy Larson, Ashley Leal, Lindsey Maund, Brook Sandahl, Nikki Seale, Lauren Sterling, Jenny Sultemeier, Stephanie Williams

2000-01: Amanda Bickman, Lauren Blackshare, Lindsey Blanck, Rosie Kanetsky, A. J. Klusman, Katie Marchand, Lindsey Maund, Bethany Nelson, Heather Poehl, Whitney Shriver, Scarlett Wright, Christie Zeiter

2001-02: Amanda Bickman, Lindsey Blanck, Jamie Dredla, Rosie Kanetsky, Katie Marchand, Bethany Nelson, Hannah Nelson, Audrey Quijano, Ashli Wittmuss, Scarlett Wright, Christie Zeiter

2002-03: Holly Armstrong, Alicia Bickham, Amanda Bickham, Jamie Dredla, Jenni Farmer, Gianna Fleahearty, Allina Pokorny, Amanda Prater, Ashley Wendel, Ashli Wittmuss, Meagan Wood, Scarlett Wright

School Mascots: Students elected to be the school mascot and wear a costume in the likeness thereof started catching on, and Dripping Springs joined the trend in 1966-67. One of the Beta Club's projects this particular year was to raise funds for the purchase of the Tiger uniform. However, Dripping Springs has had problems with continuity in this area. After beginning the tradition, it continued for over a decade and then took a hiatus for almost a decade before taking it up again. Then again in 2002-03, no one cared to run for the honor. Although not listed, it was a practice for many years for some elementary youngster(s) to serve as a mascot for the team. Below are the high school students who served as the school mascot.

1966-67: Becky Boone
1967-68: Debbie Belvin
1968-69: Donna Pittman
1969-70: Diane White
1970-71: Kathy Pittman
1971-72: Peggy Gravenor
1972-73: Jody Seitz
1973-74: Sherry Glosson
1974-75: Paula Allen
1975-76: Cindy Reid
1976-77: Sylvia Garza
1977-78: Jackie Smith
1978-79: Carol Bankston
1987-88: Bobbi Hohmann
1988-89: Kristian Henderson
1989-90: Hannah Ballard
1990-91: Nikki Harmon
1991-92: Natalie Till
1992-93: Nicole Bainum
1993-94: Kelly McGraw
1994-95: Jamie Edwards
1995-96: Abby Robbin
1996-97: Abby Robbin
1997-98: Veronica Ramirez
1998-99: Kara Malott/Chris Roberson
1999-00: Andria Marsh
2000-01: Suzanne LeClair
2001-02: Melissa Crecraft

FFA Sweetheart/FHA Beau: Shortly after each organization became established at the school, they began to elect sweethearts and beaus. The FFA continued the tradition the longest, mainly because the sweetheart had defined duties during the year, while the FHA beau was just an honor bestowed upon a boy. Both organizations began to lose their traditional roots in the 1980s as both began to take in members of the opposite sex. Finally, both dropped the selections altogether. These are ones we have records of.

1951-52: Mae Francis Sansom
1952-53:
1953-54:
1954-55: Carolyn Phillips, Charles Stephenson
1955-56: Patsy Harber, Oran Hill "Pug" Rippy
1956-57: Wanda Glass, Bobby Shelton
1957-58: Becky Shelton, Lee Jones
1958-59: Clara Rippy, Wesley Ruston
1959-60: Ora Mae "Scooter" Montague, Jimmy Shelton
1960-61: Sandra Rippy, Cecil Jenkins
1961-62: Sandra Cauthen, Dixie Smith
1962-63: Linda Holweger, Don DuPuy
1963-64: Lynn Kingsbery, Malcolm Key
1964-65: Robin Brown, Paul Herrera
1965-66: Linda Brizendine, Marvin Myers
1966-67: Rosie Collier, Sid Spillar
1967-68: Debbie Belvin, Lynn "Rocky" Weihrauch
1968-69: Becky Schenck, Ray Whisenant
1969-70: Elizabeth Madsen, Ricky Schieffer
1970-71: Anita Metcalfe, Cecil McIntyre
1971-72: Lynda McCarty, Howard Bryant
1972-73: Melody Jones, Gene Czimskey
1973-74: Melody Jones, Bill Hyde
1974-75: Cindy Reid, Tommy Moore
1975-76: Cindy Reid, Tommy Moore
1976-77: Melony Chandler, Calvin Lynch
1977-78: Melony Chandler, Tim Fitzharris
1978-79: Melony Chandler
1979-80: Keli Luedecke
1980-81: Laura Willhoite
1981-82: Misty Spencer
1982-83: Misty Spencer
1983-84: Misty Spencer
1984-85: Traci Purcell
1985-86: Sabra Till
1986-87: Cari Sawyer
1987-88: Cari Sawyer
1988-89: Christy Cayce
1989-90: Christy Cayce
1990-91: Jennifer Shults

D. W. "Weebud" Cauthen has seen every Tiger football team play.

Tiger fans leaving football stands, 1960s.

Information Sources

Every community deserves to have a record of their heritage and thanks to the citizens and descendants of Dripping Springs, this labor of love was made much easier.

Anytime anyone takes on a project like this, there are so many people and sources which need to be recognized. Since I moved to Dripping Springs only in 1965, there is not that much information that would come from my first-hand experience. Therefore, I spent many hours going over various written works to come up with as much accurate information as I could. I also have to give thanks to many people. It seems that everyone was interested in having this project done. I had so much cooperation. I am so glad that some were very patient with me because I know I made a nuisance of myself in coming back time and again with questions to get some-thing straight in my mind. I just hope the finished project does them and the history of Dripping Springs justice. Below is a list of the various sources of the information found within this book. Despite my best efforts, no doubt someone deserving of mention will be left off. If so, please accept my sincerest apologies.

Newspapers: I tried to read every newspaper on microfich that I could find that might have some mention of Dripping Springs. The San Marcos Library had many rolls of what I was looking for and I spent many hours pouring over tiny newspaper print on the screen. There would be times when the papers would be a gold mine of information and then either the newspaper issues ran out or people reporting on Dripping Springs would stop doing it. Nevertheless, it was very interesting just reading about things that happened many, many years before. Below is a list of the newspapers that provided me with reading time and information to help pull the entire story of Dripping Springs together.

San Marcos Free Press, 1874-1890; *Hays County Times*, 1886-1900; *Dripping Springs Pointer*, 1905 (two issues); *Kyle News*, 1905-1957; *Hays County Citizen*, 1957-1965; *San Marcos Record*, 1922-1965; *Dripping Springs Dispatch*, 1983-; *Dripping Springs Springer*, 1985-1990; *Dripping Springs Century-News*, 1990-; *Blanco County News*, 1906.

Reports: Much time was spent perusing original documents at the Hays County Annex in San Marcos. Again it was very time-consuming but very interesting to fight through the various degrees of penmanship to find the information I was looking for. Many of the old records were piled in heaps in the upstairs storeroom and one had to literally dig through the piles to find reports that would be of benefit for this book. Luckily I found some very valuable original reports that could have stayed in this disarray and lost to researchers. They are now housed in a vault upstairs. Here listed are some of the reports that occupied my time over the years.

Hays County Deeds Records 1854-1995

Hays County Tax Rolls (on microfich at San Marcos Library) 1854-1910

Hays County Elections Book 1848-1919

Hays County Commissioners Court Minutes 1848-1920

Hays County School Board Minutes 1911-1955

Hays County School Superintendent School Reports (all that I could find)

Hays County Treasurer's Reports (all that I could find)

Dripping Springs School Board Minutes

Publications: I tried to read as many publications as I could that would help fill in all the spaces to the puzzle I was working on. Some had specific information I could use and others would give me ideas to pursue. As my research dug deeper and deeper, it was obvious some of these publications had much erroneous information that, at times, would throw me off track. Nevertheless, they were all helpful in one form or another. Some would cause me to spend a lot of time reading to come up with maybe just one idea or bit of information. At no time did I ever consider any time spent as wasted time. Below are some of the publications that aided me in the information I am passing on to you.

Clear Springs and Limestone Ledges. A book written about Hays County which included a section on Dripping Springs. It has much misinformation but good for some general information.

Prophet of the Pedernales. A book written by native son and lifelong Baptist minister, Jasper Newton Marshall, about his life which included things that happened in Dripping Springs.

History of the Dripping Springs Methodist Church. This book was researched by Miss Ennis Follis and covered the history of the church from 1854 to 1984.

History of Driftwood. This book followed the history of Driftwood and since its close proximity to Dripping Springs gave insight to the goings on around the area.

Dripping Springs Church of Christ History. This publication was researched by one of their preachers, Don Prather, and gave a good history of the church.

Dripping Springs First Graded School Handbook. This publication was put out for the school year 1905-06, giving information about the upcoming school year.

Dripping Springs School Handbook. This covered the school year 1910-11.

Dripping Springs School Yearbooks: The first one was published in 1945. They can really be a good source of what is going on during that year of activities. I was able to get my hands on all the yearbooks published and was able to duplicate all those that I did not have in my library.

The Tiger Cry. Was the school newspaper produced by the students and began being published in 1941. Read as many copies as I could get my hands on. Good information at times.

Historical Collection of Dripping Springs and Hays County. These books are a result of the freshmen English classes at Dripping Springs High School. The students pick topics to do a research paper on and the best of these papers are published each year. The first was published in 1991. Although they had some of the misinformation expected from novice freshmen, their research was most valuable in coming up with correct information and good leads. Two teachers have been responsible for this project over the years. Janie Botkin originated it and later Lea Anne Haydon Schroeder continued it.

The Times of Hays County. This was a 100-page newspaper edition published on the 150th anniversary of Hays County in 1998. It was a collaborative effort by the

San Marcos Daily Record, *The Free Press* and *The News-Dispatch*, headed up by Bob Barton. It was chockfull of history and pictures of Hays County up to 1880. It is a good read, with good research by many.

Hays County, Texas Cemetery Inscriptions. Two ladies took the time to go to most, if not all, the cemeteries in Hays County to gather the names of all buried in them. Along with the history and location of each, the people buried in Hays County are listed in alphabetical order with the cemetery given as well as dates of the deceased. Is a good resource.

Wimberley...A Way of Life. Written by Linda Williams Allen, this book was used as a source for the beginnings of the EMS organization in North Hays County.

TEXAS, Land of Contrast, Its History and Geography. This is a school text taught in the seventh grade and written by Reese and Kennamer.

University Interscholastic League Athletic Records #6912. This book brought the UIL records up-to-date to 1969 and also gave the history of each of the sports sponsored by the UIL.

Texas Schoolgirl Basketball. This book written by James McLemore gives a very thorough history of girls basketball in Texas.

A History of Texas Boys' Basketball. This book was written by Harold Ratliff and gave a good account of the history of boys basketball in Texas.

Interviews: As I have mentioned many times before, this book is a compilation of many people's help. There are some who I had to rely on time and time again. They were my sounding board. I would find some information and go to them to see what they knew about the subject and whether I might be on the right track or not. They were invaluable in giving me insight. There were many things that I read or heard over the years that I really did not understand. I could always turn to them and get an answer. And sometimes I would have to keep coming back for that little bit of understanding that I could not quite grasp. For sure, each question answered, no matter how many or how few, was invaluable for my understanding. I will not be able to mention everyone I came into contact with and if I missed anyone, then just know you are included in the *all I have missed* category.

Cannon, Katherine Berkley. Her interest in the history of the area and her encouragement to keep plugging was a big help. She was a source in general for all my questions.

Haydon, Charlie. Charlie has a good mind for remembering stories others had told him and I could bounce my stories off him for some verification. He was also responsible for researching the history of the First Baptist Church and some of the early history of the Masons.

Davis, Bradley. He was born in Dripping Springs in 1909 and was my oldest living source when I began to work on the book. Answers to my questions and articles in which he had been interviewed were good sources in covering many of my loopholes.

Haydon, Alva. Mr. Haydon had a very uncanny ability to remember very accurately most of the details of the history of the area. He was very gracious and patient with me as he willingly sat down and answered my hundreds of questions over the period of years.

Haydon, Betty Butler. Her experiences concerning the telephone company helped enhance that history. She was responsible for the history of the telephone operators and in particular, Mrs. Horner.

Barton, Patricia Lawshe. In several instances, I could not believe my luck. Mrs. Barton was one of those. She is the great-granddaughter of John L. Wallace and another great-granddaughter, Mrs. Louise Patton Labenski, of Buda gave me her name as another source. Lo and behold she had done extensive research on the Wallace family and this plugged another giant hole in the history.

Lee, Francis Patterson. Another stroke of luck. She is the granddaughter of J. L.

Patterson. She was a retired teacher that just happened to live in Temple and went to the Methodist Church in Rogers with my father. In one of their conversations, the name of Dripping Springs came up and my dad mentioned that I lived there and the connection was made. She, too, had valuable information on her family.

Dickey, Dan, Jr. He is the great-grandson of George Dickey. In researching the Dickey house, Mrs. Anton Allen gave me his name and telephone number. He had moved a couple of times but I was able to track him down and he shared some of what he knew about his family.

Glosson, E.B. "Pete." Pete and Naoma have lived in the area for over 80 years and have been instrumental in living the history of Dripping Springs.

Hohman, Alfard. Alfard and Ann go way back as well and could recall many of the things necessary to fill in some of my gaps.

Cobb, Clarence. Clarence and Betty Dean are interested in the history of the area and could be counted on to provide information, verbally, as well as, many publications to peruse.

Rippy, J. N. His experience in the world of the wool and mohair business allowed us to get a very important lesson in that industry in the history of Dripping Springs.

Hudson, John. His research allowed me to have a more complete history of the Rambo Lodge of the Masons of Dripping Springs.

Owens, Marjorie Hammack. A great-granddaughter of Dr. Pound, she was very cooperative in giving very complete information about the Pounds. She wrote an article on the history of Dripping Springs education as well.

Haralson, Rebeccah. Her research on the Moss family for a freshman English project in 2000 unearthed facts about the Moss family that was previously unknown by anyone around Dripping Springs and allowed their history to not be presented erroneously, as it was about to be.

Kokernot, Dr. Robert. Another stroke of luck, thanks to Miss Haralson's research. She gave me the name of John Moss' only surviving grandson, Gloyd Moss of Alpine, Texas. He in turn, gave me the address of Dr. Kokernot, a great-grandson. He had spent much time researching the Moss family and graciously shared the information with me.

Michelle Fischer and Ginger Faught. Michelle, the City Administrator, and Ginger, the City Secretary, were very cooperative in providing city maps and other information that made putting together the final land ownership pieces much easier.

Other VIPs. James Hall, Travis Garnett, Billie Garnett, Fred Garnett, J. F. Glosson, Jr., Mrs. Haskell McNair, Ernest Williamson, Louella Williamson McNair, Bill McNair, Loretta McClaferty Watson, Mrs. Enoch Needham, E. E."Nookie" and Hazel Bell King Myers, Delores Conn, Willie Edna Baird Crow, Jack Lyle, Mike Rose, Don Prather, Pat Gibson, Ennis Follis, Mrs. Flemmie Cauthen Felps, Mrs. Rosa Lyle Spaw, Mike Davidson, John and Lila Gillespie, Geronimo Garza, Joe Ramirez, Zilman Piland, James Hurlbut, Knox Williams, Francis Ragland Rhodes, and many, many others too numerous to name who patiently fielded my questions.

About the Author

Carl Woodson Waits was born in Durango, Texas, a small community in Falls County, on January 22, 1942. He is the eldest of five sons born to Charles Woodson and Hazel Douglas Clowers Waits. The family moved to a ranch southwest of Rogers, Texas, in the community of Joe Lee on August 5, 1942. The 1,800 acre ranch, located along the Little River in Bell County, belonged to his dad's uncle and his dad managed this property for the next 35 years.

Carl's formal education began in September 1948 at the Joe Lee County School. It was a two-room school, plus a lunch room, that held seven grades. Never more than 50 students ever attended. The two rooms were divided by a folding wall. Grades 1-3 were in one room and 4-7 in the other. The classroom for the older children had a stage.

Because second and third graders were roomed together, second grader Carl was found to do as well as the regular third graders. He was formally moved to the third grade for the second semester. The next year he moved to the fourth grade. It was a move that did not affect him socially or academically. After completing the seventh grade, students at Joe Lee had to transfer to Rogers ISD to complete their education. He graduated from RHS in May 1959. Thanks to the influence of two of his high school coaches, he enrolled at Sam Houston State Teachers College (now Sam Houston State University) in Huntsville, Texas, in the fall of 1959. He graduated from there with a Bachelor's degree in 1963 and a Master's degree in 1965. He was then ready to pursue a career in education.

In 1962 he married Carolyn Sue May, a 1963 graduate of Rogers High School. They were blessed with a son, Timothy Wayne, on June 24, 1963. After a trip to Dripping Springs in June 1965, to meet with the school board, he began a 30-year teaching/coaching career at Dripping Springs.

In 1990, he began the project of writing the history of Dripping Springs and the P. A. Smith survey. This just goes to show how fragile history can be. Had he not been double-promoted or decided to pursue a Master's, then the opportunity to land in Dripping Springs probably would not have occurred and he would not have undertaken this project.

After retiring in 1995, the project continued until completion in the spring of 2003. Today, Coach Waits continues working for the school district as a bus driver.

www.ingramcontent.com/pod-product-compliance
Lightning Source LLC
Chambersburg PA
CBHW060309240426
43661CB00059B/2701